Eisenstadt, Shumel
Israeli society

DATE DUE

#47-0108 Peel Off Pressure Sensitive

Israeli Society

Publication Series in
the History of Zionism and the Yishuv,
The Institute of Contemporary Jewry,
The Hebrew University of Jerusalem

Israeli Society

S. N. EISENSTADT

Professor of Sociology, Hebrew University of Jerusalem

Basic Books, Inc., *Publishers*

New York

© 1967 by S. N. Eisenstadt

Library of Congress Catalog Card Number: 67–16886

PRINTED IN GREAT BRITAIN

Contents

Preface

The work presented here is the product of many years of research and teaching. The first specific beginnings of this book lie in the seminars and courses on the social structure of Israel which I have been teaching for the past fourteen years at the Hebrew University. Its research foundations were laid in the Research Seminar on the Social Structure of the Yishuv, which was established within the Department of Social Sciences at the Hebrew University in 1946. This Seminar continued after the War of Independence, until 1951 when a fully-fledged research programme was established in the Department of Sociology of the Hebrew University, founded with the help of Dr G. S. Wise, then Chairman of the Board of Governors of the Hebrew University and now President of Tel Aviv University.

The book is heavily indebted to many researches undertaken by my colleagues and myself at the Department of Sociology of the Hebrew University, as well as to the research of other institutions, and especially those of the Central Bureau of Statistics, the Falk Foundation, the Israel Institute of Applied Social Research, the Szold Foundation, and the Research Department of the Bank of Israel.

Although many aspects of the social structure in Israel have not yet been explored, it has been possible, in the last three or four years, to crystallize the existing data sufficiently to present some systematic picture and to pinpoint the areas in which future research seems most urgent. When, therefore, Professor M. Davis, Director of the Institute of Contemporary Jewry at the Hebrew University, approached me about three years ago, with a suggestion that I publish my lectures in book form under the auspices of his Institute, I very much welcomed his suggestion. This was, indeed, the final impetus needed for preparing this book on Israeli society which is at present under preparation by a team consisting of myself, Dr Ch. Adler, Dr R. Bar-Yosef, and Mr R. Cahanna, and which has been of great help also to this book.

Needless to say, this book owes much to many people. First of all, I would like to thank all my students over the past fifteen years who have suffered in seminars and lectures during which I experimented with some of my ideas. I owe an equal debt to my colleagues in the Department of Sociology for general discussions on problems of Israeli society as well as for the results of their varied researches. I would like to mention especially Professor J. Katz and his work on the Traditional Jewish Society and the Beginnings of Jewish

Nationalism; Professor J. Ben-David and his work on the professions, as well as our joint project on youth movements; Professor Y. Garber-Talmon and her work on the Kibbutzim; Dr Ch. Adler's research on the educational system; Dr D. Weintraub and his work on the Moshavim; Dr Moshe Lissak's investigations into occupational aspirations; Mr E. Cohen and his work on development areas and Mr A. Zloczower's work on mobility and status aspiration.

Beyond this, I also wish to thank several colleagues for reading this manuscript at different stages in its preparation. They include Mrs Y. Atzmon, Professor R. Bachi, Dr H. Barkai, Professor M. Davis, Mr D. Gollan, Professor Elihu Katz, Professor J. Katz, Dr I. Kolatt, Professor A. Morag, Mr B. Schachar, and Mr A. Zloczower.

During my stay as Carnegie Visiting Professor at the Massachusetts Institute of Technology, and while teaching at Harvard University, I inflicted drafts of this paper on several colleagues; on Professors Daniel Lerner, Talcott Parsons, Lucian Pye and Leonard Fein. I greatly benefited from their remarks and from the very detailed remarks of Professor S. M. Lipset on the pre-final draft of this book.

Several people helped in the preparation of the material. Above all, I would like to thank Mr Reuven Cahanna whose devotion and help in the preparation both of this book and the source book have been indispensable. Other invaluable helpers include Mr Shlomo Deshen, Mr Gur Offer, Mrs Z. Stup, Dr D. Weintraub, and Mr Yohanan Wosner.

I would like also to emphasize especially the patient help of Professor M. Davis and Mr Hagai Lev, Secretary of the Institute of Contemporary Jewry.

Mr M. Gradel and Mrs A. Shapiro have done marvels to improve the English and the general composition of the original draft – but are certainly not responsible for those 'original sins' which cannot be corrected later. Mrs P. Gurevitch helped with the proof reading.

Lastly, I owe thanks to the Central Bureau of Statistics (for the tables), the Bank of Israel, and the Falk Institute, to the *New East Quarterly*, *New Outlook Quarterly*, and Dr J. Ellemers for permission to quote, and to Dr J. Matras and my colleagues at the Department of Sociology, for permission to quote from some of their reports and articles.

One major problem which I faced in preparing the book was how to bring together both the basic data on Israeli society as well as the more specifically sociological analysis. The book intended primarily to present a sociological analysis of Israeli society and institutions. As there is, however, no book which gives the major relevant historical, institutional, and contemporary details, I felt it necessary to include in it many details which could have been perhaps otherwise omitted – although even here I left out many others which I assumed to be of general common knowledge. Obviously this always calls for finding the proper balance between the presentation of all these details and of the analysis. There is probably no single best way to do it and I certainly do not claim to have found it. I would like only to claim the indulgence of the reader for the way which I chose according to the best of my ability and judgement.

Most of the work on this book was finished by the end of 1963. However, various technical aspects of its preparation have delayed final publication. It was not, however, possible to 'update' all the material and only in some very special cases (especially in the internal political field) was more recent information added, although I have indeed attempted to do so for most of the tables.

Jerusalem,   S. N. EISENSTADT
The Hebrew University,
The Eliezer Kaplan School of
Economics and Social Sciences.
December, 1965.

This book has been prepared with the editorial assistance of Aliza Shapiro.

Part 1

THE HISTORICAL BACKGROUND

1

An Analysis of Israeli Society – The Problem and the Setting

Introduction

The aim of this study is to provide a systematic analysis of the development of the Jewish community in Palestine[1] from its beginnings in the late 1880's up to the present day. Such an analysis can, of course, be attempted from several diverse points of view. It seems to us that its focal point should be the development of the country's society as a modern society with specific problems and characteristics of its own.

The broad socio-demographic and structural results of modernization developed in the major institutional spheres have, by now, been studied in social science literature. Perhaps the best overall summary of the socio-demographic indices of modernization has been coined by Karl Deutsch in the term 'social mobilization'. He has defined it as 'the process in which major clusters of old social, economic and psychological commitments are eroded and broken and people become available for new patterns of socialization and behaviour.' He also indicated that some of its main indices are exposure to aspects of modern life through the development of machinery, buildings, consumer goods etc., reponses to mass media, changes of residence, urbanization, change from agricultural occupations, literacy and growth of per capital income.[2]

Similarly, the major structural characteristics of modernization have been identified as the development of a high extent of differentiation, of free resources which are not committed to any fixed, ascriptive (kinship, territorial, etc.) groups; the development of specialized and diversified types of social organization and the development of wide non-traditional 'national', or even supernational, group identifications. The concomitant development, in all major institutional spheres, of specialized roles and of special wider regulative and allocative mechanisms and organizations should also be mentioned here. This includes market mechanisms in economic life, voting and party activities in politics, and diverse bureaucratic organizations and mechanisms in most institutional spheres.

But beyond these varied socio-demographic or structural characteristics of

[1] Also referred to as the 'Yishuv'.

[2] K. W. Deutsch, 'Social Mobilization and Political Development', *American Political Science Review*, 55, Sept. 1961, 494–5.

modernity there looms a larger and more crucial problem. Modernization implies not only the development of the various aspects of growing structural differentiation but also the development of a social system capable of generating and absorbing continuous change. It must be capable of absorbing changes beyond its own initial institutional premises.

The central problem of modernization can therefore be seen as the ability of any system to adapt itself to changing demands, to absorb them in terms of policy-making and to assure its own continuity in the face of new demands and new forms of political organization.

In other words, modernization creates problems of sustained social, economic, and political growth and the ability to deal with continuous social changes is the crucial test of such sustained growth.

The vital importance of this problem can also be seen in the fact that most modern societies and political systems have developed through some kind of revolutionary act or movement.

It was invariably some such revolutionary act or movement that constituted the crucial signpost in the breakthrough from the more traditional to the modern, or in the transistion between different stages of modernization. Such revolutionary events were usually heralded as the beginnings of a new era – an era of greater freedom and creativity and of the establishment of a social, cultural, and political order capable of continuous growth and development.

In each such case the specific characteristics and orientations of the revolutionary breakthrough greatly influenced the specific characteristics and the course of modernization of any given society.

As with other such cases, Israeli society displays some characteristics of its own – arising from its specific historical antecedents, social features, and cultural orientations. At the same time, however, many aspects of its historical and social development can be compared with those of other societies. Such comparison will contribute greatly to a better understanding both of Israeli society's unique characteristics and of its place in the broad framework of modernization.

The Jewish community in Palestine and the State of Israel have developed out of the activities of the Zionist groups which evolved from the late 1880's in Eastern and Central Europe and which forged their specific revolutionary orientation. This rebellion was part of the general Zionist upheaval against Jewish life in the modern *diaspora* and also, to some extent, a rebellion against the official Zionist movement which had to compromise the pure tenets of their ideology in order to strike roots in Jewish communal life. The general Zionist rebellion was directed against the supposition that a full Jewish life and tradition could be maintained within the framework of an alien modern society. It was a fundamental tenet of Zionist ideology that, within such a framework, the Jews would be threatened either by spiritual

2

and cultural annihilation, owing to the undermining of their traditional and communal life by modern economic, political, and social forces on the one hand, or economic, political, and physical annihilation on the other hand, due to incomplete assimilation and the inability of modern society to digest this alien element.

The Zionist ideology assumed that the Jews would not be able to participate fully in the new modern societies and would become, despite their assimilation, an alien element – an element which might perhaps be ultimately expelled or destroyed.

Hence they thought that only in Palestine a new, modern, viable Jewish society could be established and thrive. But what kind of society did they envisage?

On the purely intellectual and ideological level the different answers to be found in Zionist literature are numerous – as are the variations in emphasis – on traditional, revolutionary, religious, secular, or socialist aspects. Perhaps clearer than the positive contents of these ideologies are their common negative elements – i.e. what kind of society they did *not* want. They were against the traditional medieval Jewish society which still existed in many places in Eastern and Central Europe and against the various types of assimilationist Jewish communities as they developed especially in Western and Central Europe. They looked, in different ways, for a synthesis between Jewishness and enlightenment or modernity. But they did not reject either Jewish tradition or modernity as such. Extremists, such as Brenner or Berditschevsky among others, did, indeed, attempt to deny large parts of Jewish tradition but even they tended, on the whole, to look within Jewish history for new elements to be revived. And there were but few who rejected any form of modernity – although very often what they wanted was a 'socialist utopian' society orientated against the 'mass society'. Often these new ideas stemmed from the *Haskala* (enlightenment) period in Germany and especially in Eastern Europe, which also aimed at a modernization of Jewish life and at a synthesis between the modern and the Jewish. But now these attempts became reformulated in a national vein, as against the more assimilationist tendencies of the *Haskala*. They resembled closely the intellectual trends and movements which, at that time, began to develop in many Eastern European countries and which were later destined to spread to Asia and Africa.

There were few who knew exactly which of the many proposed solutions to choose and which to reject, or how exactly to combine the old and the new – the 'specially Jewish' and the 'generally-human'.

The relative emphasis on each aspect of this ideology changed with time and place, but, as a whole, it represented the Zionist position and, in particular, the rebellion manifested in the various waves of immigration (*aliyot*) to Palestine.

Unlike the general run of modern Jewish immigrants, the attainment of economic goals or personal security was not a prime importance for the immigrants to Palestine. These goals were largely subordinated to social and cultural aspirations – to the establishment of a new type of wholly Jewish society, modern, mainly secular, autonomous, and economically independent. The objective of the new community was not economic betterment and a rise in the standard of living, but rather the normalization of the community's economic and social structure and the complete reversal of the usual Jewish economic structure in the *diaspora*. Hence the great emphasis on the 'return to the soil' as an essential agricultural basis for the community, as its primary occupational foundation. Hand in hand with these attempts went a strong emphasis on social justice and security, especially among the various socialist sectors of the movement. These sectors also tended to subordinate economic considerations to certain basic premises of social solidarity and to weaken the individualist and competitive aspects of modern economic activity. Thus, although the establishment of a modern, economically adequate community was strongly stressed, this was not envisaged in purely economic or technical terms but was rather set within the framework of a new national entity.

These orientations shaped the endeavours of the pioneering immigrant groups and laid the foundations of the first nucleus of modern Jewish settlement in Palestine out of which the State of Israel was to grow.

It is the task of this analysis to clarify the facts pertaining to the society emerging in Israel: What kind of Jewish society is developing; what are its basic cultural orientations and characteristics; in what way is it distinct from other types of Jewish societies, or from other modern societies; what new traditions, values, and symbols did it create; what old ones did it perpetuate; and how did the various sectors of the Israeli population participate in the creation, perpetuation, and changes of old traditions? In what way is the Jewishness of this society different from other Jewish traditions and ways of life? In what way could it be different from other modern societies?

Some Comparative Starting Points

This book constitutes an attempt to answer these crucial questions. Throughout it we shall attempt not only to describe and analyse the concrete development of the Jewish community in Palestine and of Israeli society but also to set a broader frame through which this development can be compared with other modern societies. First among such comparisons must surely be that of the new colonizing societies.

Colonization in Israel may be compared to other attempts at transplanting Western social institutions into a new, non-Western setting. In the case of Israel, however, the attempt was not made in a cultural vacuum as, for instance, in Australia, but in a part of the traditional setting of the Middle

4

East, which contained all the major characteristics of the so-called under-developed countries. The Jewish pioneers, on the whole, tended to segregate themselves from this setting and attempted to transplant into their own frameworks various European institutions. Moreover, this colonizing movement was not, as we have already indicated, primarily motivated by economic considerations but by the desire to bring about a national and social renaissance – a transformed and modern society.

Thus, Israeli society may be compared to other societies which developed from religious, national, or political movements.

However, unlike many purely religious sectarian movements, the Zionist pioneer groups did not intend to establish monastic orders or sects on the fringes of a broader society, They aimed, instead, at a new and fully-fledged society. In this respect they were more like the Puritan colonists in North America in the seventeenth and eighteenth centuries. Unlike most modern social or political movements, Zionism and aliya were aimed not at the overthrow of an existing regime but at the establishment of a new society through colonization.

The development of Israeli society can also be analysed from the point of view of an immigrant community. The Yishuv and the State of Israel were built up by waves of immigrants in a continuous process of absorption and expansion. This process may be compared to other immigrant countries and will be analysed in greater detail later. It suffices to point out here that the traits which distinguish it from other modern migration movements are closely connected with the strong national and social emphasis mentioned above.

A further criterion of comparison is that with 'underdeveloped' or 'developing' nations and with 'new states'. This comparison is twofold. Firstly, it is concerned with the problems of economic development which are of great importance also in Israel, particularly in view of the flow of immigrants from traditional backgrounds. Secondly, the development of Israeli society may be compared with that of other 'new' sovereign states which emerged through the institutionalization of socio-political movements, the transformation of the leadership of such movements into a ruling elite, and the establishment of a new political regime, stemming from various colonizing and 'social movement' beginnings.

These broad trends enable us to analyse the development of Israel as one among the crystallizing modern societies.

The development of Israeli society can be seen as the encounter between these initial starting points and three crucial social processes.

The first of these was the 'natural' development of a different and complex social structure emerging from pioneering beginnings.

Second were the changes in this structure, caused by the establishment of the State of Israel and its transformation into a full-fledged state and society.

The third process was the influx of immigrants with new attitudes and motivations and their encounter with the emerging social structure.

Thus it is the encounter between the new immigrants and the institutional structure rooted in the pioneering ideology that constitutes the central theme of our analysis.

It is the conflict between the social and national movements on the one hand, and the waves of immigrants from economically more traditional backgrounds on the other hand, that provides the main characteristics of Israel's crystallization into a modern society.

These considerations also explain the plan of the book. In the first part, consisting of Chapters 1–4, we shall analyse the emergence of the social and institutional structure of the Yishuv and of the State of Israel as it has developed through the various phases of immigration until the establishment of the state. In Chapter 5 we shall briefly describe the major changes in the basic institutional and population structures that took place with the establishment of the State of Israel.

Part 2 will analyse the major institutional spheres of Israeli society today – the political and economic structure, education, youth and family, social organization and stratification and, lastly, the sphere of 'culture' and value orientations. In each of these chapters analysis will focus on certain recurring themes. One part of each chapter will, of course, present the basic facts and outlines of the given institutional structure, to help in the analysis of the different trends of institutional development. Two major considerations will prevail. One will be an attempt to understand how the initial pioneering ideology influenced the development of any given institutional sphere, while the second major point will be the transformation that took place in those institutional spheres with the establishment of the state and the encounter with the new immigrants.

The Major Stages in the Institutional Development of the Yishuv – The Background

This and the following chapters will attempt to analyse the major institutional developments of the Yishuv and of Israeli society without, however, giving a full historical description of these developments. The main purpose here is to emphasize those factors which are most important for an understanding of the main characteristics and problems of Israeli society.

Background – The Old Yishuv

The Old Yishuv is the term used for the traditional Jewish society of Palestine, whereas the New Yishuv is the term for the society that developed along nationalist lines beginning with the first aliya of the 1880's.

Historically, the Old Yishuv goes back to remote antiquity as, with the exception of two centuries of Crusader domination, Palestine always had a Jewish population. The immigrations beginning in the thirteenth century with the disintegration of the Frankish kingdoms set the pattern for the Old Yishuv as it appeared in the ensuing centuries and marked the beginning of Jewish mysticism connected with the Kabbala lore that emerged in Spain. This intensified the yearning for Palestine as the Holy Land, which was further heightened by the central event in Jewish medieval history, the expulsion of the Jews from Spain in 1492. By the middle of the sixteenth century communities of Spanish immigrants had sprung up, mainly in Jerusalem and Safed, centred around sages who composed some of the classics of Jewish lore and who devoted their lives to 'working' for the speedy coming of the Messiah by living in holiness in the Holy Land.

It was a common belief that the Jewish community of Palestine was an élite drawn from the Jewish people in exile. The Jews of the Holy Land with their prayers and religious acts were believed to be nearer to God. These ideas attained particular impetus in the sixteenth century. They were related to the ancient Jewish concept which envisaged a few chosen men in each community who spend their time in study and prayer and are wholly or partly supported by the community and hereby elevated the whole of the Palestinian community to the status of the religious élite of world Jewry.

Economically speaking, this religious ideal meant that the Jews in Palestine were totally dependent on Jewry in the *diaspora*. This support was very similar to the giving of alms in other religious societies where the giver did not consider himself superior or self-satisfied, nor did the receiver feel grateful or inferior in accepting support. Each party regarded itself as fulfilling a religious duty. This support was as institutionalized as it was ideological. Funds were usually collected by men of eminence and religious prestige, often famous rabbis sent from Palestine. For their part the communities abroad often made systematic collections even without prodding from the recipients. In Palestine the money was appropriated not so much according to the needs of the families as in keeping with the religious status of its head.

This system functioned virtually unchanged until well into the twentieth century. However, important internal modifications were made from the late eighteenth century onwards. Religious developments in the Jewish centres of Russia and Poland brought in their wake a stream of Jewish immigrants from Eastern Europe. Although these were basically motivated by the same religious reasons as the oriental immigrants, their appearance in Jerusalem and Safed marked a change. The communities became more heterogeneous and diversified into European (or *Ashkenazi*) communities and oriental (or *Sephardi*) communities, the latter being more homogeneous than the former. Every *Ashkenazi* immigrant group organized itself according to its European town or origin, and its appeals for economic support were mainly directed to its home town.

More basic changes were introduced around 1830, when several upper-class Western European Jews (such as Sir Moses Montefiore and Adolphe Crémieux began to advocate a more productive Jewish economy. At first these efforts were mainly directed towards religious activities, such as the setting up of printing presses (for religious books), but later they also included attempts to set up primary services such as flour mills and even the beginnings of agricultural production. All these services were connected with religious ritual and could thus be justified on religious grounds.

By 1870 two periodicals existed in Jerusalem, one of them openly agitating for productivization. In the same year the *Alliance Israélite Universelle* founded an agricultural school near Jaffa. A modern secular school was set up by German Jews in Jerusalem and, though promptly banned by the rabbis, it nonetheless found pupils. In 1878 the first agricultural colony was established in Petah Tikvah.

During the nineteenth and early twentieth centuries immigration of the traditional type continued, consisting especially of those who literally fled from the ancient Jewish communities of Europe which, they felt, were disintegrating. They hoped to find, in Jerusalem, a last bastion of traditionalism, but were paradoxically already affected by the economic life and ideas of

8

the modern world. Thus, in the end, they strengthened the tendencies towards economic modernization and were prominent in the Old Yishuv's colonizing ventures.

However, the Old Yishuv still lagged way behind the mainstream of the European nineteenth century; and with the beginnings of the nationalist aliyot, the gulf between the Old and New Yishuv became clear.

The Basic Characteristics of the Modern Aliyot

The aliyot to Palestine took place simultaneously with the major Jewish migrations of the late nineteenth century which led to the establishment of the Jewish communities in the US, the Dominions, and Latin America. A brief comparison of the aliyot to Palestine with the wider Jewish immigrations may provide a helpful starting point for analysis.

Until the 1920's the various aliyot to Palestine were of little numerical significance. From 1880 to 1930 they comprised no more than 4 per cent of total Jewish migration. It was only after 1930, and the imposition of severe restrictions on immigration into most Western countries, that the aliyot mounted to more than 50 per cent. From the beginning, however, they exhibited special and, sometimes, unique characteristics.

Before 1930 immigrants consisted mainly of young unmarried people or of young couples without children or parents. They did not constitute, contrary to the general trend of Jewish migration, whole communities or even family groups. These characteristics were most pronounced before the First World War and in the early 'twenties but tended to persist throughout the 'thirties.

The nature of the aliyot changed only in the late 'thirties and 'forties, with the stream of refugees from Nazi persecution.

As mentioned, immigrant groups were composed mainly of younger people, often high school pupils, university students or 'externs', who had decided not to undertake their chosen careers. They displayed, in many ways, the characteristics of a young 'intelligentsia'. Most of them came from economically stable backgrounds and from families who, though still attached to traditional Jewish life, did not oppose more modern trends. They tended, on the contrary, to encourage their children to study at secular schools and universities. There was relatively little friction in these families between the older and the younger generation on the question of religion versus secularism.

Ideological formulations in general Jewish migration groups usually tended to concentrate on the problems of absorption in the new society and attempted to justify, explain, and to some extent alleviate the process of adjustment.[1]

---

[1] Only the Bundists and some of the territorialists attempted to give more thorough ideological guidance, but their influence in shaping and forging the waves of immigrants was very small.

Only in the Zionist movement did ideologies precede the actual migration or 'transplantation' and guide the initial stages of settlement in the new country. Although a great deal of the pioneering ideology crystallized only as a result of the immigrants' encounter with Palestinian reality, it was firmly rooted in the ideological orientations developed by the Zionist movement in the *diaspora*.

The ideology of rebellion played an important part in the aliyot to Palestine and the structure of the immigrant groups. The 'rebels' usually formed themselves into small, cohesive groups, connected by various informal and semi-formal ties to associations, social movements, and political parties, in which they prepared themselves, both ideologically and socially, for aliya. In these groups they underwent also training in the various vocations, which they wanted to follow in Palestine concentrating on agricultural training. The various *hachshara* (preparation) groups, through which practical experience in communal living was gained, were the most outstanding example of this. However, there was also preparation for work in industry, building, or the professions. The groups dissociated themselves sharply from the surroundings and adopted a new and intensive mutual social identification. This was shown in the immigrants' primary group relations, aiming at a new social reality. Although they were in fact only small, highly cohesive groups of young people lacking definite social roles or institutional commitments, they had everything needed to make them the nuclei of newly established, institutional frameworks. They were similar to various Central European rebel youth movements in that they tended to dissociate themselves from adult society. Unlike those movements, however, their rebellion was not nullified by the necessity to compromise with that society as they became older. Owing to the migratory nature and direction of their rebellion, they could detach themselves from the existing territorial and institutional structure and realize their rebellion fully by creating an entirely new one. We find in them the peculiar combination of a rebel movement with a migratory and colonizing trend, a combination which gave rise to a predisposition to change in all the main directions of social activity – economic, cultural, and political.

These characteristics distinguish the main aliyot from the usual trend of modern Jewish migrations and from modern European migrations in general. They were most clearly shown between the 1920's and up to the first half of the 1940's, particularly in the various pioneer groups which turned towards agricultural settlement, the 'conquest of labour' and the rejuvenation of Hebrew culture and education. While it would be a gross exaggeration to suggest that all immigrants who came to Palestine during this period showed these special characteristics, there is no doubt that the most active, those who left their mark on the whole country, did so. It should also be remembered that throughout this period a selective process was in operation in Palestine, by virtue of which those who differed most from the general pattern tended

10

to leave the country. Only in the late 'thirties the demographic composition and the social orientation of the immigrants tended to become increasingly similar to the general pattern of Jewish migration. More and more older married couples with children came, often in clusters of family groups or parts of communities. Their basic motive being the achievement of economic adjustment, or freedom from persecution. Yet they were absorbed within a social setting created by the pioneering groups.

Brief Description of the Main Aliyot

Following is a numerical analysis of the various waves of immigration since 1882:

	Years	Immigrants
First Aliya	1882–1903	20,000–30,000
Second Aliya	1904–1914	35,000–40,000
Third Aliya	1919–1923	35,000
Fourth Aliya	1924–1931	82,000
Fifth Aliya	1932 and onwards up to 1948	265,000 (up to the end of 1944)

The first aliya was initiated by the first Zionist movement, *Hovevei Zion*, in Russia and Romania, which had the wave of pogroms which flooded South Russia in 1881 as its main driving power. These immigrants looked on land settlement as a primary condition for the rejuvenation of the Jewish people. During this period of the first Jewish agricultural settlements, such as Petah Tikvah, Rishon LeZion, Rosh Pina, Zikhron Yaakov, and Hedera, were established and the foundations of the Yishuv were laid. The second aliya consisted mainly of members of various Zionist labour groups in Russia, who had become disappointed with the social reform movement there (in which they had taken an active part) and with the October Revolution of 1905 which ended in pogroms. They came to Palestine in a period of crisis both in that country and in the Zionist movement. Although 'workers' were in the minority during the second aliya, it is nonetheless considered as a labour immigration, since the workers' initiative and energy changed the whole structure of the Jewish community. New methods of land settlement were adopted, and the foundation was laid for the whole structure of the labour movement in Palestine. It was during this period that the World Zionist Organization started work in Palestine (1908), and the first mixed farming villages were established. This period also witnessed the beginning of urban development. The foundations were laid for the all-Jewish town of Tel Aviv (1909) and here and there even rudimentary beginnings of industry could be found.

The third aliya began while the First World War was still raging. This was in 1917 after the Balfour Declaration, which the Jewish world interpreted as the creation of a new start towards the establishment of the Zionist ideal. In this aliya, the pioneering element predominated. It consisted of young people who had been trained through the *Halutz* (pioneer) organizations prior to their departure for Palestine and who were ready and willing to do any work the country might require of them, no matter how hard.

The fourth aliya, which began in 1924, was partly actuated by improved economic conditions in Palestine, which made the absorption of further immigrants possible, and partly by the worsening economic position of the Jewish community in Poland, which was caused by the Polish Government's policy of eliminating Jews from many trades. The main factor in this immigration was middle class with small means and most of them settled in the towns and entered commerce or industry, or became artisans. However, if account be taken of the absolute number of immigrants, the pioneer element predominated this period also. This aliya was followed by a considerable exodus from Palestine as a result of the acute economic crisis which broke out during that period influx.

The fifth aliya began in 1929, but did not reach its peak until 1932 when a large volume of immigration was resumed which resulted in great economic prosperity. Up to 1935 about 150,000 Jews – many of them from Germany – came in; they brought considerable capital and helped to develop industry, trade and agriculture on a large scale. From 1936–40, a period of severe troubles in the country, immigration was limited by the Government, and only about 100,000 Jews, including about 15,000 'illegal' immigrants, entered.

3

The Major Stages in the Institutional Development of the Yishuv – Specific Characteristics of the Major Aliyot

This chapter will deal with a detailed analysis of the impact of the major modern aliyot on the institutional structure of the Yishuv.

The First Aliya

The year 1882 is usually given as the beginning of the modern Jewish migratory movement which brought millions of Jews from Russia to the West. The immediate cause of this movement was the anti-Semitism of Tsarist Russia which culminated in the May Laws of 1881. Most of the emigrants made their way to America and Western Europe, but a small minority (twenty-five to thirty thousand in the course of twenty years) came to Palestine. The best-known of these were the Biluists whose members founded the colony of Gedera. Considerable colonizing went on in the early 1880's when Rishon LeZion, Zikhron Yaakov, Ekron and Yessod Hamaala were established.

The new settlers faced great economic difficulties and could not, at that time, obtain any real and continuous help from the various Zionist societies in Europe. Only at a later stage did Baron Rothschild come to their aid with a comprehensive programme administered by Jewish-French officials who were brought to the country for this purpose and dealt with all administrative details in the fields of finance, agricultural planning, and even culture. They based the economy of the new colonies almost exclusively on vineyards, after experiments in various branches of fruit growing and processing had failed.

These officials were, in the main, lower middle class, assimilated French Jews, unacquainted with the nationalist ideals of Eastern European Jews whom they generally considered uncouth and provincial. At the same time the settlers were more or less at the mercy of these officials and had no means of public control over them. With administration in the hands of the Baron's officials and agricultural work carried out by hired Arab labour, the nationalist ideals of the Biluists were practically stifled and only survived in settlements like Gedera, which were not administered by the Baron. Even religion and education were deprived of their ideological impetus, as a largely French-Levantine school system developed which put but little stress on Hebrew culture. Efforts made to gain some independence failed, and the more independent elements and many of the younger generation left the Baron's settlements.

A second wave of immigrants came in 1891, and the colonies of Rehovot and Hadera were established with strong financial backing given by Russian Jewry. Thus Baronic bureaucracy was less marked and development somewhat more autochthonic. In 1900 Rothschild transferred his interests to the Jewish Colonization Association (ICA). Though this too was basically a philanthropic organization with no specific nationalistic interests, its public character and more restricted resources made its officialdom more prone to control. In its many ventures ICA also attempted innovation in agricultural and social planning. Especially noteworthy among these were the farms it set up for agricultural training. At the end of the first aliya the stagnation resulting from Rothschild's policy had given way to limited change. Nevertheless, the agricultural population was demoralized, rates of emigration were very high, and the overall picture a dismal one.

At the same time, however, there were marked developments in the urban sector. The Jewish population in Jaffa, previously quite insignificant, had grown considerably and was almost exclusively of the New Yishuv, unlike the traditional elements that made up the population of the old holy cities. The lack of an old-established Jewish element in Jaffa gave its new population a totally novel character and Jewish Jaffa became, in a way, the social and cultural centre of the new colonies. The town absorbed many who had initially tried and failed to settle on the land. Palestinian branches of various pre-Zionist and Zionist nationalist organizations were set up in Jaffa, the most important being the establishment of the first office of the Anglo-Palestine Company (later Bank) in 1903. Meanwhile many local institutions such as a library (1885) and a hospital (1891) had also been established. The development of a number of Jewish quarters drawn from those previously scattered throughout the old Arab city, and with a flourishing modern Hebrew culture, began in the 'eighties. The immigration of 1891 also brought professional and commercial elements which achieved an important position in Jaffa's economic life. The beginnings of citrus exports at the end of the 'nineties enhanced this group's standing. Jewish Jaffa also became an important development centre for a secular Hebrew school system, very distinct from the 'French' character of the Baron's colonies.

Although considerable simultaneous expansion took place in Jerusalem during these years, the town nevertheless retained its traditional character.

The Second Aliya – Introduction

Although the first aliya showed at least some characteristics of an embryonic social movement aimed at continuous expansion, it mostly reached a stage of potential – and even actual – stagnation within a period of twenty years.

One of the basic manifestations of this stagnation was the very rapid normalization and stabilization of the immigrants' economic and social structure. Had the trends of the first aliya continued, they would have led to a total absorption of the colonists as merely another small, stagnant privileged group within the pluralistic setting of Ottoman-Arab society.

The importance of these factors becomes apparent when we compare them with the developments of the second aliya which constitutes one of the most decisive and formative stages in the history of the Yishuv.

The importance of the second aliya is reflected in the fact that ever since their arrival its members were prominently active in the affairs of the Yishuv. This prominence continued well into the first stages of statehood, with members of the second aliya represented in the various élites but especially in the political élite of the country, in percentages out of all proportion to their actual members. The ideology forged by them has, moreover, become the starting point of the social and institutional transformation of the Yishuv, while the various attitudes towards the second aliya still pervade the social and political atmosphere in Israel.

The influence of the second aliya was, of course, not due to numerical strength – it consisted originally of a small group (or groups) of not more than ten thousand persons, many of whom left the country after a short time.

It would be misleading to assume that the members of the second aliya could have by themselves achieved anything essentially different from the first aliya under the conditions prevailing in Ottoman Palestine. Events that occurred during and after the First World War – the breakdown of the Ottoman Empire, the Balfour Declaration, the giving of the Mandate and the changes that took place in the structure of the Zionist Organizations in Europe and the United States – were the key factors that enabled them to grasp the institutional, political, and economic opportunities for more dynamic development.

But the significance of the second aliya lies in the fact that its members were ready and able – in conjunction with general world Zionist leadership – to seize the opportunities created in order to develop new social and political realities.

The ideals and organizational patterns created by them were not only maintained and perpetuated in the social structure of the Yishuv, but were to guide and shape its further development. Although the importance often attributed to the second aliya is exaggerated, the very prevalence of this myth constitutes an important aspect of Israeli society.

Unlike the first aliya, members of the second never aspired to normalization as peasants or workers. Instead, they considered themselves as pioneers, as pathfinders not interested in their own immediate settlement but only in the future of the entire national community.

In order to understand this vital aspect of the second aliya it is necessary to delve into its background.

Social Origins and Ideological Orientations of Second Aliya Groups

The second aliya was influenced by several factors: the Revolution of 1905, the anti-Jewish riots which were at that time part of the revolutionary and anti-revolutionary fervour in Russia, and the disappointment of part of the Jewish youth regarding the possiblity of solving the problem of the Jews in the *diaspora*. This disappointment was due to the realization that even the revolutionary movements did not put an end to anti-Semitism or anti-Semitic outbreaks and that, in fact, the revolutionary groups often abetted – if they did not outspokenly encourage – such outbursts. Many of them thus concluded that no solution to their specific Jewish problems could be found through socialist revolution or reform. This conclusion was reached fully only by a handful of students and intellectuals who were caught in the mesh of revolutionary activity, continuous economic expansion, and the consequent increase of assimilationist trends within the Jewish community. They conflicted with many of the official trends within the Jewish community and the Zionist movement, particularly where such trends aspired to participate in the general democratic movement in Russia and in the Austro-Hungarian Empire in the hope that the Jewish community might be enabled to take its place as one of the autonomous communities.

These attituudes were greatly intensified by the internal crisis that enveloped the Zionist Organization after the death of Herzl when dreams for an easy and quick diplomatic solution to the Palestinian problem through attainment of the Charter from the Ottoman Empire were shattered. The movement further underwent an acute crisis in the wake of the Uganda proposals which found the majority of the Russian and Eastern Zionists, and especially of the younger intelligentsia, in sharp opposition to Herzl.

Under the leadership of Wolfsohn, Herzl's successor as President, the Zionist Organization had to find new meaning for its activities. Energetic efforts were therefore directed towards attracting new members and to infusing new meaning into the colonizing work in Palestine, which had been somewhat neglected during the early period of diplomatic negotiations.

These new efforts curbed, to a certain extent, the resentment felt among young intellectuals in Russia and Austria against the official, apathetic attitude of the movement.

In 1905 groups of these young settlers began to arrive in Palestine in search of a new solution to the Jewish problem. Their fires of rebellion were fanned by the reality of Jewish Palestine at that time – especially the Baronial settlements and colonies and the incipient urban centres in Jerusalem and Petah Tikvah. The young rebels saw these as stagnant and negative symbols of

16

quick and easy settlement and of complacent satisfaction with the existing social structure in Palestine. For them this could well spell the end of further progress. Rebellion was further aroused by daily encounters and clashes with the older settlers to whom the new immigrants turned for work. The veterans saw in the new arrivals an alien and dangerous element.

Naturally these pioneers of the second aliya could not compare in terms of economic or organizational power, knowledge or resources with the older settlers – it was only in the forging of ideas that they could come into their own.

Their attempts to find organizational solutions to practical problems were made in conjunction with their ideological orientations, and not as a consequence of the daily, concrete problems of adaption to the existing environment. This approach reached out to the broader problems of collectivity whose vanguard the groups felt themselves to be.

Even the most realistic tasks which these groups took upon themselves – the finding of appropriate conditions of work as agricultural labourers, the establishment of the Hashomer defence organization, or the initiation of various mutual-aid activities would not have made much practical sense. In the given circumstances these concrete problems could have been better solved by finding some *modus vivendi* with the older settlers or with the various bodies of the Zionist organization. This ideological attitude, which embraced even the most menial of their realistic tasks, makes sense only when seen in the light of wider and more radical problems. This also explains the fiery debates, recorded in many printed pages, that raged among the various components of the second aliya – the *Hapoel Hatzair* and the *Poalei Zion*, and between them and the Zionist officialdom and the older settlers.

These discussions have to be viewed as basic disputes about the ultimately correct solution to fundamental social and cultural problems for a future society and not as solutions to the concrete problems of the existing groups.

The Image of the Pioneer (Halutz)

The combination of ideological and potentially practical attributes produced the second aliya's major cultural creation: the image of the ideal type of the pioneer. The contours of this type were mainly forged during this period. Later formulations, although more articulate and subject to much dispute and interpretation, all drew upon the less coherent but much more vivid image as it developed in the period of the second aliya.

Common factors inherent in the 'pioneer' type include first and foremost an element of social and personal self-sacrifice. The pioneer is a man ready to deprive himself and to live the life of an ascetic. This deprivation is however not for its own sake – although very often asceticism became a very strong secondary element – but for the sake of performing a task important to the community. Hence the pioneer's lack of interest in direct, immediate rewards of position, wages, material comforts, or even political power.

The second major aspect of the pioneer image is its strong emphasis on agricultural work – or on manual work in general – and on non-exploitation of others. This is seen as an essential, particularly in the philosophy of A.D. Gordon, for creating, through physical labour, a 'new' human being and a new national entity.

Emphasis therefore tends to be placed on the importance of living in a special type of community conducive to the development of the ideal society, envisaged in terms similar to those of the utopian socialists and, to a smaller degree, also of Marxists.

Next to manual work very strong emphasis is placed on self-defence and self-reliance, in short, on the achievement of independence from external protection.

The third point of emphasis is cultural creativity and rejuvenation of the Hebrew language and culture, as expressed in literary, scientific, or semi-scientific activities (such as history or archaeology). Closely related to this is the stress placed on active participation in social and political activities and in the life of the community.

'Self-sacrifice' for the sake of the (future) community underlies the pioneering spirit – the fact that the *Halutz* is an *avant-garde* who goes (in the literary Hebrew meaning of the *Halutz*) *before* the collective.

This futuristic orientation was basically a combination of élite and egalitarian ideologies in that it stresses the equality reigning within the élite groups of pioneers – thus strengthening their sectarian tendencies.

At the same time, however, the wider 'constructivist' orientation in the pioneer image helps it to become a basic focus of personal and collective identity not only for the members of the groups but also for future waves of immigrants.

The asceticism inherent in the pioneer image did not entail an escape from the social world. On the contrary, it was closely related to working for a concrete, albeit, future and as yet unformed, community. The fact that this pioneer ideology was focused on a future society envisaged, yet unachieved, and at the same time represented social ideals and values beyond any given reality, enabled it to transcend situations of 'here and now'.

It was this combination of different elements that provided the most dynamic aspects of the pioneer image and emphasized its strong élitist nature.

There were, however, contradictory possibilities inherent in the strong emphasis on an élite on the one hand and in regarding any given group of pioneers as necessarily representing pioneering values on the other hand.

Tension emerging between the various orientations were likely to become acute once the social structure which they themselves helped to create became more differentiated, and the struggle for power became inevitable. However, none of these tensions developed fully in the period of the second aliya.

Organizational and Institutional Developments during the Second Aliya

Fundamentally the second aliya was composed of a mass of sectarian groups of young people attempting to forge new symbols and find new solutions to broader social and national problems, who saw their own practical activities as symbolic expressions of such solutions. Their own attempts to set up various organizational and institutional frameworks were regarded mainly as experiments in expressing the basic problems of the emerging future society.

Paradoxically, this was why they were not really ready or willing to implement fully any organizational and institutional forms or to endow them with fully symbolic value and legal status.

The history of the Yishuv's development shows that the second aliya period was that period in which social, political, and organizational activities were most dominated by the creation and interpretation of values.

Nonetheless, many institutional and organizational nuclei were established – some of the sectarian 'pioneering' groups themselves and some in conjunction with other groups in the Yishuv.

Among the organizations set up was the rudimentary defence organization *Hashomer* (1909), comprised of a few dozen workers. Considering its very restricted practical duties, the symbols and slogans of *Hashomer* assumed a surprisingly broad national character.

An Information Bureau established in 1909 was designed as an elementary labour exchange. The appearance of *Hapoel Hatzair* (1907) and *Ahdut* (1910) heralded the development of periodical journals. Also established at about this time were *Avoda* – a forerunner of the *Work Battalion* (1909–10); *Kupat Poalei Eretz Yisrael*, the workers' fund (1909); *Misrad Haavoda*, forerunner of the labour exchange (1913); the organizations of workers of Judaea and Galilee (1911); and the *United Committee of Palestinian Workers*, a possible nucleus of the future *Histadrut* (1913). Some attempts at a general assembly representing the Yishuv as a whole were also made during this period.

However, the most outstanding organizational development of the period was the establishment of the first *kvutza* (collective settlement) in Degania and the nucleus of a moshav (co-operative settlement) in Merhavia.

This type of pioneering, destined to become one of the major symbols of the 'right' way of life, was not at first conceived in such terms. It was seen as a solution to the problem of how to organize some form of settlement for young people with strong socialist and nationalist aspirations, without capital and with little experience and know-how – a settlement which would

19

at the same time fulfil their aspirations for a decent standard of living and of cultural life within the reality of Ottoman Palestine.

Although the *kvutza* was upheld as an important way of life, some such as A. D. Gordon, who preached the religion of labour, saw, as a semi-prophetic vision, that the general attitude to the initial form of the *kvutza* was rather one of experimentation. It was only later, during the third aliya, that the more sacrosanct attitudes to the kibbutz and *kvutza* tended to develop.

As mentioned, an embryonic form of co-operative settlement, developed under the guidance of Franz Oppenheimer, was established in Merhavia. But this did not, in itself, become a pattern for continuity; and the moshavim that developed later – from the Nahalal on – were not inspired by it to any great extent.

Another extremely interesting development that took place during this period was the influx of Jews from Yemen. Sh. Yavnieli, one of the leaders of the second aliya, went to the Yemen and returned with many immigrants who formed the main nucleus of the 'old' Yemenite settlement in the Yishuv.

Beside the somewhat romantic idea of the ingathering of far-flung brothers one of the important motives for this activity was the importation of ('real' proletarian) elements more accustomed to work in conditions such as those in Palestine.

Institutional Developments in the Urban Sectors during the Second Aliya – Tel Aviv, Education and Health Services

The agricultural pioneers were not the only ones to establish institutional and organizational nuclei during the period of the second aliya. The first urban nucleus of Tel Aviv was established in 1910 by a group of old-established Jaffa residents, led by Meir Dizengoff. These people were mainly middle class and some had immigrated with the first aliya. About one quarter of this project was financed by the settlers themselves, with additional help from the Zionist Organization and various banking institutions. These residents of new Tel Aviv continued, at first, to work in their businesses, offices, or schools in Jaffa. It took some years until Tel Aviv lost its purely suburban and residential character and saw the beginnings of various professional and economic organizations which also developed in Jerusalem and, to a lesser extent, in Petah Tikvah.

However, the most dynamic development of that period was, no doubt, in the educational field with the establishment of the Hebrew Gymnasium (secondary school) in Jerusalem and the Herzlia Gymnasium and Levinski Teachers' Training College in Tel Aviv. Diverse Hebrew nursery and elementary schools had already been established by then with the backing of external agencies. Education was an important field in which many ideological battles were waged, most outstanding among them being the battle of the languages.

It was a crucial issue eventually won by the Hebraists whether instru should be given in Hebrew or in German, as the *Ezra*, the German-J philanthropic organization wanted. Thus the establishment of the H and the other gymnasia were not isolated events but rather the crown a much wider cultural effort.

Certain paradoxical characteristics of great importance for an standing of the whole institutional development and structure of this emerged among the various educational and cultural groups.

The new educational aims were directed not at the transmission of cultural heritage but at creating new cultural elements of Jewish (though mostly in a non-religious form) with the best in universal, heritage.

Moreover, while obviously of benefit to the younger generation of Palestine, the increased educational facilities now available reall rather beyond this group at an educational pattern for much wider potentially all Jewish youth in the *diaspora*.

Thus the educational system developing clearly shared the pred features of the pioneering ideology. It was also within this context image arose of the teacher as a 'cultural' innovator and pioneer.

Similar incipient developments took place in the fields of he medicine. First attempts were made to establish national medicir form of a workers' sick fund. The image of the pioneer doctor jected as distinct from the normal family doctor.

Parallel with these developments afforestation projects were u by the Zionist Organization, land was purchased through the Jewisl Fund, and banking activities were directed at helping the differen settlement.

The Future Orientation of Second Aliya Groups – Developme Institutional Nuclei

The developments enumerated perhaps best epitomize one o differences between the institutional and organizational struct first and second aliyot.

Instead of planning exclusively for the needs of the existing emphasis during the second aliya was placed on developments fe with special stress on ideological aspects.

Contrary to the first aliya this orientation stressed the dev broad functional institutions – defence, education, and, to colonization, and health – designed for an, as yet, non-existent offering only inadequate services to the needs of the existing co is significant that attempts to establish an overall territorial of the Yishuv failed completely.

Some of the emerging patterns proved to be of great importance for the future institutional development of the Yishuv and in many ways foretold this development. Although, for instance, the actual number of settlements established by the second aliya was, in fact, smaller than that founded by the first aliya, their relationship with the Zionist Organization and other colonizing agencies was of a very different nature and was also an indicator of future possibilities. In both periods colonization was necessarily dependent – in terms of capital, manpower, and political protection – on external resources. In both periods the initial providers of these resources were the various bodies of the Zionist organizations. However, in the first aliya most of these functions were taken over after a short period by the Baronial administration. In the second aliya they were carried out by the Zionist Organization and by its representative in Palestine, Dr A. Ruppin; by the Land Settlement Company (*Hevrat Hachsharat Hayishuv*) and by the Anglo-Palestine Bank. Dr Ruppin's conception of his functions was much more sympathetic to the settlers and their national aspirations than the Baronial administration had been. Admittedly there was no lack of tension between the pioneers and Dr Ruppin and other officials – especially as Dr Ruppin was on the whole indifferent to the socialistic aspirations of the settlers. Nonetheless, the settlers were no longer objects of a paternalistic administration – well intentioned and generous though it might be. They were instead active members of parties or groups comprised within the very organization whose officials administered the colonizing activities in Palestine – the Zionist Organization.

Because of this – and because of their strong ideological concepts – they were always ready to fight out their differences with officialdom not only through personal contacts but also through political propaganda and pressure within the framework of the global Zionist Organization common to them all.

Relations among Second Aliya Groups – Nuclei of a Federative Structure

Despite the relatively small number of people involved in the second aliya, many groups and parties – or rather nuclei of social movements – arose. The most outstanding of these were *Hapoel Hatzair, Poalei Zion,* the various professional organizations of labourers in Galilee, Judaea, and Samaria, and later *Haavoda,* the separatist organization of the veteran bourgeois farmers of the first aliya, which advocated a rudimentary synthesis of agriculture and collectivism.

In their ideological disputes as well as, to some extent, in their personal relationships, most of the second aliya groups exhibited all the sectarian intensity and exclusivity of extreme social movements. In spite of their common aims each believed that it had the unique solution to all major problems, and the various groups' antagonism towards each other was only

somewhat mitigated by the fact that all of them were dependent on external resources for the realization of their common aims and were therefore forced to act within the common framework of the Zionist Organization.

This essential co-operation in turn helped to shape the federative nature of the Zionist Organization. Help was allocated on a parallel though not always equal basis, thus enabling each group to remain largely autonomous, while co-operating in some common tasks.

This willingness to co-operate on essential issues was furthered by the basically positive ideology of each group. They wanted not only to establish the right doctrine but also to carry out constructive colonizing work and to see themselves as forerunners of wider national colonization and development. Further, their revolutionary zeal could not be directed at the overthrow of a − non-existent − political regime, but had to be aimed at the development of new social and economic forms. Their need for capital and additional manpower tempered the relationship between the pioneering groups and the various budding educational, medical, and banking organizations and institutions which developed along much the same lines.

The officials of these institutions and of the major urban groups, differed socially and individually from the pioneers. More akin to the older settlers, they were mostly quiet professionals and businessmen. Yet they were close to the pioneering spirit in that they shared many of its future aims and saw their own roles in a parallel, though not identical, way. Serving as a social bridge between the pioneering groups and the older settlers of the first aliya and the older Yishuv, their activities − especially in the cultural field − gave them a common denominator with the pioneers. The very fact that such organizational nuclei existed and that they tended to emphasize common goals shared by most sectors of the Yishuv, weakened the exclusiveness of the pioneering groups. This also applied to some of the common political activities within the Yishuv − especially in relations with the Turkish authorities or on the establishment of Jewish schools.

Another factor in cementing relations between the different bodies was the migration to and from Palestine during the period of the second aliya. This migration was caused by internal political reasons, friction with the Turkish authorities, or personal reasons.

The fact that rebellion against their former background was connected with territorial transplantation and severance from their families, and that this rebellion was often in the name of ideals shared − though less intensively − by their parents, mitigated the tensions between the pioneers and their families and enabled social relations on a broader plane and, in turn, also weathered the totalistic orientation of the pioneering groups.

It is doubtful, however, whether any of the new, embryonic institutional and organizational forms were strong enough to create conditions in which future developments could materialize. Such conditions were only created by the more sweeping external events after the First World War. The great strength of the second aliya period lay in the fact that, once new patterns and opportunities had been created, internal ideas were strong enough to give guidance to new developments and to leave their imprint on most of the later ones.

It is this combination of strong ideology and potential realism that contained the real promise of the second aliya. Its whole potential, as well as its problems, fully developed only in the later, mandatory period.

The Mandate–Its Organizational and Institutional Framework–The Third and Fourth Aliyot

With the end of the First World War and the establishment of the British Mandate over Palestine, incorporating the promises of the Balfour Declaration, the Yishuv entered on a new period of development. If the period of the second aliya was the period of ideological emphasis, the Mandate ushered in a period of stress on the practical implementation of the major goals of the Yishuv and on the development of its main institutional frameworks. This phase began with the third aliya (1919–23) and continued until the establishment of the State of Israel.

The social and institutional history of the Yishuv throughout this period was mainly shaped by the interaction between four basic elements. Firstly the Mandate and Government; secondly the different organizations of the World Zionist Organization and the Jewish community in Palestine; thirdly the various waves of immigrants to Palestine; and lastly the ideological and institutional framework established during the periods of the first and especially of the second aliya.

We shall start with a brief description of the interrelationship between the mandatory government, the Jewish Agency (or the Zionist Organization with the establishment of the Jewish Agency in 1929) and the other institutions of the Jewish community in Palestine – especially the *Vaad Leumi* (National Council) and the various bodies of local government.

The mandatory framework encompassed both the Jewish and Arab sectors. Within the Arab sector, however, no equivalent of the Jewish Agency emerged (although later an equivalent of the *Vaad Leumi* in the form of the Higher Arab Council developed) and the general extent of internal organizational development was smaller. In the Jewish sector internal organizations developed both in the form of the *Vaad Leumi*, which was elected by most of the adult members of the Jewish community, and in the form of numerous local government bodies.

The *Vaad Leumi* was a continuation of attempts to form a general organization representing the whole Yishuv which had hitherto failed. During the Palestine Campaign of 1918, the foundations were laid towards paving the way for Jewish representation under the new regime. During the ensuing mandatory period general elections were held every few years, whereby the *Knesset Israel*, as the organized Yishuv was formally known, elected its representative to the *Asefat Hanivharim* (the 'elected assembly') which, in turn, chose the *Vaad Leumi* as its governing body. In 1927 the mandatory power accorded the *Knesset Israel* official recognition as a voluntary body representing the Jewish population of Palestine. This representation was qualified only by the refusal of the Old Yishuv to register in the *Knesset Israel*, thus formally becoming a body distinct from the Yishuv.

In time there developed a more or less clear-cut division of labour between these different institutions and organizations. The various national institutions of the Yishuv, the Zionist movement, and the Jewish Agency dealt mostly with the following matters: (1) development of Jewish colonization, both rural and urban; (2) arrangements for immigration into Palestine from various countries of the *diaspora*; (3) maintenance and development of Jewish defence – the illegal *Hagana*, various semi-legal and legal police groups and, during the Second World War, mobilization in the British Army; (4) development of an active 'foreign' policy – mainly with regard to the mandatory government and the League of Nations – with the object of increasing the scope of immigration and colonization, to maintain the political autonomy of the Yishuv and, ultimately, to create the Jewish State; (5) maintenance of an autonomous system of education; (6) maintenance of an autonomous religious organization; and (7) maintenance of some social services, especially a wide network of health services. Significantly, the first four tasks were primarily in the hands of the Zionist Organization and the Jewish Agency, while the others were mostly in the hands of the *Vaad Leumi* or of the various Jewish municipalities. In this way the fact was emphasized that the Yishuv itself was, at any time, only one stage in the constant development of the Zionist enterprise.

The various routine tasks of administering the country and maintaining communication services, police, a legal system, and, to some extent, local government were mostly in the hands of the mandatory government. Tension developed between the government and the Jewish national institutions both on major issues of policy (immigration, etc.) as well as in spheres where activities overlapped. As the Jewish institutions, and especially the Jewish Agency, dealt mostly with 'colonizing' tasks which were strongly characterized by their connexion with future development, the Jewish institutions had no great dealings with routine economic and administrative matters nor with the maintenance of order. The only major exceptions to this were the Jewish municipalities and the allocation of the various funds for colonization and 'constructive' works.

Financial resources of the Jewish institutions were derived mainly from voluntary contributions by Jews all over the world and in Palestine. The main moral and social basis of these institutions was the readiness of most groups in Palestine to accept their political authority and to co-operate in the voluntary participation of common tasks such as in the defence force (*Hagana*), in colonization work, and in various types of passive resistance to the mandatory power. The national institutions could also rely on the Zionist movement abroad and on Gentile and Jewish public opinion as a potential source of influence, if not of direct power.

The most salient characteristics of these institutions were quickly developed in the late 'twenties and it was within their framework that the third to fifth aliyot found their feet in Palestine.

Developments during the Third and Fourth Aliyot

The third aliya, which was similar in many respects to the second aliya, consisted mainly of young proletarian pioneers from Eastern Europe, deeply influenced by the impact of revolutionary social change.

In addition to establishing a large number of agricultural settlements of both the kibbutz and moshav type, mainly in the Jezreel Valley, they also began the colonization of more mountainous areas. The pioneers were very active in road and rail building as well as in the draining of marsh areas situated mainly in the north of the country, and eventually turning these activities into the epic expression of an ideal.

The *Histadrut* (General Federation of Labour) was established in 1920 and its various subsidiary organizations and settlements were also developed during this period. Among these, brief mention should be made of *Solel Boneh*, the general construction firm, *Hasneh*; a general insurance company; the Workers' Bank; the Centre for Co-operation, and *Kupat Holim*, the health insurance organization.

At the same time the urban sectors developed continuously, and a proletariat began to emerge in the towns. Tel Aviv and Haifa grew steadily, as did the new urban and semi-urban quarters and independent town units. Some growth was also maintained in the earlier type of moshava, or private village.

The economy of the Yishuv continued to grow and diversify. Mixed farming developed steadily, in contrast to the single product farms (at first vines, later citrus) of the first aliya. In the industrial sector, factories were established as against the small workshops prevailing from pre-colonization times. Thus, electric power plants, a salt factory, grain mills, the Shemen factory for oil products, the Nesher cement plant, and several textile plants were set up. In addition, a large number of smaller but modern factories were established, particularly during the fourth aliya.

Development was hindered by economic crises due to internal and external causes. The most serious crisis (beginning at the end of 1925) was caused by the Polish government's restrictions on the flow of capital to Palestine, by mandatory regulations discouraging capitalist immigration, and by the pace of immigration which was above the abortive capacities of the Yishuv. The building industry was most affected – many firms collapsed, unemployment was high, and for three years (1927–9) emigration exceeded immigration.

The growing development of the economic structure of the Yishuv was given new impetus by the immigration of the fifth aliya in the late 'twenties and the 'thirities. This aliya, which consisted of a new type of immigrant and produced more private and public capital, did much to overcome the difficulties besetting the settlers of the fourth aliya.

Although the pioneering element in this new wave of immigration diminished, it was nevertheless within this period that the workers' groups and organizations gained predominance. To understand this process it is worthwhile analysing the various developments in the 'worker-pioneer' sectors from the third aliya onwards.

Social and Ideological Developments and Colonizing Activities of the Third Aliya

The social and ideological characteristics of the third aliya with its socialist pioneering activities made it in many ways a continuation of the second. However, in terms of concrete social organization and ideological formulation it went far beyond the second aliya. It had a wider popular composition, with a less intellectual tinge – although many intellectual elements participated in it. It was also much more heterogeneous. We find, almost from the beginning, a relatively large variety of pioneering groups, social movements, and parties, many of which had already been organized in the *diaspora*. There arose, for example, the *Gdud Haavoda* (Work Battalion) in which hundreds of pioneers working on the roads of the Tiberias district were organized. Its ideals were to form a community of workers in both town and village who would undertake pioneering tasks by conquering new spheres of work. The *Gdud*, which aimed at economic self-sufficiency, wanted to forge itself into an instrument that would be at the disposal of the Zionist movement. Permeated by socialist idealism, the *Gdud* aimed at equality in consumption and production. It also believed in the establishment of larger settlements capable of developing industrial branches. It thus differed from the Degania-type kibbutz which restricted itself to agricultural work and emphasized the ideal of the small intimate commune where everyone has first hand knowledge of all branches of activity. The *Gdud* eventually founded Ein Harod, the first of the large kibbutzim.

The *Kvutzat Haemek* was another group whose ideals and organization were similar to the *Gdud Haavoda*. Yet a further type of settlement developed with the emergence of the *Hashomer Hatzair* movement. This originated in Poland as a kind of boy scout movement drawing its members who were strongly influenced by radical socialism, from middle-class families. The settlements founded by them had the socialist aggressiveness of the *Gdud Haavoda* but were without its emphasis on the immediate occupational, demographic, and organizational development of the kibbutz. These were relatively small communes which put considerable emphasis on the socio-political goals of the movement. Beginning with kibbutz Beit Alfa, *Hashomer Hatzair*, set up a considerable number of small, radically communal, kibbutzim with strong socialist-Marxist orientation.

During these years of intensive colonization the second aliya also re-organized itself into new settlement communes. Some members merged with new immigrant groups in founding new settlements, while others remained comparatively self-sufficient in the process of settling down. The villages they founded included small and large kibbutzim, as well as the new moshav type of collective.

The differences between the various kibbutz movements were not only socio-ideological but concerned the conception of tasks to be performed – especially with regard to colonization and the creation of a new Jewish community.

As a result of these differences a federation of all kibbutzim was dissolved shortly after its establishment in 1925. A few years later three different kibbutz federations with distinct ideologies and political programmes were founded. They were the *Hakibbutz Hameuhad* which fostered large, open kibbutzim tightly organized in a centralized federation, and *Hakibbutz Haartzi shel Hashomer Hatzair* both of which were founded in 1927. The latter upheld the traditions of the small and autonomous *kvutza*; its autonomy restricted to economic and social affairs. There was complete political and ideological accord between these two federations in matters relating to the overall movement which maintained a democratic centralism.

The third *Hever Hakvutzot* was founded in 1929. It was a federation of the original, non-ideological, autonomous kibbutzim. It was, to some extent, a compromise between the original principles of kibbutz autonomy and opposed to fully crystallized and ritualized ideology. It was recognized, however, that without the support of a youth movement and some repre-sentative organization, kibbutzim of the *Hever Hakvutzot* would lose their élite position to the other organized missionary kibbutz movements.

There was a very real difference in the social atmosphere of the small kibbutzim of the *Hever Hakvutzot* and *Hakibbutz Haartzi* whose average membership per kibbutz in the early 'forties was ninety-three and one hundred and twenty-three members respectively (not including their children, parents or members of *Hachsharot* training at the kibbutz, etc.) and the larger kibbutzim of *Hakibbutz Hameuhad* whose membership averaged two hundred and sixty-four, but allowed for much greater variation (one kibbutz had more than six hundred members by 1942).

Yet another conception of colonization was developed by the founders of the *moshavim* – Nahalal and Kfar Yehezkel – and by their ideologist E. L. Jaffe. They strongly emphasized agricultural pioneering and the peasant family unit as a national and social rejuvenation, but their 'élitist' element was more moderate and put less stress on collectivism as such.

The *moshav ovdim*, like the kibbutz, was located on land owned by the Jewish National Fund (*Keren Kayemet*). But the internal structure of the moshav was distinct from the communal arrangements of the different kibbutzim in which all 'means of production' were owned collectively, all work was collectively arranged, and where even housing, eating, and the raising of children were done on a communal basis.

In the moshav, land was divided equally between the families. Hired labour was banned and the farm planned in such a way that all work could be done by the members of the household. Part of the land, however, remained under common cultivation – and while the families worked their own plots they also had to contribute work to the common land.

Marketing was organized on a co-operative basis, and there were arrangements for mutual aid, provident funds, the provision of services, and usually also for credit facilities and the purchase of equipment and consumer goods.

Certain basic concepts were common to all these movements: All land was 'nationally owned' (i.e. bought by the *Keren Kayemet* and rented to the pioneers) and 'national' capital, collected and allocated through the Zionist Organization and the Histadrut, financed their activities. The workers had no capital, but their ideological commitments made them the only reliable element suitable for the development of national enterprise without considering profits or shirking personal sacrifice.

In the name of these principles the groups fought within the Zionist Organization for greater allocation of funds for colonization through the National Fund against those who claimed that quick colonization of Palestine could best be effected by settlers with private capital.

The Shift from Ideological to Task Orientation during the Third Aliya

The major, main characteristic of the third, as compared with the second, aliya was that, due to changing social circumstances, it was much more goal- and task-orientated, although formulation and crystallization of ideological dogma, discussion on the right type of settlement, or on problems of urban workers, did not abate. However, all these disputes became more geared to concrete tasks. The new approach was also expressed by most of the leaders of the second aliya who later wielded much influence in all the organizations and movements of the third.

This change in emphasis was partly due to the changing circumstances in East and Central Europe and in the Jewish communities and partly to the increased number of immigrants who lent this aliya the contours of a social movement. Many of the broader social movements, like the various *Hechalutz* groups, had already been organized in the *diaspora*.

The new trend was also furthered by changing circumstances in Palestine where the possibilities for concrete activities created by the new political-legal framework of the Mandate was encouraged by the Zionist Organization

Due to this the major pioneer groups changed from sects and discussion groups into *magshim* (attainment) type of movements that dealt not only with ideology per se but also with its translation into practical terms.

During this period the various labour groups and movements had to compete for their place in the emerging society, emphasizing the increasing need for regulated interrelations between the different groups and sectors in the Yishuv.

The Development of 'Private' Sectors during the Third and Fourth Aliyot

As mentioned, the 'private' sector in agriculture, especially in the *moshavot*, developed simultaneously with the collective settlements. Thus, several *moshavot* were established in the Sharon Valley at this time. Moreover, the older settlements of the first aliya progressed and the urban sector expanded greatly, sometimes with the help of the National Institutions. In these years considerable numbers of new agricultural settlements of the private type were set up. In 1922 a private company of American Zionists started work on the new colony of Raanana. In the years following, similar settlements such as Binyamina, Ramatayim, Herzliya, Magdiel and Kfar Hasidim to name only a few were founded. The last two mentioned introduced a new element in the Yishuv. They were villages founded by religious orthodox Zionists of the *Mizrahi* type. The orthodox element had been prominent in the old settlements of the New Yishuv but had been almost non-existent in the second and third aliyot. The older *moshavot* – Rishon LeZion, Petah Tikvah, and Rehovot expanded considerably during these years, both in size and prosperity, Petah Tikvah reaching 5,760 inhabitants in 1927.

The citrus industry grew with the introduction of modern techniques and formed the economic basis of the *moshavot*. Development in the towns was considerable, with Tel Aviv in particular absorbing the greater part of the fourth aliya. The flourishing building industry helped in establishing new towns with private capital – such as Afula, a grandiose project to build a central town for the Jezreel Valley.

This period also saw the organization of the Manufacturers' Association (1925), the central organ of private industry. Soon after its own foundation the Manufacturers' Association set up important subsidiary bodies, such as a bank to help finance new industries, and a central import firm for raw materials. The small manufacturers long in the country and organized as far back as 1909 now ramified their organization and in 1923 established a bank of their own.

These developments continued and became intensified during the 'thirties and early 'forties – the period of the fifth aliya and the Second World War.

The Fifth Aliya

The fifth aliya began in 1932 and had reached 265,000 immigrants at the end of 1944. Its importance lay not only in its numbers – although this gave a very strong impetus to economic and organizational expansion – but in the changing nature of the immigration itself. It constituted an important land-mark in terms of immigration of urban elements and the development of urban sectors and left its imprint on these sectors as well as on the rural economy.

Although the older types of pioneering groups continued throughout the period, the fifth aliya (and partly even as early as the fourth) saw a marked change in the basic motivation of immigration. The clear pioneering-socialist pattern shifted to more accommodating types of motivation.

Perhaps the most important innovation of this period was the acceptance of 'bourgeois' professional standards and occupations within the Yishuv.

The greater part of these immigrants went to the urban centres developing new sectors and new types of economic enterprises. It was at this time that the bigger private industrial concerns like the Ata Textile Plant and several banking institutions were established or expanded.

New types of agricultural settlements developed where the socialist and communal elements were much weaker. In spite of a strong emphasis on the contributions of farming to the national effort, more bourgeois orientations, with the emphasis on private farming, prevailed.

These changes, as well as the numerical growth and the demographic development of the Yishuv, necessitated regulations for the interrelations of the different sectors.

Economic and organizational activities in the Yishuv greatly increased during the period of the Second World War, when the economy of Palestine took on the general features of a war economy. The outcome was a general inflationary trend, full employment, and increasing wage rates. Most import-ant was the increasing self-sufficiency of the Yishuv's economy, which became more and more varied due to the military needs of the Allies. Contrary to the citrus industry which suffered from the temporary loss of European markets, industry developed with other Middle Eastern countries turning to the Yishuv due to the blockade of routes from other countries. Restricted immigration caused a slump in the private building industry. On the other hand, irrigated agriculture grew very fast, the area being worked in 1945 being four times that worked in 1936.

Intensification of External Tensions

It was during the fifth aliya that external political problems intensified to the extent of a gradual breakdown of relations between Jews, Arabs, and the mandatory power. The international situation worsened: the Abyssinian war, the pre-Munich period, and the growth of militant Arab nationalism all contributed to this development. Within Palestine the deterioration was reflected in the riots which started early in 1936 and which intensified the conflict between Arabs and Jews.

The British tried to find various solutions to the Palestine problem. The first of these was that of the Peel Commission, which recommended the division of Palestine into an Arab and a Jewish sovereign state with an enclave in Jerusalem. Due to Arab pressure and the weakness of the British Government, this proposal was shelved and a series of other makeshift proposals – all of them aimed at the restriction of Jewish immigration and colonization – culminated in the White Paper of 1939 which restricted immigration and the transfer of land to Jews. At the time this did much to intensify the antagonism of the Yishuv to the British Government.

The outbreak of the Second World War temporarily shelved the problem and reduced some of the bitterness. The Jewish community participated intensively in the war effort. Over 130,000 volunteers enrolled with the Yishuv authorities at the beginning of hostilities, but the British did not accept these large numbers. Eventually 24,000 volunteers, mainly Hagana members, trained for duty in what were planned to be mixed Arab-Jewish units enrolled in the British Army. Due to the small number of Arab volunteers, however, the Palestinian units were, in fact, almost exclusively Jewish. In September 1944 permission was finally given for the establishment of a purely Jewish-Palestinian Brigade with its own specific, Zionist, emblem.

The end of the war, when the full extent of the holocaust of European Jewry became known, brought an immediate worsening of the conflict between the Yishuv and the British. An intensive struggle over immigration began which, ultimately, gave rise to the series of events culminating in the establishment of the State of Israel. It was then that the intensive struggle over immigration took place, the so-called (by the British) illegal immigration was organized, many such immigrants were brought to the shores of Palestine, 'smuggled' in and settled overnight while other import ships – such as Exodus – were turned back by the British, some back to Europe, most to special camps for them in Cyprus, all of them becoming symbols of the great struggle.

All efforts including illegal immigration were intensified during this period of growing external pressure. Public opinion was mobilized to the full and all available diplomatic and power pressure was used in the struggle with the

the British to gain concessions on the vital issues of immigration, colonization, and defence.

Simultaneously, colonization expanded greatly during this period and many new settlements were established.

While the kibbutzim had grown at about the same rate as the moshavim until 1936, their expansion was much greater between 1936–45.

With their growth the social orientations of these settlements changed emphasis. Their pioneering impetus became political and quasi-military implying organized defence, and the extension of Jewish settlements into new areas before their closure by the Arabs and the British became the main object. The purely social elements became secondary, although they were taken for granted as an essential part of the settlement.

Side by side with the development of the settlements the importance of the Defence Organization (*Hagana*) also greatly increased. It crystallized in its organizational form and, with large numbers in its various services, became an important focus of national collective identification.

At the same time there developed various dissident military organizations (the *Ezel* and *Lehi* groups), whose membership was composed of nuclei of devotees of revisionist groups in the *diaspora* (especially of the *Betar* Youth Organization).

These more militant groups also absorbed many dissatisfied elements within the Yishuv. Amongst them were some second generation Oriental groups and some of the younger element of the rightist or private sectors who were not satisfied with the limited political activities of their fathers but who, at the same time, were ideologically and by tradition opposed to the workers' groups and movements.

The rift and struggle between these groups and the 'organized Yishuv' constituted, as we shall see in greater detail later, a crucial aspect of the history and development of the Yishuv of the State of Israel.

4

The Institutional Pattern of the Yishuv

The Development of Institutional Patterns – The Basic Structure. Cultural Premises of Modernity, Modernity and Religion; The Renaissance of the Hebrew Language

The preceding chapter described the major stages of development in the Yishuv. It dealt only briefly, however, with the institutional and social patterns of the mandatory period.

The Jewish community developed within the framework of the Mandate and the Arab population and was closely interwoven with both. However, it was never fully integrated into this background, its very reason for existence being the possibility of relatively independent development.

To understand the nature of this development it is important to look at some of the salient cultural premises as they developed during the second aliya and crystallized during the Mandate and in which the first embryonic answers to the nature of the modern society which developed in the Yishuv were given.

Two features of crucial importance for the understanding of the new modern community are, firstly, the relation of the cultural orientations to the Jewish religion, and, secondly, the renaissance of the Hebrew language. Although the formation of cultural institutions was in the hands of secular, irreligious groups, these were not militantly anti-religious. Further, although religious ideologists were among the important exponents of Zionism, they had little bearing on the religious climate of the country. Only a few religious personalities – such as the late Rabbi Kook – attempted some relatively new religious interpretations. Although there were attempts, especially among the religious *kibbutzim*, to introduce practical religious innovations, these did not amount to very much in terms of the internal religious sphere or its potential influence on the more secular groups. Later on, especially after the establishment of the state, even these relatively limited innovations became suspect within religious circles and only few adjustments in traditional law, well within the limits of orthodoxy, took place.

The general lack of militant anti-religious sentiment was due to many factors, only some of which can be dealt with here. The revolt against *Haskala* (enlightenment) and assimilation necessarily involved the romanticizing of tradition and united, often within the span of one generation,

34

relatively traditional parents with secular sons. This is true of the lives of almost all the great leaders of the Zionist movement.

Beyond this the institutionalized and organized 'church' with deep vested interests among Jewry, opposed all new trends and served as an easy target for denunciation. Moreover, many of the rabbis participated – though not as prominent leaders – in the Zionist movement from its beginning. Due to this, the secular orientation and ideologies of the great majority of the Zionist movement did not turn into full-fledged anti-religious symbols and attitudes, although such symbols were certainly emphasized in many of the writings and some of the patterns of collective behaviour. In the industrial field, the religious groups were part of the structure of the Zionist movement and of the Yishuv and hence had to be accommodated. Only the extreme left wing groups sometimes negated the validity of religious claims.

This explains, at least partly, the *modus vivendi* that developed within the Zionist movement and the Yishuv between religious and non-religious groups. It applied not only to the institutional side, i.e. in the various arrangements of the Chief Rabbinate and in the acceptance of various religious activities and limitations by the public, but also extended to the acceptance of the legitimacy of religious groups and orientations within the framework of the Zionist ideology and movement. At the same time, lack of internal innovation in the religious sphere limited cultural innovation mostly to the secular field.

The second major characteristic of the cultural sphere whose importance can hardly be overrated is the renaissance of Hebrew and its establishment as the common language of the Yishuv. It is beyond the scope of this analysis to explain the social and linguistic reasons for this success. The crucial fact is that this renaissance and modernization succeeded in a way probably unprecedented in the annals of modern societies. Whatever linguistic curiosities arose in the process, the adaptation of Hebrew to Western problems and life succeeded in a relatively short time. This meant that a crucial medium of communication was created which, far from remaining merely on the level of national symbolism, became fully integrated into the life of the people. It was the first generation that created this renaissance, the second and third used it as their natural mother tongue. This proved to be an immensely powerful instrument of national unification from the early periods of the Yishuv but even more so since the establishment of the state and the influx of new immigrants. It was probably also the most important contribution to ethnic identification with the different ethnic symbols and tensions being expressed in Hebrew. If for the first generation the revival of the language was an ideological-collective aim and a facet of special cultural creativity, it later became a natural phenomenon – a language used in daily life as well as a subject for the philologist. In fact, linguistic innovations in Hebrew are a national pastime to this day.

But Hebrew became more than a medium of communication. It prevented or at least minimized the development of a rift between modernity and tradition that is so often found in other societies. Once its predominance had been established, foreign languages ceased to be competitors or symbols of alienation and turned into mere supplements. The establishment, under the Mandate, of English as the major foreign language facilitated this process, since it was not the language of any of the major groups of immigrants to the Yishuv. True, on the daily level many groups maintained their linguistic habits, but these became secondary and private, not public, institutionalized patterns.

As well as being the modern language, Hebrew was also the 'traditional' one, and the struggle against the *Yiddishists* was to no small extent motivated by the unwillingness to extend folk or populist values to Yiddish or any other language but Hebrew. Once this fight was over and Hebrew became the only common language, both Yiddish and other dialects found ways to maintain some of their traditions, losing, however, any overall, national or ethnic symbolic significance.

Thus whatever social, cultural, and political rifts developed in the Yishuv, they were expressed in a common tongue. All controversy between religious groups and secularists, conservatives and radicals, took place in the same language, with only the ultra-religious groups adhering to Yiddish. Moreover, Hebrew became the language of all strata of society and of all levels of communication. It is now the language of instruction at school, University and Technical School, the language of daily discourse, no longer a folk tongue nostalgically treasured by intellectuals fully imbued in the languages of other countries and traditions. Curiously, although the renaissance of Hebrew was the product of ideological endeavour, it was also the medium whereby, through the anti-verbalist trend of the second generation, this same ideology, its values and premises became fully accepted and, to some extent, deflated.

The Institutional Structure of the Yishuv

The most important social characteristics of the mandatory period consisted of the continuous expansion of Jewish urban and rural colonization and the establishment of basic institutional patterns with their predominance of workers' groups.

Also during this period, internal relations between the major groups of the Yishuv and the Zionist Organization crystallized, emphasis being placed on common goals in both politics and colonization.

Furthermore, the predominance of the Zionist Organization and the Jewish Agency over the various other institutions in the Jewish sector gradually emerged at that time.

Among the issues that furthered the development of these arrangements, was the Yishuv's fundamental political and economic relationship with both the mandatory regime and the Arab sector. The primary question here was whether the Yishuv and the Zionist Organization would be willing – as suggested in some British circles – to become part of the upper class pluralistic colonial society or Western 'colonizers' in an Arab economy.

The decision to create a completely independent Jewish economy was perhaps the most fateful step in the development of the Yishuv. Emphasis on political independence produced an uneasy, basically antagonistic, relationship with the mandatory power, which was accentuated by the expanded immigration and colonization which had become major political objectives common to all sectors of the Yishuv – and a bone of contention with the mandatory government. It also raised self-defence from a matter of local security to a vital political problem.

These developments became closely connected with the search for the best ways of building up the national home, and developed the colonizing drive, based on national capital as mobilized through the *Keren Hayesod* and the *Keren Kayemet*.

Several alternative ways of settling the country were considered in the early 'twenties, the first of which planned rapid colonization by large-scale private investments, as proposed by Justice Brandeis and the Zionists of the United States. This approach was strongly and successfully opposed by Professor Weizmann.

The second possibility was the simple expansion of immigration based on private capital and aimed at quick economic normalization. Here the experience of the fourth aliya was decisive. It proved that, while such immigration could be important, it did not in itself have enough significance to ensure continuous development in face of adverse economic conditions, nor could it develop economic or political power quickly enough to assure continuous absorption of new manpower.

Somewhat later the Revisionists under Jabotinsky attempted to create a political climate suitable for the development of a national home through a purely political movement, concerned with political agitation, organization of the masses and immigration, but not by means of colonization which would, it was asserted, only weaken the intensity of political activities.

The unwillingness of mass immigration by Jews settled in the *diaspora*, in order to boost the independent economy of the Yishuv and its political power, turned the balance in favour of a pioneering solution, epitomized by the policies of Weizmann and gradually crystallizing in the late 'twenties and early 'thirties.

It is not easy to settle the historical debate whether all these – and especially the last two – possibilities were doomed from the beginning. Nor whether the personality of Professor Weizmann captivated the more dynamic elements as claimed by both the Brandeis group and the Revisionists. As with many historical disputes, the answer will probably never be known.

It is a fact, however, that the shifted emphasis in favour of national pioneering and colonizing created the conditions necessary for the pre-dominance of the workers' groups. This did not mean that other sectors failed to play a crucial role in the economic development of the Yishuv. Rather, the continuous expansion of the country in its political-economic sectors and political organizations became dependent on the combination of national capital and colonizing movements.

Through this change the Zionist Organization gradually became more powerful than the *Vaad Leumi,* and, within the Zionist Organization, the labour groups gained predominance. This trend first manifested itself when Chaim Arlossoroff assumed command of the political department of the Jewish Agency in Jerusalem and when, in 1935, Ben-Gurion became chairman of its executive.

Major Changes in the Workers' Sectors – The Trend Towards Unification

The success of the workers' groups was dependent on significant changes in their orientation and activities, with two contradictory developments taking place simultaneously: These were a process of splits and secessions, coupled with a growing unity of organization.

The differences between the various labour groups were sharp and often bitter. The totalistic and semi-messianic ingredients inherent in these groups from the period of the second aliya grew in intensity. This showed itself in increasing competition for manpower and capital and in the fear that many of the new developments in the urban and private sectors were undermining and possibly drawing away resources from the workers' sectors and sapping the pioneering spirit.

Paradoxically however, many new unifying organizations grew up side by side with these tendencies. Perhaps the most important of these was the establishment in 1920 – after prolonged negotiations between the major labour groups – of the Histadrut, the General Federation of Labour, which encompassed all groups and organizations and soon became powerful and influential in many spheres.

Basic Characteristics of the Histadrut

From its inception the Histadrut was more than a trade union or a federation of trade unions. Working conditions and labour disputes were of some importance in its initial phases, but they were not predominant or primary in its basic conception. The purpose of the Histadrut was more to create conditions beneficial to the development and organization of a new, privileged working class, rather than to protect the interests of an existing under-privileged one.

The creation of a working class drawn from middle-class elements necessitated first of all the preparation and training of manpower. This meant the setting-up of various groups of immigrants in the *diaspora*, and their training for agricultural and physical work in various *hachsharot* (preparation) and *hehalutz* (pioneering) groups and training camps. They eventually obtained immigration certificates from the total quota given by the mandatory government when the Zionist Organization arranged their actual immigration and ultimate settlement in the urban or rural sectors of Palestine.

While these activities were at first mainly concerned with preparation for agricultural settlement, they extended to the urban sectors to which the emphasis of Histadrut activities was soon shifted.

The need to create a working class necessitated the creation of economic sectors in which it could function. Despite, therefore, the bitter accusations against exploiters and capitalists voiced in the writings and speeches of Histadrut leaders, the need for continuous employment and capital for the extension and creation of various economic sectors, such as public works and transport, was a much more acute problem than the fight against the weak or non-existent capitalists. The Histadrut itself became one of the focal points for the mobilization of capital. Naturally its first efforts were directed towards the agricultural sector where it continuously fought for allocation of funds from the Zionist Organization. This gave rise to the paradoxical conception that members of kibbutzim and moshavim could become independent peasants as members of the working class – a paradox which was seemingly resolved by their emphasis on collective, 'working-class' movements and organizations.

But the main impetus to Histadrut activities in the middle 'twenties came from the growing recognition of the importance of the urban sectors for the colonization and economic expansion of the Yishuv. Coupled with this was the realization that the kibbutz and *Gdud Haavoda* conception of organizing urban sectors into a quasi-expanded kibbutz was inadequate.

The establishment of various contractor and semi-industrial units within the Histadrut itself was therefore of great importance. These units emphasized the development of some public concerns in public works and industry – which might otherwise not have been developed at all or would have been left to British or Arab enterprise.

The first and most important of these concerns was *Solel Boneh*, established in 1921, originally as a contracting firm for road laying. By the middle 'twenties it was engaged in major building activities and has been expanding ever since with its activities becoming even more diversified during the Second World War.

Parallel to *Solel Boneh*, many transport co-operatives developed within *Hevrat Haovdim* as the Histadrut's economic overall organization was called.

The most important of these, *Egged*, for interurban passenger transport, was organized in 1933. The following year of disturbances and riots saw the continuous development of such transport concerns both for passengers and goods.

The inflow of private capital helped to create *Hevrat Haovdim's Mekorot* concern (1936), which became the Yishuv's all-important surveyor and supplier of water. In the same year, because of the general Arab strike, the shipping company *Zim* was founded.

The establishment and maintenance of a working class necessitated more than the creation of work outlets. They also required adequate living, working and cultural conditions, in spite of the ascetic element of the pioneering class.

Here the pure trade union activities which expanded with the growth of the urban sectors gained in importance but were as yet not important enough to constitute the central activity of the Histadrut.

The latter therefore aimed to provide relatively cheap, long-term housing facilities, as well as a broad network of consumer co-operatives to transfer agricultural products from the rural sectors to the cities ensuring certain minimum prices to the producers.

Parallel to this the Histadrut developed social security and insurance schemes. Sick and Unemployment Funds were organized, growing from relatively small beginnings into the major health and medical service in the country.

Most of these organizations were established experimentally over a relatively short period of time in the 'twenties, as organizational solutions to mainly ideological problems which yet affected the lives of relatively large groups of people.

The same ideological goals also explain the development and importance of the Histadrut's educational and cultural activities, ranging from *hachshara* to the various special educational and cultural organizations, and pioneering youth movements. All of these were directed towards training a pioneering labour force, assuring it adequate standards of living, and winning loyalty for the workers' organization.

The Histadrut as a Political Body

The establishment of this wide network of activities created one of the most powerful economic and political organizations in the Yishuv. Already in the initial phases, a special holding company, *Hevrat Ovdim*, was established as the overall co-ordinating body of the Histadrut's economic enterprises. Much later these enterprises became so powerful as to escape any real control by *Hevrat Ovdim* and special efforts had to be made to control them effectively. But at the time and for a long time to come, the most important characteristic of the Histadrut was unification under central leadership – even if this leadership was composed of representatives of differing groups and parties.

Thus, from its very beginning the Histadrut was a political body, aiming at collective and political goals, and most of its decisions, policies, and activities were shaped by political considerations. Purely economic problems were subordinated to political conceptions, which were rooted in the basic pioneering Zionist ideologies.

The main aim of the political activities and struggles of the Histadrut was to gain manpower which clearly involved getting maximum allocation of immigration certificates for its members and increasing its attraction for new immigrants.

The necessity of maintaining a framework of common activities greatly changed the totalistic and sectarian orientation of the major pioneer groups and broadened the scope of activities. This often resulted in ideological conservatism and enhanced sectarianism on the part of some groups.

In 1930, *Mapai* (the Israel Workers' Party) was created and emerged as the major political party within the Histadrut, composed of *Ahdut Haavoda*, *Hapoel Hatzair* and a sprinkling of non-partisans. The establishment of Mapai as a unified party marked the beginning of the hegemony of the workers' groups in the political organization of the Yishuv and the Zionist Organization.

Organizational Difference Between Workers' and Private Sectors

The strength of the workers' groups within the Yishuv and the Zionist Organization was rooted in the fact that they were able to mobilize political support among people who were also willing to emigrate to Palestine and establish strategically important settlements, which could serve as bases for the absorption of further immigrants and for the extension of colonization.

Their effectiveness depended on strong emphasis on occupational changes and on the lack of members' own adequate capital for settlement, which necessarily made them rely much more on the various organizations of the Histadrut and the workers' parties. These organizations constituted an important bridge between the *diaspora* and the Yishuv.

Among immigrants who were not prepared to change their professions and who also had some capital of their own, there was no such need for new frameworks and organizations. Relations between them and their respective parties in the *diaspora* were more tenuous and not based on strong ideological or organizational identification. With the exception of *Hapoel Hamizrahi* (the religious workers' party), these groups' connexion with Palestine, both as regards manpower and organization, was much looser and their internal organization much weaker.

While especially the General Zionists and *Mizrahi* parties upheld some broad political and ideological goals, they were not engaged in the pursuit

41

of concrete political aims such as organized co-operation with the various private non-labour sectors in Palestine.

Private groups such as farmers and commercial interests were to be found mainly within local and municipal organizations and were primarily concerned with the economy of the country.

The local groups did not regard the General Zionist parties as representing their interests, nor did the General Zionist leadership attempt to weld these divergent groups into a common party system.

At the beginning of 1940 attempts were made to consolidate these varying interest groups into a general right wing federation, *Ihud Ezrahi*, intended as a counterweight to the Histadrut. Its success, however, was limited.

The various General Zionist groups also bred many independent, free-thinking members of the intelligentsia. Some of these were also connected with the labour groups, but they were related to political groups on an individual basis only.

It was only with the development of the *Aliya Hadasha*, a broadly-orientated party organized in 1943 mainly by middle-class German immigrants and free professionals, that a more comprehensive political organization was set up.

None of this however could halt the decline of General Zionist groups within the Zionist Organization as a whole. From being the most important numerical element in the Zionist Congresses (73 per cent at the Karlsbad Congress of 1923 and 57 per cent at the 1931 Congress in Basle), they lost their lead in the 18th Congress at Prague in 1933 when they constituted only 44 per cent of the delegates.

A similar pattern developed within the religious groups comprising the *Mizrahi* party, with the exception of *Hapoel Hamizrahi* (the religious workers' groups) which was more akin to the workers' parties.

The pattern developed by the Revisionists was different. This group, created in 1925 as a result of dissatisfaction with Weizmann's leadership, left the Zionist Organization in 1935. It was much more of a political movement which, by its very nature, was opposed to pioneering and colonization and did not develop any marked network of interest groups.

On the fringe of the workers' political parties were such groups as *Beit Shalom* or later *Ihud*, composed of independent intellectuals (such as J. L. Magnes, S. H. Bergman, and I. Epstein) and of figures prominently connected with the professional rather than the ideological and political problems of the Yishuv such as A. Ruppin and H. M. Kalvarisky. Their main aim was the establishment of good relations with the Arabs and they were highly critical of the policies of the Zionist Organization.

The differences in the political organization of the various Zionist groups and parties were also reflected in the developing political leadership. Typical for the private or General Zionist sectors were the 'movement' leaders –

personalities of high calibre in the fields of oratory, diplomacy, and culture, part of the General Zionist élite and the élite of the Yishuv but virtually removed from practical, day-to-day problems which were dealt with by the various local economic, professional, and municipal leaders.

However, lack of a common framework of activities and interests necessarily restricted the scope and range of problems these leaders could deal with.

In the workers' sector the overall development of leadership was different. Initially various types of leaders and levels of political activity also existed within this sector, but the pure type of movement leaders only persisted in the more sectarian groups. In most cases the different levels of political activities and types of leaders became closely interwoven, and their activities extended specifically over movement problems as well as over concrete types of activity. These characteristics indicate the main reasons for the strength of the workers' groups and for their growing ability to play a crucial role in the absorption of even non-pioneering new immigrants. Their absorption necessarily turned the workers' groups and organizations away from their sectarian origins.

Thus, while the workers' groups did not necessarily constitute a numerical majority, their organizational strength grew continuously and they attracted more and more newcomers.

In 1920 the Histadrut encompassed 11 per cent of the adult population, the percentage in 1949 was forty. The curve of growth of the Histadrut runs generally parallel to that of the Yishuv as a whole, thus stressing the close connexion between Histadrut membership and the trends of immigration. This fact became more and more evident from the period of the fifth aliya onwards.

Growth of the Institutional Structure of the Yishuv

Having analysed the nature of the broad organizational developments of the Yishuv we can proceed to an analysis of the overall institutional structure that developed until the end of the mandatory period.

This evolved out of the interaction of two major trends. The first, during the 'twenties and early 'thirties, was the development of the basic pattern crystallized in embryonic form during the second aliya. This was characterized by the federative nature of the different groups and by the discrepancy between purely ecological groups and the nuclei of functional institutions and organizations.

The second trend developing simultaneously was the growing interdependence of the different sectors of the Yishuv despite the federative nature of their organization.

This became evident in the growth of common internal markets, in labour problems and relations, in the growing scope of municipal affairs, and in the development of various economic and professional organizations.

Additional points of common interest which became of central importance to the development of the Yishuv were the stand on external political relations, the struggle for continued immigration, defence, and the expansion of the national home.

Yet, despite these numerous points of contact the Jewish community in Palestine was not, even in the late 'forties, an independent, self-sufficient society.

The interdependence of the various sectors and groups on some issues did not preclude their independence in their access to external sources of power and capital, in their internal organization and, to some extent, in their internal economy and regulative mechanisms. With the growth of such areas the points of contact also increased and with them potential conflict between different groups, so that the problem of regulative mechanisms to deal with these problems also emerged.

Institutionalization of Pioneering Ideologies – Selection of Élites, Crystallization of Common Symbols

The best way to approach the problem of these regulative mechanisms is by analysing the clash between the basic pioneering ideology and the continuous growth of the Yishuv's institutional structure – or, in other words, by analysing the process of institutionalizing this ideology.

As shown, large parts of the institutional structure of the Yishuv were created by ideologically-motivated colonizing movements. These ideologies provided much of the impetus for further development.

Quite obviously, however, the pure ideology could not be retained after the development of a manifold institutional structure especially as the very strength of this ideology was due to the restricted scope of the various groups, to their non-involvement in the concrete needs and problems of the existing social structure, and to the purity of their future orientations and aspirations. A progressive, growing and differentiated social structure necessarily created new groups and problems of its own, making its own demands on the resources of the population.

Side by side with these developments the ideological purity was also weakened and challenged by the changing patterns of motivation among new immigrants and by the growth of the new generation in the Yishuv – all of which accentuated the problem of how to adjust new manpower, with its different social motivations and orientations, to some of the tenets of pioneering ideology.

There therefore developed a selective entrenchment of protagonists of ideology in strategic parts of the social system who attempted to influence and control many of the important aspects of institutional structure. Such selective entrenchment was first effected through the formation of different élite groups and individuals singled out as bearers or effective symbols of the ideology. One such type of élite were members of the various kibbutzim and moshavim who were acknowledged by large sections of the community as representatives of the pioneer ideology.

Another manifestation of this type was the predominance of the pioneers among the political and, to a smaller extent, economic and cultural élites. With the growing strength of the workers in the political setting of the Yishuv, their leaders succeeded in planting the myth of pioneer leadership in most of the strategic places of the institutional structure. Adherence to this prototype was demanded, even of those who, in their own lives, did not or could not maintain the ideal. The demands made were strengthened by the important fact that no counter-myth of any overriding validity was developed by any of the other groups. The need for such a myth was apparently also felt by many of the immigrant groups, in the process of transition, who needed some framework of continued collective identity.

A symbol in the search for self-identity by the new community was thus provided.

The establishment of different workers' educational 'trends', saw to the successful dissemination of the pioneering ideology within the Yishuv's educational system. This was particularly evident in the various youth movements which upheld the ideal of pioneering in a kibbutz as the only worthwhile way and as the major symbol of identification.

A second way in which the selective permeation of the pioneer ideology took place was through the continuous crystallization and maintenance of collective symbols based on the pioneer image. This tendency was furthered by the struggle with the Arab population and the mandatory government – and the consequent necessity to expand the settlements.

The influence of the pioneering ideology affected the whole way of life in the Yishuv. It showed itself in the emphasis placed on group outings, exploration of the country, return to nature, youth movement activity, and in the relatively simple way of dress and general style of living which prevailed at the time among most groups.

Criteria of Social Allocation

In addition to selective entrenchment, the pioneer ideology also became the criterion for the allocation of positions and rewards in the major institutional spheres. In this way the leaders of the workers' groups attempted to resolve the problems created by the continuously expanding and changing institutional structure.

Membership in the various movements and adherence to the collective symbols and values became basic prerequisites for the allocation of jobs or funds.

Again, in the political field this membership of the workers' movements became a prerequisite for accession to élite position and for participation in political activities.

In the social sphere voluntary associations were geared to broader movement goals. This was most clearly shown in the professional organizations established for teachers, doctors, and, to some extent, lawyers, in which the prime purpose was to create, as it were, new Hebrew professions which would serve the new community. It was only with the growing development of the Yishuv and the gradual normalization of its social and economic structure that purely professional and economic interests became predominant.

Economically, this institutionalization of an ideology was seen in the emphasis put on collective (i.e. Histadrut, co-operatives, etc.) ownership of economic enterprises. Membership in the Histadrut or another collective organization was an important prerequisite for obtaining facilities such as housing.

This process was perhaps most marked in the wage policy adapted by the Histadrut and to a smaller extent the national institutions (the Jewish Agency, the *Vaad Leumi* – the National Council of Jews in Palestine – etc.). Within the Histadrut a basic family salary prevailed; that is, the basic salary was roughly equal for all workers and employees, with very minor additions for specialization, education, etc., and varied mainly according to family status, number of children, and seniority of employment.

The national institutions were not quite so extreme but, nevertheless, there were only six or seven grades, based not only on specialization but also on seniority and including large family allowances. It sometimes happened that the caretaker of a Histadrut institution with six children and sufficient seniority earned more than a director with only two children. While this system of renumeration did not hold good in the free market, it is significant that it existed within those organizations that bore the main responsibility for national and social prestige and power.

In view of this, an analysis of the different standards of living in the various strata of the Jewish population becomes significant and shows a double trend. Economic differences grew with the development of the Yishuv. While they were not very great compared to those in other countries, even at the close of the mandatory period, it should also be mentioned here that discrepancies were even smaller within the non-oriental majority, and that it is the oriental Jews who form a large part of the lower income brackets.

Immigrant Absorption – Patterns of Immigrant Dispersion

Perhaps the most far-reaching way in which the pioneering ideology manifested itself was in the absorption of immigrants.

The Yishuv was a community created by immigrants who arrived in waves at comparatively short intervals. Its institutional structure was in a continuous process of formation and development. Throughout, the country was faced with the problems common to all immigrant countries as well as having to cope with its specific problems which, as in the case of the oriental Jews, it did not always fully succeed in solving.

This process of absorption is therefore worthy of examination from several points of view, beginning with the extent to which immigrant groups dispersed or were concentrated in any specific institutional structure, a criterion which has often been used as the basic index of immigrant absorption.

With the partial exception of oriental Jews and some European refugee elements, the degree of dispersion within the institutional structure was exceptionally high. There was no strong and continuous concentration of any particular group of immigrants – whether classed by country or origin or by period of immigration. On the whole, occupational, political, and social differentiation within the Yishuv came about through the continuous redistribution of the various waves of immigration among the emergent institutional positions and strata. The immigrants' social and cultural heritage was, to a large extent, neutralized, and important positions were not monopolized by any one type of immigrant group. Truly enough, there were several exceptions: the political élite was for a long time in the hands of people of the second and third aliya, i.e. mostly from Russia and Eastern Europe; while on the other hand, some immigrant groups were for some time at least predominant in some occupational spheres, like the German aliya in professions and finance. But even these were only partial and to some extent temporary exceptions, and the continuous expansion of the social and economic system minimized the cleavages and tensions attendant on this process. Therefore 'ethnic' belongings did but rarely become a focus of separatist identity within the Yishuv.

Patterns of Formal and Informal Absorption

Closely connected to this process was the relation between formal and informal absorption patterns.

The purely formal framework of the process of absorption of new immigrants was less significant in the Yishuv than in many other important immigrant countries, due, mainly, to the fact that this framework was often merely an extension of the immigrants' primary groups, containing their basic social orientation. The development of the various formal organizations was brought about by the first groups of pioneer immigrants; and gradually extended with the intake of new members and the continuous merging of various primary groups but was never really fully realized. This was due partly to the strong identification between different immigrants' groups and partly to the absence of an overall, political, coercive system, which enabled basic solidarity to be maintained by more informal means. Difficulties of adjustment were thus lessened through the continuous re-formation of various primary groups and strong connexions were developed between all facets of these groups, i.e. family, friends, and co-workers, as well as political and social activities. The co-existence of such varied but interconnected groups also allowed for the constant redistribution of power between different groups and for the maintenance of their solidarity and identification with the overall structure.

The overlapping of primary groups and the institutional set-up of the Yishuv can be traced both historically and sociologically in almost every sphere. This is evident in the history of the labour movement and of the co-operative settlements, as well as in the professional and semi-professional organizations, in the illegal defence organizations, and even in the schools and youth movements.

To some extent these varied organizations served as channels of social selection and mobility, facilitating institutional dispersion among the immigrants.

Absorption within these organizations involved no incompatibility between primary and formal relations and left little room for 'deviationist' tendencies.

Institutional Patterns of Absorption

With the growing differentiation of the country's social structure, the scope of the various formal associations grew and entry into them became more difficult.

Nonetheless, the original premises of the social structure greatly influenced the absorption of new immigrants, as can be seen in the actual ways in which this was effected.

(a) Joining existing co-operative and communal settlements as new members, with the same initial advantages and rights as those given to the old-timers, and sometimes even slightly better ones such as better housing conditions, a higher general standard of living, etc.

(b) Establishing new settlements – either alone, or together with members from earlier old or new-type settlements. With the help of national capital and aid from the main colonizing agencies, these new groups were given the same if not better facilities than older settlements.

(c) Absorption in the towns which was numerically the most important aspect. Here there was no strict emphasis on equal allocation of facilities and participation in existing primary groups.

By its nature the city was more open to the free play of economic forces and to their impact on the growing development of a free industrial and commercial market. Yet many institutional arrangements aimed at mitigating the impact of these forces developed, the most important of which were the following.

There were, above all, the various social security schemes and workers' organizations such as trade unions, collective bargaining schemes, etc., which were set up by the Histadrut and similar, smaller bodies. The growing strength of the trade unions assured a decent, sometimes even high, standard of living. Only a very short probationary period – about six months – was required for full membership in the Histadrut so that most of the new immigrants could quickly enjoy the benefits available.

Secondly, many enterprises in the urban sectors such as co-operatives and small workshops received assistance from the main colonizing agencies or from national capital. This tended to soften the impact of competitive economic forces.

Lastly, the various economic and social sectors of the Yishuv (with the exception of the working sector) established different concerns, such as banks, loan societies, etc., whose purpose was to aid their members – especially new members – in establishing themselves. In this connexion the aid societies and activities of the *Landsmannschaften* should also be mentioned.

All this helped to provide incoming immigrants with various amenities and minimized the effects of any discrimination against them. It did not, of course, nullify the growing social and economic differentiation within the Yishuv but blunted the differences between the various strata, always leaving the main sectors open to new immigrants.

This process of absorbing immigrants, almost unique among modern migratory countries, can be explained by two basic features in the social structure of the Yishuv. The first was the pioneering motivation and identification of the initial groups of immigrants, the continuity of this motivation throughout the thirties, and the compatibility between the immigrants' aspirations and the demands made on them by the absorbing societies.

This compatibility was partly the result of predisposition on the part of the immigrants to change in all directions of social action with great flexibility in the emerging institutional structure, and partly of the broad similarity in motivation and social orientation of most of the immigrants. This similarity was shown not only in external characteristics, cultural traits, etc., but also in the continuity of identification between the different groups and in their continuous need for contacts and guidance in the new society.

A second feature was the fact that the Yishuv's social structure was in continuous need of new immigrants for its basic collective tasks. Since it lacked overall coercive power, it had to minimize any inequalities inherent in the relations between old-timers and newcomers in order to attract new immigrants.

Together these two factors explain the unique nature of the absorption process, its smoothness and the strengthening of the 'federative form' of the social-political structure of the Yishuv. To a certain extent, however, it hindered the full crystallization of the Yishuv's institutional structure and the development of various dynamic and progressive forces.

The Oriental Groups in the Yishuv

The so-called oriental groups proved to be a partial exception to this pattern. They comprised individuals of wide ethnic diversity, including almost all the Jews who came to Israel from Middle Eastern countries, and especially from the former Ottoman Empire. Chief among these were the following communities (*edot*): Sephardim, Persians, Kurds, Babylonians, Yemenites, Moghrebites (from Morocco), as well as Jews from Bukhara, Haleb, Urfa, Georgia, and Afghanistan. The term Sephardi originally applied to all the Jews originating from Spain (*Sepharad*), who lived in various parts of North Africa, Turkey, Greece, and Egypt. They made up 20 to 25 per cent of the population of the Yishuv, forming a category in themselves, and exhibiting marked differences from other oriental Jews. The main part of the 'old' Jewish community which lived in Palestine before the beginnings of immigration in the 1880's consisted of Sephardim.

Many Sephardim, however, and most of the other oriental groups mentioned above, came later, with at least 70 per cent arriving in Israel after the First World War and about seventy thousand after 1918, to add to the approximately twenty thousand who were already there. Their arrival, therefore, more or less coincided with the main waves of immigration. Though there were many important differences among them, the common denominator 'oriental Jews' was not only geographical but also had a specific sociological meaning. Despite their differences, they formed a more or less unified sociological bloc as compared with the rest of the Jewish community in Israel.

Their first specific characteristic was that, unlike other groups, they were not institutionally dispersed. They concentrated disproportionately in certain strata of the institutional spheres. This can be seen from the data on their ecological concentration, economic and educational structure and extent of endogamy, as compared with other sections of the population. These data show an undue concentration of oriental Jews in the lower and lower-middle classes, living especially in certain, sometimes slum, quarters of Jerusalem and Tiberias. They also show the maintenance, to a great extent, of their own educational structure. We also see the emergence of a few political parties based on ethnic consciousness, such as the Yemenite party and the Sephardic bloc, though by no means all oriental Jews were identified with these parties. Thus we find that they were an exception to the general high rate of social integration of the Yishuv.

Side by side with these characteristics certain behaviour patterns, symptomatic of non-integration and tension, became apparent. These were juvenile delinquency, criminality, and instability of family life.

The main reasons for the relative mal-integration of the oriental Jews in the Yishuv are rooted in their specific motivations for migration on the one hand and in their cultural educational background on the other. While it is true that many Sephardim and oriental Jews (particularly those who came in later years) were inspired directly or indirectly by the secular Zionist ideal, this was not the case with the majority. The two main urges were economic and political persecution of the recurrent type, traditional in the various countries of the Ottoman Empire, and vague Messianic aspirations, which were revived by the Balfour Declaration, the establishment of the national home, etc.

Although Jewish identity was very strong, it was not typical of the modern, secular nationalism with strong social orientations characteristic of the Zionist movement. It was rather of the traditional-religious kind of medieval Jewish communities. Contact with modernization in their countries of origin served mostly to intensify this type of traditional identification, since immigration to Palestine did not imply for them a break with the traditional social and cultural structure. They came hoping to be able to follow their own way of life fully and securely and did not envisage any drastic change. They were not consciously prepared to alter either their economic and occupational structure or the basic tenets of their social and cultural life and their traditionally religious Jewish consciousness. They did not lack positive identification with the new Jewish community in Palestine – their traditional Jewish faith and Messianic aspirations embraced all Jews. But this identification, while close enough to establish general contacts and ecological clusters, concentrated usually in certain larger towns. Most of them intended to perpetuate their former ways of life, without social segregation or political subjugation. This, however, proved impossible within the framework of the Yishuv.

The oriental Jews' basic participation in the Yishuv, together with their strong adherence to old patterns of life, accounts for their special position in the Yishuv's social structure, where they formed a separate social group. The fact that their educational and vocational levels were usually below the relatively modern standards of the Yishuv forced them mainly into the lower economic sectors, and the impact on them of modern conditions can be compared, in some ways, to the contact between a modern, advanced economy and a 'backward' people (peasants, etc.). Their old structure was continuously undermined, but nevertheless this did not result in their complete integration.

This is seen most clearly in the break-up of the oriental Jews' old pattern of élites. Their main criteria – wealth, long family standing, and traditional learning – were either declining or undergoing a process of social transformation. Wealth was still valued – perhaps even more than previously – but the ways of achieving it were no longer confined to the traditional social pattern. Those with wealth were not necessarily interested in close relations by marriage with other traditionally rich families of their own origin. Nor did they wish to remain confined to their former social structure. On the contrary, wealth was often seen as a means for establishing wider social contacts. Traditional learning, for its part, declined very quickly as a goal of social achievement.

The fact that this disintegration of traditional patterns did not always give rise to complete and successful integration was due mainly to the strong influence which the old values still held. Though in themselves no longer realizable, they still prevented the acceptance of different roles in the new society.

Not all the oriental Jews, however, exhibited these symptoms of social disintegration. Although exact statistics are not available, it is well known that many of them succeeded in adapting successfully to new conditions even if they did not attain the highest social positions. To achieve this, three different, though interconnected, ways were possible. First was the complete and unqualified immersion of a given family or group of families within the Yishuv. The second possibility was the purely formal attainment of adequate social status while maintaining their specific traditions and patterns of life in their private lives and cultural patterns. Thus, while not sharing fully in the expressive integration of the Yishuv through the creation of new patterns, they also did not form a disruptive element; and their private customs were accepted as legitimate alternatives within the social structure.

A third type of relatively successful adaptation was found among some of the more conservative and stable elements in the oriental communities, usually closely connected to the families of the second type. Their way was to try to establish the whole oriental (usually Sephardi) body as a legitimate associational group within the Yishuv's social structure. Thus, for instance, within the religious sphere Palestine had two Chief Rabbis – one Ashkenazi and one Sephardi. Parallel phenomena could be found in communal activities, councils, etc. However, only the more conservative elements adhered to these institutional arrangements: attempts to re-organize the crumbling traditional pattern of life were not usually very successful.

Inherent Tensions of the Yishuv's Social Structure. The Institutionalization of the Pioneering Ideology

The preceding sections analysed some of the major institutional features of society in the Yishuv with special emphasis on the institutionalizing of the pioneering ideology.

These developments caused the ideology to become 'routinized', more diffused, and less vivid in its direct bearing on daily activities.

Side by side there developed a growing discrepancy between the symbolic expression of the ideology and its general impacts on daily life, and the more expressly ideological formulations in the sense of full doctrinaire expression.

This doctrinaire expression was carried out in the form of 'codification' of the ideology and in the literary and political interpretation of its 'meaning'. No longer part and parcel of the life of the pioneering groups, this codification of the ideology became the prerogative of the leaders who had, by now, achieved élite positions within the changing social structure.

This process of dissemination naturally created many problems and tensions. These stemmed from the encounter of the ideology's proponents with other sectors in the Yishuv, from the development of inherent contradictions in the ideology, and from the attempts of its proponents to overcome these contradictions and to extend the scope of their power and influence.

The major contradiction was between the general, diffuse ideal of the pioneer and his orientation toward a differentiated economic and political structure, entailing a high degree of specialization and individualism. It became obvious that one could attain greater success by not devoting oneself exclusively to collective goals, as many who had done so found out when they saw the more lucrative positions taken by those who had followed a different path.

This contradication was accentuated by the continuous development of the private sectors and the encounters between them and the developing economic and professional bodies within the workers' sectors.

In the wake of these activities strong competition and conflict developed between the different sectors of the Yishuv. The workers' sector, by its nature much more unified and militant, used its growing power and influence more and more widely. This militancy increased when its own internal developments and the growing interlinking and competition with other sectors brought out some of the contradictions and tensions inherent in the process of ideological institutionalization.

The first sphere of competition was youth, and this manifested itself in the establishment of various school 'trends', each belonging to a different party or sector. In addition, youth movements (particularly pioneering) emerged as the main focus of culture and tried to infuse all the youth with their ethos.

A second major focus of competition and conflict developed in the occupational and professional organizations, which became an important meeting point between the different sectors.

As we have seen, many of these professional organizations originated as pioneering groups. However, with the growing development of the Yishuv, the importance of professional and economic activities also grew. The professional groups drew manpower from different sectors and so naturally became a sort of political battlefield between the different political and social groups interested in exerting their influence.

The workers' leadership attemped to solve the problem by developing two, sometimes complementary, sometimes contradictory, policies.

The first aimed at reinforcing those trends in the social structure which weakened the normalization of the social and occupational framework.

This was effected through continuous extension of the colonizing sectors and various national organizations. Among the latter, defence rated high in importance and occupied large numbers of the younger population for certain periods – often at a crucial time from the point of view normal occupational development.

The second major set of policies was characterized by extending the scope of their organizations and power and by a monopoly on the major power positions in the Yishuv.

This tendency was most clearly shown in the attempts to maintain preferential allocation of political power and social prestige for those groups which were connected with the collective economic interests. Accordingly, these groups developed many vested interests which were furthered by their political representatives. Such activities were justified on grounds of collective ideology and national service they performed in the development of the country. The accruing benefits (housing, land, even household effects, etc.) gradually came to be accepted as basic rights due to participants in collective enterprises, with the groups themselves competing over the extent of privilege due to each other.

Second, and perhaps even more important in transforming the ideology to the changing society, was its linkage to power and position, inherent in the constructivist emphasis of the 'twenties and 'thirties. It became even more pronounced with the growing competition between the different sectors for allocation of resources and power positions.

This necessarily led to growing ideological formalism and conservatism in the adaptation of older values to the continuously changing reality. The full implication of these developments was not realized during the period of the Yishuv – it became articulated only with the establishment of the State of Israel.

The Institutional Structure of the Yishuv – A Summary

Thus we see that the overall institutional structure of the Yishuv was not yet fully crystallized at the end of the mandatory period. While the separateness of the different sectors still persisted, the interlinking sectors had nevertheless greatly expanded. This very expansion created new meeting points, tensions, and cleavages, which called for new, as yet unformulated, principles and mechanisms.

The need for regulation became more and more important for the internal structure of the Yishuv and constituted, albeit perhaps unconsciously, an important driving power for the attainment of statehood.

Of special interest in this context are the recommendations of the Peel

Commission which recognized the potential maturity of the Yishuv for the assumption of full-fledged political responsibility and development into an autonomous society.

This recognition was not based mainly on the existing structure of the Yishuv, but rather on the evaluation of its potential as a full-fledged society. However, despite these meeting points, conflicts, and problems, no regulative mechanisms comprehensive enough to deal with all problems developed.

As we have seen, the top political institutions of the Yishuv and of the Zionist movement were more concerned with external politics than with the regulation of internal conflicts and interests, and the amount of internal legislation was relatively small. Universally-binding norms developed only gradually out of the constant interplay of the various groups and were maintained mostly by the intensive identification and cohesion of the various groups and only to a much smaller extent by formal discipline. Where such formal discipline did develop (e.g. the Histadrut, or the various local councils), it did not affect relations between the various groups where identification and loyalty were largely maintained by informal pressures and disciplines. This state of affairs assured the continuity of intensive identification and solidarity of most groups with the major collective symbols but did not make sufficient provision for a unified system of regulation and norms.

Private or group interpretation of norms was always possible. The great dependence of these norms on the mutual agreement of the various groups was a potential danger to the existence of a unified interpretation of the various rules, written and unwritten, and also strengthened the tendency towards relative ideological exclusiveness on the part of these groups and their development as centres of vested interests.

These tendencies were not fully developed or clearly realized in this period, mainly because the Yishuv was not a fully unified society and existed within the framework of the mandatory government which, on the one hand, regulated many of the more instrumental aspects of social and economic life and, on the other, enabled the Yishuv to maintain, to some extent at least, its overall solidarity.

All these problems became, however, much more acute with the establishment of the state.

At the same time there developed the great rift between the 'organized Yishuv' and the 'dissident' groups (*Ezel* and *Lehi*). This struggle constituted one of the major aspects of the history of the Yishuv in the 'forties. The focus of this struggle was the relations to the British on the one hand, and the acceptance of a common political framework on the other. The organized Yishuv (and its unofficial 'illegal' army – the *Hagana*) and the dissidents shared, to some degree at least, the ultimate political goals – the removal of restrictions on purchase of land by Jews, on immigration and ultimately the attainment of political independence. But they differed greatly with regard to the relative emphasis on these ends – the dissidents stressing more the attainment of political independence and especially the 'means' used; the organized Yishuv stressing more the combination of diplomatic settlement, immigration and defence of the minimization of direct military action, while the dissidents put greater emphasis on the latter. Moreover – and this in itself was of great importance – the dissidents did not accept the common voluntary political framework of the Yishuv and its implied collective discipline and responsibility.

While there can be no doubt that the activities of the *Hagana* and the *Irgun* alike ultimately contributed to the decision of the British to give up the Mandate and to quit Palestine, yet at that time the conflict between the dissidents and the organized Yishuv threatened to rip it apart and seemed sometimes to be leading towards fratricide. The great intensity of this conflict could be partially explained by the fact that the members of dissident groups were, as we have seen, recruited to no small extent from the groups 'marginal' to the dominant institutional structure. But, it is significant for the understanding of the social structure of the Yishuv that these conflicts became focused not on social or economic issues but within that very sphere – that of political solidarity which provided the focus of the common identification and overrode many of the social and economic conflicts. Basically, the dissidents, both from the revisionists who left the Zionist Organization and from the marginal groups of the Yishuv, defied the validity of the 'federative' structure of the Yishuv and hence of its political discipline.

No wonder therefore that the split was of great significance later on, after the establishment of the state and the first clear-cut political division established the major dividing line between those who were accepted (by the official leadership) for coalition and those who were excluded from it and who, for a long time, saw themselves as opposed to this basic political pattern.

As has been mentioned several times, the social structure of the Yishuv developed within the mandatory framework. The relations between the Yishuv and the mandatory, as well as with the Arab population had several important repercussions which survived all pending changes such as the establishment of the State, the change of the basic institutional framework, the abolition of British rule and the exodus of large parts of the Arab population from the new State of Israel.

With both the small ruling British community as well as with the Arabs, there developed many informal, daily relations. Those with the English community were usually confined to the intellectual and political élite as well as some of the older Sephardi notables.

Those with the Arab community were much more widespread and ranged from traditional daily contact between Arab villagers and Jewish settlers to economic relations between the two communities, including long-established relations between Sephardi and Arab notables and covering co-operation in local administrative matters.

These varied contacts continued throughout the mandatory period despite the growing tension between the communities, but – especially in the later period – they were of course greatly influenced by these conflicts.

Beyond these informal contacts, relations between the various communities also achieved a far-reaching impact.

The impact of the British was felt mostly in the institutional and cultural scene. It was most clearly evident in the legal system, which is maintained in many of the basic aspects of the legal institutions in Israel to this day, and, to no small degree, in the administrative and political spheres.

Beyond these points, the most important impact of the English was in the cultural sphere, and especially in the contacts and orientations of the Yishuv with the 'outside' Western world. These contacts focused more and more on English-speaking countries – despite the predominance of an Eastern and Central European background among the pioneers and immigrants during the Yishuv and, later, the growing importance of more 'Latin' or Mediterranean patterns evolving through the so-called oriental immigration.

English became and, despite some advances of French, continues to be to this day, the major foreign language not only in the schools but also in the institutions of higher learning.

The number of cultural contacts with English-speaking countries increased continuously.

In many circles the conceptions of citizenship, civil order and propriety, were modelled on the English pattern. Though they did not become established and institutionalized in the Yishuv, their overall importance certainly cannot be minimized.

Needless to say, this influence was greatly reinforced by the fact that after the Second World War only very few Jewish communities were left in Central and Eastern Europe (except in the Soviet Union, with which contacts are almost impossible) and that the most important Jewish community was in the United States, with the second largest living in England. For at least the first post-war decade centres of scientific, political, and economic power were shifted to the United States, a fact which enabled the further development of tendencies which had begun under the influence of the Mandate.

Relations with the Arab community were very different – more diffuse and less articulated.

Because of the very modern orientations of the Zionist movement bent on development and because of the growing hostility between the Arab and Jewish communities, there was but little positive identification with the major aspects of Arab culture or ways of life.

Yet, in many ways and on many different levels activities related to the Arab culture and community did tend to develop.

One of the most important developments in this area was the upsurge of oriental-Arab and Muslim studies in the Jewish educational system, ranging from the University level, where the Institute of Oriental Studies was one of the first and most important schools, to the high school where Arabic was one of the two (French being the second) essential foreign languages.

Beyond this, the younger generation of *Sabras* and especially those from agricultural regions and settlements tended to acquire a variety of characteristics in dress, daily demeanour, and linguistic expressions, closely akin to their Arab equivalents.

Among many of the oriental communities patterns of dress, leisure, and cultural activities often tended to be rather close to those of the Arab communities, becoming even more marked with the growing influx of 'oriental' immigrants after the establishment of the state.

Although only a few of these patterns became fully recognized, they no doubt constitute a focal point for some of the pluralistic developments in the cultural mosaic of Israel which we shall analyse later.

5

The Establishment of the State of Israel

Social Transformation of the Yishuv

The establishment in 1948 of the State of Israel was not only a major political and historical event but also constituted a turning point in the development of the Yishuv's social structure.

Its most important single effect was, of course, the fact that the Yishuv now became self-sufficient and ceased to be part of a triple – mandatory, Jewish, and Arab – society.

The mandatory power withdrew, leaving many functional gaps in the social structure which had to be filled. The Arab community decreased because of the partition of Palestine, as well as to the large exodus of the Arab population. The fleeing Arabs left behind them many deserted towns and villages and many vacant places in the now greatly diminished economy.

All these gaps had to be filled immediately by the authorities of the new state, though in fact the state's undertaking of these many functions greatly changed their sociological nature – even if this was not fully recognized at the time or even at present.

These changes were rooted in the fact that the old division of functions between Yishuv and mandatory authority, as well as between the different sectors within the Yishuv, ceased to exist.

This was most clearly seen in the political field, where the new state now had to deal not only with the implementation of political goals and with the mobilization of resources and manpower but also with the extension of administrative services in all spheres.

The establishment of the *Knesset* (Parliament), therefore, and of the judiciary, as well as the unification and extension of administrative services, were not merely technical or administrative events but had profound overall social consequences. They shifted political emphasis to the internal scene where the struggle for power and for the allocation of resources was being waged; and, minimized the direct approach of different groups to external resources and manpower.

Approaches to external resources for money and loans which are vital to this day now became regulated through the central state organs. Similarly the attainment of statehood effected a change in the relative importance of the Israeli, as compared with the World-Jewish, organizations. In pre-state days the Zionist Organization and the Jewish Agency representing world Jewry were of much greater importance than the territorial organizations of the Yishuv. This was now changed. The focus of power shifted to the state organs, while most of the functions of the Zionist Organization became secondary.

A similar unification of various aspects of the institutional structure took place in the fields of economics, culture, education, and social status. All these became increasingly geared to the needs and problems of the continuously developing and expanding population.

Most significantly, the different agencies which had dealt with the needs of the existing and future social structure were now brought together. Though both activities continued, they were no longer institutionally separated.

This unification had important repercussions on values and ideology. The strong future orientation, so important in the past, greatly abated, and its structural place in the society became transposed.

The establishment of the state might have been – and sometimes was – interpreted as the realization of the major goals of the past, while state implementation of further goals weakened relations between the various groups in the Yishuv and their dedication to these goals. It also necessarily increased the claims being made on the State by the various groups and organizations for allocation of resources and, to a great extent, changed the bases of solidarity within the Yishuv. From being part of a network of closely-knit primary groups, their new identification entailed a weakening of the intensive orientation towards collectivism and, in the beginning, even of civil morale, with individualist orientations coming more and more to the fore.

Similarly, the establishment of the state gradually transformed the federative nature of the different groups and sectors in the Yishuv into elements of interest and pressure groups.

All these developments also necessarily accentuated the problems, tensions and contradictions inherent in institutionalizing the ideology as the proponents of the official – though transformed – ideology became the rulers of the state.

The establishment of the state in a situation of war, plus the continuous enmity of the Arab States towards Israel and their constant declarations of intent to destroy the state, added another dimension to the Jewish community in the State of Israel.

The continuous awareness of this threat, and the consequent necessity for constant alertness, gave predominance to considerations of security in many fields such as foreign policy, economic policies, and even certain aspects of development.

Changes in the Patterns of Immigration

These changes did not entail complete self-sufficiency for the new society which continued to be dependent on external resources for its membership and its explicit ideology stressed the ingathering of the exiles. The country opened its gates to the great mass immigration that took place. Since independence the population of Israel has more than tripled. It was this unique mass immigration that constituted the second major cause of social change, its effects being felt, as we shall see, in all institutional fields.

Tables 1–3 provide us with the basic demographic data on the changes in the Jewish population.

TABLE 1

The Sources and the Percentage of Growth of the Jewish Population (Percentages) 15 May 1948–31 December 1964

Year	The total population at the beginning of the period (thousands)	Percentage of growth	Percentage of increase	
			Increase from immigrants	Natural increase
Total 1948–64	2,155·6	211·1	67·6	32·4
1948	649·7	16·8	95·8	4·2
1950	1,013·9	18·7	84·8	15·3
1952	1,404·4	3·3	23·3	76·7
1955	1,526·0	4·2	48·3	51·7
1958	1,762·7	2·7	30·7	69·3
1960	1,858·8	2·8	33·0	67·0
1962	1,981·7	4·4	63·1	36·9
1964	2,155·6	3·8	56·8	43·2

Source: CBS Statistical Abstract of Israel, No. 14, 1963, pp. 16, 17.
  Op. cit., No. 16, 1965, p. 21, Table 2/B.

Note: The calculations for the years 1948–60 are based on the present population, while the calculations for 1962–4 are based on the permanent population.

TABLE 2

Jewish Immigrants and Tourists Settling by Continent of Birth
(Absolute Numbers and Percentage)
1919–62

	Percentage				Absolute numbers		
Period	Europe-America	Asia-Africa	Total	Not known	Europe-America	Asia-Africa	Total
	IMMIGRANTS						
1919–48	89·6	10·4	100·0	22,283	385,066	44,809	452,158
1948–62	45·4	54·6	100·0	19,432	479,605	575,755	1,074,792
1948	85·6	14·4	100·0	11,856	77,032	12,931	101,819
1949	52·7	47·3	100·0	5,199	123,097	110,780	239,076
1950	50·4	49·6	100·0	1,471	84,638	82,296	169,405
1951	28·9	71·1	100·0	248	50,204	123,449	173,901
1952	28·4	71·6	100·0	3	6,647	16,725	23,375
1953	24·9	75·1	100·0	13	2,574	7,760	10,347
1954	11·3	88·7	100·0	12	1,966	15,493	17,471
1955	7·1	92·9	100·0	5	2,562	33,736	36,303
1956	13·3	86·7	100·0	3	7,305	47,617	54,925
1957	57·5	42·5	100·0	609	39,763	29,361	69,733
1958	55·7	44·3	100·0	1	14,428	11,490	25,919
1959	66·8	33·2	100·0	4	15,348	7,635	22,987
1960	71·0	29·0	100·0	2	16,684	6,801	23,487
1961	52·7	47·3	100·0	3	24,564	22,004	46,571
1962	21·5	78·5	100·0	3	12,793	46,677	59,473

Source: Op. Cit., No. 16, 1965, p. 96, Table D/4.

The Jewish population increased by 211 per cent from 649,700 in 1948 to 2,115,600 in 1964; and the non-Jewish population by about 67·5 per cent – from 156,000 to 286,400. About 68 per cent of the increase in the Jewish population was due to the migratory balance and in particular to immigration, with 32 per cent being due to natural increase (the difference between the number of births and deaths). In the non-Jewish population the increase is almost entirely due to natural increase.[1]

[1] The 1961 Census showed that the Jewish population constituted 89 per cent and the non-Jewish population 12 per cent of Israel's total population as compared with 82 and 18 per cent respectively in 1948.

Of the non-Jewish population in 1961, 69 per cent were Moslems, 20 per cent Christians, 10 per cent Druze, and less than 1 per cent 'Others'.

Nearly 38 per cent of the Jewish population enumerated in 1961 was born in Israel as compared with over 35 per cent in the 1948 registration. The proportion of Israel-born Jews decreased from 1948 until the end of 1951 when it was only 25·2 per cent; this was due to the mass immigration during that period. Since then due to the reduced volume of immigration and an

TABLE 3

The Jewish Population in Israel according to Continent
of Origin (Percentages)
1948–64

Year	Total	Place of Birth			
		Israel	Asia	Africa	Europe-America
1948	100	35·4	8·1	1·7	54·8
1950	100	25·8	15·7	6·7	51·8
1952	100	27·1	20·2	7·4	45·3
1953	100	29·2	19·7	7·4	43·7
1954	100	30·9	19·2	7·9	42·0
1955	100	32·1	18·4	9·6	39·9
1956	100	32·9	17·6	11·8	37·7
1957	100	33·4	16·8	12·4	37·4
1958	100	34·6	16·7	12·2	36·5
1959	100	35·9	16·3	12·1	35·7
1960	100	37·1	15·9	11·9	35·1
1961	100	38·1	15·2	11·9	34·8
1962	100	38·5	14·7	13·3	33·5
1963	100	38·9	14·2	14·2	32·4
1964	100	39·4	13·8	14·9	31·9

Source: Op. cit., No. 14, 1963, p. 44, Table 20.
Op. cit., No. 16, 1965, pp. 46, Table 18/B.

increasing birth rate, the Israel-born in the Jewish population has been rising steadily to 39·4 per cent in 1964, (Table 3).

More than 49 per cent of the Jewish population born abroad immigrated between 1948 and 1951, 27 per cent coming before 1948 and about 24 per cent arriving after 1951.

While during the years 1919–48, 89·6 per cent of 452,158 immigrants were from Europe and America and only 10·4 per cent from Asia and Africa, during the years 1948–62 only 45·4 per cent of a total of 1,074,792 immigrants were from Europe and America and 54·6 per cent were from Asia and Africa. (See Table 2).

Accordingly, the proportion of the various groups in the entire population of Israel changed. The proportion of European and American immigrants decreased from 54·8 per cent of the population in 1948, to 31·9 per cent in 1964; and the proportion of Asian and African immigrants increased from 9·8 per cent of the entire population in 1948 to 28·7 per cent in 1964. (See Table 3) If we add to this figure those who were born in Israel to parents of Asian and African origin, who comprise more than 17 per cent of the entire population (in 31 December 1964), we shall get a slightly different picture. More than 45 per cent of the Jewish inhabitants of Israel are from African and Asian origin, 6 per cent are children whose parents were born in Israel, and the other 49 per cent of the Jewish inhabitants of the country are from European-American origin.[1]

Of all the immigrants who came to the country between 1948 and May, 1961, 14·6 per cent came from Roumania, 13 per cent from Poland, 13·3 per cent from Iraq, 12·8 per cent from Morocco and Tangiers, 5·2 per cent from Yemen and Aden, 4·5 per cent from Algeria and Tunis, and the others came from other countries in smaller numbers.

In the period under discussion, less than 1·1 per cent of all the immigrants came from the United States.

While the great immigration appeared to perpetuate the basic characteristics of the Yishuv as an immigrant-absorbing society, this is only partially true. The whole pattern of absorption and motivation for migration has greatly changed, and the analysis of this change is of great importance for the understanding of the new structure.

The mass migration movement to the State of Israel differed greatly in character from immigration during the time of the Yishuv. The best starting point for its analysis is the nature of the crisis in the various Jewish societies abroad, which formed the background for their motivation to migrate. We have seen that the early aliyot developed out of a relatively successful transition from traditional Jewish society to a modern, assimilationist setting, a transition which influenced only a small and highly selective group sufficiently to attempt to create a new Jewish society in Palestine. This crisis cut across the different Jewish communities but did not embrace them all. The nature of the crisis immediately before the Second World War and especially after it, out of which immigration to Palestine and Israel developed, was of a quite different kind. Although the various crises greatly differed, there were some common characteristics which were reflected in the main motives for immigration. The most important of these were: firstly, there was usually all-round social, economic, and political insecurity; secondly, the crisis usually affected entire communities or sectors thereof and not merely a selected group; thirdly, the perpetuation of existing communities and patterns throughout the crisis period necessarily bound them closely to their existing values and

[1] According to op. cit., No. 16, 1965, p. 42.

ways of life, preventing a new set of values, directed towards creating a new community.

All these characteristics had their obvious repercussions on the motives for migration. Nowhere do we find so great a predisposition to change or so great a fusion of national, social, and economic orientations as in the first aliyot. Their most common motive was not the creation of a new kind of community and culture but the attainment of economic and social security and basic solidarity with the existing Jewish community, and in this respect the relation between occupational aspirations and changes, and the specific identification with the Jewish nation that developed is very significant. We have seen that in the pioneering aliyot occupational standing was – at least initially – valued in terms of its contribution to the economic structure of the Yishuv and not in purely intrinsic economic technical or professional terms. Among the new immigrants occupational aspirations were not as directly connected with national identification. Their evaluation of occupational possibilities was usually made in terms of social and economic security or was rated by what may be called the usual modern social prestige of an occupation. This change in occupational motivation was most clearly seen among those immigrants who chose to join the various agricultural settlements. During early immigrations settlement on the land was usually due to strong collectivist feeling, connected with the high value placed on agriculture as a factor in national rebirth, etc. Among the new immigrants the change to agriculture was usually motivated by its conception as (a) providing relative economic security; and (b) conferring relatively high prestige within the Yishuv.

Accordingly, among the new immigrants, the predisposition to change was more restricted and less intensive than in the earlier periods, being generally limited to an adaptation to the existing structure and its demands and not to the creation of a new society.

Changes in the Patterns of Absorption

The changes in the social structure of the Yishuv – the absorbing society – were neither smaller nor less important than the changes in the immigrants' motivation and predisposition to change. In many ways both sets of changes went hand in hand. The new immigrants' reluctance to change was simultaneous to the bureaucratizing of political and economic power and the weakening solidarity of the pioneer groups in the Yishuv. Together they produced the initial conditions for absorption, some of which have already been indicated and will now be elaborated on in somewhat greater detail.

The first important characteristic in the changing absorption pattern was the fact that it was accomplished under the aegis of bureaucratic, formal agencies. From their very beginnings, most of the immigrants were met by various officials – of the Jewish Agency, the Government, the Histadrut, etc. – whose function it was to direct them to their various places of settlement, to afford amenities such as housing, furniture, rations, medical help, and to assist generally. Special rules were laid down for allocating these facilities to the immigrants who, from the purely bureaucratic point of view, were but impersonal groups to which these rules could be applied. A formal, bureaucratic relation, therefore, was the first which most of the immigrants experienced in their new country, and for a long time it remained – and in some instances still is – the main one for many of them. Even the introduction to the basic roles incumbent on them as citizens were usually effected through bureaucratic channels – whether concerned with education, military service, or economic rights. Power was an element that was very quickly added to this bureaucratic dimension. In the later stages of absorption, many of the contacts with the country's representatives were extended to officials of the various political parties and organizations – all of whom began to compete for the potential political value of the immigrants as voters. Beyond that there existed only minimum contact. Except for those who had relatives, old acquaintances, or friends in Israel, few immigrants could enter the more informal setting of the country in the beginning.

A second characteristic was the change in importance of the different types of settlements as places of absorption. Settlements of the kibbutz type where absorption was effected through incorporation into existing primary groups decreased in importance. The relatively large proportion of smallholders' settlements indicates not absorption into already existing settlements but, almost entirely, the creation of new moshavim by the immigrants. This changing pattern can also be seen from the fact that many of the immigrants tended, at least in the beginning, to settle in special, segregated areas where they usually maintained a high degree of social homogeneity, especially among the older inhabitants. Not only did many of them settle in entirely new places – such as abandoned Arab villages and towns – but even those who settled in existing towns or villages usually did so in new neighbourhoods where they were more or less concentrated and, ecologically, relatively segregated. This segregation was most pronounced at the start of mass immigrations, and although it has since been somewhat lessened through various housing projects in which old and new inhabitants participated, it still persists as the main institutional feature of the new immigration. As immigration increased, new types of special transition settlements for immigrants were built all over the country – the immigrant camp and the *maabara* (or transit camp). Composed of tin and wooden huts, the *maabara* constituted a striking contrast between old and new inhabitants. Such ecological segregation also implied, of course, that even the separate services which the immigrants often received, such as schools, local government organizations, etc., were not necessarily points of contact with the older inhabitants.

At first the economic distribution of the new immigrants also showed strong institutional concentration in special sectors. New fields of economic activity were developed for them, such as public works (afforestation, repair of abandoned property, and so on); and in general the new immigrants occupied lower economic positions than did the old inhabitants. There were, of course, differences between the various groups of immigrants, and in time some degree of occupational mobility and integration came about. But the initial picture persisted as the basic set of conditions within which absorption took place.

The Dynamics of Immigrant Absorption and the Institutional Development of the Social Structure

As has been indicated the initial patterns of absorption can be explained through several interacting facts, such as the numerical strength of the immigrant population, their motives for migrating, and the changes in the Yishuv's social orientation.

However, this situation was somewhat paradoxical. While the immigrants were given some primary rights and privileges on the criterion ascribed to them as citizens or Jews, their place in the social structure was a relatively low one, and they were initially but passive objects of the bureaucratic agencies. This paradoxical connexion between the two aspects of absorption meant that this situation did not remain static. Basic equality and universal civil rights granted to the immigrants were fully legitimized within the social structure, and the initial relative segregation had no basis in either law or the ideology of the state, which emphasized the complete equality of all citizens, and their dedication to the task of the ingathering of the exiles.

In addition to this ideology, and strongly connected with it, were other factors tending to mitigate the initial segregation inherent in the process of absorption. First among these were the various agencies, such as the schools, the army, etc., which made important demands on the immigrants and directed them into new, universal roles. Secondly, in the developing economic structure of the state additional manpower at various levels of specialization was needed. The old Yishuv could not provide the full extent of this manpower, and as no legal discrimination existed, many of the immigrants were drawn into the various economic strata of the Yishuv. Although generally immigrants tend to be more susceptible to economic retrogression, unemployment, etc., a general tendency towards economic advancement and occupational mobility gradually emerged.

Third, and most important, was the fact that the immigrants were granted basic political rights which enhanced their political value to the different social groups, parties etc. All these groups began to be active among the immigrants, extended their organizations to include them, and thus necessarily drew many people into their orbit.

The impact of all these factors gradually broke the initial segregation of the immigrants and gave rise to various processes of mobility and integration which will be discussed later. It should be emphasized here that all these trends operated within the framework of a formal, institutional setting; but although lessening segregation, they were not based on the intensive solidarity and collective identification that had previously existed in the Yishuv. No complete fusion between groups of immigrants and old inhabitants therefore took place, and each immigrant group was left to work out its own way according to its own dispositions and the specific conditions of absorption in which it was placed.

Summary

The establishment of the state brings us to the central part of our analysis – that of the development and crystallization of the major institutional spheres in Israeli society. It is with the establishment of the state that the institutional structure, developed from the pioneering groups, became differentiated, crystallized, and confronted with a population with new motivations and orientations.

This brings us to the second – and longer – part of our analysis which deals with the development and crystallization of Israeli society in its main institutional spheres – in economics, in the social organization and stratification, in education, politics and the cultural spheres. The following chapters – each of which will deal with one of these spheres – will, at first, briefly describe the major features of each sphere and will then proceed to analyse these developments in terms of the problems incumbent in the transition from Yishuv to state.

Lastly, we shall analyse the additional problems evolving and shall then study the strengths and weaknesses of Israeli society in coping with its entrance into new phases of development and modernization.

Part II

THE EMERGING SOCIAL STRUCTURE

6

Economic Structure, Problems and Developments in the Yishuv and in the State of Israel

1

Introduction

We shall start with a brief outline of the demographic, physical, and basic organizational structure of the economy in the period of the Yishuv. The tables and descriptions presented in the first part of the chapter will deal with basic demographic data, then with the development of the major economic branches, their basic institutional and organizational features and their distribution between the different sectors (i.e. private, Histadrut, government).

We shall analyse the changes in all these spheres attendant on the transition from Yishuv to state.

In the second part of this chapter we shall analyse the major economic policies of the government, while in the third part we shall deal with the overall impact of the developments and policies discussed in the preceding parts and on the performance of the economy in terms of production and consumption and the relation between them.

Composition and Dispersion of Population

In tables 1–3, pp. 61–63 some of the basic data on the development and composition of Jewish population in the Yishuv and in Israel were given, and they may serve as background for the following discussion.

Dispersion of Population

Until the establishment of the state, the Jewish population was predominantly concentrated in the three big urban centres which in 1948 comprised nearly 60 per cent of the total. The remainder were mainly dispersed in small agricultural settlements. There were thus almost no middle-sized towns.

In 1951 a plan for the dispersion of the population was evolved. Stage I, which related to a future population of 2,650,000, stipulated:

    (1) Division of the country into twenty-four districts – for each of which 'the future urban and rural population' was separately planned.

71

(2) The planned urban population was to reach 2,050,000 and the planned rural population 600,000, or nearly 23 per cent.

(3) The plan emphasized the development of two new types of urban centres:
    (i) An urban-rural centre with a population of six to twelve thousand.
    (ii) A middle-sized town, serving as a district centre, with a population of forty to sixty thousand.

These two new types were to fill the gap between the big urban centres on the one hand and the small rural communities on the other, and thus provide a focus for regional integration.

(4) The plan assumed that further expansion of the three big towns would be stopped and demanded the dispersion of the population into the two types of middle-range urban settlements.

(5) Seventy new sites of urban settlement were fixed, some of which were wholly new, some abandoned Arab settlements, and some settled only by a small nucleus of Jewish settlers.

In 1957 Stage II of the plan was evolved. It was based on a population of 3,000,000 Jews and 325,000 (changed to 360,000 in 1961) non-Jews. Of this population, 750,000 people, or about 23 per cent, would be settled in the new development towns.

What were the results of these plans? The percentage of Jewish urban population in fact rose slightly in the period 1947–61. Rural population rose from 18 per cent in 1948 to 20.1 per cent in 1964, or 120,000 as against 507,000. Jerusalem grew by 98 per cent, Haifa by 87 per cent, and Tel Aviv by only 55 per cent. Thus it seems as if the main object of the disperson of population – lessening of pressure in the coastal plain – was accomplished. But such a conclusion is unwarranted owing to the enormous growth of the smaller towns around Tel Aviv, forming with it a solid urban block of about 900,000 people. All these towns grew by between 200 per cent and 1,250 per cent: Ramat Gan – 425 per cent, Holon – 403 per cent, Bnei Brak – 433 per cent, Bat Yam – 1,244 per cent, Herzliya – 407 per cent, Giv'atayim – 220 per cent.

Nevertheless, there was a disproportionately stronger growth of the southern districts. In the period 1951–61 these grew by 169 per cent while the central districts grew by only 28 per cent, and Tel Aviv by 41 per cent. But the northern part of the country, Galilee, grew by only 40 per cent, and remains as yet sparsely populated by Jews.

In 1961 the twenty-seven development towns (twenty-three of which are formally so designated, while four are considered immigrant towns) comprised 12·5 per cent of the total, with a population of 273,000.

There was almost no change in the ratio of urban to rural population, in of the stipulation of the dispersion plan.

The growth of the central areas was slower than the growth of the south but not of the north. But the proportional growth of the south is in part an artifact of the extremely sparse population in these parts in the first period after the establishment of the state.

The growth of the big towns slowed down – partly because of geographical limitation – but their satellite towns increased at a disproportionate rate.

The growth of the new development towns is as yet far from attaining the proportions planned for a Jewish population of three million.

The Development of the Major Economic Branches of the Yishuv and of Israel – Basic Data

The following tables give us some of the basic data on the composition of the economic activities in the Yishuv and the State of Israel (See Tables 4 and 5.).

TABLE 4

Distribution of National Income Between Jews and Non-Jews by Economic Branches

	A. Distribution in each branch						B. By branch			
	1936			1944			1936		1944	
	N. income /mill. P.P.*	Jews (%)	Others (%)	N. income /mill. P.P.*	Jews (%)	Others (%)	Jews Millions	Others	Jews P.P.*	Others
Total	33·8	52·6	47·4	123·0	59·7	40·3	17·8	16·1	73·4	49·6
Population (in thousands)	1,366·7	28·1	71·9	1,739·6	30·4	69·6				
							Per cents			
	—	—	—	—	—	—	100·0	100·0	100·0	100·0
Agriculture	5·6	30·1	69·9	29·5	30·8	69·2	9·4	24·2	12·4	41·1
Manufacturing, Electricity	5·6	64·4	33·5	28·2	88·3	11·7	21·9	12·4	33·9	6·7
Construction	1·9	83·2	16·8	5·6	48·2	51·8	8·7	2·0	3·7	5·8
Trade, Transport, Finance[a]	13·9	59·2	40·8	37·2	64·2	35·8	51·7	35·2	32·6	26·8
Health and Education[b]	0·9	80·3	19·7	—[c]	—	—	4·1	1·1	—[c]	—[c]
Government, Municipalities	3·8	23·3	76·7	7·5	36·0	64·0	5·0	18·2	3·7	9·7
Other Services	1·9	—	—	8·8	77·3	22·7	4·5	6·9	9·2	4·0
Armed Forces	—[d]	—	—	6·2	53·2	46·8	—[d]	—[d]	4·5	5·8

* Palestine Pounds.
[a] and rents.
[c] Included in other services.
[b] Non-Governmental.
[d] Included in Government.

Source: R. R. Nathan, O. Gass, and D. Creamer, *Palestine Problem and Promise.* Washington, D.C.: Public Affairs Press, 1946.
Jewish Agency for Palestine, *Statistical Handbook of Jewish Palestine, 1947.* Jerusalem, Jewish Agency, 1947.

TABLE 5

National Output Product and Income
Net Domestic Product (National Income)[a] at Factor
Cost by Major Industry Branch 1936–60 (Per cent)

	1936	1939	1945	1950	1953	1955	1959[b]	1960
Total (in millions P.P. or IL)*	33·85	75·89	82·0	337·0	1,139	1,812	3,211	3,552
Per cent	100·0	100·0	100·0	100·0	100·0	100·0	100·0	100·0
Agriculture, Forestry and Fishing	16·4	19·1	11·8	9·5	11·2	11·5	11·7	11·0
Mining, Quarrying and Manufacturing	16·0	19·9	36·6	24·0	20·5	22·0	22·2	24·1
Construction	5·5	6·1	4·4	11·9	6·5	7·6	7·2	6·6
Public Utilities (Water, Electricity)	1·4	—[c]	—[c]	—[c]	2·1	1·6	1·7	—
Transportation and Communications	2·4[d]	5·9	6·2	6·2	7·4	6·7	7·2	7·4
Trade	23·5[e]	12·3 ⎤	⎫ 20·8	12·5	10·4	11·3	20·5[f] ⎤	⎫ 28·8
Banking and Finance, Real Estate	15·2	14·3 ⎦	⎭	2·4	8·4	7·9	8·1 ⎦	⎭
Other Services	5·6	7·4	12·6	18·7	11·4	10·3	—[f]	
General Government and Non-profit Institutions	14·0	14·9[g]	7·5	14·8	21·4	21·1	21·4	22·2

* Palestine Pounds, Israeli Lira.

[a] For 1936–9. [b] Early estimates. [c] Includes part of transport.
[d] Railroad Transport and Communications only.
[e] Water for irrigation in agriculture. Electricity in Mining etc.
[f] Includes 'Other services'.
[g] Includes in per cent: 1936: Central Government 9·4 per cent, Municipalities 1·9 and Health and Education' – non-governmental – 2·7 per cent; 1939: 8·2 per cent, 3·3 per cent and 3·4 per cent respectively.

Sources: 1936: R. R. Nathan, op. cit., Chap. 12, Table 1, p. 148.

1945–50: D. Creamer, Israel's National Income 1950–4, Falk Project and Jerusalem, CBS, Special Series No. 57, 1957, Table 10, p. 30.

1953: CBS Statistical Abstract 1957/8, No. 9, Table F3, p. 113.
1955–9: CBS Statistical Abstract 1959/60, No. 11, Table F6, p. 126.
1960: CBS Statist. Bull. Vol. III, No. 1, Table c, p. 72.

TABLE 6

The Share of the 'Histadrut Sector'[a]
in Total Industry by Branches

	1939		1959	
		Per cent of total		*Per cent of total*
	Total No. (thousands)	Histadrut total	Total Mill. IL*	Histadrut total
Total	156·0	18·7[a]	1,964·9	23·3[a]
Mining, Quarrying	3·7	37·8	37·5	36·8
Food, Beverages, Tobacco	20·6	19·9	347·1	33·0
Textiles ⎫ Clothing ⎭	38·0	2·4	266·9 / 184·9	2·2 / 0·3
Wood Products	13·2	16·7	116·4	29·9
Paper, Publishing	10·0	8·0	98·7	7·1
Leather and Products	b	b	73·4	4·9
Rubber and Plastic ⎫ Chemical Products ⎭	10·2	19·6	51·0 / 169·1	41·2 / 20·4
Non-metallic Minerals	8·3	47·0	116·9	67·3
Diamonds	4·1	c	92·0	c
Metal Machinery Electrical Machinery Equipment ⎫	43·6	12·2	179·8 / 52·0 ⎱ 51·4	23·6 / 14·2
Transport Equipment ⎫ Miscellaneous ⎭	4·2	21·4	106·6 / 21·1	d / 4·7

* Israeli Lira
[a] Include 50·250 Mill. IL and 7,140 persons employed in workshops in Labour Settlements and 'own industry' which are not included in the separate branches.
[b] Included in 'Textiles and Clothing'.
[c] Included in 'Miscellaneous'.
[d] Included in 'Metal'.

Sources: Total output: *Bank of Israel Report*, 1959, Table 1, p. 128.
Total persons employed: ibid., Table 2, p. 129.
'Histadrut' data: *Industry in the Labour Economy 1959* (Facts and Figures), No. 7/CFJL, Economic and Social Research Institute, Tel Aviv, August 1960 pp. iii and 5.

TABLE 7

E . *Size of Industrial Establishments by Numbers of Persons Employed, 1943–58*

	1943ᵃ		1955ᵇ		1958	
	No. of estab-lish-ments	No. of persons em-ployed	No. of Estab-lish-ments	No. of Persons em-ployed	No. of Estab-lish-ments	No. of Persons em-ployed
Total	2,120	45,049	6,996	92,000	9,271	118,300
	%	%	%	%	%	%
1–4 Persons employed	19·4	2·9	44·6	10·1	52·8	11·6
5–9 ,, ,,	37·0	11·6	27·9	14·1	23·8	12·2
10–14 ,, ,,	—	—	9·1	8·3	7·8	7·2
15–24 ,, ,,	36·1	32·8	8·5	11·9	6·6	9·7
25–49 ,, ,,	—	—	5·9	15·5	5·0	13·3
50–99 ,, ,,	3·8	12·8	2·3	11·6	2·3	11·9
100–299 ,, ,,	3·7	39·9	1·4	18·0	1·3	16·8
300+ ,, ,,	—	—	0·3	10·5	0·4	17·3

ᵃ Only Jewish industry, and without Handicrafts.
ᵇ Total industry – of establishments which employ at least one worker.
Sources: 1943: *Statistical Handbook*, op. cit., p. 217.
1955: CBS *Statistical Abstract: No. 9*, p. 174, Table 14.
1958: CBS *Statistical Abstract: No. 11*, p. 192, Table 6.

The Development of the Economy in the Period of the Yishuv

We shall now proceed to a brief description of the basic economic branches, starting with agriculture.

As we have seen above, the main monetary activities (about 70 per cent of total public investments) of the Jewish National Institutions were directed to agricultural settlement. On the establishment of the State of Israel the Jews cultivated some one million dunams, of which less than a third was irrigated. This cultivation took place in about 280 agricultural settlements, half of which were moshavot (small villages) and moshavim, and the other half kibbutzim.

The main farming method was that of mixed farming. The mixed farm was based on livestock (cows and laying hens) and fodder crops. Secondary crops were fruits and vegetables. 'Fish ponds' were another typical Jewish branch. The mixed farm developed from both economic and ideological reasons.

The mixed farm did not grow traditional international market crops, such as sugar, cotton, and wheat; but it supplied most of the Jewish community's needs in many foodstuffs. It made possible the maintenance of the family unit and did not depend to any large extent on wage labour – thus facilitating the maintenance of the ideology of 'self-labour' and economic political self-sufficiency of the Yishuv.

Side by side with mixed farming, the citrus plantations developed as a monoculture type of farm. This crop, which had a considerable comparative advantage comprised most of the Palestinian exports. The branch was mainly in the hands of private farmers. The Second World War caused a severe contraction of citrus plantations and production, which diminished to a third of its pre-war size in the whole of Palestine. It took about fifteen years to reach the 1939 planted area.

Deficiency of natural resources and of capital for investment purposes, external free trade policies of the mandatory government, and a small domestic market, prevented the development of large-scale industry in Palestine. The enterprises established worked under conditions of lack of capital and poor equipment, on the one hand and overcapacity on the other. Industry received its first push in the 'thirties when new waves of immigrants and capital came from Central and Western Europe. They also brought with them the knowledge required to operate modern industrial enterprises. For some branches – such as diamond polishing and the textile industry – the imported knowledge was the main factor in their establishment. The Second World War gave the second great impetus to industry by protecting the frontiers from competition and by widening demand owing to the needs of the armed forces and the regional population. Textiles and clothing, metals, and chemicals were the main branches which expanded in this period. When Israel was established, Jewish industry had the typical structure of a young industry in a developing country, the important part of production consisting mostly of consumer goods, such as foodstuffs and clothing.

The food industry employed some 20 per cent of all employed persons in industry and produced about 30 per cent of the total product. Other main branches were: metals (which were smaller than what is considered usual in industrial countries), chemicals (mainly from the Dead Sea resources) and construction materials (which decreased in size during the war).

The average size[1] of Jewish industrial enterprises (not including handicrafts) in 1943 was twenty-one employed persons. About half of all the employed persons worked in factories which employed more than fifty persons. More than half of the establishments employed less than ten persons.

About 80 per cent of the establishments – which employed about 40 per cent of the total industrial employees – were organized as private ownerships or partnerships. Private and public limited companies comprised less than one fifth of total establishments but employed more than half of the industrial labour force. The co-operatives' share was not more than 5 per cent of total industry according to the two criteria. (See Tables 7 and 11.)

[1] Number of persons employed.

At the end of the mandatory period (1943) the Histadrut sector owned about 70 per cent of the mixed farming, 6·8 per cent of the citrus plantations, about 10 per cent of industry, two thirds of the construction branches, and a similar share of road transportation. (See Tables 6 and 10.)

The Impact of the Ideological Orientations on the Structure and Organization of the Yishuv's Economy

Thus from the purely descriptive point of view the Yishuv's economy was not greatly different from a relatively small-scale colonizatory and urban economy. But owing to their specific ideological and social starting points, its major social and organizational characteristics developed some very special features.

The major ideological orientations in the economic field – as in most institutional fields – were shaped in the period of the second aliya and then further developed and crystallized in incipient institutional forms under the Mandate, especially in the period of the third aliya.

The first ideological emphasis was on what may be called national economic creativity – the creation of branches essential from the point of view of the establishment of a normal occupational and economic structure. These orientations resulted in several institutional implications. First, they entailed a strong emphasis on creation of those parts of the economy which characterize any normal economic structure and which were especially lacking among the Jews in the diaspora – in particular the primary productive branches. Here, as we have seen, agriculture stood out as one of the most important and crucial branches which became a symbol of the process of national regeneration.

Second, these orientations also entailed the input of national capital and effort into strategically important branches. Strong emphasis was placed on the creation of conditions appropriate for the development of manpower from among Jews in the diaspora who would be able to maintain these sectors of the economy.

Most of the general ideological tenets in this field were, to a large extent, shared by a large majority of the Zionist movement – even if not necessarily of all the settlers in Palestine. So also were some of the more general institutional derivations of these tenets – such as the strong emphasis on work on the land, on some national colonization, and to some extent also on the nationalization of land. This last emphasis was reflected in the establishment and working of *Keren Kayemet* and of the *Hevrat Hachsharat Hayishuv* and to a smaller extent also in the various banking activities of the Zionist Organization in the promotion of colonization. But the more specific socialist elements were confined mostly to the workers' sector.

As with all these institutional spheres, the development and crystallization of the economy was not built up according to the ideological blueprint or according to its initial organizational derivatives. The concrete contours of economic organization and institutions developed through the interaction between these ideologies and the initial organizational forms on the one hand and the more stychic forces which developed in the economic sphere, on the other. These forces did not, from the very beginning, identify themselves with the basic tenets of the ideology.

The growing differentiation of the economy as well as of the indigenous forces within the workers' sectors of necessity greatly undermined the purity of the ideology and the possibility of its becoming fully implemented.

As in all the institutional spheres the ideology left its imprint on the institutional structure through a process of selective entrenchment and permeation which took place in different ways – first in the development of sectors in which the institutional derivatives of the ideology were more or less strictly adhered to, and second, in the strong influence of the ideology on more general strategic points of the economy.

The purest expression of this ideology was to be found, of course, in the specific forms of the collective and co-operative agricultural settlements and in the different types of co-operatives and public and semi-public corporations.

The more general impact of the ideology in the economic sphere was manifest in the maintenance of the primacy of socio-political considerations in allocating national economic resources and regulating economic activities. This was first seen in the strong emphasis on colonizing activities and in the development of those sectors of the economy which were important from the social-ideological and political points of view. Second, it was manifest in the relatively large concentration of national and public capital in certain public sectors, especially agriculture; third, it was evident in the predominance of social and political considerations in the internal distribution of public economic resources.

One of the most general institutional derivatives of the ideology could be found in the great prevalence of public ownership in land. This had its roots in the activities of the *Keren Kayemet* and became even more intensified in the period of the state.

About 92 per cent of the total area of Israel is owned by the Government and the Jewish National Fund and is managed by the Israel Land Authority, founded in 1958. More than 80 per cent of all farming land and over 90 per cent of the areas now cultivated by Jews are administered by the company. The land rent policy of the company is thus the dominant system in Israel. The Israel Land Authority[1] charges the farmers rents which are far less than the average economic rent, and the differences in rents charged do not always reflect in land qualities and vice versa. The rent for lease of land to permanent settlements (for forty-nine years) is calculated per land unit – which is determined by the concept that each family should be given only that area

[1] Or the government and the Jewish National Fund before 1959–60.

which it is capable of cultivating without outside help; therefore the size of the family, the availability of irrigation facilities, and the anticipated main farming activity of the new village, determine the size of the land unit. In this way the land unit varies from seventeen to fifty dunams. Until recently the rent per land unit was IL 12 – which is between IL 0·25 and IL 1·50 per dunam. According to some calculations, the rent on land constitutes about 0·6 per cent of the gross value of agricultural output, or something below this rate, when public lands only are taken into account.

All this gradually gave rise to the crystallization of vested interests around many of the groups which originated through these processes. One of the most important outcomes of these processes was the division of the Yishuv's and later Israel's economy into the various sectors – the private sector (the sector within which most enterprises were owned by private individuals and corporations) and the Histadrut sector (all the different enterprises of the Histadrut such as co-operatives, agricultural settlements, and public companies belonging, officially at least, to the Histadrut).

The Development of Economic Entrepreneurship in the Yishuv

The institutional impact of the ideology was also evident in the nature of economic entrepreneurship that developed in the Yishuv.

Perhaps the most important single type of new entrepreneur that developed in the Yishuv was what may be called the institutional entrepreneur colonizer. Such an entrepreneur usually held some key position in a settlement, in a co-operative enterprise, or in one of the public or semi-public economic enterprises (for example, some of the Histadrut-owned factories and the public water companies). His main concern was to maximize the scope of economic activities and the assets and profits of his own group and organization through the best manipulation of both the market possibilities and the different sources of capital, credit, and so forth – especially from the different colonizing agencies. His conception of the role was not, however, a purely economic one. He saw himself as furthering the general social values of society, helping the general colonizing movement and expansion through the enlargement and development of his own organization – an assumption which usually contained some elements of reality. He was not, generally speaking, a bureaucrat of the usual type – although gradually more and more purely bureaucratic managers did develop and from the beginning there was, in most of these groups, some lower technical and bureaucratic staff. He saw himself rather as an elected representative of his group or organization, its emissary, and in general as an economic pioneer.

At the same time two general types of capitalist entrepreneur arose in the Yishuv. One was a big entrepreneur who was able – through appropriate use of his own financial resources, of some of the liquid capital in the country, and of some of the credit facilities extended by the main colonizing agencies – to exploit strategic possibilities of the developing internal market, export outlets, and so forth, and establish relatively big industrial enterprises in key areas. Good examples of this are the Ata Textile Industries and some of the industries processing agricultural produce.

This type of entrepreneur, too, had to take into account many of the social values found in the semi-public enterprises, though in somewhat different ways. In the first place, most of these entrepreneurs subscribed to the basic tenets of social security, collective bargaining, and family and cost-of-living allowances. Secondly, they sometimes found it beneficial to their interests to go into partnership – usually on a limited basis and in subsidiary companies – with some of the public or semi-public enterprises. This tendency has increased since the establishment of the State of Israel. Third, most of these enterprises availed themselves of the various facilities (especially financial credit) of the colonizing agencies and later of the state, and paid service to the pioneering ideology. This showed itself in their relative concentration in industries of strategic importance for economic development.

The second very general and heterogeneous type of capitalistic entrepreneur that developed in the Yishuv was the small industrialist, merchant, or businessman whose activities were mostly oriented towards the growing internal market. His range of activities was not very wide and on the whole he was rather conservative in his approach. He was not usually in close contact with the main colonizing agencies, although quite often he would enter into some competition with groups like the public co-operatives.

The Major Organizational Changes in the Economy Attendant on the Establishment of the State

The overall importance of the various political considerations in the economic system greatly intensified after the establishment of the State of Israel with unification of the economic institutional frameworks, the growing interdependence of the various sectors of the economy, the coming to power of the ideology's proponents and the increased tasks facing the economy.

The establishment of the state brought with it several important structural changes in the regulative mechanisms of the economy. The most important of these were the growth of central planning, and the direct and indirect intervention of the government in economic life.

The mandatory government virtually refrained from interfering in the economic life of the country. Its policy was expressed in laws, acts, and decrees, and in the real economic activities of the government itself through budgets. The monetary system was essentially identified with the 'Gold Standard' system in its extreme meaning and thus restrained any protection of domestic production.

81

The government budget as a whole constituted little more than one-tenth of the total national income, which is usually considered a relatively low rate for developing countries. The budget was administrative in character, with almost no investments for economic development. The share of the public services was also relatively small. Furthermore, these were generally surplus budgets and therefore had a deflationary impact on the economic activity of other sectors. About two-thirds of government services eventually went to the Arab population.

In the main this policy naturally injured the more dynamic Jewish sector. It was mainly in one area – public works – that the mandatory government was active, and to the extent that this activity was devoted to roads and public buildings it contributed to the improvement of the external economic framework.

The independent institutions of the Jewish community in Palestine tried to fill in some of the gaps of the mandatory authorities. Most of their budgets were devoted to economic development (mainly in agriculture) and public services. They were, however, hampered by lack of money and by the impossibility of executing an effective independent economic policy.

During the Second World War the acuteness of the problem was to a large extent blunted; on the one hand, the stopping of the main world trade routes protected domestic production, and on the other hand, this production was also stimulated by the demand arising from the wants of a large army. This situation also forced the government to enter economic life as an effective consumer, regulator, and supervisor.

With the establishment of Israel all relations with the immediate geographic surroundings (including the part of Palestine which was not included in Israel) ceased and the Israeli Government took over the management of a new and independent economic policy.

The economic policy of Israel's government was in many crucial ways the opposite of that of the Mandate. The government saw itself, in principle, as the supreme economic agent both in the planning, encouraging, and supervising of economic life and also in many cases as a direct participator.

The government erected a strong customs barrier which was strengthened by quota restrictions on imports, and thus encouraged, by these and other means, domestic production in all sectors. By a series of acts and decrees, the government regulated production, consumption, and most other economic activities.

The change stands out especially in the composition of the government budget which accounts for about 40 per cent of the total national income and a quarter of the total resources. A third of all expenditure is generally spent on economic development projects. The government's share in total investments in Israel had reached 80 per cent, and even now, after several years of a diminishing share, it is more than 50 per cent. (See Tables 30a and 30b.)

82

The establishment of the state has created an almost entirely new sector – the government one. This sector consists in the main of:

(1) Enterprises established to serve the government itself. In this category may be named the Government Printer and the Public Works Department. These are departments in the relevant ministries, and their budgets are part of the regular governmental budget.

(2) Business enterprises. In this category we find most of the economic public services of the government: transport (railways, ports), communications (post, telephone, telegraph), and the Development Authority which is responsible for abandoned property. These enterprises operate as separate economic entities and have a special budget.

(3) Government corporations, which are separated from the government budgets, and operate as independent limited public companies. The government owns a part of their total stock (in the majority of cases most of it) and has its representatives in the Boards of Directors (also in most cases a majority of total votes). In 1960–1 there were more than forty corporations of this sort – in mining, industry and handicrafts, water and power, transport, housing, finance, and others. These corporations employed more than 17,000 persons in 1960.

(4) In addition to the former we find various statutory, autonomous, governmental-public bodies, such as the Port Authority and, in a somewhat different way, the National Insurance Institute.

In 1960–1 the government employed 58,434 persons in permanent work (about 8 per cent of the total labour force). This figure includes all the workers in ministries and in governmental business enterprises. It does not include temporary workers, municipal workers, employed persons in the Government Development Companies, and the armed forces.

The Development and Crystallization of Major Economic Problems

The establishment of the state gave rise not merely to a change in the regulative organization of the economy. The most important feature of economic change was the great influx of new manpower, the growth, and change in the composition of the population (see Tables 1, 2, 3, 10, 12, 13, and 14).

The most important single new problem was that of absorbing the new immigrants as productive elements in the economy – a problem which became more acute both because of the relatively low education and skill level of many of them and because of the initial lowering of the capital reserves of the Jewish sector of the economy.

The second problem was that of attaining economic independence – i.e. a favourable balance of payments – a problem which was obviously not of central importance in the preceding period but which became very important with the state's responsibility for economic welfare.

This problem was very closely connected with two additional ones. One was the ability of the developing Israeli economy to attain a high level of economic modernization, of technological change and development beyond the first relatively embryonic form of such modern development attained in the period of the Yishuv. The second problem here was the striving for a higher standard of living which became, as we shall see later in greater detail, a major social goal and economic problem alike.

In order to understand how the Israeli economy dealt with these problems it is first necessary to describe the basic physical details of the growth of the Yishuv's economic structure.

Growth of the Economy and of its Major Branches

Tables 8, 9, 30a, and 30b show the continuous growth of the economy and most of its branches.

TABLE 8

Net Domestic Product at Factor Cost[a]
by Major Economic Branch (Percentages)

	1952 (1)	1954 (2)	1958 (3)	1962 (4)	1964 (5)
All Branches	100·0	100·0	100·0	100·0	100·0
Agriculture, Forestry and Fishing	11·5	12·1	13·0	9·7	9·4
Industry, Crafts and Quarrying	21·8	22·3	21·6	23·2	24·3
Construction and Public Works	9·0	7·6	7·8	7·9	7·8
Services and Public Administration	57·7	58·0	57·6	59·2	58·5

[a] Before adjustment for inventory changes, depreciation and net interest of government and Jewish national institutions.

Sources: Cols. (1)–(4): CBS, *The National Income and Expenditure of Israel (1950–62)*, Table 59, pp. 106–7.
Col. (5): CBS, *Statistical Abstract*, No. 16, 1965, Table F/14, p. 176.

TABLE 9

Net Domestic Product and National Income at Factor Cost by Major Economic Branch (IL million) 1952–62

	1952	1953	1954	1955	1956	1957	1958	1959	1960	1961	1962
Agriculture, Forestry and Fishing	97·0	127·8	176·1	200·0	244·0	315·7	370·5	384·9	411·8	468·5	507·6
Manufacturing, Mining and Quarrying	184·0	255·2	324·1	398·5	465·4	533·6	615·2	719·8	835·8	1,017·4	1,216·7
Construction[a]	75·6	84·8	110·5	144·7	155·6	191·4	220·8	234·8	247·6	312·7	412·8
Public Utilities (Water and Electricity)	14·4	24·3	27·3	29·3	38·2	46·6	53·9	67·0	74·5	87·8	100·4
Transportation and Communication	59·0	76·3	104·5	122·9	150·0	178·5	203·4	237·6	266·0	314·8	400·4
Finance, Insurance and Real Estate	19·1	26·3	34·3	45·1	54·0	63·6	75·5	95·5	118·9	154·0	201·0
Ownership of Dwellings[b]	44·4	56·0	73·3	96·4	128·7	141·5	155·8	180·1	208·2	251·6	326·2
General Government and Private Non-profit Institutions	157·6	222·2	292·9	372·4	452·4	504·6	563·4	651·6	719·3	839·3	1,023·5
Trade	106·1	134·7	170·4	208·0	248·7	291·2	328·5	360·5	729·0 }	872·0 }	1,060·0 }
Other Services	86·3	112·0	141·6	166·8	192·2	222·1	260·7	289·7			
Net Domestic Product at Factor Cost (before adjustment)	843·5	1,119·6	1,455·0	1,784·1	2,129·2	2,488·8	2,847·7	3,221·5	3,610·3	4,318·1	5,248·6
Less: Inventory Adjustment[c]	—	—	—	(−)29·0	(−)30·0	(−)32·0	(−)7·7	(−)8·7	(−)12·5	(−)52·2	(−)63·4
Less: Depreciation Adjustment[a]	(−)10·0	(−)26·0	(−)38·0	(−)34·0	(−)51·0	(−)60·0	(−)63·0	(−)59·0	(−)68·0	(−)79·0	(−)191·0
Plus: Net Interest Paid by Central Government and Jewish National Institutions[e]	7·3	11·7	19·2	13·4	16·5	6·2	5·2	5·2	20·8	34·8	48·1
Net Domestic Product as Factor Cost (adjusted)	840·8	1,105·3	1,436·2	1,734·5	2,064·7	2,403·0	2,782·2	3,159·0	3,550·6	4,221·7	5,042·3
Less: Net Factor Payments to Abroad	(−)17·2	(−)29·0	(−)34·2	(−)31·5	(−)33·1	(−)46·3	(−)54·3	(−)66·9	(−)68·3	(−)97·0	(−)148·8
NATIONAL INCOME (=NET NATIONAL PRODUCT AT FACTOR COST)	823·6	1,076·3	1,402·0	1,703·0	2,031·6	2,356·7	2,727·9	3,092·1	3,482·3	4,124·7	4,893·5

[a] Contract construction only.

[b] Imputation.

[c] Adjustment for capital gains and losses included in the estimates of returns to capital, as a result of the systems of inventory evaluation employed by enterprises.

[a] Adjustment for the difference between depreciation estimates based on balance-sheet data and estimates at replacement cost.

[e] Imputed subsidy payment to non-government sector.

Source: CBS *The National Income and Expenditure of Israel, 1950–62*, Jerusalem, Table 7, 1964.

TABLE 10

Establishments and Persons Employed by Type of Ownership 1933–58

	1933		1943		1955		1958		1964	
	No. of establish-ments	No. of persons employed	No. of establish-ments	No. of persons employed	No. of establish-ments	No. of persons employed	No. of establish-ments	No. of persons employed	No. of establish-ments	No. of persons employed
Total	—	—	2,120	45,049	6,996	92,900	9,271	118,300	10,430	178,308
Percents	100·0	100·0	100·0	100·0	100·0	100·0	100·0	100·0	100·0	100·0
Single-Owner Establishment	89	75	48·8	20·5	50·2	18·2	51·8	18·0	50·7	15·1
Partnership			29·9	21·4	27·2	18·8	23·5	16·3	22·0	11·5
Private Limited Company	5	18	16·9	52·4	16·2	39·6	14·8	39·7	22·2	47·2
Public ,,					1·2	13·7	1·2	12·9	1·6	15·0
Co-operative Society	6	7	4·4	5·7	3·2	5·5	1·8	5·7	1·8	4·7
Establishment in Collective-settlement					1·7	2·1	1·0	2·2	1·2	3·4
Others (Government esta-blishment and not stated)					0·3	2·1	5·9	5·5	0·5	3·1

Sources: 1933–43: *Statistical Handbook*, op. cit., p. 219.
1955: CBS *Statistical Abstract*, No. 9, Table 16, p. 177.
1958: Ibid., No. 11, Table 8, p. 193.
1964: Ibid., No. 16, Table C/11, p. 416.

86

TABLE 11

Size of Industrial Establishments by Branches

Average Size
(No. of Persons Employed)

	1930	1943	1955	1958	1965
Total	12	21	13	13	9
Mining and Quarrying	—	—	28	31	34
Food, Beverages, Tobacco	9	19	15	16	15
Textiles	18	23	17	21	26
Clothing	9	15	6	7	5
Wood Products	10	9	7	7	5
Paper and Cardboard and Their Products	13	12	13	15	15
Printing and Publishing					11
Leather and Products	11	15	8	7	3
Rubber and Plastic	—	—	22	24	19
Chemical Products	25	27	24	28	24
Non-metallic Minerals	19	27	18	19	15
Diamonds	—	112	14	23	11
Basic Metal Industry	11	30	13	14	227
Metal Products					9
Machinery	—	20	16	8	7
Electric Machinery and Equipment	32	40	20	12	9
Transport Equipment	—	—	48	13a	10
Miscellaneous	12	18	9	7	4

a Includes for the first time 'repairs to vehicles and motor bicycles' and this is the main reason for the reduced average.

Sources: 1930–43: Statistical Handbook, op. cit., p. 219.
1955–8: CBS Statistical Bulletin, Part b, Vol. 11, No. 10, October 1960.
1965: CBS Establishments and Employed Persons in Industry, by Branch, Census of Industry, and Crafts, 1965, Table 8, p. 58.

87

TABLE 12

Number of Establishments and Persons Engaged by Size of Group
(*in Absolute Figures and Percentages*)

Size group/years	1955		1960–1	
	Establishments	Persons engaged	Establishments	Persons engaged
Total in Absolute Figures	6·996	92·900	9·754	138·800
Total in Percentage	100	100	100	100
1–4	44·6	10·1	51·7	10·7
5–9	27·9	14·1	22·6	10·4
10–14	9·1	8·3	8·6	7·2
15–24	8·5	11·9	6·7	9·0
25–49	5·9	15·5	5·8	13·8
50–99	2·3	11·6	2·6	12·4
100–299	1·4	18·0	1·5	18·0
300 and more	0·3	10·5	0·5	18·5

Sources: 1955: CBS *Statistical Abstract*, No. 9, 1957–8, p. 176.
1960–1: Ibid., No. 14, 1963, p. 282.

TABLE 13

Number of Establishments and Persons Engaged by Year of
Commencement of Production (*in Absolute Figures and*
Percentages)
1961–2

Year of Commencement of Production	No. of Establishments	No. of Persons Engaged
Total	9,754	138,800
Total Percentage	100	100
Until 1939	20·6	27·2
1940–47	13·3	17·0
1948–51	22·2	19·4
1952–55	18·1	20·6
1956–57	8·8	6·0
1958–60	13·5	8·6
Not stated	3·5	1·2

Source: Ibid., No. 14, 1963, p. 283.

TABLE 14

Employed Persons by Occupation
(Percentages)
1955, 1961, 1964

	November 1955	1961[a]	1964
All Employed Persons	100	100	100
Professional, Scientific, Technical, and Related Workers	10·4	11·5	12·3
Administrative Executive, Managerial, and Clerical Workers	15·8	14·1	16·0
Traders, Agents, and Salesmen	11·3	8·6	8·5
Farmers, Fishermen, and Related Workers	17·1	16·9	12·5
Transport and Communication	6·0	4·8	5·0
Construction Workers, Quarrymen, and Miners[a]	—	8·0	9·5
Craftsmen, Production-process Workers, and Related Workers[a]	29·0	23·8	24·1
Services, Sport, and Recreation Workers	10·4	12·3	12·1

[a] In 1955 building workers were classified and included in the category of workers which included artisans and workers in industry and building. From 1961, a new classification of occupations was used. The chief difference is that in the new classification workers are a separate group and warehouse employees are classified as clerks, while in the old classification they were classified with craftsmen, production-process workers, and related workers.

Source: Ibid., No. 16, 1965, Table K/16, pp. 316–7.

TABLE 15

Distribution (Per cents) of the Net-Domestic Product by Type of Establishment and Economic Branch 1953 (Percentages)

	All types (mill. IL)	Hista-drut enter-prises	Collec-tive and co-op. settle-ments	Other co-oper-atives	Propriet-orships & private com-panies	Govern-ment sector
All Branches	1,141	7·9	10·3	3·3	53·9	24·7
Agriculture	140	2·0	61·5	—	35·7	0·8
Industry, Quarrying	242	12·6	3·6	3·4	79·0	1·4
Construction	7·6	18·9	—	—	71·6	9·5
Public Utilities	18	—	—	—	100·0	—
Electricity for Light and Power	7	—	—	—	—	100·0
Regional Water Systems	—	—	—	—	—	—
Transport, Communication						
Roads, Buses	17	—	—	100·0	—	—
Other	38	—	2·7	4·8	92·2	0·3
Trains	4	—	—	—	—	100·0
Harbours	5	—	—	—	38·4	61·6
Merchant Fleet	5	—	—	—	100·0	—
Air Transport	5	—	—	—	4·5	95·5
Post, Telephone, Telegraph	9	—	—	—	—	100·0
Wholesale Trade	45	20·6	—	—	78·2	1·2
Retail Trade	77	0·5	—	5·8	91·6	2·1
Commercial Banking	15	7·7	—	18·2	71·4	2·7
Insurance	6	20·3	—	—	76·2	3·5
Government and non-profit organization	250	8·8	—	—	—	91·2
Other Service	134	—	16·4	0·7	82·4	0·5

Source: D. Creamer, *Israel's National Income 1950–4*, Jerusalem, Falk Project and CBS Special Series, No. 57, 1957, Table 15, p. 36.

Footnotes for Table 16.

[a] Line 1 is Creamer's data adjusted for differences in the definitions of sectors. Line 2 is Creamer's data adjusted for differences in sector definitions and in estimating procedures. The figure for NDP in 1953 is according to the revised series for NDP for 1950–62. Creamer's original estimate for NDP in 1953 was IL 1,141 million.

[b] The alternative estimate for 1959 (line 11) was obtained by applying Creamer's estimating procedure for net product in agriculture and manufacturing in 1953 to the comparable 1959 data. For agriculture this involves the use of gross output data for each sector and the assumption that the relative share of net product originating in the relevant groups and sectors is equal to the relative share of gross output of each of the respective groups and sectors. For details see Creamer, op. cit, p. 110 and Appendix B below.

Source: H. Barkai, op. cit.

TABLE 15A

Distribution (Per cents) of the Net-Domestic Product by Sector
and Industrial Origin
1959 (Per cents)

	Total	Public sector	Histadrut sector	Private sector
Net Domestic Product[a]	100·0	21·5	20·3	58·2
Agriculture, Forestry, and Fishing	100·0	0·8	32·0	67·2
Mining, Quarrying, and Manufacturing	100·0	4·3	22·2	73·5
Construction	100·0	10·6	31·9	57·5
Public Utilities (Water and Electricity)	100·0	100·0	—	—
Transportation and Communications	100·0	40·3	37·0	22·7
Banking, Finance, and Real Estate	100·0	1·1	9·1	89·8
Trade and Other Services	100·0	1·7	15·8	82·5
Non-profit Institutions	100·0	—	37·6	62·4
Government Services[b]	100·0	97·0	3·0	—

[a] Since the net domestic product figure for 1959 derived by using a global depreciation adjustment (cf. NAU, *Israel's National Accounts, 1950–62*, forthcoming), we used the figure that appeared in the provisional summary of the NDP for 1959.

[b] In the case of the Histadrut sector, the term 'government services' applies to services produced by the Histadrut Administration mainly by the personnel of the Executive Committee and Local Labour Councils.

Source: H. Barkai, *The Public, Histadrut, and the Private Sectors in the Israeli Economy*, Jerusalem, Falk Project for Economic Research, Report No. 6, 1961–3, 1964, Table No. 4, p. 33.

TABLE 16

Net Domestic Product by Sector 1953–60

Year	NDP (1)	Public sector (2)	Histadrut sector (3)	Private sector (1)–[(2)+(3)]= (4)
	IL millions (current prices)			
1953[a]–(1)	1,120	217	227	676
1953 (2)	1,120	217	201	702
1957	2,489	521	513	1,455
1958	2,848	570	571	1,707
1959	3,222	695	653	1,874
1960	3,610	761	737	2,112
	Per cent			
1953 (1)	100·0	19·4	20·3	60·3
1953 (2)	100·0	19·4	18·0	62·6
1957	100·0	20·9	20·6	58·5
1958	100·0	20·0	20·0	60·0
(1959)[b]	(100·0)	(21·5)	(22·3)	(56·2)
1959	100·0	21·6	20·3	58·1
1960	100·0	21·1	20·4	58·5

Footnotes for Table 16 on facing page.

91

Concomitant changes also took place in the organization of different branches of the economy. Agriculture became the most planned branch. Instead of planning the individual settlements, as in the pre-state period, the planning institutions passed to overall planning and most of the changes in the agricultural structure are the results of this planning. The planning was accompanied by a system of subsidies whose aim was to guide production and maintain a minimum income level to the farmer.

The physical growth of agriculture since the establishment of Israel has been very great, as the enclosed table shows. Production grew fourfold; the cultivated area reached four million dunams, and the irrigated area 1·3 million dunams; heavy investments were made in water enterprises and irrigation, machines and equipment, and land redemption. The number of

TABLE 17

Value of Agricultural Production at 1948–9 Prices
(Including Intermediate Produce) 1948–9—1963–4

From	1948–9	1950–5	1952–3	1955–6	1958–9	1961–2	1962–3	1963–4
	Value							
Total	44,413	61,189	81,446	126,730	87,880	236,195	238,674	249,145
Field Crops	6,698	7,951	16,730	27,571	36,693	41,703	40,011	51,423
Vegetables and Potatoes	5,338	9,105	13,085	16,245	18,391	19,814	20,519	21,415
Citrus Fruit	6,924	8,402	9,507	12,770	16,532	15,362	21,343	20,657
Other Fruit	3,252	2,661	5,350	9,393	13,541	23,960	24,224	31,132
Milk	7,213	9,900	12,735	17,083	24,667	31,267	31,208	32,414
Eggs	6,663	10,766	10,147	14,549	29,337	36,988	32,947	37,448
Honey	123	96	167	241	234	211	202	286
Changes in the Livestock Inventory	1,433	1,411	1,012	1,525	2,937	1,532	0	106
Meat (Live Weight)	3,775	5,144	6,016	17,853	32,766	49,839	52,582	58,060
Fish	1,584	3,303	3,439	4,988	5,954	7,716	7,753	9,028
Miscellaneous	1,410	2,450	3,250	4,512	6,828	7,803	7,885	7,176
	Index							
Total	100.0	138	183	285	423	532	537	606
Field Crops	100.0	119	250	412	548	623	597	768
Vegetables and potatoes	100.0	172	245	304	345	371	384	401
Citrus Fruit	100.0	121	137	184	239	222	308	298
Other Fruit	100.0	82	165	289	416	737	745	957
Milk	100.0	137	177	237	342	433	433	449
Eggs	100.0	162	152	218	440	555	494	562
Honey	100.0	78	136	196	190	172	164	233
Changes in the Livestock Inventory	100.0	98	70	106	205	107	0	7
Meat (Live Weight)	100.0	136	160	473	868	1,320	1,393	154
Fish	100·0	208	217	315	376	487	489	570
Miscellaneous	100.0	174	230	320	484	553	559	509

Source: CBS *Statistical Abstract*, No. 16, 1965, Table L/18, p. 390.

agricultural settlements grew to about 730 and the number of agricultural units to 80,000. Of the 450 new settlements, about three hundred were moshavim and villages and only one hundred kibbutzim, so that the share of the family farms rose. In addition, administered farms became an important new form in agriculture. Most of this extensive enlargement took place in the first years of the state, when agriculture was the main source of the mass immigration-absorption. After a period of relatively low rate of growth (1952–5), came another period of rapid growth, mainly on the intensive margin. In the course of a few years agricultural production turned from deficiency to saturation, surpluses, and decreasing prices.

This last trend was one of the causes of the production directives, especially with regard to composition of crops. Another reason was recognition of the fact that water and not land (as in the pre-state period) is the real limited production factor, and that plenty of cultivable land would remain when all water resources had been fully exploited. It thus seemed necessary to plan more extensive farms. Another factor in changes in agricultural planning was the great dependence on feed imports for livestock. All these factors combined against adherence to the mixed farm and as early as 1953 gave rise to many discussions on the planning of new types of farms – especially the administered farm – and on transition to other crops, mainly industrial crops, sugar, and cotton. This was possible since subsidies and high customs duties protected domestic production. But the share of the family in agriculture had increased during the last decade in spite of the criticisms of irrationality in dividing the cultivated area into small fields, especially where industrial crops were concerned.

It has already been noted that the citrus plantations expanded in area, production, and export over the state period and were about to reach the 1939 level. Citrus fruit is now the main, but not the only, agricultural export (and about 25 per cent of total exports). In recent years exports of some other agricultural items have developed, the main ones being eggs, poultry, and some fruits and vegetables.

The direct and indirect activities of the government of Israel and the influx of capital also changed the structure of industry. One main factor – that of natural resources – changed but little. At the same time it became increasingly clear to economic authorities that the absorption capacity of Israel and its economic fortune are dependent on the success or failure of industrialization. As an outcome of the intensive efforts in this direction, the real output of industry grew by two and a half times, and net domestic product by about 170 per cent during the state period. The annual rate of growth of output was 12 per cent and of the net product 6–8 per cent. The annual rate of workers in industrial enterprises increased from 77,000 in 1949 to about 160,000 in 1960. After a transition period, productivity also began to rise. In the composition of sub-branches, we note a relative decrease in the share of food, which in

1960 constituted only one-fifth of output and employed 15 per cent of the industrial labour force, a greater emphasis on textiles in the textile and clothing branches, an increase in the metal sector (up to a fifth in output and a quarter of the total labour force) and in other branches, such as rubber, paper, chemicals, and minerals. But not until recently did all these trends give rise to basic changes in the composition of industry, non-sequitur about 20 per cent of total industrial output is now exported.

It is hard to compare the average size of industrial enterprise in the two periods, because of many changes in the definitions used in the surveys and in the population investigated. The average size of an industrial enterprise was about thirteen employed persons during the state period. This remained constant throughout the period and is the result of a simultaneous increase in the number of both very small and very big enterprises. More than 40 per cent of the industrial labour force are employed in enterprises which employ more than fifty persons; whilst more than half of total enterprises employ about 10 per cent of the industrial labour force, in groups of one to four persons per enterprise (see Tables 12 and 13).

During recent years a small revolution has taken place in retail trade, mainly in food – with the rising share of the supermarket and the self-service systems. The pioneers of these new selling methods were the consumers' co-operatives, which have recently been followed by private enterprise. About two-thirds of co-operative food shops were organized in the self-service system in 1960. Some of them are now much bigger than regular shops. Other big supermarkets have been established in the last few years by private owners. A rough approximation of the share of all supermarkets and self-service foodstores in total revenues from retail food sellings gives about 20 per cent. This development – which is still going on – spurred the small food retailers to experiment in organizing their shops as chain-shops, but this did not succeed. In any event, they were forced to raise the level and quality of their services.

The great physical expansion of the economy outlined above did not, however, give rise to far-reaching changes in the branch structure.

Intra-Branch Structure of the Economy

A comparison of the intra-branch structure of the Jewish economy before the Second World War with its development up to 1962 (see Tables 5, 8, 11, 14) shows only relatively small changes in the distribution of employed persons among the branches and in the share of each branch in total national production. The impact of the war caused several changes in this structure which were, however, cancelled out within a few years.

This may be seen in several important spheres:

(1) About half of all Jewish employed persons work in primary and

secondary branches, i.e. agriculture, mining, industry, and handicrafts, construction and public works. The share of these branches in national production is about 40 per cent. This rate has been quite stable over the last three decades, with the exception of the Second World War when it was a little higher. This was mainly due to the rapid growth of the industry.

(2) Agriculture generally employs around 15 per cent of all employed persons, and produces somewhat more than 10 per cent of national production. The share of agriculture in the economy diminished during the war, with an upward trend in the first years of Israel and a drop again in recent years.[1]

The share of industry (including mining and handicrafts) both in total labour force and national income is slightly above one fifth. This increased to about a third during the war boom and returned to its normal size in 1953. There exists a very slight growth trend in recent years. Decrease in the share of agriculture and increase in the share of industry will supposedly take place in the near future as a result of the relative saturation of agricultural products and of the large investments in industrial projects.

The construction branch was throughout the period 1930–60 – with the exception of the war years – large relative to its size in normal countries. It employed at times one-tenth of the total labour force and originated a similar part of national product. This branch is the most unstable in the economic structure since war or mass immigration can (respectively) cause a halving or a doubling of its size. Of total investments, 40 per cent in the early 'fifties and about 30 per cent in recent years were invested in housing, a fact which increases the relative importance of the branch in the economy.

(3) Services (including transport and communications) employed throughout the period about half the total labour force and produced some three-fifths of the total national product. These rates are very high relative to other countries in a similar degree of development.

Distribution of Economic Activities Between the Major Sectors

It would be interesting to see how this development was divided between the different sectors – i.e. between the private, Histadrut, and Government sectors.

In Tables 15 and 16 above on type of ownership, we find a decrease in the percentage of privately-owned enterprises and partnerships and an increase in the proportion of government corporations, while the share of co-operatives and limited companies remained more or less unchanged.

Many government companies have been established during recent years.

[1] This last trend is the outcome of a large increase in production and a large decrease in prices.

But the importance of the government in this sphere is not to be measured in per cent of ownership but in its share in total investments (see below) of which 40–75 per cent was direct investment and the rest loans and grants. However, the share of direct government investment has been diminishing over time.

The Histadrut sector comprised *more than a fifth* and the government sector about a fifth of total net domestic product in 1953.[1] In the Histadrut sector only 40–50 per cent in 1960 of output originated in enterprises owned directly by *Hevrat Haovdim*, the rest originating in the communal agricultural settlements and in other co-operatives.

In the productive branches we find that about two-thirds of output from agriculture came from the Histadrut sector (mainly from kibbutzim and moshavim) in 1953, but only 32 per cent[2] in 1959.

The Histadrut sector's industry produced in 1953 about one-fifth of total industrial production and in 1959 about 22 per cent. In 1953 about two-thirds of this production came from enterprises which are directly owned by *Hevrat Haovdim*, but in 1959 only 49·4 per cent. Among the secondary branches the Histadrut concentrated its enterprises mainly (and relatively to other sectors) in building materials and minerals where its share in output was about four-fifths of the total, in the metal-machinery industries (one-quarter), in the food industry (15 per cent) and in the paper and publishing industries (20 per cent). The share of the Histadrut in clothing and textiles and in diamonds is very small. In the building and public works sector, the Histadrut's share was about 20 per cent of total output.

The proportion of the government sector in the productive branches is rather small, and it does not show the real share of the government in financing investments in these branches. The government share (in 1953) in the chemicals industry's output was 11 per cent, in paper and publishing 6 per cent and in minerals about 5 per cent. Some of the big firms which were owned by the government in 1953 have since then transferred to other public or to private hands.

In the building and public works branch the government sector produces about 10 per cent of total output (mainly through the Public Works Department of the Ministry of Labour).

The transport and communications branches are divided among the sectors in an interesting manner: the government owns all the railways, most of the air transport, and all the means of postal communication. The Histadrut sector owns the bus transport and haulage services. The private sector manages most of the road transport other than buses. The harbours were recently transferred to the hands of a public authority, and the merchant navy is distributed among all three sectors. The public services of electricity and water are now owned by the government.

[1] Source: H. Barkai, op. cit. D. Creamer, op. cit. Falk Project and CBS Special Series, No. 57, 1957.   [2] Cf. Barkai, op. cit., p. 33.

Among the other services let us mention briefly trade and banking. In wholesale trade the Histadrut sector participated with about 20 per cent of total net domestic product, but in the retail trade its share was about 6 per cent only.[1] The government's share in these branches is insignificant.

The Histadrut sector comprised about a quarter of the total output of the banking branch, about 20 per cent of the insurance branch and about 80 per cent of provident and other social funds – in all about one-quarter of these financial branches. The government's share in the output of the above branches was about 3 per cent.

In general we witness, after several initial attempts by the Government to create its own direct investments and enterprises, a shift towards greater indirect participation, through partnership or subsidies, in the economy.

Another interesting development in the Israeli economy has been the undertaking of activities in various Asian, African, and South American countries, in the form of shipping, or transport companies, various types of public works (especially construction), and widespread technical aid. (In 1963 there were about 870 Israelis serving as technical experts in these countries). While no exact data on the scope of these activities are available, it seems that the Histadrut and the government sector are predominant.

Housing in Israel – Illustration of Public Enterprise

Of special interest in the context of the distribution of economic activities between different sectors is the housing organization. As we have seen, the population of Israel has more than tripled since the foundation of the state, so that the housing question during this period was one of the main problems of the public authorities. The mass immigration which took place in the first years, together with little experience in this sphere and lack of resources, caused mass building of small dwellings of low quality and planning and of numbers of temporary housing units (of wood or even canvas) which were erected up to 1951. The density of persons per room built also reached its highest point in those years.

The housing problem would have been much more difficult if the possibility of housing a considerable part of the new immigrants in the deserted houses of the Arab refugees had not existed. On the other hand, building for new immigrants was accompanied by a strong building demand for veteran families who had not previously had suitable housing conditions.

When immigration slackened and more experience was gained in the sphere of public housing, considerable improvements took place in the areas of quality, sanitation, and electricity; interior and exterior architecture were also improved. The temporary housing units were replaced by permanent ones and the density of dwellings diminished.

[1] Its share in the food branch is greater.

Most of the building for housing was in the hands of public authorities. Almost all the housing for immigrants and part of the housing for veteran families was carried out by the Jewish Agency and the Housing Department in the Ministry of Labour. Another considerable part was undertaken by other authorities and organizations, such as the Histadrut and housing companies connected with political parties and movements.

The share of private enterprise in housing was relatively low throughout this period, even in the great urban centres where it was concentrated. Private building has been increasing in recent years, but even in 1959 about two-thirds of the newly-built housing units were financed by the Government (and the Jewish Agency) and a considerable part of the rest by other public factors.

Almost all the new-built houses for veteran families (or immigrant families who changed apartments) were built for sale and not for renting. As for building for new immigrants, the aim has also been to sell the flats to the families if at all possible. In this way more than half of the dwelling units in Israel are now owned by the families who live in them, and this rate will doubtless grow.

The buying of flats brings with it the problem of credit arrangements and credit institutions to help ordinary families to bear the heavy expense. For this purpose several housing-mortgage banks were set up and several saving-for-housing programmes were organized. The efforts of the Government to transfer the burden of financing credit for the acquisition of houses to private hands have not so far succeeded much.

However, the fact that a large part of housing is under the aegis of various public companies does in fact often restrict the individual's rights of ownership.

Almost all the public housing in Israel was organized in the form of public associations. The rules of these associations imposed, in the first years, severe restrictions on their participants and on the owners of houses – especially on the use of their ownership-rights.[1]

---

[1] A number of these associations did not really give full legal right of ownership of apartment, mainly in matters of selling or transferring it to other hands. The main restrictions (in the housing associations of the Histadrut) were:

1 Every transfer was subject to the approval of the committee of the association;
2 Preference was given to members of the association to buy any vacated apartment;
3 In any event the transfer was restricted to members of the Histadrut only;
4 The selling price was determined by a special committee of the association; the prices so determined were in general lower than the relevant market prices.

One of the members of the committee of every housing association was a representative of the Histadrut and had a veto right in some of the questions.

A second problem was a result of the fact that the land on which the houses were built was not under the ownership of the houseowners, so that every transfer had also to get formal approval from the land owners (the JNF, or afterwards the Israel Land Authority).

In recent years the restrictions on the ownership of dwellings have been relaxed to some extent – but not, as yet, completely. As to the land, there has recently been a trend to sell it to the owners of the houses, but this step has not made much progress till now – although more general sale of land to the public has, as we have seen above, given rise to intensive speculation and increase in prices.

The Development of Social Services and the Relations Between the Major Sectors

The relations between the different sectors were also well illustrated in the distribution of various social services.

Of the major social services only primary education came early under purely governmental jurisdiction (see later). Compulsory and free elementary education was established in 1949 and a unified national system of education in 1953.

The housing and settlement of immigrants quickly became, as we have seen above, the Government's and the Jewish Agency's responsibility, and the latter has also built homes for war veterans and civil servants. The Histadrut and political parties have also subsidized housing projects for their adherents.

The picture is much more mixed in the broad area of the social security. The first phase of a comprehensive scheme of social security was enacted by the National Insurance Law of 1953, which made provision for old-age and survivors' benefits, maternity grants, and insurance against industrial accidents. This compulsory insurance covers all inhabitants between the ages of eighteen and sixty-seven, the salaried, self-employed, and non-employed as well as wage-earners. The insurance fund is composed of contributions by employers and employees, with a subsidy from the State Treasury. Old-age pensions are paid generally at sixty-five for men and sixty for women; encouragement is given to continue working for an additional five-year period. The pensions are linked to the cost-of-living index, so that a rise in prices does not undermine the value of the benefits (see Table 18).

The employment of women is regulated by law. The Minister of Labour is empowered to prohibit or restrict their employment in certain industries, and night work is forbidden, save in exceptional cases.

National unemployment insurance has not yet been introduced because of financial stringency. The Government attempts to estimate in advance anticipated unemployment and provides public works programmes to absorb it.

A national health scheme has not been instituted, mainly because of the pressure of the Histadrut which did not want to give up its *Kupat Holim*, thus leaving this crucial area outside direct Government ownership and control.

Both the Histadrut and the voluntary agencies (such as *Hadassah*, the pioneer of social medicine in Israel; and *Malben,* instituted by the DC[1]) have continued their health services, nominally under the supervision of the Ministry of Health. *Kupat Holim,* the sick fund for the Histadrut, has, with government subsidies, expanded its facilities so that it serves about two-thirds of the population, most of the remainder being served by one of the smaller

TABLE 18

Claims for Benefits Allowed During the Six Years 1954–60
—National Insurance
(in round figures)

Type of Benefit	1959–60	1954–60
Old-age Pensions	8,000	47,000
Survivors' Benefits	2,000	7,500
Burial Grants	5,500	17,500
Birth Grants	51,000	274,000
Maternity Benefits	12,000	57,000
Allowances for Large Families	42,000	42,000
Injury, Disability, and Dependants' Benefits	51,000	222,000
Total	171,500	667,000

Expenditure on Benefits (in million IL)
—National Insurance

Type of Benefit	1959–60	1954–60
Old-age Pensions	26,900	64,400
Survivors' Benefits	4,300	10,600
Burial Grants	400	1,000
Birth Grants	4.600	19,800
Maternity Benefits	3,800	14,900
Allowances for Large Families	3,500	3,500
Injury, Disability, and Dependants' Benefits	6,900	24,600
Rehabilitation (medical expenses, etc.)	3,800	16,200
Total	54,200	155,000

Source: Appendix to National Insurance Institute Report 1959–60.

sick funds or private health insurance schemes (see Table 19). The government has supplemented the efforts of the private agencies in all fields of

[1] Joint Distribution Committee.

public health, and it has concentrated attention on anti-malaria work, sanitation, and food hygiene, the control of epidemics through testing and quarantine, the expansion of hospital facilities and public health laboratories, and mother and child care.

Table 18 presents the major expenditures of the National Insurance Institute.

TABLE 19

Insured Population (including Dependants)
of the Sick Funds

Year			Absolute Numbers					
	General Sick Fund	National Sick Fund	People Sick Fund	Sick Fund Maccabi	General Zionist Sick Fund	Total	Total population	Insured population per cent of total population
1951	783,000	100,000[a]	30,000	—	—	913,000	1,578,000	57·8
1952								
1953								
1954								
1955	1,013,000	133,000	12,000	—	—	1,158,000	1,789,000	64·7
1956								
1957								
1958								
1959								
1960								
1961	1,478,000	171,000	35,000	76,842	43,200	1,804,042	2,234,000	80·7
1962	1,570,000	—	—	—	—	—		

[a] 1952

Computed on the basis of CBS *Statistical Abstract,* No. 14, 1963, pp. 156–9.

One of the interesting and important outcomes of this situation was that despite all the claims to a welfare state, there is in Israel no over-all universal health service, and that certain strata of the population – especially some of the lower or the lower-middle self-employed groups, such as small pedlars, or handworkers were left out of any type of health insurance.

Another important area of such policies was that of relief and rehabilitation which have received a great deal of government attention with major emphasis upon wounded or handicapped veterans and their families. Provision has been made for hospitalization, medical care, convalescence, education and retraining, and housing and pension payment for the seriously disabled.

The Transformations in the Nature and Interrelations of the Private and Histadrut Sectors

We thus see that the development of governmental regulations did not obliterate the older – Histadrut and private – sectors. It is therefore necessary to examine to what extent these different sectors persisted after the establishment of the State of Israel and what they signify in present day Israeli economy – to what extent they denote differences in economic interests, approaches, and types of organization.

This question is especially pertinent because of the growth of problems common to all the sectors – such as the problems of manpower and organization – which have given rise to common activities and organizations. This was reflected in the establishment of the Institute of Productivity, joint production boards, and organizations covering the same branches though in different sectors (e.g. the Citrus Marketing Boards).

Moreover, the very establishment of the administrative and political organs of the state as an important regulator of economic life has increased the recourse of *all* sectors to these frameworks, and therefore necessarily homogenized many of their approaches to economic problems. Such homogenization, however, often increased competition over scarce resources, while emphasizing the growing importance of political pressure as an instrument of economic activity.

The decreasing difference between sectors was not only due to growing recourse to government administration but also to the fact that several important changes took place in the whole structure of the economy. There were several reasons for this.

First, some of the foundations had already been laid previously by colonizing agencies or activities or, as with railways, were taken over from the mandatory power. Of crucial importance has been the change in the place of agriculture in the economy – in the sense that after the great initial drive by the Jewish Agency to absorb the various new immigrants in moshavim, agriculture has more or less reached its point of economic satiation.

Second, the government has established a sector of its own which has taken over several – though certainly not all – of the former colonizing or development functions.

Yet all these common features have not obliterated the differences between the various sectors – although some of these differences have become greatly transformed since their historical and ideological beginnings. Obviously one of the basic inter-sectoral characteristics is the competition for various scarce resources within the economy.

This rivalry goes beyond the usual economic competition between enterprises or groups of enterprises and embraces wider considerations of the size of each sector and its ability to gain preferential treatment through the accumulation of political influence and power.

These political considerations are, of course, very prominent within the Histadrut where some concerted action is always easier. It may also be discerned in some of the activities of the private sector or in activities common to both sectors, as in the organization and activities of the Citrus Board which maintains very strict monopolistic supervision, with full legal sanction, over the production and distribution of this vital part of the Israeli economy.

However, beyond these similarities some differences between the different sectors in their basic approaches to several problems of economic activity and organization can perhaps be discerned.

One alleged difference is the emphasis on 'development' and the readiness to engage in 'colonizing' or national activities. The Histadrut and lately also the governmental development sector often claim that they tend to emphasize development and are more ready than the private sector to invest in unprofitable (at least in the short-run) branches – such as enterprises in development areas or abroad (development companies operating in various African and Asian countries).

This may be seen as a continuation of the older colonizing tradition – especially in its emphasis on the preferential allocations of national capital to those branches which are of special importance from the point of view of national economic goals.

According to this premise, the private sector does not generally engage in such activities to the same extent and goes only where its profits are assured. The representatives of the private sector tend on the whole to deny this allegation, claiming – with particular reference to the Histadrut – that apparent devotion to national goals serves only to extend the powers of given political groups. It is further asserted that the risks are mostly taken by the government and the national economy and that, given the same preferential treatment by the government, private enterprises would be willing and able to undertake such ventures.

This claim seems of late to have been substantiated, to some extent at least, in that it has been mostly private enterprises – with the help of the government development budget – that have flourished in the various development areas (especially in the south). This has also shown up some of the more paradoxical aspects, namely the growing dependence of both sectors on the protective barrier of the government and their great fright – especially evident among manufacturers after the 1962 devaluation – of attempts to open the local market to international competition.

The success of the private sector in the sphere of development has caused no little apprehension within the Histadrut. In 1961 its Secretary-General – Mr Becker – announced a plan of great expansion of the Histadrut's economic enterprises in all the development areas.

Although liberalization and the growing dependence on government protection and subsidy mean that the differences between sectors become less pronounced, these are still often stressed in the basic conceptions of the leaders and entrepreneurs in the different sectors.

Perhaps one of the important manifestations of these differences may be seen in the debates within the Histadrut on the role of profit and the serious claims of some – even if not the most effective – economic leaders that the Histadrut should not undertake new enterprises for profit and should even abandon old ones once they have become economically viable.

Differences between the sectors have been often emphasized in the ideology and – to a smaller extent – the practice of labour relations and labour participation in industrial management. The most important feature has been the attempt in the Histadrut industrial sector to achieve broader participation of the workers in management.

These attempts have on the whole been confined to ideology rather than practice, except perhaps with regard to the lower levels of plant-production committees and departmental committees.

Only in very few cases was full participation of the workers in the central management of a company achieved. One of the most prominent examples of this – within the government sector – has been the Electricity Company and it was not very successful. The inclusion of representatives of the workers in management led to growing politicization, continuous tensions, and lowered efficiency.

But if, in the sphere of workers' participation there have been undertaken in the Histadrut sector some special attempts in the sphere of work-relations, the situation seems to be, paradoxically enough, obverse. A recent survey has shown that workers in Histadrut enterprises think that their local unions and committees are less effective in achieving various benefits for their employees because of the very fact that the enterprises are owned by the Histadrut and hence the trade unions are not willing to accede to their demands.

The Sectors as Political and Economic Frameworks

But if the differences in concrete economic activities and mentality between the sectors have become somewhat blurred, there still exist some basic differences in overall economic organization. Within the government and the Histadrut – albeit in different ways – there is great emphasis on political control and on internal political considerations and allocation while in the private sectors these play a somewhat lesser role. In this respect there are also many differences between the government and the Histadrut – the latter depending *more* on internal, political control and much less on purely economic mechanisms.

The nature of the political direction prevalent in the Histadrut may be seen mainly in the fact that considerations of relative economic profits are to some extent overruled by internal and external political considerations. The interests of any one branch may be, in principle at least, sacrificed in the interests of overall political considerations or in favour of general social or national considerations.

However, this very wide range of Histadrut activities has obviously another aspect. With the development and extension of the various concerns, their managers have necessarily developed a strong preponderance for autonomy and have often tried to exploit the wide political backing of the Histadrut for the expansion of their own concerns.

At one point (in 1959) the Histadrut reacted very strongly against this tendency to escape from the overall political direction of *Hevrat Ovdim*. The Histadrut has not, however, always been successful in its attempts to supervise all the economic enterprises formally belonging to it.

One of the most important examples of this has been the relative lack of success in maintaining effective control over the transport co-operatives, especially with regard to the employment of hired labour prevented by the prohibitive cost of a share from entering the co-operative as members.

In many cases the co-operatives maintained monopolies which could not be fully curbed either by the Histadrut or the government. The bus service in Israel which constitutes the major part of the transportation system is owned almost totally by three big co-operatives which divide the major service areas amongst themselves. This is a result of a gradual absorption of smaller companies.

The main problem is not the direct price of the service to the consumer (which is relatively cheap) but the overall efficiency of the co-operatives and especially the extent to which the co-operatives undertake the replacement of vehicles and machinery from their own profits – or conversely, the extent to which they have to be subsidized by the government in this respect.

As with most of the co-operatives in Israel, the bus companies are also part of *Hevrat Haovdim*, but the latter's authority here is very weak, especially in matters of practical policy. The bus co-operatives have, as a matter of fact, achieved a high degree of independence as a result of their size and monopolistic power. The outcome is a situation where a public service is in the hands of private owners, with but little effective inspection by any public authority. Many conflicts occur between the co-operatives and the public authorities on the problems of the level of service, prices, and the high wages and emoluments of the owners. In recognition of the need for effective public control of such a monopolized service, some proposals were made in recent years by public bodies or authorities (mainly *Hevrat Haovdim* and the government) to purchase a considerable portion of the companies' capital and so get real control of these services. The co-operatives opposed these proposals on the grounds that the members of the co-operatives would become more or less salaried workers, the general productivity of the service would diminish, thus causing a burden to the public. Despite many attempts, none of these proposals materialized. As a sort of compromise, the following steps were taken (some of them before the rejection of the said proposals):

(1) A representative of *Hevrat Haovdim* was appointed to the managing body of the co-operatives;

(2) It was agreed that no increase in the wages or other contributions to the members of the co-operatives would take place without the agreement of the Histadrut;

(3) A 'Public Tariff (Fares) Authority' was organized to supervise the co-operatives' accounts and decide on changes in fares.

Since then the problems both of members' wages and of fares have been a continuous subject for public dispute – without any real structural change having taken place. While no doubt this is a very extreme case of monopoly, it is indicative of some of the problems arising from the sectoral structure of the Israeli economy.

In other cases, such public monopoly tends to develop not only within a given sector but through mutual arrangements between the sectors. The best example of this may be found in the Citrus Marketing Board – which was set up by law to regulate the whole of the citrus industry.

We thus see that to some extent the differences between the sectors have tended to persist in the period of the state, but that at the same time the extent of these differences has diminished and their nature changed. The relatively simple dichotomy between 'colonizing' and 'private' sectors – a dichotomy which has always been exaggerated and which in its purity existed probably only as an ideological tenet – dwindled even further in importance.

The sectors have perhaps retained some of the emphasis on different types of economic activities, but above all their importance can be understood in political terms. They constitute important political divisions within the Israeli economy, the very existence of which is, as we shall see, of great importance for the functioning of the economy.

2

THE MAJOR ECONOMIC POLICIES

Introduction

The preceding discussion has continuously emphasized the great importance of political and administrative regulation, within different sectors – and especially within the central framework of the economy as a whole. It is therefore now worthwhile analysing in greater detail the mechanism of this control and the way in which it operates within the Israeli economy and shapes its contours.

From a broad typological point of view the Israeli economy is a pure market economy in the sense that it contains almost no subsistent, self-sufficient autarchic units and that – with the partial exception of some agricultural produce – all products are produced for internal and external markets and are not consumed within the production unit.

Hence it is a series of markets that constitute the most important regulatory mechanism of Israeli – as of any other modern (even if small sized) – economy. The most important among these are markets for labour, commodities and money.

In the pre-state period the very structure and nature of the economic activities of the Jewish sector created, as we have seen, several specific types of regulative mechanisms within different sectors and especially within the Histadrut. With the establishment of the state and the unification of the economic and market structures, these various regulative mechanisms became much more important.

Several of the internal sectoral regulative mechanisms – especially those of the Histadrut which we have briefly described above – persisted, but even they became necessarily more and more drawn into the orbit of the central markets and of the central political regulation of these markets.

Israel's economy is subject – even after the so-called policy of 'liberalization' initiated in 1952 and which abolished various physical controls – to a considerable degree of political regulation. This control is not effected – as has been already seen above – through the direct ownership of various enterprises by the state, but mainly through strategic control in the majority of markets and through the close co-operation – despite many disputes over details – between the state and the Histadrut.

The Major Types of Economic Policies

Among economic policies the most important are, first, monetary policy in general and credit policy in particular, effected mainly through the Bank of Israel and through the control of foreign exchange in terms of multiple exchange rates (until the devaluation of 1962).

The second major economic policy is, of course, fiscal policy, implemented by the Treasury and dealing with various direct taxes (the most important of which is income tax) and various indirect taxes, such as customs, excise duties, and purchase tax.

The following tables show some of the most important aspects of tax development in Israel (see Tables 20 and 21).

TABLE 20

The Structure of Taxes in Mandatory Palestine (in Total Governmental Incomes) 1934-44 in Per cents

	Five Fiscal Years 1934-9	Five Fiscal Years 1939-44
Total Taxes (% of Total Incomes)	*83·8*	*69·6*
Income Tax „ „	—	7·7
Land and rural taxes „	13·9	12·5
Licence fees and fines „	15·6	12·3
Customs and excise duty	54·3	37·1
Other Incomes	*16·2*	*30·3*
Grants	9·8	20·2

Source: R. R. Nathan, op. cit., p. 343.

TABLE 21

Income Tax Receipts by Status of Tax Payer (*Including Defence Levy*)

Year	Total Income Tax IL millions	Percentage	Employees	Self Employed[a]	Companies
1949-50	9·3	100	47·3	39·8	12·9
1955-6	152·9	100	38·0	39·5	27·5
1960-1	319·8	100	44·5	35·1	20·4
1964-	900·9	100	40·6	33·8	25·6

[a] As from 1961-2 income from interest deducted at source has been included.
Source: CBS *Statistical Abstract*, No. 16, 1965, Table R/7, pp. 554-5.

Analysis of tax policy shows that:

(1) The share of taxes in total budgetary income has been continuously increasing.

(2) The share of direct taxes (of which the main one is the highly progressive income tax) increased over the period 1949-57 and diminished afterwards. The share of indirect taxes decreased until 1953 and has increased since then. Among the indirect taxes customs duties decreased in the early years and have been increasing since 1956. This is the outcome of the 'liberalization' programme by which the quota system for imports was replaced by free imports with high customs rates. This is also the outcome of the process of widening the gap between the real and nominal exchange rate.

(3) The increase in the share of customs duties during recent years is one of the causes of the diminishing share of the direct taxes. This decrease is not an outcome of fiscal policy but of foreign trade policy.[1]

The third major area of economic policies is the regulation of production and trade through import and export licences, subsidies, and differential allocation, which, of course, entails preferential treatment of different enterprises and also potentially at least (and probably also in practice) of different sectors.

Fourth are the basic social policies, dealing with the whole field of services to the population, extending from education and health to housing. Here also the great outlay on defence must be mentioned.

Fifth is the field of wage-policies. Officially this policy is not in the hands of the government but of the Histadrut and the Employers' Associations (especially the Manufacturers' Association). But it is greatly influenced by the government both as one of the biggest employers in the country (about 59,000 employees) and as one of its basic economic problems.

In 1959 the former Employment Departments of the Histadrut were transferred to the authority of the Employment Service which is part of the Ministry of Labour but is managed by a special public council. According to the law, every wage- or salary-earner (not including some senior officials) and every employer has to obtain employment and labour through the service. The Employment Service is organized on the basis of geographical and occupational distribution.

Special labour employment offices for youth are scattered throughout the country which, in addition to their basic task of finding suitable work for their applicants, try to direct young persons to training courses and to borrow for their education and take care of their conditions of work. On the other hand, there exist departments for old as well as for handicapped workers. Offices of the Employment Service also serve the Arab population.

In addition, the Employment Service arranges for the training of unskilled workers and deals with the problem of vocational training in general – both for adults and for young persons who have completed elementary school.

Special machinery has been set up by law for the settlement of labour disputes. While the right to strike is not curtailed, collective agreements in labour relations are encouraged and registered with the Ministry of Labour. A state inspection service has been set up and charged with the supervision and promotion of work safety and saniary conditions.

The last major type of economic policies are the direct development policies of the government. Formerly (in 1950–1) governmental regulation of the economy was also effected through many direct physical control policies –

[1] Later on (see page 213) we shall deal to a greater extent with some of the social implications of tax policy and structure.

such as rationing of food – but the importance of these activities has become smaller in recent years.

Fiscal, Administrative, Social and Political Forces Influencing the Formation and Implementation of Economic Policies

In order to understand the effect of the varied policies described above on Israel's major economic problems and their efficacy in solving them, it is necessary to analyse the basic considerations and criteria according to which these policies were formulated and executed.

Several such criteria can be discerned operating throughout the implementation of economic policy in Israel. The actual policy in any given case is usually the outcome of some compromise between the different economic orientations and political and administrative considerations and pressures.

The first, and in a way the simplest, factor in economic policy has been fiscal necessity as determined by the budgetary needs of different ministries and the demands they make on the Treasury. These comprise personnel (salaries), allocation funds for building and maintenance, and money for subsidies and for the development of their own enterprises.

Within these general needs several constant ones – beyond those of maintenance of personnel – stand out. The demands for defence are necessarily a heavy burden on the Israeli economy. Second, there are the various demands of social policy – education, housing, and health services. Lastly, there are the continuously growing demands for various subsidies, funds for payment of interest on loans and for repayment of loans.

These constitute together the demand or expenditure side of the budget and the problem of the Treasury has been to finance these expenditures through taxes, loans, and external resources, and to determine the scale of priorities for different demands.

What are then the basic considerations according to which such priorities are established? First, consideration of budgetary solvency, i.e. keeping the expenditure, insofar as possible, within the framework of the budget. But these are only starting points and in fact varied social, political, administrative, and economic considerations and factors are operative in the implementation of economic policies.

These considerations or criteria of policies can be found in all the different spheres of economic policy, some of them more prominent in one sphere than in the others.

Thus within the field of fiscal policy several such considerations always operate beyond the purely fiscal needs, which are themselves often greatly influenced by the demands of various ministries. Considerations of social policy and ideology are also clearly operative. Among them are, first, egalitarianism, evident in a relatively strong emphasis on progressive income tax.

These ideas of social justice are also evident in other taxes, such as those on foreign travel, cars, and petrol, or the newly-proposed taxes on large flats, beauty parlours, and driving lessons – whose fiscal utility may be small – but which are administratively convenient since they can be taxed at source. At the same time the social orientation is also evident in the exemption from purchase tax of food, books, newspapers.

More recently several new taxes with 'social' (i.e. mostly egalitarian) aims were instituted. One such tax – aimed at curbing both excess profits from speculation in land and at curbing such speculation – was the 'improvement tax' of 1963 which, after some initial administrative difficulties and inefficiency proved to be relatively successful in its aim.

Another, somewhat more problematic, 'social' tax was one on capital gains, instituted in 1962 whose effectiveness is as yet to be proved – as perhaps its first effect was mainly to affect adversely the young Israeli stock exchange.

The third one is a new (1964) inheritance tax which seems to hit especially the middle echelons or income groups.

A second condition is the potential influence of different types of taxes on the economic motivation and behaviour of different groups – whether in terms of providing incentive to work or increasing propensity to save as well as the influence of taxation policy on public morals and honesty. But on the whole these considerations did not seem usually to be of paramount importance.

Beyond these the demands of different groups (such as agriculturalists or professionals) for special treatment may also play a role – according to their political or economic importance. Of no lesser importance in the actual implementation of taxation poliyc is the relative efficiency of the tax system as regards each group of taxpayers – and here the major weakness has been the self-employed sector and companies.

Such varied social, political, and administrative criteria operate also in monetary and wage policies. In monetary and credit policy we find that considerations of curbing inflation on the one hand and the needs of development on the other (see below) greatly influence the regulation of credit and the various attempts to curb consumption.

These factors are, however, very often mitigated and sometimes even nullified by political pressures of varying groups for growing wages and for extension of credits and subsidies.

Of some significance here are ideological and political considerations of the importance of state and administrative control over the economy. In addition these monetary policies, and especially that of foreign exhange, were also – initially at least – influenced by the fiscal needs of the government.

Wages policy is perhaps even more determined by the different pressures of various groups, by the ideology of egalitarianism and by attempts to find some compromise between these factors and the need to absorb new immigrants and provide incentives for technical and professional skills.[1]

[1] For the major social implications of this policy see in greater detail (Chapter 7).

TABLE 22
Subsidies by Authority and Type
(IL million)
1952–1962

	1952	1953	1954	1955	1956	1957	1958	1959	1960	1961	1962
Total Subsidies	7·4	39·1	30·3	76·6	82·9	111·8	128·7	157·6	218·1	257·9	211·7
Central Government Subsidies	—	26·9	9·9	61·2	63·9	102·6	120·2	149·5	194·0	220·1	161·1
Subsidies Paid by the National Institutions	0·1	0·5	1·2	2·0	2·5	3·0	3·3	2·9	3·3	3·0	2·5
Net Interest Paid by Central Government and National Institutions	7·3	11·7	19·2	13·4	16·5	6·2	5·2	5·2	20·8	34·8	48·1

Source: CBS, *The National Income and Expenditure of Israel, 1950–62*, Special Series No. 153, Jerusalem, 1964, Table 44, pp. 82–3.

The whole policy of subsidies – the range of which is given in Table 22 – is also greatly influenced by some broad social-national considerations, most clearly seen in the heavy emphasis on agriculture and to a somewhat lesser degree by special help to enterprises which are willing to absorb new immigrants by going to development areas. Allegedly here also political considerations of preferential treatments to different sectors might be operative.

Further, policy is guided by considerations of the necessity to expand trade and exports, as a means towards economic independence, as well as by considerations of 'protection' of local industries.

Thus, for instance, the aim of subsidies to agriculture has been:

(1) To maintain a reasonable level of prices to the consumers (and sometimes reasonable price levels for c.o.l. index calculations). In this category we include also subsidies on imported food (such as cereals and beef).

(2) Encouragement to produce several crops, to maintain a fair income-level to the farmers in general or to certain of their groups or to stabilize the prices of certain crops (vegetables in particular) during the surplus season.

The special policies of housing, rent control, education, etc. are determined by the practical needs of immigration and are moulded according to conceptions of social rights and the ideology of the ingathering of the exiles – if possible within the framework of existing social institutions.[1] Lately, much emphasis has been given to the closing of the economic and educational gap between the old-timers and the newcomers (especially oriental).

In these spheres, as well as in that of health insurance and services, basic socio-ideological considerations were coupled, on the administrative and implementative level, with considerations arising out of the vested interests of various powerful organizations which dealt with these problems and were not ready to give up their positions in this realm.

Major Dilemmas of Economic Policies

Cutting across these varied political, social, and administrative considerations, some basic problems or dilemmas of economic policy have continuously stood out. These dilemmas are closely connected with the ways of dealing with the major economic problems outlined above.

The first major dilemma is that between what may be called the distributive aspects of the economy and the emphasis on attainment of economic independence. The distributive aspects emphasize the increase of consumption, the allocation of various services and goods, and the provision of various services and amenities to the population. Ideological tenets which emphasize

[1] See in greater detail in the next chapter.

113

the basic social rights of various groups and pressures are closely interwoven here.

In contrast to these distributive goals of economic policy stands the goal of economic independence in which a much greater emphasis is laid on the accumulation and investment of capital instead of on consumption.

These goals of development and attainment of economic independence contain varying, sometimes parallel, sometimes contradictory, orientations.

Important contradictions may develop between the different sub-goals of economic development and independence and between the main goal and the emphasis on the distributive aspects of the economy.

Such contradictions may arise, for example, between growing investment and growing public consumption – although sometimes developmental investment may bring its own inflationary trends and pressures. In such cases the emphasis on physical development may very easily become combined with the distributive orientations of the economy.

Cutting across these orientations are the different emphases on the basic conceptions of economic policy – planning and centralization versus free economic mechanisms.

Of no smaller importance were the dilemmas or contradictions between some of the major social goals implicit in economic policies – and especially those between continuous economic expansion, rise in standard of living and social equality and maintenance of the political predominance of the existing élite. We shall deal with the problems arising out of these dilemmas in the next chapter.[1]

The Implementation of Economic Policies

As already pointed out the actual policy undertaken has, of course, been a compromise between the different economic orientations and political pressures on the one hand and the various administrative conceptions and vested interests on the other.

The concrete deliberations and decisions and their execution are in the hands of the cabinet, ministerial committees, and the different economic ministries (the Ministries of Finance, Trade and Industry, Development, Agriculture) each of which constitutes in many ways an empire of its own with its own vested interests. The disputes between them are relegated to the Cabinet and the Committee of Economic Ministers, while others – especially those dealing with wage policies – are discussed in central committees of the major parties (especially of Mapai) and the Histadrut or between the government and these bodies.

The deliberations and decisions of these various bodies are obviously

[1] See Chapter 7, Part 3.

114

greatly influenced by pressures exerted on them by various groups – from different economic enterprises and representatives of different sectors up to the various governmental bodies and ministries themselves – and by broader considerations of economic policy.

Obviously these decisions are made on different levels – ranging from middle echelons of the administration where many of the most important routine decisions are made, up to the more general decisions on principles of policy, which are made in the upper echelon of the administration through inter-ministerial discussion and committees.

To what extent did the Government pursue a clear-cut, consequent policy? Let's first survey the actual development of its major policies.

Major Stages in the Development of Economic Policies: 1949–62

Throughout the development of the State of Israel we may discern both some basic continuity as well as some important shifts in economic policy.

The major features of continuity may be found in the general emphasis on physical development, maintenance of full employment, and provision of services (here also the huge expenditure on defence may be included), and on the overall strategic importance of the Government in the direction of the economy.

Four stages may be discerned in the economic development of Israel. Mass immigration and extensive – though mainly improvised – economic activities marked the period from the establishment of the state in May 1948 to the end of 1951. This was followed by the New Economic Policy of 1952–4, which achieved greater economic stability. Since 1955 the country has been slowly grappling with conditions and problems similar to, but less acute than, those of the first period. It was only in about 1960 that the overall economic situation again became rather critical and a new economic policy was put into effect in February 1962, when the Israeli pound was devalued to IL 3 = $1 from IL 1·80 = $1·00.

The strain of settling masses of immigrants, fighting a war, building up defence forces, and promoting extensive development projects, was too much for Israel's economy. The weaknesses showed especially in inflation and in an unfavourable balance of trade.

The immigrants became consumers as soon as they arrived in Israel, because they had to be supplied with a minimum of food, clothing, and shelter. But the majority arrived without means and did not immediately contribute to the production of goods. This created an increased demand for the available supply of commodities. Large defence expenditures likewise increased purchasing power without adding to the supply of consumer goods. The long-range programme of economic development added to the pressure on the goods desired for current consumption. Finally, unbalanced budgets and credit expansion created a spiral of inflation, with increased prices, costs, and wages, and a decline in the value of the Israeli pound

The pattern of foreign trade was equally discouraging. During 1949–51 exports amounted to only 11 or 12 per cent of the value of imports, and the annual trade deficits increased steadily, reaching a total of some $333,000,000 in 1951. During this period the government attempted to repress inflation by means of rationing, price controls, and other direct administrative measures. But these efforts were nullified by black market operations and by waning public confidence, especially after clothing and footwear rationing was introduced in the summer of 1950. The drought of the following winter aggravated the situation, threatening collapse of the entire currency and price structure. A change in policy became imperative.

The first New Economic Policy is generally associated with the official devaluation of the Israeli pound on 13 February 1952. In fact, however, it was more far-reaching, and some of the measures were adopted as early as the spring of the preceding year. The New Economic Policy gradually abandoned direct controls such as rationing and sought to curb inflation and improve the balance of payments by indirect means. The issue of Treasury Bills was stopped and an attempt was made to balance the regular state budget. Basic wages were frozen, except when justified by higher productivity, and a compulsory development loan was levied. These measures helped to reduce imports, and varied policies served to stimulate exports.

The effects of the New Economic Policy were evident – although not immediately – in increased agricultural and industrial production and in the development of local raw materials. Although in the beginning there was a rise in unemployment and in prices, average daily unemployment fell sharply during 1954. The foreign trade deficit fell from $333,000,000 in 1951 to some $198,000,000 in 1954. Greater stability in prices and costs was achieved during 1954, and public confidence was restored.

From 1955, however, various factors again disturbed the trend toward economic stabilization. Mass immigration – although not at the rate of the initial wave of 1948–50 – occurred as a result of disturbances in North Africa. Military expenditure mounted to meet the threat of the arms agreement between Egypt and Soviet Russia and its satellites in September 1955, and the Sinai campaign of October–November 1956 further strained the Israeli economy. Dependence on foreign imports again increased, and greater purchasing power intensified inflationary pressures.

The main purpose of the economic policy of the government from 1955 on was to achieve – by high rates of investment – rapid development and growth in the different economic branches, so as to deal effectively with the problems of immigration absorption, economic independence, and raising the standard of living of the population. Secondary aims were the dispersion of the

116

population, especially into the southern regions, and the attainment of self-sufficiency in some essential commodities.

To achieve these main purposes side by side with rapid development, the government employed four main lines of policy.

(1) A policy of balanced budgets – an effort to achieve surpluses in the regular budgets – for financing expenditures in the development budget. This policy was generally successful in spite of a steady growth of public services.

(2) A policy of wage restraints was attempted and was partially successful.

(3) Encouragment of the population to save (by several means[1]) and an effort to restrain the rapid growth in the level of consumption.

(4) Supervision of credit and monetary expansion.

The main policies in the sphere of development were:

(1) The encouragement of exports by increasing subsidies and by other means.

(2) Regulation and laws to encourage foreign capital investments, accompanied by big loans on good terms from the government development budgets.

(3) Direct investment by the government – mainly in basic enterprises and services such as mining, power, irrigation programmes, transport facilities, etc.

In almost all areas of governmental activity we may discern a clear trend of liberalization and diminishing direct interference of the Government in economic life.

In spite of the Sinai campaign and the many expenditures on security and defence, we can say that in general the Government succeeded to some extent in achieving its aims. The main failure was in savings and consumption. Because of this and because of the development of autonomous monetary expansion, the general stability began to falter and ultimately gave rise to yet another change of policy to what may be called the second New Economic Policy.

The (Second) New Economic Policy – 1962

On 9 February 1962 the Israeli pound was devaluated and instead of the rate of IL 1·80 = $1, a new rate of IL 3 = $1 was introduced. Together with the devaluation, a plan aimed at stabilizing the Israeli economy was proclaimed.

During the preceding years (after a short period of stabilization) inflationary pressure had increased and brought about an increase in demand. The automatic linking of wages and salaries to the cost-of-living index (as was explained above) caused an increase in salaries, and this, coupled with a

---

[1] Saving programmes, tax reductions, high interest rates on savings, incentives in the stock market.

growing demand, created a vicious price spiral. The government tried to tackle this state of affairs by a creeping devaluation, imposing higher customs tariffs and granting premiums to exports and capital transfers. The main motivation for this approach was the relatively big unilateral capital transfers. A devaluation would have brought tremendous additional sums of Israeli pounds into the economy and thus increased the inflationary pressure. From this point of view there was no need for an immediate and severe restriction of imports, especially since the share of capital goods in total imports increased. On the other hand, with the help of premiums, exports showed a steady upward trend; and there were debates and differences of opinion as to whether there was need for devaluation to stimulate exports.

There were, however, several reasons why the government decided on a change of policy:

(1) It became exceedingly difficult administratively to control the labyrinth of exchange rates. It reached a stage where even the officials dealing with these matters could hardly find their way about (not to mention the public). The profitability of an enterprise or a commercial transaction often depended on an official's decision and was influenced by the power of persuasion of the interested party.

(2) The government reached the limit of its ability to finance the premiums and subsidies by non-deficit financing.

(3) The cost and price structure of the economy was considerably distorted.

This last reason was probably the most important one. Israel is developing at an accelerated pace. Leaving the distorted cost and price structure as it was would have deprived the economy of any objective criterion for determining the profitability of investments and establishing a scale of priority. Devaluation was intended to avert misinvestment on a large scale.

As mentioned; there was a real danger – due to these specific circumstances in Israel – that devaluation might increase the inflationary pressure.

To restrain demand, an increase of money supply had to be avoided. The main source of this increase was (and still is) personal restitution money from Germany which has flowed in during the last few years at a rate of over a hundred million dollars a year. In addition to the current flow, there were foreign exchange deposits from this source on the day of devaluation of approximately 130 million dollars. The Minister of Finance issued an appeal not to convert foreign currency into Israeli pounds. It was a tremendous risk on the part of the Government because a mass conversion could have been disastrous to the new economic plan. The appeal has proved successful to some extent – at least in the initial year or so.

The Government succeeded in having a surplus budget in 1962–3. Among other things a compulsory saving law was enacted with the intention – maintained during the first year – of immobilizing the money thus received.

Loans in foreign currency were reduced to a minimum and are restricted to import requirements. The conversion of such loans into Israeli pounds is entirely forbidden.

There was no relaxation of banking credit, in spite of the fact that devaluation meant that a greater volume of credit was needed to achieve the same volume of imports and production.

But the most important aspect of this policy was the initial ability by the Government to curb, to some extent at least, the rise in prices in agreement with the Manufacturers' Association, despite the necessity of paying additional cost-of-living allowance, and in agreement with the Histadrut not to make overall demands for wage rises in 1963–4. Contrary to many expectations the government was successful, up to 1962–3 at least, in implementing most of these policies and achieving stability.

The situation changed to some extent in 1963–4. True enough, expansion has taken place in almost all the major branches of the economy, unemployment has been greatly reduced, and a shortage of skilled labour has become almost endemic in the economy. Similarly, the standard of living continues to advance rapidly, and there was on the whole relative price stability, expansion of consumer credit and a general feeling of economic security.

But as a survey of 1963–4 in a leading English newspaper indicated, the feeble efforts made under the New Economic Policy to arrest the boom and to divert more of the nation's resources to improving its balance of payments have been tacitly dropped in view of the continuing high tide of capital import – both from personal restitutions and from private investments – on top of which substantial amounts have been obtained by way of long-term loans.

As a matter of fact, the trade gap widened, due to a bad citrus season and a general slow-down of export expansion, while the import bill has swelled considerably. This development, however, was inevitable if price stability on the domestic market was to be maintained in the teeth of soaring demand. Public deficit financing was maintained. While the Government firmly resisted wage increases beyond 3 per cent (in order to keep the advance of money incomes within the range of productivity gains) and blocked any expansion of bank credits, credit expanded instead in the form of bills negotiated outside the bank control, system and after dramatic conflicts and many strikes – most of which were disowned by the official trade unions – wages were also raised by more than the safe margin of 3 per cent. The results of this wage rise, however, will not be immediately felt.

Thus new inflationary pressures were building up in the economy which did not seem to be geared to any far-reaching structural changes.

Thus if we survey the broad trend of development of economic policy in Israel, we find that in the first stage the major emphasis or goal was that of securing full employment; in the second the main goal was the improvement of balance of payments; while in the last stage there was the rather vague aim of what has been called 'stability' – i.e. the maintenance of some

119

continuous development without inflation and many far-reaching structural changes in the economy.

The aim of the maintenance of full employment and of physical expansion continued to be predominant throughout all these periods and constituted, together with the maintenance of the stability of the existing political frameworks, the major guiding lines of economic policy. But even these seem to be only guiding lines and not principles of clear-cut, consequent policy.

In this respect the picture is a rather mixed one. While in some spheres, such as education, a relatively uniform policy has developed and been implemented by a relatively cohesive administration, this has not been the case in most spheres.

One reason for this is the division of policy aspects between different ministries, each dealing with a different area, often merely allocated to it by the exigencies of party politics.

Second, there is not always effective co-ordination between ministries. Very often the criteria of administrative activities employed by different ministries are contradictory – for example, help to social cases through self-employment (especially by providing them with private shops as is sometimes done by the Ministry of Social Welfare) may contradict the criteria of productivization of the Ministry of Labour.

Third, as mentioned, many crucial areas of social policy, such as health, are not – mainly for political reasons – in the hands of the Government, while at the same time they necessarily impinge on many areas dealt with by the Government – in this way only increasing the lack of co-ordination and the high costs of social policy.

Last and most important is the 'surrender' of the authorities to various political or local pressures – immigrant groups, political parties, economic vested interests – which very often obviates the possibility of maintaining clear-cut policies.

It seems that the overall picture has been more one of continuous adaptation to changing political and social and economic pressures, situations, and exigencies rather than of a continuous overall policy. This adaptation has been mainly guided by several interconnected considerations – continuously increasing fiscal needs, attempts to assure maximum employment (even if at a relatively low level of remuneration), continuous physical development aimed at ensuring places of work, keeping social and political conflicts and tensions at a minimum, assuring the political control of the ruling élite, and the implementation of some of its social goals, and last and often least, the goal of economic independence. The former considerations seem to have been paramount and have necessarily minimized the possibility of the implementation of clear-cut, consequential policies in general and of giving to considerations of economic independence and productivization a high level of priority, in particular.

THE PERFORMANCE AND PROBLEMS OF ISRAELI ECONOMY – PRODUCTION, CONSUMPTION AND THE GAP BETWEEN THEM. THE PROBLEMS OF BREAKTHROUGH

The Gap Between Production and Consumption – the Major Problems in Israeli Economy

The preceding discussion attempted to analyse the criteria guiding the major economic policies and their implementation. What is the overall outcome of these various policies?

On the one hand we witness a tremendous economic development, a process of sustained economic growth, which is especially remarkable in view of the great number of immigrants who entered the country. The ratio of this growth has been variously estimated at around 11 to 13 per cent but all agree that it is very high.

On the other hand, however, Israeli economy is continuously – as Tables 23 and 24 show – plagued with a gap in its trade balance.

This gap has been held in check mostly by external sources – Jewish contributions from abroad, US government loans, German reparations, etc.

TABLE 23

Excess of Imports over Exports
(Thousands U.S. $)

	Net Imports	Net Exports	Excess of Imports Over Exports	Exports as Percentage of Imports
1949	251,906	28,495	223,411	11·3
1950	300,325	35,147	265,178	11·7
1951	381,682	44,754	336,928	11·7
1952	322,261	43,489	278,772	13·5
1953	279,929	57,636	222,293	20·6
1954	287,248	86,300	200,948	30·0
1955	334,453	89,056	245,397	26·6
1956	375,593	106,501	269,092	28·4
1957	432,829	140,127	292,702	32·4
1958	420,930	139,102	281,828	33·0
1959	427,291	176,383	250,908	41·3
1960	495,646	211,276	284,370	42·6
1961	583,912	239,082	344,830	40·9
1962	620,473	272,256	348,217	43·9
1962	626,222	271,403	354,819	43·3
1963	663,506	338,285	325,221	51.0
1964	804,102	351,821	452,281	43.8

Source: CBS *Statistical Abstract*, No. 14, 1963, p. 422; No. 16, 1965, Table I/1, pp. 239–9.

TABLE 24

Excess of Imports over Total Resources, 1950–1963[a]
(Million Dollars)

Year	Total Resources	Excess of Import	Percentage of Total Resources
1950	1,045	338	32·3
1955	1,529	289	18·9
1960	2,203	292	13·2
1963	3,061	515	16·8

[a] In fixed prices of 1955: $1 = 1·80 IL.

Source: D. Horvitz, *Trend and structure in Israel Economy* (Hebrew), Tel-Aviv, Massada, 1964, p. 39.

This problem has constituted a continuous topic of public debate which is evidence of its great *political* importance.

As may be seen, for instance, from the tables, the reason for the gap does not lie in stagnant production – although this could probably have been expanded much more – but in the inability of production to catch up with the continuously increasing consumption.

TABLE 25

Population aged 14 and over by Labour Force Characteristics
(Absolute Numbers and Percentages)
in September 1955;[a] Yearly Averages 1960 and 1964

Year	Total Population	Civilian Labour Force (Per cent)	Total Civilian Labour Force (100 Per cent)	Employed Persons (Per cent)	Unemployed Persons (Per cent)
1955	1,073,800	54·4	100	92·9	7·1
1960	1,258,100	54·1	100	96·1	3·9
1964	1,506,000	54·0	100	96·6	3·4

[a] In November 1931, the civilian labour force and armed forces comprised 30·3 per cent of the total population of Palestine.

Source: CBS *Statistical Abstract*, No. 16, 1965, Table K/2, p. 296.

In order to understand the reasons for this persistent gap it is necessary to analyse the major components of the economic process – especially the processes of production and consumption. As a detailed technical-economic analysis would be out of place here we shall concentrate only on some of the broader aspects.

Manpower Composition in Relation to Productivity

Let us attempt to analyse some of the major aspects of the production process and some of the broader economic, social, political, and ideological factors affecting increases and decreases in productivity.

Let us begin with an examination of the structure and distribution of manpower and its relation to productivity.

TABLE 26

Population (14 Years age and over) by Labour Force Characteristics, Religion and Sex, 1959–62

Year	June 1954			Av. 1958			Av. 1960			Av. 1962		
	Total (·000) (1)	Civ. labour force (% of total) (2)	Unemployed (% of civ. labour force) (3)	Total (·000) (1)	Civ. labour force (% of total) (2)	Unemployed (% of civ. labour force) (3)	Total (·000) (1)	Civ. labour force (% of total) (2)	Unemployed (% of civ. labour force) (3)	Total (·000) (1)	Civ. labour force (% of total) (2)	Unemployed (% of civ. labour force) (3)
Total Population	1,145·1	49·0	8·6	1,313·7	53·2	5·7	1,391·9	52·9	4·6	1,513	54·1	3·7
Males	578·0	76·5	8·7	661·6	78·7	5·3	700·2	78·1	4·5	760	78·7	3·3
Females	567·1	20·9	8·2	652·1	27·3	7·0	691·7	27·3	4·9	753	29·2	4·8
Jews:												
Total	1,046·8	49·4	8·3	1,190·1	54·5	5·6	1,258·1	54·1	3·9	1,369	54·5	3·6
Males	528·1	76·6	8·3	599·3	79·3	5·1	633·0	78·4	3·6	687	78·5	3·1
Females	518·7	21·7	8·4	590·8	29·4	7·0	625·1	29·5	4·9	681	30·3	5·0
Others:												
Total	98·3	44·0	9·0	123·6	40·0	7·1	133·8	41·5	13·3	—	—	—
Males	49·9	75·8	10·1	62·3	72·7	7·3	67·2	75·5	14·2	—	—	—
Females	48·4	11·4	1·8	61·3	6·8	4·8	66·6	7·2	4·2	—	—	—

Sources: 1954: CBS *Statistical Abstract* No. 6, 1954–5, Table 1, pp. 117–8.'
1958: Op. cit., No. 11, 1959–60, Table 1, pp. 300–1.
1960: CBS *Statistical Bulletin* (Hebrew), Part B, Economics, Vol. 12, No. 4, April 1961 Tables 1–6, pp. 385–90.
1962: CBS *Statistical Abstract*, No. 19, 1963, pp. 486 and 488.

TABLE 27

Jews in Civilian Labour Force
By Sex, Continent of Birth and Period of Immigration
(Percentages)
(Averages 1958–1963; November 1955)

Continent of Birth and Period of Immigration	Civilian Labour Force as Percentage of Total Population Aged 14 and Above, in Each Continent of Birth and Period of Immigration Group					Labour Force-Absolute Numbers (1,000)
	Nov. 1955	1958	1960	1962	1963	1963
Total	54·4	54·5	54·1	54·5	53·6	774·9
Israel Born	51·8	50·5	49·7	51·9	50·5	136·7
Born Abroad—Total	54·8	55·3	54·9	55·1	54·2	430·2
Immigrated up to 1947	60·2	60·3	61·3	61·3	60·7	201·5
Immigrated since 1948	51·2	52·6	52·0	52·8	51·7	436·7
Born in Asia and Africa—Total	48·9	49·2	49·7	51·0	50·2	259·3
Immigrated up to 1947	52·9	52·4	53·6	54·7	51·7	30·7
Immigrated since 1948	47·9	48·6	49·2	50·6	50·1	228·6
Born in Europe and America—Total	58·2	59·0	58·5	58·1	57·3	378·9
Immigrated up to 1947	61·7	61·7	62·8	62·8	62·7	170·8
Immigrated since 1948	54·4	56·3	55·1	55·2	53·6	208·1
MALES	80·3	79·3	78·4	78.6	76.5	557·5
Israel Born	64·9	62·9	62·5	65·8	62·7	86·0
Born Abraod—Total	83·1	82·6	81·4	81·1	79·8	471·5
Immigrated up to 1947	89·4	88·6	88·4	88·5	87·5	150·2
Immigrated since 1948	78·8	79·2	78·0	78·3	76·6	321·3
Born in Asia and Africa—Total	77·3	77·1	77·2	77·6	76·0	198·1
Immigrated up to 1947	81·5	84·2	85·2	84·4	80·8	25·6
Immigrated since 1948	76·3	75·9	76·0	76·8	75·3	172·5
Born in Europe and America—Total	86·4	85·7	84·4	83·8	82·7	273·4
Immigrated up to 1947	91·0	89·4	89·1	89·4	89·0	124·6
Immigrated since 1948	81·2	82·3	80·3	80·1	78·1	148·8
FEMALES	27·9	29·4	29·5	30·3	30·3	217·4
Israel Born	27·4	37·8	36·8	37·7	38·0	50·7
Born Abroad—Total	26·3	27·7	28·1	28·9	28·5	166·7
Immigrated up to 1947	29·6	30·5	31·6	32·6	32·0	51·3
Immigrated since 1948	24·2	26·2	26·6	27·6	27·1	115·4
Born in Asia and Africa—Total	20·2	20·8	21·8	23·8	24·0	61·2
Immigrated up to 1947	21·8	18·4	19·2	23·1	18·3	5·1
Immigrated since 1948	19·9	21·2	22·2	23·9	24·7	56·1
Born in Europe and America—Total	29·8	31·7	32·5	32·6	31·9	105·5
Immigrated up to 1947	31·2	32·6	34·1	34·7	34·8	46·2
Immigrated since 1948	28·3	30·9	31·3	31·4	30·0	59·3

Source: Op. cit., No. 16, 1965, Table K/7, p. 302.

TABLE 28

Labour Force Characteristics of Jewish Population (14 Years and over) – Veterans and New Immigrants[a] – by Place of Birth and Sex (1954–60) (Percentage)

Year: Sex	Total	Born in Israel	Veter-ans	New immi-grants	Veterans Europe and America	Veterans Asia and Africa	New immigrants Europe and America	New immigrants Asia and Africa
A. Civilian Labour Force of Population:								
June 1954:								
Both Sexes	49·4	43·5	52·8	46·3	60·3	50·2	51·6	43·8
Males	76·6	59·1	78·1	75·2	91·5	83·2	83·8	74·5
Females	21·7	27·4	25·8	18·1	27·9	15·2	21·5	14·8
June 1957[b]:								
Both Sexes	55·3	52·2	61·8	52·4	62·5	58·3	56·1	48·6
Males	80·0	64·6	89·8	78·8	90·3	87·0	83·6	74·1
Females	28·3	—	—	—	—	—	—	—
1960:								
Both Sexes	54·1	49·7	—	—	62·8	53·6	55·1	49·2
Males	78·4	62·5	—	—	89·1	85·2	80·3	76·0
Females	29·5	36·8	—	—	34·1	19·2	32·0	22·2
B. Unemployed of Civilian Labour Force								
June 1954:								
Both Sexes	8·3	10·7	5·7	11·1	3·4	7·7	7·9	15·4
Males	8·3	10·5	5·7	10·9	3·6	7·9	7·8	14·7
Females	8·4	11·2	5·4	12·0	2·6	6·5	8·1	18·3
June 1957:								
Both Sexes	6·6	8·7	2·9	8·6	(2·5)	(5·5)	6·5	11·2
Males	8·9	(7·3)	(2·6)	7·7	(2·1)	(5·0)	5·1	10·6
Females	8·9	—	—	—	—	—	—	—

[a] Veterans: born in Israel and immigrants who arrived up to the end of 1947; New Immigrants: arrived from 1948 onward.

[b] Veterans: as a, but excluding those who were born in Israel.

Sources: 1954: CBS Labour Force Survey, June 1954, Jerusalem, April 1957, Tables 5, 7, 8, pp. 10–14.
1957: CBS Labour Force Survey, 1957, Jerusalem, January 1959, Table 10, pp. 20–1.
1960: CBS unpublished data.

The various surveys of manpower summarized in Tables 25–29 indicate that:

(1) During the period 1931–59 the rate of growth of the labour force was about the same as that of the total Jewish population (10·5).

(2) As a result of the large number in the armed forces in 1948 and the mass immigration in 1948–9, the ratio of civilian labour force to population was extremely low in 1948, quite low in 1949, and only in 1951 did this ratio reach its former level.

(3) From 1931 to about 1944, the demographic composition of the Jewish population became increasingly more favourable to a large labour force. In about 1944, this trend was reversed. This is the cause of the continual reduction in the ratio of civilian labour force to population.

(4) Generally speaking, the large-scale immigration did not lead to extremely high unemployment (apart from the direct effect in 1949) although during the first six to seven years the rate of unemployment was certainly not low. At the same time (during most of the period 1949–58) real wages increased.

(5) Very low rates of labour force participation are to be found, first in the group of males aged fifty-five and over – who had immigrated after 1948 from Asia or Africa – and second among women of thirty-five and over – new immigrants from Asia and Africa.

(6) On the other hand, among the fourteen–seventeen-year-old group in the Jewish population, we find a relatively high unemployment rate.

(7) It seems that housewives are the major future source of the civilian labour force.

(8) Non-Jews, who constituted about one-tenth of the Israeli population from 1948–59, had a higher ratio of children per family than the Jewish population, a lower level of education, higher unemployment, and a lower specific ratio of labour-force participation, particularly among women.

(9) A projection of the population of Israel to 1970 – based on present demographic composition and on the assumption that the rates of participation for each group by age, sex, continent of origin, and period of immigration will remain more or less stable – leads to the conclusion that the ratio of civilian labour force to the population will decline from 34·9 per cent in 1958 to 30·9 per cent in 1970[1] – but this may of course change if the composition of immigration changes.

This survey also shows that in comparing the industrial distribution in Israel's economy with that of other countries (distribution of persons employed as well as national product), the low percentage in agriculture and manufacturing and the extremely high percentage in the service industries stand out.

[1] Source: The Falk Project, Fifth Report 1959–60, Project Report 1, pp. 133–8, and see A. Hovne, *The Labour Force in Israel*, Jerusalem, Falk Project for Economic Research, 1961.

These findings show that the main assets of Israeli manpower from the point of view of production have been the large reservoir, especially among the old-timers, of people with higher education and skills. But these findings also indicate certain problems.

These problems may be discerned from the two poles in the composition of Israeli manpower – the older manpower (i.e. those who came before 1948) and the new immigrants. We may as well start with the latter. Here the major problem was the composition of manpower which shows the relatively low participation of immigrants in the labour force. This phenomenon is related to the low level of education and technical skills and the consequent low level of earnings and is also related to some extent to age structure. Although all these factors are constantly improving, yet, on the whole, the productive level of this manpower is relatively low. It has always contained some structural unemployment, and society is faced with the threat both of continuous gaps in available skilled manpower and of inadequate levels of skill.

The Effects of Absorption Policies on Productivity

One of the most important questions with regard to this whole area is the influence of the policy of absorption on the productivization of the immigrants. In the first stages this policy was guided by two interconnected principles – first, the provision of a minimum level of security to the immigrants in terms of housing and economic needs and second, mitigation of open competition between the newcomers and old-timers in the labour market, so as to protect the immigrants and old-timers alike.

The most important single continuous device of this system was the provision of special public works for the immigrants in road construction, afforestation, etc. At the same time, this kept them out of the regular labour market.

In the later stages of absorptions, more diversified policies were developed to deal with this problem – the most important perhaps being the various policies dealing with direction and education of labour and with vocational guidance and training.

In this context we should mention the various training facilities provided by the Employment Service.

Only a few of the new immigrants had, prior to their arrival, been industrial workers; many, coming from underdeveloped countries, did not even know the meaning of a factory. As the new immigrants constitute the only reservoir of labour, it is important for the success of Israel's expanding industry to turn them into a trained labour force.

Because of this, the single plant has itself to educate the immigrant and socialize him into the role of an industrial worker. The plant is somehow doubly responsible for the job and livelihood of the new immigrants as well as for their vocational training. In the meantime there is not much sense in trying to impose strict standards of efficiency.

Moreover, though the industrial labour force is still in the process of formation, it has already has a strong organizational framework in the form of the Histadrut. The trade unions have considerable strength and any change in personnel has to meet with their approval. It is of special importance for the selection of workers that in fact, if not formally, neither hiring nor firing are in the hands of management (although lately there has been a tendency to give more leeway to the single plant in this respect). As the Histadrut is itself one of the largest entrepreneurs and a basic factor and participant in development, it sees itself as the chief representative of the general national interests – an approach which makes management's bargaining with the trade unions quite complicated. Moreover, at least in the first stages of absorption in industrial enterprises, there has been a more or less explicit policy of maintaining a relatively slower level of productivity per worker so as to enable the absorption of a larger number of workers.

What is the overall influence of the various policies of absorption – on the countrywide or local level – on the productivization of the immigrants? Although no full and systematic data are available, some indications may be discerned.

One basic facilitating factor was the social security given by the absorbing institutions. This reinforced those internal forces among the immigrants inclined to change and willing to acquire new skills. Also very important in this context was the fact that these various services – if properly administered – could quickly raise the general standard of health and physical ability. But this basic security was only the first step – and one, as we shall see, which had dangers of its own. It was only insofar as reinforcing factors did develop that the potentialities of this basic security could be maximized.

The second facilitating factor was that the absorbing structure sometimes provided social settings in which the new types of skills, activities, and attitudes could be learned. The best examples of this are the agricultural settlements and some of the most general social and political organizations concerned with economic and labour relations, such as local trade union councils and local workers' committees. In all these cases the immigrants were not thrown into the open market, with its impersonal relations and possible lack of organization, but were able to participate in relatively stable social groups which incorporated many of the new types of economic activities and motivations within a framework of new social values and incentives. In this way the immigrants could be spared some of the anomic experience of rapid urbanization or modernization.

But these various factors and policies did not only facilitate the process of productivization of new immigrants. They also often included several impeding factors.

The most general impeding effect was due to the ascriptive allocation of various services, rights, and facilities for consumption without any clear or basic relation to productivity. While this could at a certain stage provide minimum security and various other prerequisites for the acquisition of new skills, such as certain standards of health and education, beyond this level it could easily – if no steps were taken to avoid it – impair productivization. This could happen in several ways. The immigrants could be unwilling to work more than was necessary for the maintenance of their present level of needs and would be especially unwilling to work to pay taxes, and so forth. Or they might use their settlement, factory, and so forth, as a base for less productive activities yielding easy money, such as various black market activities, peddling, or small-scale speculation.

Closely connected with this was the problem of dependence on various bureaucratic absorption agencies. This often gave rise to passivity, apathy regarding advancement, and strong aggressive demands on the agencies on the part of the immigrants.[1] All these problems were likely to be especially acute when, as was usually the case, the capital available to the absorbing agencies was not sufficient to effect a rapid productivization of the immigrants – who for their part were unwilling to invest their own funds – and had to be spent on maintaining a given level of consumption.

A second major impediment – especially in the initial stages of absorption – was connected with certain tendencies inherent in Israeli bureaucratic administration. Power and authority were concentrated in the hands of the absorbing sector, while the immigrants had only the more passive functions and were thus extremely dependent on the former. This state of affairs was particularly conspicuous in the various immigrant reception camps, transitional work settlements, etc. Such a formal bureaucratic and authoritative relationship usually constituted one of the decisive factors in the creation of social and vocational apathy and in the development of various other negative phenomena, such as peremptory demands, aggressiveness, and unwillingness to persist in any job seemingly imposed from above.

These problems were accentuated by the fact that with the passage of time there developed in the later stages of absorption many loopholes which prevented the absorption of many immigrants in productive activities.

A very important instance of such loopholes has been the lack of adequate vocational guidance for various groups – especially for the younger immigrants – or their lack of ability to avail themselves of the existing provisions and facilities. This became evident in the late 'fifties when quite a lot of unemployment among these groups was due to such conditions.

Though some of these loopholes have recently been taken care of by the development of special vocational guidance courses, gaps probably still exist.

[1] See, for fuller analysis of these problems, S. N. Eisenstadt, 'The Process of Absorption of New Immigrants in Israel', *Human Relations*, Vol. 5, No. 3, 1954.

Entrepreneurship and Overall Problems of Productivization among New Immigrants

Another problem was connected with the type of entrepreneurship most strongly favoured by the absorbing structure. Quite obviously there existed many formal and informal pressures on the immigrants to produce types similar to those that existed in the Yishuv – and especially the more specific institutional type. Although no reliable statistical data are as yet available, some general impressions can be given. Of the three main types of entrepreneur in the Yishuv, only the first (the institution) and the third (the petty capitalist) seem to be prevalent among the immigrants. The second type, that of the large-scale colonizing capitalist, is rare – largely owing to the very small number of new immigrants with adequate capital resources of their own. The few who had such resources did not greatly affect the whole structure of development of the immigrants' economic activities. Moreover, some of them tended to use their capital in various financial ventures instead of in productive investments.

Many immigrants continued their old pattern of activities, becoming small-scale entrepreneurs of the third type. Some continued to be artisans of the traditional type, while many others were drawn into the less productive section of the economy which expanded during the inflation and the rapid growth of the population.

The most original development among the immigrants was the institutional type of entrepreneur – the secretary of a co-operative settlement, the small-scale agricultural organizer, the director of a co-operative plant, the foreman or official of one of the bigger existing agricultural or industrial enterprises, an official of one of the public or semi-public enterprises. Few of these entrepreneurs in fact attained top economic positions, but their very development was significant. It is also significant that, in a way, this type is being given greater chances for productive activity than the other types, although quite often a more mixed type of entrepreneurship may arise and develop.

Perhaps the basic problem here has been the latent, but nevertheless very real, competition existing between political mobility and purely vocational mobility. In many immigrant settlements – especially those composed of oriental immigrants – we may often observe the following phenomena: because of the pressure exerted by the various absorption bodies – local government institutions, political parties, and so forth – many of the most active immigrants choose public activity as the trade affording greatest security and are not inclined to learn to settle into any primary vocation. The influence of this attitude also penetrated beyond the active stratum into wide circles, especially of the oriental immigrants who regard office work in the public sector or political activity as the most important advancement.

But whatever the success of the various concrete measures of absorption, it has become more and more clear that the most important single problem within this context is that of raising the ultimate productive skill of sections of the population by raising their educational level. It is only relatively recently – in the last three years – that the full importance of bridging the gap between the oriental (new) immigrants and the older ones has been understood and special measures taken to counteract the low educational level of these groups (see Chapter 7).

It is on the ultimate success of these measures that the solution of one of the most crucial problems of Israeli manpower depends.

At the same time, with continuing absorption of the immigrants in the economy, many of the specific problems of the new immigrants have become blended with the more general problems of Israeli manpower. The most important of these has been, as we shall see in greater detail in the following sections, the ability of the Israeli economy to develop higher levels of professional and technological know-how which can ensure the breakthrough of Israeli economy to a higher level of economic development.

Here, paradoxically enough, the relative success of the economy to absorb many new immigrants at its lower and middle levels, as well as mainly through the older channels of entrepreneurship, may prove a very important stumbling block to the attainment of such a breakthrough.

Structural Impediments in the Veteran Sectors of the Population

We may now proceed to the analysis of the various factors affecting problems of manpower and productivity within the veteran sector of the population.

Here several basic problems have developed – all connected with the needs of the expanding economy for different types of skilled manpower and of adequate levels of skill – and the overall picture is rather complex. On the one hand we find a continuous development of new skills, new economic and professional activities, and new enterprises – as Tables 29 and 30 show. On the other hand, several very important bottlenecks have developed in all these areas.

The first bottleneck is that of the distribution of occupational manpower. One central problem here, as has been seen above, is the continuous growth of services – especially of what may be called administrative service – and the relatively small percentage of people in manufacturing and agriculture. This is to some extent a natural phenomenon in a highly developed economy – and especially in one which depends mainly on import of manpower. There is, however, a rather general consensus of opinion among the experts that this development has in Israel extended beyond what may be called normal economic expectations. It has distorted occupational development and retarded the development of productivity through the concentration of too large a part of manpower in these services and through the (consequent) relatively low efficiency of many of these services.

The reasons for this over-expansion of services are usually not merely economic (such as the great import surplus in Israeli economy) but also related to social and political factors. The most important of these seem to be the high demand for public services, the high degree of politicization and bureaucratization in the government and in many public agencies, the continuously expanding proliferation of bureaucratic organizations within various parties and public bodies and the consequent competition of such different organizations to assure for themselves as many positions as possible.

To this is added the necessity of absorbing personnel unwilling or unable to enter other occupations and able to exert direct or indirect political or semi-political pressure by constituting a potential clientele or hostile group from the viewpoint of different parties.

But beyond these reasons the strong predilection to service occupations was also greatly influenced by the occupational composition of immigrants on the one hand and changes in occupational motivation, especially in the first period of the state, on the other.

This was manifest in the general trend in mobility after the establishment of the state in the direction of services and political jobs.

Though the last few years have seen changes in the direction of more technical and professional activities, these have not as yet sufficiently counteracted the former trend.[1]

Impediments to Productivity in the Development of Professional Manpower and in Work Morale

The specific problem analysed above was only a part of a broader framework of structural impediments to productivization. One area in which impediments to productivity might occur is that of industrial organization.

We have seen that many new enterprises have developed, particularly in the direction of larger and more complex units. But it seems that this development was impeded not only by the parallel development of smaller units but also by the inadequacy of the techniques of organization and management.

Here the lack of managerial manpower and tradition, the specific types of entrepreneurship which developed in Israel – those of relatively small enterprises – combined with traditions of family units and management on the one hand and of various 'institutional' (kibbutz, Histadrut) enterprises with very intensive political orientation and management on the other hand, have

---

[1] A most comprehensive economic analysis of this problem can be found in *Gur Offer, Service Industries in Israel*, Advisory Council for the Israel Economic and Sociological Research Project – in co-operation with the List Institute, Basle, July 1964.

133

TABLE 29

Employed Persons[a] by Economic Branch and Religion 1931–62

Economic Branch	PALESTINE				ISRAEL									
	1931 Total	1931 Jews	1942 Total	1943 Jews	1948 Jews	1954 Jews	1957 Average Total	1957 Average Jews	1957 Average Others	1960 Average Total	1960 Average Jews	1960 Average Others	1962[c] Average Total	1962[c] Average Jews
Total (Thousands)	338·3	66·7	595·9	212·0	315·3	474·4	642·2	599·5	42·7	701·8	653·7	48·1	787·9	719·4
Per cent	100·0	100·0	100·0	100·0	100·0	100·0	100·0	100·0	100·0	100·0	100·0	100·0	100·0	100·0
Agriculture, Afforestation, Fisheries	58·8	18·4	46·7	13·2	14·0	14·7	16·3	14·0	48·8	17·3	15·0	48·4	16·0	12·4
Mfg., Crafts, Quarrying	10·2	21·9	11·8	29·0	30·9	23·4	21·7	22·1	16·5	23·2	23·8	14·4	24·8	26·0
Construction, Public Works	3·6	7·6	10·6	9·2	6·1	9·2	9·8	9·5	14·9	9·3	8·9	14·2	9·6	9·0
Electricity, Gas, Water, Sanitary Services	—	—	—	—	—	2·0	2·4	2·5	0·7	2·2	2·3	1·0	2·0	2·2
Commerce and Banking	—	16·3	—	14·6	13·4	13·1	13·0	13·5	5·4	12·3	12·7	7·5	12·5	13·1
Transportation, Storage, Communal Services	12·6	5·0	11·1	3·8	6·1	6·7	6·9	7·1	3·5	6·2	6·4	3·3	6·1	6·4
Services[b]	14·8	30·8	19·8	30·2	29·5	30·9	29·9	31·3	10·1	29·5	30·9	11·4	29·0	30·9
Government, Public Administration	—	—	—	—	—	—	8·1	8·5	2·1	7·9	8·3	3·1	7·4	7·8
Health, Welfare, Education	—	—	—	—	20·1	—	14·1	14·8	5·4	14·1	14·8	5·0	14·0	15·0
Religion, Judiciary, etc.	—	—	—	—	—	—	—	—	—	—	—	—	—	—
Personal Services, Recreation	—	—	—	—	9·4	—	7·7	8·0	2·6	7·5	7·8	3·3	7·6	8·1

Note: '—' *data not available.*

[a] 1931–43 'Gainfully employed'; 1948 'working Population' (Includes unemployed). [b] 1931–43 'Includes among other Professions' and 'Others'.

Sources: 1931–43: R. Nathan, O. Gass, D. Creamer, *Palestine: Problem and Promise*, Washington, Public Affairs Press, pp. 144–5. 1948: *Registration of Population*, op. cit., Table 26, p. 50. 1954: *Labour Force Survey*, op. cit., Table 15, p. 24. 1957: CBS *Statistical Abstract*, 1958–9, op. cit., Part P, Table 3, p. 295. 1960: CBS *Statistical Bulletin*, op. cit., Table 6, p. 390.

[c] Sources: CBS *Statistical Abstract*, No. 14, 1963, pp. 498–501.

constituted important impediments for a breakthrough to higher levels of technological enterprise.

Many attempts have indeed been made to transmit managerial and organizational skills and know-how – initially by the Institute of Productivity and the Management Centre. But the effectiveness of these attempts – the importance of which should not be belittled – were often weakened by various aspects of social and wage policy analysed above and also by overall economic policy which subsidized enterprises regardless of their productivity – emphasizing rather their function as providers of work places for new immigrants.

Another crucial bottleneck in this sphere which seems to arise continuously is that of the inadequate supply of skilled managerial, professional, and scientific-technical personnel on the one hand, and the inability of the economy to absorb some of the existing manpower on the other.

Closely related to this is the parallel tendency to 'make do' with lower standards of training.

These problems are also related to the attempt of the government and the Histadrut to counteract the development of a more differentiated conception of professional activities. Here also the policy of the Histadrut (and the government) with regard to wage differentials between skilled and non-skilled and between manual and intellectual labour may be relevant. This policy tended, because of its egalitarian premises, to favour the established, veteran, skilled manual workers, as against the more technical and professional groups.

Though this policy did not generally impede the development of differentials between skilled and non-skilled labour, it has often been claimed that it was nevertheless not sensitive enough to the needs of various professional and technical groups.[1] It has also been asserted that these policies and the restrictive organizational atmosphere of many enterprises cause technical manpower to escape abroad where they may easily find much better conditions. While no exact research on these problems exists, there are many indications that these allegations are not without some foundation.[2]

A more general manifestation of such structural impediments may be found in the area of work morale, which has been a central subject of many recent public debates.

Most of these debates have shown not only that there is a recognition of the existence of these problems in a general way but that it is closely related to the whole context of social, economic, and wage policies of the Histadrut.

---

[1] See for instance the report in the *Jewish Observer and Middle East Review*, 20 October 1961.

[2] A very interesting sideline on this problem is the importance of the varied economic and technical activities in various African and Asian countries. These activities provided temporary opportunities for technical, professional, and administrative manpower.

TABLE 30

Gross Domestic Capital Formation

	1950 (1)	1954 (2)	1958 (3)	1962 (4)	1964 (5)
1. Gross Domestic Capital Formation	127·4	415·3	1,024	2,120	2,885
2. Gross National Product (M.P.)	474·8	1,828·9	3,574	6,652	9,341
3. Import Surplus	100·7	367·1	624	1,368	1,649
4. Import	—	—	1,046	2,802	3,592
5. Export	—	—	422	1,434	1,943
6. G.D.C.F. as per cent of G.N.P.	26·83	22·71	28·65	31·87	30·88
7. G.D.C.F. as per cent of Import Surplus	126·51	113·13	164·10	154·97	174·95

Sources: Col. (1) and (2), Rows 1–3. D. Patinkin, *The Israel Economy in the First Decade*, Jerusalem, Falk Project Report, No. 14, Falk Project for Economic Research, 1957–8.
Col. (3). Bank of Israel, *Annual Report, 1963*, Table II–1, pp. 12–3.
Col. (4). Bank of Israel, *Annual Report, 1963*, and *Annual Report, 1964*.
  Row 1. *Annual Report, 1964*, Table V–1, p. 67.
  Row 2. *Annual Report, 1964*, Table II–8, p. 23.
  Row 3, 4, and 5. *Annual Report, 1963*, Table II–1, pp. 12–13.
Col. (5), Rows 1–5. Bank of Israel, *Annual Report, 1964*, Table II–1, p. 9.

TABLE 30A

Resources and Uses of Resources

(Percentages)

	1950	1954	1958	1962
Private Consumption Expenditure	57·9	55·4	53·7	48·4
General Government Consumption Expenditure	15·5	13·4	14·7	14·9
Gross Domestic Capital Formation	24·1	21·4	21·8	21·7
Exports of Goods and Services	2·5	9·8	8·9	14·7
Subsidies on Exports	—	—	0·9	0·3
Total Uses of Resources	100·0	100·0	100·0	100·0
Gross Domestic Product	77·9	74·3	74·0	69·2
Imports of Goods and Services	20·2	24·0	21·1	26·7
Net Taxes on Imports	1·9	1·7	4·9	4·1
Total Resources	100·0	100·0	100·0	100·0

Source: CBS, *The National Income and Expenditure of Israel, 1950–62*, op. cit., Table 2
pp. 6–7.

137

Though there are but few studies which systematically analyse the effect of these policies on productivity – by their very nature such studies are not easy to make – there are indications that there exists in Israel a rate of fringe benefits in wages, although these are not necessarily balanced in the best way. The difficulty of tying wage increases to increased efficiency, the practice of granting permanent status after a relatively short probation period (six to twelve months), and the virtual impossibility of dismissing employees, may have detrimental effects on work morale. They may also have detrimental effects on the mobility and flexibility of manpower and their ability to adjust to an expanding technology.

Economic Policies and Their Bearing on Productivization

Among further alleged impediments to increased efficiency and productivity, reference may be made to the tax structure, with its heavy emphasis on direct taxes. This is of special significance in view of the relatively low level of earnings and the scanty encouragement given to the professional and managerial sectors. Another major impediment to efficiency is claimed to be the extensive political control and the consequent exaggerated restriction of economic competition and other mechanisms. Such restrictions on competition operate not only because of pressure of labour demands but also be-because of the competition between sectors in which political considerations are paramount; the centralized system of allocation of economic resources necessarily mutiplies the possibility of preferential administrative treatment in general.

Another allegation commonly stressed is the vagaries of development policy. Public funds are not only allocated to some major development scheme which can perhaps be developed only with government financing, they are sometimes also granted – in the form of concessions – to various private or public investors in enterprises of doubtful economic viability. This system often gives rise to excessive speculations, as for instance in land where uncurbed price rises have been very frequent during recent years. One of the paradoxical outcomes of this policy – paradoxical especially from the point of view of the social or socialist orientations of the élite – was the growing tendency to give preferential treatment and encourage large-scale economic enterprises. There seemed to develop here an interesting coalescence between the public sectors and the large-scale entrepreneurs within the 'private' sector. The tendency of the Government to control indirectly most of the economy, coupled as it was with the abandonment – after some initial attempts to undertake such activities itself – and the pressure of the Histadrut sector, all these have created a situation in which the big enterprises and entrepreneurs were given great preference over smaller ones – even co-operative ones.

138

Moreover, the profitability and efficiency of many government development enterprises often come under severe criticism by the State Comptroller.

The lack of adequate co-ordination between the different economic ministries, each with its own clientele and vested interests, is also often pointed out as an impeding factor, as are also the continuous shifts in the details and execution of economic policy which were already mentioned above.

The Social and Ideological Roots of the Relation Between Policies and Productivization

What then are the broader structural roots of various impediments to growing productivization?

One of the most important common denominators may be found in the lack of the development of the different economic occupational roles – especially of producers – be they workers, managers, or professional workers. As we have seen above, in most of these roles the intrinsic activities or goals were of relatively small importance and it was mainly their contribution to collective values and tasks that were emphasized in their role-definition. We have seen how this approach could enhance development of various ascriptive criteria of belonging to certain collectivities (i.e. to a party or movement or settlement) as more important than criteria of work achievement.

This approach has spilled over in various ways into many areas of work and could greatly impede the development of occupational identification and motivation. This problem has become more acute with the growing differentiation of the economy and the need for more skilled and professional manpower, and may affect negatively the possibility of a breakthrough to a higher, more modernized, level of technological performance and development.

Such negative influences on the breakthrough to higher levels of development are often combined also with some of the major organizational derivatives of the major ideological and political orientations in the economic sphere – namely by the tendency to governmental, administrative, and varied internal political regulations of the economy, by the weakness of long-range – as against a variety of short-range – considerations in the setting up and implementation of such regulations, and by the continuous shifts in the details and implementation of policy.

One continuous source of shifts and inconsistencies in economic policy was the ambivalent attitude of the élite towards those of the aspects of development, related to growth of consumption and especially differential consumption, which went against some of the ascetic and equalitarian elements of the official ideology.

The continuous expansion of consumption often gave rise to attempts to curb – or at least tax – some of the 'extravagant' or 'visible' aspects of such consumption. While in some cases, like the imposition of travel tax, the direct economic implications were not great – although the fiscal limits of such attempts became very quickly apparent – in others, such as in the raising of the charges for postal or telephone services or taxes on cars, these activities often weakened certain important technical aspects or facilities of economic development.

These activities often undermined the efficiency of such technical services, diverted the attention of policy-makers from some crucial technical problems (such as the planning of transportation and loads suffering under the over-crowding of cars). They also increase the tendency to shift more and more of such taxes to expense accounts and the continuous shifts of policy probably had bad effects on incentives for saving and the possibility of long-range economic planning by various entrepreneurs.

Planning of Agriculture – A Crucial Instance of Socio-Ideological Impacts on Economic Policies

Some of these ideological and social orientations, relating to both the older and newer sectors of the population, may be found in agriculture and its place in economic development.

We have already seen that when the State of Israel was established agricultural policy continued as before. For four years at least (that is, up to 1952) agricultural settlement continued at full speed – mainly through family farms and mixed farming – in every part of the country and on every type of land. The large expansion of the population in the course of those four years also enabled a large expansion of agricultural output without any serious price falls or other crises. The agricultural sector enjoyed a period of relative prosperity and of course the question of profitability did not arise.

From 1953 onward the first signs of a saturation crisis in almost all the products of mixed farming were seen. The profits of the farmers began to diminish together with prices, and the government had yearly to increase its direct support to the farmers in the way of overt or disguised subsidies.

This crisis brought about a gradual revision in the agricultural policies of the government and the Jewish Agency. In 1953 the time had come to consider more economic factors (and not only such 'natural' factors as availability of land), such as the alternative costs of the high valued products of mixed farming (which were found to be higher than those of other crops). Account was also now taken of the differences in climate, fertility of land, and availability of water in the different regions of the country, the advantages of specialization, and other factors.

The crisis in the production of mixed farming – and the acknowledgement of the new conditions – brought with them the planning of other types of farms with the following common characteristics: contraction of the live-stock branches (and consequently the area under fodder crops) and of vege-table growing; and a change-over to several low-value industrial crops – mainly cotton, sugar, and peanuts. This change in the crop patterns brought with it savings in water per unit of land, while the land unit per family had to be enlarged. Another need of industrial crops is large-scale production, which opposes the small unit settlement patterns. The planning authorities did not submit to this factor, since they wanted to continue family farming. They tried, however, to find ways to concentrate large enough areas for the grow-ing of the industrial crops. The administered farm, already mentioned above, is one of these new ways.

There is no doubt that this change in the agricultural policy of the govern-ment stopped the downward trend of agricultural profitability, although the need for government support did not yet disappear.

The general saturation of agricultural production of recent years has also caused a major change in settlement policy. In contrast to the general purpose of settling as many new immigrants as possible on the land during the mandatory period, it is not now generally intended to increase the agri-cultural labour force (now about 12·5 per cent).

All these changes in agricultural policy were not effected without much debate a large part of which was not confined to technical and economic aspects but extended to many ideological problems – such as the importance of the family farm, and above all the general importance of agriculture in the social and economic system of Israel. The most crucial point of this debate was reached when the problem of agricultural profitability in general and of specific forms of settlement (kibbutz or moshav) was raised. Whilst some advocated a relatively matter-of-fact evaluation of the various problems, others claimed that agricultural settlements had to be maintained and ex-panded – because of their social-national importance – beyond any calcu-lations of profitability and that it was not up to the settlements to prove their viability at all. While such an extreme view was seldom expressed, in a more diffuse way it has certainly pervaded large areas of agricultural planning.

A very interesting and significant transformation of agricultural policy could be found in some recent years. One of the major avowed aims of the official policy of the Ministry of Agriculture has become to manipulate subsidies and prices in such a way as to ensure for the agriculturists the same average use or level of income as has been attained by other parts of the labour force.

According to this policy it is not the relative productivity or rentability of agriculture and its contribution to the national economy and growth, which are the main considerations. Such levels of productivity or rentability are, as it were, attained by other productive sectors, and the major aim of agricultural

141

policy seems to become to adjust the peasants' income to these developments seemingly irrespective of their own direct contribution.

This transformation of policy gives Israeli agriculture a political status with regard to the assurance of certain levels of income – not dissimilar to that which can be found in other countries, such as the US – but here in Israel with a much stronger ideological and political bent or overtone.

Rising Consumption – The Achilles Heel of Israeli Economy

The preceding analysis has attempted to show some of the structural impediments to raising productivity in the Israeli economy.

However, production in itself has not been, as has already been indicated, the Achilles heel of Israeli economy. Whatever the limitations to its expansion there has been a continuous rise in efficiency and in growth.

Truly enough Israeli economy faces, in the field of production, the problem of a successful breakthrough to a higher level of technological production and it has not yet become geared to the attainment of a breakthrough. But at the same time it has been continuously developing within the framework of its existing level of capital, output, productivity, and physical expansion.

The real Achilles heel of the Israeli economy is consumption. It has been rising consumption that has eaten up most of the increase in productivity.

These factors have been continuously stressed by the Bank of Israel, both in its annual reports and in the special reports which the Governor of the Bank has to submit to the Financial Committee of the Knesset in time of inflationary trend.

In all these reports, as well as in economic research studies, it has been pointed out that expanding consumption has been facilitated through expansion of credit, and by relatively non-effective curbs on inflation, which have greatly contributed to the continuous gap in the balance of trade.

Such growing consumption is greatly influenced by the continuous rise in wages and the standard of living on the one hand and by public spending on the other. Table 31 shows developments in this field.

7

Social Organization and Stratification

1

SOCIAL ORGANIZATION AND STRATIFICATION IN THE YISHUV

Introduction – The Problem and the Setting

This chapter will analyse the basic patterns of Israeli society. We have seen that one of the major aims of Zionist ideology was to create a new type of modern society – one in which some of the pitfalls of other societies would be avoided. As it developed, however, more and more problems similar to those of other modern societies became apparent and varied social groups and organizations, with different styles of life, values, and traditions emerged. The activities which crystallized from them had to be evaluated – in terms of the major social rewards – money, power, and prestige. Israeli society – as any other – was therefore faced with the problems of organizing different social positions, and the allocations of people into these positions.

This chapter will attempt to analyse these aspects of Israel's social structure, starting from the small 'sectarian' groups of the first and second aliyot and developing into the much more differentiated social structure of the late 'thirties and early 'forties.

In one important aspect the development of the Yishuv differed from normal, peasant or traditional societies, and even from most colonizing societies: in the initial stages of development ecological units and basic ascriptive solidarities such as kinship groups, territorial or class divisions, etc., did not constitute the most important or binding factor from which the more specific groups developed and crystallized.

Initially, the basic groups within the Yishuv were the various pioneering groups and sects. Some ecological groups of the older Yishuv existed throughout the initial period, and most new ones – whether agricultural settlements or new urban quarters – were, at first, offshoots of these sects and did not develop any strong traditions or symbols of identification of their own.

Moreover, the special nature of the migratory movement to Palestine implied that no strong ascriptive solidarities such as kinship or ethnic groups or social strata developed initially. It was only much later that such different collectivities – sometimes of a rather special type – developed, and ecological seetings as well as ascriptive solidarities acquired some autonomy and tradition of their own. But even these were greatly influenced by the

143

characteristics of the sects from which they stemmed and the most important of which was perhaps that these sects and groups were orientated towards complex social, economic, political, and cultural activities which soon outstripped their concrete needs.

Trends of Development in the 'Private' and 'Workers' ' Sectors

From these beginnings, the social structure of the Yishuv developed in two 'ideal-type' directions which, though greatly differing, had some common characteristics.

One can be seen in the rural and urban settlements of the first aliya and in what came to be called the 'private' sector of the Yishuv. The second trend, developed from within the more sectarian groups which comprised the 'workers'' camp. In between these two, several meeting points existed in various cultural, educational, and even professional activities.

Even as early as the first and second aliya, and though tempered by their orientation to national service and by the development of the working sector, the 'private' sector developed relatively strong inclinations to a 'normal' social organization, i.e. one based on economic attainments and family tradition.

This brought stronger emphasis on functional groups and on relatively small ecological settings, such as the moshavot and some of the urban quarters which developed traditional symbols of a rather diffuse solidarity. But, due to the small size and great dependence of all the groups on external resources, even these orientations were weak and not fully crystallized. The various developing economic, professional, and administrative organizations within the private sectors were restricted by the small scope and very minor differentiation of these groups. Similarly the various voluntary philanthropic or 'local' cultural associations that developed were necessarily also of a limited scope, unless connected with wider Zionist principles.

The patterns of social organization which developed within the so-called labour or working sectors out of the sectarian groups of the second and the social movements of the third aliya were of a markedly different type from those described in the previous section.

Crystallization of ecological units was relatively slower in this sector. Even in the kibbutzim and moshavim, where very definite identification with localities developed, these traditions were at first strongly embedded in a wider, non-ecological, movement and ideological framework.

The same was to a large extent true of the more specialized units and organizations, whose aims were, at least initially, envisaged as general, collective pioneering goals. Membership in the general sects and movements was therefore much more important than any specific qualification needed for participation in the specialized groups.

Attempts at more independent development of each organization were strongly discouraged within the sects the more so as the natural development of these groups tended to generate autonomous new goals and evolve various possibilities of co-operation with different groups in the private sector.

Concurrently with these tendencies the workers' groups developed their own ascriptive solidarities. Unlike the private sector which based its criteria on kinship, ownership, and economic and educational achievement, those of the workers' sector were mainly based on membership in the sects and movements, and, to some extent, on common immigration background and common political affiliation and activity. They were of great importance in the development of the Yishuv's social structure.

The Structure of the Major Roles

To understand the special features of the social organization of the Yishuv more fully, it is worth analysing the structure of the various roles and role images and the way in which these were defined by the different groups and their élites.

Once again, the roots of these tendencies and orientations were in the basic Zionist and socialist pioneering ideology and its derivatives.

Initial Zionist ideology, common to a large extent to the different branches of the Zionist movement, envisaged the full development of all occupational, economic, social, cultural, and political functions, as being permeated by a spirit of national identification and social justice and equality.

In this image the only real role was that of the pioneer with its basic dedication to national goals and pioneering movements.

More autonomous demands of such functions – their claim for prestige, for technical competence, or for intrinsic achievement and performance – were very often looked down on as infringing on the purity of the pioneering role. In more ideological formulations this lack of emphasis on any concrete task was seen as a manifestation of the lack of 'human self-alienation', characteristic of so many modern, and especially capitalist, societies. In the more realistic-political terms which developed during the third aliya, such demands for the autonomy of different functions were considered as weakening political ardour and identification with the various sects and parties of the workers' sector.

Ideological orientations against such tendencies were also greatly reinforced by the fear of 'premature normalization' – as in the case of the first aliya.

This fear of premature normalization coupled with strong ideological orientations was seen most clearly in one of the most vital roles of the period – that of the agriculturist which crystallized as early as the first aliya, matured in the period of the second aliya and fully developed in the mandatory period.

145

The most important characteristic of this 'peasant' role was the de-emphasizing of occupational and 'traditional' aspects of peasant life, at the expense of the more élitist conception of agricultural work as the main symbolic expression of pioneering.

Later, during the third aliya, these élitist orientations were consolidated in the various kibbutz movements, which placed greater importance on ideological orthodoxy than on agricultural activities or a rural way of life.

Although the moshavim established during the third aliya placed greater emphasis on agricultural activities and family life, these tendencies were yet part of a socio-political movement and ideology.

A similar, though perhaps less intensive, tendency developed within the cultural and educational sectors, in which the role of the teacher was defined and developed so as to include the cultural ingredient in the general image of the pioneer.

Evaluation of Roles

Closely related to the definition of different roles was their evaluation and the status levels that developed in the various sectors of the Yishuv.

The criteria of evaluation in the private sector were in many ways the 'usual' criteria of economic and professional competence with somewhat stronger emphasis being placed on family status by economic standing and family lineage. But even within this sector strong emphasis was placed on national goals and service, although several of the basic assumptions of the pioneer group were rejected.

The situation was necessarily different in the pioneer groups and in the workers' sector. There, the basic criterion of status evaluation was devotion to pioneering-collective tasks with prestige in the eyes of the community the main reward. It was assumed that material rewards – and especially *differential economic* (and even prestige and power) rewards – were not only unimportant but even dangerous and potentially disruptive to the solidarity of the pioneering group.

These evaluations of activities in the workers' groups and in the first settlements were, in their pure form, much more adapted to the small avant-garde élite groups than to wider and functionally differentiated settings. Hence it is no accident that the fullest manifestation of these criteria of evaluation was to be found in the collective settlements. Because of this, the maintenance of these criteria by the élite groups was greatly dependent on the minimizing of the occupational and status aspects of their peasant orientations and on the stress of the élitist orientations to the settlement and the movement. Within these groups such criteria and rewards could be upheld in all their purity.

It is significant that this ideology did not deal with the problem of access to any of these roles. Its implicit assumption was that access to all the roles – and especially the role of the pioneer – was equally open to all who were willing to undertake them. Only later, with the growth of the Yishuv's social structure, did this problem become important and the fact that the predominant ideology was not ready to deal with it significant.

The Image of Society

These variations in social stratification were closely related to the image of a society developed by these groups and derived from their basic ideology.

Most of the available data is limited to clear ideological expressions – which necessarily means those of the workers' sector rather than the private one.

The views as expressed there are mainly concerned with a 'classless' society, composed of different groups and movements, and bound by common aspirations and activities, in which there is but little division of labour and small difference in wealth. However, these images were purely ideological and utopian, and bore few connexions to existing society.

It is significant that neither in the basic ideologies nor in this embryonic image of society was there any reference to the problems of distribution of power, or of power as a basis for social status. This omission was due to the limited scope of the settlements and groups, to the strong utopian elements of their ideology and to the fact that the main resources of most groups came from outside the Yishuv. This fact had many important repercussions on the developing social organization and stratification.

Interrelations Between the Scale of Collectivities, Role Structure and Criteria of Status

The three major aspects of social organization – the nature of collectivities, the definition of roles, and the criteria of status – tended to complement each other in controlling incipient social differences.

This was due to various factors. One was the relatively small degree of differentiation in the Yishuv's social structure, a tendency which was re-inforced by the fact that the Yishuv was at that time composed of many small 'parallel' settlements and organizations, allowing little occupational or economic differentiation to develop. Little specialization took place among the many similarly composed yet different groups, and even the activities of the professional and cultural bodies were not geared to any specific needs but rather to those of a 'future' society. Only gradually a more concrete inter-relationship between the various groups developed and with it a growing change in tasks.

The second major reason for the limited differences was rooted in the ideology of the pioneering group.

147

Historically, these two conditions were closely connected. However, each was more strongly operative in one sector than in another and hence their development varied between the sectors and probably influenced later developments in the Yishuv's social structure.

These initial tendencies left their imprint in several crucial areas. The first important characteristic, common to the Yishuv as well as to many other colonizing countries, was the absence of an aristocracy. This was due not only to lack of special family tradition but also to the fact that much of the land, and the available capital, was vested in public hands, often abroad. The second characteristic was the concentration of wealth in various public bodies and organizations. Thirdly, the strong egalitarian emphasis in the social structure of the Yishuv became apparent even at this stage; and fourthly, side by side with the strong egalitarianism, there was also the emphasis on the élite inherent in the image of the pioneer. This combination had many interesting repercussions on the social structure and organization of the Yishuv.

Growing Differentiation in the Mandatory Period – Competition Between the Sectors. Patterns of Voluntary Associations

With the mandatory period the relatively homogeneous social structure became more complex and diversified and distinct from older types of homogeneous sects and small, 'under-developed' ecological communities.

With the growing expansion of the Yishuv's economy, many new occupational activities – industrial, professional, and clerical – developed. These were connected with the growth of more diversified ecological settings, with the many new types of organizations and groups, and with the growing interdependence of the different sectors of the Yishuv. The growth of autonomous functions and specialized groups as well as the growing importance of monetary and economic rewards also influenced this development.

These developments created new tendencies in the distribution of wealth and power, giving rise to growing differences between economic groups and between the incipient occupational groups.

Concomitantly, ascriptive solidarities began to develop in the private sector, based on kinship, and ecological and occupational traditions, with more widespread emphasis on criteria of economic status, occupational achievements, and differential remuneration.

Within the workers' sector these developments constituted a challenge to the basic ideological pioneering premises.

To understand the difference between the sectors more fully we shall analyse briefly the characteristics of voluntary associations in the Yishuv and the patterns of mobility within it.

The differences between the sectors can perhaps be most clearly seen in the nature and development of the various voluntary associations. The aims of such associations were manifold – cultural, literary, sporting and recreational, ethnic, etc. No exact statistics on them are available, but it is well known that their number was considerable. One preliminary survey of voluntary associations in Jerusalem has shown that, at the end of the mandatory period, there were about 1,146 different voluntary organizations, ranging from simple philanthropic aid societies for children of students of the *Yeshivot* (schools devoted to religious study) to countrywide associations of different kinds.

There were many similarities in the official aims of the associations of the different sectors. Some of the purely philanthropic or cultural ones drew their membership from both sectors. But most of the central associations were separate, and each sector developed a somewhat different pattern of activities and orientations. On the whole the workers' sector evinced the following characteristics:

(a) Most of their associations were closely related to, and often a part of, various general social movements and organizations (the labour movements, the Zionist organizations, etc.), and political parties.

(b) Most of them performed certain vital functions within the community, such as guard duty and defence (as in the case of the *Hagana*, the semi-legal defence organization which consisted mostly of voluntary groups), medical aid (the Red Shield Society), social welfare, propagation of the Hebrew language, help for co-operative settlements, furthering the consumption of local products, developing various professional and cultural activities, etc.

(c) Due to these functions most of the groups were closely connected with the central social and political activities of the community and its centres of power and influence.

(d) Most of the groups considered themselves to be contributing to the Zionist ideal of national rebirth.

In the majority of cases, just as in the dominant value system of the Yishuv, there was usually little differentiation between social, political, and cultural aspects and ideals, although one or another of these would obviously receive stronger emphasis according to the group.

Most groups enabled their members to participate in the political and social life of the community, making them feel that they were contributing directly to its development and sharing in its power and influence. In this connexion it is important to note that a large proportion of the social and political élite participated more or less actively in some of these groups, and exercised influence within them. Thus these associations served as important meeting points between the élite and the socially and politically more active strata of the population. Through participation in these groups, members received recognition and prestige in the community and established and maintained their status.

The structural pattern of association activities was somewhat different in the private sector and in the lower status groups. In these sectors the connexion between the purely 'social' side and participation in the central sphere of society was much weaker. On the higher strata of the purely economically-orientated groups there existed certain forms of social, philanthropic, and cultural activities (e.g. lodges and clubs) through which wider interests and cultural orientation were expressed without, necessarily, close relationship to political groups. In the lower echelons more purely social bodies prevailed and there was relatively little contact between associations of different strata. It is important to note here again that only very few 'ethnic' associations developed in this period, and that the scope of their activities was more or less restricted to mutual-aid purposes or to the commemoration of their places of origin in the *diaspora*.

Patterns of Mobility

In order to understand fully the competition between the sectors it is essential to study the methods of mobility, and especially of occupational mobility, at that time. Unfortunately, exact and systematic data on this process are scanty and analysis has perforce to be based mainly on assessed information.

Even so, some characteristics stand out. The two most important facts seem to be the extent of one-generational (intra-generational) mobility, especially among the first generation of immigrants on the one hand and the extent of inter-generational continuity on the other hand.

The measure of intra-generational mobility among the first generation of immigrants was caused mainly by continuous economic expansion. This created many channels of occupational mobility – drawn especially from the relatively non-defined pioneering tasks, such as building, etc., to more crystallized positions like those of industrial workers, clerks, etc. – which developed both in the workers' and in the private sectors.

It is, however, quite possible that such mobility was somewhat smaller in the private sector where members settled in more 'final' positions from the beginning.

Data available on the inter-generational span tends to show some degree of continuity between the 'final point of occupational arrival' of parents and the aspirations or real achievements of the sons – at least until the establishment of the state when a new upsurge of mobility took place.

Information on this problem is merely illustrative but indicates that even at this time incipient tendencies towards some 'freezing' of inter-generational occupational continuity and some initial crystallization of status groups developed in all sectors.

There were, of course, several mitigating factors in these tendencies. One was the continuous emphasis on joining the kibbutzim prevalent in many youth movements which direct some – although seemingly a relatively small percentage – of young people to these settlements.

Second was the fact that, due to the need for national service – such as the *Hagana, Palmach* and, later, the Jewish Brigade – there was a period of occupational moratorium, with young persons being taken out of the usual channels of occupational mobility to which they often had to, or planned to, return.

Thus the problems stemming from the growing social differentiation and from the competition between the sectors also became apparent in the processes of mobility sharpening mutual awareness and competition of the sectors.

Patterns of Institutionalization of Ideology

The challenges of growing social differences were taken up by the leaders of the working sector in several ways, some of which have already been analysed in the section on methods of ideological institutionalization where it was made clear that ideology became institutionalized partly through the selection of élites and partly through affiliation by the élites with the pioneering groups as well as by allocating symbolic élite status to the settlements. (See Chapter 4, p. 44–45, 52–53.)

Similar problems arose on an organizational level where there was continuous striving among professional and economic groups towards autonomy.

The labour leaders dealt with these tendencies in several ways, bearing in mind the fact that many functional organizations existed within the labour sector, which could 'absorb' these tendencies towards autonomy whilst keeping them within the limits of the general monolithic structure of the movement.

The ability of the Histadrut to maintain its overall structure was greatly facilitated by the fact that these organizations were in a very strong position with regard to allocations of material rewards and symbolic prestige.

Of special interest in this context is the way in which the problems connected with the development of industrial workers and the labour force were tackled.

A body of semi-skilled and skilled industrial workers employed in construction work, public works, and agriculture gradually emerged. This greatly increased the trade union activities within the Histadrut as well as the development of specific organizations and 'sectors' dealing with their problems.

On the organizational level this was tackled by the development, *within the Histadrut*, of special sectors and organizations dealing with specific problems on both local and central levels. Ideologically, many attempts were made to define the industrial workers as individual or group pioneers whose duties and image did not differ greatly from those of the older pioneer type.

Of equal interest were the only partly successful attempts made to define the various professional roles and organizations according to the pioneer image and within the limits of the movement's framework.

Thus, teachers were comparatively highly rated while less value was placed on the functions of doctors and – even less – on lawyers who appeared the least related to collective goals. Although no systematic survey data about the relative prestige of the different professions at the time is available, existing information indicates that, certainly on the 'ideological' level, this evaluation was true.

The worker's function was defined more and more in collective terms of social and political identification and, even less than in the case of the agricultural pioneer, in terms of occupational or technical contribution.

Criteria of Allocation and Organizations in the Workers' Sectors

Attempts to institutionalize the pioneering ideology brought to light some of the structural implications and potential contradictions inherent in this ideology.

Access to different functions and resulting rewards became important at that time.

Although official formulation of the pioneering ideology emphasized the importance of free access by all to the pioneering tasks, strong selectivism was in fact practised within it. This was stressed by the importance placed on membership in the various collective organizations and was inherent in the nature of élitist orientation. With the growing problem of adapting the ideology to the developing social structure, this became even more general, applying to the allocation of rewards, the organizational patterns within the movements, and the different ways of life in the workers' sectors. Such ways were based on membership of different élitist groups and movements centred in the communal settlements, the youth movements, and the workers' quarters in the cities, but showed few autonomous class or strata orientations.

Leaders of the workers' sector aimed at maintaining the older homogeneity of status criteria. Membership in these associations became an important means of access to different positions and resources.

The Social Structure at the End of the Mandate – Social Differentiation and Ideology

By the end of the mandatory period, social organization and stratification in the Yishuv was already much more complicated than in the incipient stages of its development. A greater variety of collective bodies existed, as did ecological groups, functional organizations, voluntary associations, broad movement organizations, and fraternities, as well as various types of latent ascriptive solidarities – and the differences between urban and rural settings continuously increased.

However, gradually a greater number of more specific occupational, political, and cultural functions and functional groups emerged which, although as yet embedded in the collective and ideological definitions of the pioneering image, acquired growing autonomy and began to cut across their initial collective sectors. As a result of these developments the differences in standards and ways of life between groups grew.

Most of these differences were still small compared to those in other modern countries, but nevertheless 'lower-class' areas or even slums developed as, for instance, in the Hatiqvah quarter of Tel Aviv. These were mostly composed of groups from a lower class and educational background with little pioneering orientation.

Adherence to the sects of the official pioneering ideology as the major framework to all social developments, and the continuous expansion of the social structure, prevented these inequalities and incipient social problems from being fully perceived; one by-product was the slow, and initially inadequate, development and recognition of social work.

Various factors unrelated to the pioneering ideal, such as occupation, profession, and education, began to assume importance in organization and stratification and in determining the social and occupational status of various groups.

Of special importance here was the fact that the fifth aliya brought in its wake not only growing economic differences and specialization but also fuller recognition of professional and managerial functions.

Only within some oriental groups the relation between low occupational standing and low educational attainment became relatively clear. But even in other sectors the influence of these criteria grew continuously and was only partly offset by the continuity of both the older pioneer groups and the worker immigrant groups.

Moreover, the attempts made by leaders of the workers' groups to institutionalize the ideology gave rise to new tensions and problems, as well as to many paradoxical and unintended consequences.

Among these was the growing and yet not fully-recognized importance of power and power positions in the system of social organization and stratification.

Few clear norms therefore emerged to deal with the distribution or regulation of power. Most economic and organizational frameworks constituted important power positions, and the gradual transition of the Yishuv from a series of groups connected mostly by 'mechanical' solidarity and ideological orientation to a more differentiated social structure necessarily enhanced the power positions and value of all these groups and enterprises. The growing importance of power positions was only partly offset by the 'federative' nature of the expanded social structure, and by continuous preoccupation with the implementation of collective goals. This naturally changed with the establishment of the state.

2

SOCIAL ORGANIZATION AND STRATIFICATION IN THE STATE OF ISRAEL – EMERGING TRENDS

The Establishment of the State – Major Changes in Social Organization

With the establishment of the State of Israel, the trends, tensions, and problems of social organization and stratification described in the preceding section were thrown into greater relief. In many ways national independence proved to be a turning point in development and crystallization, highlighting several factors of crucial importance:

(1) The first was the growing unification of different sectors with their often separate 'systems' of stratification and social organization. This was accompanied by a weakening of relative autarchy and the dissolution of the 'federative' nature of relations between the sectors.

This unification was caused by the establishment of a central political framework and by the growing importance of political considerations and criteria in the allocation of 'material' and prestige rewards.[1]

(2) The second major development which influenced social organization was the great influx of new manpower in the form of new immigrants, with their special social, cultural, and educational backgrounds and with their specific motivations for immigration (see in detail, Chapter 5). This influx created great problems in terms of pressures on various resources, the extent of mobility open to these groups, and in tendencies to maintain or develop their own styles of life and traditions.

(3) This process of absorption was closely connected with continuous economic development and social and economic differentiation. The very establishment of the state with its administrative and political frameworks created new occupational and prestige positions, which were enhanced by the expansion in the economic structure, giving rise to new occupational roles, organizations, and patterns of mobility.

---

[1] The growth in importance of overall political considerations in the allocations of material rewards was most clearly shown in the fact that major problems of wage policy as well as labour conditions were decided by the central political authorities on a more or less country-wide basis, thus becoming a focal point in the central political struggle.

154

Equally, new problems of differential mobility with regard to both old and new immigrants emerged.

(4) The fourth major development was the growing importance of political power as a social reward, a criterion of social status and position, and as a means of access to major occupational and economic positions.

(5) This development also brought out important changes in value-orientations among the different sectors, the most important of these being a weakening in the 'forward-looking' outlook and, instead, a growing emphasis on the present as an important dimension of social action. Growing emphasis was therefore placed on a wider spectrum of rewards and on the struggle and competition for these rewards.

This greatly changed relations between the various groups and strata of society and also affected major collective goals and values. A process of some dissociation took place between these goals and the private domains of many groups (with the partial exception of some of the settlements with strong élite orientations), and the transfer of these goals to official political and administrative bodies.

(6) All these trends necessarily sharpened the conflict between the official pioneering ideology and the developing social reality. The establishment of the state brought the bearers of the pioneering-socialist ideology to power but, at the same time, a new reality resulted from their own policies and their change into a ruling élite.

Growing Differentiation of Roles and Organizations

The processes described above provided the background to the development in social organization and stratification.

The most general trend in this period was a growing change from the predominant pattern (whereby various functions of society were performed by the same people in a given group) through a process of gradual emphasis on separate tasks which crystallized into distinctive roles and organizations.

Many new industrial enterprises developed, bringing with them a growing managerial and professional class and increased differentiation between technical, skilled, and semi-skilled jobs. In addition, the army and the civil service provide conspicuous examples of entirely new or previously underdeveloped functions.

Similar developments took place in other spheres. In the field of public services banking was greatly expanded and new sectors, such as a growing hotel trade, evolved. Continuous expansion also took place in the older professions such as law, medicine, and teaching while engineering and architecture which had not developed much in the previous period grew very rapidly. Relatively 'underdeveloped' professions such as social work also gained in importance. Moreover, there was a continuous inclination towards professionalization in many new occupations. This showed itself in a growing emphasis on formal educational standards for the attainment of occupational grades in the civil service, in the army, and in business, as well as in the growing tendency of such groups to organize themselves in relatively autonomous professional organizations.

Closely connected with this was the development of new forms of large bureaucratic, administrative and economic organizations – a tendency which could also be found in agriculture. Although officially the basic unit remained the single village (kibbutz or moshav) much of the overall planning was in fact done by central bureaucratic agencies, like the Jewish Agency, and on a regional or 'sectional' (i.e. kibbutz movement) basis.

The continual influx of population caused certain multiplication of collective functions both in agricultural and urban settings.

However, much of this was absorbed by the growing specialization and differentiation of factions. Thus, side by side with the expansion of the scope of Durkheim's 'mechanical' solidarity, a strong shift to a more 'organic' structure with a more complicated division of labour took place.

This multiplied the number of new functions but also enhanced the tendencies towards autonomy within them. One such tendency was the growing emphasis on the intrinsic standards of any role, be it technical, economic, profit, or professional. This greatly increased the importance of professional and managerial roles, compared to the former overall preponderance of 'movement' orientations and functions.

However, the most important structural result of this growing occupational differentiation was perhaps that it created a situation of irreversibility of occupational roles. Unlike the original pioneer-ideology which assumed that a person can easily shift his occupational role according to collective demands, the economic development after the establishment of the state caused commitment to an occupational role to become more set.

People could and did retrain, but the time spent and the specialized demands of most jobs were such that the possibilities of continuous shifts in occupation by adults became more difficult.

This growing occupational specialization constituted the most important breakthrough to economic modernization in Israel.

However, all these changes and trends to differentiation did take place within the framework of a relatively small-scale society. Although the population of this society has, since the establishment of the state, been almost quadrupled – yet its absolute numbers were yet relatively small in terms of comparison with other modern facilities.

This fact had, as we shall yet see, many repercussions on the very direction of these processes of differentiation, on their structural repercussion and on the relations between the élite and the broader groups of the population.

Patterns of Occupation and Mobility, Standards of Living

All these developments greatly affected occupational distribution, mobility, and the living standards of different occupations.

The data on occupational distribution and mobility show a double trend of growing occupational diversification and new channels of mobility, as well as growing differences in the access to the various positions, by different 'ethnic' groups.

Almost all researches indicate that the major factor explaining occupational status today is education. Thus for instance the occupational history of a sample on research[1] shows that entry into the labour-market in Israel was, typically, into manual occupations during the pre-state period irrespective of the educational level of the entrants but the percentage of 'matriculated' entrants into manual occupations was lower than that of 'non-matriculated' entrants.

The differential between the two educational levels in this respect has increased constantly:

Percentage Entering Manual Labour

	1938	1947	1952	1958	1964
Non-matriculated	78%	79%	73%	68%	67%
Matriculated	52%	40%	32%	27%	23%

The research was carried on a sample of residents of Haifa aged 25–55.

These data show that the longer a person has been in the labour-market the less likely he is to remain in a manual occupation. This is especially pronounced for 'matriculated' individuals.

This research has shown about 60 per cent of all respondents were in 1964 in the same occupational class (manual/non-manual) as their fathers. Inter-generational mobility was greater for non-matriculated (about 43 per cent changers) than for matriculated individuals (about 31 per cent). More than 80 per cent of the downwards mobile (manual sons of non-manual fathers) are non-matriculated (compared to 66 per cent non-matriculated in the sample).

Examination of these facts shows great general scope of mobility – mostly explained by the continuous economic expansion, although some special characteristics stand out. We find relatively great emphasis – common to most modern countries – on mobility into the higher echelons of professional and technical occupations and, to some extent, into 'big business'. In the middle echelons we find a limited movement towards the white-collar

[1] See A. Zloczower – materials from fieldwork for – *Mobility Patterns and Status Conceptions in an Urban Israeli Setting*, Ph.D Thesis, The Hebrew University, 1966.

occupations often concentrated in small-scale commercial units, and a greater trend to the skilled and semi-skilled occupations which enjoy the benefit of large-scale trade union protection in Israel. The data on mobility also shows the continuous coalescence between mobility and countries of origin.

A similar pattern can be discerned in the development of the standard of living which encompasses most population groups.

An interesting aspect of this development is the growing emphasis placed on consumption, which caused the ever-growing equalization of standards of aspiration between the various groups most of which began to strive for the same material comforts and emoluments – such as better housing, radios, refrigerators, furniture, etc. Such material benefits also became important status symbols, in many cases conspicuously displayed.

Although the most extreme manifestation of these tendencies is to be found in the so-called 'Golden Circles' of the urban society it has, to some extent, penetrated to most groups and strata, and the level of conspicuous consumption has become a continuously expanding feature of Israeli life.

Many material benefits, such as housing and education, as well as relatively scarce articles like refrigerators, were initially allocated through the various collective-political organizations although they were also available on the 'open market'. The differences between the 'sources' of these articles became relatively immaterial, with the growing demand for such goods increasing the importance of the market.

Standards of living of almost all groups have thus been rising continuously though in varying degrees and the consequent growth of demands for the same types of goods cut across all groups and sectors with the more extreme manifestations to be found among the higher groups of the private sector as well as among some of the public executives.

Many of these aspects of 'higher living' were, at least indirectly, helped by the government renting land at specially low rates to foreign or local investors, or, more indirectly, through various subsidies. This fact helped to legitimize these tendencies and patterns.

Growing Differences in Occupations and Standards of Living

The growing occupational diversification and the expansion of the standard of living raised the problem of access to various positions and to the different levels of consumption. It also accentuated the growth of income and the variations between different occupations and between 'older' and 'new', 'western' and 'oriental'.

An analysis of the data on mobility, mainly in the distribution of the population by occupation, shows the importance of country of origin and seniority of settlement in Israel. In determining this distribution, however, the importance of these factors is not equal in all professions. Thus, for example, there is a much greater concentration of new immigrants from Asia and Africa than from European countries in agriculture. This combination of country of origin and seniority of settlement can also be found inversely, in industry where fewer new immigrants from the oriental groups in comparison with the early settlers are found. In construction work the same combination of seniority and origin reappears although, in this case, the former carries more weight than the latter, and so it is possible to find many new immigrants of European origin in this category. This also applies in the commercial sphere. Country of origin carries the greatest weight in the field of public services, which contains numerical predominance of the oriental population but a very high concentration of the Ashkenazi population in the middle and higher echelon of service.

Sometimes length of residence is more important in this selective index, than country of origin (European as opposed to Middle Eastern). However, in both cases the process of selection in the labour market has led to a concentration of new immigrants from Asia and Africa in the most under-developed professions and occupations. Veteran settlers of European origin dominate the administrative and professional sphere, and while new immigrants from Europe and America and earlier settlers from Africa and Asia hold intermediate positions, those of the former are usually higher than those of the latter.

A similar picture can be found with regards to levels of consumption and standards of living. (See Tables 31 and 32.)

Thus, that share of total expenditure devoted to the purchasing of food, declined amongst Jewish employees from 30·1 per cent in 1950–9 to 26·8 per cent in 1963–4 (in 1963–4 prices) while expenditure on health, education, cigarettes, transportation, and personal services was continually rising.

This was also the case with respect to durable goods. The percentage of families in Israel owning an electric refrigerator rose from 34 per cent in 1958 to 70·8 per cent in 1964. The percentage of families having gas ranges and ovens for cooking and baking rose from 35 per cent in 1958 to 84·5 per cent in 1964. The use of electric washing machines has remained less extensive but is also continually rising. Thus in 1958 only 9·1 per cent of families owned a washing machine and this figure rose to 23·6 per cent by 1964.

A study of a number of other items presents a similar picture:

radio	1959 – 76·2 per cent	1964 – 89·3 per cent
gramophone	1959 – 11·8 per cent	1964 – 20·9 per cent
electric mixer	1962 – 9·2 per cent	1964 – 14·4 per cent
vacuum cleaner	1963 – 8·7 per cent	1964 – 10·3 per cent
automobile	1962 – 4·1 per cent	1964 – 6·9 per cent

Source: CBS *Statistical Abstract* of Israel, No. 16, 1965, Charts Nos. G 21, G 23, pp. 213–14.

TABLE 31

Average Monthly Expenditures for Consumption (excluding Housing) for Jewish Wage-earning Family and the Percentage of Expenditures of All the Expenditures for Consumption, according to Real Expenditure Groups (1959–60, 1963–4)

	Expenditure in current prices		Percentage of change				Percentage of expenditure of the entire consumption	
	1959–60	1963–4	Nominal expenditure	Prices	Real expenditure	Real expenditure monthly average	1959–60	1963–4
Primary Expenditure Groups								
Total Expenditure for Consumption (excluding Housing)	369	574	55	24	26	6·3	100·0	100·0
Food (excluding Fruit and Vegetables)	118	154	30	15	13	3·3	32·0	26·8
Fruit and Vegetables	34	51	50	41	6	—	9·3	8·9
Household Upkeep and Budget	33	48	43	23	16	4·0	9·1	8·3
Furniture and Household Appliances	35	62	79	20	48	11·0	9·5	10·8
Clothing and Shoes	44	66	48	13	31	7·5	11·9	11·4
Health, Education, and Culture	54	93	70	35	26	6·3	14·7	16·1
Cigarettes, Transportation, and Personal Services	42	90	112	33	60	13·4	11·4	15·6
Organizational Taxes and Donations	8	11	45	—	—	—	2·1	2·0

Source: CBS (Hebrew), *Study of Family Expenditures 1963–4*, Special Publication No. 175, 1965, Table A, p. viii.

TABLE 32

Indexes of Expenditures for Consumption for Families,
according to Continent of Birth and Length of Residence
in Israel of Heads of Family (Average 100)

Expenditure by continent of birth and length of residence in Israel of heads of families	Per Family		Per Person	
	1959–60	1963–4	1959–60	1963–4
Average Expenditure of Population	100	100	100	100
Asia and Africa	97	90	73	70
Europe and America	100	104	115	120
Israel	109	—	112	123
Immigrated before 1947	113	114	119	121
Asia and Africa	104	96	84	82
Europe and America	114	118	127	131
Immigrated after 1948	86	92	85	85
Asia and Africa	95	89	71	68
Europe and America	84	95	103	108

Source: CBS *Study of Family Expenditures 1963–4.* op. cit., Table B, p. x.

Thus we see that the standard of living in Israel has been steadily on the rise. For instance in the years 1959–60 and 1963–4 the real expenditures for a family increased by 26 per cent.[1]

This absolute rise in the standard of living was connected to the relative decrease in expenditure for those born in Asia and Africa. While among this population the expenditures per person went down from 73 per cent to 70 per cent of the average expenditure of the entire population, the expenditures of those born in Europe and America went up from 115 per cent to 120 per cent, in comparison with the average expenditures per person of the entire population.

A similar picture emerges with regard to educational standards and occupational distribution. A comparison made between persons in Israel who are of Asian and African origin and those originating in Europe and America shows a concentration of the former in the lower educational levels. In 1961, for instance, the per capita educational investment (in thousands of pounds) was 2·4 for immigrants from Asia, as compared to 5·9 for European and American immigrants. The same discrepancy appears among persons born in

[1] *Study of Family Expenditures 1959–60.* First Results.
The Central Statistics Bureau, Special Publications 175, 1965, pp. 7, 8.

Israel. The per capita educational investment for children of persons originating in Asia and Africa was 3·8 (thousand of pounds), while its investment for the children of persons of European and American origin was 8·9, as was its investment for children born of native Israelis.[1]

A study of the development trends between 1961 and 1963 indicates that the sum total of educational investment for immigrants from Asia and Africa went down from IL 2·400 to IL 2·200 per capita and that the educational investment for native Israelis went down from IL 7·300 to IL 7·000 per capita, which best is explained by the increase in percentage of children of Asian and African percentage amongst its population.

A partial comparison between its 1954 and 1961[2] data indicates that while the number of years of education acquired by native-born Israelis between 15 to 29 years of age was 8·1 years in 1954, in 1961 the number of years of education pertaining to *all* native born Israeli males was 10·2 years.

A similar increase manifested itself amongst native-born Israeli females.

As for immigrants from Asia and Africa, the number of years of education acquired by males aged 15 to 29 increased from 5·1 years in 1954 to 6·5 years in 1961. Concerning the number of years of education acquired by female immigrants from Asia and Africa, it increased from 3·6 years for females aged 15 to 29 in 1954 to 4·3 years for females of *all* ages in 1961.

The percentages of increase pertaining to immigrants of European and American origin are slightly less than those pertaining to native Israelis.

Similarly a breakdown of Jewish employees – according to profession, continent of origin, and length of stay in Israel – indicates a difference in the distribution of the members of the various ethnic groups amongst the various professions. Native Israelis and immigrants of European and American origin are employed in the scientific, executive, and clerical professions above and beyond the national average. On the other hand, immigrants of Asian and African origin are employed in these professions to a degree which falls below the national average. The opposite picture emerges with regard to the semi-professional skills and manual labour (agriculture, building, mining, industry) where a high concentration of immigrants of Asian and African origin (compared to the national average) may be found, with a correspondingly low occurrence of native Israelis and immigrants from Europe and America.[3]

In accordance with this trend, for example, the percentage of native Israelis (this being a percentage of the total number of native-born Israelis) employed in the 'professional' scientific and technical professions increased

---

[1] Investments in education and human reserves in Israel. Bank of Israel Survey, 23 December 1964.

[2] Standards of education. The Central Bureau of Statistics, Special Publication No. 66 (Table 11).

[3] Source: Statistical Abstracts of Israel, 15, 1964, p. 274 (Table 16).

from 18·5 per cent in 1958 to 21·2 per cent in 1963. The corresponding figures for immigrants of European and American origin also show an increase (veterans: from 14·3 per cent to 16·6 per cent; newcomers: from 11·1 per cent to 14·4 per cent). On the other hand, the percentage of immigrants of Asian and African origin (of its total number of such immigrants in Israel) employed in executive and clerical positions went down from 7·5 per cent in 1958 to 7·1 per cent in 1963, while going up in the industries' workshops and mines from 38·6 per cent in 1958 to 42·8 per cent in 1963.

It should be noted, however, that in the 'professional', scientific, and technical professions, for the purposes of which a higher standard of education is necessary, the percentage of employment of immigrants from Asian and African countries moved in the opposite direction, rising from 3·9 per cent in 1958 to 4·8 per cent in 1963. This rate of rise is lower than the corresponding rate pertaining to immigrants from other countries, which also indicates a different trend.

As for veteran immigrants from Asian and African countries, their change trends are exactly opposite to those of newcomers from the same countries (while in 1958, 6·2 per cent of them were concentrated amongst the professions under discussion, this percentage went down to 4·1 per cent in 1963).

A research undertaken in 1960 has summarized the pertinent findings on these problems in the following way:[1]

Considerable inequality between Israeli families was found to exist in every year during the last decade. While half of the poorer families in 1957–8 received only one-quarter of total income, the richer half received three-quarters. Nevertheless this inequality is narrower than that found in West European countries, and is probably one of the narrowest in the world. To a large extent, this phenomenon is due to the homogeneity of the pre-state Jewish population of Palestine and to its strong ideological background. Since the establishment of the State things have changed, and we have witnessed a significant widening of inequality, along with the rise in the average real income of the population. This is a process contrary to that taking place in most of the developed countries, where inequality has tended to narrow during the last decades. It is reasonable to expect a reversal of this trend in Israel in the long run, with the full absorption of immigrants, the spread of education and the removal of social and economic barriers.

First of all, the longer the period of residence in Israel of any group the higher its income. The differentials between the duration-of-residence groups are explained in part by the fact that the occupational composition and the educational level of the new immigrants are lower, on the average, than those of the veretans, with the result that their average incomes are also lower. We also found that the differences in the composition of the duration-of-residence groups by countries of origin lead to income differentials. There is a greater percentage of persons of Asian and African origin among the new immigrants than among the veterans, and this reduces the

[1] G. Hanoch, Income Differentials in Israel. Falk Project, Fifth Report 1959 and 1960. Jerusalem, 1961, pp. 117–19.

average income of the immigrants. But these factors provide only a partial explanation for the income differentials according to duration of residence. Such differentials also exist among wage earners of the same age, who came from the same country, and have a similar level of education, or belong to the same employment status group and the same occupational group. Moreover, it appears that the differentials between immigrants who came during different periods do not disappear or even decrease with the passage of time, and in recent years they have apparently tended to increase.

There are also considerable income differentials between persons from different countries. As has been stated, persons of oriental origin have lower incomes, while persons from the West, as well as native-born children of European families, have higher ones. The gap in the standard of living between these communities is still wider than the gap in the incomes of earners, as may be seen from the data on per capita income and expenditure. This is because persons of oriental origin have larger families and must support a larger number of children and dependants. In addition the gap between origin groups has increased in recent years, so that the real income of persons of European and American origin has risen considerably more than the real income and standard of living of persons of Asian and African origin. Because of the extreme changes that have taken place in the composition of the population by continents of origin, the inequality arising out of differentials by origin tended to widen even more than these widening differentials. Indeed, the rapid increase in the proportion of the Asian-African group, which has a lower income and standard of living, would have widened total inequality considerably even without any widening of the differentials.

Again, the greatest part of the differentials between the wage earners in these groups is explained by the differences in age structure, educational level, and occupational composition. The lower average duration of residence of persons of oriental origin is another cause of their relatively lower incomes. But all these factors do not completely eliminate the net differences in incomes on the basis of origin. Even within groups of wage earners who came to the country during the same period, who are of the same age and have the same education, or belong to the same employment status group and occupational stratum, there are net differentials of the type described. However, it seems that these differentials and particularly those of education, are much narrower in the groups with the longest duration of stay. We may therefore conclude that even if there exists some sort of direct discrimination between immigrants from Eastern and Western countries it is eliminated in the course of time, when the newcomers become veterans. Nevertheless, the relative economic status of the oriental groups is lowered owing to their low educational levels and their lack of appropriate occupational training.

In comparing the differentials in the averages with the total inequality among families, individuals or wage earners, we find that only less than half of the total inequality can be explained by these factors.

As for comparison of inequality within the groups, it was found that it is wider among Asian-Africans and new immigrants than among European-Americans and veterans, even after adjustment for occupational and family size differences. After eliminating an estimate of the transitory variation of incomes, it was found that the veteran Europeans have a narrower inequality than the other groups. It appears that the new immigrants from Asia and Africa suffer from a considerable instability in the flow of their incomes, in addition to their low average incomes and standards of living.

Changes of Criteria of Status; Weakening of Elitist Orientations

Developments in occupational differentiation and growth in standards of living were closely connected with significant changes in the field of status evaluation.

In many spheres, and with many occupations, a higher degree of status insecurity emerged than is to be expected in a modern, differentiated society. This became evident in the uncertainties about the criteria of evaluation to be applied to different activities and occupations.

Perhaps the best starting point for an analysis of these changes is the development in the image of the pioneer, in which a general weakening especially of the emphasis on the 'settlement' pioneer took place. The attachment to this image and its derivatives, however, did not weaken, rather it underwent a series of transformations.

One such transformation was the increasingly widespread denial by different groups of the right of any single group – be they members of the settlement or the political élite – to monopolize this image. Thus, military men, professionals, industrialists, and other groups now also claimed to be pioneers with equal contributions to some common goal.

Many groups rejected the limitations on rewards inherent in the pioneering élitist premises or the right of any group to monopolize the distribution of such rewards. This reluctance developed despite the many attempts made by the political élite to exercise such rights and to maintain, often through legislative and political action, its monopoly to set up relatively rigid and uniform criteria according to which the various status professions and rewards should be allocated.

Relations between pioneering and ascetic values and orientations also weakened with the former becoming a basis for claiming the various emoluments of status.

The developments described emphasized different types of rewards – economic, prestige, and political – and stressed the awareness of the different groups to the possibilities inherent in these rewards.

Changes in the Structure and Organization of Kibbutzim – Consumption and Production

All these changes have necessarily greatly affected the whole system of stratification of the Yishuv and have especially weakened its élitist components and orientations. Therefore, before analysing the repercussions of

165

all the new developments in the fields of social organization and stratification, it is worthwhile describing the changes that took place in the centres of these élitist orientations – the kibbutz and the moshav – and their place in Israeli society. Many developments changed the place of the settlements in Israeli society.

Many of the national tasks, such as defence and settlement, on the performance of which the settlements, and especially kibbutzim, based their claims to élite status, were taken over by state agencies. The same applied to an even greater extent to the absorption of new immigrants.

The weakening in their élite positions was greatly accentuated by the split among the kibbutz movements which took place in the early fifties. At the same time the settlements had to adapt themselves to the growing economic differentiation and specialization.

Side by side with these external factors many internal factors of change took place.

These changes were manifold. One of the main developments here was the transition from groups of young men and women to established communities of middle-aged family units, accompanied by a strata of old people, members' parents or aged members and retired persons. At the same time there was continuous growth in the groups of the second and even third generation born and educated in the kibbutz. By this process, kibbutz population changed from a uniform to a diversified population, and from a young to a higher average age.

These changes in turn affected the main institutional derivatives of kibbutz values, namely (1) equality – 'allocation of rewards according to needs, and work according to capacity;' (2) simplicity and modest consumption; (3) manual labour; (4) collective production and consumption; and (5) government by direct democracy.

These tendencies are clearly discernible with regard to the allocation of consumer goods to members of the settlements. The original method of distribution made for a high degree of uniformity among wide categories of members on the basis of age and sex, and assured equality in the goods which a member received. But even this method already overlooked the principle of 'everybody according to his needs', or, more correctly, in the very first stages of the kibbutzim, gave it the interpretation of equal needs for everybody.

By 1960 the dominant method of distribution functioning in most of the kibbutzim allocated equal yearly budgets, defined as a certain monetary sum to its members within the limits of which each member had a free hand to obtain goods amounting to the ascribed sum from the kibbutz general store.

The main changes resulting from this method of distribution concern the principle of uniformity in consumption. This principle declined in the transition from 'norm' to 'personal budget'. An important change also took place in the degree of austerity that kibbutz members imposed on themselves. The method of personal budget implied that the kibbutz allocated relatively meaningful sums and stocks diverse items for consumption. This also increased the range of individual choice.

In the sphere of productivity continuous change has been taking place; moving from agricultural and manual labour as goals in themselves, to growing recognition of material achievements and hence to the establishment of agricultural diversification and industrial plants right up to stressing the profitability of an enterprise.

Another structural change revolved around the allocation of different positions to kibbutz members. According to general kibbutz values, members rotated their duties and were expected to carry out a specific task for a limited period only. No identification between a member and any special type of work should therefore result. This arrangement broke down when the need for specialization by different persons suited to the different demands arose. An increasing degree of functional stability developed in most branches except those which demanded central, managerial qualities on the one hand, or low prestige and service functions on the other hand. By now even this distinction is breaking down. Positions of leadership, many of which are allocated by elections, still rotate – but among a small group of members. The main tasks in the service branches – kitchen, laundry, general store, children's house, and schools – are being filled by the same persons for increasing periods of time. Only arrangements for work on Shabbat, in the evening, and other extra duties are arranged by rota. This change proved to be a structural turning point because it necessitated a redefinition of many tasks along more specialized lines. It gave precedence to the needs and demands of the functional-economic structure and neither to the person fulfilling the task, nor to the persons or groups who are its users. Growing identification and continuity among the different work-groups therefore developed and distinct trends of rationalization, specialization, and centralization emerged, especially in older kibbutzim.

There are many mitigating factors derived from overall kibbutz values. Work is regarded as an aim in itself as is the readiness to work without a time limit such as eight hours a day. Hence, when conditions demand it, kibbutzim are prompt to subordinate economic interests to wider social and economic considerations, delegating experienced members to help the younger kibbutzim or to take a part in the élite-roles – such as in government or the army.

A central issue here is the question of hired labour in the kibbutzim, which is strictly forbidden by kibbutz ideology. However, as most of the kibbutzim have expanded economically and suffer from a constant shortage of manpower, settlements have no choice but to use the hired labour to be found in the surrounding areas. There is, however, no kind of legitimation for this, not even from the national point of view of providing work for the unemployed. Employment of hired help in kibbutzim is a result of urgent need and, having no legitimized status, creates a very real anomaly.

Many attempts have been made to find more suitable solutions to the shortage of manpower such as establishing *ulpanim* (language courses) combining part-time work with part-time studies, and offering groups of neglected city children hospitality and work for a small wage. Summer work camps, where city children and members of youth movements voluntarily donate their vacation to work in the kibbutzim, are also of value from this point of view. But nevertheless this continues to be one of the most difficult problems in the kibbutz.

Side by side with these internal developments various types of new economic activities have arisen which have proved the kibbutzim capable of great flexibility to many fields. Although no exact figures exist, reliable estimates indicate that about a hundred industrial enterprises have been established in the kibbutzim – mostly of medium or small size requiring high levels of technical competence. Some of the larger enterprises are owned jointly by several kibbutzim in the same region or by the kibbutz movement – and in some cases private capital is mobilized. Most of these enterprises are in the wood and furniture, food, metal, and plastics industries and comprise some 30 to 40 per cent of the total output of the kibbutzim.

Regional arrangements and enterprises deal with various service needs. There are common educational institutions (especially high schools and seminars) and various economic, marketing, and industrial enterprises, most successful in cases where the kibbutzim using the service belong to the same political movement.

Changes in Internal Kibbutz Social Organization

Similar changes have taken place in the internal government of the kibbutz.

With increased membership and development the running of the kibbutz has become complex and diverse, so that the 'general assembly' of members used in the past, has lost much of its operating ability and authority. While the general assembly is still the highest authority for most members, it now serves as a source of information and a means of communication, which is under the influence of specialists and elected managerial functionaries, for the purpose of decision-making.

The whole field of family relations in the kibbutz has equally changed. In the beginning most kibbutzim tried to diminish family functions. It was believed that by weakening the family unit the kibbutz would be strengthened and that direct identification of the second generation with the kibbutz would follow. Today, however, more and more kibbutzim are giving the family new functions and values. Though in most kibbutzim they still do not sleep at home, the children are nevertheless closer to the parents. The belief now is that, if the child identifies itself with the family and the family with the kibbutz, the child will identify itself with both kibbutz and family, thus strengthening the kibbutz.

This has also become evident in the growing importance of 'private' or family consumption of meals (especially afternoon teas, snacks, etc.) more and more of which are being prepared in private rooms where also most informal entertainment takes place.[1] The main dining hall continues to serve as the centre of all major daily meals and especially for festive (Shabbat and holiday) occasions.

Education is the same for all children in the kibbutz. All have to finish high school even if their talents are not academic. Only after completion of high school are the selected best sent to receive higher education and often return to become the kibbutz's own teachers.

On the whole the second generation stays in the kibbutz and identifies with its ideals. There are some exceptions: some of the young generation prefer to establish their own, new kibbutzim, feeling that this is the only way to realize their pioneering values. Others leave the kibbutzim for town as a result of conflicts either with the kibbutz or with their parents, or in order to attain a higher standard of life and 'better' and more specialized careers outside. But most of the younger generation stay and continue their parents' way of life, taking full part in all activities.

Growing Importance of the Moshavim, and Changes in their Internal Structure

No less important than the changes that took place in the kibbutzim with the establishment of the state is the fact that, at the same time, the moshavim gained preponderance over the former, reversing the situation of the pre-state period.

As a form of settlement for new immigrants the moshavim proved to be more successful than the kibbutzim for European and, even more so, for oriental immigrants. One of the major reasons for this success is their greater flexibility, their diminished emphasis on ideological and élitist principles, and their stress on what has earlier been called the 'instrinsic' or 'stratum' aspect of peasantry.

With the onset of mass immigration it became imperative, for security and economic reasons, to settle large numbers of immigrants on the land available, overlooking ideological motives. Most of these new immigrants did not choose voluntarily to go there but were directed by the settling authorities. But within this general framework they had relatively great choice. In spite

---

[1] An interesting recent innovation in this sphere is the establishment, in many kibbutzim, of communal coffee-bars, which attempt to restore the more public consumption, but on a more personal and informal basis than in the dining-hall.

169

of considerable efforts, the kibbutz did not succeed in attracting sufficient immigrants because they lacked the ideological background without which kibbutz life is meaningless. Nor could the kibbutz adapt themselves to the needs of the immigrants. The moshavim therefore absorbed the bulk of rural immigration and directed it into agriculture. Thus, whereas in 1948 there were only some sixty moshavim in the Yishuv, by 1953 there were one hundred and eighty, of which one hundred and nine were composed exclusively of new immigrants. Dozens more have since been established. In 1957, 70 per cent of the new villages were composed of oriental immigrants, as against 30 per cent of Europeans. Though the kibbutz movement established a number of new settlements composed mainly of veterans and demobilized soldiers immediately after 1948, it has since been generally on the defensive – both as regards numbers of settlements and population.

In 1965 there were 367 moshavim in Israel, numbering 124,102 members. Of these, eighty-three were 'veteran' moshavim numbering 28,194 members and 284 'new' moshavim (the majority are immigrant moshavim) with a total of 95,908 members.

Seventy per cent of the moshav population in Israel belongs to *The Moshav Movement* (influenced by Mapai and Rafi) and the other moshavim are divided between *Hapoel Hamizrahi*, the *Haichud Hachaklai, Haoved Hazioni, Poalei Agudat Israel*, and *Hitachdut Haicarim*.

In the same year there were 230 kibbutzim and kvutzot with a total of 80,939 members. Of these, 135 were veteran kibbutzim, numbering 61,528 members and 95 new kibbutzim, with a total of 19,411 members (mostly Israelis and groups from abroad).

Of the total number of kibbutzim, seventy-four belong to Hakibbutz Ha'artzi (Mapam), seventy-six to *Ichud Hakibbutzim* and *Kibutzot* (Mapai and Rafi) and five hundred and eight-one to *Hakibbuz Hameuchad* (Achdut Haavodah). The others are divided between *Hapoel Hamizrahi* (Mafdal) *Haoved Hazioni*, and *Poalei Agudat Israel*. Only five kibbutzim are not politically connected to any movement whatsoever.

The moshav movement, having trebled in size, has also undergone important internal changes, originating primarily in the immigrant villages, in which several new sub-types of moshav have evolved. Some of these processes in turn influenced the veteran sector, itself increasingly susceptible to overall social, ideological, economic, and political developments.

The most universal change directly due to the settlement of immigrants is undoubtedly the appearance of hired labour, including Arab labour. This was caused by lack of socialist and pioneering ideology among the new settlers as much as by their new external and internal circumstances.

The most important factor, however, is no doubt the ecological situation. Most new villages are in mountainous and semi-arid or arid areas, not suitable to the mixed farming characterizing the older settlements but rather to vegetable growing, fruit orchards, or industrial crops. This agricultural transformation has resulted in an uneven work-curve, and particularly in a very heavy seasonal requirement which cannot be met by family labour alone. Recourse to hired labour was further made imperative by lack of previous demographic selection of the settler families. The villages thus include households which lack sufficient manpower even for the more balanced mixed farming and have to call on outside help, more intensive mechanization, or both.

The uneven work-curve has affected yet another principle of the moshav, namely that the settler should make his living only or mainly in agriculture. The existence of long slack seasons implied the need for considerable outside work – a tendency strongly reinforced by the slow development and low income of the new farms. This situation intensifies with the growth of children, who have neither a farm of their own nor can inherit that of the parents, but who are merely attached to the village and wish to continue living in it. Many households have consequently become only partly agricultural, and many villages contain a large population not locally employed. The problem of integrating this element into the community has created great difficulties.

Social differentiation is also increasing in the administrative sphere. In the old moshav officials were elected for a fixed period, either combining their duties with farming or returning to their farms after completing their public service. Tours of duty were usually short and the rotation large. Now the growing complexity of municipal and economic problems, together with progressive withdrawal of national protection from agriculture, have combined to require administrative specialization and the creation of distinct 'bureaucracies'. In the veteran villages, these quasi-permanent functionaries are still members, though usually non-agricultural ones, of the community. In the immigrant villages, however, they are mostly not of the settlements themselves, but are either representatives of the absorption and colonization agencies, or simply officials hired on the labour market.

Marketing in immigrant villages has also undergone important changes. Originally, the whole co-operative agricultural sector established and utilized a co-operative marketing concern, known as *Tnuva*. This served as a marketing agent for the producer, with the latter retaining all responsibility for the quality of the product and the risk of surplus. However, increasing complexity and bureaucratization have loosened the ties between the villages and their agent, with relations between the farmer and *Tnuva* being largely formal and interests often conflicting.

Immigrant settlers have often encountered difficulty in growing and shipping choice or strictly-graded produce, and have been unwilling to run the risk of loss. Hence the necessity of establishing a further marketing agency (*Nuv*, in which *Tnuva* is a partner) arose which buys the product wholesale,

171

takes care of grading and selection, and underwrites the marketing balance. Marketing is thus becoming increasingly differentiated and detached from production.

However, other types of marketing are also developing in the new villages, along the officially-sanctioned pattern. In some, all marketing is individual, with the farmers selling either to wholesalers or directly in the market. In others marketing is organized through the village co-operative, but not necessarily through *Nuv* or *Tnuva*. Finally, combinations of these systems often operate in one village, according to seasons, or different branches. These trends can be traced to cultural, social, and practical reasons: most new settlers do not profess any specific ideology of co-operation, some even finding it contradictory and encroaching upon their individual responsibilities and autonomy; some villages – mostly those composed of heterogeneous traditional groups – are simply unable to maintain a common overall social organization; many find *Nuv* less flexible, tardy in payments, and offering worse conditions than other channels; finally, settlers often object to marketing through the village co-operative as such, because this enables the moshav to deduct members' debts and taxes from the proceeds of the sale.

Obviously, all these forms of 'irregular' marketing are resisted by the moshav movement, for ideological reasons, and by the settling agencies, on economic and administrative grounds. Completely individual marketing is fought with particular vigour, as this form is associated by the movement with social disorganisation and considered as undermining the foundations of the co-operative village. It also creates difficulties in the collection of internal taxes – especially in those places where there is no civic sense and discipline – and thus affects the scope and standard of the various services maintained by the moshav.

The social sphere is another field in which the immigrant villages have developed new important characteristics. Originally, the moshav was based on carefully-selected members, with close ties and intense identification with common egalitarian and pioneering values. The new immigration and the melting-pot policy of settlement combined to produce villages which are often ideologically varied and culturally heterogeneous. A high degree of social integration and mutual help and responsibility still exists in the traditional moshavim. Such moshavim are, however, a small minority, most of the oriental villages being composed of conflicting groups. The new European village, while having a viable municipal and co-operative structure, is often more in the nature of an association than a community. This loosening of communual ties, a process in which co-operation becomes a technique rather than a value, is slowly also affecting the veteran sector.

Politically, the classical moshav was based on pure democratic doctrine and practice, both in the election of officers and their responsibility. This pattern of internal government was largely taken over by the new villages with Western traditions. The oriental population, however, finds democracy foreign, their prevailing political set-up having been based on traditional criteria of age, sex, kinship, and religious leadership. These moshavim are therefore often still influenced by patriarchal principles, with family and kinship groups forming the political units and frames of reference, and the elders constituting the political élite. The ensuing result is a kaleidoscopic variation of different mixtures of traditional-democratic blends of local government.

Overall Changes in the Structural Placing of Kibbutz and Moshav in the Israeli Social Organization

The vital changes that took place in the settlements obviously affected their place in the overall social structure of the country.

Internally the kibbutz and the moshav have shown great flexibility and adaptability, seen in their ability to absorb most of the internal developments previously described above, as well as in the growth of new – especially industrial – branches in the economy, and in their acceptance of various regional arrangements.

Thus both within the kibbutzim and the moshavim there developed a very far-reaching adaptibility and capacity for innovation. But the nature and scope of those innovating tendencies varied greatly between the two movements. Within the kibbutzim the capacity to innovate was set within the limits of ideological legitimation. Insofar as new activities could become legitimate by the ideology, they were accepted and more or less fully institutionalized. It was only with regard to hired labour and to some regional enterprises that ideological evasion was practised.

Within the moshav unit, there was, on the other hand, a tendency to what may be called a segregation between the ideological and practical sphere. The older official ideology remained, on the whole, rather unchanged, but entirely segregated within the leadership of the movement.

This permitted a much longer extent of adaptation in practice – but an adaptation of innovation which again was rather segregated and unrelated to the ideological fields. But the flexibility of the kibbutz should not be underestimated. The kibbutz continued to form a very important part of Israeli society and its collective values proved a continuous centre of social and ideological discussion and ferment. It was, however, no longer the sole repository of national values and symbols.

Some of the elements of élitist orientation still persisted – as for instance the fact that most of the leaders of the workers' groups came from the kibbutzim. But on the whole, the scope and importance of this selection in élite positions has greatly diminished – as has the importance of the settlements as the main reservoir of pioneering manpower.

173

Instead of maintaining crucial structural positions as the reservoirs of élite, the settlements – and especially the kibbutzim – have become a symbol of the major pioneering values and an arena of significant social experiments.

At the same time, however, the orientation towards such élite positions was fostered by various cultural and political activities.

This self-perception, while not affecting their flexibility towards available opportunities, did affect the settlements' attitude towards the 'outside world'. The kibbutz felt a lack of sufficient support by state and government agencies. The non-enforcement of youth-movement activity in the schools, and the policy of setting up *Nahal* (mixed agricultural and military) settlements, appeared to detract from the pioneering status of the kibbutz. Members also felt that less than their due share of arable land was being allocated to them. Moreover, the kibbutz movement asserted that the government was not sufficiently upholding the pioneering values cherished as part of the state's image.

Demands for special treatment on the basis of their pioneering status began to be made by the settlement groups. Their claims were of two interconnected types. One was to receive special material benefits in terms of subsidies, special allocations, tax exemptions, etc. The second – of broader structural and social implication – was for special legal standing and protection by the state.

Demands and proposals for special legislation by the *Knesset* (Parliament) were made which would, in effect, give special legal powers to the settlements and their movements. While members would be able to appeal to the High Court against such decisions, judgement would largely be taken out of the effective jurisdiction of the state, giving the settlements partial 'legal' extra-territoriality and minimizing the venues of direct access by the members to the legal institutions of the state. Such proposals would necessarily weaken the continuity of the voluntary element in the settlements and tend also to strengthen broader political-bureaucratic elements and orientations.

These two laws involve the structure of the movements concerned (kib-butzim and moshavim) and were, within them, accepted by a large majority. In both instances there was, however, some resistance to the law within the movement itself and outside it.

In the moshav movement there was a relatively strong resistance by a large group of moshav people who organized themselves within the framework of 'The Organization for the Preservation of the Basic Rights of Moshav Members in Israel'. This organization received support from the Farmers Association and the Herut and Liberal Parties, while the majority of the other parties, the Histadrut and its Agricultural Centre, opposed them. In this way, the argument around the moshav law became, to a large extent, a public political battle. Supporters of the proposed law saw in it a guarantee for the preservation of the moshav way of life and the opportunity of aid through the law in the prevention of 'deviation' from this type. Those rejecting the law saw in it a regulation which would loosen the volunteering foundations of the moshav by giving authority to the movement or the collective at the expense of the freedom of the individual.

The argument regarding the law was more limited in the kibbutz movement because of the prominent collective orientations prevalent in this sector but here, too, the contention was heard that the law preserves rights of movement more than it preserves the rights of the individual.

It is as yet difficult to predict to what extent these proposals may become law. However, the fact that they were drawn up by a committee headed by the Minister of Justice despite strong opposition from some moshav elements indicates their strength.

Changes in Status Conceptions – Occupational Aspirations

These manifold changes in the system of local organization in general and the weakening and change of its élitist orientations in particular had many repercussions on the status system, on status evolution, and perceptions. These could be seen in many ways – one of which was that of occupational aspirations.

Research on the occupational aspirations of the young in the period of the Yishuv indicates a strong emphasis on agriculture and other 'pioneering' occupations. In the 'fifties more varied tendencies developed.

One of the very few systematic studies available in this field analyses some of these changes.[1]

Investigations delved into the hierarchy of occupations, as perceived by the members asked (subjective hierarchy) as well as held by the public (objective hierarchy).

This research has shown that the upper portion of the 'objective hierarchy' includes most of the academic professions and those holding power in the political sphere (members of Parliament and diplomats but not professional politicians who occupy a rather low rung on the ladder). At midpoint there is a variegated group of professional categories, including those characterized as able to afford a high standard of living, such as bankers and industrialists or occupations connected with artistic abilities in the broad sense of the term (painters, musicians), and officials of intermediate rank whether in government or private employ. Manual labour is at the bottom of the ladder, in particular occupations not involving extensive training. Perhaps the most

---

[1] The empirical research on which this analysis is based deals with the various trends in choice of vocation prevalent in 1957–8 in a sample of urban male youth in Israel. It constitutes part of M. Lissak's 'Tendencies in occupational choice among Israeli urban youth'. Ph.D. Dissertation, Dept of Sociology, The Hebrew University, 1963, from which the presentation here is based.

important indication of the changed values that came with statehood is the fact that agricultural labour whether performed in kibbutz, moshav or moshava, moved to the bottom of the scale. In general, greater agreement was found regarding professions included in the upper and lower quarters of the ladder than with those found in the centre.

Even greater uniformity of opinion was found in the personal ('ego') stand on the prestige rating of the different professions. However, here too, this unity is not the same with regard to all parts of the hierarchy. For reasons already mentioned, differences of opinion recur regarding the professions in the centre of the scale.

Comparisons between the two hierarchies are particularly interesting and show very high correlations, as well as systematic deviations, from the core of identification. Thus, for example, the kibbutz member and the mechanic are always placed higher in the 'ego' than in the 'public' hierarchy, while the banker, the lawyer, and the rabbi are placed lower. The tendency also exists among the lower classes of the survey population to ascribe higher prestige to the professions in the lower quarter of the objective hierarchy. On the other hand, those in the upper classes tend to look down on the 'lesser' occupations.

Substantial agreement was found to exist in the population studied, about the criteria for success in Israeli society. Although there were several exceptions, the order of importance found was as follows:

(1) Personal standards (individual qualifications, talent, education, etc.).
(2) Economic means.
(3) Social connexions.

These findings seem to hint at a change of values among the younger generation related to the degree of prestige attached to different occupations.

Investigations revealed four basic criteria determining the stratification of Israeli society: (1) the economic factor, (2) profession or occupation, (3) education, (4) political power.

Criteria which were typical of the pre-statehood period, like 'service' in a collective framework (individual realization) and 'pioneering way of life' seem to have lost their prominence and are now of secondary importance.

At the same time, however, the study indicates a relatively high degree of uncertainty developed in the perception and evaluation of different occupations.

A very important indication of such uncertainty seems to be the significant discrepancy between one's own evaluation of occupations and the perceived standing of these occupations in the public esteem, as reported in the study.

Changes in Structural Placement and Evaluation of Different Professions

The change in the relative importance of different occupations is well illustrated by the changes in their placement and evaluation.[1]

While both teaching and medicine were accepted in varying degrees into the 'movement' framework of the Yishuv and developed professional ideologies in accordance with collective values, this was not so with the legal profession.

We do not have adequate data on the supply or demand in different periods, and it would be only natural to assume that this also influenced, to some extent at least, the evaluation or at best the 'drawing' power of different professions. But the major structural and ideological changes in the position of different professions – and some of the structural repercussions of these changes – may be discerned.

Since the establishment of the State of Israel, the general trend in most professions has been to emphasize the importance of technical and professional training and individual responsibility. Only in teaching was this trend, to some extent, reversed. Teaching continued to be regarded officially as a pioneering task, where the general spirit and right approach were more important than formal qualifications.

Nonetheless, the teacher's social status rapidly deteriorated, and the social gap between him and the political and administrative élite or the other professions seems to be on the increase. In contrast to teachers, the doctors reacted to the changing conditions of the state with a vigorous campaign for recognition of their professional status. The Israel Medical Association has been campaigning much more openly than is usual with professional associations at defending and furthering the economic and status interests of its members.

But perhaps the most dramatic change took place in the marginal status of the lawyer. As the law was regarded as not properly belonging to the semi-autonomous structure of the Yishuv, the status of the lawyer was rather marginal.

With the establishment of the state, the status of the legal profession changed with unexpected suddenness. It was not only incorporated into the social structure of the Yishuv, but became a highly respected calling. The judiciary gained a position of independence and respect, which the lawyer in time came to share. The status of the legal profession was raised and its internal cohesion and morale were strengthened.

This development culminated in the establishment in 1962 of the Israel Bar Association, which has wide legal power of supervision – such as control of

---

[1] The analysis here is greatly indebted to various papers of J. Ben-David on the professions in Israel, and especially to his Ph.D. Thesis 'The Social Structure of the Professions in Israel' Hebrew University, Dept of Sociology, 1956.

admission to the profession and jurisdiction over professional behaviour and ethics.

In other professions demands for higher educational prerequisites, attempts at legal recognition, and corporate organization, also took place. This trend developed among some of the 'older' professions – engineers, social workers, technicians, and accountants – and also among many new ones, such as economists and psychologists.

Many professions became organized with admission regulated by law. Some, such as the Medical Association and to a smaller degree the engineers, have received some measure of corporate organization – although smaller than that given to the Bar Association.

Repercussions of Status Insecurity – Development of Voluntary Associations

Status insecurities and consequent mobility aspirations had many structural repercussions manifest in the search for new functions and organizations which will be dealt with later. At this stage we shall examine one important field of structural development, that of the voluntary associations.

The most important changes in this field after the establishment of the state seem to have been the following:

(1) Multiplication of purely social associations among many social groups and sectors;

(2) A very strong decline in semi-voluntary associations which had performed various civic activities in the community, coupled with a relative increase in purely philanthropic associations;

(3) The transformation of many of these associations into pressure-groups to force governmental bodies into granting various facilities;

(4) Development of several new types of associations and groups.

Among the latter the following were found:

(1) Variations of the social clubs, whose activities usually combine leisure-time activities with talks and discussions of a topical or intellectual nature;

(2) Ideological clubs or groups interested in developing an intellectual orientation in contemporary society, and dealing with various problems of Zionism, government, education, etc.;

(3) Formal clubs combining ideological discussions with more or less explicit political orientation, and aiming at some degree of influence in the political life of the state.

It might not be out of place to mention some groups (such as *Shurat Hamitnadvim* (Voluntary Service Group) aimed at giving new impetus to voluntary work, improving relations with new immigrants, and fighting corruption, official bureaucracy and general apathy in public life.

The new associations differed from those that existed during the Yishuv in several aspects: firstly, with the exception of some, the ideological groups were not related to any existing social movement, or party, etc., and usually emphasized their dissociation from such groups. Even those with strong activist tendencies (like the *Shurat Hamitnadvim*) tried to draw adherents from various political parties, and in this way to cut across them; secondly, most groups became detached from the élite. The élite, in turn, separated and formed groups of their own. The composition of these associations reflected the various status incongruities and insecurities.

The two levels on which such associations and groups did not develop were the lowest economic stratum, where there was no background for organized activity, and the upper élite groups of the country, especially the holders of political power in the government and in the main political parties. These did not usually participate in such groups, and would merely sometimes appear as guests or passive participants for purely social or personal reasons.

While no common socio-economic denominator could be found among members of the purely social and cultural groups, they evinced certain common characteristics from the point of view of their status positions and aspirations. One was that most members of such groups felt no contradiction between their status positions and their own status evaluation. Thus most of them either evaluated their status positions in terms of only one set of criteria (generally economic), or saw no contradiction or discrepancy between their status as measured by power and by collective values. Most of them derived satisfaction from their status positions, and identified with them to a large extent. However, as most of these positions were relatively new, they looked for security by expressing their solidarity and attachment to them.

Among those who, on the other hand, felt some contradictions in their status positions and who were in some marginal position within the various status systems and evaluations which developed in Israeli society, there developed a greater predisposition to more active participation in cultural, ideological, or semi-political groups. The following types were found to be most common among them in the early 'fifties:

(1) People in relatively high official positions who emphasized the old collective values but who had, to a large extent, lost their power and influence.

(2) Members of various political parties, especially intellectuals and semi-intellectuals, who found themselves deprived of influence and power.

(3) Young people (generally aged 25–35), mostly former members of youth movements and the *Hagana*, who had fought in the War of Independence, now in government and other public services, usually in relatively high positions.

Most of these people had university degrees and entered public service mainly on the basis of their professional achievements. The group to which they belonged did not include those who had entered the civil service through the influence of various parties and pressure groups. By virtue of their education and background, most of them were collectively orientated and their enlistment in government service was at least partly motivated by ideals and national service. However, their positions were usually relatively weak, since they carried with them little power of decision; and, the people concerned, were therefore unable to regard their positions as fully compatible with the common values of society and as conferring unequivocal status.

While some of the specific types of associations were prevalent only during the first years of the state, some of the broader types still continue.

Thus it can be seen that the activities of these last two groups were also related to the peculiar status incongruities.

Membership of these associations has been continuously changing and shifting and, while new groups develop continuously, older ones tend to die out. Although no exact data exist, it seems that these shifts are connected with the growing stabilization of status aspirations among the higher social groups and with the continuous status insecurity among many of the more mobile groups.

3

SOCIAL DIFFERENTIATION AND POLICY. CONFLICTING CRITERIA AND ANOMIC AREAS IN ISRAELI SOCIETY

Changes in the Composition, Social Placement and Orientations of the Elites

Most of the important developments in the social organization of Israel analysed hereto were connected with the continuous growth in social and economic differentiation and constituted problems of the manifold social policies undertaken by the élite groups. The emerging pattern of social organization can be understood only in terms of interaction of these policies and their historical background.

It is the combination of the various broad structural changes and the changes in the composition and orientation of the élites that provide the dynamic focus of the emerging pattern of Israeli social organization and stratification.

The very term 'élite' is, of course, not easy to define. Each sector of the Yishuv had its different élites, and only gradually differentiations increased within each sector, and common interests among the different sub-élites – especially the administrative and the professional ones – grew.

With the establishment of the state several crucial changes took place. The most important among these were: the loosening of close structural ties between the élites and the settlements, growing unification of the major élite groups, and growing differentiation between and within the major élite categories.

In the period of the Yishuv connexions between the élites and the settlements were very close; large parts of the political élite were drawn from the settlements which served as the reservoir for the élite image, a tendency which was reinforced by the performance of many national tasks through the settlements. With the establishment of the state and the transfer of many crucial national tasks such as defence and settlement to the army or the Jewish Agency, this tie weakened.

The kibbutz changed from being one of the main tools in the realization of national goals, to being a group which, while often contributing to various pioneering functions, no longer had a monopoly of such activities. With the exception of the more extreme 'leftist' parties (such as *Mapam* and *Ahdut Ha-avodah*) the extent to which leadership was rooted in the settlements, decreased.

The establishment of the state accelerated the unification of different élites; they became more conscious of one another and both co-operated and competed with each other. But within this common framework growing differentiation between the various élite types developed, accompanied by a strong shift in the contents and image of élite activities and, above all, a change in the structural position of the different élites.

This differentiation developed in several directions. There was continuous change between the political, cultural, intellectual, and various professional élite groups. In addition new military and bureaucratic élite groups also developed.

Many professional, more specialized sub-élite groups such as the administrative management élite emerged in the field of politics.

The same applied to the various academic, professional, and scientific groups, as well as the more general literate élites.

A growing distinctiveness of institutional, organizational, and social setting developed, as did a growing tendency to more autonomous concepts and images.

Although many attempts were made to maintain some common identity of the different élite groups, these were already based on a much greater structural differentiation and on growing self-awareness.

The common 'roots' of social background were no longer based only on participation in different movements, but also on common schooling and professional backgrounds. Moreover, many of these new contacts gradually became crystallized only after an initial period of social dissociation, tension, uneasiness, and potential conflict.

In each institutional sphere different images with their own symbols, identifications, and career patterns developed. While these images continued to stress the importance of collective orientations and often maintained some orientations to the older image of the pioneer, varied differences and changes in the way in which their self-image was conceived emerged.

Within the political élite loyalty and service to the party and manipulative ability became more important for one's career and 'official' biography than participation in cultural activities or overall ideological activity. Within the cultural élites differentiation between the literary and the academic grew and increasing professionalization and differentiation took place.

Similarly, the economic, professional, and administrative fields began to demand greater concentration on more specific problems, and increased competence in the performance of respective tasks.

Collective goals and values were no longer fully crystallized into an overall 'master-image', and the right of any single élite group to monopolize and interpret the image of the élite was increasingly challenged.

These developments gave rise to important changes in the structural position of the élite and its relations to the wider strata.

Perhaps the most important dissociation between the élite and the wider groups from which it developed was the growing bureaucratization which changed the basic relations between them, without, however, diminishing their mutual sensitivity.

In addition, the influx of immigrants faced the élite with a new type of population whose basic values and orientations were different from their own.

The common outlook and values as well as the tensions that existed between the élite and the older population were almost entirely lacking, except in terms of general, Jewish identification. This created a complicated set of relations between the élite and these new groups.

It changed these new groups into objects of political, economic, and socio-educational effort to be moulded according to the values and interests of the élites. The élite however, also developed an attachment to the newcomers who were as yet thought to be uncontaminated by recent changes in the older society.

A further aspect of structural transformation important in the development and institutionalization of new norms, is related to the small size of Israeli society, and especially to the many primary groups held together by informal controls.

With the transformation of the élites into ruling groups and their growing dissociation from the wider groups, an important transformation took place in their relations to these primary groups.

The mutual informal controls weakened and the élite easily took recourse to more formal controls and organizations. At the same time, however, demands were made on the élite by the wider groups in terms of primary expectations of solidarity, while, no matter how far relations towards them had changed the élite expected the same type of identification, loyalty and support that was characteristic of former times. But although the new norms and activities developed both by the élite and by the wider groups were no longer based on such close identification yet, because of the small scale of Israeli society, the groups and the élites still remained within very close perceptive orbit of one another – the illusion could be often maintained that the old relations still persisted. This often created new types of tensions which we shall analyse later in greater detail.

The small size of Israeli society posed yet another problem – namely the extent to which it would be able to bear the strong tendencies to differentiation which developed within it – and what would be the specific structural characteristics which would develop as a result of this tension between small scale and the strong impetus to differentiation.

Basic Elite Policy Towards a Changing Society

Major policies evolved out of the changes in the structural placement of the élites.

The main developments in social organization already analysed and the growing structural differentiation had many repercussions on the distribution of power and wealth and on the values prevalent within most groups of society. As in similar cases of growing modernization, these phenomena were closely connected with the development of concomitant tensions and conflicts. Repercussions on the political demands and ambitions as well as on the basic social orientations of different groups necessarily affected the whole image of society and their relation to the major élites. They posed new problems for the élites and called for policies on economic, social, educational, cultural and immigrant absorption problems. The continuous encounter with these policies and the incipient tendencies of different groups constituted the dynamics of institutional developments in the spheres of social organization and stratification.

These policies were guided by a series of ideological, social, and political considerations. The élite emphasized that its own legitimation was greatly dependent on adherence to the various 'movement' symbols and collective goals and that its function was to implement these goals. Because of this, it maintained and intensified adherence to the pioneering-socialist ideology despite the fact that its own pattern of activities and positions had greatly changed.

Elitist policies aimed at the allocation of rewards through the major collective organizations, such as the government, the Histadrut and the various settlement organizations, and tried to minimize and counteract attempts at autonomy by the different professional and occupational groups.

Although these policies were seemingly guided by the pioneering ideology, their structural implications were complex and often paradoxical. They were basically rooted in the changes in social structure and in the fact that the implications of social changes at which the policies aimed, were not fully perceived and understood by the élites.

One of the most important aspects of these changes was the fact that the élite became a ruling class and that, therefore, political power became a criterion of status, prestige, and economic rewards.

As stated, the élites did not fully perceive the nature of this change. They insisted on continuity of and even identity between their positions in the older federative system and their new political positions.

As these multiplied, the growing struggle over positions and power necessarily reinforced these orientations and the implementation of social policies greatly increased the power of various competing bureaucratic organizations, the importance of political criteria in the status system, and the intensity of the power struggle. This, in turn, gave rise to a shift in the basic aims of social policy. Ideological orientations, considerations of equality, and pioneering ideals were accompanied by growing considerations of political power and stability discernible throughout the development of the state.

The changed orientation of the political élite itself with its ambiguous criteria of power was, of course, connected with this shift, which also brought strong monolithic tendencies to the fore.

Their new aims were to monopolize the allocation of status, occupational positions and economic rewards, to impose an egalitarian, 'homogeneous' system based on the assumptions of the pioneering ideology and to absorb the new immigrants and assimilate new developments in the older section, according to these two principles. In the new reality of the state this necessarily implied increased power for the various bureaucratic and administrative bodies as well as greater bureaucratization of the access to positions of power.

These manifold contradictory developments in the élite policy gave rise to important points of stress, i.e. gaps which presented severe contradictions between several norms or in which lack of any definite, binding norms emerged.

While such anomic gaps or situations are inherent in the development of any modern society their degree of acuteness varies greatly from one society to another. With the rapid ecological expansion and mobility in Israel these anomalous situations could be seen in almost every aspect of life.

These tendencies became noticeable in a variety of 'daily' occurrences – as for instance in the great congestion on the roads and the rate of road accidents due both to the inadequacy of the roads and to the impatience and lack of courtesy among drivers. They were evident in the general impatience of people and the lack of simple manners. But grave and often very annoying as all these were, some diminished with time or could perhaps be explained away as manifestations of Israeli dynamism.

Beyond these however, there were 'reactions' and consequences which crystallized in new structural arrangements, and it is here that the specifically Israeli characteristics of these developments could be seen, often closely connected with unintended consequences which also developed from the encounter between these policies and the reaction of various groups. The specific manifestations and structural repercussions differ, of course, between different societies, and in the following section we shall analyse some of the developments peculiar to Israeli society.

Contradictions in Economic Development and Structural Repercussions

The various contradictory orientations of the élite and their often paradoxical results were apparent in all major spheres of social and economic policy, affecting economic and social development, wage policies, labour relations, allocation of public funds, and absorption of immigrants. These fields were of crucial importance in regulating the access to the continuously expanding positions of control over economic resources. Hence developments within them had wide repercussions on the stratification in Israeli society.

The contradictory policies of the élites in this field can be discerned in two major areas: firstly, in the basic ideological orientations towards consumption and institutional derivation, and secondly, in the implications of the broader development policies.

While the basic ideological premises contained a strong 'ascetic' orientation which emphasized the importance of curbing consumption, the ideology equally emphasized the egalitarian rights of various groups to a decent standard of living. The combined effect of these ideological orientations was to reinforce political demands for continuous pay-rises and cost of living allowances and to stress various ascriptive components such as seniority and size of family in the composition of wages.

As a result of this relative weakness in the regulation of these growing demands many attempts were made by the élite to channelize the allocation of goods and services through various collective agencies.

Very often the broader economic policies of the government encouraged the demands of the private and the public sectors while, at the same time the government's ability to regulate such demands was not sufficiently effective. Thus, paradoxically, the development policies of the government encouraged the growth of conspicuous consumption by new groups of nouveaux riches and brought about the crystallization of new class-styles among wider sectors of the population.

The contradictory policies of the élite led to a dilemma between physical development, coupled with central political and administrative direction, and the government's inability to either undertake or effectively regulate the activities of all sectors according to some clear-cut economic criterion.

The emphasis on development therefore not only released new economic resources and created inflationary pressure, it also encouraged the growth of many speculative enterprises and of conspicuous consumption.

Direct and indirect encouragement enhanced the ambivalent and contradictory attitudes towards growing spending, with government policies legitimizing the conspicuous consumption indulged in by parts of the élite.

However, as these developments were not fully perceived or acknowledged, there were continuous attempts to deny their existence and to justify them on ideological grounds. Egalitarian principles were underlined without taking into account the newly developing reality. As a result of this both effectiveness and legitimization of many of these policies became greatly weakened.

This can be clearly seen in the structural repercussions of those aspects of social policy which aimed at the regulation of income, wages, and developing economic differentials.

The policies aimed at minimizing the differences between various occupational categories and social strata in the hope of maintaining the egalitarian premises of the predominant pioneering ideology, and the high evaluation of 'manual' – as against professional and commercial – activities. Two important aspects of policy here were the regulation of wages and wage-scales and various taxation policies. The most important social aim of the wage-policy was the continuation of limited differences between echelons and types of workers (i.e. professional and non-professional) and, if possible, the minimization of such differences in favour of the lower middle class and salaried groups as against the higher middle class and professional or academic grades. But, as in many other fields of social policy, unanticipated, paradoxical results developed.

Above all, the government and the Histadrut did not succeed in uniformly regulating wage differences among the various sectors, even in their own companies.

This tendency was reinforced by the stress laid on the capacity of employment in all industries irrespective of their suitability and by the fact that, despite declarations to the contrary, they could not withstand pressures from the more 'aggressive' groups.

A similar tendency could be discerned with regard to tax-structure and policies, where two factors of great importance are seen. The first was the acknowledged difficulty of imposing effective controls on the larger private and public companies, made even more difficult by several legal injunctions favouring these sectors and resulting in administrative failure in the implementation of tax policies. The second was that the structure of many taxes tended to affect the middle income groups far more heavily than the higher 'expense account' income groups, the public sectors – government, Histadrut companies – and the various settlements.

Two mutually reinforcing tendencies developed as a result of this: a

186

prevailing acceptance of tax evasions caused by the feeling that normally binding standards did not exist, and the exertion of pressure to obtain greater benefits or, at least partly, to legitimize the many existing policies and legal injunctions.

This also led to far reaching structural repercussions with paradoxical results as far as the aims of the élites were concered. Although the wage and taxation levels did not counteract the general tendency to increased differentials, it cushioned some such differences as could have developed with the impact of free market forces. But, paradoxically, the differences between skilled and unskilled labour increased more than those between skilled and professional and technical groups (especially as the former were often large in terms of seniority and length of time in the country).

Even more important is the fact that the government's and the Histadrut's influence on distribution of income among the independent self-employed was much smaller than their influence on the salaried groups and, in particular, on the public sectors. This led to a certain drain of skilled and professional manpower from public bodies to the private or semi-private ones. Together with the success of various active pressure groups this often tended to distort the wage structure and to discourage the direction of manpower to professional and technical, as against more speculative sectors of the economy.

These developments also encouraged the pressure for higher levels of consumption, thus creating a vicious circle in the social and economic field. Equally, these policies caused repercussions in the social organization of class structure which will be analysed later.

Labour Relations and Professional Activities

A similar development of paradoxical tendencies took place in labour relations and professional organization and activities.

With the establishment of the state the majority of the Israeli labour force was organized in the trade unions, mainly in the Histadrut. Collective bargaining rights were in the hands of the Histadrut's Trade Union Department, thus giving it the means to uphold its wage policy.

However, the growing differentiation in the labour market and in standards of living created new trends, problems, and controversies. The main issue involved, which first arose among the professional groups, was the right to organize separate groups within existing organizations and the right to separate wage negotiations.

In almost all professional groups demands were made for adequate financial recognition of professional standing. Continuous strikes were declared by secondary school teachers, engineers, and sometimes groups of doctors against the decisions of the Federation of Labour, and separatist trends developed. A specific department of the Labour Federation, the Department for Academic Workers, was established in 1956 to deal with these problems. However, the Department's activities and policy did not always conform with the ideas of its 'clientele'.

The basic attitude of the élite was to minimize differentiation and any attempts at professional autonomy although both continued to grow. In fact, while there was growing de facto recognition of such discrepancies, they were never fully acknowledged and continuous attempts were made to combat them.

In the wider field of incomes regulation the declared aims of the government and the Histadrut were to uphold the egalitarian orientation of the élite and to minimize wage differences by increasing the cost of living and family allowances, and through progressive taxation. As in the field of professional organization, so also here the policy of the élite was one of continuous ad hoc adjustments with little overall change in the basic conception and ideology.

But in general, the solutions prepared by the leaders of the Histadrut and the government, consisted of a mixture of ad hoc flexibility and acquiescence to some of the demands made, accompanied by a strong ideological and official disavowal of such tendencies.

The Horowitz Report – 1963

Whatever the extent of these ad hoc adjustments, the basic orientations outlined above guided the official policies and declarations of the élites in varying degrees after the establishment of the state.

One of the most far-reaching attempts to regulate these problems according to the basic socio-political orientation, was the so-called Horowitz Report, i.e. the 'Report of the Public Committee on Wages and Salaries of Civil Servants and Employees of Local Authorities and Religious Councils'. The committee was appointed by the government on 12 November 1961, and its recommendations were published in April 1963.

Besides dealing with administrative and technical problems, this report had several broader implications, the most important of which was the abolition of special professional grades in government service. A further implication was to reduce the importance of professional seniority over general seniority, and the consequent possible blocking of avenues of mobility within the services. Lastly, by handing over the right of representation to a single professional organization (i.e. the Histadrut) the report legitimized and increased the monolithic, administrative-bureaucratic tendencies and minimized the scope of more flexible arrangements.

Publication of the report and its acceptance by the government aroused a great deal of unrest and protest among academic and professional groups.

Under pressure of these protests the government then tentatively agreed to modify some of the recommendations, especially those dealing with the abolition of the academic grade. The impression remained, however, that the report represented the basic social orientations of the government and the Histadrut. As such it contained a very interesting ideological transformation. The strong pioneering emphasis on manual work and on the activities of the primary sectors of the economy, was changed into the defence and even exaltation of the non-professional clerical grades in the public sectors, while the strong egalitarian emphasis on sanctity of labour became transformed into a de-emphasis of professionalism and an emphasis of rights of seniority and length of service.

Changes in Professional Organization and Labour Relations

The translation of these newly evolved orientations into continuous policies, coupled to the empirical approach which tried to facilitate adjustment to changing developments, was not, on the whole, successful.

The combination of the rather strong monolithic orientations and rigidity of social orientations together with the ad hoc empirical approach and giving in to varied pressures created first a situation of relative lack of clear norms and the feeling that application of indiscriminate pressures was the best way of achieving results. This led to continuous tensions and, more important, to new and often overlapping organizations and structural developments.

One such development was the growing dissociation by certain professional groups from the Histadrut, the most prominent of these being the Secondary Teachers' Union. At the beginning of 1957 academically-qualified secondary school teachers, who belonged to the general Teachers' Union of the Histadrut, demanded equalization of salary grades with other academically-trained personnel.

This demand had previously been opposed by the General Teachers' Association (affiliated to the Histadrut) which did not recognize the right of secondary school teachers to separate wage agreements, until January 1958 when the secondary teachers formed a separate section within the GTA. Long disputes and strike-threats ensued with the secondary teachers refusing to dissolve their separate organization, and a general strike of secondary teachers was declared on 7 October 1958.

On 29 October a general meeting of secondary teachers' representatives decided to withdraw from the GTA and to create an independent Secondary School Teachers' Association within the Histadrut's Professional Section. On 31 October the secondary teachers returned to work, but the threefold struggle between the GTA, the Histadrut, and the new Secondary School Teacher's Association continued on the aspects of wages and their right to a separate organization.

Despite existing opposition the new association elected its officers on

10 December and, at the same time, declared its right to belong to the Histadrut's Professional Section as 'an integral part of the workers' community'. The new organization continued its struggle for wage rises, and was gradually recognized de facto by the Ministry of Education.

In 1962-3, almost all major professional groups joined in organizing a special Co-ordination Committee, outside, and, in fact, against the Histadrut. These included Histadrut bodies, such as the Engineers' Union, the *Kupat Cholim* (Sick Fund) doctors, the government's academic employees, and various smaller groups; as well as those not belonging to the Histadrut, such as the Medical Association, the Secondary School Teachers' Association and the newly-established organization of Teachers of Institutions of Higher Learning.

After publication of the Horowitz Report the activities of these bodies intensified and, despite the opposition of the Histadrut, a one-day protest strike was called in November 1963, by almost all the 25,000 professionals and civil servants. About two weeks later the General Union of State Employees – which constitutes a part of the Histadrut – declared a one-day strike against the explicit directives of the Histadrut in opposition to the demands of the academicians and the possible non-implementation of the Horowitz Report. The professionals in government service did not participate in this strike.

Thus one of the paradoxical outcomes of the report, whose main aim was to minimize differences between professionals and non-professionals, was a growing polarization of the cleavages between them – symbolized by these two conflicting strikes.

This situation in which both the Histadrut and the Co-ordination Committee claimed to represent the academics' group, continued throughout the latter part of 1964 when the necessity to establish new patterns of settling labour disputes through arbitration became clear – without much being done in this respect.

New wage-agreements showed clearly that the government was unable to keep increases within the 3 per cent range which alone, it claimed, could assure 'stability'. It gave in, and salaries rose by up to 18–20 per cent while, at the same time, the government indicated that, with the exception of some technical aspects of the Horowitz Report, no new principles in the regulation of labour would be instituted. At most, therefore, the continuous ad hoc arrangements made, became partially institutionalized.

New Patterns in Labour Relations and Strikes

These developments can be seen as part of a wider trend that grew in the field of labour relations, in which the manifold position of the Histadrut as employer and as representative of the workers, as well as a political body was of particular importance.

With the establishment of the state and the access to power of the former labour leadership, basic changes in the structural activities of the Histadrut took place. Both the Histadrut and the government attempted to regulate the Israeli economy in a unified, centralized way, which gave way to the growing unification and subjugation of decisions on economics and labour relations to considerations of overall policy. This could be seen in the fact that most decisions on wage-disputes were made through central, country-wide negotiations between the Histadrut and the major employers – the government, the Histadrut itself, and the Association of Industrialists. Most crucial decisions in these areas were made in the central committees of *Mapai* (Workers' Party).

But this very centralization, and the growing identification of the Histadrut and the government, had several important results.

First, the very tendency to monolithic decision-making, in which consideration of political power played a very important part, weakened its flexibility and its ability to control the new situation and to work out any new long-range principles of policy. Second, it necessarily weakened several other functions of the Histadrut – especially those of representing the workers in any given disputes.

As a result of these trends there developed within the Histadrut a rather ambivalent attitude towards strikes. While the basic ideology of the Histadrut as a trade union necessarily included the sanctity of the right to strike, this was upheld more strongly with regard to privately-owned industry where, owing to country-wide arrangements between the Histadrut and the Manufacturers' Association, it was exercised only rarely. When it came to upholding the right to strike in the public service in which the government and the Histadrut were the main 'owners', their support was much less outspoken. It discouraged such strikes but, at the same time, was unable to find a way to represent the interests of different groups of public employees and to evolve a new pattern of regulations of labour relations.

In recent years strikes not approved by the Histadrut have been on the increase in particular among the academic professions, and even the strikes by some of the lower echelons, as for instance by postal employees, were based on semi-ideological demands for higher differentials, trade union autonomy, etc.

A further significant fact about many of the strikes was that they were seldom directed against the employer but against the Histadrut, which in its *overall* policies seemed to neglect the interest of specific groups. In some cases the employer – i.e. the state – would even assume the part of mediator between the employer and the employees.

All these developments gave rise to the spread of a new pattern of labour organization and activity.

'Action groups' composed of local leaders developed, sometimes joined by leftist parties who did not accept the authority of the official workers'councils. These developed among the more privileged workers' groups as well as among the lower echelons of skilled or semi-skilled labour.[1]

This was seen as a grave threat to the authority of the local labour councils which were usually dominated by Mapai. On the whole, they proved effective in pressing their immediate demands, as they were composed either of strong privileged groups of skilled workers or of wider groups of lower echelons whose potential threats to political power were often very high.

These developments intensified during May–June 1964 (and again in early 1966) when a series of 'unauthorized' go-slow strikes broke out in some of the public services (postal and tax services) and others were threatened by various professional groups.

While this happened, no new perception of reality or *new* continuous policies developed and thus the scope of anomalous gaps, feelings of uneasiness and uncertainty, and a general need for some new structural arrangements and norms, increased. This feeling seemed to be especially acute with regard to the necessity to improve the structural relations between the government and the Histadrut on the one hand and among the different components of the Histadrut on the other.

TABLE 33

Days Lost in Strikes and Lock-outs by Economic Branch
(Percentage) 1963

Economic Branch	1963	1964
Total	128,001	100,912
Total Percentage	100	100
Agriculture	1·6	0·8
Industry and Quarrying	23·4	42·1
Construction	0·1	0·2
Electricity, Water, and Sanitary Services	0·1	11·1
Trade	1·0	0·6
Transportation, Storage, and Communication	12·3	7·8
Government Commercial and Public Services	61·5	35·1
Personal Services	0·0	2·3

Source: CBS Statistical Abstract cf Israel, 16, 1965, Table K/31, p. 336 and Table K/33, p. 337.

[1] *The Jerusalem Post*, 20 July 1962; 30 November 1962.

TABLE 34

Types of Strikes 1961–4

Nature of strikes	1961 (1)			1962 (2)			1963 (3)			1964 (4)		
	No. of strikes	Work days lost	Percentage work days lost	No. of strikes	Work days lost	Percentage work days lost	No. of strikes	Work days lost	Percentage work days lost	No. of strikes	Work days lost	Percentage work days lost
Approved strikes	60	25,979	38	53	18,610	11	55	12,984	10	46	29,635	32
Strikes that were not approved	52	41,915	62	85	216,484	89	68	111,289	90	800	62,988	68
Total	121	83,894	100	138	235,094	100	132	1,124,273	100	120	92,584	100

Sources: (1) Histadrut Yearbook, p. 177. (Available only in Hebrew.)
(2) Op. cit., p. 177.
(3), (4) State of Israel, Ministry of Labour, Department of Labour Relations. Review of Labour Relations and the Activity of the Department 1964–5, Jerusalem, 1965, p. 13. (Available only in Hebrew.)

Conflicting Norms and Gaps in the Regulation of Power and in the Upholding of Legal Norms

The concomitant development of her anomic situation in relation to new structural developments can be seen most clearly in the institutionalization of norms regulating the use of power, the access to positions of power and in the maintenance of the new legal norms promulgated by legislation.

Needless to say, this cuts across most concrete areas of life, and it would not be possible to analyse all of them. We shall therefore select only some cases, each of which will illustrate different aspects of this problem.

The first important area was the allocation of public benefits to those near to positions of power, where additional emoluments (especially among the political and administrative élite) caused a problem particularly acute during the first five or six years of the state. Arrangements for various special emoluments (cars, etc.) for different grades of officials tended partly to legitimize evasions of the official wage policies in this field.

A somewhat similar situation of ambiguity and semi-official evasion of norms developed through the provision of various facilities granted by the government and various public organizations to their own officials, in order to overcome complaints against the low level of earnings and to avert the potential threat of leaving public service.

This lack of clear definitions of norms was equally apparent in the allocation of various benefits to the public by different authorities. Public facilities or benefits were often allocated in such a way that people close to the allocating agencies could obtain them more easily and often had sole access to them.

A somewhat similar situation developed up till recently (1963) with regard to land speculation, encouraged to no small degree by the lack of a clear policy, and by the help given by the government to various special groups such as foreign and local investors or politically influential people or groups.

In several cases the State Comptroller intervened and established norms. In other cases, although there was no formal legal infringement, there was widespread public feeling that such arrangements were not 'in order'.

The significant aspect of this was not the mere occurrence but that it became an accepted pattern of evasion, by various public authorities, of the norms and injunctions developed and nominally upheld by them.

Public suspicion was prevalent that many of the rules were often made for the convenience of those making them. The absence of clear norms led to the use of position to evade regulations and to the formation of pressure groups aimed at the subversion of these laws, legitimizing evasion in a variety of ideological terms and symbols. Many attempts to implement far-reaching changes – and especially slum clearance programmes – were met by strong

194

local opposition. In many cases such attempts were directly of, or indirectly encouraged by, political groups or leaders who hoped to further their own interests and to receive wider support. One of the most striking cases in point seems to be the general evasion of municipal building laws by building contractors – often with the convenience of the municipal bodies who demanded only special payment. Again, there were allegations of acceptance of personal or institutional bribes by officials able to allocate various benefits or resources to the public.

Side by side with these events, many areas developed in which the law was not upheld and in which non-enforcement of legal norms and injunctions was rampant.

In some cases – as for instance, in the case of the Kanowitz anti-smoke fuel law of vehicles – vested interests have been active with the alleged co-operation of parts of the administration, creating a situation in which the law became almost entirely ineffective. Until recently the uncontrolled boom in land-speculation provided another area for such evasions. Many attempts to implement far-reaching changes – and especially slum clearance programmes – were met by strong local opposition.

Some of the more outstanding fields affected were those dealing with cleanliness and street begging in some of the big cities (especially, but not only, in Tel Aviv) and with the control of hawkers on the streets.

While these areas were not necessarily closely or directly related to the institutional centres of society, their overall impact was to increase the scope of anomic situations and to emphasize that legal injunctions in which various powerful groups were not interested did not have the best chances of being enforced.

A similar problem was that of regulating the co-operatives (such as transport) which had effective monopolies in their respective fields. Within this area a sore point, closely related to the tendency of many of the co-operatives to develop into 'closed shops' and to escape effective public control, was that of hired labour and its frequent strikes. Many of the co-operatives were unwilling to accept Histadrut rulings in this field and the Histadrut was unable to enforce its injunctions or to formulate new policy. In extreme form this could be seen in the events that occurred in the Haifa meat co-operatives in 1962.

The public's special sensitivity to such occurrences within the public and co-operative sectors was due to the predominance of these sectors in many spheres and also to the attempts made by many groups within these sectors to avert outside criticism through ideological justification.

Even more far-reaching in their structural implications were the attempts made by many groups and parties, as well as by the various settlement groups, to maintain their own internal jurisdiction and to limit access by their members to the general juridical organs of the state as well as to shield their members from the activities of these organs. We have already alluded briefly to such attempts above, in our discussion of the kibbutzim and moshavim and of various professional organizations, and will return to this problem in greater detail later.

Basic Policies of Immigrant Absorption

While the preceding analysis was mostly confined to developments in the 'older' sectors of the Yishuv, parallel developments also took place in the new sectors of Israeli society, and it not surprising that most of the unexpected results of various social policies developed in the absorption of immigrants.

This chapter will firstly analyse the basic policies that developed with the absorption of immigrants and will then proceed to an analysis of their repercussions and results.

The basic policy orientations of the élite were evident also in the most important single set of new problems – that of the absorption of immigrants.

Absorption policy was guided by a series of inter-connected basic orientations and considerations. One such consideration was the shaping of the immigrants' social life as far as possible along the lines of existing social values and institutions and to minimize their potentially disruptive effects. An important instance of this was the emphasis on primary absorption in agriculture, and only then on 'general' development, which in practice meant the initial directing of immigrants into development areas.

Initially, great consideration was also given to minimizing the immigrants' competitive value with the older population in the labour market and to the possibility of their becoming a factor of social unrest. In later stages of absorption, once the problem of educational and occupation achievement for new immigrants had become important, a whole series of policies were promulgated to deal with it.

While the authorities attempted to provide immigrants with their basic minimum requirements, they also made – consciously or not – their progress much dependent on recourse to the principal collective agencies for the allocation of rewards and facilities. Many special agencies and services were established to deal with problems of absorption. The Departent of Absorption of the Jewish Agency dealt with the initial stages of housing and household facilities. The Ministry of Labour developed a widespread net of housing schemes for immigrants and organized emergency work in afforestation, construction, and public works until suitable productive work could be found. Two further institutions dealing with the absorption of immigrants were Youth Aliya and the Settlement Department of the Jewish Agency; the latter dealing with the settlement of new immigrants on the land, mostly in co-operative villages (moshavim). Moreover, many of the usual public services such as health (mostly provided by the Sick Fund of the Histadrut), education, and social work agencies, set up special services for immigrants, which often meant that they were in fact given preferential treatment.

Similarly, immigrants were gradually absorbed through the normal channels of society – the school system, the army (which was of crucial importance in this process), and economic and occupational selection. Here the effects were more complicated and many new policies had to be developed aimed at giving preferential treatment in order to alleviate the immigrants' socio-economic and educational disadvantages.

For a relatively long period basic absorption policies which were undertaken within these frameworks were guided by 'homogeneous' approaches, rooted in basic official ideology. The strong tradition of rebellion against the diaspora prevented full awareness of different cultural and social backgrounds and explains the initial tendency to treat all immigrants as a uniform whole.

Probably the strong pioneering emphasis on occupational change prevented the absorbing agencies from studying different vocational traditions and potentials and from developing a flexible policy of vocational selection, guidance, and education.

The emphasis on agriculture and development often resulted in neglect of the urban sector, which had to absorb all those who did not succeed in agriculture. Accordingly, co-ordination between services in the urban sector within which the majority of the immigrants were ultimately absorbed was small and no 'guidance' system developed similar to the one developed in the agricultural settlements.

In the later stages of absorption (since about 1959), when the danger of perpetuating 'two nations' gained prominence in the public mind, various special economic, political, and educational policies were adopted which gave rise to a new, though closely connected, problem.

While many of the new policies constituted departures from the homogeneous earlier approaches, their ideological terms minimized their socio-economic aspect but tended to stress the cultural differences between oriental and Western, thus often emphasizing ethnic problems and symbols of ethnic distinctions and separateness.

Contradictions in the Absorption of Immigrants. Development of Partial Absorption

These varied and often contradictory policies created structural repercussions and problems of crucial importance to the social pattern in Israel.

The most crucial manifestation of these problems was the continuous coalescence between ethnic and (especially low) occupational status, which could often lead to the crystallization of different immigrant groups into new structural units with a high degree of mutual tension, and of conflict and opposition to the absorbing society.

The ensuing tensions and conflicts were not due to quantitatively insufficient absorption, but rather to 'partial' absorption, to social forces generated by the very success of the initial stages of absorption but not fully recognized and dealt with by the absorbing society.

Manifestations of such partial absorption became evident on the administrative as well as on the socio-political level. In the administrative field these developments were particularly evident in the beginning, while in the socio-political field they became apparent in the more advanced stages of absorption.

Most administrative agencies dealt mainly with the preparation of immigrants for adjustment in Israeli society, but not with continuous help and guidance. The immigrants were first given financial help, housing on easy terms, and some help in finding work – but after that they were left more or less to their own devices, with little continuous guidance or help.

Only in the agricultural settlements (moshavim) and through Youth Aliya did the absorbing agencies attempt to co-ordinate different services on a local level and continue to help immigrants beyond the initial stages. The political structure of the various agencies, each of which was often identified with a separate party, and the consequent lack of overall planning, often created many difficulties and problems for the immigrants.

The fact that most of the initial absorption work was left to the Jewish Agency (which became less important than the government, but at the same time attempted to maintain its autonomy) also probably contributed to these problems.

As a result of these facts, a paradoxical situation developed when absorption policy extended from agricultural to semi-urban areas of development.

The initial basic aim of this programme was the direction of as many new immigrants as possible into new development centres or towns.

However, the more active elements among the immigrants often refused to stay in these centres, while many others became passive, neglected and almost delinquent elements within them, thus negating the aim of this policy.

Lack of co-ordination was also felt acutely by some immigrants, when they found themselves lost among the many different administrative agencies without having proper understanding of their functions. In the field of education and vocational guidance for example, it often happened that certain groups (like those in the fourteen–eighteen age-group, who were between the end of compulsory education and military service) were not fully covered by any law or agency and if unable to find their own way could not turn to anybody for guidance or help. This was also felt acutely by those released from military service who, even after some preparatory vocational training in the army, found themselves with few occupational skills and no ability to find permanent work.

In order to assure manual work for all immigrants who could not find productive work, a system of emerging public works *Avodot Dahak* was initiated to keep them in development areas until industry reached them, and to prevent their swamping the labour market. However, both for general economic and administrative reasons, these works often became permanent and many of the less 'successful' immigrants, or those who were sent to far-away places of development, found themselves during the fifties 'stuck' in jobs, where the father of a family would sometimes only obtain sixteen days of work per month at the rate of IL 6–7 per day for several years.

A somewhat different range of problems developed at the socio-political and ideological level. Although the ingathering of the exiles was one of the main goals of the state and the Zionist movement, its implementation was largely concentrated in the hands of various bureaucratic bodies, and absorption no longer came about through direct contact between old-timers and newcomers as was the case in the pre-state period.

Neither the informal groups in Israel's social life nor the political organizations contributed much to the *direct social* absorption of immigrants. The former became more and more closed socially, with membership confined to people of similar occupations, seniority in the country, or housing vicinity. Only those newcomers who had relatives or friends among the old-timers were able to participate fully with them.

The homes of old-timers were not closed, in principle, to the new immigrants. On the contrary, once immigrants reached the thresholds of these homes they were usually well received. But most of the veterans did little to bring new immigrants to their door.

The political parties, which became more and more centralized and bureaucratic, regarded the new immigrants mainly as potential voters or supporters who had to be 'organized' and made 'safe'. The considerable help given to immigrants by the various parties was therefore mostly extended with this aim in mind.

The same applies to the Histadrut and its various subsidiary organizations, which gave great economic and vocational help as well as trade union protection for those who had reached some level of occupational skill.

Political pressure, especially at local levels, was often imposed on immigrants by the officials of these agencies and was enhanced by the many administrative agencies dealing with absorption which were closely related to the different centres of political power.

It is important to stress that the same applies to most of the old Sephardi organizations. Despite their claims to be the leaders of the oriental immigrants, the social gap between them and these immigrants was as great as in the case of most other organizations or parties.

Thus, though the ideology of the absorbing society emphasized the ideas of full equality, brotherhood, and common enterprise, it was nevertheless assumed, at least in the initial stages of absorption, that the existing social

199

and political groups were adequate and sufficient for the needs and aspirations of the immigrants.

All these factors – the discrepancy in the political and social field between ideology and social reality, the relatively small extent of social guidance given to immigrants, the gamut of administrative problems, ideological rigidity, and the later symbolization of the ethnic problem – tended to create some of the major problems of absorption.

Failures, Tensions, and Conflicts in Immigrant Absorption

The first major problems in this sphere developed in the moshavim in the early 'fifties.

At that time the absorption policy in the moshavim, guided by 'homogeneous' ideological orientations, attempted to settle people of different countries of origin in the same moshav, assuming that the process of integration would thus be speeded up. The assumption that this would assimilate the newcomers to the pioneering ethos was quickly disproved. The immigrants developed no spontaneous pioneering spirit. Their main motives for settlement were those of security, and their predisposition for change was small. The disruption of their primary groups therefore usually gave rise to anxiety and lessened their ability to adjust to new settings. The level of their performance in the moshav was, accordingly, very low; conflicts developed between different groups, and many moshavim became disorientated.

Resulting from these failures a new, more flexible, approach was developed and first crystallized in the Lakhish area. There the tendency was to set up several moshavim in one region, each composed of people from the same country of origin, with minimal services such as kindergarten, synagogue, etc. in each village, but with most of the municipal and state services, such as schools, health services, etc. placed in the centre of the region. In this way a common framework was provided to which people adjusted and which served as an important channel for their absorption. Experience proved that this approach was, on the whole, much more successful than any of the former ones.

Even more acute problems of absorption arose later in the various 'unstructured' regions which developed in the very midst of Israeli society and of its absorptive agencies as well as in the new structural crystallizations which developed within these regions. Immigrants drifted into these regions after getting initial help from the absorbing agencies and after going through some of the channels of Israeli society (like schools and the army) and still found it impossible to stand on their own feet or to advance in their economic and social life.

These regions tended to develop in some of the more neglected development areas, in Galilee or in some parts in the South to which the immigrants were directed, but where real development lagged behind.

They also appeared in some of the main urban centres – Tel Aviv or Haifa – into which many immigrants drifted from agricultural settlements and development areas, in the hope of getting easy jobs. Some of these were gradually absorbed on certain occupational levels and developed new social groups but, at the same time, they also often became more demanding and restless.

Structurally, more advanced and crystallized types of new groupings of immigrants developed in the new towns and development areas, like Beersheba Ashdod, or Dimona, where immigrants constituted a large part, if not the majority, of the population and where they were eventually drawn into local politics.

The more successfully these specific groups were absorbed in the initial stages, by attaining housing, work, and possibilities of advancement, the more they crystallized and impinged on the country's social structure, making new demands on it and changing it continuously.

Patterns of Absorption – Traditionalism, Cultural Differences and Predisposition to Change

The preceding analysis does not imply that this structure of absorption was necessarily detrimental to all groups of immigrants or that all drifted into unstructured, marginal spheres within society. Many groups of immigrants successfully found their way into Israeli society with the help of the existing absorbing agencies. They advanced economically, merged socially with the old-timers, and became 'absorbed' at different occupational and social levels, and, in their turn, greatly influenced social life in Israel.

However, the extent to which different groups became mobile within the new frameworks varied greatly.

One central factor which influenced integration, and which became crucial especially in later stages of absorption, was the cultural and educational affinity of different groups of the predominantly European culture of the old-timers which moulded most Israeli institutions. These factors and the concomitant level of educational achievement were naturally important in facilitating occupational absorption and the advance of respective groups of immigrants.

On the other hand the level of 'traditionalism' which existed in any group of immigrants was not always an impeding factor in absorption.

Another crucial variable which influenced the degree of successful absorption, especially in the initial stages, was the extent to which immigrants proved flexibile and ready to change their social orientations and occupational patterns.

The most important general factor found to influence such predisposition to change was the extent to which the old social structure was able to provide social and emotional support for its members to develop new activities

201

appropriate to the new setting. Two more factors within this context are, firstly, the internal cohesion and flexibility of the family structure, and secondly, the system of stratification of a given immigrant community and its élites. Here the flexibility of their status system, the interchangeability of different élite tasks (e.g. economic, political, cultural), and their acceptance of subgroups as well as the extent of both basic solidarity and relatively small differentiation between the élites and other strata of the population, were of very great influence.

The existence of these factors did much to facilitate the absorption of different immigrant groups, while their absence greatly impeded such absorption.

When the two broadest factors, the 'educational' level and predisposition to change went together, as was the case with many Bulgarians, Yugoslavs, some Eastern European, and some oriental immigrants, the speed of absorption and social and economic advance was fast. The process of productive adjustment, however, was more difficult. When immigrants differed culturally from the predominant pattern but had some flexibility in vocational matters, as was the case with many Yemenites and rural North Africans, they were usually absorbed and adjusted in agriculture, handicrafts or in the lower echelons of industry. The greatest difficulties arose in cases, where, as with some of the North Africans, cultural dissimilarity was coupled with great occupational inflexibility.

The Transformation of Traditional Groups

It was within this framework of broad social forces that the transformation of all major immigrant groups took place. Among the more traditional oriental groups, this process was necessarily connected with changes in their traditional groupings and patterns.

Total obliteration of traditional settings did not take place within any group, it was rather a continuous re-shaping of traditional elements within the new framework. With almost all groups, the family as a unit continued to play some role either in the economic sphere (i.e. to hold common property, obligations, etc.) or in the political and cultural sphere (i.e. it became one of the main informal media through which political influence and direction could be exerted).

Similarly, within almost all groups and in various spheres, older patterns of authority still held good to varying degrees. This is seen in the relations between generations, in the acceptance of the authority of elders in cultural and religious life, in family life and welfare and, in some moshavim, in the visible predominance of the traditional élite in political life and in relations with the absorbing society.

Behaviour patterns took on a variety of forms often overlapping. Families re-crystallized into new economic and political frameworks, special sections dealing with immigrants developed within existing political parties and organizations, as did a variety of special 'ethnic' voluntary associations devoted to mutual help and leisure time or political activities.

While the existence of 'traditional' and 'modern' spheres could be found in varying degrees among most groups, the need to maintain relative harmony and contact between these two spheres emerged, and priorities between the traditional and the modern sectors had to be devised in a manner which emphasized their mutual interests. Good illustrations of such interlinking activities and organizations are the various moshav committees in which both old and young participate (although to different degrees in different committees).

The successful working of such interlinking spheres is closely connected to the development of a status image oriented towards the traditional as well as the modern sphere and attempting to integrate the two.

Where such a flexible status image does not develop either because of lack of internal cohesion or because of negative conditions of absorption, cleavages and tensions develop between the traditional and the modern spheres. The traditional structure itself becomes disorganized – while the possibility of divisive ethnic symbols increases.

The extent to which each of these ways of transformation of traditional groups develop, greatly influences whether their crystallization in Israeli society comes about peacefully or through tension.

What then are the conditions which influence the different types of transformation of different immigrant groups? One such set of conditions can be found in those aspects of their structure which were analysed above. Another set, related to the first, are the processes of selection of leaders from within them.

Leadership Selection Within Immigrant Groups

The interaction of absorbing conditions naturally influenced the selection of leaders and had great bearing on the transformation of immigrant groups.

Both automatic selection through general mobility and more formal selection through education, training, political courses, etc. are continuously taking place among all immigrant groups and have produced different types of leaders. They include leaders of purely ethnic associations or groups, various types of 'influentials' (such as community leaders, professionals or members of the various bureaucratic organizations of Israeli society) and local social and political leaders.

Until recently bureaucratic and political leaders were confined mainly to the lower and middle echelons of their respective organizations. But lately more political-ethnic leaders in municipal and local posts as well as in central party organizations have emerged. Some of these created new types of ethnic organizations – both clan groups in the moshavim, and politically active and even militant ethnic cliques.

Several interconnected variables seem to determine the influence of these leaders on their groups of origin. One of these variables is the continuity of relationship between the leaders and their groups. The closer this is the more can such leaders help in the gradual integration of their groups in the absorbing societies – provided they are themselves successful in the realization of their aspirations within it.

When such continuity does not exist the groups tend to become depleted of their more active members. Apathy is likely to develop and communicative gaps between them and the absorbing society may breed tensions and outbursts.

A further variable in this context is the nature of power relations between leader and group, and especially the extent to which the group shares in the new attainments of its leader and the leader directs new rewards towards the group. From this we can distinguish between two main 'ideal' types: the democratic and the authoritarian leader.[1]

In addition to the pure authoritarian or democratic attitude to the group, the distinction between these two types includes a different evaluation of relations between the groups of origin and the absorbing society and this, in turn, affects his functions as mediator between them.

The effects of these two types of leaders on their groups are, of course, quite distinct. Authoritarian leaders usually provoke a negative attitude and passive or even active opposition to the values of the society. Their authority is not willingly accepted and, when forced upon the group, evasions and rebellions ensue. The group usually feels that these leaders adversely affect their economic and political positions and use the groups for their own ends. The ramifications of such leaders' activities are, however, much wider. They give rise to a sharp power-orientation on the part of the people themselves, who, in turn, try to exploit the leaders in utilitarian and power terms, without much regard to the norms regulating such relations. The strong emphasis on power therefore gives rise to a cumulative series of deviating activities.

---

[1] The first type has the following characteristics: (a) His positive identification with the group of origin; (b) He wants to serve the group, and sees himself as its representative who must help in its relations with the 'outside'; (c) He wants to be accepted by the group yet does not force himself on it; (d) He aspires to transmit new values to it – but only in a peaceful way; (e) He does not want to exploit or use the group directly as a means of personal aggrandizement (although in reality he may, of course, be helped by it). The second type is characterized by the following: (a) His negative attitude towards the values and members of the group of origin (although usually connected to it with a strong emotional attachment); (b) He wants to force the values of the new society on it and demands obedience and power in terms of his holding of these values; (c) He aspires to a strong position of authority within the group and uses it as a means of self-aggrandizement (e.g. by procuring votes, etc.).

Nevertheless, the autocratic leader can often become popular or at least successful in influencing and organizing groups of immigrants that are uprooted, dissatisfied, and caught in the various 'loopholes' of absorption.

The more democratic leaders are usually willingly accepted and their authority is legitimized. Their success in attaining new goals is usually approved of by the groups, which hope to share in it. Consequently they become good mediators and enhance both the positive identification of the group with the values of the absorbing society and the group's participation in political, cultural, and social spheres.

The conditions under which these different types of leaders emerge crucially affect the importance of their selection and here the basic variables of absorption mentioned previously come, once more, to the fore.

Of primary importance are the internal structure of the immigrant groups and their cultural-educational traditions as well as their internal group and family cohesions. Professional and economic leaders are therefore more prominent in groups with an appropriate educational background. However, the relation between the internal cohesion of the group and the tendency to develop democratic or autocratic leadership seems to be even more important.

The conditions of absorption are no less important than the initial conditions in which the immigrant groups find themselves. Accordingly, autocratic leaders, often found in bureaucratic and party-political positions, are more prone to develop when the absorbing agencies are excessively bureaucratic or political and in situations where criteria of power are emphasized – in the various 'loopholes' of absorption or in the 'unstructured regions' of society.

Structural Crystallizations and Tensions in the Advanced Stages of Absorption

The importance of different conditions of absorption became even more pronounced in the advanced stages when larger groups of immigrants were drawn into the more central spheres of activity.

New active, articulate, professional, and especially political-ethnic leaders appeared instead of the low-level organizers or 'clan mediators', but their basic influence though more lasting was still similar to those previously described.

The broad aspects of group transformation, especially in the more advanced stages of absorption, constituted the focus for new structural crystallizations among the different groups of immigrants.

Where such transformation was smooth, the 'positive' leaders predominated and the internal cohesion of the changing groups was not greatly disturbed. The re-crystallization of these groups and the consequent continuous change of subcultures within Israeli society were relatively smooth and accepted.

205

When such smooth transformation did not take place, it was the combination of ethnic clusters in their new setting with the various alienated leaders that was most conducive to ethnic tensions and outbreaks.

This has been demonstrated on many occasions, starting with the troubles at Wadi Salib in 1959 and going on to more recent and articulated disturbances. (See later, Chapter 9.)

It is significant that such outbursts did not occur in the first years of absorption when most immigrants, and especially the oriental ones, were very badly off, but at a much later stage when the lot of most of them had greatly improved.

Furthermore, participants in these outbursts were generally not completely destitute but belonged to those who had already benefited from the services provided by the absorbing agencies though they had not 'made good' afterwards. Especially important was the age group twenty to twenty-five, who had been in Israel for from five to ten years and had served in the army where, according to all testimonies, they felt no discrimination. On leaving the army they found themselves with insufficient skills or without permanent work and drifted into various emergency jobs, unable to find a stable livelihood. The fact that even these part-occupations provided a standard of living much higher than they could have enjoyed in their country of origin made no difference. Comment of this sort only made them angrier as, in the meantime, they had acquired the values of Israeli society and felt themselves entitled to live accordingly. These situations bred various types of autocratic leaders who were very important in the crystallization of these outbreaks.

Immigrant Subcultures in Israeli Society

The incorporation of the various immigrant groups into the framework of Israeli society meant that any previous 'closeness' or self-sufficiency on their part were necessarily weakened, limited, or transformed. The major areas in which such incorporation into Israeli society took place were those of occupational and economic life, education and, to some extent, politics.

The institutional spheres in which the continuity of their own way of life was greatest were the family, social life, friendships, and relations with neighbours, as well as some aspects of cultural traditions such as leisure-time activity or religious and folklore traditions.

However, it was in the same sphere of cultural values and traditions that immigrants' customs were largely undermined through the impact of the absorbing society.

In general, the higher the degree of ecological concentration, the greater were the possiblities of maintaining some continuity of tradition, and in such cases these traditions could easily become the centre of wider, even country-wide social and political activity. Here, also, lay the greatest potential for extremist, populist ethnic incitement which could easily lead to disturbances and foster separatist tendencies.

The process of absorption and the concomitant internal transformation of immigrant groups could both facilitate the continuous absorption of these groups in Israeli society as well as further the development of inter-group tensions and points of conflict.

The transformation of the immigrants' social structure greatly influenced cultural change and gave rise to two contradictory tendencies.

In some cases these subcultures integrated successfully into Israeli society, stressing their identification with it and their satisfaction with the attainments achieved in it while, at the same time, developing their own specific social and cultural traditions.

In other cases the immigrant groups were disorganized by inter-group tensions, with ethnic symbols indicating negative group identification and alienation from the absorbing society. As will be seen later, these disorganized groups were potential foci for political tensions.

Whatever tendency becomes predominant, the very emergence of such subcultures – and especially of the more alienated ones – on the one hand, and of the continuously growing coalescence of ethnic and class situations on the other, was certainly an unanticipated and to a great extent paradoxical development considering of the major social policies and their implications.

In the preceding paragraphs we spoke about the effects of the absorption policy on the crystallization of ethnic and community groups primarily among immigrants from oriental countries. It was these groups which were concentrated in the low levels of the educational and occupational ladder, and therefore their ethnic and community identification could easily have become a separatist focal point in the existing social structure. Though among the immigrants from various European countries there also developed a tendency to continue many of their former customs and though many tensions arose also among them within the absorbing structure, yet the lack of that educational-culture distance with all its implications and results did not turn their communal identification into a focal point of tension and crystallization of continuous social and political cleavages. The main influence and implication of the absorption policy with regard to these groups was, on the whole, in stressing the political and organizational aspects in the stratification structure.

But beyond these implications the absorption policy did also have a certain influence – which is perhaps difficult to estimate accurately – on the very process of immigration. The basic statistical data indicate clearly the meagre immigration from what are called 'prosperous countries', i.e. from North and South America, Western Europe, and the former English dominions. The main body of the non-oriental immigration came from Eastern Europe and to a small degree, lately, also from Latin-American countries. There is no doubt that the main reason for this meagre immigration from the 'prosperous countries' is due to the lack of sufficient motives for immigration and to the inability of the Zionist Organization to find new ways to overcome this lack of desire to immigrate.

But beyond these general reasons which, of course, also indicate some basic problem in the building of the Israeli society, there are also quite a lot of data showing that the absorption policy was not – at least until lately – planned to deal with the problems of immigrants from these countries. The same non-differential method of approach, which we have seen in the early stages of absorption towards the oriental immigrants, has found expression also in the approach to immigrants from these countries. To a certain degree these approaches were rooted in the same sources even if their concrete expression differed greatly.

In relation to oriental immigrants the absence of differential approach was expressed in the lack of consideration of the social cultural background which is permissible in the tradition and of the social problems resulting from it. In relation to immigrants from the prosperous countries and to a certain degree also to other, non-oriental immigrants, this approach was mainly expressed in the non-recognition of the existence of 'non-pioneering' motives for immigration and with only a slight understanding of the problems of immigration and absorption of independent middle-class and of professional immigrants. The system of absorption was more adapted to people who accept voluntarily or necessarily the organizational implications of the pioneering approach, their dependence on the absorption organizations, and the fact of their being in the first stages guided, in their economic activity, to a great extent by these organizations. Only lately, a certain change has taken place in this matter, mainly as a result of the problems raised by the immigration of Latin Americans. However, it is still difficult to estimate the degree of success.

Difficult as it may be to estimate the influence of the absorption policy on the immigrants who did not come, there is no doubt that the absorption policy, to a large extent, increased the importance of political and administrative factors and distinctions in the organizational structure and stratification of the Israeli society.

Contradictions and Problems in Social Policy and Social Welfare

Another important field in which major contradictions of official policies developed was that of social welfare.

The basic assumption of most social policies in Israel was that broad welfare considerations are a necessary part of the country's institutions. The absorption of immigrants, many of whom were social cases, was also seemingly oriented to the assurance of a minimum living standard.

However, reality did not live up to the basic ideological assumptions, and special welfare became one of the most problematic issues in the range of Israeli social policy. This is especially true of the more marginal groups – the social cases – the unemployed, destitute, old, sick, etc., which constitute a not inconsiderable part of the population.

Although many different agencies – the Ministry of Social Welfare, *Malben, Hadassah*, and various private bodies performed important functions in this area, yet many 'loopholes' developed.

Thus, side by side with institutions of high levels of performance and professional standards, those with much lower ones also developed – a situation which can, admittedly, be found in any society. Beyond this, however, a more acute problem existed in the fact that the minimum allocation due from the Ministry of Social Welfare was and still is often neither fully nor continuously given. Moreover, this allocation does not take care of the special problems of different groups and the different categories of social cases. The following survey on economic assistance illustrates these problems.

Direct economic assistance is based on 'minimal subsistence' and consists only of the cost of food. Water, electricity, fuel, clothing, education, special needs for children, medical care, as well as rates of taxes, are not included in this sum. These other needs are not ignored, but there are no clear-cut instructions concerning eligibility, the amount, or even the ways in which these services are to be supplied. If it is judged necessary, and if means are available, the municipal welfare agency extends these services in various ways. Thus people whose main or only income is derived from public assistance are usually exempted from the payment of municipal rates upon recommendation of the welfare department. Quite often the same department also pays part or all of the rent. Medical care, i.e. hospitalization, is given by the Ministry of Health, on recommendation of the welfare authorities; clothing is supplied if available (clothes are usually donated from private services). Various educational needs are covered by additional provisions in the welfare budget, but water, electricity, and fuel are not included in any of the above-mentioned provisions. It should be stressed again that there are no clear-cut criteria for eligibility to any of the above services. The only service administered with the help of strict directions concerning the amount of money to be spent per household is that of direct economic assistance, where the directives are as follows (1965):

IL 61 a single person per month

IL 95 a couple per month

IL 175 for 5 persons per month

    and IL 35 per each additional person.

The budget of the Ministry of Social Welfare is based on the assumption that these sums cover minimal subsistence needs (food only). This quota which was accepted over five years ago is ratified by the Knesset each year. Total expenditure on social welfare in 1962–3 amounted to IL 120,000,000 and in 1963–4, IL 143,000,000.

The Ministry of Social Welfare has a fixed budget for this purpose, whereby 30 per cent of the money is granted by various Jewish welfare agencies and 70 per cent derives from government services. The number of families who received aid in 1962–3 was 106,300, distributed as follows :

Regular economic assistance	27,400
Other material assistance	31,000
Care without material assistance	47,800

Thus from these data it can be seen that more than 5 per cent of the whole population are dependent on these allocations, while the 'Maximalists' argue that the total number of persons who received welfare aid in 1961–2 was 241,000, which is 11 per cent of the total population.[1] Fifteen thousand people who benefit from old-age pensions should further be added to this number.

In 1961 the government statistician prepared a survey of families living on assistance. Some of the data obtained is worthwhile mentioning here:

(a) 95 per cent of the families concerned immigrated after 1948.

(b) 80 per cent of families came from Asian or African countries.

(c) 17·5 per cent of the families consisted of 8 or more persons.

(d) The average size of family was 4·7 persons.

Thus we see that this field produced paradoxical results. The lowest strata of the population rose in such a way that perpetuated in their positions.

One of the reasons for this is the proliferation of different organizations and institutions and the vested interests which developed and which make a unified policy difficult.

A second reason is the paucity of clear definitions of standards and guiding principles in this field. These were never firmly laid down either by the social workers or by the Ministry of Social Welfare. This Ministry is not among the strongest and could not easily overrule and co-ordinate the various agencies and institutions – many of which are related to strong political groups in the country. The Ministry itself also suffered from political pressures and inadequate professional manpower which was not easily co-ordinated.

Closely related to these were the difficulties in developing adequate professional standards in social work and hence of attracting high-level manpower to it.

The ambivalent attitude to social work already commented upon was due to the fact that in the social pioneering ideology there was no place for social cases or problems. All these were meant to be taken care of by the full implementation of the ideology. Hence also, the policy which was based on the assumption of 'total' absorption could paradoxically not easily provide for different needs of immigrant groups. Accordingly one of the basic loopholes

---

[1] Source: Y. Kanev, *Social Policy in Israel*, Institute of Social and Economic Studies (Hebrew), *Kupat Cholim*, 1964, Tel-Aviv.

of this policy developed around such social problems and spread over wide groups of social cases.

Because of the strong political vested interest of the Histadrut Sick Fund no overall health insurance developed. Similarly, there is as yet no unemployment insurance. A hidden assumption beyond this state of affairs is that most groups of the population can provide these for themselves, either directly or through joining one of the socio-political organizations. This attitude, coupled with the organizational state of the services, discriminates against those 'weaker' social groups which cannot take care of themselves in these ways and which therefore tend to remain beyond the pale of these services.

While continuous administrative advances are being made, these problems still persist. They provide one of the interesting, paradoxical, and unexpected results of social policy and of absorption.

4

EMERGING PATTERNS OF SOCIAL ORGANIZATION AND STRATIFICATION

Trends in Crystallization of Status

The continued impact of the various social, economic, and occupational differences and the policies evolved by the élite produced some lasting, if unexpected, tendencies in the Israeli social organization.

The most obvious change was in the manifestations of different styles of life and in the ways in which accessibility to basic resources became organized.

It is in this context that both the importance of different, older movement settings and the tendencies towards new ascriptive solidarities could be most clearly discerned.

Perhaps the most important general development here was the weakening of the 'movement' style of life. The growing emphasis on common standards of consumption diminished the differences between private and collective sectors, but accentuated the differences between occupational, economic, and ethnic groups and strata.

This gave rise to a blurring of differences between the major formal or semi-formal sectors in the Yishuv and affected all sections of the population.

At the same time relations between the different sectors accentuated the stress on power and greatly increased in importance as a basic element in the system of stratification. This was part of the wider process of proliferation of the various centres of power in Israeli society, rooted in the establishment of the state, in the diversification of administrative-bureaucratic agencies, and in the growing importance of political positions within the social organization.

Such competition developed not only between the major sectors but also between sub-groupings and enterprises within each sector and increased the scope of such competition as well as the number of people and spheres of life affected.

This weakening of the élitist and movement orientations intensified the problems of access to various positions and resources – partly because this development went against the egalitarian assumptions of the élites and partly because the process of differentiation itself was apt to weaken the control by the élite over access to major positions and resources.

The most important transformation in stratification developed around economic differentiation and the diverse styles of living.

These transformations were neither smooth nor simple. They were very closely connected with the development of various anomic areas and with various new, often unintended, structural consequences and cleavages.

While the growing importance of consumption as a criterion of status strengthened the class or stratum in the social stratification at the expense of the older élite movement ideologies, yet within it new trends specific to the Israeli scene developed.

Trends in Class Crystallization

An analysis of the trend of occupational, positional, and income differentials may well be the best approach to these developments.

In order to analyse the specific characteristics of Israeli society it is not enough to indicate general trends; rather it is essential to analyse the constellations and coalescence between criteria of status – education, occupation and income – as they developed.

Some peculiar characteristics emerged, closely related to some of the aspects of social mobility analysed above.

The data in Table 35 give a preliminary view of this problem.[1]

Analysis shows a high discrepancy between the different scales, and the lower grades, especially people at the lowest educational level, emerge with a fair chance of achieving a relatively high-level income.

Thus, whereas 51·1 per cent of all Israelis belong to the lowest educational grade, only 33·2 per cent belong to the lowest income level. Unlike the USA where we find a high correspondence between occupational prestige and income in the upper grades of the two scales, in Israel the trend seems to be the opposite. The upper grades show a marked discrepancy between occupational prestige and income: 10·5 per cent of Israelis are in the higher occupational prestige grade but only 3·9 per cent are counted in the highest income level.

This means that when distributing the population on an income scale, the

[1] Bar-Yosef, R. and Padan, D., "The Oriental Communities in the Class Structure of Israel," *Molad*, Vol. XXII, Nov. 1964. pp. 195–6,

TABLE 35

Status Crystallization (Percentage of Population) in Israel

	Income	Occupation	Education
High	3·9	10·5	12·2
Upper Middle	19·5	34·0	35·1
Lower Middle	43·4	24·7	—
Low	33·2	25·5	51·1[a]

[a] The following criteria were used to characterize the class scale:—
Education: Low   = no schooling – elementary education.
                Middle = high school.
                High   = university or its equivalents of after high school education.
Occupation: Low   = unskilled manual work services.
        Lower   Middle = skilled workers, semi-skilled workers, minor clerical positions
                        and minor business and sales groups.
        Higher Middle = white collar employees in middle range positions.
                High   = business men, self-employed and employed professionals, high-
                        est managerial grade.
Income: the grade frontiers are based mostly on the socially accepted evaluation of low,
middle, and high income:
                Low   = 1,000–1,999 IL
        Lower   Middle = 2,000–3,999 IL
                High   = 7,500–10,000 + IL
Source: R. Bar–Yosef and D. Padan, op. cit.

slant is towards the lower grades, whereas in the occupational scale this distribution points towards the upper ones.

As most of the statistical data are more reliable with regard to wage-earners than to self-employed, these findings and implications have, to be corrected accordingly, even though exact data for a full correlation are not yet available.

Among recent trends in the Israeli economy and society the most significant is the continuous rise in earnings and standards of living in the private (industrial, banking, and commercial) sector and to some extent among self-employed professionals (lawyers, architects, some doctors). This also applies to many employees of government companies, all of whom managed to break through the official wage restriction.

Hence, while probably a larger percentage has to be put in the upper income echelons, it is doubtful whether this could greatly change the lesser importance of education in the upper echelons – especially as most professionals are still publicly employed. It is possible that this indicates a discrepancy between income and occupational prestige in the higher levels which may be somewhat smaller than assumed, especially with regard to non-professional occupations in the private or semi-public sectors.

However, whatever the extent of these cleavages, the class system in Israel tends towards a strong emphasis on the lower middle and middle class, a fact which is also borne out by the preliminary data on mobility quoted above.

An interesting paradox of this is the fact that the economic situation of the lower groups is very low indeed and that they form a marginal group within the society.

Even more important, the relative percentage of these lower groups has not decreased, despite the heavy emphasis of official social policies on minimizing inequality. Some of these policies, such as the lack of full-scale health insurance as well as the importance of political pressures in their implementation, may well tend to reinforce and perpetuate this stituation.

On the other end of the scale, the various middle classes greatly stressed differential symbolic consumption and encouraged the continuous growth of a small, but continuously expanding, 'upper' class of millionaires or very affluent groups of industrialists, bankers, foreign investors, and some professionals.

It was also partially legitimized by the general emphasis on conspicuous consumption, by the participation of many public figures and officials in such consumption, and by the fact that this was an unanticipated but also uncontrolled result of the government's economic policies. This, in its turn, greatly influenced the direction of the processes of mobility in Israeli society.

This overall trend towards middle-class crystallization becomes even more evident in the self-evaluation of Israelis in terms of status and class criteria. One preliminary research[1] has shown that, in spite of the fact that Israel is known for strong ideological and political orientation towards labour movements and although the USA is regarded as the stronghold of capitalism, the data on class identification in the two countries shows a reverse picture. Interestingly enough even a third of the members of socialist collective settlements (kibbutzim) considered themselves as belonging to the middle class.

Another research[2] which used a somewhat different questionnaire indicates what at first glance may seem to be different results but are basically rather similar ones. This research used the following status categories, derived to some extent from the 'pioneering' ideology: (1) middle class; (2) working intelligentsia; (3) labour class; (4) working class.

It was found that self-identification with one of these class-categories is closely connected with objective occupational status and educational attainment. Fifty per cent of the non-matriculated wage-earners who were investigated identified with 'working class' and less than 20 per cent with 'middle-

[1] A. Antonovsky: *Social and Political Attitudes in Israel*, *Allot*, June–July 1963.
[2] Adapted from fieldwork for: A. Zloczower: *Mobility Patterns and Status Conceptions in an Urban Israeli Setting*. Ph.D. Thesis, The Hebrew University of Jerusalem, 1966.

class'. Fifty-one per cent of the non-matriculated and 62 per cent of the matriculated self-employed identified with 'middle-class'; while 50 per cent of the matriculated wage-earners categorized themselves as 'working-intelligentsia', an additional 22 per cent as middle-class and only 10 per cent as 'working-class'.

Thus here also there seems to be a strong emphasis on the 'middle' strata – even if defined by somewhat different categories – than on the 'truly' proletarian or 'low' ones.

All these data indicate an interesting trend of development of the Israeli status system. They do indeed indicate that occupation has become an important, even if not a single, determinant of socio-economic status in Israel. During the pre-state period the objective process of downward inter-generational mobility was recognized and idealized ('proletarization', 'normalization of the occupational pyramid'). Formal education was devaluated and the stereotype of the 'cultured worker' fostered by the 'halutzic sector' enhanced the self-image of the 'class-conscious worker' (at least so we are told). Remnants of this idealization are probably still operating today. Yet no doubt there exists today a greater variety of significant status components than in the past competing with 'class', occupation, and ideology as potential foci of identification and solidarity.

In the research quoted above[1] it was attempted to evaluate the solidarity-potential of some of these categories.

High solidarity-potential was shown (among others) by those identifying themselves as 'religious' (74 per cent of those placing themselves in this category gave it high rank in their solidarity preferences), 'working-intelligentsia' (65 per cent), 'working-class' (52 per cent), 'matriculated' (46 per cent), 'native-born' (44 per cent), 'self-employed' (46 per cent), 'active party-members' (52 per cent), 'oriental ethnic group' (43 per cent), 'socialists' (47 per cent).

Low solidarity-potential was shown by the following categories: 'non-religious' (15 per cent), 'middle-class' (27 per cent), 'non-matriculated' (18 per cent), 'new immigrant' (20 per cent), 'wage-earners' (31 per cent), 'rich – well-off' (11 per cent), 'public sector' (17 per cent), 'moderate socialists' (19 per cent), 'unpolitical' (i.e. not member of party) (13 per cent).[2]

The plurality of status components and the relative absence of congruity between the various criteria prevents the emergence of a status-consciousness based upon the primacy of a single deprecatory factor even of the most basic kind. Through increasing the salience of status-enhancing factors, low-status individuals are enabled to form a relatively favourable status-image for

[1] A. Zloczower, op. cit.

[2] The percentages above refer to the number in each category which placed that category among the first five ranks of solidarity choices. Occupational categories showed the highest solidarity potential of all (57 per cent average).

themselves. Whatever the limitations of these data, they do reinforce other findings on the relative predominance of middle-class orientations, aspirations and identifications in Israeli society.

This overall tendency may also explain the continuous trend to measure status in terms of wealth and occupation and the steady upsurge of aspiration to mobility, as well as the development of many tensions, cleavages, and structural changes in the professional and labour fields, analysed in the preceding sections.

New Status Crystallization: Occupational, Ethnic, Political, and Religious Affiliations

These crystallizations of 'middle class' orientations indicate the growing importance of occupational criteria in evaluation of status. But in spite of this, there also developed growing differences in hierarchies of prestige according to various non-professional criteria, among the most important of which were religion and ethnic background. Simultaneously, the older movement orientations became transposed into political and administrative ones which became a very important and distinct additional criteria of prestige and points of access to different positions and resources.

All these developments pose several problems. First, what these hierarchies stand for, what different styles of life they tend to develop, and to what extent they impinge on other aspects of social stratification. Second, the problem of to what extent each criterion indicates objective factors impeding or facilitating access by various groups to different occupations, positions, and resources.

The Ethnic Element in the Transformation of Traditional Structures

Due to the basic characteristics of the various immigrant groups and because of the initial conditions of absorption described in Chapter 4, some of the major 'ethnic' groups tended to concentrate, at least temporarily, in special clusters.

Although these groups maintained some of their traditions and ways of life, they were naturally strongly affected by the impact of the absorbing society – the educational system, the army, and economic and occupational pressures.

These clusters were indicative of the common 'fate' of the different immigrant groups in the process of absorption.

In this context the extent of coalescence between economic 'class' and 'ethnic' criterion, achieved a special importance.

It was mainly the interplay between original traditions and the conditions of absorption that caused these ethnic clusters to form separate patterns and social identifications. Even if external manifestations, such as housing, dress,

216

speech, and demeanour, were not entirely dissimilar from those of the older groups, the feeling of separation and alienation was very often quite remarkable. This obviously created new foci of social identification and social tensions.

Ethnic background and identity were most strongly articulated among the oriental, but, to a smaller degree, also among some European groups – and became an important new factor in the pattern of social organization. Effects were also felt in the re-crystallization of the avenues of access to different occupational and political positions and to economic and political resources.

The development by the oriental immigrants of specific subcultures within the Israeli system of stratification is indicated by several different reinforcing trends and is closely related to the continuous coalescence – especially within oriental groups – of low occupational, educational, and economic status.

Among oriental groups the less differentiated images of society seem to be more prevalent. Similarly, they evince patterns of mobility aspiration, which emphasize larger incomes rather than the attainment of advance education. This is related to findings that, at the same level of income, the oriental group tends to invest less in education and more in direct consumption. The continuous educational backwardness of many of these groups, to be dis-discussed in the next chapter, is, of course, closely related to this.

The crystallization of the specific ethnic element as distinct and divisive also becomes apparent in the data on intermarriage between groups of different origin. These show that in 86 per cent of all marriages performed in 1959, partners were of similar ethnic origin, whereas in only 14 per cent were their origins 'mixed'.

Moreover, most 'mixed marriages' followed the pattern of hypergamy, i.e. marriage between an Ashkenazi bridegroom and an oriental bride. During 1952, 17 per cent of Ashkenazi bridegrooms married oriental brides, whereas only 10 per cent of all Ashkenazi brides married oriental husbands. The inclination towards hypergamy has increased since 1952, showing that identification of ethnic differences with class differences has grown.[1]

We see thus that the ethnic and especially the oriental element could crystallize as a specific new ascriptive element in the Israeli social structure, a development which constitutes one of the most important within Israeli society and a challenge to it. In addition, the ethnic factor also caused new cleavages and tensions in the social and political fields.

Closely connected with these developments were the many attempts made to change the negative relationship between ethnic background and access

---

[1] In 1955, 4·3 per cent of all the marriages were between grooms from Asia and Africa and brides from Europe-America and 7·5 per cent of all the marriages were between grooms from Europe-America and brides from Asia and Africa. In 1963 the first marriage pattern increased to 6·5 per cent and the second type increased to 8·9 per cent.

(CBS: Statistical Abstract of Israel: 16, 1965, Tables 12/c, p. 65.)

to occupational and educational positions. One attempt was a demand for more help in acquiring the resources (especially education) necessary for the achievement of various positions and occupations.

The other attempt made was to increase demands for more direct access to such positions by virtue of belonging to a given ethnic group.

These directions combined through the political organizations of various ethnic groups and reinforced several broader tendencies of crystallization of status in Israeli society.

Politics and Power in the Crystallization of Strata and Status

A similar picture emerges with regard to the second new criterion of status – the political-administrative one.

Of the many organizations which, increasingly, affected the life of the Israeli citizen, the most important, encompassing almost every sphere of life, was the Histadrut. This organization controlled areas of work (and until lately also access to work through the various labour exchanges), health services (through *Kupat Cholim*), and a large part of the access to housing and other basic necessities.

The various government departments and agencies constituted another important conglomeration of organizations dominating the access to basic areas and facilities. For many of the new immigrants the Jewish Agency and the different parties constituted the all-important sources of allocation of resources and goods. These various organizations often competed among themselves and had to take recourse to the central political and administrative organs of the state to develop some *modus vivendi*. This greatly increased the importance of power in the context of social organization – as a criterion of status, as a resource, and as a focus of conflict within the social structure.

Many of the élite policies tried to enhance the value of power and the prestige of political position and their control over access to resources. The growth of large-scale economic organizations in both private and public sectors, encouraged by the government's economic and tax policies, reinforced the importance of political and organizational criteria in the state system.

Seen from the political and administrative criteria of stratification, the Israeli population divides according to differences in access to the various facilities and according to the channels through which such access is organized.

Since the various political groups largely control access to major facilities, membership in one of them may be virtually essential. While it is relatively easy to evaluate different groups according to relative standard of living, wealth, and education the picture becomes more complicated with additional criteria. In many cases the lack of affiliation to any collective, party, or bureaucratic organization, is a sign of the lowest possible status group. Among many groups of new immigrants, however, while access to collective agencies certainly mitigates low status a too exclusive dependence on only one organization may freeze different groups of the population at a relatively low occupational level.

There is no doubt for example that a very large percentage of those who are not members of any sick fund belong to the lowest strata of the population for whom the attainment of full rights in the *Kupat Cholim* of the Histadrut would mean a very great advance.

As in many other welfare societies, social services in Israel tend to discriminate in favour of the more powerful or rich, so that the lower rungs who have neither additional income nor the pull of membership in other organizations, receive only minimal attention which may well minimize their possibilities of advancement. Therefore the access to a number of more active organizations may be of crucial importance for the achievement of higher mobility.

On the other hand, especially among the higher occupational groups, constant recourse to such organizations becomes a constricting factor which may impede the possibility of further social mobility and participation.

Among these groups, especially among the professional ones, more autonomous hierarchies of prestige emerged and with them important tensions and cleavages in reaction to restrictions imposed by political and administrative bodies – although many of these groups (especially the non-professional ones) may still be largely dependent on the economic policies of the government for their relative status and may not wish to undermine this dependence.

The first cleavage appeared between the salaried and self-employed sectors, and was particularly pronounced among the upper and middle groups. The second cleavage seems to be developing within the salaried professionals, between those employed in sectors (like government service) where official wage policy is more or less maintained and those private sectors and government companies where this is not the case. These cleavages explain the growing conflicts and tensions between professionals and non-professionals in the public service.

These tensions produced two broad tendencies of structural crystallizations of great importance for the merging patterns of stratification in Israel. The first such tendency found expression in growing occupational and social differentiations, in multiplication of avenues of mobility, and in heterogeneous points of prestige and status.

The second tendency developed in the direction of growing concentration on and restriction of access to resources, positions, and prestige, affecting members of various, either new political, or ethnic (or religious) organizations.

Thus, within the professional groups, attempts were made to break the monopoly of the Histadrut, while at the same time new ascriptive groups were organized which could become a second Histadrut, assuring members of various benefits.

Similarly, the new proposed laws on moshavim gave rise to attempts to 'liberalize' those of its regulations which gave overall control over access to membership to the movement, while also developing strong support for these very attempts. Similar contradictory tendencies can be found in many other instances.

The Religious Element in Israeli Society

The change in the place of the religious groups and the growth of new religious patterns have been quite remarkable since the period of the Yishuv. These changes will be dealt with in greater detail in the chapter on culture and values, but some comments are not out of place here. During the period of the Yishuv the ultra-religious groups (*Agudat Israel* and the even more extreme *Neturei Karta*) were, socially and politically, almost entirely outside the general society and constituted a sector of their own. Only the 'religious Zionist' groups, represented mainly by the *Mizrahi* and *Hapoel Hamizrahi*, were part of the 'federative', sectoral arrangement of the Yishuv.

While the religious kibbutzim formed the most crystallized religious way of life, the more general religious elements contained in the *Mizrahi* dispersed mainly within the urban population and their special interest was the system of religious education which constituted one of the educational streams in the country.

In daily life the religious elements were not concentrated in any specific framework, but intermingled with other groups. Although some nuclei of distinctive groups existed, their religious observance was, on the whole, a private matter.

Since the establishment of the state, several important changes in the composition, orientation, and activities of the major religious groups have taken place.

These changes related mainly to the following factors:
(1) the inclusion of *Agudat Israel* in the first government;
(2) the consequent changes in the legitimation of the state and the relative weakening of the *Mizrahi* Party as the sole upholder of religious values;
(3) the political controversies around the Chief Rabbinate;
(4) the influx of new non-Zionist Orthodox immigrants, both from traditional (oriental) and European countries.

As a result of these processes, religious strongholds which stressed their traditional ways of life, developed. Although they were often absorbed in modern economic activities, they did not necessarily share the major social values and orientations of the Yishuv in its 'movement' phase, such as pioneering, Zionism, etc. Instead, they often developed into relatively closed religious group centres in which an autonomous, separatist orientation was maintained and perpetuated.

These groups ranged from the more extreme, like *Neturei Karta*, through the various orthodox groups and institutions, such as the *Yeshivot* and the *Hassidim* who settled in special ecological units in various cities, up to the more 'modern' orthodox groups. In many of the more extreme groups, this separatist tendency went hand in hand with a lack of economic productivity. Fostered by various political and philanthropic organizations, this pattern was not unlike the one prevalent within the 'old Yishuv'. But even the more modern orthodox groups showed greater cohesion and developed their own, relatively separate, ways of life.

Some of the most important factors of this separateness were the development of special religious-educational institutions, such as the special *Yeshivot-Gymnasia*, and the growth of 'aggressiveness' or militancy among religious youth movements. Often the younger elements were even more militant than their elders on issues between the secular and the religious sectors of the Yishuv.

This distinctiveness was emphasized and, in a way, legitimized by the fact that students of *Yeshivot* are de facto exempt from military service.

Due to these developments, the religious element and its criteria have become much more important in the general context of the Israeli social organization.

The religious element achieved an important and specific pattern of life and framework of prestige. It also aimed at becoming a distinct pressure group with distinct new channels of access to political and occupational positions and economic resources. In all these ways the religious factor tended to become a focus of continuous cleavages and conflicts, as we shall see in greater detail in Chapter 9.

Ecological Patterns of Stratification

It may be worthwhile to describe briefly some of the major social organizations that crystallized in different ecological settings.

As a result of factors analysed above, different social patterns and groupings are in constant development. The strong movement patterns as seen in the kibbutz and the moshav are at one extreme, with new immigrant settlements – especially the moshavim – constituting a special sub-category within this framework. These patterns are mostly characterized by a more positive attitude to agriculture, by growing interests in urban patterns of life, and by more organized leisure activities, interwoven within different patterns and traditions. In the non-movement rural sectors and in the older moshavot, a wealthy suburban peasant type developed with close family tradition, connected with economic and occupational orientations, around which the new semi-urban immigrant groups tended to settle.

However the most varied development took place in the various urban centres of Jerusalem, Tel Aviv, and Haifa.

It is here that the different occupational, professional, and economic groups changed and crystallized most dramatically. Here also many of the religious groups are concentrated, and the most conspicuous 'ethnic' problem areas developed.

The cities developed different patterns of social life. Jerusalem is characterized by academic groups in and around the University, by the civil service in various government offices, and by religious and ethnic groups concentrated in closed quarters. Its industrial activities are not very developed and most of the economic activities are centred in public service, trade, small industry, and handicrafts.

The older groups of oriental immigrants in Jerusalem are still concentrated in some of its quarters while new religious groups and immigrants concentrate in others. These different neighbourhoods are relatively segregated from one another and only in the centre of the city do some leisure-time activities take place, especially on Saturday nights.

Tel Aviv is the most dynamic of all the urban centres. Side by side with commercial groups, many government officials, army officers, and professional groups – lawyers, doctors – are concentrated in different quarters. Industrial workers of different social levels also constitute an important part of the social structure.

Around Tel Aviv the most luxurious and conspicuous suburbs of the upper crust of Israeli society have sprung up, continuously new groups and quarters develop, while many new immigrants concentrate in some of the slum areas nearby. Haifa developed a rather different pattern, and in its various suburbs a predominantly worker-urban style of life has taken shape. Some professional academic (teachers and students of the Technion) and business groups, concentrate in certain quarters, but the predominant pattern is that of the workers – skilled and semi-skilled, organized in trade unions and parties, and guided by the labour predominance in the city. Haifa is characterized by many facilities for collective entertainment, such as public gardens, public shows, etc., and a relatively highly organized recreational life with less informal private recreation. In the port district some more transitional elements concentrate. Within some Haifa quarters – as in Tel Aviv and Jerusalem – there are also some of the most wretched concentrations of new immigrants – the most notorious of which is at Wadi Salib.

An entirely new pattern of social organization in which some of the 'new trends' have crystallized can be found in the various development towns and areas, such as Beersheba, and the much less urbanized development areas, such as Kiryat Shmona and Kiryat Gat.

Within these frameworks the criterion of occupation and origin – as well as the length of stay in the country – is gaining increasing importance, and different groups and strata tend to crystallize according to occupation, education, ethnic origin, etc.

While many variations exist in the development areas, the following survey[1] of one of these medium-sized towns may give an indication of some of the emerging trends in the development areas.

The town under study was established as the result of a twofold policy: development of arid areas and settlement of the numerous immigrants who entered Israel in the 'fifties. The construction of the town was part of a plan which included the establishment of agricultural settlements. An industry based on agriculture was to be set up, and the town was also intended to serve as an administrative, commercial, and cultural centre.

The first settlers were new immigrants from North Africa who came to the town directly from the port. Within a few years more North African immigrants followed, mainly from Morocco, as well as some immigrants from Egypt, Eastern Europe (mainly from Poland and Roumania), and a small group from English-speaking countries.

From the beginning these groups were joined by veteran citizens who came from all parts of the country, and at the time the study was undertaken, the population of the town was about 10,000.

The main criteria of social differentiation in the town are length of stay in the country and ethnic origin. Ethnic origin also determines affiliation to different communities with their own cultural and religious traditions: the Ashkenazi community which includes mainly European Jews, and the Sephardic community which includes Jews of Spanish descent and oriental Jews. The differentiation among these various groups embraces all spheres of life, including politics.

At first the old settlers filled all the central roles in the occupational sphere. They were sent to the town in order to function as an administrative and cultural élite, to teach, to instruct, and to build up the municipal and public institutions. Their occupational concentration, relatively high standard of living, and common culture and way of life, made them into a rather closed social stratum in which members enjoy high social status.

This strata contains the senior officials in the municipal institutions and in government service, such as social welfare and health, as well as the first political party officials sent there as the population grew. In this way the veterans were at the head of the political organization from the very beginning.

In contrast to the veterans, the new immigrants generally lack economic resources and means of obtaining employment, and are dependent on various

---

[1] This is based on: E. Cohen, L. Shamgar and Y. Levy. Research Report: *Absorption of Immigrants in a Development Town.*
The Hebrew University, Department of Sociology, 1962.

governmental and municipal agencies for such basic needs as housing and work.

After the first difficult period of adaptation, differences among the several groups of new immigrants became apparent, mainly in their economic situation and way of life.

Highest average incomes and occupational positions are held by the immigrants from English-speaking countries, who form a small group. They live in the best part of the town, together with many veterans and some prosperous immigrants from Eastern Europe. They are active mainly in the economic field, whereas in public-political life their impact is hardly felt. In general, the situation of the East European immigrants is less good, particularly as regards the many elderly persons who have difficulties in getting re-established. The situation of the Hungarian immigrants who are active in the economic life of the town is better than that of the Poles and the Roumanians, a rather high number of relief workers being found among the latter. Among Polish immigrants, a considerable number have succeeded in bettering their income, obtaining administrative and professional posts, and procuring adequate housing.

Socially, the Hungarian as well as the Anglo-Saxon immigrants form comparatively cohesive groups. Among the Polish and the Romanian immigrants, who constitute much larger groups, there is a lower degree of social cohesion.

Due to their higher level of education and professional training, and because of their cultural closeness to the Old Yishuv, as well as their personal ties with the old settlers, the European and Anglo-Saxon immigrants have access to many avenues of individual social mobility.

The situation of the oriental immigrants who lack the above mentioned characteristics is much harder. Among the Egyptian immigrants there is a small nucleus of persons whose educational and professional formation is European. They occupy relatively good positions and form an élite at the centre of their group.

The North African immigrants who constitute half the town's population are the most backward of all newcomers and form the greater part of unemployed and relief workers. The average income of a Moroccan family is often inadequate even for minimum food requirements. Their level of formal education is usually very low. Most Moroccan families are large and a considerable number of them are under the care of governmental social welfare. Many of these immigrants live in the oldest housing quarters which are now near-slum areas. The older Moroccan immigrants are traditionalists and the synagogue to them is a social institution of prime importance. However, they lack central traditional – or other – leadership, and they are socially divided into a number of rival groups.

The study has shown that the various ethnic groups, and the veteran residents, form distinct social units with major social ties. Nevertheless these groups are not homogeneous from the point of view of stratification, and within each group economic and educational differences exist. Indications show that different ethnic groups, of a relatively high economic or educational level, tend to tie up in 'status-groups' which cut across ethnic barriers and create new social units whose bases are economic and cultural. However, they do not, normally, cut across the boundaries between the two community formations: the Ashkenazim and the orientals.

Thus economic and cultural criteria gradually assumed increased importance in the more developed groups of the population, which, in turn, led to greater emphasis on divisions among the communal groups.

Naturally, the organizational settings of the various development towns differ in many details, especially in those towns where the original political or administrative élite was composed of 'oriental' settlers who received the newcomers, among them also European groups. But nonetheless, the crystallization of status and ethnic groups with concomitant ethnic tensions was of equal importance.

The Importance of Ascriptive and Power Elements

It is interesting to see to what extent the new patterns of 'strata' crystallization and the growing importance of power and ascriptive criteria, influenced the perception of the social structure.

Several recent research projects arrived at the conclusion that, in modern industrial societies, most stratification images can be classified into one or two types, or into a combination of the two. These two types are: (a) The hierarchic image, in which society is seen as a composition of usually three groups forming an 'open-class' system. These groups differ in their functions and in their way of life, but together they are conceived as constituting a relatively harmonious social entity with few overall conflicts. The various groups are usually arranged as a hierarchy, but there is a great measure of mobility from one group to another. (b) The power image, in which society is seen as a dichotomy of two sharply distinguished classes.

Some studies undertaken in Israel[1] substantiated these findings and have shown that here, as in most other societies, the more hierarchic image is characteristic of the higher social groups, while the second is typical of the lower. But some specific characteristics seem to emerge.

The survey mentioned above showed that the most common images of social structure among the dwellers of our development town were found to be the following:

(1) A non-hierarchical, multi-group image, in which the groups differ in the ethnic origin of their members (18·1 per cent of the total answers). According to this conception, the community is made up of a number

[1] E. Cohen, L. Shamgar, Y. Levy., op. cit., 1962.

of ethnic groups of equal status and without conflict. No possibility of mobility between them exists since the distinguishing criterion is ascriptive and one simply 'belongs' to the group. As these groups have equal status, this image was named 'the egalitarian image'.

(2) A hierarchical, multi-class image, in which classes differentiate according to economic criteria (12·8 per cent of the total answers). According to this conception, the community is a hierarchy of economic groups, mostly occupational, income-bracket groups. The distinction between them is not as clear-cut as in the previous image, for, together, they constitute an organic entity without contrasts or appreciable discrepancies. Since the distinguishing criterion is one of economic achievement and the groups form a hierarchy, mobility from one group to another is possible.

(3) A hierarchical, two-class image in which distinction is made along the lines of economic criteria (17 per cent of the total answers). According to this conception the community is made up of two groups whose economic situations differ sharply. The existence of social conflict is inherent in this image. Thus, free movement between the two classes is more limited than in the previous image, although the distinguishing criterion is one of economic achievement. Here the differential *economic power* status of the groups is emphasized.

(4) A hierarchical, two-group image, in which the groups are differentiated by the criterion of origin (26·9 per cent of the total answers). With this approach, the community is also made up of two groups, but these are distinguished either by length of stay in the country or by ethnic origin and communal affiliation (veteran-new immigrant; Ashkenazi-oriental). The groups constitute a dichotomy, and there is a conflict of interests between them. As the distinguishing criterion is ascriptive, there is no possiblity of mobility between the groups; and this image may be labelled as the 'caste image'.

The project concludes that the egalitarian image which is non-hierarchic, is characteristic of those of higher status. The extent of hierarchization increases as status decreases, and, among those of lowest status, we find the 'caste' image, which is extremely hierarchical by nature. The usual two images – 'the hierarchic image' and 'the power image', are therefore placed between the two new images which were encountered in our research; they are characteristic of the groups which occupy the highest and the lowest positions in the social structure of the town. It is also interesting to note that both groups have ascriptive bases of valuation, while the common base of the two intermediary groups is achievement.

These findings are based mostly on material gleaned from development areas and necessarily reflect some of the specific problems of these areas. Tentative comparison between the stratification images of the town and of the whole country shows that, on the national level, both the 'conflicting' images (the 'power' and the 'caste' images) and the ascriptive images (equality and caste) were stressed to a smaller, but not insignificant, degree.

The picture of Israeli society as perceived by some groups, differs greatly from the more official ideological view of a 'classless' working society – the ideological image of the élite.

Our picture indicates not only the emergence of growing differences between various groups but also the growing importance of several new elements of power and ascription, both in the actual processes of crystallization of social stratification and in the perception of the social structure.

Major Patterns of Change in Social Organization

The trends and developments described indicate that a double process of change has developed in the social organization in Israel. One such process was the multiplication and diversification in the structure of different groups and the widening of emphasis on different status criteria. The second change was the development of new principles and mechanisms regulating inter-relations between these groups and their problems. These changes constitute the major framework of development in the country, forming new patterns of social organization and structure.

In the continuous striving for predominance, the political and ideological considerations of any given groups or party, as determined by its élite, are the major criteria of action. A second mechanism is political bargaining in which agreements and bargains are worked out between different groups according to the balance of power among them.

Yet another mechanism is the legal one, which bases regulation on general legal principles and enforcements. These legal mechanisms can be divided into legislative, judicial, and bureaucratic. While each of these emphasizes some general public regulation encumbent on all groups, the bureaucratic and to some extent the legislative ones may come closer to the various bargaining mechanisms.

Lastly, there are various types of self-regulation and public representation by different professional groups, voluntary associations, and organs of public opinion as well as market mechanisms which are, of course, most prominent in the economic field.

Specific characteristics in the development of these mechanisms during the first stages of statehood in Israel, are the great emphasis placed on political mechanisms, the continuous ideological justification of overt and covert bargaining, and the continuous, if slow, expansion of legislative, judicial, public, and professional regulations. Recently, however, additional new tendencies and combinations have appeared.

Development of these varied regulative mechanisms impinges on more general trends which constitute the central problem in the system of stratification – the allocation of status, wealth, and power.

The continuous physical expansion, development, and mobility of the old and new groups tended to break up older ascriptive groups, giving way to new possibilities and frameworks, often based on achievements and institutional and legal norms set up according to universalist criteria.

The growing importance of educational and occupational criteria in the determination of social status has greatly enhanced the scope of universalist and achievement orientations which in turn were reinforced by the growing specialization and by the growing tendency to autonomy of occupational and professional roles and organizations.

But development and mobility were not always solely connected with the establishment of universalist and legal norms. The development of mobility and differentiation also created the problem of differential access to new positions and resources, and it was mainly here that several possibilities of new particularistic and ascriptive criteria emerged.

The first and most closely interwoven with the more universalist criteria of achievement is the amelioration of the negative beginnings of the different and especially oriental groups, through special aid programmes and the 'usual' technique of modern social policy: provision of social services and progressive taxation.

The second possibility was the widespread attempt made by the various groups to preserve their interests, whether by de facto acknowledgement of a status quo, or simply through different methods of bargaining. Many of the co-operatives' activities to establish unilateral monopolies and maintain their positions, are among the most important examples of this tendency.

These various activities did not in themselves constitute or initiate any new structural developments, since they found themselves in a situation of growing differentiation and competition.

Side by side with them, attempts developed to regulate the new and structurally more differentiated environment according to new types of particularist norms.

These attempts mitigate the criteria of achievement by narrowing or negating the scope of their applicability and by enhancing the importance of various ascriptive criteria, thus not only changing the initial conditions of entry into different markets, but also the structure, operation of, and access to these markets, as well as the positions held in them. The distribution of different facilities through various collective agencies was continually expanded, thus often making membership in such collectives more important than criteria of achievement or of universalist citizenship.

Attempts were made to establish differential norms of access to different facilities and rewards, such as housing, health service, education, work, and salary-scales, according to criteria of seniority,[1] ethnic data (country or origin), or membership in different collective agencies, parties, or movements.

Even more significant, of course, are the attempts made to establish different norms of achievement for those belonging to these categories.[2]

On the organizational level, these tendencies become evident in attempts made to establish and 'freeze' the links between different groups and to organize access to them according to various ascriptive and particularistic criteria. Attempts were also made to achieve some measure of legal extra-territoriality, one instance of this being the effort made by the religious groups to claim certain extra-territorial rights for their neighbourhood with regard to the observance of various religious laws, particularly those connected with Shabbat. The proposals put forward to give the kibbutzim and moshavim special legal rights limiting access of their members to the legal organs of the state is another instance of such attempts, as are the efforts made by the various political parties and movements to achieve effective monopoly in the development of new settlement regions. The tendencies of various professional bodies to establish strong corporate autonomy and supervision over their members also constitute important indications of this trend.

The common denominator of all these attempts was the tendency to organize the emerging differentiated activities and groups on the basis of new, more flexible, but still particularistic criteria, which were to serve as foci of autonomous – but separate and closed – hierarchies of prestige, as well as of organization of access to different positions and resources.

The new criteria were not simply evolved for the defence of existing vested interests. They contained rather more dynamic orientations which attempted to divert the process of mobility according to more particularistic criteria, sometimes making group membership the basis for development and differential achievement. At the same time, they also offered many possibilities of 'freezing' development in the patterns of social stratification.

Summary: Coalescence of Ascriptive Orientation and Criteria of Achievement

There are several ways in which the ascriptive and particularist criteria became interwoven with universalist principles and with criteria of achievement, three major trends of development being discernible. One such trend was the development of a continuously changing focus of ascription, interwoven in many ways with criteria of achievement and changing the extent that different groups crystallized around them. The ascriptive criteria became

---

[1] One very important aspect of this tendency was the growing importance, since about 1957, of seniority components in the pay of almost all public servants – whether professionals or officials.

[2] See also chapter on education.

evident in the attempts made to facilitate entry into different markets by various measures of social policy and in the changing focus of general ascriptive solidarities – whether based on family, class, movement, sector or country of origin – without crystallization into closed particularistic units.

This trend was sometimes connected with attempts made to combine development, differentiation, and mobility according to more particularistic criteria. Efforts were made to direct and regulate the creation of new groups according to various ascriptive and particularistic criteria, at the same time maintaining some openness of movement among them.

However such attempts were prone to develop into the third tendency – that of 'freezing' the various ascriptive (ethnic, political, class or religious) criteria and minimizing the possibilities of change and continuous differentiation.

In a way this was the outcome of the coalescence of social groups both among the highest and the lowest strata of Israeli society. The very importance of these problems transformed them into points of political pressure and greatly reinforced the potential 'freezing' aspects of these criteria. Thus, the various ascriptive symbols and solidarities became the focal points of political activity and demands, strongly interwoven with problems of social policy. They tended to weaken, circumscribe, and contravert the various criteria of achievement and dynamic (particularistic) orientations.

These different ways of crystallizing relations between ascriptive and achievement orientations were also closely related to the predominance of different and complex regulative mechanisms. The prevalence of criteria of achievement and ascriptive orientations necessarily enhanced the importance of market, legal and public mechanisms, and, to some extent, of bureaucratic bargaining.

The predominance of more 'dynamic', particularist criteria, could be effected through a combination of legal (especially legislative) and administrative mechanisms, and bargaining.

These continuously increasing tendencies have provided the dynamics of Israeli social development and have also created the major anomic gaps within it. The very existence of such gaps proved to be a challenge to new norms and institutional frameworks. This underline the problem of the extent to which Israel can continue its dynamic development and modernization, and whether it will develop and institutionalize its more stagnative aspects.

This chapter analysed these possibilities in the broad field of social organization and stratification. However, these problems are also manifest in other parts of Israeli society. Perhaps the most important among these spheres are those of education and politics, to be analysed in the forthcoming chapters.

8

Education, Youth and Family

1

DEVELOPMENTS IN THE YISHUV

Introduction

This chapter will deal with the inter-relating factors among family, youth and education as they developed in the Yishuv and in the State of Israel. Most of the tendencies, problems, and tensions analysed in the preceding chapter, crystallized and focused on education.

We shall first analyse the development of educational institutions during the formative period of the Yishuv, when they were under the impetus of the pioneering ideology, and shall then see what problems developed from the encounter between them and the developing social structure.

The second part of this chapter will analyse the developments of educational institutions and problems in the State of Israel, with the changes in the overall social framework and the influx of new immigrants. In the third part we shall analyse the major responses to these new problems.

The three areas of education, youth, and family span the process of socialization: the preparation of the young to become full adult members in their society, replacement of membership in a society from generation to generation, and transmission of the social and cultural heritage of a society.

From this common focus more specific contacts with other social spheres branch out. Family and youth are closely related to stratification and social organization, while the educational institutions serve both as extensions of this system and as agencies of social mobility and change. They are, of course, also closely related to whole areas of cultural creativity and tradition and to various professional organizations.

Among the most important factors that complicated the relatively simple relations between these spheres was the fact that the initial educational system in the Yishuv was not geared to the transmission and elaboration of a given social and cultural heritage, but that it developed rather as a cultural and social innovation.

Also, as in many other immigrant communities, the family could in most cases not serve as the focus of social and cultural continuity for the younger members in the society. In Israel, this factor was greatly alleviated by the fact

231

that the Yishuv was a colonizing society, created largely by young pioneers who established their new families. Due to the youth of the pioneer-immigrants, the generational lack of continuity and tension shifted largely to the pre-migratory period and to relations between the immigrants and their families in the countries of origin. Only with some of the oriental families was this lack of continuity between the generations rather more acute.

Similarly, the relation of the educational system of social stratification and mobility was greatly influenced by the expansion of the social and economic structure of the Yishuv and the continuous creation of new sectors and social groups.

Because of these factors, the central problems of these spheres in the Yishuv developed in rather special ways.

Three problems stand out:

(1) How did an educational system initially viewed as an agency of cultural innovation and creativity become transformed into a normal educational system – and what were the effects of this transformation on its organization, contents, and functioning.

(2) How were the paradoxes inherent in the continuation and perpetuation of pioneering, innovating, and rebellious ideologies resolved or dealt with.

(3) How did the rather fluid family structure of the young immigrants crystallize into a fixed pattern relevant to the developing social structure.

Underlying these problems were several issues of central importance: The crystallization of social and *cultural* continuity; the nature of the newly created cultural collective identity; the transmission of this identity to the new generation, and its transformation at the hands of this generation.

Educational Institutions Established during the Second Aliya

As shown earlier, the initial stages of the educational system were laid down during the period of the first aliya through various schools and seminaries. However, the great upsurge of cultural creativity and institutional innovation occurred during the second aliya, when both specific educational institutions and professional organizations were established and the basic educational ideology was formulated.

This culminated with the establishment of the Gymnasia – Herzlia in Tel Aviv and the Rehavia Gymnasia in Jerusalem. The main professional organization established at the time was the Teachers' Association, which did not serve predominantly as a professional association but more as a cultural-pioneering group. The basic educational ideology of the period evinced a close affinity to the basic pioneering ideology of the second aliya – even if it was never fully identical to it.

In the development of the somewhat paradoxical curriculum, considerations of cultural creativity and innovation were given much greater importance than purely pedagogical-technical problems or problems of the practical preparation of the young for adult life. Similarly the educational system, of which this curriculum was a part, was more oriented towards drawing new recruits from abroad than to the simple transmission of a given cultural heritage to the sons of the Yishuv's middle-class families.

Also within this framework, the teacher was defined as a pioneer, the main stimulator of cultural creation and innovation, and a leader of youth. During this time, the school, together with the ideological pioneering groups, was almost the only focus of youth culture in Palestine. This youth culture was without a specific ideology or even organization of its own beyond the confines of the school and the pioneering group.

Changes in the Educational Institutions after the First World War

The first marked shift in educational institutions occurred soon after the First World War, with the establishment of the Mandate, and largely shaped the development of the Yishuv's educational system until the establishment of the State of Israel – and even afterwards.

The main manifestations of this shift were as follows:

(1) A country-wide organization for educational institutions of the Jewish community, especially in the field of primary education, established with the help of the Zionist Organization, the *Vaad Leumi*, the mandatory government, and the local councils.

(2) The growth of institutions of secondary education, which were not, however, part of an overall system but were mostly privately owned.

(3) The political influence on the primary educational system asserted through the various 'trend' schools (*zramim*) i.e. the workers', the religious, and the general trend.

(4) The development of autonomous and distinct educational systems within the kibbutzim evolved in spite of the fact that officially they were part of the workers' trend.

(5) The growing incorporation of the school in the crystallizing social structure, and, with the development of autonomous youth movements, the school's narrowing scope as the focus of youth culture.

(6) The gradual narrowing and specialization of the teachers' role, together with some lowering of their status, and the growth of political and economic emphases in the teachers' professional organization.

(7) The consequent decrease in importance of the teacher as a youth movement instructor (*madrich*), whose role became more diffuse and general, in contrast to the increasingly specialized function of the teacher.

(8) The concentration of educational changes in the secondary schools, the kibbutzim, and Youth Aliya.

(9) The establishment of an institution for higher education (The Hebrew University), only partially related to and incorporated in the existing social structure.

(10) Great expansion in adult-education activities in the settlements and towns, organized by workers' councils, municipalities, and various groups and movements.

Transformations in the Educational Institutions during the Mandatory Period

The reasons for such transformations were rooted in the changing social structure of the Yishuv during this period. There was the influx of diverse groups of immigrants, whose dedication to pioneering principles was very uneven. As they comprised more families with young children of school age, their demographic pattern also differed from that of the former pioneering groups.

Parallel to this, an autogenic, second generation, grew up in the twenties and thirties which increased the demand for schools and other educational facilities. Under these changing circumstances, the educational system could not continue to deal only with the creation of new cultural activities and with the absorption of selected youth groups. It had to concern itself also with more routine aspects of education and with the socialization of the expanding youth sector.

This formalization of educational activities then became involved in the competing sectors of the Yishuv for control over 'body and soul' of the second generation from among the waves of new immigrants.

In this competitiveness each sector, but especially that of the workers, attempted to maintain the continuity and self-sufficiency of its own population. The most extreme manifestation of such attempts developed in the kibbutzim and the moshavim, where the educational system tried to keep the younger generation entirely within the fold and framework of the kibbutz.

In the urban sectors, this competitiveness was focused on a more aggressive goal, i.e. the attempt of each sector to draw as many children as possible into its own educational framework.

This system had many opponents, especially among the uncommitted teachers and educationalists. Yet, many of these were subsequently integrated into the general trend. Several primary – and almost all secondary – schools however succeeded in keeping free of any official trend.

These developments caused the initial emphasis on general cultural creativity to be transferred mainly to the political and ideological spheres – with less consideration on pedagogics and education. It was mainly within the secondary schools and in the kibbutzim (and later in *Aliyat Hanoar*) that a relatively serious concern with pedagogical problems and educational-cultural creativity developed.

The Embedding of the Educational System in the Social Structure of the Yishuv

These developments attest to the growing integration of the school system into the crystallizing social organization and stratification in the Yishuv. This growth may, to some extent, be reflected in the importance of educational criteria for the attainment of economic and occupational positions.

Available data on this subject are not systematic enough to warrant anything but an overall picture. Although the educational system was not a crucial factor in regulating occupational positions, the relation between educational levels and economic standing was continuously growing, tempered by the expansion in the institutional structure of the Yishuv, the parallel expansion of its rural and urban sectors, and the consequent pattern of mobility that developed at this stage.

Relations between the educational system and the occupational structure were further affected by the fact that 'dropping out' of school was relatively great, especially in the higher classes of secondary school. This was probably due less to economic reasons than to the influence of youth movements, the pioneering ideology, the calls to national service in the various defence formations and the continuous establishment of new settlements. Although these ideological orientations did not negate the importance of cultural and educational activities and, in fact, greatly contributed to the network of adult education, they tended to under-emphasize the importance of *formal* educational criteria and weaken the relationship between these criteria and socio-economic status.

Among oriental Jews, the picture was entirely different. Here a continuous relation between low-educational level and equally low-occupational level developed, initiated and accentuated by the 'culture conflict' in which the oriental Jews found themselves. As many of them were not fully identified with the pioneering values of the Yishuv, they did not take recourse to the various adjustive mechanisms – such as participation in youth movements or in adult education classes – for raising their status.

The Educational System of the Kibbutzim

A special educational system, closely interwoven with its own, specific, social structure developed in the kibbutzim and, to a lesser extent, in the moshavim.

It did not crystallize fully and in the same way in all the different kibbutzim, but it evolved rather quickly into a distinctive system which aroused great interest from the point of view of educational practice. Whatever the differences between the kibbutzim, some of the characteristics of this system were common to them all.

The basic tenets or assumptions of these systems were put by one of their protagonists in the following way:

The milieu of collective education is a society which strives for the simultaneous solution of social, economic, and cultural problems on the basis of co-operation, equality, and mutual aid. Such a society, even though it takes the existence of the family unit for granted, cannot leave education within the sanctuary of the family as a single, isolated entity. The responsibility for the education of the child is thus, in part, taken away from the family, and becomes the responsibility of the kibbutz society.[1]

The emphasis on collective ideals constitutes an important factor in the development of the educational system in the kibbutz. Another is its so-called feminist ideology, i.e. the ideology which stressed the importance of freeing women for equal work with the men. Out of the combined effects of these orientations and the special organizational problem of the kibbutzim its distinctive educational system developed.[2]

[1] See Golan, S.: 'Collective Education in the Kibbutz', *Psychiatry, Journal for the Study of Interpersonal Processes*, Vol. 22, No. 2, May 1959.

[2] The formal organization of the educational system of the kibbutz is usually based on the following divisions:

1 The infants' house
2 The toddlers' house
3 The kindergarten
4 Primary school (or the Junior Children's Community)
5 The Secondary school.

In these separate though continuous frameworks, the kibbutz child receives his education. The infants' house handles about 20 babies – ranging from a few days after birth until about one year of age. During this time specially-trained nurses take care of the babies, in close co-operation with the mothers who, of course, nurse their own children. Mothers are released from all other work during the nursing period, up to six weeks, and thereafter work only half days until weaning takes place.

From the infants' house, the one-year-old child moves to the toddlers' house. Here he remains until his fourth year, in a group of six children, with a permanent nurse. He meets his parents in the afternoons, when he is taken for a few hours to their room. The toddlers' house, much as the infants' house, is furnished with the maximum of facilities designed to make a child happy and to give him a psychologically-stimulating environment for intellectual and emotional development.

The kindergarten is located in a separate building, where the children live from the age of four to about seven. 'The kindergarten makes methodical efforts to develop the child's senses and physical skills – by gymnastics, calisthenics, musical education, verbal self-expression, painting, clay-modelling, and acting.' (Golan and Lavi, "Communal Education," *Ofakim*, Vol. XI, 4, 57.)

'The kindergarten enables the children to strike roots in the landscape of their home district, brings them close to the work and production processes of the various farm sectors, and educates them in accordance with the principles of the adult community.'

The instruction given to the pupils is shaped by social, economic, and political needs, as well as by the ideological orientations of the kibbutz and the larger movement to which it belongs. The curriculum contains humanities, sciences, art, and physical education. The techniques of instruction have developed into a special method, somewhat akin to the American project method.

While this method constituted one of the major pedagogical innovations of the kibbutz educational system, and became identified with this system, it did not prevail in all kibbutz movements. Lately, as we shall see, it has been undermined by tendencies to adopt the formalized education, prevalent in the rest of the country.

Kibbutz education aimed mainly at the interweaving of individual and community – the development of an adult in whom personal initiative and maturity would combine with devotion to the community and with the acceptance of the communal way of life. Its special features were shaped by the division of labour and by the kibbutz ideology.

However, while some of these pedagogical devices and innovations – like the 'project' system or the organization of youth working groups – were taken over elsewhere in Israel and aroused general interest, this educational system, as a whole, remained confined to the kibbutz.

Development in the Urban Centres – Relations Between Educational Activities and Pioneering Ideology; the Development of Youth Movements

The problems of adjusting the pioneering ideology to the changing society were focused in the general urban educational system and in the school system in particular. The school system no longer continued to be the bearer of the more dynamic, and revolutionary orientations, aimed at changing society through continuous colonization and spreading of the pioneering ideal.

Even within the workers' trend, the schools had to concentrate more and more on scholastic performance. The emphasis on pioneering values changed

---

From the age of seven to twelve the kibbutz child attends the equivalent to the Western primary school. During this period he also enters the children's community. He lives in special quarters among a group of 20, with a teacher-leader and a matron who stay with the group until high school. At the age of twelve, the youngsters study and live in a secondary school, which is usually set up in a special compound within the kibbutz. In each group (class) there are about 25 members, taking part in academic and social activities. Each group has its special instructor who performs functions similar to those of a youth-movement leader. Thus the youth group is closely interwoven in the more formal education – and it is in this area that some of the most important educational innovations of the kibbutz can be found.

Perhaps the most characteristic feature of the kibbutz school system is that it is non-selective. Every child is entitled to the educational facilities provided by the kibbutz. Consequently, in most cases, no grades are given and no examinations are held.

into identification with more general values, instead of remaining a concrete educational task within the school itself.

At the same time, however, demands for pioneering activities were being continuously made by leaders of the working groups, by the different kibbutzim and, above all, by the growing needs of defence and national-political colonization in the thirties. Attempts to maintain their élite status reinforced the wish of the workers' sectors to maintain the pioneering ethos and to imbue at least part of the new generations with it. It is here that the different youth movements played an important part.

Most of these movements started in the diaspora and were transplanted to Palestine, where they were linked to the major socio-political movements and parties[1].

With gradually increasing immigration, more members of these youth movements came to Palestine, and even the new Palestinian generation began to be drawn into the transplanted movements.

The character of these movements changed considerably with trans-plantation. Originally they were mostly autonomous youth movements, with clear-cut demands for right of self-determination.[2]

With their transplantation and the gradual realization of many of their pioneering ideals, the originally rebellious movement lost the gist of their rebellion, and the principle of self-determination changed to self-differentiation from other youth movements. Their connections with general (adult) social and political movements tightened, and the indoctrination of new members became a basic matter of interest for the leaders, who thereby hoped to create a generation of followers.

[1] The first two Jewish Zionist movements, the 'Blue and White' in Germany and *Hashomer Hatzair* in Poland and Russia, were organized about 50 years ago. They were the forerunners of the other youth movements which were to emerge during the course of the colonizing process taking place up to the foundation of the state.

The various non-religious youth movements can be divided into (1) the socialist movements such as *Gordonya* (1924), *Boruchov Youth, Hashomer Hatzair*; (2) the Revisionist *Beitar* (1923); and (3) the Zionist Youth Movement of the General Zionists. The most important religious movements in the diaspora were *Torah Ve'avodah* and later *Bnei Akivah* (1929).

A rather extreme orthodox movement came into existence in Germany – *Ezra* – inspired by Jewish Neo-Orthodoxy, later becoming Zionist, and now affiliated with the labour branch of *Agudat Israel*.

[2] It is rather interesting to note that these developments among Jewish youth in both Central and Eastern Europe occurred concomitantly with similar movements in Europe at large, mainly in Germany (the historic rally of the Free German youth groups, demanding the right of self-determination, took place on the Hohe Meissner in 1913). A number of similar features appear in the German and Jewish Youth movements: the idea of changing a stagnating society, the struggle against the symbols of authority, hope for the rejuvenation of society through youth, etc. We also find that some of these movements, e.g. *Hashomer Hatzair*, were also influenced by scouting, adopting it as one of their major educational tools.

238

In 1923 the Organization of Working Youth, closely related to the General Federation of Labour, was founded. Originally formed as a trade union organizing Jewish working youth in Palestine, it adopted the ideology of the other youth movements, emphasizing life in the collective settlements.

In 1927 *Mahanot Haolim* was founded as a movement aimed mainly toward secondary school youth. In 1946 this movement joined the *Gordonya* movement first founded in Eastern Europe in 1925, and together they formed the *United Movement* (*Hatnuah Hameuhedet*), closely connected with Mapai. *Hatnuah Hameuhedet* and the Organization of Working Youth did not unite until 1962.

Hashomer Hatzair was reborn in Palestine in 1929, where it affiliated to the *Kibbutz Haartzi* movement and, later, to the United Workers' Party (*Mapam*).

The religious youth movement *Bnei Akivah* was founded in 1929 in conjunction with *Hapoel Hamizrahi*, and was followed soon after by *Ezra*, the youth movement of *Agudat Israel*. The aim of these movements was to base the new Jewish society in Palestine on the laws of the Tora, blended with a socialist approach to labour relations. Their ultimate goal was the foundation of collective settlements in which these ideals could be implemented.

The General Zionist trend incorporated two main youth organizations. One was *Hanoar Hatzioni* (Zionist Youth) founded in 1934 as a pioneer movement in the diaspora and linked to the more liberal, labour-oriented and lower middle class General Zionists (later Progressives), with their labour groups – *Haoved Hatzioni*.

The second General Zionist movement was *Maccabi*, a movement with roots both in the diaspora and in Palestine. Although mainly a scouting-sporting movement, not connected to the pioneering trends, even this group could not withstand the ideological pressures of the period, and a nucleus of pioneers came into existence and founded a collective settlement.

The extreme right-wing movement, *Beitar*, was founded in Riga in 1923 by the Revisionist Party. A para-military youth movement, in opposition to the official Zionist movement on questions of foreign policy and Arab relations, it could, however, not entirely disregard the general tendency to the foundation of new settlements.

Beside these movements, the more independent Scouting Movement was founded in 1919, with a general organization of all Scout groups then functioning in Palestine being established in 1921. Two years later, at the General Assembly of the Jewish Scouts in Jerusalem, two different trends emerged also within this movement. One advocating the ideology of collective settlements while the second favoured a more general pioneering approach. The more extreme wing broke away and merged with *Mahanot Haolim* in the late twenties. The controversy between these two trends went right through the movement's development until, in 1936, the Education Department of the *Vaad Leumi* took the Scouting Movement under its wing, and widespread overall organization largely supplemented the national-pioneering and socialist orientation.

The Scouts became as active as any other group in the country. Service in the *Palmach* imbued them with both kibbutz ideology and socialist philosophies, and they too started a chain of settlements (three before the foundation of the state – nine altogether), whilst their pioneer groups joined existing settlements – mainly after the foundation of the state. Party politics were also inevitable here; and since most leaders were graduates or members of kibbutzim, the Scout influence diminished and the kibbutz influence grew. Growing Mapai influence has been felt since 1951, when the movement underwent a political split.

Basic Characteristics of the Youth Movements

Some characteristics are common to all movements: firstly, they all operate outside the family, school, or place of work; and secondly, they all attempt to organize their members in specific, formal groups. Their activities are geared to goals not contained in either family, school, or workshop, thereby fostering new identifications.

They differed mainly on the extent of their social activities and the corresponding degree of formalization and the extent to which set goals implied a change in their members' social status, or permitted a certain degree of continuity with the parents' life.

The different youth movements can be divided into three sometimes overlapping major types: (a) the pioneering type, emphasizing Zionist and socialist ideals and aiming to contribute members to co-operative settlements (b) the working-youth movements whose aim was the educational and occupational advancement of their members; (c) the recreational movements, which emphasized sport and leisure-time activities and had no definite social aim. This latter type, least organized, tends to shade off into informal groups.

It has been estimated that between twenty to thirty per cent of the youth in the Yishuv were members of the youth movements. However, it is well possible that the number of those who passed through them at one time or another was in fact greater.

The Youth Movements and the Pioneering Ideology

The development of the various youth movements cannot be seen only as a device to lure youth into the ranks of the different parties. They were a dynamic part of the wider world of youth cultures that developed in the country, a widespread phenomenon in all modern societies but especially in immigrant countries.

Interaction between the cultural and social setting of the home background and the various adult-sponsored activities and organizations in the country, helped to develop the distinctive qualities of the youth groups and movements.

A cursory examination shows that a specifically organized youth culture developed predominantly among the different professional middle-class and upper working-class sections of the urban population, in the communal settlements (kibbutzim), and among those sections of the oriental Jews which were going through rapid processes of cultural contact and change. It was far less evident among those oriental families who persisted in their traditional setting; in the co-operative settlements (*moshav ovdim*, a co-operative village consisting of family farms); in the moshavot, and among some of the lower urban classes.

Collective values and ideologies played an equally important part in the growth of the youth movements, and a close relationship developed between those sectors of the Yishuv in which such values existed and the more organized youth movements.

Where orientation towards collective values was weak, youth culture developed neither a strongly organized character nor distinctive goals, but took the shape of loose cliques, with only recreational goals and activities.

From the above analysis the peculiar position and features of the working-youth movements become clear. Their purpose was not only to change the status and economic welfare of their members, but also to ensure that such change would be concomitant with their transition towards common values.

The more deviant types of youth culture were mostly concerned with situations where a discrepancy existed between social orientations, the values of the family and the possibility of these values being realized within the social structure. This was intensified only in specific situations, and occurred mainly in two typical instances: In families lacking economic stability, who could not offer their children the realization of these goals, and, to a larger extent, among some sections of the oriental Jews where the new cultural contacts were most acute and where juvenile delinquency occurred more frequently.

Relations Between Youth Movements and the Yishuv

Within this context, relations between those sectors of the Yishuv closely identified with collective values and the organized pioneering youth movements need further analysis.

Several studies have shown[1] that considerable correlation exists between the youth movement joined by adolescents, their school, and the social status of their parents. Thus the Scouts recruited most of their members from the old

[1] The following analysis is based on S. N. Eisenstadt and J. Ben-David – *Inter-generational Tensions in Israel*. From: International Social Science Bulletin, Vol. VIII, No 1, pp. 54–75 (1956), UNESCO.

established secondary schools, whereas the members of *Mahanot Haolim* came mainly from technical high schools and the less fashionable secondary schools. There was, of course, a corresponding difference in the status of parents, although the objective status is, in fact, not always decisive. The members of *Hashomer Hatzair* seem to come from a more varied background, including both higher and lower class families and, quite often, children from broken homes. The atmosphere of this ideologically intensive movement and the thorough and efficient organization of its members' lives appear to be substitutes for a stable home life.

Even closer correlation was found between the parents' status identification and aspirations, and membership in different youth movements.

Children of families identified closely with their status tended to choose a politically neutral type of movement (such as the Scouts and Guides); or, as in the case of participation in *Mahanot Haolim*, they stressed the non-political elements of the movement's ideology, often expressly denying the importance of the political factor.

More active identification and participation in the pioneering youth movements was displayed by children from harmonious homes, but whose identification with their status was relatively passive.

These investigations give interesting results on the relation of these youth movements to the emerging social structure of the Yishuv.

It was the avowed aim of the youth movements to bring about social change through transferring urban (mainly middle-class) youth to the rural settlements. Nevertheless, the choice of movement was, to a large extent, influenced by the status, security, and aspirations of the family. Similarly, the child's role in the movement reflects the family status.

It was this comparatively harmonious co-operation between parents and children which paradoxically precluded the full realization of the movement's avowed ends. Only a small proportion of members established communal settlements – the path prescribed by the movement and strongly supported by almost all members. The actual meaning of membership, therefore, became, not education for this particular type of social and occupational change but the inculcation of idealistic socialism, which acquired its place in the central symbol system of the society. Seen from this point of view, the functions of the movement complemented those of the family.

In other words, the youth movements provided an important channel for the continuous transference of identification from the family to the wider social structure, insofar as the family identified itself with collective, pioneering values.

In this way youth culture became deeply embedded in the developing and crystallizing social structure, legitimized by, and closely connected with, collective values. The possibility that it would take on disruptive or even strongly innovative characteristics and oppose the values of the adult world has, thus, not materialized. Although psychological tensions between children and parents may arise, the degree of structural incompatibility between the family, the total social structure and the youth movement is minimized.

Youth Movements and the Social Structure – Summary

We now see that not only more informal youth culture but even the more radical youth movements were gradually woven into the social structure of the different groups and strata in the Yishuv. It is possible that the extent to which these movements really effected social and occupational change was much greater in the late twenties and early thirties. But with the gradual crystallization of the Yishuv's social structure, their ideology and emphasis on change became in many ways a mechanism of social and cultural selection and of the articulation of common values, rather than of continuous social change and innovation.

These functions of the youth movements were performed in ways very closely related to the more general process of selective institutionalization of the ideology analysed above. They gradually developed a certain style of life, evident in fashions (the simple khaki dress, the open shirts), in the great emphasis placed on tours and explorations of the land, in spending some time doing manual agricultural work, and in songs and festivals. All of these quickly spread throughout the Yishuv. Similarly, the youth leaders and instructors quickly became important figures in Israeli culture.

In addition, the youth movements also performed important functions of general socialization and social selection. Within the general content of family–school–youth, they constituted a very important – if not *the* most important – avenue of identification with some of the major collective pioneering symbols of the society. By virtue of these functions, the movements succeeded in mobilizing their members for various national tasks, such as defence or seasonal help in the kibbutzim.

They also served as channels of social mobility for some strata of the population, as meeting points between different sectors, and as important agencies for the absorption of immigrants.

They served, morever, as selection agencies for some of the élite positions, and, in this way, contributed to the perpetuation of the élite status of the pioneering values and their bearers.

Here also the special position of *Aliyat Hanoar*, the Youth Aliya, is of great interest. Youth Aliya was founded in 1934 to facilitate the immigration of children without parents from Germany and Central Europe. Most Youth Aliya groups were educated in agricultural settlements, with a view to permanent settlement there. Although most of them did not settle permanently in the agricultural settlements, the sociological importance of Youth Aliya cannot be overestimated. For the younger immigrants it provided the framework for strong pioneering tendencies and afforded an institutionalized setting in which the basic pattern of pioneering motivation was recreated. At the same time, it also provided a channel of absorption, through which young immigrants were given equal opportunities to take part in existing informal and semi-formal groups. Youth Aliya constituted a distinctive mechanism through which the selective institutionalization of the pioneering ideology was effected, in ways not dissimilar from those of the youth movements and the high schools. It also served as a channel of selection to higher occupational echelons.

In the later stages of the Yishuv, especially during the war when the influx of immigrants receded, *Aliyat Hanoar* also started some activities among lower-class, underprivileged urban youth.

Changes in the Teacher's Role

The teacher's role was greatly affected by these developments and changed from that of cultural creator to technical transmitter of knowledge, skill, and tradition. This process of change began in the early twenties and gathered momentum in the thirties.

Though many possibilities for creative work remained, especially on pedagogical aspects, this change implied a weakening of the teacher's élite status.

Moreover, due to the faults in the financial situation of the educational system, monetary problems (salaries, endowments, social security rights, etc.) became predominant, and in the late thirties and forties teachers were among the most strike-prone groups in the Yishuv.

The altered role of the teacher, and the lowering of his status, were connected with the emergence of new types of educators who became the bearers of more dynamic, social-educational roles. One was the youth movement instructor – the *madrich* – who often came from a kibbutz and symbolized educational pioneering ideology. The other was the *madrich* of the Youth Aliya groups – also often a kibbutz member.

The Development of Adult Education

It is important to mention here the development of a vast network of adult-education activities in the Yishuv. While many of these activities were limited to practical objectives such as learning the Hebrew language or technical subjects, the general impetus to adult education was the basic ideological orientation which emphasized its importance in the process of cultural creativity, but, at the same time tended to belittle formal education.

Organizationally the first nuclei of adult education were set within the framework of the Histadrut, which even in the early twenties engulfed existing activities and initiated new ones. Starting in the thirties, the Hebrew University undertook a continuously growing programme of activities.

The aim of these educational programmes was not so much attainment a degree or diploma, as raising the general level of culture and increasing knowledge of the land, its history and geography. Ideological roots were drawn from the popular education movements in Europe, and from the strong emphasis on the importance of the general spread of knowledge, stressing the potential cultural creativity of all groups. Lectures were given in remote settlements, as well as in specially-created educational centres. Study groups were formed in each neighbourhood and settlement, and local libraries were founded.

The Development of Higher Education

At the same time as primary and secondary schools and the various adult education activities developed in response to the actual needs of the growing population, there emerged also the institutions of higher learning – the Hebrew University and, to a lesser extent, the Israel Institute of Technology (Technion). The Technion was founded in 1912 but full-scale teaching only began in 1924. In its initial phases the Technion did not develop much beyond the scope of a technical school, geared to the concrete needs of the Yishuv. As these were relatively few, and catered for by skilled immigrants, the Technion did not prosper or attract many of the younger local generation who often went abroad to study.

The development of the University was different. Established in 1925, it was, at first, mainly a research institute, with teaching as a secondary role. Only growing demands led to the development of a teaching programme and the establishment of regular faculties.

It was the original aim of the University to serve not only the needs of the Yishuv, but also the more general needs of a Jewish cultural renaissance.

The emphasis on research and relative lack of emphasis on the practical needs of the Yishuv, reinforced each other in maintaining relations with the Jewish communities abroad and encouraged the segregation of the University from the more organized Yishuv. Although the establishment of the University was deeply rooted in the Zionist ideology and the University was seen as the cultural apex of this creativity, it never became part of any social or political movement or groups within the Yishuv. In this way it maintained its autonomy to uphold universalistic criteria of achievement and to escape the politicization of the educational system.

Moreover, while many members of the University staff participated in the political parties as individuals, others served on the independent centres of public opinion. The University also provided a meeting point for people from entirely different movements and political sectors of the Yishuv who jointly served on its Boards.

Only gradually did the initial University nucleus expand, and in 1935 a Department of Education was established which aimed at the training of secondary school teachers, thus responding to a growing need in the Yishuv. Similarly, an Institute of Agriculture was set up in Rehovot to ensure the agricultural development of the Yishuv through scientific activities and research. Gradually some of the science departments became connected with the developing industry and undertook some industrial research. By 1939-40 the number of Israeli students had grown to about one thousand.

The University always served as a formal apex of the educational system, in as far as it supervised the standards of the secondary schools, and recognized matriculation as a condition of entry, thus giving it wider, international status. These functions became even more important with the growth of the second generation in the Yishuv.

The Educational System in the Yishuv – Summary

By the end of the period of the Yishuv, the educational system had developed a variegated complex in which different and often contradictory trends and orientations were closely interwoven. Its primary impetus was rooted in the initial ideological orientations to social and cultural change and creativity, but this impetus changed and modified with the growth of the Yishuv and its needs for educational services. These needs facilitated the development of educational creativity in secondary and higher education, and in the kibbutzim and *Aliyat Hanoar*, but at the same time, they minimized the extent to which the basic primary educational system could continue to be an instrument of social change and cultural creativity.

Some of the impulses to cultural creativity crystallized in the secondary schools, in the kibbutzim, and in some of the institutions of adult education, while the more ideological orientation to change crystallized in the youth movements and the various institutions of adult education and aimed at undermining the connexion between educational and occupational standing, at the same time maintaining the élitist conception of general education.

The combined impact of the continuous normalization of the educational structure and the growth of different political sectors in the Yishuv gave rise to a growing politicization of primary education, to stagnation in ideological and pedagogical creativity, and to the development of several contradictory orientations in the educational system.

The educational structure tended to emphasize collective-ascriptive criteria of activities and motivation and to minimize the importance of occupational motivations. This was, of course, very much in line with the élitist conception inherent in the image of the pioneer, but at the same time, it created important problems in various institutional spheres.

2

EDUCATION IN THE STATE OF ISRAEL

Development of Education in the State of Israel

The establishment of the State of Israel profoundly affected the nature and development of the educational as of all other institutions. The first important manifestation of change was the expansion and administrative unification of the educational system on the one hand, and a growing functional differentiation on the other.

The State Education Law was passed by the Knesset (Parliament) in the summer of 1953, thus abolishing the previous multi-trend educational system.

The promulgation of this law implied wide reorganization of the existing system, with dismissals and appointments of teachers and principals, and a general technical and administrative overhauling. The country was divided into six districts, each headed by a District Inspector with a number of Deputy Inspectors working under him. But even within the new organization the division between non-religious and religious state schools remained. The National Religious Party supervises the latter system which, in effect, constitutes a continuation of the 'trend' system. In accordance with the Compulsory Education Law, every child from the age of five to the age of fourteen is obliged to attend school.

Secondary education is not compulsory. These schools are mainly semi-private, supported by various public agencies, local authorities, and, to some extent, by the state.[1]

The secondary school system consists of the following:

(1) Secondary academic schools.
(2) Secondary evening schools.
(3) Secondary agricultural schools.
(4) Vocational schools.
(5) Continuation classes in collective settlements.
(6) Two-year secondary courses for children in remote settlements.

Only the first two types and some of the vocational schools lead to the matriculation examination, which is held after four years of study from the ages of fourteen to seventeen inclusive. These examinations are set by the Ministry of Education and enable successful graduates to enter any institution

---

[1] There are many schools in which the strict division between elementary and secondary is not maintained internally – but officially this is the major dividing line.

of higher learning. A special agricultural matriculation for enrolment in the Faculty of Agriculture of the Hebrew University has recently been instituted.

The evening schools often prepare their students for the 'external matriculation', i.e. a matriculation which is not taken within the school (and where the marks given in the school are not taken into account), but which is entirely under the auspices of the Ministry of Education.

On the whole, the strongly centralized educational system deals with all problems pertaining to the curriculum as well as the employment of teachers, while problems of finance and administration are dealt with in conjunction with the local authorities.

The only schools not fully incorporated into this framework are those of *Agudat Israel*, the extremely religious sector, which has its own curriculum with very minimal – and rather negligent – supervision from the 'outside'. It has its own teachers and teachers' training institutions which are only partly supported by the state.

The following tables show the development of the educational system in Israel:

TABLE 36

Indices of Pupils in the Educational Institutions
according to Type of Institution (1949–64)

Type of institution	1949–50	1954–5	1959–60	1964–5
All the pupils[a]	100	202	307	376
The entire education system[b]	100	203	303	363
Higher education	100	215	338	550
Other institutions	100	140	407	667
Total Hebrew education	100	207	318	383
Educational system (compulsory)	100	207	310	364
Kindergartens	100	167	232	253
Elementary schools	100	218	333	370
Special schools	100	254	470	716
Schools for working youth	100	267	240	104
Secondary schools	100	160·5	273	517
Evening high schools[c]	—	167	263	192
Continuation classes	100	389	605	829
Vocational schools	100	161	272	687
Agricultural schools	100	225	209	320
Normal school for teachers and kindergarten teachers	100	155	279	—
Other post-primary schools	—	—	100	97
Other institutions[d]	—	—	117	145
Total Arab education	100	156	222	317
Educational system (compulsory)	100	162	226	355
Kindergartens	100	1,353	3,783	5,790
Elementary schools	100	148	199	298
Special schools[e]	—	—	—	111
Schools for working youth[f]	—	—	42	53
Secondary schools[g]	—	467	637	924
Continuous classes	100	156	—	—
Vocational schools	—	—	—	127
Agricultural schools	—	—	100	282
Normal schools for teachers and kindergarten teachers[h]	—	—	288	280
Other post-primary schools	—	—	100	94
Other institutions	100	140	185	212

Calculated according to:
　1 CBS *Statistical Abstract of Israel*, 9, 1957–8, p. 325, Table 6.
　2 CBS op. cit., 14, 1963, p. 634, Table 7.
　3 CBS op. cit., 16, 1965, p. 575, Table D/20.
　[a] Includes all the pupils in all the educational institutions, Hebrew and Arab, and also higher education.
　[b] Includes Hebrew and Arab primary and post-primary education with the exception of higher education and other educational institutions.
　[c] 1951–2 = 100.　　　　　[f] 1951–2 = 100.
　[d] 1959–60 = 100.　　　　[g] 1963–4 = 100.
　[e] 1963–4 = 100　　　　　[h] 1956–7 = 100.

Thus we see that the number of pupils in the educational system increased from 140,817 in 1948–9 to 711,274 in 1964–5 – almost fivefold. The number of pupils in the post-primary education in the same years increased almost tenfold (9·6) (from 10,218 to 97,937).

In this period the number of primary school teachers increased fivefold (5·3) (from 6,469 to 34,340), and in the post–primary more than ninefold (from 941 to 8,847).

The number of primary-school institutions increased three-and-a-half fold and the post primary five-and-a-half fold (5·4). The greatest rate of increase of students was in the higher education, having increased elevenfold (from 1,635 to 18,363).

Developments in Religious Education

As we have seen, the religious groups maintained a high degree of separateness in their educational system, but, at the same time, interesting innovations have taken place within this sphere. Perhaps the most interesting of these was the adjustment of the yeshivot or orthodox religious educational institutions to the demands of the new situation. These schools were formerly (and some of them still are) solely dedicated to all-day study of Jewish traditional writings, Talmud, etc. Recently, however, a combination of modern secondary education and the traditional course of study emerged in the secondary-school yeshivot which are run as boarding schools. Most of them now prepare their students for matriculation, though some do it in five instead of the usual four years.

Similarly, the vocational yeshivot and the agricultural yeshivot now combine the traditional studies with the learning of a vocation.

The number of pupils in state religious primary schools increased from about 56,000 in 1953–4 to 115,000 in 1964–5. In 1964–5 they constituted twenty-eight per cent of all the primary education, in comparison to 18·5 per cent in 1952–3 (see Table 37).

In the independent educational system (of *Agudat Israel*) the number of pupils increased from 15,438 in 1953–4 to 27,907 in 1954–5.

In the post-primary schools the State religious education decreased from 18 per cent in 1962–3 to 16·7 per cent in 1964–5.

The post-primary independent education increased from 1,137 pupils in 1959–60 to 3,000 in 1964–5. (See in detail Table 37.) The total number of students is divided as follows: secondary yeshivot 12,198 students; vocational yeshivot 1,900 students; and agricultural yeshivot 1,657 students.

All these data indicate the tendency of many extreme, especially non-Zionist religious groups, to find their own way of coping with the problems of modern society. Sometimes this may be combined with attempts to assure for themselves more influence and autonomy but more often it seems that this indicates a trend of segregating themselves from it.

250

TABLE 37

The Development of State Religious Education in Israel in the Years 1952–3 to 1964–5

(The Number of Students and Percentages – Hebrew Education)

Year	1952–3 No. of Students	%[a]	1953–4 No. of Students	%[a]	1962–3 No. of Students	%[a]	1964–5 No. of Students	%[a]
Primary Schools[b]	40,601	18·5	56,372	22·4	111,734	28·2	115,544	28·0
Post-Primary Education Total[c]	4,391	16·0	5,645	15·0	15,138	18·0	19,005	16·7
Municipal High Schools (including Yeshivot)	2,704	16·0	3,941	16·5	11,281	19·0	13,880	21·9
Vocational Schools	283	6·7	300	5·8	1,900	15·0	3,145	12·2
Agricultural Schools	1,404	27·2	1,404	45·3	1,675	17·0	2,000	26·0

[a] Percentage of the total number of students in Israel in the appropriate school.
[b] The part played by the 'Independent' (*Agudat Israel*) Stream in the primary education system was 7·5 per cent in 1953–4 and 6·9 per cent in 1964–5.
[c] This does not include grade 13 and beyond in the normal schools.
Calculated according to:
1 Elementary Education, Y. Kil, 'Ten Years of State Religious Education', in *Year by Year*, Heichal Shlomo, 1964, pp. 341–2, and CBS op. cit., 16, 1965, p. 582, Table T/11.
2 Post-Primary Education Y. Kil, op. cit., and A. Yehudah 'The Religious Post-Primary Education, in *Year by Year*, Heichal Shlomo, 1965, pp. 414–29; CBS op. cit., 16, 1965, Table T/10, p. 581.

Extracurricular Activities – Recreation, Special Education, Adult Education, and Education in the Army

Side by side with the schools, a mass of extracurricular activities developed including recreational and special educational organizations and those dealing with problem (especially retarded and disturbed) children.

Great expansion and change also took place in the field of adult education, largely because of the new immigrants. Organizations and activities to cope with these problems were developed by the government, the Jewish Agency, the Histadrut, and various other institutions, such as the local authorities and *Malben*.

Of special importance here were language and vocational courses. Among the schools which concentrated on language teaching the most outstanding are the *ulpanim* (a school for adults in which the Hebrew language is taught very intensively) which are of several kinds: One is the Boarding-Ulpan which lasts five months, with classes five hours a day. A second type is the Work-Ulpan, organized in various kibbutzim, which is planned for younger people. Here students work four hours a day and study the rest of the time. A third type is the Day-Ulpan, where students come for the day only and study thirty hours a week. Still other types are the Popular-Ulpan, where the classes are held in the morning or evening, and which is usually maintained by the local authorities; the Ulpanit or small Ulpan, where studies take place from four to eight hours a week, planned especially for people who cannot get away from their daily activities.

In addition there are different types of less intensive courses such as 'Learning a Month', for people who are extremely backward. In these cases the teacher visits a home where a number of adults meet.

In 1965 there were 16,249 students in the Hebrew language courses (including ulpanim), 5,185 students in adult institutions in 1963–4 and 10,827 students in the vocational courses. The main development was in the rural and new urban centres.

Within this context the educational activities of the Army should be given special attention. Many enlisted men are inducted into the army very shortly after their arrival in Israel, a fact which posed several educational and cultural problems, and called for the organization of considerable educational activities for the recruits. The Army Department of Education organizes courses ranging from the study of the Hebrew language and basic arithmetic to geography, history and more general subjects of cultural and educational importance, in an effort to raise the educational level to that of the general cultural atmosphere of Israel.

The Army also gives great help to discharged personnel, training them in various mechanical skills and performing functions of vocational guidance.

Between 1948–63, 43,000 students attended the Hebrew and basic educational courses in the Army.

Changes in Adult and Kibbutz Education

The general field of adult education not specifically connected with problems of new immigrants has also greatly expanded since the establishment of the state, and has shown some marked changes and shifts of emphasis. The greatest increase was in courses leading to direct results, either in terms of the language, specialized skills or the obtaining of some degree, although many general 'informational' and recreational activities also expanded.

However, adult education with the ideal of learning for its own sake weakened somewhat, a trend which also influenced the internal educational system of the kibbutz, where the demand for official matriculation caused serious controversy. While the kibbutzim were always interested in giving their members 'as high a level of education as possible', their intrinsic ideology has been that there is no need for external recognition or acknowledgement of such education, as the children stay in the kibbutz in natural succession to their elders. The demand for matriculation is therefore seen as an indication of other possibilities, and this is by no means acceptable to the kibbutz. On the other hand, withholding achievement from its talented children, and the realization that some of them have – even from the point of view of the kibbutz – to continue to higher education, has placed many kibbutzim in a dilemma.

No uniform solution to this problem has, as yet, been found. Some kibbutzim permit external matriculation examination, some hold them in the fourth grade of secondary school (or, as they call it, at the end of the twelfth class), some still stop formal education after ten classes (two secondary) but give an informal opportunity to able pupils to study further.

During the same period the activities of *Aliyat Hanoar* have also greatly expanded. The number of pupils in the Youth Aliya was 9,736 in 1965 (the total number from 1950–62 was 31,623).

In comparison with the early years of the state more than fifty per cent are in educational institutions not in rural settlements. The rate of pupils from Asia and Africa increased till 1957 (67 per cent); from 1957 there took place an increase in the rate of pupils from Europe and America (41 per cent in 1962) and Israel.

Pioneering Education – Army Youth Formation

Side by side with these developments, important changes took place in pioneering-educational activities.

Political youth movements were banned from schools and only partially reinstated in 1961, and various state-sponsored youth organizations devoted to the implementation of pioneering goals were developed. One such organization is *Nahal* (Pioneer-Fighting Units), which was founded a few years after the establishment of the state.[1]

Another is the *Gadna* (Army Youth Corps), an army-sponsored paramilitary organization for youth between the ages of fourteen and eighteen. Its aim is to train and prepare youngsters for national service and imbue them with concepts of responsible citizenship. In 1964 there were in the *Gadna* 61,200 children between the ages of fourteen and eighteen.

Developments in Higher Education

The sphere of higher education has also greatly expanded and changed. Institutions of higher learning which, till the establishment of the state were

[1] Every Israeli recruit has the possibility of joining a so-called *garin* (nucleus) of a youth movement, which enlists en bloc in this special formation of the army, the *Nahal* or Pioneer-Fighting-Youth. This formation combines military training with agricultural work, especially in collective settlements. Its underlying aim is in a way a continuation of the older ideology of the pioneering youth movements – i.e. that after national service this nucleus should found new settlements. Usually this aim is not fully attained. Many, if not most, of the groups tend to dissolve after service and only a very small part of the original nuclei joins an already existing settlement. However, there are instances of these nuclei having founded new settlements.

not primarily geared to the needs of the Yishuv, soon transferred and faced the problem of combining research with educational and professional needs.

While, in 1950–1, there were 1,250 first-year students in the institutions of higher learning, there were 3,022 in 1958–9. In 1948–9 there were 405 first-year students, while in 1964–5 there were 6,055 such students, the increase being thus fifteenfold.

From Table 38 we see that the total number of students in the institutions of higher learning increased elevenfold in sixteen years (from 1,635 in 1948–9 to 18,368 in 1964–5). The rate of the students in the total population (per 10,000) increased from twenty-one in 1950–1 to eighty-eight in 1964–5, while the rate of the graduates per population (per 10,000) in this period increased from two to eleven.

The following table shows us the enrolment in the available institutions.

TABLE 38

Students and Graduates of the Institutions of Higher Learning

(Absolute Numbers and Rates per 10,000 Persons in the Population from 1950–1 to 1964–5)

Students	1950–1	1955–6	1961–2	1964–5
Total Number of Students in Institutions of Higher Learning	2,892	587	11,814	18,368
Rate of Students per 10,000 persons in the population	21	37	52	88
Graduates in the Institutions for Higher Learning (BA, BSc, MA, MSc, Ph.D, MD)	313	946	1,844	2,491
Rate of Graduates per 10,000 persons in the population	2	5	8	11

1 CBS, op. cit., 14, 1963, Tables 25–31, pp. 648–53 (1950–1 to 1960–1).
2 CBS, op. cit., 16, 1965, Table T/25, p. 593.

The proportion of holders of the matriculation certificate (including externs) amongst those enrolling for advanced studies, is known only with regard to the Hebrew University and the Technion. In 1951 only fifty-seven per cent of new students accepted by the University had received Israeli secondary education. Since then, this percentage among university students (including those in the later years of study) increased – varying between sixty-five and seventy-five per cent in the years 1951–6. In the Technion it was found that the percentage of Israeli secondary school graduates among new students was around seventy per cent.

This numerical expansion brought with it the growth and diversification of faculties and subjects.

Among the main developments at the Hebrew University during the years 1949–59 was the establishment of a Law Faculty (formerly law classes were given by the mandatory government), a complete Medical Faculty and, in conjunction with it, a School of Dentistry and of Pharmacy. Two additional new faculties were those of Agriculture and the Social Sciences.

In addition, Departments for Public Administration and Business Administration were established, as was a School of Social Work and a Graduate School of Librarianship.

These new professional departments produced graduates necessarily more orientated to the needs of the country, while the new programme of general higher education, in the form of BA courses, took the place of the outright academic specialization predominant before.

These developments were closely related to the growing demands for trained manpower and to the increasing tendencies to academic professions and occupations.

In all these ways the institutions of higher learning became closely interwoven with the demands of the country, as can be seen in the growing number of Israeli-born-and-educated students.

The Technion, on its side, expanded from a technical school to a full-fledged academic institution providing adequate professional technical manpower for the country's needs.

The Weizmann Institute of Science developed as an important centre of research in the natural sciences. There are ten departments and five sections[1] in the Institute which was formally dedicated in 1949.

The great demand for education, coupled with the pressure of local political forces, also gave rise to further new institutions of higher learning, such as the Tel Aviv University, established under the aegis of the Tel Aviv Municipality, and the Bar-Ilan Religious University in Ramat Gan, founded under the auspices of the religious groups, especially that of the National Religious Party.

The Academic Staff of the institutions of higher learning comprised in 1948–9, 293 members and in 1964–5, 2,504, thus increasing ninefold as compared with an elevenfold increase in the number of students.

[1] The departments are: Applied Mathematics, Nuclear Physics, Nuclear Induction, Electronics, X-Ray Crystallography, Isotope Research, Polymer Research, Biophysics, Organic Chemistry, and Experimental Biology. The sections are: Photochemistry and Spectroscopy, Infra-red Spectroscopy, Biochemistry, Virology and Genetics, and Plant Genetics.

The staff comprises about 650, including 222 scientists, research students, and Visiting Fellows and others working temporarily on grants, special projects, or fellowships. The permanent academic staff consists of (by rank) 14 Professors, 10 Associate Professors, 36 Senior Scientists, 43 Research Associates, and 34 Research Assistants.

Source: *Israel Government Yearbook* 1960–1, p. 168.

Changes in Family and Youth Cultures

Developments in the scope and organization of Israeli education went hand-in-hand with changes in the sphere of family and youth, which occurred among both older settlers and new immigrants. Although the changes in the two scetors were sociologically parallel, they tended to widen the differences between population groups through integrating education into the social structure.

In the older sectors a general weakening of pioneering youth movements and ideologies occurred, in favour of more formal activities and organizations.

Although exact information is not available, the general impression indicates a decline of active participation in such movements – even if not in their actual numbers – and especially of identification with their pioneering ideals. The following Table indicates some of these trends (see Table 39).

Thus we see that the rate of members in youth movements within the population age group between ten and nineteen was in 1947–8, 47 per cent. In 1949–50 it decreased to 28 per cent and from 1957 there seems to be a trend to increase.

In 1963–4 the rate was, according to official data, 37 per cent (see Table 39).

TABLE 39

Youth Organized in Youth Movements

	Year	No. of organized youth (approx.) (1)	General number of youth between 10–19 (approx.) (2)	Youth organized (percentage) (3)
1	1947–8	37,500	80,000	47
2	1949–50	52,500	148,000	28
3	1955–6	67,300	295,000	23
4	1960–1	129,500	406,000	32
5	1963–4	191,982	525,000	37

Sources:
Rows 1, 2, and Row 3 Col. 1:
H. Barzel, *The Youth Movement – History in Israel and among the Nations*, Jerusalem, 1963, p. 103 (Hebrew).
Row 3 Col. 2:
CBS, op. cit., No. 9, 1956–7, Tables 11–12, p. 12.
Rows 4, 5 Col. 1:
According to the Deputy Minister of Education: A. Yadlin, *Davar*, 23 July 1964.
Row 4 Col. 2:
CBS, op. cit., No. 12, 1961, Table 11, p. 39.
Row 5 Col. 2:
CBS, op. cit., No. 15, 1964, Table B/12, p. 28.

Although officially the movements themselves still clung to the ideals of pioneering, they, in fact, lost much in importance for most members and even instructors, and purely social activities gained prominence.

Moreover, many collective tasks gave way to more 'philanthropic' activities – such as aid to new immigrant children and to kibbutzim.

Side by side with these changes in the youth movements, numerous informal youth groups became increasingly prevalent among the veteran sectors of the Yishuv; and the difference between the pioneering youth movements and more informal youth culture became somewhat blurred, although at its extremes – in the more ideological, sectarian youth movements on the one hand, and in the groups of 'Teddy boys' or 'gilded youth' on the other – the differences were yet very marked.

Changes in the Youth Movements – Participation and Aspirations

These changes can be seen in the patterns of participation in youth movements and of aspirations of their members. Although no full-scale research has been undertaken, partial investigations point unequivocally to the following conclusions.

A survey of 600 youths from one particular movement showed[1] that the majority of members of this, officially pioneering youth movement, came from homes where the parents identified with Histadrut or Mapai and generally favoured the movement, a fact which increased the children's own social identification with it.

The main attractions of the movement were its intellectual, social, and sporting activities. Little emphasis was placed on ideological or 'movement' commitments, which were expressed in a somewhat vague 'kibbutz-orientation', often coupled with aspirations to professional and academic occupations. Most members were aware of the fact that their parents would prefer a more definite occupational future for them. Forty-six per cent of the subjects believed that their parents expected them to enter an urban academic profession, 21·4 per cent thought that their parents did not care, 14·5 per cent felt that their parents would like them to be skilled urban workers, 16·2 per cent did not know, or mentioned 'some other profession', and only 1·7 per cent thought that their parents expected them to join a kibbutz. As, on the whole, there is little evidence of overall disagreement or tension between parents and children, these findings would appear to be significant.

The emphasis on 'academic' occupations appeared further reinforced by the positive relations between school and movement. Scholastic success increased the member's 'academic' orientation and satisfaction with the movement, and detracted from his self-image as a future kibbutz member.

[1] See M. Lotan, *Values and Attitudes among Youth Movements*, (Hebrew) Berl Katzenelson Institute, 1964.

Rebellious or change-orientated attitudes were expressed by many members in a general feeling that 'things' should be improved and that the movement should perhaps do something about it. However, such feelings were usually related to a low evaluation of the movement and held little expectation of action.

While these data are only very partial and preliminary, they do indicate the growing consolidation of the youth movements within the style of living of the different social strata and show the growing emphasis on social and educational activities as well as on professional and academic occupations.

Changes in the Functions of Youth Movements

Whatever their exact membership, many of the youth movements' functions considerably changed or weakened. They no longer constitute the main mechanisms of élite-selection or orientation towards the major collective values of society.

If, formerly, the youth movements constituted the focus of youth culture, this focus has now shifted to the family and to the schools. Extracurricular activities and the pre-military services which serve as important channels of identification with collective values also play their part in this change.

This has led to an even greater integration of the youth movements in the patterns of social organization and orientation of different groups and strata and to the weakening not only of their role as agents of social change but even of that as channels of orientation to the common values of the society, and consequently to a blurring of the earlier sharp differences between movement youth and the less organized and less ideologically orientated type of youth culture.

At the same time, the possibility of *personal* and social tensions between parents and children because of the children's non-acceptance of many of the parents' placid ideology or conservatism was perhaps more acute. But these tensions tended to be more personal than ideological.

It was possibly the transformation of the inter-generational relations among the older sector that explains the slight manifestations of 'Teddy Boys' among what have been called *Bnei-Tovim*, i.e. sons of good families.

This phenomenon first appeared in the form of small groups of juvenile delinquents from higher middle class families with a 'cultural' and 'ideological' background. Since then this phenomenon has reappeared several times, with high school students engaged in anti-social activities 'just for kicks'. They were found mostly in Tel Aviv, and in a few economically well-established smaller towns, spreading later also to other socially lower groups which at the same time were thriving in conditions of full employment.

Youth Culture Among New Immigrants

Structurally parallel developments took place among various groups of new immigrants, where new forms of youth culture developed, equally embedded in the styles of life of the parents, and consisting mainly of semi-organized and informal youth groups or clubs on the one hand, and of membership in the older type of youth movements on the other. Although these youth cultures were greatly influenced by formal education and extracurricular educational activities, their impact was largely absorbed by the different immigrant groups according to their specific ethnic or ecological patterns.

A basic part of the youth culture of different immigrant groups was their strong orientation towards occupational and economic adjustment and advancement in the absorbing society, and the extent of success in this field greatly influenced the nature and scope of their activities and organizations.

The place of the youth movements (and especially of *Tnuah Hameuhedet* and *Hanoar Haoved* – or as they are called today 'The General Federation of Working and Learning Youth', and of the religious youth movement *Bnei Akiva*) among immigrant groups is of special interest here. Although exact data is not available, there are many indications that these movements tended to draw many members from the immigrant groups. Possibly they were more popular there than with the more established section of the population. They appear to attract the more élite elements among the immigrants, especially children who are successful in the upper classes of the elementary and high schools and whose families are relatively mobile. In such cases the youth movements serve either as channels of mobility for the children or as confirmation of their newly achieved status. Here too, the emphasis on the pioneering ideology seems to be very small, and the movements serve to channel the activities and orientations of their members within their social strata.

These developments necessarily changed the nature of the various youth movements which turned more and more into youth clubs, organized by different adult-sponsored agencies, and thus becoming part of the wider scheme of extracurricular activities.

Development of Juvenile Delinquency

Within this context the problems of juvenile delinquency occupy a central position in the framework of educational problems. From being a problem relating mostly to 'marginal' groups, it has become a much more general one. In 1957 the rate of juvenile delinquents per 1,000 in the population of relevant age was 6·5. In 1959 it was 8·5 and in 1962, 10·5.

In 1962 the rate of Jewish juvenile delinquents per 1,000 born in Israel was 6·4, in comparison to 6·7 among those born in Europe, 13·5 born in Asia; and 18·9 in Africa.[1]

[1] CBS: Statistical Abstract of Israel No. 16, 1965, Table V/6, p. 624.

Delinquency is closely related to vagrancy and the early school-leaving which seems to be concentrated in the higher classes of elementary schools and, especially, in new immigrant schools both in the villages and cities, and among children from an oriental background.

Conditions of Absorption and Patterns of Youth Culture

Conditions of absorption in the emerging social structure are apparent in the varied degree of youth culture among groups generally, and in the development of delinquent youth groups in particular. Although these conditions are most apparent among the immigrant groups, their influence is similar among the older groups.

Developments emphasize the close relation between different types of youth culture and the life-style and occupations of different groups and strata. Studies of this problem indicate that the extent and scope of immigrant youth culture was greatly influenced by incongruities between conceptions of social status of immigrant parents and their actual position in Israel. Such incongruities tended to develop where the parents had rigid conceptions of their own status, which were mainly influenced by their old social and cultural setting. In such cases occupational change meant loss of status and, correspondingly, new demands on the children – whether in schooling, leisure-time activities, etc. – were met with hostility. A further factor in the changing youth cultures were the conflicts of authority between the traditional (older) and the new setting and the consequent undermining of parental authority. In such cases the children's ability to perform new social roles and achieve full status within the new environment, was jeopardized by old authority norms forced on them, and the ensuing conflict predisposed the youths towards the formation of delinquent groups.

Next, the extent of family solidarity in face of the hardship of immigration plays its part. This was generally found to be the most important internal factor determining the extent of continuous or delinquent group formation. Insofar as great internal solidarity existed, the family could absorb the many shocks and changes, as well as the new kinds of behaviour among young people. If emotional ties within the family and its internal solidarity could withstand these changes, few delinquent activities developed.

In other words, the predisposition towards delinquency is minimized where parents and children and adolescents can find new, permanent, and recognized social roles and can participate in their new setting.

Lastly, the discrepancy between the parents' aspirations and the possibility of their realization is of importance. This applies mainly to those immigrants or groups from the older population who were initially more predisposed to change their social roles and aspirations but did not succeed in realizing these changes in the new social setting. In this context, cultural differences become of greater dynamic importance, since the lack of skills and knowledge necessary for the performance of these new roles may seriously impede their realization.

These varied social conditions could be found among all the strata of the population although they were necessarily more visible among some of the new immigrant groups. With the growing integration of these groups their special visibility became lessened and the various more extreme manifestations of youth culture, such as the various types of 'Teddy Boys', could be found among old and new, and among most of the social strata alike – among all of which the different conditions of absorption or integration analysed above could be found.

3

NEW PROBLEMS AND RESPONSES

Overall Changes in the Social Function of Education

The combined effect of the developments and changes described was the growing integration of the educational system into the existing social structure and the minimization of its functions in social change, creativity, and innovation.

The different juvenile subcultures which developed among different social strata, the schools, youth organizations and activities, all became more closely related to the pattern of social life and minimized the culturally and socially innovating function of the educational system.

Similarly, the shift in the functions of the educational system weakened its role as bearer of social change and innovation. Instead, it became a channel of occupational and social selectivity, a transmitter of the existing social and cultural heritage to new generations, and a channel of absorption for new immigrants.

The impact of the educational system on the new immigrants was twofold: It served to unify the different groups of immigrants, performing important functions of educational and social change. It encompassed most groups and brought them, within a very short time, into the orbit of a common culture and society.

On the other hand the system absorbed new immigrants into the existing social and economic structure and no longer served as a mechanism through which social and cultural frameworks were created by immigrants and old-timers. This greatly enhanced the function of the educational system as a channel of social selectivity.

The reasons for these changes in the educational system are easily seen.

261

Their roots were, to some extent, in the pre-state period, but they matured with the establishment of the state. One reason was the growth in differentiation of the social and economic structure of the Yishuv and its development and crystallization into a full-fledged society. A second one was the growing need for skilled manpower, and a third, the great influx of new immigrants, especially from oriental countries.

As a result of these factors, the actual (as distinct from the official-ideological) demands of society on the younger generation – as well as the opportunities opened up to them – were mainly in the direction of growing occupational mobility and advancement: the adjustment of the new generation to the developing structure.

These changes in the organization, orientation, and functioning of the educational system, gave rise to many new problems in all major fields of educational activity.

Cultural, Ideological, and Pedagogical Problems: Crystallization of Traditions

The establishment of the state and the need to absorb new immigrants greatly emphasized the cultural heritage into which they would be received and the extent of its crystallization, flexibility, and accessibility.

The educational system was faced with the fact that the pioneering ideology had lost much of its vividness and drawing power for the new Israeli generation, that it could not be upheld by the teachers, did not appeal to the new immigrants, and did not provide enough common bonds between the old and the new parts of the population.

At the same time the often contradictory pressures on the institutional frameworks also diversified resulting, on the economic side, in a great variety of occupational needs and in the necessity of drawing on existing as well as on incoming manpower for these tasks. But this complexity goes beyond purely economic or occupational problems – the basic human and social conceptions and the images underlying the educational process also became more ambiguous and varied.

The first dilemma, arising from the encounter between the existing educational system and the changing Israeli reality, was the choice of élitist or more democratic and even populist education for all. Though both conceptions are rooted in the pioneer ideology, the contradictions between them have, of late, become greatly accentuated.

Closely related to this was the dilemma of differential emphasis on either religious, ethnic, or movement orientations, or the more technological, occupational, or professional ones.

Lastly, although collective values in educational ideals continued to be of importance, and though the importance of civic education was widely acknowledged, conflict developed on the issue of whether or not the old pioneering orientations and organizations (such as the agricultural settlements or youth movements) constituted the best vehicles for such education.

Similar conflict arose over the school curriculum which, hitherto, conservatively stressed specific Eastern European Jewish tradition without greatly emphasizing broader literary and aesthetic criteria.

Such debates and conflicts were indicative of the lack of certainty in the ultimate aims of both primary and secondary education.

It is significant that these discussions have not yet crystallized into a clear approach, the most important achievement still being the matriculation examinations which seems to outweigh any other in the evaluation of schools – reinforcing the general trend to emphasize academic education.

Major Social and Economic Problems, Frictions, Selectivity, Drop-outs and Bottlenecks in Education

The first major problem in the educational system developed in the socioeconomic sphere. It arose from the growing interrelation between the educational, occupational, and economic systems, from the integration of the educational system into different strata patterns, and out of the system's increased importance as a mechanism of social and occupational selection and placement.

The first such problem was that of selectivity, i.e. the extent to which the educational system was open to all or only to selected parts of the population, and the extent to which such selection helped to bridge the gap between immigrants from different countries.

A second, and closely related, problem was the general efficiency of the educational system and its ability to provide adequate manpower for the growing economy.

Although, in this context, the oriental immigrant children have been and still are the most important problem of the Israeli educational system, theirs is, in fact, part of a wider problem, that of the various bottlenecks that tend to develop within this system.

Let us first present some general data. On the whole, the rate of the graduates of primary schools who continued in post-primary schools from the population age group fourteen to seventeen (Jews) has been on the increase. Thus in 1951–2 only 42·8 per cent of these continued to study,[1] while in 1964–5, 63 per cent continued in post-primary education.[2] At the present time 47·2 per cent of all the population of the age group fourteen to seventeen study in post-primary schools supervised by the Ministry of Education, 26 per cent of these continue in secondary schools; 12·4 per cent in the

---

[1] CBS: op. cit., No.14, 1963, p. 636.
[2] Z. Aran: *Bahinuch Uvatarbut* (in Education and Culture), June 1965.

vocational schools; 3·6 per cent in agricultural schools, 4·5 per cent in the continuation classes, and 6·7 per cent in part-time post-primary schools.

Let us look, first of all, at the process of educational selection. Upon conclusion of primary school studies (i.e. at the age of fourteen) a nation-wide examination is held for all children on the same day. Success in this examination entitles the student to benefit from the graded scale of tuition fees.

Only 83 per cent of the potential population of pupils reached the survey examination. Of these 33·2 per cent reached Norm A level in 1957–8, in comparison to 29 per cent in 1963–4.[1]

The rate of the pupils who reached Norm A[2] remained more or less the same (23 per cent), and the rate of the pupils who succeeded only in attaining lower marks increased from 44 per cent in 1957–8 to 48 per cent in 1963–4.

In general the selective process is severe. Thus out of a total of 18,600 primary school graduates in 1957, only 3,000 students (or 17 per cent) reached matriculation stage in 1961.[3]   Of those who had successfully passed the selective examination in 1957, 40 per cent only reached matriculation stage in 1961. These percentages are no higher than those from the period before the existence of the selective examination.

In 1964–5 only 19·4 per cent of the relevant age group in the Jewish population came up to the matriculation examinations, and only sixteen per cent of these age groups in the Jewish population had successfully passed it.[4]

The rates of success of those born in Asia and Africa were lower in comparison to the others. In 1957–8, 43 per cent of the children born in Europe and the U.S. attained Norm A; 30·4 per cent of those born in Israel and only 16·8 per cent of those born in Asia and Africa attained Norm A, but in the lowest degrees the rate of those born in Asia and Africa increased to 63 per cent.

Success in this examination originally determined which students should proceed to an academic secondary school with state-aid. Although the successful examinee may now apply for financial state-aid for all types of post-primary education, the examination still strengthens the traditionally great pressure on the academic secondary school as the main avenue to white-collar occupations. Of the IL 8,500,000 allocated under the graded tuition fee scheme in 1961–2, 64·5 per cent was channelled into academic secondary schools and only 35·5 per cent into vocational and agricultural secondary schools.

---

[1] Manpower forecast, Post Primary Education. Manpower planning authority, Labour Office, July 1965, pp. 23–30.

[2] Students who pass their examinations with grades of more than 80.

[3] The following is partially followed from H. Adler – The Role of Israel's school system in Elite Formation (mimeo.), 1964.

[4] Manpower forecast, post primary education, op. cit.

Students who fail the examination have considerable difficulties in being accepted by an academic secondary school, even if money is no obstacle, and turn mainly to either vocational or agricultural secondary schools. As a result, the existing ambivalence towards technical occupations is accentuated by the pattern of directing students of lower intellectual abilities into them.[1]

The problem of drop-outs has thus become central on the educational scene. Its specific acuteness, however, was intensified by the high percentage of drop-outs among oriental children – i.e. children of immigrant families from Asian–African countries – from the lower as well as the higher echelons of the educational system. The following tables give the basic data on this problem (Tables 40-42).

These Tables and various investigations prove that new immigrant children (mainly of oriental origin) have a higher drop-out rate:

(1) According to one of the researches in this field,[2] in 1957 students of oriental origin comprised 52 per cent of the 13–14 age group (comparable to the final year of primary school) and an average 55 per cent in the 14–17 age-group (comparable to post-primary education). However, they constituted only 32 per cent of the final primary grade, and 17 per cent of the post-primary school population.

In 1961–2 the children from oriental groups constituted 40·5 per cent of all the Jewish students of eight grades, while their proportion in the entire population was more than fifty per cent. In 1963–4 this rate increased to 45·5 per cent.

The increase is explained mostly by the increase of their proportion in the population, and partly by the success of the various new educational experiments and methods (see Tables 40–42).

In the post-primary schools the proportion of the oriental children increased from 25·9 per cent in 1963–4 to 28·3 per cent in 1964–5. The major concentration of the oriental pupils constituted 54 per cent of the students in evening classes; 75·8 per cent of the students of part-time schools; 41·2 per cent of agricultural schools; 38·6 per cent of those of vocational schools and 20 per cent of those of secondary schools. (See Tables 40–42).

(2) In academic secondary education, oriental children constituted no more than 7·8 per cent of the population of the fourth (final) grade. Thus whereas these young people comprise about one-half of the secondary school age-group, they constitute only 7·8 per cent of the candidates for the crucial matriculation certificate.

[1] This is also strengthened by the nature of the examination. The examination is of an academic character mainly of a multiple-choice type, based on the knowledge gained in the last two years of primary school.

[2] See M. Smilanski – The Social Aspect of the Educational Structure in Israel, (Hebrew) *Megamot*, Vol 8, July 1957, pp. 2–33.

TABLE 40

School Pupils, by Type of School and Place of Birth (Percentage)
(Jewish Education) (1956–7 to 1961–2)

Type of School	Born in Asia and Africa as % of born abroad			Born in Europe and America			Born in Asia and Africa			Israel born		
	1956-7	1958-9	1961-2	1956-7	1958-9	1961-2	1956-7	1958-9	1961-2	1956-7	1958-9	1961-2
ALL SCHOOLS	61·4	65·2	69·0	12·1	14·5	14·4	19·3	27·1	32·2	68·8	58·3	53·4
Primary schools[a]	68·4	64·6	68·8	8·4	14·6	14·5	17·9	26·7	32·1	73·7	58·7	53·4
Grade I	71·6	79·0	89·3	3·8	3·5	3·1	9·4	13·4	26·3	86·8	83·1	70·6
II	72·1	78·6	83·2	4·4	4·9	6·3	11·2	17·8	31·2	84·4	77·3	62·5
III	70·5	79·2	68·6	4·6	6·8	17·3	10·8	26·0	37·9	84·6	67·2	44·8
IV	74·2	74·5	58·0	4·9	10·9	24·3	14·0	32·0	33·6	81·1	57·1	42·1
V	74·6	61·4	58·8	6·2	22·6	24·0	18·2	36·0	34·3	75·6	41·4	41·7
VI	74·3	52·5	67·4	8·4	28·9	16·5	24·3	31·9	34·1	67·3	39·2	49·4
VII	68·7	53·3	70·8	13·2	27·5	12·1	28·8	31·5	29·5	58·0	41·0	58·4
VIII	54·9	61·1	66·4	24·8	19·5	12·5	30·3	30·6	24·7	44·9	49·9	62·8
Schools for handicapped children	85·7	81·5	77·5	5·7	9·9	11·5	31·8	43·6	39·7	2·59	46·5	48·8
Schools for working youth	84·8	93·7	95·2	13·4	5·7	4·4	74·1	85·4	87·9	12·5	8·9	7·7
Post-primary Schools—Total	39·7	52·3	50·3	29·9	16·2	17·0	19·8	17·7	17·1	50·3	66·1	65·9
Secondary schools	25·6	43·4	36·0	37·4	16·5	18·6	12·8	12·6	10·5	49·8	70·9	10·9
Secondary evening schools	63·1	69·2	59·0	21·0	15·1	19·4	36·1	33·9	28·0	42·9	51·0	52·6
Continuation classes	40·2	50·8	47·8	16·4	13·4	14·5	10·9	13·8	13·3	72·7	72·8	72·2
Vocational schools	41·2	56·7	51·8	30·5	16·1	16·1	21·4	21·1	17·3	48·1	62·8	66·6
Agricultural schools	51·7	64·8	77·4	27·1	20·4	12·9	29·1	37·5	44·0	43·8	42·1	43·1
Teachers' training colleges	50·5	42·4	24·6	17·0	15·7	18·8	17·3	11·6	6·1	65·7	72·7	75·1
Other post-primary schools	65·0	—	—	23·8	—	—	54·0	—	—	22·2	—	—

[a] Including primary school classes with no clearly defined degree.
Source: CBS., op. cit., 14, 1963, Table 16, p. 641.

TABLE 41

*Pupils in Primary Schools of the Hebrew Education, by Type of
School, Grade and Continent of Birth (Percentage)
(1961–2; 1963–4)*

Type of School and grade	Per 100 Foreign born Pupils				Israel born				Total
	Immi- grated since 1955	Born in Asia- Africa as % of born Abroad	Born in Europe- America	Born in Asia- Africa	Father born			Total	
					Europe- America	Asia- Africa	Israel		
1961–2									
Primary schools— Total*a*	50·0	68·4	8·4	17·9	34·6	31·9	7·2	73·7	100·0
I	84·2	71·6	3·8	9·4	30·5	47·3	9·0	86·8	100·0
II	77·3	72·1	4·4	11·2	31·7	44·3	8·4	84·4	100·0
III	71·2	70·5	4·6	10·8	35·2	41·7	7·7	84·6	100·0
IV	65·3	74·2	4·9	14·0	36·3	37·6	7·2	81·1	100·0
V	54·0	74·6	6·2	18·2	37·1	31·5	7·0	75·6	100·0
VI	44·2	74·3	8·4	24·3	38·4	22·5	6·4	67·3	100·0
VII	36·9	68·7	13·2	28·8	38·4	13·4	6·2	58·0	100·0
VIII	29·3	54·9	24·8	30·3	29·2	10·2	5·5	44·9	100·0
Special schools	20·0	–84·7	5·7	31·8	16·4	40·8	5·3	62·5	100·0
Schools for working youth	46·4	84·8	13·4	74·1	3·2	7·2	2·1	12·5	100·0
1963–4									
Primary schools— Total*a*	72·4	75·1	5·8	17·4	31·5	37·7	7·6	76·8	100·0
I	85·1	78·9	3·0	11·1	26·3	50·0	9·6	85·9	100·0
II	86·7	77·4	4·0	13·9	27·4	45·9	8·8	82·1	100·0
III	86·7	76·1	4·9	15·8	28·5	42·4	8·4	79·3	100·0
IV	79·0	76·1	5·4	17·0	29·8	40·1	7·7	77·6	100·0
V	75·3	75·4	5·8	17·9	31·9	37·6	6·8	76·3	100·0
VI	71·4	74·5	6·2	18·3	34·1	34·8	6·6	75·5	100·0
VII	61·8	73·8	7·5	21·1	35·8	29·2	6·4	71·4	100·0
VIII	52·9	72·0	9·7	24·9	38·7	20·6	6·1	65·4	100·0
Special schools	32·7	86·0	4·4	27·0	11·8	52·0	4·8	68·6	100·0
Schools for working youth	63·5	86·4	10·9	69·4	5·7	12·1	1·9	19·7	100·0

a Including pupils in class without clear grade.
Source: CBS, op. cit., 16, 1965, Table T/17, p. 587.

TABLE 42

Pupils in Post-Primary Schools of the Hebrew Education,[a] by Type of School and Continent of Birth (Percentage) (1963–4; 1964–5)

Type of School	Foreign born		Born in Europe America	Born in Asia-Africa	Israel born				Total
	Immigrated since 1955	Born in Asia-Africa as % of born abroad			Father born			Total	
					Europe-America	Asia-Africa	Israel		
1963–4									
TOTAL	33·3	41·2	28·0	19·6	39·7	6·3	6·4	52·4	100·0
Secondary schools[b]	31·4	29·1	31·3	12·9	44·9	4·9	6·0	55·8	100·0
Preparatory classes for teachers' training colleges	21·5	39·0	–24·4	–15·6	42·0	5·4	12·6	60·0	100·0
Secondary evening schools	25·2	54·5	24·8	29·7	25·3	13·5	6·7	45·5	100·0
Continuation classes	40·9	30·1	23·1	10·0	57·4	4·4	5·1	66·9	100·0
Vocational schools	35·4	49·4	28·7	28·0	28·7	7·9	6·7	43·3	100·0
Agricultural schools	38·8	60·3	21·5	32·7	33·1	5·9	6·8	45·8	100·0
Post-primary schools for part-time evening courses	36·6	85·9	10·6	64·7	5·8	14·8	4·1	24·7	100·0
1964–5									
TOTAL	43·1	45·7	22·1	18·6	42·8	9·7	6·8	59·3	100·0
Secondary schools[b]	41·3	32·0	25·8	12·2	47·4	7·8	6·8	62·2	100·0
Preparatory classes for teachers' training colleges	19·8	49·5	17·9	17·5	46·2	7·6	10·8	64·6	100·0
Secondary evening schools	20·4	67·3	16·9	34·7	19·4	19·7	9·3	48·4	100·0
Continuation classes	49·9	42·4	13·0	9·6	63·9	7·7	5·8	77·4	100·0
Vocational schools	46·2	54·5	21·9	26·2	33·1	12·4	6·4	51·9	100·0
Agricultural schools	51·0	63·2	17·7	30·5	33·3	11·1	7·4	51·8	100·0
Post-primary schools for part-time evening courses	41·9	84·0	11·6	60·5	9·6	15·3	3·0	27·9	100·0

[a] Education system only, excluding seminary schools and teachers training colleges.
[b] In 1964–5, included 15 secondary Yeshivot.
Source: CBS, op. cit., 16, 1965, Table T/18, p. 588.

(3) At the higher education level, therefore, young adults of oriental origin are even less represented. The percentage of oriental-born students at the Hebrew University in 1957 was between 5 and 6 per cent, and at the Israel Institute of Technology about 3·4 per cent. Thus, the new immigrant population of Middle Eastern origin does not yet occupy its proper position within the élites.[1]

Paradoxically, the success of the educational system in the initial absorption of immigrants emphasizes the special problems of the various groups and accentuates the severity of this problem by interweaving the educational system with the occupational and economic one.

These results are due, above all, to the great initial differences in educational levels and cultural backgrounds between most oriental immigrants and the rest of the Yishuv. However, to some extent, these results were also due to the initial lack of recognition by the educational authorities of the problems stemming from the great variety and heterogeneity of the immigrant group.

The problem of 'drop-outs' is not, however, confined to the general schools nor to the children of oriental immigrants only. It can also be found in various agricultural and vocational schools and in the more general bottlenecks that developed in the educational system.

It is closely connected with several crucial problems in the structure of secondary education – the scarcity of secondary schools and the relatively low level of the different types of (non-humanistic) secondary schools.

This low level is mainly due to the fact that these schools were often regarded as second-best by those who failed to get into the humanistic schools; they were used as springboards to overcome such failure and were not found attractive enough to hold their students.

Thus, for instance, the average drop-out in 1961–2 in grades one to two of the agricultural schools was sixteen per cent, in grades two to three, twenty, per cent. Out of the pupils finishing the third grade in 1956–7 only forty-five per cent continued their studies in the fourth grade, and only forty per cent took the agricultural-matriculation examinations.

A similar picture emerges in the vocational schools. The results of a study by Smilanski show that forty-eight per cent of the students starting vocational-secondary education do not finish it. This drop-out varies from institution to institution according to the selective devices used at the time of accepting pupils and according to the vocational training programme in the specific institution. Thus for instance, in one school with no selection at all, the drop-out was seventy per cent, while in an institution giving training in one specific occupation only thirteen per cent dropped out. This latter school runs a three-year course and is located in a big city, while the former is situated in a small town.

[1] M. Smilanski – Ibid. According to the Ministry of Education there were 12.3 per cent students of oriental origin in schools of higher education in 1962–3 (see *Bahinuch Uvatarbut* 11, p. 20, June 1964).

Thus we see that this problem is connected to the whole structure of Israeli post-primary education – to the relations between the general (humanistic) and the vocational high schools on the one hand and to their relations to occupational selection on the other. On the one hand the general humanistic school constitutes the major channel of selection to 'good' occupations, while the other – vocational or technical schools – are often seen as substitutes for those who did not succeed in getting into the general high schools and often serve as springboards for later entrance into them – thus giving rise to a very high rate of drop-out.

Thus, for instance, one of the manpower surveys predicts the drop-out from agricultural high schools in 1965–6 to be fifty-four per cent and from vocational high schools as forty-eight per cent.[1]

Several factors have been singled out as contributing to this situation, all of which point to some central problem in the educational system.

(1) Inadequate selective methods.
(2) Ambivalent attitude of the parents toward vocational high schools.
(3) Inadequate curriculum in the vocational schools.
(4) Economic difficulties.
(5) Unsatisfactory treatment of the individual in the schools.

The general tendency to underestimate vocational and agricultural schools and to overstress general, humanistic education is also evidenced in the great number of students taking 'external matriculation examinations' and in the growing pressure on vocational schools to offer a curriculum preparing for matriculation.

These circumstances had some very interesting results on the ability of the educational system to provide that kind of skilled manpower which the economy seems to need. The general high school became a channel of selection mostly into white collar and professional occupations and is not seen as promoting a general educational background for a wider range of occupations. In this way several such occupations – especially many of the more technical ones which the economy seems to be in need of – are deprived of that status-legitimation which the general high school seems to confer.

The various vocational schools, which did not have the appropriate prestige, tended to prepare their students only for the lower, or at most middle-level, occupational levels. Moreover, even the vocational training which they gave seems to be relatively narrow, i.e. orientated to rather specific jobs with but little transferability to other jobs while their general educational level has not, on the whole, been of the highest and most flexible nature.

Thus the process of selection now raises new problems: (a) the probability of considerable loss of talent along the educational ladder; (b) the growing

---

[1] Manpower forecast post primary education, op. cit.

pressure on only *one* channel of post-primary education may have negative effects on the diversification of possible occupational avenues.

Problems in Higher Education

The two most important problems in the sphere of higher education are, firstly, the extent to which the continuity of the high level of scientific productivity can be institutionalized and, secondly, the extent to which adequate professional manpower for the developing economy can be provided. Some aspects of the first problem are connected with the cultural contours of the country and will be analysed later.

Cutting across these two problems is the question of investment in higher education and the extent to which such investment will enable a combination of educational extensions and the development of further organizations and departments with high levels and standards of scientific productivity.

The problem of providing adequately trained manpower for the economy has several aspects, an important one among them being the shortage of teachers. But on the other hand no less important is the scarcity of academic manpower in the Israeli economy – a scarcity which is indicated in several surveys which also envisage that it will even increase in the 1970's.

This scarcity is explained by the increase in the demands for more skilled manpower in the economy and by the decrease of potential academic manpower, due to the expected increase of students from oriental countries[1] and to their greater tendency to drop-out from secondary schools.

The most general problem which arises here is the extent to which the growing response of the institutions of higher learning to the needs of the economy and to the demands for higher education will enable them to raise or even maintain their standards.

Perhaps the most crucial aspect of this problem is the relative scarcity of science and technology personnel and departments and the inadequate investment in basic scientific education.

The rate of students in sciences, agriculture, medicine, and technical studies has decreased from 48 per cent in 1961–2 to 41·9 per cent in 1964–5.

Another indication of this problem is the fact that a large part of research in Israel is financed by outside – especially US – sources. While this attests to the relatively high standards of the existing research institutions, it also points to the inadequacy of local interest in this field.

Truly enough the part supplied by the government in the budgets of institutions of higher learning increased from 40·3 per cent in 1955–6 (IL 4,900,000 to IL 12,400,000) to 50 per cent in 1964–5 (IL 40,000,000 to IL 80,400,000) and further increases are envisaged for 1966–7.

But the budget of the higher institutions increased during this period only

[1] An estimated 57 per cent in 1970 in comparison to 52 per cent in 1964–5.

ninefold, while the number of students increased fifteenfold – a fact which stresses the acuteness of the problem of whether it will be possible to maintain the standards of these institutions.

The close relation of the development of secondary and higher education to the growing problems and needs of the economy may create a rather dangerous vicious circle. On the one hand the educational system may be unable to provide the economy in general, and institutions of higher learning in particular, with the needed academic manpower. On the other hand there may arise the situation in which the Israeli economy and institutions of higher learning would be unable to absorb the professional and academic manpower which is coming out of its secondary and higher schools. The relatively high percentage of graduates of these institutions among those who emigrate from Israel is an indication of this problem.

The extent to which such problems can be overcome, will be of crucial importance for the continuation of high levels of scientific endeavour in Israel.

Contradictions in Policies attempting to Solve these Problems

It became a recognized fact that Israel's future was in danger if the gap between old and new immigrants were to create two nations and/or if the general educational level of the population were to be lowered.

To find the right solutions however was not easy. Older ideological preconceptions coupled with a number of vested interests might easily impede the understanding and solving of new problems, and contradictions could easily develop between solutions to different problems and between the pressures of various groups in the society.

These contradictions were rooted in the great potential political importance inherent in the gap between Western and oriental immigrants, either of which could become objects of pressures by the 'underprivileged' parts of the population. One way of giving in to these pressures and of minimizing the differences between groups, was the lowering of educational requirements for certain groups.

Contradictory attitudes to selectivity in the educational system also developed, i.e. the extent to which the educational system should serve as a channel of social and occupational selection.

Here two different pressures worked side by side. One was the socio-political and ideological pressure to provide general primary, secondary, and even higher education for all, irrespective of means. The other was and still is the economic need for differentiated and trained manpower.

An important contradiction developed in the ideological and political emphasis on education, which largely underestimated the connection between educational and economic problems.

To quote Patinkin:

Some preliminary investigations have shown that the mass immigration into Israel noticeably reduced its per capita level of educational capital in the first years of the state's existence. A less-expected finding is that this downward trend probably continued until 1955–6. Furthermore, despite the probable reversal of the gap, the trend at that time (as a result both of the operation of Israel's educational system and of the higher educational levels of the 1957–8 immigration), the per capita level of educational capital in 1958 had still not succeeded in climbing back to its 1950 level. This should be compared with the per capita level of tangible capital – which grew steadily over the same period at an annual rate of 3–8 per cent. This decrease in the relative importance of intangible 'human' capital in Israel stands in sharp contrast with the view that investment in the intangible capital represented by human resources is an even more essential component of the economic growth process than investment in tangible capital.[1]

Later data indicate that the total per capita capital invested in education did not change in 1963 in comparison with 1961, and it remained IL 4,000 (in 1957 prices).

Among the oriental immigrants investment in education decreased from IL 2,400 per capita in 1963 to IL 2,200 in 1965. Among the European and American born we may discern a trend of increase. Among the Israeli born, the investment per capita in education was in 1961 IL 2,400 higher than the average of the total population and reached IL 7,300 (1957 prices). But for the Israeli born whose fathers came from Asia and Africa, the investment per capita was only IL 3,800 (in 1957 prices).[2]

Shifts in Educational Policies

Though often intermittent and not fully grasped, all these developments combined to cause a growing shift in educational practice and ideology.

As has already been pointed out, the various new problems were accentuated by the encounter between the educational system and the new immigrants. It is natural therefore that most new policies aimed at some of the consequences of this encounter.

One partial response to these problems was the inclusion in the first three years of the state of parts of the traditional literation (e.g. liturgy) of the oriental groups in the school curriculum.

But the influx of immigrant children also posed many more specific educational problems, taking into account their varied traditions, social background, and problems.

[1] See D. Patinkin – *The Israel Economy: The First Decade*; Falk Project, Jerusalem, December, 1960.

[2] Y. Barruch – Investments in Education and the Human Capital Stock in Israel, Bank Israel Survey, (Hebrew), 23 December 1964.

The attitude prevalent at first was that the best way to assure swift absorption of the children would be by enforcing the older 'rebellious' or pioneering ideology.

In the initial stages of absorption it was often assumed that, in order to attract youth to various occupations, their family and ethnic ties had to be weakened. In reality, however, this proved to be neither the best nor the most expedient way.

It was quickly found out that a rebellious educational ideology, based on pioneering, was not easily applied to children coming from backgrounds where this was not indigenous.

The ineffectiveness of this ideology was further stressed by the fact that the occupational demands made on these children were in keeping with the existing and developing occupational structure.

These problems were accentuated by the fact that the educational system quickly imbued the immigrant groups with aspirations to a general, humanistic education as against a more vocational, technical, or pioneering one.

Pedagogical Experiments

Naturally, the most far-reaching problems arose within the general school systems, and it is here that different pedagogical organizations and social problems were attempted.

In the pedagogical field a good deal of experimentation took place on the part of some select groups, combined with a relatively high degree of general conservatism and organizational rigidity.

Among the most important pedagogical innovations were the numerous attempts to develop special teaching methods to cope with the cultural background of the oriental children.

The teaching of the Hebrew language, as of arithmetic, geography, and history, contained its own intrinsic difficulties for pupils coming from an environment where abstract study and historical understanding were not an integral part of their cultural heritage.

New text books were published, turning from the older 'content-centred' type to the newer 'psychological type' 'child-need centred'. These experimental activities, started by individual teachers, are now under the aegis of the 'Pedagogical Secretariat of the Ministry of Education'.

'Special' Educational Problems

The shift in pedagogical practice and ideology also affected the development of extra-curricular activities.

The prevalent educational ideology, rooted as it still was in the political and pioneering orientation, did not fully acknowledge the autonomy and

274

central importance of these new trends which, accordingly, suffered from lack of finance and inadequate manpower.

Moreover the prevailing ideology has also greatly limited the possibility of crystallization of new types of extracurricular activities for youth and adolescents beyond the scope of the 'traditional' youth movements, and of the possibility of development of new educational professional roles in this sphere. This has created many lacunae in this field – which are probably related to the development of the new types of youth outbreaks previously described.

However, whatever its limitations, the expansion described above, constituted an indication of possible changes in these parts of the educational system.

Changes in the Educational Pattern of Youth Aliya

After the establishment of the state several drastic changes took place in the educational activities of Youth Aliya. A great number of children without families, many of them from oriental countries, came under the auspices of Youth Aliya; and in order to cope with the growing number of children, special youth institutions were founded to supplement the collective settlements. As before, the main emphasis of Youth Aliya was on settlement in kibbutzim and moshavim.

However, these children lacked the ideological background necessary for this pioneering orientation. Especially in cases where parents joined their children, a deep conflict among the children, the parents, and the educational institutions developed. Resulting from this, Youth Aliya's educational practice was changed, in the first instance, by more differentiated educational and vocational training. This was of great importance for children whose socio-economic and family circumstances made it impossible to provide them with regular basic education.

Thus Youth Aliya became transformed from an agency whose main aim was the preparation of pioneers to a multi-purpose educational and training agency, working in close co-operation with other institutions, such as the Ministry of Social Welfare or the youth services of the various municipalities.

This brought several organizational changes in its wake. Rural vocational centres were established to give intensive courses to about six hundred youngsters a year. The subjects taught in these six months' courses are agriculture, plumbing, electrical-maintenance, and metal work, whilst girls are trained in baby and child care, sewing, and cooking. A second new innovation was the multi-purpose youth centres, established jointly by the government and the Jewish Agency. Training a total of about 1,700 pupils in twenty such centres, they combine paid work with general and vocational studies and recreational activities.

Although the changes within Youth Aliya were more far-reaching than those of any other sector of the educational system, they were not whole-hearted. They were more on the practical than the ideological-pedagogical level and were often coupled with a yearning for the older, simple, and unequivocal educational ideology.

Obviously, whatever the success of Youth Aliya or of the special educational organizations, they could affect only small parts of the young population of Israel and only selected aspects of their activities.

Socio-Economic Aspects of Integration in the Educational System

Side by side with the various pedagogical policies and experiments described, a series of policies evolved during the past five to six years, aimed at overcoming the initially low educational achievements of oriental children and at raising the level of these groups.

One such policy was the lowering of the compulsory age for kindergarten children from low-class families. According to this policy there were 17,000 children in the ages of three to four who attended compulsory kindergartens. Second, a long-day school was instituted for children from low-income families. In 1964–5 there were 50,000 children who participated in this arrangement in 2,900 classes. Third, 120,000 children were defined as in need of extra help and their schools received additional manpower.

Within this programme the Ministry of Education added 694 classes with 20,000 children in 1964–5 and a special month in summer time; seventy special classes were also opened to help children who had difficulties in studies owing to the psycho-social background.[1]

Another such policy was the abolition of class repetition as a solution to the scholastic failure of oriental students even in the first grade. The Ministry of Education decreed that only four per cent of any class should be permitted to repeat it. However, this system did not alleviate failure. On the contrary, it accentuated it by creating accumulated failure without remedy.

A programme of aid and scholarships initiated by the state in co-operation with the Jewish Agency was a more positive move. This programme was especially established for children of oriental background or for children who immigrated during the last four years. Altogether 5,236 full or part-scholarships were granted in 1960–1 for academic, vocational, and agricultural high schools, etc. The system of graded fees was broadened in 1964–5, 83,000 pupils participating in it, more than half of them (45,000) in general secondary education. About IL 21,000,000 were invested in this programme. More than forty per cent of children from development towns enjoying this graded fees system.[2]

[1] Z. Aran. *Bahinuch Uvatarbut* (Hebrew) (In Education and Culture) June 1965.
[2] CBS: Statistical Abstract of Israel, 16, 1965, Table T/21, p. 590.

The extension of special facilities to new immigrant children, especially aimed at the reduction of the number of children in a class, has also been envisaged. The Ministry of Education's plans for 1962–3 was to add 940 more classrooms for elementary schools, 52 classes for vocational and agricultural studies, and 180 classes for academic secondary schools – all giving priority to children of new immigrants and of oriental families.

Extracurricular activities are mainly concentrated in slum-areas and in districts where the population is mainly of oriental descent. Altogether 596 institutions exist in which 77,500 children of elementary school-age are given help. Similar facilities for older youth (pupils of schools for working youth) were used by 11,800 young persons.

In addition, programmes of selective intensive education were established for especially gifted children from a low socio-economic background or from remote settlements where no secondary education is available. About sixteen boarding schools are planned for these children where they receive regular secondary school education in the morning and are engaged in various recreational and educational activities in the afternoon. In 1960–1, there were eighty students in such schools, in 1961–2 – 250, and in 1964–5 – 900.[1]

This policy of creating special institutions for gifted oriental children has evoked twofold criticism. One was that, by taking them out of their natural settings, they might develop strong feelings of resentment towards their groups of origin, thus depriving the groups of effective leadership. A second criticism was that, by segregating these children in special institutions instead of spreading them among the general schools, their separatist 'ethnic' self-identification may be enhanced and its symbolization may receive partial legitimation.

While it is too early to evaluate fully the validity of these criticisms, they certainly point to potential contradictions and problems inherent in these policies. An additional measure taken in this context by the educational authorities was the institution of Norm B.

The main directive of Norm B was that, whereas a regular student had to score about 7·5–8 (out of ten), the oriental student with a score of about 6·5 plus was entitled to state-aid in post-primary education.

While this measure was intended to facilitate the absorption of these children, it also tended to weaken the universalistic achievement approach of the test by putting it on a particularistic-ascriptive (ethnic) basis, containing many possibilities of lowering the general educational level.

Moreover, the beneficial effects of Norm B on the oriental children has also proved doubtful since it artificially advances non-qualified students into

[1] Data received from the Ministry of Education on 11 January 1966, based on research on 387 pupils from these schools, indicate that 85 per cent of them are successful in matriculation examination.

post-primary education, where no special allowance is made for them. They then face problems of adjustment and are bound to rate high among students who drop out later. The high levels of aspiration are thus first raised – and then frustrated.

Further, this policy is likely to attach the stigma of 'second-rate'[1] to most of the oriental children, most particularly on the few who could achieve Norm A by their own efforts.

Policies Dealing with Organizational Bottlenecks

Other closely connected policies aimed at overcoming the various organizational bottlenecks in the educational system. They recognized the inadequacy of existing facilities in catering for the needs of the various groups, and tried to provide the services needed by the developing society and economy.

Among the many attempts made two are worth mentioning here. One was the introduction, in 1956, of a new scheme of pre-vocational training into the syllabus of the upper two classes of some elementary schools. This called for twelve weekly hours of workshop training and three hours of related subjects (technology and technical drawing) in addition to the time devoted to general education.

The aim of this scheme was: firstly, to prepare pupils for their chosen trades reducing the period of apprenticeship; and secondly, to divert some of the pupils from secondary to vocational schools. However, the scheme did not work out. Pupils falling into the first category were not prepared for the varied demands of the labour market, for which their training was of little help. Failure was mainly caused, however, through those in the second category who, in spite of vocational training and guidance, continued to aspire to academic training by any means. Thus, though some pupils no doubt gained technical know-how through this scheme, its function as a guiding agency, channelling pupils into various fields before formal selection, was ineffective.

But whatever the intensity of these problems, a continuous trend of expansion of vocational education can be discerned.

Thus the number of students in these schools was in 1964–5 twenty-three per cent more than in 1963–4, while the number of graduates grew by thirty-per cent. At the same time there took place a great expansion of vocational schools under the auspices of the Ministry of Labour.

[1] In general some conclusions based on a follow-up of the first group that went through the entire post-primary education according to the scheme of a graded scale of tuition fees (including Norm B) – seem to indicate that Norm B was not of very high value: only 7·7 per cent out of all students who qualified in 1957 under Norm B, reached the stage of matriculation in 1961. In 1957 students of oriental origin constituted 33·6 per cent of the graduating class in primary school. However, they still made up only 12·4 per cent at the stage of matriculation in 1961, in spite of Norm B.

The available data seem to indicate that about forty-two per cent of all the pupils in post-primary education attend all the vocational schools.

This overall expansion of vocational education, which is greatly helped by the government, indicates that an alternative channel of education and occupational mobility has been developing lately.

A more recent attempt to reform secondary education is called 'streaming' or 'grouping', this aims at the establishment of two different martriculation examinations, one certifying that the holder of the matriculation certificate is a graduate of a secondary school and the second enabling the holder to attend institutions of higher learning.

According to this system, the pupils of the sixth, seventh and eighth classes are divided into three levels of studies – the criteria being their achievements in arithmetic, English, Hebrew, and sometimes also biology. Homogeneous groups are thus formed in the different study-subjects, which contain pupils coming from various classes or even various schools.

The aim of this new system is two-fold: first to differentiate the pupils according to their achievement level, so that one group will not suffer from the presence of the other levels. Secondly, it aims to maintain the class as a social unit with a high level of cohesiveness in spite of the differences in the educational achievements.

It is hoped that these innovations will improve the quality of secondary schools and will provide pupils with a comprehensive curriculum adjusted to the actual demands of the market. It is also felt that, as the curriculum will not be solely directed towards the achievement of matriculation, there will be more time for other subjects and activities.

This plan recognizes and accepts the fact that any homogeneous and uniform approach to special problems was doomed to failure and that only a differential individual approach could hope for success. It also signifies a growing emphasis on a school system akin to the English 'comprehensive' school, instead of the more specialized school for the gifted.

In 1964–5 this 'setting' system comprised approximately 1,500 classes with 42,000 pupils. According to the programme, this method will comprise some 45,000 pupils. It was observed from the study of the distribution of the pupils by country of origin among the different levels that the pupils whose parents came from Asia or Africa are concentrated heavily in the lowest level, in smaller rates in the second one, and the least in the highest level.

Till now it seems that this system is most successful mainly in the high and the low levels but not in the middle level, in which there was no improvement in the scholastic achievement of the pupils.

This aim to change the structure of the educational system in the direction of an increasing differentiation became even more manifest in the appointment of a committee (January 1963) which had to examine 'the necessity of and the possibilities for adding two years of free compulsory education' (the

Prawer Committee). In 1965 this committee recommended the addition of one year to the existing free and compulsory education. It made such a change conditional on the structure of the educational system so as to create a mid-unit comprised of the seventh, eighth, and ninth grades, the first stage of the secondary education, and independent unit in what concerns administration, teaching-programmes, and staff. The committee took into consideration the necessity of long preparatory work for the realization of this aim, such as the preparation of teachers, text-books, buildings, etc. Therefore it proposed postponing its complete execution for four to five years.

The assumption behind this recommendation is that the programme will enable a higher differentiation and a better possibility for a choice in accordance with the tendencies and abilities of the pupils, beginning in the higher classes of the elementary school.

The reactions to these proposed reforms – e.g. the initial strong opposition expressed by the Teachers' Union to the Beersheba experiment, to the new 'setting' system in general, and to the conclusions of the Prawer Committee – indicate one of the major weak points of the educational system in Israel, namely, the conservative character and great strength of the powerful Teachers' Union. This strength is derived from the historical fact that the Teachers' Union was in a way the creator of the Hebrew education, and therefore enjoyed a position of very great power, which even increased with its growing trade-unionization.

It is, as yet, difficult to evaluate the effect and success of these various policies. They do show however the severity of the Israeli educational problems and the fact that educational policy was often guided by contradictory ideological and political considerations.

Shortage of Teachers and Attempted Remedies

Among the many tasks and problems facing the educational system, the shortage of adequate manpower, with the consequent lowering of the status of the profession, was one of the most arduous.

The shortage of teachers could be seen in the growing drop-out from the profession, in its growing feminization, in the number of unqualified teachers employed, and in the difficulties of recruiting new staff from high school and university graduates.

Whilst in 1950–1 there were 5,367 male teachers out of 10,945 teaching posts, there were in 1954–5 only 8,331 male teachers out of 17,337, and 9,006 female teachers. In 1958-9 there were 24,826 teaching posts, out of which 10,664 were male teachers and 14,162 female. This proportion is more prominent in the elementary schools, in which, in 1958–9, out of 13,336 teaching posts there were 4,924 male teachers and 8,512 female teachers. In the same year 8,431 were qualified teachers, 4,024 unqualified teachers, and 881 whose qualifications were not known.

In 1959–60 there were 4,074 unqualified teachers in vocational, agricultural, and evening schools. There are no data available concerning schools for working youth and for retarded children, but they also lack teachers. In 1963–4 there were 17,514 teachers in the elementary Hebrew education – out of which 11,923 (68 per cent) were female, and 5,591 (32 per cent) were male. The number of unqualified teachers was 5,850 (33 per cent). 32·7 per cent of the teachers had experience of four years or less, 59 per cent had experience of between zero and nine years. 42·1 per cent of the teachers were born in Israel (compared to fifteen per cent of the same age group in the population that is Israeli born). Only 13·1 per cent of the teachers were of Asian or African origin, while their relevant age group in the population is 35·4 per cent.[1]

In addition the results of a follow-up study of teachers' training college graduates for the years 1956–7, 1958–9, and 1959–60, show a drop-out rate of about twenty per cent.

Researches into the drop-out of teachers show that these tendencies are closely connected with the narrowing of the teachers' role and the growth of tensions between the pioneering ideology and the demands of the changing occupational scene.

In order to overcome this grave shortage, special preparatory classes were introduced in secondary schools, and special training colleges for rural teachers running one or two year courses were established. In 1964–5 a reform aiming to increase the number of pupils in teaching training colleges by more then twenty per cent every year was undertaken. The budget for the training of teachers by the Ministry of Education was increased from IL 4·5 million to IL 16 million in 1964–5.

The Ministry decided to offer to students who were willing to be trained as teachers in post-primary schools scholarships at the rate of IL 1,500 to 2,500 a year.

In 1964–5 600 students from among 1,100 candidates were chosen to be trained as such teachers – 35 per cent in sciences and 65 per cent in humanities.

A comparison of the total number of teachers in 1959–60 on all levels of the educational system shows[2] 18,056 teachers,[3] with the existing teaching posts for the same year being 22,354,[4] indicating that there is still a lack of manpower in spite of the 41,251 students attending the various teachers' training colleges between the years 1948–9 to 1960–1.[5]

[1] Manpower forecast. Teachers in the Primary education. Manpower planning authority. Ministry of Labour, 1964.
[2] Except higher education, but including Teachers' Colleges.
[3] Source: CBS Stat. Abstr. No. 12, 1961, p. 450, Table 5.
[4] Source: CBS Stat. Abstr. No. 12, 1961, p. 450, Table 5.
[5] Ibid., p. 448, Table 3.

Equally, one cannot as yet estimate the efficiency of the measures taken and especially the extent to which they may help to overcome the broader social impediments of the teaching profession. There are some signs, for instance, that the growing feminization of the profession has to some extent been halted.

Many complications were caused by the teachers' associations' concentration on political, organizational, and wage disputes, rather than on pedagogical matters. The internal struggles between different teachers' organizations were of special importance here, as was the rift between the General Teachers' Association and the teachers in secondary schools who formed a separate organization not fully recognized by the GTA.

Similar contradictions and conflicts also developed in the field of higher education.

Various administrative devices were attempted to assure high standards of scientific creativity and to increase the country's investment in education. The most important of these was the reorganization of the former Research Council of Israel into the National Council for Research and Development in 1959. Attached to the Prime Minister's office, this agency was 'designed to augment scientific contribution towards the development of the State'.[1] It is 'charged with formulating national policy in respect of research and development and co-ordinating research projects and requirements'.

The relative proliferation of institutions of higher learning also created several administrative and policy problems, especially when related to the problems of keeping up adequate standards and official recognition.

On 19 May 1958 the Knesset promulgated the Law of the Council for Higher Studies 1958. This Council's responsibilities are as follows: to recommend any institution to be recognized by the government (actually the Council recognizes para. 9, but the government approves para. 10); to recommend the expansion of an institution, to recommend government subsidy for an institution, to withdraw recognition (also with the government's approval, para. 19), to recognize and grant degrees, etc. The law does not define the rules according to which the Council is to execute its duties – these are to be fixed by the Council itself.

It is as yet too early to evaluate the double functions of this Council in encouraging new institutions of higher learning and ascertaining that they will not be below a minimally acceptable standard. In 1965 a special committee was set up to examine the situation of higher education.

[1] Government Year Book, 1960–1, English edition.
The Council has the following sub-committees:
Agricultural Committee, Committee on Industrial Chemistry, Pharmacology Committee, Committee on Medicine, Committee on Patents, Committee for the Survey of Scientific and Technological Manpower, Committee on Oceanography. It has also an office for Graduate Personnel, being in charge of the affairs of students abroad, and a Centre for Technological and Scientific Information.

The report of this committee advised to establish a special higher education authority that would plan a basic programme for the development of the institutions without impinging on the academic freedom and the autonomy of the institutions of higher education.

This authority was to be established instead of the existing Council of High Education and was to include the representatives of the institutions of higher learning of the public and of the Cabinet.

Several aspects of the expansion of institutes of higher learning may lead to problematic results. The importance of local political pressures and the limited expansion of the natural sciences, as against the growing multiplication of arts students, do not assure either higher levels of investment or the creation of conditions conducive to higher standards of scientific creativity.

It is probably too early to evaluate the activities of the Research Council. It seems that this Council was more successful in initiating limited activities of applied research and in serving as a partial clearing house for outside sources applying to Israeli institutions for research than in planning the overall needs of the country or in assuring a higher level of investment in the educational and scientific fields.

Problems and Promises on the Educational Scene

The picture of the educational scene after the first fifteen years of the State of Israel is even more complex and varied than it was at the end of the period of the Yishuv.

The whole structure of relations between school, family, and youth movement has experienced great changes, rooted in several interconnected starting points. One was the establishment of the state itself, a full-fledged society with sovereign authority, and centralizing tendencies. Second was the concomitant crystallization of the social structure and cultural heritage. Third was the influx of great numbers and varieties of new immigrants bringing new basic motivations and attitudes and varying educational and technical skills to the country.

Fourth was the combined impact of the preceding processes and of the economic differentiation and development of the educational and occupational structure. The economic needs of the country, the expansion of the economic structure, the need for skilled manpower and the influx of immigrants of a low educational level, have enhanced the importance of educational standards in the occupational and economic spheres. It is here that the special problems of the new immigrants, and particularly of the oriental ones, begin to be acute.

Paradoxically, the absorption of the different immigrant groups into the educational system emphasized the differences between social groups and strata, and initially even increased these differences.

283

Educational, administrative, and organizational problems had to be faced as had the shaping of the system as an instrument of social policy. These problems were often new ones, reaching beyond the traditional perception of the education authorities.

Moreover, difficulties in facing these problems were intensified by the internal, 'structural' development of the educational system in its initial reaction to the changing society. Progress was obstructed by the strong politicization of a large part of the educational system and of the teachers' professional organization, and by the limited scope and incentive which the major educational framework provided for pedagogical and cultural innovation.

Further impediments were caused by the preponderance of professional vested interests in different echelons of teachers, by the instability and ambivalence of the teachers' roles, and by the lowering of their status.

The ideological-pedagogical difficulties to forge out a more flexible combination of the initial ideal with an orientation to more specialized tasks and activities, may reinforce the more stagnant tendencies in the development of Israeli economy.

A similar range of problems developed with regard to the social consequences of educational selection. Here the attempts to overcome the cleavages between different social and immigrant groups also tended to develop in two contradictory directions.

At the same time, several important trends developed from within and without the educational system constituting important innovations.

Thus we see that while the educational system shared the great impetus of continuous expansion, differentiation, and ability to absorb the new immigrant groups, it also shared the impediments within Israeli society to deal effectively with these new problems.

On the one hand many of these policies and measures facilitated possible changes and improvements, but, on the other hand, some of the policies may reinforce the more ascriptive and freezing tendencies in the system of social stratification and organization.

9

Political Structure and Institutions

1

Introduction

The many tendencies and developments analysed in the preceding chapters converged in the political institutions and structure in Israel.

The political institutions and organizations have been, and to some extent still are, the centre of contemporary Israeli society. The chapter on economic institutions showed the importance of state and government policy in the economic field. In the chapter on social organization we saw the criterion of power acquired in the stratification of Israeli society, as well as the importance of government agencies in the absorption of immigrants. This chapter will deal with some of the causes for the importance of these political institutions.

It must be remembered that the implementation of such collective goals as colonization, security, and keeping the gates of Palestine open for new immigrants, constituted the *raison d'être* for many major groups and institutions in the Yishuv, an orientation which was in many ways enhanced by the establishment of the State of Irael. The state was not only the culmination of a prolonged political struggle and countless diplomatic endeavours, but it was also seen as the redemption of the Jewish nation and the fulfilment of Zionist endeavour.

The symbols of sovereignty and statehood – the flag, the presidency, the government, Parliament, and especially the army – became the foci of strong national identification both in Israel and in the diaspora.

In its first stages the state also became the focal point for the ideologies prominent in the various social movements of the Yishuv. The weakening of these ideologies in the private spheres of life, caused by the feeling that they had been largely achieved through the establishment of the state, reinforced attempts to portray the state's symbols, organs, leaders, and officials as the embodiment of these values.

Yet the crucial importance of the state and of the political institutions have never been without problems or taken for granted, for, unlike most other institutional fields, the political one was not clearly formulated in basic Zionist and pioneering ideology.

The goal of statehood was one of the basic tenets of Zionist ideology, but this was envisaged mainly as an external framework for national collectivity and as the external manifestation of a new collective identity.

Most concrete political organizations developed during the mandatory period when the implementation of collective goals became more prominent than pure ideological formulation. Moreover, the Zionist ideology – as many other utopian, socialist, and nationalist ideologies – shied from dealing with problems of power and often implicitly assumed that such problems would be solved when the major collective aims were attained.

Hence, the proliferation of political functions and organizations in the new state produced problems which ideology was not equipped to handle.

The Formal Structure of Israel's Political Institutions

The state, established on 14 May 1948, very rapidly developed its main formal institutional characteristics and features.

To this day Israel has no constitution – only a series of basic laws, with much political controversy raging on the problem of a constitution. The main formal features and characteristics of Israel's institutional and governmental structure may be described as follows:[1]

The structure of government consists of the executive, legislative, and judicial branches, with a President, a Parliament, a Cabinet, and a legal system. The President is the titular head of the state, whose functions are mainly ceremonial and formal. He is elected for a five-year term by a majority vote and secret ballot of the Knesset (Parliament). The first President of the state was Chaim Weizmann, the outstanding leader of the Zionist movement during the period of the Mandate. He was elected on 16 February 1949 and died on 9 November 1952. His successor, chosen on 8 December 1952 and re-elected on 30 October 1957 and again in 1962, was Yitzhak Ben-Zvi, Chairman and President of the *Vaad Leumi*. On the death of President Ben-Zvi in April 1963, Zalman Shazar (a veteran Mapai leader, orator, and scholar) was elected to the Presidency.

The Knesset (Parliament) is the formal (but not actual) supreme government agency. It is a one-chamber parliament consisting of 120 members, whose powers are not limited either by presidential veto or by the Supreme Court. It is elected for a four-year term by direct, equal, and secret ballot, on the system of proportional representation. Formally, the government is responsible to the Knesset and cannot be formed without majority support in the Knesset and must resign when it fails to command the latter's confidence.

Special provision has been made for close and continuous scrutiny of state financial and economic activities under the aegis of the Knesset. A State Comptroller, named by the President upon recommendation of a committee

[1] Adapted from O. Janowsky – Foundations of Israel, N.Y., 1959, pp. 88–92.

of the Knesset, reports to the Finance Committee of the Knesset on the legality, economy, integrity, and efficiency of government affairs. The State Comptroller is responsible to the Knesset and is not dependent upon the government.

The cabinet, or government, is the functioning executive body. The Prime Minister, a member of the Knesset, is charged by the President with the task of forming a government and he negotiates with the various party leaders on the choice of his colleagues, who may not be members of the Knesset. When approved by the Knesset by vote of confidence, the government is constituted.

The principle of collective responsibility officially governs the Cabinet system, although the exact interpretation of this responsibility has constituted a bone of contention in many of the coalition governments.

The judicial branch of government comprises religious as well as civil courts. The hierarchy of civil courts includes many municipal and magistrates' courts (including two juvenile courts) with minor civil and criminal jurisdiction; three district courts where appeals from the lower tribunals are heard and which serve as courts of first instance in major civil and criminal cases. The highest court of the land is the Supreme Court, comprising seven justices, a president, and a deputy president. While the Supreme Court cannot declare as unconstitutional laws passed by the Knesset, it can invalidate administrative actions or interpretations of statutes which it regards as contrary to the rule of law.

The rabbinical courts exercise exclusive jurisdiction on matters of marriage and divorce in the Jewish community. In other matters of personal status, such as alimony, probate, and succession, they may hear a case only if all parties consent. The ecclesiastical courts of the Christian communities have exclusive authority in marriage, divorce, alimony, and confirmation of wills of the members of their respective communities; and they may judge other matters of personal status with the consent of the parties concerned. The Moslem courts have exclusive jurisdiction in all matters of personal status of the Moslem community. Tribunals also exist for special cases, such as rents, profiteering, speculation, and national insurance, and there are tribal courts for the Bedouins.

The independence of the judiciary is assured by special safeguards against political appointments and by tenure, subject only to good behaviour.

The body of law administered by the courts consists of enactment of the Knesset and laws inherited from previous regimes. These include Ottoman survivals, especially in private and land law; the emergency regulations which obtained under the Mandate, English common law and equity, Rabbinical law, and the religious laws of the Moslem and Christian communities.

Local government, initiated cautiously during the Mandate, has been extended and democratized since the establishment of the state. The owning of property as a qualification for voting has been abolished. The franchise has been extended to women in all local elections; and mayors and vice-mayors, appointed under the British regime, are now elected by the local representative bodies.

The Major Parties in Israel

The most important political parties in Israel were, to a great extent, also predominant during the time of the Yishuv. Within them all, the transformation attendant on the establishment of the state, brought about the development of new unified organizations uniting the different movements, sects, and interest groups and with a marked shift in orientation towards the absorption of new elements.

Mapai

The greatest flexibility in absorbing new elements, varied interests, and different political orientations took place within Mapai. The most important older groups of which Mapai was composed were the various agricultural settlements – the kibbutzim (especially those belonging in the *Ihud Hakibbutzim*) and the moshavim and, in the urban sectors, the trade union and labour groups. At the same time Mapai, which was in a good position to face the changes of mass immigration, also attempted to attract many of the new immigrants. It was better organized for the absorption of immigrants than many other parties and was traditionally the party that led Zionism to statehood. Even immigrants who could not distinguish one party platform from another, recognized the dramatic figure of Ben-Gurion, Prime Minister and leader of the party that won independence. In the elections to the Sixth Knesset (1965), Mapai and *Ahdut Haavoda* founded the Alignment (*Maarah*) which received together 37 per cent of the votes. At the same time the Rafi group headed by D. Ben-Gurion split off from Mapai and received 8 per cent of the votes.

The Left – Mapam and Ahdut Haavoda

The more sectarian elements of the labour movement with a purer, élitist conception of pioneering developed among the left wing of Mapai (in some of its kibbutzim) and, outside it, in Mapam and *Adhut Haavoda*.

Originally both of these latter groups were relatively closed sects based mainly on the kibbutzim. They only developed into full-fledged political parties with the establishment of the state, when they also attempted to attract and organize broader non-sectarian elements.

In August 1944, some parts of *Poalei Zion* broke away from Mapai, under the older name of *Ahdut Haavoda*. In 1948 they merged with *Hashomer Hatzair* to form Mapam (United Workers' Party). Controlling 60 per cent of the governing body of the party, *Hashomer Hatzair* was easily able to outvote *Ahdut Haavoda* consistently. Finally in 1954, *Ahdut Haavoda* broke away from Mapam and organized its own independent party. The final split was hastened as a result of the anti-semitic Prague trial in 1951, and the trial of Jewish doctors in Moscow in 1952. In Israel's labour politics, *Ahdut Haavoda* occupies a position between Mapai and Mapam.

Although the majority faction of Mapam, *Hashomer Hatzair* refrained from forming a political party until statehood was imminent and its activities were, in fact, those usually associated with political parties. Its programme and leadership still retain their pioneer (*chalutz*) appeal and continue to reflect a rural and collectivist approach to domestic issues.

During the life of the Second Knesset (1951–5) three separate splits cut Mapam's voting strength in half and reduced it from the third to the sixth ranking party. Two of its delegates formed a splinter group that joined the Communist Party, two joined Mapai, and four left in 1954 when *Ahdut Haavoda* seceded from Mapam. Until 1965 when *Ahdut Haavoda* founded the Alignment with Mapai, no great changes took place in these 'leftist' groups.

The Centre – The General Zionists, Progressives, and Liberals

Similar changes – perhaps even more pronounced than those within the labour groups – took place among the different General Zionist groups.

Two major parties developed from the General Zionist movement, the Progressive party and the General Zionists which, in 1961, merged into the Liberal Party.

Until then the Progressive party was Israel's closest replica to a Liberal Party, and, though small, it carried considerable moral influence. Evolved partially at least from *Aliya Hadasha*, a party made up mainly of Central European immigrants who came to Palestine after 1933, the Progressive party was founded in 1948. Its aims were a national educational system, an independent civil service and judiciary, guarantees of personal liberty, state rather than Histadrut control of public transport, health services, labour exchanges, encouragement of private investment, and more liberal treatment of Arabs living in Israel. With the brief exception of one year, the Progressives formed part of all government coalitions from 1948–61.

The General Zionist party is made up of a merger of different interest groups, such as the Manufacturers' Association, the Citrus Growers' Association, various merchant groups, and the leaders of some municipal groups.

With statehood, this party emerged as a champion of private enterprise in an economy dominated by the Histadrut. In 1949 it polled only 5 per cent of the vote and won seven seats in the Knesset. However, it grew tremendously between 1949–51, becoming the second largest party in the Knesset with twenty seats, which were later augmented to twenty-three through the affiliation of three minor party delegates. From 1952 until June 1955 the General Zionists were members of the government. However, in the 1955 elections they lost strength, mainly to the right-wing *Herut* (Freedom party).

The main strength and appeal of the General Zionists were its opposition to government economic controls and its effort to curb the power of Histadrut enterprises and activities. Its domestic programme emphasized maximum freedom from any restrictions that might hinder free enterprise and a unified educational system devoid of partisan indoctrination. The party called for the conversion of the health services (*Kupat Holim*) of the Histadrut into a national health service, nationalization of labour exchanges, and greater differentiation between unskilled, skilled, and professional workers as an incentive to increased productivity.

Trying to broaden its appeal by organizing a special wing within the Histadrut, this party also has its own women's organization.

One of the important results of the 'Lavon Affair' (see later page 126) was the merger of the Progressives and General Zionists into the Liberal Party, which gained about 14 per cent of the votes and seventeen members in the Knesset in the 1961 elections. In 1965 there took place a split in the Liberal Party. Its great majority (almost all the former General Zionists and some former Progressives) founded a parliamentary block with *Herut* which received about 21 per cent of the votes. A minority – consisting mostly of former Progressives – founded the 'Independent Liberal Party' which received about 7 per cent of the votes.

Herut

One of the main developments in the period of the state was the growth of the *Herut* party – the only full opposition party in the spectrum of Israeli politics. It developed from the older Revisionist groups, the 'terrorist' groups of the *Irgun Zvai Leumi* and members of the Revisionist party. (The other dissident group, *Lehi*, sent one member to the first Knesset only).

This is the most extensive right-wing anti-government opposition party, being opposed to any economic role by the state, and to the economic preponderance of the Histadrut. Like the General Zionists, it demands unfettered free enterprise, elimination of Histadrut monoplies, uniform national education, and state labour exchanges. By and large it favours a written constitution, abolition of censorship, and an impartial civil service. It has emphasized – at least officially – an actively expansionist orientation in its foreign policy and was for a time identified with a policy of preventive war against the Arabs as being the best assurance of Israel's survival.

In the 1949 election *Herut* emerged as the third largest party with fourteen seats in the Knesset and 11.5 per cent of the popular vote. General Zionist growth in 1951 was largely at the expense of *Herut*, which dropped to eight seats with 6·7 per cent of the vote. The opposite happened in 1955, when the two parties reverted to their earlier positions. As the major opposition party it has learned to exploit the dissatisfaction mainly stemming from high taxation of many middle-class and lower middle-class groups, as well as the resentment felt by many new immigrant elements who were not fully satisfied with the pace and extent of their absorption. In 1965 *Herut* founded together with a great part of the Liberals a parliamentary block (*Gahal*) which, as we have seen, received about 21 per cent of the votes.

The Zionist Religious Parties

Similar developments occurred within the National Religious Party, with a growing shift from *Mizrahi* (based mainly on diaspora elements) to *Hapoel Hamizrahi* (more firmly rooted in Israel).

In 1949, *Mizrahi* joined the United Religious Front (comprising *Agudat Israel* and *Poalei Agudat Israel*).

Due to its success in absorbing oriental and North African immigrants in its rural settlements, the position of *Hapoel Hamizrahi* has improved in recent years. Though formally merged into a single party known as the National Religious Front in 1956, in fact *Hapoel Hamizrahi* still maintains its own organization for trade union purposes. The two groups have been throughout the period of the state receiving about 10–11 per cent of the votes.

The Extreme (Non-Zionist) Religious Parties – Agudat Israel and Poalei Agudat Israel

Poalei Agudat Israel, the labour wing of *Agudat Israel*, was founded in Poland in 1922. Its objective was to counteract anti-religious feelings among the Polish workers and to defend the place of the orthodox Jew in industry. The religious base of *Agudat Israel* and its offshoot, *Poalei Agudat Israel*, was identical, but the labour wing put more stress on agricultural settlement. Their first rural settlement in Palestine was founded in 1934, on land purchased by the Jewish National Fund, an event that roused bitter conflict with *Agudat Israel*, which opposed the Jewish National Fund. Eventually, however, *Poalei Agudat Israel* controlled about fifteen rural villages and one agricultural school. Its settlement work gradually brought it into closer touch with the Jewish Agency and the Histadrut, and though not a member of the Histadrut, the party participated in some trade union activities. It helped with the organization of illegal immigration, sent workers to refugee camps in Europe, and fought in the ranks of *Hagana*. The *Agudah* on the other hand did not, till the establishment of the state, maintain too many contacts with the Zionists (except in some political activities oriented to the English) and was based on the older Yishuv.

The most extreme of the religious groups in the 'old Yishuv' were the *Neturei Karta* who to this very day keep themselves apart and do not 'recognize' the State of Israel.

Unlike *Mizrahi* and *Hapoel Hamizrahi* which have become closer together in recent years, *Poalei Agudat Israel* has become more independent of *Agudat Israel;* it now publishes its own newspaper, has its own youth movement, and works among immigrants in transit camps.

In 1960 and 1961 *Poalei Agudat Israel* participated in the government coalitions and one of their members was appointed Deputy Minister of Education.

The Communist Party

The Communist Party was founded in Palestine in the early 1920's, primarily as an instrument to encourage Arab resistance to British imperialism and Zionism.[1] Since then it was only for the short stretch dating from the UN Partition Resolution in November 1947 to the beginning of the first Knesset in 1949 that this party worked toward the Zionist goal of national sovereignty. Its orientation has, of course, been unflinchingly pro-Soviet. In domestic policy, its programme was readily predictable: opposition to any form of reliance on reactionary capitalism, including American grants-in-aid and technical assistance and the German reparations; nationalization of all enterprises, beginning with those that were built by foreign investors; and continuous demands for higher wages.

Exploiting Arab grievances, the Communist Party has become one of the champions of the rights of the Arab minority in Israel and one of its strongholds is the Arab city of Nazareth. It is not surprising, therefore, that roughly a third of its members are Arabs, many of whom drift in and out of the party at a high rate of turnover. In June 1965 the Communist Party was split in two. A new party – the New Communist List – based mostly on the Arab leaders and groups, with a strong Arab orientation, was founded and mustered enough votes for three members in the Knesset, while the old list succeeded in putting in only one member. These results underlined the fact that the major strength of the Communists was within the Arab population.

Arab Parties

At election time, lists of candidates are presented by a large number of parties all competing for the vote of the Arab minority. Of these parties or lists, four were most significant and three of them are affiliated to Mapai. In the 1955 Knesset election approximately 60 per cent of all Arab votes went to the Arab parties, and about 90 per cent of these were won by the three Mapai-affiliated parties. The rest of the Arab vote is divided mainly among Mapai,

---

[1] For an excellent brief history of the Communist Party in Israel, see Walter Z. Laqueur, *Communism and Nationalism in the Middle East*, New York, Frederick A. Praeger, 1956, pp. 73–119, 300–2.

Mapam and the Communists. The Arab parties appeared under different names in different elections. In 1965 the most important Arab parties were 'Co-operation and Fraternity' located in the Triangle (area populated by Arabs near Natanyah and Kfar-Saba) and among the Druzes, and 'Progress and Development', located mainly in Galilee and affiliated both to the Alignment and to a small group called 'Peace' which was affiliated to Rafi.

'Splinter Groups'

In addition to the major parties, several small splinter parties developed, such as the various ethnic lists – which counted five members in the first Knesset, three in the second, and none thereafter.

Some political, semi-intellectual groups also developed, mostly representing totally different views:

(1) *Hamishtar Hehadash* – a group of politically discontented intellectuals of the older Yishuv, drawn from all the parties, which was established in 1959.
(2) The Semitic League – a small group of marginal intellectuals and journalists, loosely connected with *Hamishtar Hehadash* whose special emphasis is placed on the necessity of becoming integrated with all Semites.
(3) *Shurat Hamitnadvim* (The Volunteers Group) – dealing mainly with the ethics of public issues and active during the early and middle 'fifties.

In 1965 the editor of *Haolam Hazeh*, Mr U. Avneri, founded a list called *Haolam-Hazeh* – 'New Fare' which succeeded in gathering enough votes to put one member (Mr Avneri himself) in the Knesset.

Election Results and Changes in Government

The government of Israel has changed several times, sometimes through elections (in 1949, 1951, 1955, 1959, 1961, and 1965) and sometimes through the re-organization of the government without dispersion of the Knesset. Tables 43 and 44 show the election results.

A common feature of all governments to date was the fact that they invariably comprised a coalition, i.e. they were always composed of several parties, as no one party held a majority in the Knesset, and that Mapai always had predominance within the coalition. Until now all governments were formed by Mapai, most of them by David Ben-Gurion, one by Moshe Sharett from 25 January 1954 to 29 January 1955 (during Ben-Gurion's temporary resignation) and two by Levi Eshkol, one after Ben-Gurion's second resignation in 1963 and one after the elections of 2 November 1965.

The coalition pattern evolved with the World Zionist Organization and since 1935 the major posts within the coalition have been in the hands of

293

TABLE 43

Results of the Elections for the Knesset by Parties, the Change

Party	First Knesset 25.1.1949	Second Knesset 30.7.1951	% of change
Total	100·0	100·0	
Mapai	35·7	37·3	+1·6
Rafi	—	—	—
National Religious Party	12·2	8·3	0·3
Agudat Israel and			
Poalei Agudat Israel		3·6	
Other Religious Parties	1·7	0·6	−1·1
Herut	11·8	6·6	−4·9
Mapam	14·7	12·5	−2·2
Ahdut Haavoda	(included in Mapam)	(included in Mapam)	
Progressives	4·1	3·2	−0·9
General Zionists	5·2	16·2	+11·0
Communists	3·5	4·0	+0·5
Minorities	3·0	4·7	+1·7
Others	8·4	3·0	−5·4

Source for the years 1949–61: CBS, op. cit.,1965, No. 16, Table W/1, p. 631.
^a Source: for 1965: *Al Hamishmar*, 10 November 1965.
^b Including Ahdut Haavoda (the Alignment).
^c Including a section from the Liberal Party. (Gahal)

from one Knesset to the next (Per cent) (1949–65)

Third Knesset 26.7.1955	% of change	Fourth Knesset 3.12.1959	% of change	Fifth Knesset 15.8.1961	% of change	Sixth Knesset[a] 2.11.1965	% of change
100·0		100·0		100·0		100·0	
32·2	−5·1	38·2	+6·0	34·7	−3·5	36·7[b]	+3·3[b]
—		—		—		7·9	
9·1		9·9		9·8		8·9	
4·7	+1·9	4·7	+0·8	5·6	+0·8	5·1	−1·4
0·3	−0·3	—	−0·3	—	—	—	—
12·6	+6·0	13·5	+0·9	13·8	+0·3	21·3[c]	−2·3[f]
7·3		7·2		7·5		6·6	−0·9
8·2	+3·0	6·0	+2·3	6·6	+0·9	3·8	—
4·4	+1·2	4·6	+0·2			3·8[e]	
10·2	−4·0	6·2	−0·4	13·6 (Liberal Party)	+2·8		
4·5	+0·5	2·8	+1·7	4·2	+1·4	3·4[d]	0·8
4·9	+0·7	4·7	−0·2	3·9	−0·8	3·8	−0·1
−1·6	1·4	2·2	+0·6	0·3	−1·9	2·5	+2·2

[d] Including the New Communist Party.
[e] Under the name 'Independent Liberals'. (IL)
[f] The comparison is between Gahal and IL in the Sixth Knesset and the Liberal Party in the Fifth.

Mapai, with Ben-Gurion serving as Chairman of the Executive of the Zionist Organization and the Jewish Agency.

The predominance of Mapai was apparent not only in the fact that, as the largest party, it was always called upon to form a coalition, but also in its continuous and absolute preponderance in the Histadrut – even at those times when its actual majority was relatively small (about 57–8 per cent in 1949 and 1956, declining to 55 per cent in 1960).

There is no doubt that in a way it was the strength of Mapai and its leadership – and perhaps especially of the Prime Minister, David Ben-Gurion – which constituted the major foci and symbols of continuity from the period of the Yishuv to that of the state.

To a smaller extent such continuity also existed in the other parties, especially those participating in the coalition governments in the state of Israel. Almost all these parties developed from the original Zionist and Yishuv parties although they underwent several significant changes which will be analysed presently.

The only major exception is *Agudat Israel* – the extreme orthodox party – which not only took no part in the Zionist movement, but even opposed it, at least on the ideological and cultural level. However, it has joined several coalition governments, though without necessarily accepting the Zionist interpretation of the goals and legitimations of the state.

This move, which at the time was seen mostly in terms of national unity and/or the exigencies of coalition politics, was in fact, as we shall see in greater detail later, pregnant with significance from the point of view of the legitimation and symbols of the state.

Thus, there was marked continuity of political parties throughout the various stages of the Yishuv and the state.

Changes in Power and Differences of Structure between Yishuv and State

While the continuity previously discussed also applied to the institutional structure of the government, all the formal paraphernalia of a full sovereign state could obviously not be taken over from the earlier period. The major features of these institutions however, such as the democratic framework, the maintenance of representative institutions, and the responsibility of the government to the legislature are not dissimilar from the situation as it existed at the time of the Yishuv.

Some of the most important formal changes can be seen in the presidency which, unlike the Zionist Organization, has become mainly a symbolic office with little real political influence.

Similarly, important changes were effected in the establishment and institutionalization of the judiciary, non-existent within the Jewish institutions except for the honorary court of the Zionist Congress, and in the con-

296

TABLE 44

Results of the Elections for the Knesset by Blocks and the Per Cent Change from One Knesset to the Next (1949–65)

Block	First Knesset 25.1.1949	Second Knesset 30.7.1951	% of change	Third Knesset 26.7.1955	% of change	Fourth Knesset 3.12.1959	% of change	Fifth Knesset 15.8.1961	% of change	Sixth Knesset 2.11.1965	% of change
Total	100·0	100·0		100·0		100·0		100·0		100·0	
Religious Parties (Mizrahi, Hapoel Hamizrahi, Agudat-Israel, Poalei-Agudat-Israel and the rest)	13·9	12·5	−1·4	14·1	+1·6	14·6	+0·5	15·4	+0·8	14·0	−1·4
Labour Parties (Mapai, Rafi, Mapam, Ahdut, Haavoda, Communists)	53·9	53·8	−0·1	52·2	−1·6	54·2	+2·0	53·0	−1·2	54·6	+1·6
Right-Wing Parties (Herut, Progressives, General Zionists, Liberals, Independent Liberals)	20·8	26·0	+5·2	27·2	+1·2	24·3	−2·9	27·4	+3·1	25·1	−2·3
Minority Lists	3·0	4·7	+1·7	4·9	+0·2	4·7	−0·2	3·9	−0·8	3·8	−0·1
Others	8·4	3·0	−5·4	1·6	−1·4	2·2	+0·6	0·3	−1·9	2·5	0·5

Sources: (1) For the years 1949–61: CBS, op. cit., No. 16, 1965, Table W/1, p. 631.
(2) For 1965: *Haaretz*, 10 November 1965.

TABLE 45

The Occupational Distribution of Members of Parliament
First-Sixth Knesset, 1949–65
(Percentages)

Occupation	1st Knesset	2nd Knesset	3rd Knesset	4th Knesset	5th Knesset	6th Knesset
1. Politicians and Clerks, including Mayor and Diplomats	49·5	32·5	29·0	30·0	28·8	25·8
2. Agricultural Workers	16·5	23·0	23·0	22·5	21·0	20·0
3. Professionals includes Teachers, Rabbis, etc. Owners of Factories, Merchants	23·6	35·7	39·7	39·6	42·4	41·6
4. Heads of Corporations	1·5	2·5	3·0	1·5	3·0	7·5
5. Skilled and Semi-skilled Labourers	3·0	4·0	2·4	4·1	2·4	5·1
6. Others and Unknown	5·9	2·3	2·9	2·3	2·4	—
Total	100·0	100·0	100·0	100·0	100·0	100·0

[a] Notes: (1) The table is based primarily on what is claimed by the candidate on his presentation of his qualifications for the Knesset.
(2) Several of the candidates have, from time to time, changed their occupational category.

Source: Knesset 1–5 – A. Zidon, *Parliament* (Hebrew), Aihasaff, 1964, p. 392.
Knesset 6 – *Reshumot* (Hebrew), 17 November 1965.

trolling and empowering agencies – such as the State Comptroller and the various permanent parliamentary committees.

In spite of the continuity in the nature and composition of the parties and their élites, the establishment of the State of Israel has obviously wrought far-reaching changes in the political process and institutions.

Most functions of the Mandate, the Jewish Agency, and the *Vaad Leumi* have been incorporated within the institutional framework of the state, largely ending the old division of labour that existed between them in the mandatory period (see above Chapters 3 and 4). The Jewish Agency continues to deal with problems of colonization, settlement of new immigrants, cultural activities in the diaspora, and some political and propagandist activities of its own, but most of its political activities naturally devolved on to the state.

A change, parallel to that in the institutional structure also took place in the relative importance of Israeli and World Zionist organizations and institutions. The situation predominant in the pre-state period – when World Zionists were of much greater importance than their Palestinian counterparts – was completely reversed. Now the centre of gravity shifted to Israel, with the Zionist organs in the diaspora playing only a secondary role. This could be seen in the composition of the political leadership (with most of the top leaders going over to the government) and in the division of functions between them.[1]

Beyond these and the formal changes in the organization of the political institutions, one of the most important developments was the unification of different levels and issues of political struggle into one common framework and the emergence of various new organs and patterns for the formulation of political decisions and regulations.

---

[1] The contract between the Government of Israel and the Zionist Executive, called also the Directorial of the Jewish Agency, was signed in 1954. This contract states the JA's functions, rights and duties. The underlying principle is that the JA should deal with immigration, absorption, development, etc., but all other functions undertaken previously by the JA, and especially foreign relations, are now to be under the auspices of the government. The JA is not a representative of the State. However, this theoretically clear-cut distinction was not easy to execute. Problems of international relations, overt and covert, from time to time necessitated the intervention of the JA which contradicted the spirit of the contract.

In 1960 a joint proclamation was issued which, though ending all formal dispute, still gave rise to an undercurrent of controversy between the two agencies of the Jewish people.

The declaration states (25 May 1960): 'The Government of Israel and the Executive of the ZWF, gathered for a joint meeting, thus declare of their absolute wish to establish close relations, according to the contract from 1954, and in the spirit of the Law of the ZWF's status from 1952, according to which the State of Israel sees itself as the creation of the Jewish People in total, and expects efforts from the ZWF's side to reach the unity of the nation for the State . . . .'

The framework and organization of power was, of course, greatly changed with the establishment of the state, developing new and unified institutional and political frameworks and positions and extending the scope of their activities.

But the most important change was not merely in the increased scope of political activities but in the development of new mechanisms and norms of allocation of power and political positions. The most important of these changes were the following:

(1) Establishment of unified political institutions;
(2) The establishment and institutionalization – even though only partial – of new legal and formal norms of political activity;
(3) Growing centralization of the basic frameworks of power within the hands of the government and its administrative agencies;
(4) A rise in the social evaluation of power and power relations;
(5) Re-orientation and organizaton of political activities;
(6) A concomitant growth in the differentiation between élite and non-élite groups;
(7) The development of power as an important factor in the solution of internal problems.

Among the crucial functions now taken over by the state was, first and foremost, the establishment of the Israel Defence Army as a unified military organization, subject to the directives of the government, and in place of the looser organizations of the *Hagana* and the various dissident groups. Eventually, the unification of services spread to the establishment of a unified educational system in lieu of the different trend schools and, still later, to the establishment of state labour exchanges instead of those run by the Histadrut.

Although some of the older attitudes and arrangements persisted in the newly unified institutions they did not detract from the general importance of the new central political institutions – although they influenced their functioning.

The Establishment of Basic Government Branches—The Executive, Legislative and Judiciary

Side by side with the unification of the political framework came the establishment and functioning of modern political institutions, including legislative, executive, judiciary, and administrative services.

Unlike the legislative and executive organs, which had organizational predecessors in the Zionist organization and in which a marked personal continuity could be found, the judiciary and administrative were new, both from the point of view of organization and personnel.

The establishment of a legal system was of very great importance for the unified framework of political institutions, and the courts played a continuously growing part in the regulation and adjudication of political and civil issues.

Although the courts have no actual constitutional rights in the revision of existing laws, many of their decisions (especially those of the 'orders nisi' of the High Court of Justice) carry important constitutional repercussions, and the spirit of their decisions has greatly affected the functioning of the administration.

Development of Government Administration

As seen from the following table, the development and continuous increase in personnel of government administration (see Table 46) quickly crystallized.

The following ministries were set up: Defence, Foreign Affairs, Finance, Commerce and Industry, Agriculture, Labour (containing the National Insurance Institute), Interior, Justice, Health, Social Welfare, Education and Culture, Communications, and Posts. Because of coalition exigencies a Police Ministry was also established, and the special needs of the country further prompted the establishment of ministries of Development and Religious Affairs. In addition, the Prime Minister's office embraces important administrative units, whose total personnel exceeds that of a number of ministries. Among these are the Civil Service Commission, the Central

TABLE 46

Government Employees by Grade[a] (1955–64)

Year[b]	Total		Administrative grades		Professional grades		Manual workers	
	Number	%	Number	%	Number	%	Number	%
1955	30,872	100	18,289	59·25	3,731	12·08	8,852	28·67
1957	32,889	100	19,138	58·19	4,454	13·54	9,297	28·27
1959	37,175	100	19,849	53·40	7,001	18·83	10,325	27·77
1960	38,691	100	19,637	50·76	8,174	21·12	10,880	28·12
1961	39,978	100	20,462	51·19	8,815	22·04	10,701	26·77
1962	40,738	100	20,165	49·50	10,084	24·76	10,489	25·74
1964	43,629	100	21,042	48·25	11,274	25·84	11,313	25·91

Source: CBS, op. cit., No. 16, 1965, Table K/35, pp. 340–1.

[a] Does not include Police and Prison Officers.
[b] The data relate to the situation of Government employees at the end of March of every year.

Bureau of Statistics, the Scientific Research Council and institutes of special-ized research such as the Atomic Energy Commission, Broadcasting and Press Services, Technical Assistance Liaison Office, the State Archives, and the Government Tourist Corporation, Ministries of Emigration and of War Veterans which existed in earlier years have since been integrated into other ministries.

Although some of the specific divisions and relations among the different ministries originated as points of political expediency, their bureaucratic structure spread quickly into independent, autonomous bodies representing separate interests, traditions and orientations. Many appointments to major posts were made in deference to the coalition system or to party consider-ations, and the top echelons (Director-General and his deputies, Legal Adviser, various Directors of Departments) changed with each change of Minister.

Gradually however, especially in the vital economic and legal ministries, a growing professionalization of the civil service has developed. At the same time, due to continuous social and political problems, a slow but continuous growth of administrative bodies took place, raising many problems of efficiency and often undermining professional orientations.

During the last five years considerable efforts were made to increase the 'professionalism' of the Civil Service; recruitment is made increasingly by merit, greater attention is given to post-entry training of civil servants, and efforts are made to strengthen the 'professional' orientation of the civil service through de-politicization. Out of 38,691 civil servants in March 1960 8,174 or 21·1 per cent were professionals, 19,637 or 50·8 per cent were administrative workers and 10,880 or 28·1 per cent were labourers. By March 1961,[1] out of 39,978 civil-servants (without Constables, Supernumer-aries and Warders) there were 8,815 or 22·3 per cent professionals, 20,462 or 51·05 per cent administrative workers, and 10,701 or 26·65 per cent labourers.

Despite this increase of the professional element in the civil service the overall picture is not that of a highly professional service. Rather the picture here is somewhat similar to the one we have seen in the economic sphere – continuous expansion due to the general expansion of the economy, but guided mostly by consideration of political and coalition exigencies and pressures, with but relatively little long-range planning or co-ordination, giving rise to a host of different bureaucracies each with its own vested interests, with but little professional or service orientations.

During the first years of the state, the higher and even intermediate administrative positions were considered to be the apex of the social hier-archy, mainly because of their proximity to political power. With the passage of time, however, this prestige has decreased and these posts became much

[1] Source: Statistical Abst. No. 13, 1962, pp. 424-5.

more dependent on professional criteria. Nonetheless, the criterion of political allegiance and power certainly did not abate entirely.

The situation was very different with the judiciary which, on the whole, maintained a continuous upward swing in general prestige and in professional orientation.

Naturally the civil service became the main instrument for the implementation of both major goals and day-to-day policies.

This has necessarily increased the control by the bureaucratic administration over various spheres of life and turned the civil service into a major area of political struggle, where most interest groups have recourse to political decision-making and where the concrete details of political bargaining are continuously arranged.

The central economic Ministries of Commerce and Trade, Development, Labour and, in particular, the Treasury are of special importance here, as they often form special interest groups backed by their Ministries and their parties or clientele.

While the problem of a Constitution as a basic framework of political institutions has often been a subject for general public discussion, it has not really become a matter for political party dispute.

Other Public Bureaucracies

Parallel to the civil service and, to some degree, in response to it, similar bureaucracies developed within other public bodies, especially the Jewish Agency, the Histadrut and the different political parties.

The Jewish Agency was now charged with the task of absorbing and settling immigrants, as a result of which the number of its employees increased from 759 in 1946 (the period of the 22nd Congress) to 4,437 in 1951 (the 23rd Congress), and to 4,444 in 1946, with a minor drop to 4,153 in 1960. From this time no great changes occurred.

On the establishment of the state the members of the Histadrut and their families numbered 270,750 and its administrative employees about 6,000; its budget was IL 873,213 per annum. At the end of 1964 membership was 1,388,000 and there were 24,816 employees (1961).[1] The budget had grown to IL 49,500,000 by 1965.[2]

Growing Bureaucracy in the Structure and Activities of the Political Elite

The growing importance of administration in the political field also furthered the belief in the greater efficiency of more autonomous civil and military

---

[1] We were not able to get information for later than 1961.

[2] This budget does not include the budget of the Health Services and some small subsidiaries of Histadrut.

bodies, an attitude which was supported by the continuous extension in power and scope of the administrative agencies. It changed the pattern of political decision-making, as well as the structure of the major political parties, and also affected relations between the élite and the public.

Many of these changes, especially the exaggerated emphasis on the status of the civil service, were only transitory phenomena. The overall structural effects of these changes were, however, lasting.

The political élite of the Yishuv, and especially the more active group within it – the leadership of Mapai – soon became a ruling élite group, passing through several important changes in its basic characteristics.

The relative homogeneity of the élite within the different sectors gave place to a marked differentiation between the different echelons of the political élite, while also producing growing cohesion among the élites of the different sectors. More professional élite groups developed in the bureaucratic military and diplomatic service, as well as in the judiciary, weakening the internal homogeneity and cohesion of the élite. Many problems and tensions arose between these various élite groups.

All this naturally produced many repercussions on relations between the élite and the public. The comparatively close relation between the élite and the various informal and semi-formal groups weakened considerably. Members of the élite tended to detach themselves and formed groups of their own and their whole pattern of life and association began to be different from that of the non-élite.

Thus, the roles of ministers and of members of the political élite altered. Party, government, and administrative foci emerged, around each of which different roles and groups developed to focus the demands and references of the upper ministerial or political élite. Older movement leadership became less important – and even impeded the full development and crystallization of these new roles.

Growing Bureaucracy of the Parties

The developments analysed above led to the rapid crystallization of the prominent groups and sects, causing them to emerge into more or less organized parties. Together with the different interest groups, sects, and social movements, they grew into more unified political frameworks, sharing their organization and patterns of activities and with strong orientations to wider political frameworks and to the general public.

Only the leftist and the extreme religious groups retained part of their sectarian nature based, in the case of the leftist parties, mainly on the kibbutzim – and their totalistic orientations – but even they had to look for support among the wider public.

With the spread of formal organization and growing centralization, both the central part and the branches of the parties segmented into various interest and professional cells. Recruiting activities were organized through more specific agencies adapted to the sources of potential recruits, i.e. the younger generation, the new immigrants, and other uncommitted individuals. The primary appeal to the individual member was thus made through these differentiated cells, to which he belonged either at his working place or in his home district.

In addition most parties also created a vast network of economic facilities in the form of banks, housing projects, loan funds, and, to some extent, employment-providing enterprises. All economic enterprises of the Histadrut, the Public Health (Sick Fund) Services, the many co-operatives, until recently the labour exhanges and, to some extent, even private enterprises, are in some ways closely affiliated to the parties.

Thus, whatever the formal structure of the parties, it is the upper leadership, coupled with the core of the functionaries, that wield the real power.

While there have lately been many signs of rebellion within the parties against these élitist and oligarchic tendencies, these have usually resulted merely in the co-opting of the more rebellious leaders into the central bodies rather than in any structural changes within the parties.

The extent of centralization is usually greatest in the small leftist parties and in Herut, of medium strength in Mapai and the National Religious Party, and probably weakest in the 'bourgeois' parties. However the general trend towards such centralization can be found among all parties.

Within the Histadrut the growth of economic and political enterprises and the concomitant tendencies to overall centralization and bureaucratization, were already evident in the limited autonomy of the different trade unions and local workers' councils. With increased membership and diversification of its activities, this tendency naturally grew and was strengthened by the fact that the Histadrut, a federation of different parties, attempted to use it as a means of extending their power.

The various elections to the Histadrut have maintained Mapai in its position of power – although with decreasing strength.

Political Continuity from the Yishuv to the State

Whatever the extent of internal change in the parties, there has been a marked continuity in their general controls from the pre-state period and throughout the years of the state. The only important changes were the various mergers and splits between Mapam and *Ahdut Haavoda*, in the religious bloc and, in 1961, the merger of the Progressives and the General Zionists into the Liberal Party.

The continuity is the more marked and astonishing when considering the

305

great influx of new immigrants – for most of whom the specific form of modern political organization and social movements were alien.

How then can this continuity be explained? And what has been its effect on the Israeli political system? Did the older ideologies and the programmes of the various parties really attract the new parts of the population in terms of their own problems? And did the new population – the various immigrant groups as well as the new native-born generation – identify with these goals, symbols, and ideologies? How was this continuity of parties effected within the framework of the new unified political institutions and norms?

2

THE POLITICAL PROCESS IN ISRAEL – THE MAJOR ISSUES OF POLITICAL STRUGGLE AND THE ALIGNMENTS AROUND THEM

Introduction

The starting point for any understanding of the Israeli political scene is an analysis of the political controversies between the major parties, a number of which have emerged since the establishment of the state. These issues reflect the major social, economic, and political problems of the country and the policies undertaken by the government to cope with them.

They can be divided into several 'levels', and into different 'content' areas. There are first of all the 'simpler' issues which deal with concrete aspects of relation and competition among different groups, with the differential allocation of various facilities, and with priveleged position or subsidies – be they in religion, education, or in economic or social policy.

Second are the issues dealing with more general economic or social principles (such as the problem of 'liberalization') or those concerned with relations between the religious and non-religious groups, the problem of military government in the Arab sectors, or the merits of various measures for integrating new immigrants.

These issues sometimes merge into the third level of those dealing with the definition of basic goals or orientations or the state – be they the ingathering of the exiles, the maintenance of military security or the continuity of democratic institutions.

As far as content is concerned, these issues divide roughly into economic, social, political, and religious ones.

Economic Issues

Economic problems and policies have been central topics of public and political debate in Israel throughout its existence. More specifically the main economic problem has been the large-scale expansion of public and private consumption, and whether the maintenance of a democratic system in difficult conditions made this inevitable.

Only extremists (like some of the *Hamishtar Hehadash* group) contended that problems of consumption and demands for a higher standard of living could be ignored in a democratic system. In general, there were few who were prepared to defend the existing policy without admitting that it was, to some extent, detrimental to economic development. Reports of the Bank of Israel and many other independent studies clearly substantiate such critical attitudes.

In the political sphere, the problem of economic independence was often treated as a moral issue – namely the extent to which the basic ideological tenets of Zionism made it morally justifiable to live beyond one's means.

Beyond these general issues, the details of concrete economic policies, their administration and execution were constantly under discussion, revolving mainly around the following themes:

(1) The scope of the development policy – i.e. the extent to which development should be encouraged through special government spending as against development through the usual market mechanisms. Problems of agriculture, and the extent to which it should be expanded beyond its level of profitability are of special interest here.

(2) Government or other direct supervision of the economy as opposed to the extension of more autonomous market mechanisms.

(3) Monopolization and preferences for different sectors – especially the alleged preference given to the Histadrut sector.

(4) The scope of the wage policy and especially the continuous rise of the cost-of-living allowance, contrasting with the opposition to wage differerentials.

(5) Nationalization of the major social services – especially of health services – as against the attempts of *Kupat Holim* to maintain the status quo.

These issues were often intertwined with social problems, the most important of these being related to wage differentials – i.e. the extent to which differences between skilled, professional, etc, workers should be limited or encouraged. Second in importance were problems dealing with the autonomy of various professional organizations as against the monolithic framework of the Histadrut. These issues were closely related to debates on the values and ideologies of Israeli society and spilled over into a variety of concrete issues discussed in this and in preceding chapters.

Problems of Immigrant Absorption; Wadi Salib

It is crucial for an understanding of Israeli politics that, with one exception, issues of immigration and problems of immigrant groups did not really form part of the political struggle on the central inter-party level.

General problems of absorption policy (such as immigrant settlement or selectivity – acceptance only of 'healthy' or productive immigrants) sometimes constituted a topic of dispute without clear party alignment. But, on the whole, the details of the absorption policy rarely constituted any special focus of political discussion.

What is even more surprising is the fact that (except during the 1959 election) these issues were hardly expressed by the immigrants themselves, but rather by the various party leaders. Though specific ethnic lists appeared in almost every election, they were not very successful.

But in 1959, with the Wadi Salib outbreak, new developments took place. Intergroup tensions and hostilities developed among the large number of newcomers of low economic position. The government's policy of directing these new immigrants seems to have unwittingly added to their disappointment, turning it into an overall frustration.

In July 1959 a violent demonstration took place in Wadi Salib in Haifa organized by immigrants from North Africa. This was followed by similar occurrences in other places. The main body behind these demonstrations was the *Likkud Olei Tsfon Africa* (the group of North African immigrants) led by David Ben-Haroush. They organized the demonstration in Haifa and, on the evening of the same day, distributed leaflets calling on all North Africans to keep calm but to 'leave' all established parties and 'their lackeys among the North Africans' and to trust only the *Likkud* which undertook to look after their real interests. Several days later, further disturbances occurred in other places. In most cases, the rioters claimed that it was discrimination against the North Africans that had prompted them to demonstrate, and that the outbursts were directed at the basic aspects of the system of absorption – especially at alleged discrimination against North Africans and the system of *avodat dahak* (public emergency work). It was clear from the beginning that these local incidents were symptomatic of deeper problems and the government therefore appointed a public committee to investigate the occurrences in Wadi Salib and their background.

Wadi Salib, a formerly obscure slum area on the slopes of Hadar Hacarmel in Haifa, has now become a well-known symbol in Israel. The events at Wadi Salib unleashed a stream of public debate, political recrimination as well as more serious and responsible discussion by various parts of the Israeli public.

The *Likkud* seemed to be more than a mere ethnic group. Starting as a small spontaneous group with common problems of housing and work, they soon developed into an extremist-populist organization opposed to all parties and especially to the self-interest rampant in all established parties and proclaimed a completely new and extreme ideology of 'ethnic' separateness.

In fact Ben-Haroush's extremism only played into the hands of those who wanted to treat the whole problem as one of hooliganism and political agitation by 'subversive' elements.

However, a growing sensitivity to the 'ethnic' problem resulted from the incidents at Wadi Salib. They gave impetus to several important policy innovations in the economic and educational sphere and, on a more superficial but nevertheless significant level, they led to the inclusion (often in 'safe places') of orientals and North Africans on the election candidates' lists of many parties. Several specifically ethnic parties again emerged at election time, among them the *Likkud* with Ben-Haroush heading its list and claiming that he represented not only the North Africans but all victims of discrimination.

The need to include more orientals in major public posts became generally recognized and, in the 1961 election, some of the older Sephardi groups supported Mapai which included a Sephardi minister in the 1961 Cabinet.

The awareness of the gravity of ethnic problems in the spheres of education and occupational guidance has grown ever since and policies have been drawn up to overcome them.

No new parties or alignments developed as a result of these problems and most of the interested groups were absorbed in the existing parties – the more contented elements mainly within Mapai and the religious parties, and the more discontented elements within Herut. In all parties, however, the 'ethnic' problem became increasingly important, especially on the local level. During the last two years ethnic leaders have become prominent in local and municipal politics and, as we shall see later, in many of the local elections ethnic issues gained growing, sometimes central, importance. One of the results of these developments was the doubling of the number of deputies with oriental background – the Sixth as compared to the Fifth Knesset – where they constitute now 12 per cent of the total membership.

Religious Issues – General

Religious issues constitute a very important and continuous focus of political debate. Already the drafting of the Declaration of Independence in 1948 gave rise to differences of opinion between the religious representatives and the secular majority, the religious leaders demanding that the Declaration include some religious legitimation of the state. The compromise solution adopted, which quotes 'The Rock of Israel' instead of 'God' is typical of the many compromises which mark the relationship between state and religion.

On a cultural level this problem appears as the basic definition of total collectively in terms of Jewish tradition and the extent of freedom given in the interpretation and innovation in cultural tradition. The extent to which religious law would become the official law of the land in various legal spheres developed into a broad, institutional issue.

In more concrete terms, the main bones of contention between the religious and the secular parties lay in three fields: (1) general question pertaining to the legitimation of the state and to the definition of the nature and traditions of society; (2) more concretely, the scope of the religious contours of the state or the degree of non-separation between religion and state, and the extent to which religious laws could be imposed on the population as a whole; the extent to which religious-juridical bodies, like the Rabbinate, would on the one hand have jurisdiction over the whole Jewish population, and conversely the extent to which they will be exempt from supervision by the 'secular' authorities; (3) the autonomy of the religious groups in the educational sphere, and the extent to which various religious institutions will enjoy state support.

In the discussion of the religious issues several basic facts should be kept in mind. One is the *modus vivendi* that developed between the religious and secular groups in the period of the Yishuv. As a result of this all personal jurisdiction (i.e. with regard to marriage, divorce, etc.) was vested by the Knesset in the Rabbinate (and with parallel religious institutions for the Muslim and Christian and Kurdish communities) – thus giving it full jurisdiction over all the population, religious and non-religious alike.

Thus, although the Rabbinate represents, and is fully accepted as a source of authority by only a part of the population, it has general legal power in personal matters over the whole Jewish population in Israel. It therefore tends to maintain and foster claims to universality and consequent autonomy of its own in relation to the religious groups, while at the same time its power is in fact largely dependent on the political power of these groups.

The Rabbinate developed thus a high degree of centralization and militancy demanding total autonomy from the secular institutions, and has become akin to a centralized ecclesiastical organization. At the same time it formed the focus of an intensive struggle between different religious and even secular groups, affecting the possibility and limits of their co-existence and respective overall jurisdictions.

This struggle was intensified by the fact that the National Religious Party claimed for itself the monopoly of representing in the state all religious interests and institutions (except for those of the *Aguda*) and fought very bitterly any attempts to curtail its power over them.

Religious Issues – 'Who is a Jew?'

The focus of the first question, that of the religious legitimation of the state, focused around the problem of 'Who is a Jew?'

The latent 'Who is a Jew?' problem erupted in March 1958. At the time the immigrants coming into the country included assimilated Jews from Iron Curtain countries who, in some cases, brought with them Gentile wives and children of half-Gentile parents. The then Minister of Interior, a member of *Ahdut Haavoda*, issued directives on the registration of immigrants which stated that a person be described as a Jew on his identity card on the strength of his declaration to that effect alone. These regulations caused considerable public debate. The religious groups opposed them on the grounds that the definition of a Jew should be based only on *halachic* law, according to which a person is a Jew if his mother was Jewish or else he has to be duly pro-selytized by rabbinical sanction. Under *halachic* law a number of marriage ties are forbidden, such as union between a descendant of the ancient priestly caste (*Cohanim*) and a divorcee, or between a Jew and a Gentile. But the crux of the rabbinical marriage law is the problem of divorce. Unless divorce is obtained by this law the older marriage still holds and any new marriage by any partner is considered null and void. The children born out of such a marriage are born in adultery and are considered as 'bastards' – the only type of illegitimacy in rabbinical law – and they and their descendents are ulti-mately forbidden from inter-marrying with the bulk of Jewry. Orthodox Jewry feared that any breach in the *halachic* family law would give rise to non-recognized divorces and remarriages and would thus ultimately force the orthodox minority into a virtual social and racial ghetto, as it would not be able to marry into a majority into which such illegitimates would have married. This fear was generally paraphrased by the orthodox on an ideological level – namely that the introduction of secular family law would 'destroy the unity of the nation' and that therefore they opposed the new regulations which laid down a formal separation between religious affiliation and nationality and would thus pave the way for the acceptance of 'illegitimate' children. On the other extreme the very left wing opposed the regulations because it objected to religious affiliation being registered at all. The new regulations were formally ratified by the Cabinet in June 1958 and the crisis came to a head with the withdrawal from the coalition of the National Religious Party. During the deadlock of the ensuing months Mr Ben-Gurion took an unprece-dented step by putting the problem to the forty-three so-called 'Sages of Israel' all over the world (who included personalities outstanding in religion and the humanities belinging to all schools of thought). These 'Sages' were thus asked to voice their opinions on the problem of how to register Israelis of mixed Jewish origin.

The replies of the 'Sages' turned out to be largely in favour of the orthodox point of view, a fact which helped in finding a formula acceptable to the secular side though based on *halachic* principles. The new proposal put forward was that a minor's religion should not be given as his own, but that the religion of the parents should be stated instead. On the other hand, every adult would have the right to state his own religion. This proposal solved the specific problem at the time, because the question of identification was crucial only in the case of children who were to grow up in Israel and would eventually raise the problem of intermarriage forbidden by *halachic* law.

The new provisions were carried out in 1960 when the National Religious Party was again installed in the Ministry of the Interior.

The Problem of Benei Israel

This problem erupted again, in a tense and unpleasant way, around the *Benei Israel* – a Jewish group from India.

As the family law among this group differed in some details from the general rabbinical family law, it became doubtful whether they could marry other Jews without being 'converted'. Since the *Benei Israel* had been isolated from other Jewish communities there had been de facto intermarriages in the past with other Jewish communities, on the other hand it was suspected that they might have sometimes intermarried in India with non-Jewish groups.

However, with the immigration to Israel of about a third of this community, numbering several thousand souls, the problem of intermarriage with the general population of Israel and the old rabbinical doubts now assumed a more practical form. During the early 1950's the few occurring cases of intermarriage were solved by individual rabbis giving divergent judgements, but the lack of uniform decision led the Chief Rabbinate to take up the matter at the end of the 1950's.

The Chief Rabbinate took the bold step of overruling the nineteenth century ordinance prohibiting intermarriage, and thus, in principle, now placed the community on the same footing with the rest of the Jewish people.

Nevertheless, the new ruling was supported by only a minority, though an influential one, of the Great Rabbinical Council. The Chief Rabbinate followed it up by issuing qualifying clauses, which were so formulated as to appease extreme orthodox opinions. One of these clauses ordered the officiating rabbis to enquire of the member of the *Benei Israel* entering a 'mixed' marriage whether the two generations preceding him were fully Jewish. Chief Rabbi Nissim's fairly liberal policy nevertheless aroused opposition. The *Benei Israel* community demanded that the original rulings as to their status be cancelled outright, a request which was supported by the secular sector, including President Ben-Zvi himself. The extreme circles of *Agudat Israel*, whose recognition of the Chief Rabbinate's authority is at best lukewarm, flatly rejected the ruling, whilst many local rabbis refused to obey it. As with other questions the opinion of extremist rabbis in the diaspora was also felt here.

The issue came before the Knesset, where the demand was voiced that undisciplined rabbis be brought to law. The problem has now been solved temporarily by the Minister of Religious Affairs briefing various regional rabbis (whose personal convictions are the same as those of the Minister and Chief Rabbi) on how to deal with these 'mixed' marriages. The unpleasantness of coercing various local rabbis to act contrary to their convictions was thus circumvented. However, members of the *Benei Israel* community are dissatisfied with this arrangement which does not recognize them as being categorically on the same footing as the rest of the nation. The situation is typical of Israeli life in this field, where precarious *ad hoc* arrangements prevail.

This precarious arrangement erupted once again in the summer of 1964, bringing in its wake one of the most intensive conflicts on the religious-secular front, in which the standing of the Chief Rabbinate was very much called into question.

The following newspaper excerpt gives a fairly accurate picture of these developments:[1]

On Monday the Knesset went on record by voting a resolution which called upon the Chief Rabbinate 'to mend its ways'. In a rare show of unanimity, Israel's parliament called upon the Chief Rabbinate to remove the causes for bitterness among the Benei Israel, who came to Israel from India, and who felt that they were discriminated against under the regulations laid down by the Chief Rabbinate with regard to marriages between them and other Jews.

Even the National Religious Party voted for the Knesset resolution which was based on a Cabinet decision to which all parties in the coalition government subscribed. Only two hands were raised against the resolution, those of two members of the Agudat Israel Party.

Most opposition parties – Herut, Liberals, Mapam and the Communists – abstained because they considered the resolution to be too weak. The Knesset voted the resolution by forty-three votes to two, with thirty abstentions. It declared that the Benei Israel are Jews in every way, without qualification, who have equal rights in all fields including those of marriage and divorce.

This reference was directed at the instructions given by the Sephardi Chief Rabbi Nissim which decreed a set of special regulations for the members of the Benei Israel community.

Some weeks before, a few dozen families of this ten thousand strong community began a sit-down strike in front of the Jewish Agency offices in Jerusalem. Their case was taken up by almost all political parties, both in the government and in opposition – including Mapai.

Even before the matter reached this stage, there were several behind-the-

[1] From *Jewish Observer and Middle East Review*, 21 August 1964.

scene attempts to reach some agreement. But appeals to the Chief Rabbinate and even the intervention of President Shazar failed.

The opposition parties' proposal was that the Knesset must order the Chief Rabbis to alter their stand or else adopt appropriate legislation to solve the problem itself.

For a week before the Knesset meeting there had been mass rallies in support of the *Benei Israel*, and Premier Eshkol, in his address to the Knesset, put what is clearly the majority view.

The *Benei Israel*, he said, is not the only community whose members have not always acted in accordance with the strict letter of the *Shulhan Aruch* (rabbinic law). If, for instance, the Jews of the Soviet Union were permitted to emigrate to Israel, the rabbis might reject them also as not having a thoroughbred ancestry.

The rabbinate would thus become an obstacle to the principle of the ingathering of the exiles, and this must not be permitted.

Eshkol expressed regret for some of the ugly incidents included in the demonstrations of the *Benei Israel* and their supporters – such as the burning of an effigy of Rabbi Nissim. But these were overshadowed by the seriousness of the problem

After this the Chief Rabbinate did in fact back down from its previous instruction, accepting a compromise solution suggested by the Mayor of Jerusalem, according to which the specific injunctions against *Benei Israel* were withdrawn from the directives and were substituted by more general injunction to investigate 'cases of doubtful parentage in all cases'.

The Case of Brother Daniel

A major highlight of this problem of definition was the recent High Court decision in the case of 'Brother Daniel'.

The subject of the case was almost as interesting as the question itself: Oswald Rufeisen, a Jewish-born Carmelite monk, who had fought against the Germans in the underground during the Second World War. During his youth in Poland, Rufeisen had been an active member of a religious Zionist movement and had then spent two years in Wilna preparing himself for the life of a pioneer in Palestine. When the war broke out he was arrested by the Nazis but managed to escape and succeeded in being accepted by the Germans as a *Volksdeutscher*. Thanks to his connexions with the Germans, he succeeded in saving the lives of at least 150 Jews who later joined the partisans. He was found out and arrested but escaped again and hid in a Roman Catholic convent where, in 1942, he embraced the Catholic faith out of conviction.

After the war he studied for the priesthood and, when ordained, joined the Carmelite Order because, as he said, although leaving the Jewish faith, he considered himself ethnically Jewish and wanted to emigrate to the Jewish state, the only country in the world where he could find the fulfilment of his wishes as a Jew. He joined the Carmelites because that Order has monasteries in Israel.

He arrived in Israel several years later with the permission of his superiors to join the Stella Maris Monastery on Mount Carmel, after the Polish authorities had allowed him to emigrate as a Jew.

On arrival in Israel he applied to the Minister of the Interior for citizenship under the Law of Return, which permits every Jewish immigrant to become a citizen of the country as soon as he sets foot on its soil. He also asked that in his Israel identity card the space provided for 'ethnic affiliation' (*le'um*) should be marked 'Jewish'.

The Minister of the Interior refused to do this on the basis of the government's resolution that only a person declaring himself to be a *bona fide* Jew who does not belong to any other religion is a Jew. He did, however, offer Rufeisen citizenship through naturalization. Rufeisen refused to accept this and took the matter to the Supreme Court in the form of a petition for an *order nisi* against the Minister of the Interior, which was heard before the Supreme Court on December 1962. The five judges – Silberg, Landau, Berenson, Cohen, and Manny – decided (Justice Cohen dissenting) that an apostate had no claim to be recognized as a Jew in Israel.

It is significant that not all the judges based their judgement on the *halachic* law – according to some interpretations of which even a Jew who has sinned (or has even become an apostate) remains a Jew – but rather on what they called the historic consciousness and tradition of the people.

Thus Justice Silberg summed up for the majority by saying: 'I am well aware that there are many different opinions about Jewishness – from extreme orthodox to outright heretic – but common to all the people living in Israel (with the exception of a very few) is that we do not cut ourselves off from our historic past and we do not deny the heritage of our forefathers.'

He stated that petitioner's counsel had raised the question that if Rufeisen were not recognized as a Jew, which nationality did he belong to? He was not a Jew and not a Pole. The answer, the Judge said, was that Rufeisen did not belong to any nationality, and the space provided for ethnic affiliation in his identity card should be left blank – nor did he see anything anomalous in this situation.

Justice Landau based his concurrence in the majority's verdict on an interpretation of Zionist thought.

Justice Berenson said: 'If I were able to follow the inclinations of my heart I should grant the petitioner's request. Unfortunately I am not free to do so because I have to interpret the term Jew not as I deem fit, but the way I must assume it was meant by those who coined it.' He held that when the Knesset decided by a majority vote that a Jew is only a Jew when he does not profess any other faith, it went beyond its powers because this was a matter for the Knesset to decide.

Justice Cohen agreed with Justice Silberg that, according to religious law, an apostate is still a Jew, although he would suffer from certain disabilities. He also agreed that the Law of Return must be interpreted according to secular legislation and that:

> We do not cut ourselves off from our historical past and do not negate the legacy of our forefathers ... However, I cannot agree that ... the interpretation of the Law of Return makes it obligatory, or even only possible, to deny the rights of a Jew to the petitioner.
>
> ... If I have correctly understood my honourable friend, Justice Silberg, he is of the opinion that the 'continuity' of Israel's history from the terrible days of the past until our present, prevents us from ever regarding as a Jew anyone who joins the Catholic Church, although it is no longer – either in theory or in practice – our sworn enemy.
>
> I cannot subscribe to such a kind of historical continuity. If history is indeed continuous and must not be severed from its origin, it does not mean that it does not change, progress and develop. On the contrary, it is in the nature of historical progress that time, concepts and processes of thought and cultural values should change, and that there should be a constant improvement in the ways of life and of law.[1]

While one legal aspect of the problem was settled by the judges, the diversity of opinions around the issue certainly attests to the fact that, in one way or another, this problem will be the centre of public discussions and controversy for some time.

The Place of Religious Institutions in the Framework of the State; The Religious Contours of the State

The second level of religious controversies was centred around the general religious contours of the state and of the place of the general institutional framework of the state.

With regard to the first aspect, already in the period of the Yishuv the religious groups attempted to establish some such religious contours in some aspects of public life. Some of the most important illustrations of these demands – as they crystallized in the period of the state – were the passing of a law prohibiting the raising of pigs in most (with the exception of those inhabited by Christian minorities) parts of the state; the promulgation of many local laws which prohibited in most places (except Haifa) public transportation on Sabbat and which not only decreed Sabbat as the official rest-day for Jews but also the closure of all services and places of entertainment (except restaurants) on Sabbat; the maintenance of *kashrut* (religious

[1] *Jewish Observer and Middle East Review*, 14 December 1962, pp. 16–18.

dietary laws) in most government-owned and public and semi-public establishments – such as El Al (Israel Airlines) and the Zim Shipping Company (where the religious parties opposed the establishment, in one of the ships of two kitchens – one kasher and one non-kasher). All these demands were greatly intensified in the 1965 elections where the demand was made by the religious groups to promulgate a general 'Shabbat' law which would give full sanction to these various local arrangements.

Another instance of this tendency was the demands of the religious parties for changes in the law of anatomy and pathology – directed mostly against autopsies – demands which raised the opposition on the doctors who saw them as detrimental to medical research.

With regard to the second aspect of the 'religious' contours of the state – namely the place of the religious institutions in the general framework of the state – some basic foci of controversy can also be pointed out.

One such focus was rooted in the fact that the Rabbinate had the virtual monopoly over personal law. This gave rise to demands that some ways should be found to enable marriage in those cases (like a Cohen and a divorced woman) in which marriage was not allowed according to rabbinical law; and when these demands were not favourably reacted to by the religious circles this gave rise to the more extreme demands for civil marriage.

Another controversy, rooted in the monopolistic position of the Rabbinate, could be found in its relation to the 'non-orthodox' Jewish religious organizations abroad (especially in the USA) – the Conservatives and the Reformists – whose organs and rulings were virtually denied any legitimation by the Rabbinate.

Similarly in several cases attempts were made by orthodox circles to prevent Reform congregations in Israel from being able to hire places for public worship.

A third – perhaps the most central – focus of controversy in this realm centred around the problem of the extent of the juridical autonomy of the Rabbinate *vis-à-vis* the juridical system of the state. Here the more extreme religious groups raised the claims that the Rabbinate – while having jurisdiction over the whole Jewish community (including the non-religious majority) – should be exempt from supervision by the state juridical authorities, i.e. especially by the High Court.

Two major problem areas arose here. One was related to personal law in general and marriages in particular. The High Court has since intervened several times restraining the Rabbinate from implementing various decisions. For example, it issued an *order nisi* calling on the Chief Rabbinate to show cause why it should not rescind a rabbinic judgement which permitted a man to divorce his wife, without her consent, and marry another woman. Similarly the Minister of Interior, himself a member of the National Religious Party, ordered a couple (a 'Cohen' and a divorced woman who could not be married according to the *halacha* but who were married in a private ceremony) to be registered in the population register as married, after the Rabbinical Court had decided that though, according to *halacha*, they were not validly married, they could not re-marry without prior divorce.

The second major area in which the problem of the juridical standing of the Rabbinate arose was that of kashrut.

During the time of the *Benei Israel* conflict, a serious dispute between the Rabbinate and the judiciary erupted around a new abattoir. Once more, a newspaper report will best serve to describe events.[1]

The clash between the Judiciary and the Chief Rabbinate occurred a fortnight earlier. The latter had refused to issue a nationwide *hechshar* (certificate of purity) for the country's newest and most modern slaughterhouse, Marbek, which is situated in the South at Kiryat Malachi.

The general consensus of opinion is (in the non-religious groups as well as in parts, at least, of the religious groups) that this refusal stems, not from any doubts about kashrut, but in order to safeguard the economic interests of slaughterers and others in the meat business, who could not compete with this large enterprise.

After repeated efforts to settle the matter, the company applied to the Supreme Court, and an *order nisi* was issued against the Chief Rabbinate and the Religious Council of Tel Aviv and Jaffa, to show cause why they should not grant Marbek the certificate for which it had applied.

The Chief Rabbinate refused to contest the case. Instead, it stated, in a letter signed by its secretary, that the Supreme Court had no jurisdiction to intervene in matters of *halacha* (religious law).

The Supreme Court had indeed decreed its own competence to intervene in this matter. The Attorney General said he wanted to prevent a situation wherein the Supreme Court would see itself bound to make pronouncements against the Chief Rabbinate and so aggravate an already difficult situation. He was concerned for the standing of the Chief Rabbinate within the nation and asked for a postponement.[2]

The Court agreed to an adjournment of the case for a fortnight.

The Chief Rabbinate reacted by convening a meeting of rabbis. Four hundred of them came to Hechal Shlomo (the seat of the Chief Rabbinate)

---

[1] From the *Jewish Observer*, op. cit., 21 August 1964.

[2] 'The High Court ruled as follows: The Rabbinate has been empowered by the state to establish and supervise kashrut arrangements for those Jews who are concerned with the kashrut of their foods, so that those who observe the laws of kashrut may be assured that the meat they buy from butchers who are under Rabbinate supervision is truly kasher. But this authority was not given to the Rabbinate for the purpose of imposing a regime of kashrut upon Jews who are not interested in it.'

This ruling of the High Court of Justice was one of the bases for its decision to require the Chief Rabbinate to reply to the Marbek abattoir company's application for an *order nisi* against it. The ruling of the Bench which heard the application was written by the President of the Supreme Court, Justice Y. Olshan, and concurred in by Justices Agranat, Landau, Witkon and Manny.

from all parts of the country, and heard Chief Rabbi Untermann reiterate his denial of the rights of the secular court to intervene in rabbinic jurisdiction. The meeting also expressed the rabbis' support for the Chief Rabbinate's stand on the *Benei Israel* issue.

The occasion produced a notable response in the Knesset from Mapai's Yemenite deputy speaker, Israel Yeshayahu. He said: 'Halacha is given by God, but rabbis are appointed by communities. Therefore the Rabbinate as such is a secular institution not derived from the scriptures.'

A compromise arrangement between Marbek and the Rabbinate was reached which, in fact, constituted a backing down by the Rabbinate and as a result of which Marbek withdrew its application from the High Court.

This issue underlined the severe tensions which might arise around the claim of religious groups and institutions for such an extralegal position – a claim which became relatively articulated and vocal during the 1965 elections.

Perhaps the most extreme manifestation of these claims for such extralegal standing and for an asymmetric relation to some of the most central and almost sacred state institutions, was in the exemption of some orthodox young people from military service. One such group were religious girls who were exempted from military service if they declared that their religiousness prevented them from serving in the army.

Another and more serious case in point, which was not promulgated by law but agreed to by internal arrangements with the Ministry of Defence, was the exemption of yeshiva students, the alleged reason being that military service would entirely undermine their studies and the yeshivot as an educational institution.

All these militant tendencies in the religious camp were strengthened by the continuous weakening of the Zionist elements in the religious camp, by the strengthening of the more extreme and militant orthodox religious group whose attitude to the state and its laws was very ambivalent, in their unwillingness to accede even the 'neutral' attitude often adopted toward laws of non-Jewish governments also towards the authorities of the state – and which in many ways wanted to perpetuate that type of closed minority culture which was characteristic of the Jewish communities in Eastern Europe, without taking into account the new reality of a Jewish state.

State-help to Religious Institutions; The Development of Tensions around Religious Issues

The third major level of religious issues was focused around the allocation of help to religious institutions in general and to religious education in particular, and around full recognition of a religious secondary school system in particular. This was closely connected with continuous attempts made by them to monopolize as many of the state religious services as possible, thus creating a uniquely secure political position for themselves, as the major if not the only intermediary between the state and the religious groups.

These various issues around religious problems constituted continuous foci of tensions. These tensions ran particularly high during the summer and autumn of 1963, when various militant activities by extreme religious elements aroused public feeling. Demonstrations against missionary schools took place at that time, as did continuous stone-throwing at vehicles passing near religious quarters on the Shabbat. Stones were hurled even at tourist cars passing to and from Jordan and at the attendant police, on the spot to assure the smooth progress of vehicles.

The growing tensions in the religious field were reflected in the establishment of the League Against Religious Coercion, founded in June 1950, in Jerusalem. This League, led by intellectuals of mainly German and Central European origin and younger University teachers and students, established branches in the three main cities. The rank and file of this organization were mostly from the same circles, and there were generally few members prominent in political life.

The demands of the League were: civil marriage and the minimization of religious restrictions and coercion on the life of the country. The League tried sporadically to influence public opinion by publishing pamphlets, letters to the authorities, and articles in the press on the problem of religious coercion. It also gave active support in specific cases of individual protest, such as cases where pig breeders ran into difficulties with various authorities, or where marriages could not be religiously sanctioned.

In 1960, after a series of religious crises, and especially the 'Who is a Jew?' affair, the League once more took up the cudgels on a local Jerusalem issue of closing various streets to traffic on Saturdays.

In 1963 it organized a demonstration in Jerusalem against the growing militancy of the orthodox groups, during which many 'secular' youth-groups armed with sticks marched up to the outskirts of the religious quarters.

While the influence of the League was very changeable it epitomized to some extent the growing cleavage between the religious and non-religious camps.

Political Issues – The Problem of a Constitution

Beyond the various issues analysed above there developed intensive controversies around political issues as such – mainly around the basic institutional framework of the state – and ranging over what may be called the 'state' image. These controversies come to the fore mainly during election campaigns, when a 'religious state' is advocated by the religious parties, a 'codialistic state' by the left-wing, and so forth. However these problems do not, usually, become acute except in moments of crisis, when they are reinforced by more concrete institutional issues.

The problem of the 'state' image was, in institutional terms, first focused on the possibility of promulgating a constitution, first raised during the period of the Provisional State Council. The debate on this issue was one of the most important in the history of the First Knesset. Opinions differed in three directions. A formal constitution, uniform and complete, was advocated by Mapam, Herut, the General Zionists, and the Communists. Basic laws, to be enacted as and when necessary, to regulate specific aspects of life were advocated by Mapai and the Progressives, while the religious parties claimed that the only acceptable constitution for Israel was one based on the Jewish faith.

The decision to shelve the debate and to adopt a series of basic laws left this whole question open.

After this the central issues of controversy in the political field were focused around problems of 'statehood' – but the meaning of these problems changed in the early and in the later years of the state.

Unification of the State Army, Education, Labour, and Health Services

In the very beginning of the state the focus of such political issues was the establishment of various state services and their relation to the previous more federative agencies which caused many institutional problems, the first of which concerned the disbandment of the *Palmach* in 1949. The *Palmach* originated as a semi-voluntary military organization in which members of Mapam (and later *Ahdut Haavoda*) were in leading positions. With the establishment of the state and the Israeli Army, the government decided to include the *Palmach* in the regular armed forces without granting it any special autonomy. The issue arising here was whether the new Israeli army should be controlled only by government or whether some of the older federative arrangements should be maintained. The Prime Minister strongly opposed the latter, emphasizing the importance of keeping politics out of the army.

The same problem applied to other military splinter organizations – such as the *Irgun Zvai Leumi* and the *Lehi* (Stern Gang) – which, after many doubts and disputes, were dissolved into the general army.

The factions in the defence forces having been solved, the problems of other sectoral organizations came to the fore, starting with the trend system in education. Though after much dispute a national system of education was established in 1963, the religious trend still remained separate.

Another continuous point of dispute was provided by the health services which are organized by the Histadrut and by the various political parties.

No less acute was the problem of the labour exchanges which, during the early years of the state, were organized on a political basis, each party being represented according to its strength. Since employment was dependent on party membership, the relative strength of the parties became virtually permanent. This problem was finally solved by the Labour Exchange Law, which brought all exchanges under state control.

Besides these concrete problems loomed the more general ones of whether rights and facilities of state services such as housing should be allocated directly and by virtue of civic rights, or through various groups and organizations such as political parties or the Histadrut.

While these problems persisted also in the later years of the state, they became less central.

The Executive and Its Control; the Security Problem

The second stage in the disputes on the contours of the state, and the scope of its activities, crystallized in the late 'fifties and was focused on the scope of the rule of law, the relations between the legislature and the executive, especially, but not only, in matters of security, and on some of the basic relations between the state and its citizens.

One subject for debate was the preponderance of administrative as against parliamentary legislation, which was reflected in the difficulties of the citizen to maintain his rights in face of this predominance of state, executive, and bureaucracy.

Of special importance in this context was the tendency to see in the citizen an 'object' of governmental and administrative regulation which knew better than any citizen – or group of citizens – what the ultimate good of the country and of the citizens may be, and the concomitant tendency to put the citizen in a continuously defensive position with regard to the authorities.

These tendencies were aided by government on the various drastic 'security regulations' inherited from the Mandate. And in a rather drastic basic security law which laid down that it is the duty of the accused to supply proof of innocence in matters of treason. An unsuccessful attempt was made in 1962 to promulgate a new Law of Slander.

The proposed law caused a furore among the public and especially among the press. It was claimed that the passing of the law would have given the authorities an unassailable case against unfavourable criticism at second-hand, besides depriving the public of its elementary right to know whether the accused was or was not found guilty.

The local newspapers were widely supported by the foreign press, and the proposal was withdrawn for 'reconsideration' by the ministerial committee. The revised proposal is much milder, though it still bears traces of its predecessor, and several of the more extreme and arbitrary clauses have been dropped.[1]

[1] The following is a resumé of some of the more important facts concerning the above law:

(a) On 21 July 1965 the Knesset (during its last session) approved the Anti-Defamation Law.

Footnote continued from p. 322)

Defamation consists of the publication in print, writing, figures, movements, drawings, speech, noise, or any other manner, of anything injurious to another person or to his dignity, in one of the following ways:

1 Attributes to him a criminal or hostile act.
2 Attributes to him unsuitable behaviour while holding public office.
3 Might harm his professional standing.
4 Might publicly make him the object of scorn or ridicule, or make him hated.
5 Might cause people to avoid him, or abstain from his company.

(b) The main modifications embodied in this law, as compared to the previous corresponding law, are as follows:

1 Consolidation of the civil and criminal provisions concerning proceedings for defamation. A common definition of defamation, which extends to apply both to crimes and to torts.
2 Defamation of the *public*.
3 Defamation of deceased *persons*.
4 The law broadens the scope of the direct criminal and civil liability of editors, publishers, the persons who brought the material in for publication, and in cases of *weekly and monthly publications* even that of the owner of the printing press (section 12).
5 While the defence of 'a true statement' is recognized both by the new law and by its predecessor, the new law has added two conditions: 'That the publication was of public interest, and on condition that the publication did not extend the limits appropriate to the case' (section 14).
6 The presiding justice may prohibit publication of proceedings for defamation if he thinks such a step necessary for the protection of a person's reputation. (According to the former law, the only basis for such prohibition was the possibility that publication could be derogatory to state security.)

(c) The evolvement of the law.

Upon its approval (21 July 1965) the law was strongly opposed by the newspapers, on the basis of the contention that it had been approved too hastily, without sufficient attention having been paid to the motions of criticism approved by the general assembly. The newspapers claimed that the law would have the effect of restricting freedom of expression and freedom of the press, and demanded amendment of the law while the Fifth Knesset was still in session.

The opposition, Gahal and Mapam, raised thirty-six votes in favour of the instigation of a special session for discussion of the Anti-Defamation Law (thirty votes are enough). This session was fixed for 1 September 1965, and on that date four amended versions of the law were proposed (Gahal, Mapam, Maki, Independent-Liberals) 'none of which deviate from the basic rules of the Anti-Defamation Law, and all of which are carefully composed, with the object of avoiding injury to human dignity.' (Haaretz, 1 September 1965.)

The newspapers decided to call a general meeting of the press in Israel, and it was also decided to translate the law into English and French, in order to compare it with corresponding laws in ten democratic countries.

The main points of the resolution passed at the general assembly of the press were as follows:

(a) The press will not accept those sections of the law which restrict newspapers (and which were approved very hastily).

(b) All political parties are called upon to support amendment of the law during the Knesset's special session.

(*Footnote continued on* p. 324

Similar tendencies, even if in milder forms, could be found from time to time in other regulations or proposals of law.

Problems of Security – the Place of the Army in the Political Process

It was but natural that some of the most basic political issues became focused around the problems of security. This was rooted first, in the objective facts of Israel's continuously difficult security situation – in its being since its very inception under the constant threat of annihilation by the Arab states.

But beyond this it was also rooted in the view, strongly promulgated by Ben-Gurion, that it was in the army and in security matters that the new statehood was most clearly epitomized, as well as in his view that in matters of security he was vested with special, unique personal, responsibility which in a way was beyond the usual parliamentary or even ministerial responsibility – thus vesting it with a special charismatic aura, which he shared only with those personal assistants of his whom he chose.

The first important problem that developed within this broad context was the extent to which the dangers of usurping political power by the military existed.

The establishment of a unified army and the fact that it quickly became a focus of intensive national identification, pride, and unity was a basic cause for this problem, a corollary fact being the formation of a military élite which differed in several important characteristics from the older political élite. This new élite was, initially, more predominantly Israeli, and became an important drawing point for many younger Israelis who found other avenues of public activity blocked by the old guard. It epitomized victory and efficiency as well as youth as distinct from the usual political 'muddle' of the older generation. It was further invested with the aura of pioneering and of being the mainstay of national values.

(c) No newspaperman will serve on any committee which might be constituted for the purpose of examination of the criticism of the law.

(d) In the event that the special session of the Knesset did not decide to amend the law, a strike would be called, for the period of twenty-four hours.

The press made an effort to arouse public opinion against the law, and implemented the existing political structures for this purpose.

In the course of the special session, which was held on 1 September 1965, a resolution was passed, constituting an Anti-Defamation Law Committee, to be presided over by Supreme Court Justice Dr Vitkon. Consequently, the press called a strike on 16 November 1965 – two weeks after the elections to the Sixth Knesset.

In December 1965 the 'Vitkon Committee' submitted a number of proposals concerning the law. The object of most of the proposals was to mitigate considerably the harshness of the stricter provisions of the law but it is still too early to foresee the outcome of these proposals.

In addition the army performed a very important function for the new immigrants, in terms of education and basic socialization into Israeli society.

In the early fifties these developments gave rise to great concern over the possibilities of militarization. However, for several reasons, the setting has since greatly changed.

This change was partly caused by the reorganization of the army from a war-footing to that of a beleaguered peace, with the concomitant growing importance of the reserves, and partly by the growing professionalization of many branches of the army.

The recruiting of adequate professional manpower for its 'permanent' core posed great problems as did the fact that many senior officers were encouraged to leave service at a relatively early age (though after a long period of service) and were thus capable of adapting themselves to civilian careers.

Although the army continued to perform many important functions, especially in the education, vocational guidance, and absorption of new immigrants, these non-military tasks were performed mostly within the army and not as an extension of army activities to the civilian sphere. This decreased the possibilities of the military becoming a distinct group with its own political orientations. However, in many common administrative problems the slogan of 'security' could often be used to quell an argument.

Similarly, the fact that certain patterns of life were shared by the military élite (i.e. they often lived in the same area) did not prevent them from being closely related to different political and social groups and movements. The transition of many members of this group to civilian life meant a drop to secondary importance, and military leaders who wanted to enter the political field generally had to go through the usual channels and restate their claims in civilian terms even though they continued to enjoy some of their old aura as bearers of 'security' values. They were thus sometimes seen by their opponents as representing anti-civilian or anti-democratic tendencies.[1]

This caused a marked shift in emphasis from the army to the Ministries concerned with Defence and from the threat of militarization to the dangers of seeing security problems monopolized by certain political or administrative groups, especially by the then Prime Minister, with a resulting lack of civilian parliamentary and even ministerial control.

This was a major issue during the 1961 election and its aftermaths.

---

[1] These claims were not always unsubstantiated. Very revealing from this point of view was a collective interview with all the former Chiefs of Staff undertaken in 1963 by one of the major newspapers. Almost all expressed their disappointment of Israeli political life as ridden with factionalism and unable to produce 'drastic' decisions; all of them strongly advocated the change to direct (not proportional) representation, and most of them said that they could not participate actively in politics in Israel under present conditions. But in the last (1965) elections the picture changed a bit. Three of them joined Rafi while two actively supported the Alignment.

Problems of Security – Military Government in Arab Areas

Another field of conflict in this context is that of security in general and of military rule in Arab districts in particular, and it is often claimed that the phrases 'security regulations' and 'reasons of security' are used as a magic formula for stifling discussion.

Since 1960 there has been a growing demand for parliamentary control over security matters. The discussion on the dangers of militarism, which will be discussed shortly, should also be mentioned in this connexion.

Included in 'security', but related also to the problem of state power, is the question of military government. In accordance with old mandatory regulations several border areas in Israel come under such rule. These contain a great part of the Arab population in Israel (which numbered about 285,000 in 1964). The problem of military rule, the extent of its necessity, legality, and commensurability with the democratic orientations of Israel's political system, has had special attention throughout the state's existence and has been a continuous topic of public debate.

Opinions on this issue range from the advocating of complete abolition to insistence on its preservation – the former being pressed by Mapam, the Communists, the Semitic League, and *Hamishtar Hehadash*, and the latter by the other parties, especially Mapai.

In 1959, however, the number of restricted areas in the north were reduced from fifty-four to sixteen and limitations on the movement of non-Jews to Jewish centres were lifted for work and business purposes. Similarly, long-term licences were granted permitting dwelling in restricted areas. Nevertheless, this lessening of restrictions did not solve the basic problem and agitation continued.

On 2 February 1963, a vehement debate on military rule took place in the Knesset, when most of the opposition in one way or another proposed the abolition of the military authorities. They claimed that the various security problems could be handled by the regular, civilian police, and that military rule precluded Arab loyalty to Israel, created social and political tensions, hindered contact between Jews and Arabs, and diminished world respect for the state and her foreign policy. Some also claimed that military government served to insure the ruling party's influence over the minorities.

In opposing the proposals for the abolition of military government Prime Minister Ben-Gurion relied mostly on Israel's precarious security situation, though he claimed that 'on principle' he was against such rule.

During the debate it became clear that even some members of the coalition parties opposed the continuation of military rule (all of *Ahdut Haavoda* some of the National Religious Party and some members of Mapai). Ben-Gurion threatened resignation and pressure was put on the non-Jewish members of parliament associated with Mapai. Thus, when the issue came to the vote the proposals for the abolition of military rule were defeated by a fifty-seven to fifty-six majority.

The second marked change in this area took place in 1963 on the initiative of the new Premier, Levi Eshkol.

After continuous discussion with the representatives of *Ahdut Haavoda* Mr Eshkol announced the removal of movement restrictions in all districts under military rule on 21 October 1963. The only exceptions to this rule are restrictions to be imposed on individuals considered 'security risks' and on Arab villages located right on the border. On this occasion Mr Eshkol also spoke about the 'Land Requisition Law' according to which Arabs will be assured of full compensation for property requisitioned for development purposes. On similar lines the Prime Minister made known plans for the development of Arab villages. In a vote, these plans were ratified by a majority of the coalition parties (including *Ahdut Haavoda*).

It must be stressed that these proposals did not, in fact, abolish military rule, and that the majority of its regulations still remained in effect. However even the limited change was of importance as a sign of possible future developments – some of which did indeed take place in early 1966.

The Place of Bureaucracy in the Political Process

A somewhat similar problem can be discerned with regard to the civil service and bureaucracy, which, in the first years of the state, grew continuously in strength and prestige, with major decisions being increasingly concentrated in the top bureaucratic echelons.

While the civil service may thus tend to uphold legal norms at the expense of executive-charismatic ones, it is important to distinguish between a natural tendency to extend the scope of bureaucracy, and the possibility of complete political usurpation.

The Political Symbolization of the State

The preceding issues have lately crystallized into an ideological dispute between the protagonists of two different basic political attitudes. The one side stresses the importance of political, technical, and military know-how and 'performance', while the other side emphasizes the maintenance of legal, constitutional, and institutional norms, and the rule of law.

The term 'performance' appeared again and again in public controversies concerned with the image of the state, and is, to a certain extent, regarded as the natural follow-up to the pre-state striving for *hagshama* (fulfilment of ideals). For adherents to this point of view the duties of the state require swift and competent action without over-long ideological deliberation.

The opponents of this view assert that 'performance' in itself is not enough.

327

They claim that this approach is dangerous and likely to lead to 'techno-cracy' with the aims of the state being pushed into the background while the means are in the limelight.

Such technical emphasis – often coupled with a strong charismatic tendency – thus came to be regarded as being potentially opposed to ideo-logical and movement goals, and against rule of law in political institutions.

Apart from their ideological implications these discussions also had many institutional repercussions, most obvious are the attempts made to institu-tionalize the interpretation of values vested around the then Prime Minister, David Ben-Gurion.

The most important symbolic manifestation of these attempts was the small emphasis placed on non-political (or non-governmental) state symbols. In matters of protocol this could be seen in the fact that the Prime Minister comes second after the President (taking precedence over the Speaker of the Knesset who acts for the President in his absence) and in the smaller formal place given to the judiciary, despite its enormous prestige. This tendency could also be seen in the attempts made to equate the state with the govern-ment, to minimize the full participation of the opposition, and to leave even the legitimation of opposition in the hands of the government, i.e. in the hands of the Prime Minister.

Among non-political offices only the Presidency was upheld as a relatively autonomous symbol, and it is interesting to note that many patterns of activity undertaken by the Presidency have, perhaps unconsciously, been contrary to those developed by Mr Ben-Gurion.

The Electoral System

An issue closely connected with the basic contours of the political institutions, is that of proportional as against direct representation. The latter system has always been advocated by Mr Ben-Gurion, by certain groups of Mapai, by some members of Herut, by the General Zionists, and by *Hamishtar Hehadash*.

The main arguments of those advocating this system were that it would ensure direct contact between elected representatives and the electorate, that it would end the multiplicity of small parties, and guarantee the develop-ment of a two-party system, resulting in greater stability.

Opposition to these proposals was based on the premise that direct repre-sentation would assure the monopoly of Mapai, obliterate any opposition, and thus undermine the bases of Israeli democracy.

Foreign Policy

Foreign policy attitudes were, to a great extent, inherent in the various party ideologies. Although not one party (officially not even the Communist Party) advocated alignment with the Eastern bloc, there were some parties on the left who demanded a strictly neutralist policy.

The alleged claim that the government was making little real effort to improve its relations with the Arabs was another important factor in any foreign policy debate. This claim was made on the right, where Herut often asserted that a more 'aggressive' policy was needed, as well as on the left where it was claimed that the way to attain integration in the Middle East was by neutralizing the region.

Relations with Germany constituted another important issue which cut right across usual political controversy and went into deeper layers of national identity. One central problem here was the issue of preparations.

In January 1952 the Prime Minister announced that negotiations between Western Germany and Israel were being held, concerning compensation to those Jews who had suffered under the Nazi regime before and during World War Two. This announcement caused an uproar among the public and Knesset members.

Although some individuals in all parties deviated from their party's policy on this issue, it was Herut which most actively opposed such an agreement claiming that it was tantamount to national treason. Demonstrations were held in the cities, culminating in a demonstration outside the Knesset building held whilst the debate on this issue was going on. Stones were thrown and the whole area of the Knesset seemed to be a battleground.

Relations with Germany came up a second time in 1959, on the issue of selling arms to Germany and, this time, caused the breakdown of the coalition. The Prime Minister (Mapai), the General Zionists, and the Progressives favoured the deal, while the two leftist partners of the coalition, Mapam and *Ahdut Haavoda* were against it, together with Herut and some of the religious parties.

In many different ways, Israel's relations with Germany have continuously been a matter of public and political controversy.

The Lavon Affair

The Lavon affair erupted in the autumn of 1960, though its roots date back to 1954, when Mr Pinhas Lavon was Minister of Defence in a Cabinet headed by Mr Moshe Sharett. Mr David Ben-Gurion was at that time in semi-retirement in his Negev retreat at Kibbutz Sde Boker.

During this period a major political and military blunder or 'mishap' occurred. At the outset the officers of the Intelligence Branch claimed that Lavon, the Minister, had given the original order leading to the mishap. At the Prime Minister's request a committee of enquiry was appointed consisting of High Court Judge Olshan and former Chief of Staff General Dori to clarify the issue.

It became clear later that some of the officers testifying succeeded in deceiving the committee. On the basis of its conclusions, Lavon was re-lieved of his ministerial post, and the 1955 elections brought Mr Ben-Gurion back as Premier and Minister of Defence. At that time, and probably as part-compensation, Lavon was appointed Secretary-General of the Histadrut.

Matters came to a head once more in 1960 during the trial, on another matter, of one of the officers previously involved, when new evidence indi-cating Lavon's probable innocence came to light. Mr Lavon now demanded that the Prime Minister issue a public declaration rehabilitating him. Mr Ben-Gurion however insisted that the affair was of such secrecy as to warrant not being brought before the public in any way. He also claimed that Mr Lavon's name could not be cleared without incriminating another Senior Intelligence Officer. However, the Prime Minister agreed to have a judicial committee enquire into the affair once more. The 'Cohen Committee' and later a special investigating committee consisting of seven Cabinet Ministers headed by the Minister of Justice, found that Mr Lavon was not to be held responsible for the occurrences in 1954. Far from being concluded, however, the affair then developed from a question of personal rehabilitation into a debate on some of the crucial aspects of the state. Mr Ben-Gurion considered Mr Lavon's criticism of some aspects of the Israeli Army and Ministry of Defence as being close to treason, while Mr Lavon felt that the army and security establishment should not be above criticism and public control. The issue was repeatedly discussed in Mapai's Central Committee and different factions developed within Mapai. One consisted mostly of the 'younger' elements (such as, Moshe Dayan, former Chief of Staff, and Shimon Peres, then Deputy Minister of Defence) which supported Ben-Gurion and his demands for the dismissal of Mr Lavon from his Histadrut post. The other faction consisted mostly of the old guard and, at first, opposed this arbitrary demand.

However, the matter was not left within the confines of Mapai. The whole government and the political system became closely involved in the dispute, especially when Mr Ben-Gurion refused to present the full report of the Cohen Committee to the Cabinet. It was then that the Cabinet appointed a Committee of seven ministers, which unanimously and unequivocally cleared Mr Lavon, and placed the responsibility for the 1954 mishap on the then Head of the Intelligence Branch. At the ensuing cabinet meeting Mr Ben-Gurion declared that he would not accept these findings which he declared to include 'partiality, perversion of justice, and half-truths'. He immediately left for a prolonged vacation, proposing to resume his premiership after the deposition of Mr Lavon from the Histadrut leadership.

The party machinery now set in motion a public campaign to return Mr Ben-Gurion to the government, even at the price of accepting his ultimatum. Slogans appeared, announcing the 'imminent disaster' awaiting the state should Mr Ben-Gurion retire at this stage. The coalition partners who had taken part in the ministerial committee on the affair were offended by their Premier's high-handed behaviour, and together with some veteran Mapai ministers now threatened to resign.

Mapai now made frantic efforts to reach a compromise in its internal conflict, but Mr Lavon did not agree to the compromises proposed, nor was any Mapai leader willing to take responsibility.

Finally, in March 1961, Finance Minister Eshkol was forced to decide the issue because Mr Ben-Gurion had meantime resigned and the country was without a government. In a dramatic session of the Party Executive, with pro-Lavon elements demonstrating outside the building, Mapai decided to remove Lavon from his position. The Histadrut Executive, led by its Mapai majority, carried out the Party's decision.

The final outcome of the vote in the Mapai Central Committee was rela-- tively close (159 versus 96). The motion against dismissal was proposed by Mr Sharett and the result was on the whole regarded as a moral victory for Mr Lavon.

Bowing to public pressure, the coalition partners once more decided to take part in a government headed by Mr Ben-Gurion, thus finally bringing the Lavon affair to its conclusion, with the Knesset dissolving nearly three years before time, and the nation going to the polls again in August 1961. Mapai lost four seats, but the resulting narrow coalition government contained an even stronger Mapai majority.

Repercussions to the Lavon Affair

An interesting and significant facet of the Lavon affair was the upsurge of independent public opinion, mainly among intellectuals, kibbutz members, the younger elements of various parties (especially Mapam and the religious bloc) and in the press. This latent discontent came to a head in January 1961 when a group of influential professors of the Hebrew University issued a public protest. They invited the country's academicians to voice their dissatisfaction and as a result of this call hundreds of declarations of protest made by many academic and literary figures were received within a few days. Various student groups spontaneously followed their teachers by forming a 'Committee for the Defence of Democracy' in which they voiced their protest by means of public addresses and through the press. The press took an active part in the debate, with two independent papers – *Haaretz* (which was on the whole pro Ben-Gurion) and *Maariv* (which tended on the whole to be pro-Lavon) – being especially vocal. The party newspapers were generally pro-Lavon and Mapai's internal crisis was especially manifest in the Histadrut paper *Davar*, which had no clear policy on the country's major issue of the day. Efforts were made by the party machinery to organize a group of intellectuals to support Ben-Gurion's position, but this proved a failure as no more than a handful of writers and professors accepted the party's call.

The development of such unprecedented public opinion showed that the focus of the affair had gradually shifted from being a personal issue to the wider problem of democracy in Israel.

The Lavon group as well as several others attempted to spread the controversy to some wider political issues, especially to the conflict between the power of the state versus more voluntary forms of social organization.

Several crucial aspects of Israeli political life were thrown into the limelight through the affair, one such question being the Prime Minister's power to override a Cabinet Committee's decision. This became closely related to the whole issue of parliamentary control.

Another issue brought to the fore was the right of individuals to tread on the 'sacred' ground of security, and the power of the Prime Minister to override government decisions *post factum*.

Although, institutionally, Ben-Gurion won insofar as Lavon was ousted from office and he was able to form a new government, these developments did not enhance the prestige of either himself or his government.

During the affair his popularity was at its lowest ebb, and the fact that his version of the affair was not accepted was a severe blow to his prestige. His ousting of Lavon was generally considered more a successful *coup-de-force* than a victory of justice and, significantly, his own party tried to avoid raising the issue during the elections and, instead, pleaded for growing stability, security, and dependence on the 'old man'.

The Lavon affair continued to have wide repercussions in Israeli political life, which eventually led to Premier Ben-Gurion's resignation in 1963 and Mr Eshkol's accession to power. Even afterwards it continued to serve the re-crystallization of forces in Mapai and in the country as a whole.

3

THE POLITICAL PROCESS AND THE CONTINUITY OF THE SYSTEM

The Patterns of Continuity of the Israeli Political System – The Political Parties

The preceding analysis on the major issues of political struggle in Israel indicates that while the major parties participating in this process have largely remained the same as in the period of the Yishuv, most of the issues around which this struggle was focused were relatively new, developing mostly after the establishment of the state. Even those issues – like the religious and some of the social ones – which were also of great importance in the period of the Yishuv became largely transformed within the framework of the state.

It is this fact that constitutes one of the major keys to the understanding of the continuity of the Israeli's political system, of its problems, and pitfalls. A good starting point for the analysis of these problems would be the analysis of the major participants in the forums – the various political parties.

As we have seen the initial ability of the political system to deal with new forces was epitomized in the absorption by the existing parties of most of the new social and immigrant groups, a fact which was very closely related to the major characteristics of the Israeli parties – their organization and activities.

These tendencies explain, to a great extent, the continuity of the parties since the period of the Yishuv.

Thus, most parties tried to maintain several 'federative' arrangements and especially the allocation of 'fixed' resources and manpower within the framework of both the state and the Jewish Agency. The most sought after resources were housing, settlements, educational facilities and, in many cases, the access – through the labour exchanges – to work. The health services which were in the hands of the *Kupat Holim* and which drew most new immigrants immediately into the framework of the Histadrut were of special importance in this context and constituted one of the main reasons why the Histadrut opposed the nationalization of the health services.

The various parties also attempted to assign new immigrant manpower prior to actual immigration. This was done through the allocation of 'percentages' and through the sending abroad of emissaries who could organize and direct the different immigrant groups into allotted settlements. There thus existed an unadmitted, unofficial, and yet very real, agreement within the Jewish Agency on the proportionate division of new settlers between the settlements of different parties.

The allocation of funds raised through the UJA (United Jewish Appeal) and *Keren Hayesod* (National Foundation Fund) to various party funds, was more openly admitted. This applied especially to so-called 'constructive' funds – usually used for housing and help in absorbing party members.

Even when some of these services (like housing or the labour exchanges) were transferred to state agencies which did not, officially, permit party patronage, these arrangements still persisted on a local level in the sense that the various party officials exerted considerable influence on the immigrants to become affiliated to their respective parties. This tendency to continue the 'former' federative arrangements could also be found in the plans for regional settlement of kibbutzim, moshavim or for the development areas.

Here the various parties and movements, often acting through the ministries which they headed in the coalition governments, attempted to attain complete or partial monopoly over such regions in an effort to divide the main development areas among themselves.

This was closely connected to the second major structural change in party activities, namely with the type of clientele mobilized by the various parties and its relationship to the parties.

From the beginning many of the new immigrants held no ideological identification with the various parties. Their relations were formulated either in terms of vague identification with some of the general symbols of the state represented by the parties (and especially by Mapai) and/or in terms of concrete benefits to be derived from the parties.

Nor were the activities of most parties (with the partial exception of some of the left-wing ones) directed at forging new social or ideological groups. Rather they attempted to help the immigrants to find their way in the Israeli economy by offering them agencies of absorption and by representing the given party as the main embodiment of the state.

A great emphasis on allocation of benefits, manipulation of manpower, and power positions therefore developed within most parties, with much less stress being placed on the older type of 'movement' orientation and ideologies. In spite of the many differences between the various parties, the shift to such activities and orientations was very marked in most of them.

Some of the repercussions on the structural and organizational aspects of different parties have already been mentioned above, but it is worthwhile here to dwell on some of the problems stemming from the encounter of the various parties with the new immigrants. As we have seen, special sections dealing with immigrants developed within most parties drawing the more active elements among the immigrant groups into their orbit by giving them certain power positions but, at the same time, maintaining strong control.

The various ways in which the party structure adapted itself to the more traditional leadership and settings existing among many of the new immigrants is both interesting and significant.

In many cases, and especially among the moshavim, we find that the older traditional leaders or the more active new elements among the immigrants were drawn into the parties through different agreements with their leaders, with the political leadership in rural and development areas often becoming identical with the leadership of the extended family.

The political leaders of these extended families were not, usually, men who were leaders abroad. The leadership of family heads who functioned abroad now tends to be restricted to the religious and cultural fields, while leadership in economic and political activities is now generally in the hands of younger men who, in many cases, attained standard modern education in Israel. Nevertheless the ancient traditional family framework still persists and the activities of these younger men, though personally considerably modernized, are still channelled in traditional forms.

The parties seek to influence the rank and file by way of these leaders of extended families and, in many instances, the allegiance of a whole clan is assured by winning them over to the political party. Basic political allegiance thus centres not on ideology or on a political programme, but on the attaining of concrete material benefits for the clan as a whole. The attitude of the clan and its leaders to the ideology of the parties is often cynical, stemming from the irrelevance of the ideology to many of the concrete problems or the process of settling.

To this must be added the 'traditional' dynamics of the clans themselves, as distinct from clan activities resulting from the impact of modern political parties. Thus there are numerous cases where the inner power and leadership division of a village is based on clan cleavage. In such cases one clan struggles against another for positions of power such as that of village secretary, organizer of machinery services, membership on the village board, etc. Though this cleavage is usually based on the traditional basis of differing family loyalty, these local political struggles are often caught in the wider framework of politics on the national level, with the various national parties seeking to influence the different clans, and the clans apparently belonging to different national parties. Although ideologically these parties range from the religious parties on the one extreme to the left-wing parties on the other, the ideological aspect is usually forgotten on the village level. Where the internal (village level) political struggle is between various ethnic groups, the national parties often appear as representing different ethnic interests. Only the largest parties encompass widely differing ethnic groups in the same locality and thus succeed in appearing as patrons of various ethnic groups at one and the same time.

Internal leadership selection among immigrants is, of course, greatly affected by all this, with more and more local 'bosses' and leaders being drawn into the pattern, particularly in the moshavim, where the close social structure encouraged the maintenance of traditional frameworks. However, such new leaders also emerged in the various urban and semi-urban centres where 'political bosses', encouraged by all parties, came to the fore from among the different ethnic groups.

Continuity and Change in Party Activities

These party activities explain, to a large extent, the continuity of the parties – especially as related to the new immigrants.

No new types of political parties have as yet emerged among the new immigrants. This is no doubt due to the fact that prospects for progress are more favourable within the frameworks of the older parties. Partly this is due to the fact that the social reality to which the new immigrants had to adjust was shaped by the older groups who also controlled the strategic points within the major institutional spheres.

In addition, the immigrants developed a marked identification with the more general party symbols whether of statehood, religion, or even ethnic origin – despite their lack of interest in the more ideological aspects of the parties.

Lastly there was a marked shift in the activities and orientations of the parties towards 'power activities' rather than 'totalistic' ideology – even though they often continued to develop totalistic symbols and organizations.

The same pattern also appears with regard to the 'young' generation which grew up after the establishment of the state or the various new professional and occupational groups which developed during this period.

Most parties attempted to absorb these elements, partly through the provision of leadership positions, and partly through taking care of their various concrete interests.

These developments underline the internal transformation of the major parties from sects and 'movements', into fully-fledged parties, with distinct political leadership interested in the maintenance of their positions and containing wide networks of interest groups and bureaucracy.

Among party functionaries the political boss and organizer, as well as the direct representative of the various interest groups, greatly gained in importance over the older type of movement or independent leader. At the same time, the emphasis on organizational discipline – as against ideological commitments – also grew, the new frameworks enabling the parties to accommodate new groups and absorb new adherents from both the old and new sectors of Israeli society.

The religious parties found their adherents among the more traditional elements from the oriental as well as the East European communities.

The leftist groups were mostly supported by some of the younger Israeli groups (especially from kibbutzim and urban youth movements), some ex-members of youth movements and some immigrants from East Europe.

The General Zionists had little initial success among new immigrants, but later attracted some of the more urban 'bourgeois' elements, while the Progressives were especially successful among the professional groups and the younger intelligentsia. It seems that in the last election the Liberal bloc also attracted a relatively wide section of the older and/or European urban elements.

Herut attracted some members of the older Revisionist movement, many former members of *Irgun Zvai Leumi* and many dissatisfied elements among the newer immigrants, particularly those who were already partially absorbed and not satisfied with their progress. Paradoxically this was in a way a more 'proletarian' party than any of the labour groups.

The widest and most varied spectrum could, of course, be found within Mapai.

It is important to remember that several attempts made to organize specifically ethnic parties had completely failed and that the party leaders had to turn increasingly to the existing parties to present their claims.

Herut, the only 'real' opposition party – i.e. the one that never participated in any of the governmental coalitions – succeeded in attracting many who were dissatisfied with the system, a fact which has, paradoxically, strengthened the existing system.

This ability of many of the parties to draw new groups to themselves is to no small degree based on their attempts to extend and perpetuate the relative paucity of what may be called independent centres of power and public opinion and to reinforce the tendency of different trends of public opinion to be organized in relatively 'closed' groups.

The Development of New Forces – Problems and Contradictions

The fact that the success in perpetuating the various parties was partly due to the continuation and reinforcement of the older 'federative' arrangements, indicates that this continuity implied a change in the meaning of these activities.

As these federative and totalistic arrangements are made within the framework of a state which formally upheld universalistic-legal norms, they necessarily became semi-legal, decried by some groups as deviating from the general legal norms and ideals of the state.

However, such 'deviation' in itself was less important than its broader repercussions, such as the fact that many beneficiaries of such arrangements did not remain loyal to their benefactors and often questioned the assumptions of different parties and groups to be the main purveyors of state services.

Thus the institutional arrangements created by the parties often generated new demands and political expectations not easily gratified within the existing pattern of party politics and decision-making.

Such forces already tended to develop in the period of the Yishuv, but they became much more intensive after the establishment of the state, and especially with the continuous – even if not wholly acknowledged – institutionalization of the new political frameworks.

In order to understand the ways in which the Israeli political system attempted to deal with such new forces, it is necessary to proceed to the analysis of another aspect of the political process – namely to the alignment of the various parties and the major issues analysed above.

Alignments around Religious Issues

What then is the meaning of these issues? How are they related to the forces within Israeli society and to the major problems of Israeli society?

The 'simplest' and most straightforward alignment of forces seems to be that connected with religious affairs, although this points to more basic cultural and political problems.

There, many aspects of religious tradition were seen as part of the common national heritage – even if the specific religious interpretation was not accepted by the non-religious majority.

However, this gave the religious parties a certain strength in claiming that they represented some special aspects of the national traditions or of broader national unity.

These claims of national unity, and of the upholding of national tradition also gave rise to a great variety of demands with regard to the religious contours of the state – such as the scope of public services on Shabbat or the raising of pigs. The fact that, on the whole, no overall anti-religious militancy developed within the Zionist movement has greatly helped the religious groups in their claim.

Although the different groups have shown varying degrees of extremism, even the less extreme groups have recently shown a growing tendency towards more orthodox and even militant ideas, connected to important structural changes in the religious camp and the weakening of the more Zionist elements in favour of the 'non-Zionist' *Agudat Israel*.

Although the religious groups are concentrated mainly among the petit-bourgeois groups and among the more traditional new immigrants particularly from East European countries, religious issues cut across various social and economic strata.

Throughout the period of the state, the religious groups have increased their encroachments on general aspects of life in the state and although they uphold the *status quo* in various religious matters, they have continuously widened the scope of concessions made to the religious groups.

Lately, the growing militancy of the religious groups, and the intensity of the controversy around religious issues, have become so great as to create the possibility of a situation in which there might develop a continuous increase in the non-tolerant theocratic characteristics of the state leading to a possible *Kulturkampf*.

Alignments around Economic Issues

Divisions between the different socio-economic groups on economic and social questions were not always as easily definable. Thus, for example, on questions of salary differentials, progressive taxation, participation of workers in the executive of the trade union, etc. the 'usual' division between 'right' and 'leftist' groups was clear.

The various Histadrut groups on the whole supported state regulation of the economy and the extension of welfare policies, while the liberalization of the economy was upheld mostly by the Progressives, the General Zionists, and Herut. However at the same time it should be emphasized that many of the industrialist and financial groups which developed in the last ten or fifteen years were heavily dependent on the government policies and administration to which they owe much of their success. And very often they were unwilling to give up the protection which the government policies and administration gave them although they might attempt to get better conditions from the government.

The picture became, however, more complicated with regard to the nationalization of some basic industries and services, especially of the health services. Paradoxically, the Histadrut and the leftist groups strongly opposed such nationalization, regarding it as a danger to the power of the Histadrut. It was left to the 'state-oriented' elements inside Mapai and the so-called 'centre' or 'rightist' parties such as the Progressives and the General Zionists, to advocate nationalization – especially of the health services.

The problem of economic independence was even more complicated. While the importance of this was recognized by all the major parties, the degree of priority given to this aim differed with each group, overriding priority for it being supported by the Progressives, General Zionists, and some elements in Mapai, while the leftist groups contested such urgency.

Pressures on the government and the administration for economic benefits were exerted equally by the Histadrut or private sectors – but the combination of ideological claims and vested interests might have given greater weight to the demands of the Histadrut.

Political Alignments

Even more complicated alignments developed on the various 'political' issues with the protagonists in the various disputes not always aligned according to any 'usual' divisions.

The alignments around the various political issues and especially around the problems of 'statehood' were not uniform. They varied especially between the different aspects or the stages of this problem. Thus the alignments around the issue of the universality of state services, rule of law versus the various federative arrangements differed from those around the upholding of statehood as the charismatic epitomization embodied in the executive, of the major collective values versus the view of the state as a general and central agency of the community and the consequent necessity of supervision of the executive by the legislature, public opinion, etc.

The ideal of comprehensive state-services was upheld with varying emphasis by the Progressives, by the General Zionists and by some elements within Mapai. It was opposed by the more conservative elements in almost all labour factions, especially when they benefited from the existing federative arrangements. Of late two different groups have become allied on various issues. They are the protagonists of the older sectarian groups within the

339

labour sector – such as the *kibbutzim* – and the proponents of the rule of law and of universalistic norms, together with several politically sensitive, independent public opinion groups.

The alignments around the perception of the state and of the executive as embodiments of the major collective goals were markedly different – as became especially clear in the aftermath of the Lavon affair. Here the leftist parties as well as various Histadrut-orientated groups in Mapai joined forces with the Progressives and General Zionists, as well as with various independent forces of public opinion and emphasized the responsibility of the executive to the Knesset and to the public at large as against groups in Mapai – and to some extent in other parties – which upheld the charismatic view of the State and of the executive.

Alignments on the electoral system are of great importance for an understanding of the political and social reality in Israel. This issue has been raised in the name of greater political stability and efficiency by the then Prime Minister, Mr Ben-Gurion, some sections of Mapai and, intermittently, also by parts of the General Zionists and Herut. Opposition came mostly from parties claiming that this would undermine the existing democratic structure by giving predominance to one party.

Undoubtedly, the desire to ensure predominance for his own party and its executive, played its part in Mr Ben-Gurion's insistence on this change, as it is doubtful whether a real two-party system could develop under existing conditions. But his insistence was probably even more rooted in the belief that only within the framework and ideals of statehood are the forces which can forge a new nation to be found – and that these forces are to a great extent lacking or weak within the existing groups.

Alignments on foreign policy issues usually kept close to the internal party division, and some, especially those dealing with relations with Germany, often became the subject of heated debates. However, excepting the emphasis placed on 'neutralism' by the leftist parties and, sporadically, by Herut, foreign policy was, on the whole, not very much in the public eye.

The 1961 election was the first in which foreign policy constituted a focus of public debate, with the Liberal Party (especially Dr Goldman) criticizing the government's policies on 'neutralism', and raising the issue of coming to some understanding, even if not official, with the Arab countries.

Continuity and Change in Politics

We see thus that the nature of the different political alignments cannot be fully understood in terms of the accepted distinctions between 'left', 'right', and 'centre', as these 'usual' connotations applied only to some concrete aspects of economic policy (i.e. the emphasis on progressive taxation or income differentials). Instead, the specific characteristics of the Israeli social structure give the clue to an understanding of the country's politics. It is a paradoxical fact that the Histadrut and the workers' parties and groups are from a certain point of view the conservative elements in the social-economic system of Israel. They are most interested in the perpetuation of existing structural arrangements with their emphasis on different sectors, and on 'public' planning and decision-making. The incentive to institutional change comes from the right-wing 'bourgeois' groups, and from some parts of the government administration as well, to some extent, as from some groups within Mapai.

This conservatism is not rooted only in the vested interests of power anxious to impede changes in society, on the contrary, it is also very closely connected with the emphasis on the continuous expansion of the existing social structure and on the absorption of new elements within it. Such expansion is envisaged as an extension to the existing social and economic structure and its existing settlements, co-operatives, and public companies with overall power of the Histadrut.

This conservatism may be directed against the 'bourgeois' elements in the private sector, in turn regarded as 'conservative' in the usual European sense, but it may equally be directed against the growing encroachment of the statehood – either in its legal-universalistic form or as the sole bearer of all the major collective values.

Due to these complex basic orientations, the alignment on different issues is often, as has already been indicated above, unusual and surprising.

Although in social and economic matters, both the Histadrut and the 'state' may well oppose the liberalization of the economy, though for different motives, many government circles may pursue 'statist' or 'liberal' economic policies differing from the orientation of the Histadrut.

Insofar as the government tends to pursue a long-range policy aiming at economic independence, it may act against the interests of the Histadrut as a trade union as well as against the vested interests of the private sector and the Histadrut as employers.

At the same time different cross-cutting alliances tended also to develop as we have seen, in the political field. Here of special interest are the relatively new alliances between various 'opposition' groups on the left and centre, who tend to uphold the legal-institutional framework of the state against the encroachments of the more 'militant' proponents of the state and executive as being the sole embodiment of all collective values.

While at certain stages of development the upholders of universalistic state services could be seen as innovators against the older federative arrangements, later it was the claim to supervise the executive effectively that constituted a major change of orientation.

Thus the re-alignment of conservatism versus change does not coincide with the division between left or right parties, the distinction having first become blurred by the fact that some aspects of conservatism were closely related to development and to the absorption of immigrants.

The central position of Mapai in the government and in the Histadrut provided an important focus for the political process, since it was within Mapai that most of these tendencies developed and most of the crucial decisions were taken.

The most important structural aspect of Mapai's power was the fact that it was both the ruling (majority) party in the Histadrut and the major key party in all government coalitions.

Although the Histadrut was also a federation of the main workers' parties and some smaller religious and liberal groups, the majority which Mapai held within it gave it vital power in the social structure of the Yishuv. Its influence on the Histadrut economic sector provided the crucial link between the demands of the workers and the implementation of government policies, both in the social and economic spheres especially on wage policy.

The many groups existing within Mapai included diverse economic and social bodies such as members of kibbutzim and moshavim, unskilled, skilled, and to some extent professional workers, intellectuals, and even private entrepreneurs, of whom, especially after 1951, Mapai took good – if not too good – care.

Mapai also contained many different socio-economic and political groups, the more 'conservative' such as the older Histadrut élites, as well as the more 'innovating' such as the new economic and professional entrepreneurs, managers, army officers, etc.

Its capacity to absorb these different groups and to rule effectively was dependent on three basic conditions. First, was its ability to maintain power control in the economic system through the government, the Histadrut, and the settlements. Second, was its ability to use this power for general economic expansion and development and to assure a continuous rise in the standard of living. Third, Mapai was greatly dependent on the internal cohesion of its leadership, so that political decisions could be implemented and regulated in face of the diverse and often contradictory pressures of the varied population groups.

As long as these conditions were fulfilled Mapai was able to maintain its effective rule and central political position. It was within its central committees that major shifts of policy in the economic, security, or educational fields were thrashed out and settled. In such cases all other parties acted as pressure groups or catalysts of the different forces within Mapai.

From this point of view it is very significant that on almost all major issues the other parties were usually relatively more homogeneous and unified than Mapai, within which a greater variety of attitudes could be found.

Furthermore, no matter how great the opposition to Mapai from other parties on any specific issue, such opposition was never unified over any length of time over a broad range of issues, and even changes in the coalition patterns, were not always fully indicative of the true shifts of policy.

So long as the leadership of Mapai was cohesive and capable of making decisions and executing them, this heterogeneity of attitudes was a source of flexibility and strength for Mapai.

Mapai leaders when attempting to implement certain policies tried sometimes to include in the coalition those parties which might have been opposed to these policies. Thus many of the more 'liberal' aspects of economic policy were undertaken with the leftist parties in the coalition, while the more or less continuous participation of the Progressives in the coalition often served as a useful cushion against the development of too intensive 'liberal' political demands.

Resolving Conflicts

To understand these issues it is necessary to analyse how they were resolved and what were the results of these disputes on the institutional structure of politics.

Between 1949 and 1960 many Cabinet crises arose over political, economic, and religious issues. Not all these issues toppled governments. In fact, the fall of the Israeli Cabinet was generally produced, not by votes of no-confidence, but by the resignation of the Prime-Minister (eight times Ben-Gurion and once Sharett). Apart from constitutional termination of office the issues provoking such resignations were:

(1) the proposal to establish a Ministry of Commerce and Industry to be occupied by a person not a member of the Knesset or a political party;

(2) rejection of collective responsibility by the religious parties in the coalition by opposing military service for women and unification of the four-trend system of education, and for failing to support the government in the Knesset vote;

(3) rejection of collective responsibility through abstention during a vote of no-confidence in the Knesset involving an accusation against Dr Israel Kastner, a Mapai leader, of having made deals with the Nazi, Adolf Eichmann;

(4) rejection of collective responsibility and violation of cabinet secrecy in leaking a cabinet decision to send a secret mission to the German Federal Republic for the purpose of negotiating military ties and in order to seek support for a North Atlantic Treaty Organization commitment to guarantee Israel's security;

(5) religious opposition to the cabinet's definition of the term 'Jew' for entry on identity cards;

(6) rejection of collective responsibility in connexion with the sale of Israeli-made arms to the German Federal Republic;

(7) Prime Minister Ben-Gurion's refusal to accept a ministerial inquiry on the Lavon affair;

(8) last, Mr Ben-Gurion's attempt to force the new Prime Minister, Mr Eshkol to institute such an inquiry.

Although most of these crises were focused on 'matters of principle', the changes in the government did not usually greatly affect the settlement of these problems and the new government rarely seized the opportunity of a change in coalition to upset the *status quo* in these matters.

Moreover, while the different parties often maintained these various issues of principle in the elections, they were not of vital importance in the forming of the coalition, where some *modus vivendi* between the different parties was usually attained without great adherence to the electoral platforms.

Although significant changes in economic, social, or immigration policy did occur, they were not necessarily proclaimed in the electioneering campaigns, nor even fully debated in public. The actual development of such policies was usually worked out by mutual adjustment of various interests – especially within Mapai and through the pressures of different other factors on groups within Mapai – thus reinforcing predominance in the Yishuv's and in Israel's political system.

Crises of Legitimation and Development of New Forces

To what extent were the political élite of the country and, especially, Mapai leadership able, through the working out of these varied alignments, to deal with the new problems and forces which were continuously arising on the Israeli political scene?

Needless to say this success was always only partial. In some of the more extreme cases, these developments created intermittent crises in the legitimation of the existing political system. As far as can be ascertained, most citizens identified with the state as such, and with the basic tenets of Jewish statehood and independence – although the meaning given to these goals differed among different groups. However, this did not necessarily extend to the institutional arrangements of the state.

At different stages of development, several negative manifestations to the concrete institutional arrangements of the state appeared. The first such manifestation was seen in the activities of *Shurat Hamitnadvim*, founded mostly by students in the early fifties. The declared aims of this organization were:

(1) to help new immigrants in various aspects;
(2) to uncover misdeeds and 'underhand' activities on the part of government officials within the political and economic organization of the government and of the various political parties.

The *Shura* started its vigilant activities hoping to re-create the ideological atmosphere of 'pioneering' days and to abolish corruption. Their approach was puritanical in that they denounced any manifestation of luxury, or of personal benefit from public means.

344

The summit of the *Shura's* activities was the trial during which Police Inspector Amos Ben-Gurion sued the *Shura* for libel, on the grounds that he had been accused of participating in illegal deals and suppressing certain cases before they were brought to trial.

The verdict given both in the District and Supreme Courts was against the *Shura*. However, the Supreme Court, while upholding the decision itself, decided on 4 June 1960, to lower the *Shura's* fine. It was further found that many irregularities in the presentation of the prosecution's case had taken place. The trial had some far-reaching consequences, the most important of which was the removal from his post of a former Inspector-General of the police, for giving false testimony as a prosecution witness.

The conclusions and outcome of the trial were very interesting from the point of view of the institutionalization and legitimation of the different state organs. While the existence of various irregularities in the state organs was shown, the importance of such irregularities as foci of denial of legitimation to the regime began to dwindle. In the first stages of the state they might have served various 'old-time' elements who found themselves left out of the new 'establishment' or saw a betrayal of the older pristine values of pioneering. But with the further development of the state the acceptance of such vigilante groups and their claims to serve as a substitute for the usual control activities of the state, seemed to wane. Instead, the control activities and legitimation of the courts were upheld, and it was the establishment and acceptance of these that constituted the most important outcome of the trial.

Attempts to deny the legitimation to the regime were later made by several small groups such as *Hapeulah Hashemit* and *Hamishtar Hehadash*, as well as some free lance intellectuals.

Hapeulah Hashemit was closely connected with the somewhat sensational weekly, *Haolam Hazeh*. While its wide circulation was probably largely due to its sensationalist approach, it seems that quite a lot of people also read this magazine because of its overall critical attitude to the government.

Hamishtar Hehadash was founded by various ex-prominent members of Mapai and Herut, as well as some independent intellectuals. The group, which started as a kind of 'free-lance speakers' organization', tried to establish itself as a political party but did not register as such in the elections and, shortly after the elections of 1959, the organization was dissolved.

This group called for changes in almost every socio-political and economic field. Their criticism ranged from the relationship between religion and state, to the impotence of the present foreign policy regarding the neighbouring states or the economic policy which, according to them, nullifies any prospect of economic independence.

They were, in fact, an out-and-out opposition group whose main claim was that all these problems could be solved only by a total change of the political regime and of the ruling class, whose rule they claimed was based on the continuous dependence on foreign economic sources, and on the stifling of any independent activity.

The Development of Independent Forces and of a Floating Vote

In the course of time, more and more issues and problems emerged which, in the eyes of some parts of the public, were not fully taken care of by any of the existing political parties or institutions, thus creating tensions and uneasiness.

The development of a floating vote and of independent forces of public opinion indicate public concern with issues which are not dealt with by the older, traditional totalistic claims of the various parties.

This became especially evident during the elections of 1959 and 1961 and during some of the 1961–3 municipal elections, when some of the character-istics of the floating vote became discernible.

In terms of influencing the ultimate distribution of seats in the Knesset, these shifts – which never exceeded seven to ten seats in the Knesset – were not very important. But within the context of Israeli politics they were of considerable concern to the various parties.

Analysis shows that these shifts originated among new immigrants in 'the later stages of absorption' – those already established to some extent in urban or rural settlements who felt capable of participating in the political process, mainly on the local, but also on a central level.

The second cause for floating votes was based on the various emerging professional groups. Some of the younger generation could probably also be counted among these groups although no exact statistical data on their voting behaviour is available.

In addition to the above, some 'older' 'marginal' middle and lower middle class groups also seem to have been of significance in this context.

The structural placement of these elements in Israeli society is of great importance for our analysis; it indicates that at least some of the groups are the 'product' – albeit the unanticipated product – of the policies aimed at the perpetuation of the 'totalistic', 'federative' arrangements of different parties, and especially of Mapai, but which in fact generated and created new types of political participation.

A similar partial shift also occurred in the foci of independent public opinion, which can perhaps be best seen in the development of journalism. New developments took place of special importance among them being the growth in circulation of the two evening papers, *Maariv* and *Yediot Aharonot*. In particular *Maariv*, which is owned privately by different companies, has always taken a very independent stand.

These independent attitudes became most fully articulated during the Lavon affair and its aftermath. One important indication of this development was the fact that in almost all parties – and above all in Mapai – great pressures from the rank and file, especially from young new members and professionals, developed and challenged the official party policy.

It is not easy for such groups to become independent and articulate, in view of the great power of the existing party machines. But these developments indicate the growing potential importance of such forces and of the feeling of dissatisfaction with many existing arrangements.

New Conflict, Problems, and Tensions

The aftermath of the Lavon affair, the post-devaluation economic policy of February 1962, and the continuous problems concerned with new immigrants, and last, the 1965 elections, greatly sharpened the general awareness of the issues mentioned, and gave rise to the question of the extent to which the existing political leadership was able to represent the growing variety of political demands and problems.

Various groups brought growing pressure to bear on the central political institutions, whose ability to regulate and integrate these interests and formulate effective policy diminished accordingly. These developments first became apparent in the various 'revolts' against Histadrut authority and continued in various ways throughout 1962 and 1963.

Although initial reaction to the new economic policy seemed to emphasize many of the older *ad hoc* measures and adjustments to pressures, the policy was, on the whole, successful (at least until the end of 1963) in maintaining economic stability. The wave of widespread 'unofficial' strikes among professionals and public servants, recurring continuously since 1964, is an important indication of the existing problems and difficulties and has cast serious doubts on the possibilities of continued stability.

However, the crystallization of specific 'ethnic' lists – especially in municipal elections – has, perhaps, even more far-reaching implications. The emergence of such lists can be interpreted as a further development of the occurrences in Wadi Salib – and, in fact, constitute new and very important developments in the political articulation of the immigrant groups. The two most important developments in this field took place in August 1963 during the municipal elections in Ashdod and Beersheba.

Both these towns were developed only after the establishment of the state, and in both, the majority of the population comprises new immigrants, among whom about two-thirds are 'oriental'. In both cities there is almost full employment.

Both towns were at first administered from 'above' – by the various development authorities and (especially in Beersheba) by dynamic leaders from the older Mapai élite, being, in fact, ruled from the centres of the various political parties. However, with growing economic development and stability, various groups of immigrants became involved in public activity and entered the political arena.

The revolt by the various immigrant groups and their leaders, combined with the personal conflicts that provided the main background to the crises within the Mapai-dominated municipal coalition, led to new elections in the summer of 1963.

At about the same time, a country-wide movement of oriental groups was formed by a group of well-to-do oriental Jews (mainly from Iraq) from Ramat-Gan and Jerusalem which provided moral and material support for the local 'ethnic' list in Beersheba and its leader David Chacham.

Mapai accordingly searched for a suitable candidate who would be acceptable to both old-timers and immigrants groups, and found their ideal candidate in Judge Eliahu Nawi, who had come to Israel from Iraq at the age of thirteen and had made his own way up from a working-class background. He was nominated, together with two further oriental candidates originally from North Africa and Egypt respectively.

The election results in Beersheba showed a drop in votes for Mapai, no change for Mapam, an increase for the religious parties, and success for the ethnic list which won two of the fifteen seats in the City Council.

After lengthy negotiations, a coalition headed by Nawi was formed between Mapai, Mapam and the two religious parties (the National Religious Party and *Poalei Agudat Israel*).

The elections in Ashdod took place a week before those in Beersheba. Of Ashdod's sixteen thousand inhabitants only five thousand have the right to vote and of these only two thousand had ever taken part in a previous election, the remainder being new immigrants. Ashdod, a typical development city, containing a new power station and the country's southernmost Mediterranean port now nearing completion, consists mainly of oriental Jews from North Africa. The old-timers consist of a negligible minority and usually fill professional and managerial positions.

The coalition governing the city consisted of Mapai and the religious parties and was headed by an immigrant from Egypt (Robert Haim) who represented Mapai; the second-in-command, Boskiliah, was also of Eastern origin. The older-timers in Ashdod did not mix with the new immigrants and refrained from taking part in the running of the city's affairs. In this way, a local élite of oriental Jews developed and, with party support, directed the city affairs. About a year before the municipal elections Mapai headquarters started to undermine the local administration.

In contrast to Beersheba, Mapai was up against a more or less consolidated party branch in Ashdod, likely to rally around its own local leadership.

Again, in contrast to Beersheba the Ashdod elections took place in a mood of relative indifference and in a 'give and take' fashion as local politicians changed their party affiliations from day to day.

The election results showed a drop in votes for Mapai and an increase for the religious parties (which received an equal number of votes to Mapai) and the 'ethnic' list which took two of the eleven seats.

After protracted negotiations a coalition was formed between Mapai and the religious parties, with the new 'ethnic' list joining with the Liberal Party. Once again, while the number of votes for Mapai had decreased, the party had succeeded in preserving its position of power in the city.

These developments indicate problems of great potential importance for the political scene in Israel.

In both instances the crux of the problem lay in the attempts made by the existing party to minimize the importance and independence of local leadership. In both towns and, of course, in many other places in Israel, the immigrant groups were drawn into the political arena, becoming more organized and articulate in their demands and developing their own leaders.

Their demands were various. At the least articulate level were those for larger direct economic benefits. Later, these demands became more articulate and were couched in terms of greater and more independent participation in the political scene and, when frustrated, could easily lead to outbreaks focused on ethnic symbols.

Although the 'traditional' parties continued to rule after the 1963 election, in spite of the success of the 'ethnic' lists, it became clear that it was no longer possible to ignore the opinions and influence of the majority of the local inhabitants or their leaders.

Several basic alternatives developed, based on the relative success of the older parties against the new 'ethnic' lists and the need to stop the possible development of countrywide 'ethnic' parties which, in the social reality of Israel, would quickly develop into the parties of the lower socio-economic groups, activated by populist leaders. But if the older parties were to be successful in absorbing these new elements and their demands, they would have to give in to most of the short-range, relatively non-articulated demands thus lowering their ability to socialize these groups within their own frameworks.

Another possibility was to open up wider channels of mobility and broaden the active participation of new elements and leadership within the existing parties, while at the same time minimizing purely 'ethnic' symbols and demands.

In the 1965 elections, it seems that for the time being at least, this last alternative became more predominant. The 'ethnic' parties were not successful at all at the national level and only very partially at the local level. At the same time it seems that Rafi became a channel for at least part of the 'ethnic' vote.

Transformations within Mapai

The continuous and predominant pattern of government in Israel was that of a coalition centred around Mapai, with most parties, except the Communists and Herut, being ready and willing to participate in such a coalition. Thus, none of the other parties developed into an effective opposition with an alternative programme and ready to undertake the full responsibility of forming a government.

This situation enabled Mapai to manoeuvre between the different parties, which acted as pressure groups on Mapai, claiming various benefits.

This situation also enabled Mapai and the Prime Minister to claim their indispensability and identification with the state and so to develop a cavalier attitude towards all other parties.

However, this predominance was tempered by the fact that Mapai never had a clear government majority, and therefore had to look continuously for various allies, making far-reaching concessions both to the different parties and to many interest groups within the society.

This effective though limited predominance of Mapai was rooted in the basic historical-sociological characteristics of the Yishuv analysed in chapter 4. With the establishment of the state this system changed through the unification of political frameworks and through the processes of social and economic differentiation described above.

Here again Mapai played a crucial role. Its leaders presided over the transition from Yishuv to state, and established many of the new state's frameworks and symbols.

While the bases of Mapai's predominance remained rooted in the historical background described above, it had to rely increasingly on its ability to monopolize the major power positions and to formulate flexible policies. This flexibility attracted different groups and strata of the population to Mapai and weakened the lure of other parties. Due to its relative flexibility as well as its strategic power position Mapai invariably found allies among different groups, even if not among actual coalition parties.

Mapai was thus greatly dependent on its ability to combine a certain basic conservatism with the inauguration of new policies which could further the development of new state organs and activities, and tackle new problems. These facts explain the continuity and the ability of the existing institutional structure to absorb new elements with innovating tendencies in the social, economic, and political spheres (be they new immigrants and their leaders, professionals, managers, or members of a new political generation).

Some of the latest developments show the peculiar and ambivalent position which Mapai holds in this context. Its strength was rooted in a combination of 'conservatism' and flexibility, but its freedom to manoeuvre was handicapped by social differentiations and the divergent interests which it had to placate. It also developed strong vested interests in its own power positions in the state; naturally interpreting any attempts to undermine these positions as threats to the stability of the state.

With growing pressure from different groups on its two main interests and on its power position in the state, it became more difficult to maintain its position, and Mapai's conservatism may well have become an important stumbling block to further political development.

It is possible that these developments have 'frozen' the capacity to deal with various new problems and may ultimately lower the level of political participation and the overall efficiency of the system.

This potential weakness of Mapai can also be discerned in what was one of its main strengths – the dual role of ruling party in both the Histadrut and the government coalitions. For many years this combination furthered the development and implementation of far-reaching policies and the regulation of demands made by the different workers' groups. However, it is likely to make the government and Mapai too susceptible to various pressures and demands, undermining the scope of its manoeuverability.

Similar problems naturally developed within most other parties, which had to face the alternatives of developing new political frameworks of their own, or of persuading Mapai to create such frameworks for them.

It is as yet difficult to estimate the strength of these socio-political forces with their varied demands, and the ability of the country's leadership to formulate effective new policies to deal with these demands.

Some of these problems came to a head with the second resignation of Ben-Gurion in 1963 and with the assumption of the Premiership by Levi Eshkol. The fact that the transfer of both the Premiership and the Ministry of Defence from the more charismatic personality of Ben-Gurion to Eshkol was effected smoothly, and the legitimation of the new government accepted, has greatly contributed to the potential stability of the political system. This stability, and the effective routinization of the system, will naturally be enhanced if the Eshkol government proves effective. All these problems became more fully crystallized in the 1965 elections.

The 1965 Elections

The 1965 elections marked an important turning point from the point of view of the political alignments in Israel in general, and from the point of view of relations between conservatism and radicalism within the Israeli political system in particular.

Several important developments took place. In the first place, the Alignment between Mapai and *Ahdut Haavoda* was formed, in an initial effort to effect a more complete consolidation of what is generally called the Workers' Left Wing which was, or would have liked to have been, the beginning of a trend towards complete unification of the Labour Movement, and which at first glance might seem to form a concentration of 'conservatives' within the Israeli scene. In the second place, a 'right-wing' bloc, parallel to the Alignment, was formed within Gahal: the Herut-Liberals – were joined by most of the General Zionists and a small number of Progressives. Most of the former

Progressives remained within the framework of the Independent-Liberal Party. This combination emphasized Herut's trend to move from an isolationist party towards a regular and recognized parliamentary opposition, based to no small extent upon the specific economic interest of various social groups. The Communist Party also became split (see above p. 292).

Finally, Rafi was formed. This could have seemed initially as being the most significant manifestation from the point of view of the various possibilities of change of the political structure in Israel. The formation of Rafi was connected, as we have seen, with the Lavon Affair and with the rift between Ben-Gurion and the veteran leaders of Mapai, who formed the Alignment. The formation of this party was also closely connected with Ben-Gurion's refusal to recognize the legitimacy of the existing political system – a system of proportional representation and of coalitions.

The breach between Ben-Gurion and Mapai was initiated by Eshkol's letter to the members of the *Min Hayesod* group (March 1964), which contained, in effect, a promise to return Lavon to political activity and also to avoid bringing up the Affair again. Ben-Gurion viewed this as being a miscarriage of justice and protested the lack of separation between the administrative and judicial authorities.

Following the rejection by Mapai of Ben-Gurion's request to renew investigation of the Affair and to transfer it to a judicial committee, he rejected completely the party leadership and framework. When, at a later stage, he found himself unable to obtain control of a majority within the existing party organs, he declared in July 1965 the foundation of a new party – Rafi (*Reshimat Poalei Israel* – Israel's Workers' List). The new party was formed around a number of rallying points:

(1) Ben-Gurion's personality and leadership.
(2) The demand to renew investigation of the Affair under judicial auspices (a demand which was later, in the course of the elections, largely neglected).
(3) The demand to change the system of elections (from proportional representation to personal-regional one).[1]
(4) The demand for speedy modernization of agriculture, industry, and educational institutions and for
(5) More extensive representation of ethnic groups and development areas.

Rafi hoped to receive, by means of its leadership (headed by Ben-Gurion) a high percentage of the electoral votes, so that even if it did not receive a majority, it could at least constitute a crucial factor in the formation of the government.

This combination of the contents of Rafi's platform and the background of its formation, tended to emphasize that according to its view, no real

---

[1] A demand which was some years earlier accepted by the Mapai party organs, but not implemented.

innovation was possible within the existing political framework, and that these frameworks are unable to deal with major new problems, such as modernization, absorption of ethnic groups – as every innovation is doomed to failure because of the necessity for the compromises inherent in the existing coalition-system. The comparative novelty in the appearance of Rafi was emphasized by another fact – it was the only party amongst the large and medium-sized parties which did not emanate from a party, settlement move-movement, or Zionist movement dating from the time prior to the formation of the state. It was by way of being the first purely 'Israeli' party.

A number of groups joined Rafi: part of Mapai's 'young' leaders (M. Dayan, S. Peres, S. Yizhar, etc.) who were sometimes designated as the 'doers' and who viewed themselves as representing the forces behind the political and social innovations: a small part of the veteran bloc within Mapai (chiefly from the moshavim); some groups from within the ethnic groups of Eastern origin active in party affairs in the towns (mainly in development towns).

Thus we see, that in these elections, two comparatively large blocs were formed for the first time – the Alignment and Gahal – which represented different social and economic attitudes, and to a certain extent also different political attitudes. It seemed as if in this way a possibility of formation of an alternative to Mapai's rule was approached. There also appeared, in the form of Rafi, for the first time, a political force which at first sight seemed to reject the legitimacy of the existing political system. This force was neither a marginal one (such as the *Haolam Hazeh* Party List) or other splinter groups, nor an ethnic-separatist one (although as we have noted, it did absorb a bit of the ethnic tension), but rather came from within the centre of the political arena.

At the outset of the general election campaign – which was long, bitter, and very expensive – and during the elections to the Histadrut (in September 1965, two months before the elections to the Knesset) these two forces – Gahal on one hand, and Rafi on the other – seemed quite likely to upset the power system in Israel. 77·6 per cent of the Histadrut electorate (which comprises 60 per cent of the electors to the Knesset) voted in these elections. The follow-ing seven party lists participated in the election: the Alignment, Rafi, Inde-pendent-Liberals, Mapam, Gahal, and two Communist groups. The major novelty in these elections was the appearance of a Histadrut list of candidates connected to the Herut Party – the Blue-White group, which joined the General Zionists' faction in the Histadrut, and which appeared jointly with it as the 'Herut-Liberal Bloc'. The appearance of Herut on the political scene in the Histadrut constituted an important innovation because this precarious part and its founders were among the leaders of the opposition to the Histadrut and its structure. The importance of this novelty was underlined by the fact that Herut has a workers' branch in the form of the 'National

353

Workers Organization' (about 50,000 members) which did not join the Histadrut and also opposed the formation of a Herut faction in the Histadrut. These facts were stressed by the majority in the Histadrut in order to justify its opposition to Herut's bid for a formation of a political faction within the Histadrut. The main contention was that a faction which strives to dissolve the Histadrut should not be permitted to act within it. The Histadrut organs decided before the elections, by a large majority, to reject Herut's request for admission. This decision was appealed by Herut to the courts, which decided that the Histadrut's decision was illegal, and that Herut should be permitted to form a separate faction.

The result of these elections was a considerable change in the Histadrut's political set-up. The Alignment received 50·88 per cent of the votes, 17 per cent of which were reserved for *Ahdut Haavoda*. The end result was, therefore, that Mapai received only about 33 per cent in comparison to the 56 per cent that it received in the elections to the Ninth Conference (February 1960) – thus losing its majority in the Histadrut for the first time. Mapam received less than 1 per cent more than in the previous election (from 13·9 per cent in 1960 to 14·5 per cent in 1965). The Independent-Liberals received about 4·4 per cent (in comparison to 5·8 per cent in the 1960 elections). Rafi received about 12 per cent of the electoral votes and the two Communist parties received about 3 per cent (as they did in 1960).

The surprise was in the rise of the 'Herut-Liberal' bloc, which now formed the second largest party in the Histadrut, after having received 15·2 per cent of the votes (in comparison to the 3·5 per cent that the General Zionists received alone in 1960). The sharp increase in the number of votes received by Gahal may be explained by the fact that the Herut supporters in the Histadrut were formerly forced to vote for other parties. (They seemed to have had a tendency to vote for *Ahdut Haavoda*).

However, this new trend was not repeated in the elections to the Knesset – and there may be some basis for the contention that the results of the Histadrut elections alarmed large enough parts of the public and thus influenced the results of the Knesset elections. The percentage of voters was higher than in most of the previous elections, as some 83 per cent of all the eligible voted. The Alignment (Mapai, without Rafi, and *Ahdut Ha'avoda*) succeeded in maintaining its position and even gain 2 per cent over Mapai in the 1961 elections (34·7 per cent in 1961 and 36·7 per cent in 1965). Rafi received 100,000 votes, comprising 7·9 per cent of the total number of votes cast. Rafi, Mapai and *Ahdut Haavoda* received together 3·3 per cent more votes than they received in the Fifth Knesset. Mapam lost 0·9 per cent (receiving 6·6 per cent) and the two Communist parties lost 0·8 per cent in comparison to their standing in the Fifth Knesset. Generally speaking, the left-wing bloc retained its standing, and continues to receive about 50 per cent of the total number of votes cast.

It is interesting to note that the 'New Communist Party' received almost three times the number of votes received by the 'Hebrew' Communist Party, a fact which seems to substantiate the supposition that Rafi is mainly supported by Arab voters.

The religious bloc lost about 1·4 per cent in the 1965 general elections, going down to 14 per cent. The Herut-Liberal bloc did not succeed in reinforcing right-wing representation. The 'bloc' received 21·3 per cent of the electoral votes, in comparison to the 13.5 per cent and 6.2 per cent that Herut and the General Zionists received respectively in the Fourth Knesset elections. The Independent-Liberals succeeded, more or less, in retaining 3·8 per cent

However, if we combine the percentage that the Independent-Liberal Party received in the Fifth Knesset (3·8 per cent) and compare it to the percentage received by the Liberal and Herut Parties together, we see clearly that the 'right-wing' bloc suffered a loss of 2·3 per cent. This decrease is insignificant and one may conclude that no far-reaching changes in the balance of power took place.

Finally, it should be noted that the ethnic and personal candidate lists proposed for election to the Sixth Knesset did not even succeed in obtaining the number of votes (about 10,000) necessary to secure one representative in the Knesset, with the exception of the *Haolam Hazeh* list, led by U. Avneri, who was elected to the Knesset.

Some interesting developments occurred during these elections on the municipal level:

(1) A difference between the pattern of voting for the Knesset and the pattern of voting for local authorities manifested itself in a number of local councils and municipalities. The most outstanding discrepancy was observed in Jerusalem – where Rafi received 20 per cent of the votes (as did the Alignment) – as compared to the 7 per cent it received in the elections to the Knesset. A similar discrepancy occurred in several other municipalities, but in each of them it concerned different political parties. In Hadera, for instance, Gahal received a higher percentage of votes than in the general elections.

(2) These discrepancies in the voting patterns may be largely attributed to the distinction made by the electorate between the two levels of election and to the attempt made by the electorate to vote for a candidate who seemed to be personally suitable, rather than for the party which supported him. (Again, the most outstanding manifestation of this tendency was the number of votes cast for Teddy Kolleck in Jerusalem.) On the other hand, there is no doubt that the parties are the most powerful force alive on the municipal level.

(3) Another fact which became clear after the election was the tendency to oust Mapai from its former position of control in a number of local councils and municipalities.

In several places, such as Yerucham, Hadera, Netivot, Ashkelon, Kiryat Shmoneh, and other similar locations, coalitions were formed between Rafi, Gahal, and the religious parties. This tendency was specially marked in the development towns.

The explanation given (mainly by Rafi representatives) for the reasons behind this tendency was that ousting Mapai from power in the municipal authorities would bring about the development of more independent local leadership, which would act as a sort of 'check and balance' to the central government. It is still too early to determine whether this assumption is correct or not. However, there is no doubt that a certain change has appeared in the Israeli political scene. On the other hand, it should be emphasized that Mapai succeeded in retaining its position of power in most of the municipalities in the large cities (Tel Aviv, Haifa, Petah Tikva, Givatayim, Kfar-Saba, and others).

The new government comprised of Mapai, *Ahdut Haavoda*, Mapam, the Independent-Liberals, the Mafdal and *Poalei Agudat Israel*, and headed by L. Eshkol, was formed in January 1966. The government therefore enjoys the support of seventy members of Knesset.

The process of formation of the new government entailed tiring negotiations, in the course of which pressure was exerted upon the main party in the coalition (Mapai) by all concerned. Most of the pressure exerted by the religious parties concerned religious matters, and they received promises guaranteeing further restraint of services and industries on Saturday (including Ashdod port and agricultural farms), and the prohibition of post-mortems without consent of the deceased's relations, apart from exceptional cases.

As for Mapam, its inclusion in the coalition was made possible by allowing it to reserve the right to vote independently on matters which it viewed as being of special importance (relations with Germany and atomic disarmament).

The Independent-Liberals received promises concerning wage policy, the extension of basic legislation in order to safeguard democratic principles, and also the implementation of public supervision and guidance over hospitalization through the Ministry of Health. The government was finally approved on 12 January 1966, by a majority of seventy-five votes in the Knesset. The government is comprised of eighteen ministers, five of which are newcomers.

As stated above the 1965 elections were extremely important from the point of view of the major problems of the Israeli political system, and especially from the point of view of the relations between conservatism and innovation within it on the one hand and between its continuity and its ability to deal with new problems on the other.

From the point of view of 'continuity' of the system these elections have shown the relative failure of the attempts of various groups – and especially of Rafi – to undermine its legitimacy.

Truly enough, Rafi was severely handicapped in these attempts – especially, paradoxically enough – because of the combination of appeals which it attempted to foster. There was on the one hand the personal, charismatic appeal of Ben-Gurion – denying, in its extreme manifestations, the legitimation or validity of almost the entire institutional setting of the regime, attempting to base its claims to change the regime on a combination of personal charisma and a monopoly on activism and political and technical know-how. There was the claim of the younger groups and leaders in terms of 'modernization' and innovation as against the vested interests and lack of innovative initiative of the older groups – a claim which lost perhaps some of its appeal in view of the fact that most of the leaders were until very recently members of the government, where they did not necessarily fight for the things they began now to advocate. And lastly, there was the appeal to the problem of the various ethnic groups – especially to some of the more politically and socially mobile groups among them.

While each of these claims could have appealed to some groups of the population, very often they might also have cancelled one another. Those who were seriously concerned with problems of modernization or change, and even would have liked to give credit to some of the younger leaders in this respect, did not always easily accept the upsetting of the whole institutional setting as a necessary condition for such innovation or modernization.

Others – especially the broader strata of new immigrants – while perhaps attached to Ben-Gurion's charisma might have doubts about the ability of Rafi to 'deliver' the goods as against the more massive means at the disposal of the existing parties.

Probably only the purely personal devotees of Ben-Gurion were ready to accept all these appeals blindly.

Truly enough each of these appeals – and all of them together were enough to assure Rafi ten members in the Knesset – in themselves were too few to sustain their claim to become a new force for change, especially as very soon on the municipal level and to some extent in the Histadrut they attempted to play the usual game of coalition politics.

They were especially too few in view of the resounding success of the Alignment to receive forty-five members – much above the expectations of most of the public.

This victory was first of all a victory of the institutional setting of the existing regime as such. It emphasized that the Israeli electorate was not ready to conceive the political system to be dependent on any one person, and believed that it could probably deal with most of its problems through existing frameworks – or at least that no better ones were in view.

This acceptance of the institutional setting was perhaps the most significant result of these elections. While, of course, in itself it did not negate the possibility that in the future this framework may be overthrown a great

357

crisis or breakdown would be necessary, especially as in the future even the continuity given in Ben-Gurion's personality would become weaker.

But beyond this the relative victory of the Alignment was beyond all a victory for the conservatism of the Israeli electorate and in many ways it emphasized many of the paradoxical characteristics of this conservatism.

Thus, although the Alignment was founded on a 'socialist' or 'labour' ticket stressing more and more the 'socialist' orientation and the unity of the Labour movement (which became apparent also in the fact that Mapam joined the new coalition in early 1966) yet quite a lot of its support – and probably especially that support which made the resounding victory possible – came from 'non-aligned' groups be they professional, academic, or industrial, who were very far indeed from accepting the socialist ideology. These groups voted for the Alignment either because of vested interests or general feeling of well being and/or because they were against the general upset of the regime as advocated by Rafi and to a smaller extent Gahal. (It may well be that Gahal, the paradoxically 'less radical' opposition, which presented itself as a possible alternative in terms not only of personnel but also of ideology, lost some votes because of the fear of extreme upheaval created by Rafi.)

From this point of view it was extremely significant that the vote of the well-to-do suburbs – such as the North of Tel Aviv – went to the Alignment, while in the more proletarian quarters Gahal and (especially in some of the new development towns) Rafi found greater support.

Thus the bases of the victory of the Alignment have stressed, perhaps even more than before, the great discrepancy between the ideological orientation and slogans on the one hand and the social bases of the electorate and concrete policy orientation on the other.

Here again it is significant that during the coalition talks prior to the formation of the new government in 1966, it was said that the Prime Minister was interested in co-opting, as usual, the religious parties (and was willing to give in to them on several important points – such as prohibition of work on Saturdays in the new port of Ashdod or extending the validity of municipal laws dealing with work on Shabbath) – so as to be less dependent in economic and social matters on the more doctrinaire Mapam and possible also his own Alignment colleagues from *Ahdut Haavoda* – the very groups which formed the basis of the United Labour Front. The inclusion of the small Independent Liberals also clearly indicated the same orientation,

These facts were in no way new – in many ways they were but continuations of the former activities and policies of Mapai. But the problem that arose now was whether it would also be possible to continue them effectively in the somewhat new situation created in these elections through the formation of the Alignment on the one hand and of Gahal on the other, and the possible juxtaposition between 'left' and 'right', enhanced because of the possible joining of Rafi – as it had in some cases on the municipal level – with the 'right' wing.

This brings us to the second problem, namely that of the relation between conservatism and innovation in the Israeli political system, and between the extent to which the very continuity and seeming institutional stability of the system are compatible also with the ability to cope with the many new problems – be they those of modernizing the economy, absorbing actively new types of social, academic, and immigrant groups – and to develop new approaches and policies.

The main test of such ability is the extent to which there will develop within most parties, and especially within Mapai, new ways of looking at problems, new channels for selection of leadership, and new organizational forms and settings.

We have seen that till the early 'sixties Mapai has indeed shown a relatively great ability in all these directions – even if mostly in an *ad hoc* way – but that since then many signs indicated a weakening of this ability.

This problem became even more pronounced and acute during the period of 1965 elections – despite, or perhaps because of, its great victory. On the one hand the older cohesion of Mapai leadership, which enabled it to forge out throughout the 'fifties some of these new policies, became weakened through the split of Rafi. While it is true that the organization and structure of the leadership showed great resilience to this split, it is yet to be seen whether this is also connected with the ability to forge out the new orientations and policies and to continue to absorb new groups.

Two problems seem to stand out here. One is, to what extent the growing alignment between Mapai and *Ahdut Haavoda* will weaken the more sectarian leadership elements – *Ahdut Haavoda* in such a way as to enhance the potential for innovation and creativity and of opening new channels, or conversely, the extent to which it will be immobilized (especially in the Histadrut, where it is now in a minority) by its dependence on *Ahdut Haavoda*.

It seems that this is more a question of internal cohesion, strength, and self-confidence of Mapai leaders than of purely tactical positions of relative strength – mainly because basically the dependence of *Ahdut Haavoda* on Mapai is greater than vice versa, and secondly, because it seems that in some ways there are among the members of *Ahdut Haavoda* inclinations or some readiness to some such new orientations.

The second major problem here is to what extent Mapai and the Alignment will be able to absorb new social groups and to open up new channels of political mobility.

The pre-election period has shown that the claim of Rafi to represent the 'young' and 'modern' was not substantiated, that many such groups have indeed voted for the Alignment. Moreover, under the impact of Rafi, the Alignment and other partners have included in their lists new blood –

although obviously the secession of Rafi has withdrawn some such elements from them.

But it is not yet certain to what extent such new elements will be indeed permitted to positions of leadership and will be able to participate in the forging out of new policies or will only become new pressure groups. This problem is especially acute in view of the fact that even in the past the ability to absorb new groups and to cater to their demands was greater than the ability to forge out new orientations and policies. The same problems exist also with regard to other parties – including Rafi. Truly enough the emergence of Rafi has increased the possibilities of the crystallization of new coalition alignments and hence also perhaps of a new centre alternative to the existing coalition. In this sense it might well be true that the real test of the coalition predominated by the Labour parties will come only in the next elections. But in the sociological reality of Israeli politics the possiblity of such change does not yet in itself assure an increase in the innovative ability of the political system.

It is the constellation of all these factors that brings out sharply the problem whether the institutional continuity of the Israeli political system will be connected with growing flexibility and innovation or, conversely, with growing immobilization.

4

BASIC CHARACTERISTICS OF POLITICAL PROCESSES AND
CONTINUITY OF THE SYSTEM

Basic Characteristics of the Political System – Socio-Historical Roots

The complicated political process in Israel, shows several distinct trends. We find a relatively high degree of actual *de facto* consensus on many basic issues concerned with the contours of the state, with occasional eruptions into acute political controversy, when the limits of the existing consensus of the *modus vivendi* are endangered. Such crises usually result in the restoration of the *status quo* or in the acceptance of some changes in it.

The vociferous and totalistic orientation of political discourse in Israel, combined with the ability to compromise on concrete issues, helped to prevent the various 'basic' issues which could have proved divisive from being drawn into the political debate. Some such issues, especially in the religious field, have recently emerged, but even here they are, on the whole, merely incipient.

360

The continuity of the Israeli political system was also helped by the variety of alignments on different issues, which prevented the development of serious splits, and by the ability to develop overall policies combining conservative dynamism with administrative and political innovation.

At the same time, however, the efficiency of such empirical political bargaining was limited by lack of public acknowledgement and full institutionalization of the rules and criteria instrumental for its attainment.

These characteristics to some degree explain the continuity of the system and its ability to absorb new forces, but also show the creation of many tensions and anomic gaps in the political system.

To understand the continuity and the ability of the Israeli political system to deal with new problems, it is worth while to analyse some of its characteristics as they have crystallized from their socio-historical roots.

The establishment of unified political institutions and the concomitant development of new norms and legal perceptions, necessarily constituted a great change from the frameworks of the period of the Yishuv.

Established through the impetus of 'older' values, these new frameworks and norms established the relationship between groups, parties, and leaders and greatly changed the overall political setting.

The various groups necessarily became parts of a new, wider, and more differentiated framework. But at the same time they tended to continue to proclaim their totalistic views in the new setting. The newly-developed state organs were often perceived by the groups in terms of former goals.

While the impetus to the establishment of the state was largely due to the social, pioneering movements of the Yishuv, the very creation of the state produced new political frameworks and institutions, whose basic premises and structure often opposed the values and traditions of the older movements. Most leaders were thus not prepared or able to accept and understand the changes in the institutional structure that developed with the state, particularly so since some 'blindness' to the new situation could reinforce their own positions of power within the new framework.

This situation generated many tensions and 'anomic gaps' in the political structure, focused relations of the state to the major collective goals of the community, and brought several crucial problems to the fore. One was the problem of establishing such goals, and the degree of priority to be attached to them within the setting of the new political institutions. Second, was the problem of accepting these goals as part of the basic consensus of the nation.

These problems largely developed through the fact that the establishment of the state greatly weakened the 'movement' type of legitimation causing a general weakening of ideological Zionist orientations, which was underlined by the limitation of the functions of the Zionist Organization as well as by the general inability of the Zionist movement to re-interpret the meaning of Zionism in the State of Israel.

The inclusion of clear non-movement groups within the framework of the state – the most outstanding of which was *Agudat Israel* – was another reason for the growth of these problems.

Next was the unification of the framework of political struggle, which made former movements into parts of a single, unified political entity in which they had to agree on some broad, general goals and on the principles of federative arrangements, in spite of their tendency to maintain older 'totalistic' attitudes.

Many compromises were achieved on the ways of setting the priority of different goals, but they were not fully institutionalized in terms of the political process and discourse in Israel.

Two Basic Attitudes to the State – The State as the Epitome of Collective Goals

Several basic attitudes to the state emerged from these problems, bringing important repercussions in the institutionalization of the new political frameworks and process in Israel.

The first of these was the conception of the state as bearer of the major collective future – such as Zionism, or ingathering of the exiles – and the investment of the state and its active organs (especially the government) with the task of fulfilling these goals.

The second was the perception of the state as a distributing agency whose task was to allocate facilities to the various groups and movements.

In its first aspect the state encompassed the major symbols of the nation and appeared as successor to the various movements with their strong future orientations and totalistic claims.

In the second aspect it appeared mostly as a distributor of various goods and services, as mediator between external resources and internal groups and, in a way, even as an object of exploitation by these groups.

The first set of orientations established the state and its executive organs as the main repository of the older types of goals borne previously by the various social movements.

National defence, the ingathering of the exiles, a just society, etc. derived from the basic Zionist-socialist ideology, were to a considerable degree transferred to the state and its symbols.

Some of these, such as the army, identified with the state in a natural way. Others – such as pioneering or the ingathering of the exiles – became bones of contention, and claims to represent these goals continued to be made both by the state and by other groups.

As these attempts and orientations towards 'statehood' were often interpreted as a reaction against the continuous 'haggling' over details of policy, they lent the state and the executive – and especially the office of Prime Minister – a special charismatic aura. In this way both the maintenance of strong emphasis on implementation of goals, and the removal of these goals from the daily political process could presumably be achieved especially with Ben-Gurion attempting to take over for the state, and often for himself, the monopoly representation of the major collective values and their inherent 'rightness'.

Closely related to this were the attempts, again made mostly by Ben-Gurion, to develop a new set of values directly linked by Jewish biblical and prophetic history, often by-passing, not only many periods of Jewish history in the diaspora, but also the more recent values of the Zionist and Labour movements.

One of the most important indications of this was the attempt to divest the kibbutz movement of its pioneering aura – an attitude which later changed markedly. Perhaps even more significant was the attempt, made by Ben-Gurion and some of his entourage, to stress the disparity between the *Hagana* and the Israel Defence Army, and to present the latter as an almost new creation inspired by Ben-Gurion.

Similarly oriented were Ben-Gurion's attempts – in clear opposition to the views of the government and his own party – to minimize the importance of the Zionist organization and even Zionist ideas, and to stress in their stead the more general connexion and identification with Israel of Jews everywhere.

This entailed another important structural-ideological aspect in the 'transfer' of the goal emphasis from the various social and pioneering movements to the state. The original movement goals implied the 'dedication' of members to the common goals. When transformed into the new framework of the state these often crystallized ideologically into claims of 'supremacy' of the state and of its consequent legitimacy to define and limit the activities of the subject. These tendencies had many implications on the constitutional level – such as the development of the various security regulations previously mentioned – and they were, in turn, greatly reinforced by a tendency to bureaucratization and administrative centralization.

The State as a Distributive Agency

Many of the tendencies analysed above were paradoxically strengthened by the way in which the emphasis on the state's distributive functions developed.

This attitude was ingrained in many of the 'sectarian' trade unions, which looked upon the state as provider of services or even as a potentially 'alien' institution. It was also underlined by the fact that each group could claim that the state 'belonged' to, or favoured another, or that it did not yet fully epitomoze true national values better represented by specific groups and that, therefore, the group had to be given special rights and privileges within the state.

This was seen in the continuation and even extension of the internal

363

'jurisdiction' of many public bodies – ranging from the Histadrut and the different parties to co-operatives and settlements – and their attempts to evade or circumvent the jurisdiction of the courts.

This attitude was ingrained in many of the interest groups which developed claims on the state for allocation of positions, subsidies and goods, an attitude which was, of course, reinforced by the growth of state bureaucracy.

In institutional terms the most important manifestation of these tendencies was the demand that various facilities and services allegedly vested in the state should be allocated through movement, party, or Histadrut agencies. The most important instance of this was in the area of health services. Another was in the sphere of housing, where allocation was demanded through the agencies of the Histadrut or the different parties on the basic tenets of 'social justice.'

This attitude also left its mark on the economic policy manifesting itself in the inability of the various leaders to withstand the pressures towards growing public and private consumption. On the basis of their ideological pioneering values, the kibbutzim and moshavim claimed special protection by the state, and in a more general way the Histadrut demanded almost equal partnership with the state.

In the ideological debate which arose from the Lavon affair, this problem shifted from the emphasis on the purity of older values to the more general claim of the importance of 'voluntary' associations (of which the Histadrut was presumably the epitome) as against the 'etatist' tendencies of the state.

This shift, stressing the voluntary aspect of various activities, rather than their goal, contained an important recognition of the changing social reality. However, as it was coupled with continuous totalistic claims for the Histadrut, this shift was only partial and contained many conservative elements in it.

Structural Effects of the Two Orientations to Statehood on the Legitimation of the State and Its Efficiency

The potential contradiction between these two different orientations appeared in its extreme form as opposition between different parties and, within Mapai, these different tendencies existed side by side, its leadership attempting to satisfy both to varying degrees.

Nonetheless, the combination of these two approaches to the state, weakened the legitimation of 'routine' legislative and judicial organs and encouraged the perception of the state as the framework which maintains and helps the implementation of general values and goals, but which is not, in itself, their repository or sole guardian.

Throughout this period the legislative, juridical, and state-controlled agencies became more established and accepted, and connected with the legitimation and proper functioning of state organs. The importance of various parliamentary and juridical controls in the eyes of public opinion seems to have increased since the establishment of the Eshkol government.

The interaction of these various tendencies developed several anomic gaps in the Israeli political structure; indicating both the possibilities of erosion of the existing political system and its re-crystallization. The crucial weakness of these gaps was the inability to develop the full institutionalization of new norms which could regulate new problems, issues, and conflicts.

In this way the belief in democratic institutions could easily erode through apathy, conflict and through the growing discrepancy between the high level of commitment to national goals and the strong practical conservatism rooted in vested interests.

The tendencies towards predominance of the executive and bureaucracy could very often reinforce such apathy and be in turn reinforced by the feelings of inadequacy of existing groups and parties to stand up to the executive or to deal adequately with new demands.

However, these varied gaps also contained the possibility of the development of new political orientations. In contrast to the forces eroding the belief in democracy and in the functioning of the existing system, the growth of more independent forms of public expression and concern also took place, in turn leading to increased legitimacy and acceptance of new regulative norms and mechanisms, such as those of the judiciary and the legislature.

The basic political orientation of the citizen to the state is complex and, to a certain extent, ambivalent. It wavers between overall identification in terms of ultimate symbols of statehood and a tendency to negative evaluation of the institutional frameworks, and of the demand made by the government, this being tantamount to a negative conception of the rights and duties of the citizen.

However, a counter-attitude to this also tends to develop, expressing itself in great concern with the apathy and cynicism shown, and in a feeling of devotion to the state and anxiety over concrete issues.

Sometimes these two opposing attitudes may even supplement one another in as far as a growth of cynicism may also give rise to growing concern.

These ambivalent attitudes towards the political institutions are probably the equivalent to the lack of clear definition of the roles of the rulers which were analysed above. They are also rooted in the absence of a clear definition of norms regulating the exercise of power.

Political Discourse and Decision-Making

The nature of political discourse and decision-making in Israel reinforced the tendencies previously analysed. While most parties presented different policies in terms of ultimate values, relations between them were characterized by hard bargaining for the allocation and division of concrete benefits, with relatively little dispute on major concrete problems, the existence of which all admitted.

Naturally, 'totalistic' ideological claims of different groups and parties were often used for the maintenance of power positions, 'federative' bargaining agreements, or the attainment of a more favourable position in the political sphere.

Criticism of such arrangements was often answered in terms of ultimate values and looked upon as a sort of apostasy. Only in the day-to-day work of parliamentary committees, the judiciary and, to a small extent, of some municipalities, more realistic attitudes gradually developed, though they are, as yet, only a minor part of political discourse in Israel.

This indicates that many concrete issues are either not openly discussed (as for instance matters of defence, where this is justified on 'security' grounds) or are debated in terms of ultimate loyalties and values and not on their concrete implications. Many such disputes were settled with Mapai, excluding discussions among the different parties.

Similar patterns affected the decisions made in the top executive echelons of Mapai, and in the various bureaucratic ranks.

In general, regulative political mechanisms which go beyond direct bargaining among different parties are relatively weak and only partly accepted, and apply mainly to juridical safeguards against the encroachment of the executive and bureaucracy.

While these regulative forces became, to some extent, formalized and institutionalized as they developed, they were not easily accepted, and although some marked changes and progress have taken place any attempts to control the executive in crucial areas such as security, still face many problems.

Possible Patterns of Development in the Political System

Till now the young Israeli political system succeeded in quelling all extreme-populist, ethnic, or 'vigilante' attempts to undermine its legitimacy. Whether it will continue to maintain its legitimacy and function effectively within the framework of its existing institutions is the main problem it now has to face. The real issue within this context is not so much the formal structure of the government (i.e. whether a two party system will develop) but whether the various new issues and problems can be adequately dealt with within existing institutional frameworks – both through the development of new regulative mechanisms and through the ability of old and new parties to deal with such problems.

There are several possibilities of dealing with these new problems. One is the continuation of the existing system and increase of its ability to deal with new problems, this would probably be connected with the increasing importance of the legislative and juridical bodies, the various organs of public control and independent public opinion. This can be effected in two ways. One would be to continue the existing coalition structure by re-organizing Mapai sufficiently to enable it to absorb new groups and to establish new effective leadership, while the other parties would have to be revitalized enough to exert effective pressures on Mapai.

The other possibility is that of a growing realignment of political parties and groups around the 'right', 'centre', and 'left', with the possibility of weakening the smaller parties and merging them with the bigger ones. This might enable the development of an opposition strong enough to be a real alternative to a Mapai-dominated coalition.

The development of the Israeli political system in such a direction would probably be connected with the growing importance of legislative and public opinion organs, with the growth of more dynamic particularistic orientations, and with a weakening of the 'freezing' ascriptive orientations in the social organization.

Yet another possibility is that of weakening the existing system by lowering its efficiency and level of flexibility. There are many ways in which this might be achieved, but they would all include a weakening of legislature and of the influence of public opinion, and would enhance the importance of various types of bargaining as a major political mechanism. Such developments would also probably be strongly connected with the growing preponderance of the 'freezing' ascriptive-particularistic orientation in Israel's social structure.

10

Culture and Values

CULTURAL RENAISSANCE – INSTITUTIONALIZATION OF CULTURAL ACTIVITIES

Introduction – Ideological Premises and Patterns of Creativity

The preceding chapters dealt with the historical development of Israel's basic social structure, mainly derived from Zionist and, later, Zionist-Socialist ideology which aimed at the creation of a new Jewish society. We now return to the question posed in the very first chapter of this book – what kind of society did they envisage, what society and initial tradition did they create, and how did the various sectors of the Israeli population participate in the creation, perpetuation, and changes of these traditions?

Several basic ideological assumptions on the institutionalization of ideals developed within most pioneering groups, which were part and parcel of the basic ideological-sectarian orientations and can be summed up very briefly. It was assumed that, ultimately, the national cultural renaissance would encompass all spheres of culture – arts and sciences, language and religion – with its traditional and modern elements, and that all these would thrive and develop within the new national framework. The second assumption was that the process of cultural creativity would also encompass all spheres of daily life and would permeate all groups of society. Lastly, it was assumed that all would participate fully in this process of cultural creativity, irrespective of specific inclinations. This latter assumption was personified by the great figures of the heroic age of Zionism – the poet Bialik, who was also active in politics, by leaders such as Weizmann, who combined political and scientific activities, or Sokolov, who was a litterateur of standing. It was also represented by the intense cultural activities of the various groups within the Zionist movement, and in particular by the pioneering groups.

Although some cultural specialization dates back to the first and second aliya, when various schools and seminars and newspapers were founded and professional and scientific societies established, such differentiation was usually perceived merely as a difference of emphasis within the common endeavour.

The institutionalization of the various cultural activities dates back to the second, and the beginning of the third, aliya when some crucial cultural aspects – like the revival of the Hebrew language and the relations of the

Zionist movement and the Yishuv to religious tradition – crystallized. The first full expression of these trends can be seen in the initial school curriculum previously discussed, which combined Jewish and general studies in a relatively modern pedagogical framework. Jewish learning emphasized the (mostly non-religious) study of the Bible and the Talmud, as well as Jewish history and literature. In history and literature a growing emphasis on the periods of the first and second Temples developed together with stress on the immediate precursors of the Zionist movement. Although other periods of Jewish history were not neglected, the underlining of these specific periods, as well as the secular attitude to the Bible, constituted an important shift to 'Palestinian' emphasis. In general studies the emphasis was put on history and, to a lesser extent, on general literature (most general literature was taught as part of the English and, to some extent, French languages) and science. While this basic curriculum developed many variations and pedagogical experiments, the most important single fact to emerge was that it overcame and transposed the problem of tradition versus modernity, Jewishness versus 'general' culture and, in fact, created a technical-pedagogical rather than an ideological problem.

Similar tendencies appeared in the literary-cultural sphere of the Yishuv, which was, from the very beginning, part and parcel of broader Zionist endeavours in the diaspora, and a continuation of the former *Haskala* movements. Among the important characteristics of this activity was the combination of new, original creative work in Hebrew with translations from world literature. Thus, for instance, Bialik translated Don Quixote, and Tschernikhovsky the Iliad, Odyssey, and Kalevala, as part of a much wider literary activity spread over many journals and undertaken by several publishing houses. An important part of these activities was the attempt to Hebraize great parts of *Wissenschaften des Judentums* developed in Germany.

A similar pattern appeared in the development of the theatre – with the establishment in 1918 of Habimah, the first Hebrew national theatre, greatly influenced by the modern Russian theatre, which, from the very beginning, included both foreign and original Hebrew plays in its repertoire.

Within the field of literary and scientific creativity, mention should be made of school (especially high school) textbooks, particularly in the literary and historical fields and in the various fields of science, which were very often of a high literary and cultural level. The 'popularization' of parts of the Jewish tradition was another important development, culminating in the famous *Sefer Haagadah* (The Book of Legends) in which Bialik and Ravnitski extracted the body of non-legal literature from the Talmud. Side by side with this, a spate of new, semi-scientific, semi-popular historical and archaeological activities developed, destined to flourish later.

In the early mandatory period, holy days and rest days began to be institutionalized in a somewhat similar pattern.

All major Jewish holy days – the High Holy Days (Rosh Hashana and Yom-Kippur), Succot, Pesach, Shavuot and, to a lesser extent, Chanuka and Purim (which do not entail as many religious restrictions as the full holy days) were set up as official or semi-official holy days in the Yishuv and later in the State of Israel. Similarly Shabbat (Saturday) became the weekly rest-day, with non-Jewish communities being able to opt for their own specific day of rest.

But while these arrangements were accepted by all parts of the population, they did not necessarily imply the acceptance of all the religious implications or injunctions entailed and many innovations evolved, especially in the settlements. No non-Jewish holiday became fully institutionalized within the Yishuv, with the exception of the First of May, which was recognized by the workers' sectors during the period of the Yishuv, but which has lost in importance since the period of the state. All non-Jewish communities naturally fully observed their own religious holidays. In addition to the above, the Day of Independence became an additional full holiday after the establishment of the state.

Although the institutionalization of the Jewish holy days meant that the Jewish (lunar) calendar was adopted in the religious field and, to some extent in the programme of the school-year, all other events and activities were regulated according to the Gregorian calendar without causing undue problems of co-ordination.

The Institutionalization of Cultural Activities and Orientations

Whatever the level of intrinsic value of the various cultural activities which developed on the Yishuv they integrated historical tradition as well as modernity without undue conflict. New cultural activities in the Yishuv faced the problems of provincialism and low standards, but they developed within a framework of common symbolism and communication which, with but few exceptions, overcame the problems of tradition versus modernity.

The one important factor of inflexibility in the cultural sphere was the strong totalistic 'movement' element, which saw all cultural creativity as an integral part of the national or social effort. Several institutional antidotes to these totalistic orientations developed, through the widespread connexions with the Jewish communities abroad, the various socialist or international movements, and through foreign professional groups and centres. Internally, the most important institutional development from this point of view was the University and, to a lesser extent, the Technion. Moreover, the federative nature of the institutional structure of the Yishuv, and the fact that cultural aspects were largely common to the different sectors, emphasized potentially universalistic orientations.

While all these could not negate the totalistic ingredients in the cultural orientations of the Zionist movement and the Yishuv, they did provide

370

important antidotes. Strangely enough, ideological definitions of cultural activities were not firmly maintained in the heyday of cultural creativity, limited as it was by strong ideological emphasis. Some more problematic aspects – like control of such activities by collective bodies – never became severe, apparently being blunted by the continuous cultural creativity. The success in reviving the Hebrew language, the lack of a sharp rift between tradition and modernity, and the institutional contacts which weakened 'totalistic' orientations – all these created a variegated complex of cultural activities orientated towards national effort and rejuvenation even if this heterogeneity was not fully acknowledged. Paradoxically, the search for solutions to major cultural problems was stronger than the institutionalization or acceptance of such solutions. These diverse cultural activities went beyond the confines of ideological solutions or prescriptions borne, to a large extent, by motivations and orientations rooted in the various official ideologies.

The intensity of cultural creativity obliterated, to some extent, the fact that even at the beginning of the mandatory era, some differences between cultural roles and spheres as well as between production and consumption in these spheres developed, as did a very strong and continuous recourse to external, i.e. various European or American sources and centres.

The Institutionalization of Culture After the Establishment of the State

With the growing crystallization of the Yishuv's social structure in the 'thirties and 'forties came the increasing institutionalization of the cultural system bringing to the fore many problems and contradictions which had, until then, been only latent.

The establishment of the state was a crucial turning point in the country's cultural development though, perhaps, in somewhat different ways, than in other institutional spheres. The state did not, in itself, change the basic framework of cultural traditions and problems. It did however, change the ideological and institutional aspects of the problems and traditions. As the very establishment of the state constituted an historical event, which had to be incorporated into the overall historical tradition, it necessarily added a new, significant historical dimension.

The establishment of the state posed the problem whether the future-orientated values had already been realized, or whether they had to be transposed into new contents and new types of future-orientation not fully identified with any given collectivity or institution. This transformation had to incorporate two new elements, the growing importance of non-Zionist, religious groups and traditions, and the influx of the oriental Jews, with their different manifestations of tradition and their different orientations to the Jewish and Israeli society. These developments, together with the many social changes, weakened the future-orientations inherent in the ideology and the emphasis on cultural creativeness as such. They threw the problem of different cultural 'contents' into sharp relief and thus necessarily increased the possibility of social and political conflict on these issues.

Institutionalization of cultural activities and orientations took place on several different levels, the first of which affected the 'content' and form of the new cultural symbols and traditions in the Yishuv. The second level was the definition of major roles in the field of cultural activities, while the third level was that of institutional and organizational transmission and the spreading of 'culture' within the Society. As we shall see, the developing trends on each of these levels did not always converge.

PUBLIC CONTROVERSY AND INSTITUTIONAL PATTERNS IN THE CULTURAL SPHERE

Definition of Collective Identity – Ideological, Religious and Historical Dimensions

On the level of the institutionalization of the contents and symbols of cultural identity the most important problem was the definition or nature of Israel's collective identity and tradition, i.e. the Jewishness of the society. This problem became acute on the ideological level, in the institutional, organizational, and legal fields, in literary and artistic circles, and also with regard to daily attitudes and expressions. Although a lot of interdependence naturally exists between different levels, they did not always develop in the same direction.

On the ideological, literary level this problem became evident through the emphasis on different periods in Jewish history, and the search for a clear definition of the new emerging Jewish society. The central problem was to find which aspect of ancient Jewish tradition made the most important contribution to the present, living tradition, and what were the relations between the Yishuv and the State of Israel with its different Jewish communities and their traditions. This was complicated by the specific problem faced by the Zionist ideology with the establishment of the state.

The one part of the Jewish community for which this was only a very minor, if any, problem at all was the extreme orthodox religious community. For them the common religious tradition was the most important system and the common ground for different Jewish communities. The special attachment to Israel could be expressed in terms of religious concepts but entailed no special re-definition of religious tradition as the most important and most binding force between Jewish communities.

However, for the greater part of the Jewish community which did not accept this religious view, and for those religious sections aware of the non-acceptability of this solution by wider groups, the problem existed with varying degrees of acuteness, and was expressed on the literary and ideological level, as well as in public, literary, and political debates. These debates and literary activities gave rise to various attitudes, the most extreme of which was that of the so-called Canaanites in the late 'thirties, the 'forties, and early 'fifties. The Canaanites were a small group of young Israeli writers and artists who claimed that the 'Israelis' or Palestinians had to shed all specific Jewish, diaspora-orientated historical trends and establish a direct continuity with the pure Palestinian, Canaanite past.

The intensity and novelty of the Canaanite ideology, as well as its literary expression, later subsided, but on a less articulated level it contributed some elements to self-identification, even if its importance has been exaggerated by many of its adversaries.

Beyond this, the specific Palestinian-Israeli theme was evident in the great emphasis placed on the periods of the first and second Temples, and in the attachment to archaeology and to Biblical study.

Another important and significant development in this field was the debate on 'Jewish consciousness' (*Toda'a Yehudit*) in the schools, which developed from an attempt made in the late 'fifties to teach Jewish religious tradition as a special 'secular' subject in non-religious state schools. While those advocating this proposal wanted to extend the scope of historical tradition, it was generally felt that the new Israeli generation growing up in a secular environment might lose contact with the religious and liturgical Jewish tradition and thus perhaps become estranged from the Jewish people living abroad. The proposal was crystallized in its latest form in 1959, in a directive published by the Ministry of Education and Culture which stated that the curriculum in non-religious state schools should include some instruction in religious tradition, and that students should become familiar with blessings, customs, etc., even if they did not practise them. This latter assumption contained the core of the problem. 'Is it possible to teach young pupils the content of religion without teaching religion?' it was asked, and 'Is it possible to transfer those values without transferring an attitude which, in this case, is apt to be sympathetic to religion?'

The advocates of the programme consisted mainly on the centre and centre-left secular parties – Mapai, the Progressives, and the General Zionists. Its main adversaries were the leftist workers' parties, especially Mapam, which saw in the proposal an attempt at religious compulsion, and the extreme religious parties. Ideological objections to the programme also contained Canaanite elements which claimed that the young Israeli should learn the history of the land and not the history of its people in the diaspora, as it was the land that created the new nation, the tradition and history of Jewry in the diaspora thus being of secondary importance. The extreme religious parties opposed the programme as they were against the idea that religious tradition could or should be taught by non-believers in a secular setting.

A further dimension of historical content was the most recent period in Jewish history, the period of the holocaust, dramatized by the Eichmann trial. This brought home the direct relationship between the diaspora and the Yishuv, though it also underlined the differences in mentality as evident, for instance, in the attitudes to self-defence.

Yet another attempt to find the meaning and emphasis of Jewishness, as expressed mainly by Ben-Gurion, was to find the essence of Judaism in the 'prophetic', messianic element, as distinct from the more legal Talmudic or Zionist traditions.

However, the most important debate since the inception of the state has been surely that on Zionism, its meaning in the state, and its effect on relations between the State of Israel and the Jewish communities abroad. It would be out of place here to present a full and detailed analysis of this debate, but some salient features should be pointed out.

One of the consequences of the establishment of the state was the gradual institutionalization of the Zionist ideology, and the realization that the partial fulfilment of Zionism's political aims weakened its eschatological aspects and created new needs and problems. While this was not yet fully realized during the first years of the state's existence with its mass immi-gration, the need for a new meaning or definition of Zionism gradually evolved and came to a head during the Twenty-fifth Congress of the Zionist Federation, when Mr Ben-Gurion (the then Prime Minister) declared that, in his belief, it should be the ultimate aim of every Zionist to immigrate to Israel, and that people who could immigrate but did not do so were not Zionists. The Zionist movement had finished its task, he declared, its purpose was reached, its hopes fulfilled.

His adversaries consisting mostly of the veteran Zionist leaders, including the President of the Zionist Federation Dr Nathum Goldman, maintained that the help extended by the Jews in the diaspora to the State of Israel constituted part of the realization of the Zionist idea, while the continuous diffusing and strengthening of Jewish culture, Hebrew language, and of the diaspora's ties with Israel provided another important aspect of this process.

The debate continued for a long period, at Zionist meetings and congresses, in special symposia, and in many journals and periodicals, but no final, fully acceptable solution could be found or formulated. However, the length and intensity of the debate in intellectual and veteran Zionist circles attested to the fact that the re-definition of Jewish tradition in Israel and abroad, the links between the two sectors of Jewry, the possibilities of some new form of cultural creativity, and the necessity to re-define the ideological tenets of Zionism, had become of great importance. The place of the state within this context had to be found beyond these attempts to define the newly emergent collective tradition.

While it was obvious that Zionism was not fully realized with the establishment of the state, yet attempts were made not only to incorporate the state into the framework of collective tradition but even to make it the focus and symbol of this tradition. This exaltation of the state was closely related to the attempts made to promote the priority of the state in politics and in the the field of social organization, and was equally related to the collective elements and orientations so prominent in the basic pioneering ideology. But while the ideological definition of these collective orientations has greatly weakened with the general ideological erosion, the more basic elements of this orientation still persist.

Among the elements of Zionist and pioneering identity, self-assurance, self-reliance, and self-defence were very important. Later, with the continuous tensions with the neighbouring Arabs, defence and security became the basic ingredients of collective national identity.

As in many other spheres, the overt ideological and institutional formulation, as seen in the over-emphasis on the military, was not successful in striking roots in Israeli society and self-perception, though the commitment to these values and their implications seems to be very strong.

Within this context, a new pattern of partial change and institutionalization also appears in the relations between the Jewish community in Israel and the various Jewish communities in the diaspora, with official, formal, and organized relations being maintained through the Jewish Agency and the Zionist organization, the various organs of financial help to Israel, and diverse cultural and ideological enterprises. But beyond these formal and semi-official contacts many new informal patterns tended to develop. The growing custom of many Jewish organizations such as *Bnai Brith* to organize special branches in Israel or to arrange special meetings, conventions, and symposia in Israel is of great significance in this context.

On a more informal but continuously increasing level, these contacts are maintained through visits, tourism and the growing custom of having the Bar Mitzvah ceremony celebrated in Israel.

These different patterns defy any prescription or ideological formulation. If they attest to the strength of motivations towards collective problems, they equally clearly show the development of patterns beyond any clear ideological traditional, or legalistic definition, and even indicate the possiblity of some dilution of the specific Zionist element in Israeli identification.

The developing Israeli identity consists of many basic elements and components, and its crystallization among the population has not yet been sufficiently investigated to enable the drawing-up of any conclusions. The only characteristic which stands out is that no one overall pattern crystallized and that the whole process is still in a state of flux.

Problems in the Institutionalization of Scientific, Literary and Artistic Activities.

We shall now proceed to the analysis of the second level of institutionalization in the cultural sphere – namely to the organization of various scientific, literary, and artistic activities.

With the growing crystallization of the Yishuv's social structure the scientific, literary, and artistic areas of culture and creativeness developed in different ways regarding contents and organization. The great thrust of cultural creativity that characterized the first generation continued – in science, literature, journalism, and the arts – in the second and third generations, with full institutionalization of cultural organization and endeavour emerging in all these fields. In some aspects, such as scientific research, the second and third generations even surpassed the first.

However, the exact content and organization between the major spheres of cultural activity necessarily differed in the extent of ideological orientation, and the degree to which any specific sphere developed local, Palestinian, or Israeli contents and identifications.

The 'pure', natural, and medical sciences evinced the sharpest universalistic, non-localized endeavour. In many spheres of these sciences – ranging from agriculture to medicine – strong emphasis on choice of problems of local and regional interest necessarily developed, though such emphasis was, on the whole, made with the general, universalistic criterion of general scientific endeavour in mind.

In the humanities and the social sciences the situation was more complex. Here, many enterprises in the fields of Jewish and general studies – history, philology, literature, philosophy, or oriental studies – developed mainly through the University, but also among high-school teachers and freelance intellectuals. The new social and cultural setting also caused many new *Problemstellungen*, greatly influenced by the endeavour to re-define and re-crystallize the new national tradition.

Guided by these orientations and by the many activities at the University, relatively high standards of scientific endeavour and creativity developed in many of these subjects. Some of these subjects, such as Biblical studies, Jewish history and literature, became, however, also, a point of more general public endeavour and interest, with somewhat different traditions and orientations. These were manifest, first, in the widespread popular activities developed, aimed at the spread of scientific and literary activity among wider sections of the population. Second, they were also manifest in the fact that 'national' ideological or populist orientations were consciously stressed, not only as motives for the undertaking and development of scientific activities, but also as possible aims and criteria and as having their own *raison d'être*, traditions and even organization.

These orientations were often reinforced by 'natural' inclinations of wider groups and strata and were organized by institutionally marginal intellectuals with populistic leanings, and by various official proponents of state endeavours in these fields.

The more socialist or sectarian settlements provided a special subvariant of cultural creativity, many of them establishing widespread literary, educational and publishing activities of their own. The most important of these are the various seminars held by the kibbutz groups and the publishing houses of the major kibbutz federation – *Sifriat Poalim* of the *Hashomer Hatzair*, and *Sifriat Hakibbutz Hameuchad* – which, beyond the translation of 'progressive' classics, adhered mainly to translations of socialist literature. A similar position exists with regard to *Am-Oved* (the publishing house of the Histadrut) whose repertoire is even less orthodox. In general the strong tradition of widespread translations from world literature was continued and intensified – in part by these publishers and especially by 'Mossad Bialik' and the University Press.

In the social sciences, the predominance of socialist-ideological orientations in the 'twenties and 'thirties minimized the importance of any 'scientific' (bourgeois!) social sciences and confined itself mostly to statistics, or to factual reports submitted to British, or League of Nations, commissions. Later, and especially after the establishment of the state, a relatively strong development in economics, sociology and demography took place. While the strong 'social' or 'Israeli' bias in the selection of topics continued with such problems as the absorption of immigrants or the structure of the kibbutzim and moshavim, a general scientific approach was brought to them, which incurred strong opposition from the more 'movement-ideological' elements which aimed at the continued predominance of formal, socialist ideologies.

In literature and the arts the situation was necessarily much more complicated. The most 'universal' non-local artistic sphere was that of music, a sphere which is certainly not marginal. Here both consumption and production were generally geared to universal musical creativity, a fact which is fully borne out by the Israel Philharmonic Orchestra with its string of international conductors and its own international repertoire.

Naturally, folk music and dances, etc., have also developed in this sphere and have thrived, like the orchestra of the Israeli Radio, in many other centres which maintained at the same time the traditions of classical music.

The literary field was, again, very different. Unlike science, and to some extent music, there were no fully-fledged institutional organizations with definite standards able to maintain continuous relations with broader international institutions. This sphere was more dependent on local, shifting, clientèle and markets. Moreover, these fields, by their very nature, were to become the centre of specific national or local creativity.

The possibilities of the development and overlapping of different orientations and standards became much more pronounced here, and side by side with some of the great traditions and the continuous literary endeavours of the younger generation, many demands for public and state help were made by varied, often mediocre, groups claiming to represent the new national or social spirit. A similarly mixed situation developed within the theatre and the opera.

The universalist orientations of the scientific and, to some extent, the literary and artistic fields, were maintained by continuously-expanding relations with various institutions abroad. Travel and contacts in the form of scholarships, visiting appointments, consultant posts, etc., have increased continuously since the Second World War; and ties with scientific institutions abroad have become intensified and supplemented by a growing number of visitors to the institutions of higher learning in Israel.

In many cases such contacts abroad have made scientific personnel partly independent of the local setting, thus making them less susceptible to various local pressures.

A similar, if less organized and regularized state of affairs exists with regard to literature and the arts, although this is apt to be regulated or at least influenced by various government committees and arrangements.

Crystallizations of Traditions and Patterns of Cultural Participation

The preceding discussion brings us to the discussion of the third level of institutionalization in the cultural sphere – to the crystallization of patterns of cultural participation, 'consumption' and traditions.

Many cultural activities which seem to be specific to the Israeli scene have been developed. Some of them have developed from the more central cultural traditions of the society. Among them we may mention the following:

The study of the Talmud and the 'oral' tradition have, recently, become very popular, especially among religious, but also among other groups. The two most important instances of such study-sessions are the 'Gathering for Oral Law' and the 'Month of Special Learning' organized by one of the larger Yeshivot in *Bnei Brak*.

Many public activities were organized for Bible study, and for the learning of history and archaeology. The various congresses of the learned national societies (such as the Archaeological or Historical Societies), were attended by hundreds and even thousands of people attracted not only by scientific curiosity but, above all, by the search for new links with their historic past.

Here we naturally come to the problem of the attitude of different parts of the population to the religious tradition. Before, however, attempting to deal with the problem, it must be again stressed that, within the field of fully institutionalized, orthodox religion, there was but little innovation and what there was was frowned upon by most of the official religious leaders of the country containing the elements of a *Kulturkampf.*

The influence of the extremist religious group is felt most strongly here because it is they who enjoy full religious legitimation. The absence of legitimized Reform Judaism in Israel makes the position of the modernized religious groups uncomfortable. In the debate between tradition and modernization therefore, tradition is, in general, becoming increasingly militant and intolerant; and the potentially radical innovative religious groups and religious kibbutzim movement, which forms the apex of the radical wing, have lost much of their importance in the last decade.

Till now it was the Orthodox groups who set the tone in most public debates on religious issues, although some independent but, so far, unimportant groups have developed especially among religious academic circles, which do not accept the official policy of the rabbinical leaders or of the leaders of the religious parties. The debates on religious issues have had many repercussions, both on internal Israeli life and on the relations between Israel and the diaspora.

Thus, for instance, a clash between the Ministry of Religious Affairs and the Rabbinical Assembly (the rabbinical organization of the conservative movement in the United States) over the validity of marriages performed by conservative rabbis, led to the abandonment of a special convention in Israel planned by the Assembly.

Only lately have there been some stirrings greatly aided by the Reform groups in the United States. Some Israeli Reform prayer-groups have now been established, though in the face of very strong opposition from the local orthodox groups. The precedent for greater religious freedom was set by one Reform group which won a case in the High Court against a local authority which, under the pressure of local orthodox groups, refused to rent a public place for prayer. This case clearly established the principle of freedom of religious association.

Notwithstanding these developments in the religious camp itself, several important and significant trends in the attitudes of the non-religious majority to religious traditions emerged. Thus, there was growing attachment to some religious traditions, which did not, however, imply any growth in religiosity or in the acceptance of orthodoxy.

Of the many developments in this direction, several can be pointed out. One is the growth in attendance at synagogue services – especially on the High Holy Days. The other is the growing public recourse to religious ceremonies in the major *rites de passage* with ever more circumcisions, bar mitzvahs, weddings, and funerals taking place in accordance with the full religious ritual. Perhaps the most conspicuous of these – because least necessitated by public convention – is the resurgence of the bar mitzvah and even the innovation of bar mitzvah ceremonies. Evidence also points to a growing observance of some Shabbat ritual – like the lighting of candles – in many non-religious homes.

The distribution of these patterns is, of course, uneven and with two extreme exceptions (in the religious groups and the more leftist settlements) they cannot be clearly and uniformly defined as belonging to any one social or cultural group. Side by side with these activities there developed new more peripheral types of cultural participation. Among these the most widespread and interesting phenomenon is the development of popular sports – ranging from athletics to football. Organized in local 'sectional' and national leagues the interest in sport has become widespread. Despite the comparatively low or mediocre standards of many of these teams, they evoke great popular interest and have become objects of nation-wide endeavour and organization.

Another tradition emerged from the settlements, and became evident in widespread folk-activities (folk dancing and music), as well as in new interpretations of the main traditional festivals such as the fruit picking or harvest ceremonies, or in the creation of a new Passover-Seder ceremony.

The oriental Jews, who brought their own traditions or religiosity, provide a facet of special interest and importance in this cultural mosaic.

The influx of the many immigrant groups with their different cultural traditions, and the difficulties of absorption previously described, constitute a crucial factor in the growing pluralism of the Israeli cultural scene. This was accentuated by the general ideological weakening in the country, which defied the acceptability of a homogeneous approach to cultural problems.

This emerging plurality of cultural patterns is seen in the multiplicity of languages spoken, in patterns of dress (especially on holidays), in the different intonations of Hebrew, and in the patterns of cultural consumption. It can also be seen in the transformation of many traditional patterns of social organization, in the emergence of 'ethnic' groups and leaders in political and cultural affairs, and in the persistence of familial attitudes and attachments.

Beyond this, on a deeper level of personality orientations, as yet barely touched by research, a great variety of personal attitudes are likely to develop in conceptions of time and space as well as in personal relations.

This cultural pluralism is by no means limited either to the specific 'Jewish ethnic' elements in the traditions of the different groups or to the patterns of their daily life, for differences in orientation towards European culture and traditions are of equal importance. Two major patterns of wider, general cultural orientation, the one Eastern and Central European, and the other 'English-speaking', began to develop in the Yishuv and in the formal institutional framework of the state.

These two greatly weakened the 'Latin' and, especially, the 'French' cultural orientation predominant among the older Sephardi groups under

Turkish rule and preserved more fully only by a small restricted intellectual élite. Only with the influx of new immigrants did the potential for their revival increase somewhat. However, though fostered by various attempts of the French and, to a smaller extent, the Italian governments anxious to extend the scope of their cultural activities in Israel, powerful forces worked against these efforts. One was the comparative weakness of specific intellectual tradition among these immigrants coupled with the indifference of their more articulated élite groups. A second was the predominance of other patterns in most of the major institutional areas in the Yishuv. However, there can be no doubt that some, though somewhat restricted, changes are being made and are greatly contributing to the emerging cultural pluralism in Israel, even if it is as yet impossible to assess their ultimate impact.

But several caveats should be pointed out. One is that despite the natural emphasis on the great importance or difference of the oriental cultural tradition as distinct from the occidental, or Western, ones, there is, in fact, much greater variety within each of these groups as against the relative homogeneity of the Eastern and Central European Jewish cultural orientations which were predominant in the Yishuv.

The new immigration includes many orthodox groups from Eastern Europe which had but little in common with Western culture, many of the lower classes being in touch only with the external, peripheral aspects of such cultures while the more assimilated groups had little, if any, orientation to Jewish culture. Similarly, the oriental camp did not constitute a homogeneous group, and many cultural orientations developed within it.

A last crucial aspect of the development of cultural pluralism in Israel is the strong interweaving of social and cultural transformations with political issues, and the consequent possibility of their becoming not only an important aspect of the political process at all levels but also a cultural and ethnic focus of political organizations and symbols.

These tendencies are inclined to intensify the various processes of social and cultural disorganization on which they feed, while equally tending to 'homogenize' the different oriental and Western ethnic camps. We shall be able to understand some of these problems in a fuller way by looking briefly at some aspects of participation in cultural activities and of cultural 'consumption'.

Problems of Cultural Participation and Consumption

The overall picture of the cultural scene shows great heterogeneity and recourse to very diverse cultural activities. In all spheres of cultural consumption, the different internal and external traditions conditioned by respective countries of origin or different levels of education played an important part. However, neither the diversity nor the high level of

381

consumption in the distribution of newspapers and the production and sale of books assure consistently high standards. In fact, levels of contents range from sophisticated cultural activity of a high standard to the philistine and provincial, and right down to cheap entertainment and 'mass culture', reinforced by the influx of new, especially oriental, immigrants whose own cultural activities had been largely disrupted.

Whatever the diversity of contents and levels, the general picture indicates the vitality of relatively high cultural interest, creativity, and participation with possibilities of the erosion of these orientations and of the development of anomic 'mass culture'.

This possiblity of the growth of an anomic 'mass culture' is intensified by the encounter between the older social structure and the various groups of new immigrants, many of whom bring in new cultural elements while undergoing intensive social and cultural change.

If this process of social change should become more organized and less full of tensions, some of the different ethnic and traditional cultural elements may well become foci of various new subgroups and patterns in the Israeli cultural mosaic.

Patterns of Cultural Participation and Consumption – Israeli Journalism

A good way of tracing these developments is by observing the growth of journalism in Israel.[1]

The varied demands made by the reading public and the countries of origin of the journalists themselves, are strongly reflected in the make-up of Israeli newspapers. There is the journalistic style of the pre-war Central and Eastern European press, centred round the article intended to admonish, criticize, guide, and provoke thought. There are the news features as in the English and American press, the *feuilleton* of the Swiss and German papers, the 'column' of the American press, and the near-sensational thorough reporting of the French press.

Almost all papers carry permanent columns aimed at increasing the readers' familiarity with the Hebrew language – which, to many of them is a new language – and extensive literary sections. Sports sections are on the increase, and women's pages multiply steadily. While adding these features of entertainment, the press is still deeply concerned with the maintenance of its weight as an educating and guiding factor.

Through its continuous immigration, Israel provides a steady market for foreign-language papers, though over the years many readers change to the Hebrew press. Nine out of Israel's twenty-four newspapers are published in languages other than Hebrew. Of these, one is published in Arabic, one in English (an official language in pre-state days), one in French, two in German,

[1] This follows J. Ellemers, 'Some Sociological Comments on Mass Communication in Israel', *Gazette*, V. 7, 1961, p. 89ff.

and one each in Hungarian, Polish, Roumanian, and Yiddish. All these papers serve new immigrants or tourists. The keynote however is set by the Hebrew dailies, many of which are organs of the numerous political parties in Israel, with only a minority of the Hebrew dailies being privately owned and published.

The number of papers published is dependent on the development of the political parties. Thus, for example, owing to the existence of several parties within the General Federation of Labour, five papers are defined as 'workers' papers. When the United Workers' Party split up, one section retaining the original name, and the other becoming *Ahdut Haavoda*, two newspapers appeared immediately: *Al Hamishmar* and *Lamerhav*. The Communist Party in Israel maintains its own paper, somewhat smaller in size than other morning papers. The religious parties also maintain four newspapers, two in Jerusalem and two in Tel Aviv. There are however four dailies without party affiliation – one morning paper (*Haaretz*), two evening papers and one sports paper.

The two established Hebrew evening papers are *Maariv* and *Yediot Aharonot*, with a combined circulation of over 130,000 which, considering that the country's population is only slightly more than two millions and that the combined circulation of all twenty-four papers does not exceed 250,000, can be considered as relatively large. Each of these evening papers commands a far greater readership than other newspapers in Israel, and they have also a marked influence on the general press. Both papers are independent, non-partisan and free to criticize, in contrast to the morning press which is mostly partisan and sectarian in its outlook.

Although there is no grown-up kibbutz member who does not read one or more daily newspapers, there is no national newspaper for the kibbutzim. These readers are served by the daily labour press – *Davar*, *Lamerhav*, *Al Hamishmar*, etc., all of which carry special features, sections and additions with general and specific news for the kibbutz population, and with weekly or monthly items on the kibbutzim.

However, the considerable economic and social growth of kibbutz institutions has necessitated the expansion of their 'internal press', which is characterized by its 'seriousness', and its complex and high-level style.

Five magazines now appear in Israel for children between the ages of six and sixteen, achieving a total circulation of over 50,000. The number of young readers in Israel is proportionately higher than in other culturally well-developed countries.

Needless to say this survey does not tell us much about differential consumption of communication, as the heterogeneous population of Israel causes very special problems.

Relatively little is as yet known about the influence of mass communication media in Israel, and the information obtained from a survey into radio listening habits held in 1955 among a representative sample of the adult Jewish population in Israel is not very comprehensive. It was found that, about two-thirds of regular radio listeners questioned belonged to the more educated classes, the old-timers, the immigrants of European origin, and to those born in Israel. These same categories were also more interested in topical programmes than were the listeners coming from countries in the Middle East and North Africa, those recently arrived in Israel, and those with little education or who were over sixty years old. It was found that regular listeners consisted mainly of those born in Israel and people of European origin, with the exception of the Roumanians. Ninety per cent of listeners in the kibbutzim showed regular listening habits – among the urban population almost two-thirds were found to listen regularly, with this figure decreasing to less than half for the moshavim and the moshavot. These differences according to type of settlement can be traced partly to the country of origin, and partly to the length of time that inhabitants have been in Israel. They can also be explained by the differences in social structure between the various types of settlements.

The Ideological Format of Israeli Society

A further sphere around which serious conflict arose was the ideological format of Israeli society, and the consequences of attempts to institutionalize certain crucial aspects of the pioneering-socialist ideology.

On the ideological level the central problem was the extent to which Israel could continue to be an ideological society, finding the full meaning of its cultural tradition, creativity, and identity in a clearly crystallized and form-ulated ideology, or whether it would have to find such meaning in terms of other symbols and value formulations.

In the debate that developed around this issue, this problem was often defined as the decline of ideology which spells the erosion of commitment to collective goals, and encourages the creation of an anomic 'mass' society.

The major structural-institutional trend with direct bearing on this whole area was here, as in other fields, the growing differentiation of the different roles and their growing tendency to organizational and professional autonomy.

Great ideological stress was placed, initially in the period of the Yishuv, on the necessity of treating culture as part of the pioneering image with concomitant emphasis on overall participation in general cultural activities.

Most other cultural and communicative roles were defined in terms of movement or cross-movement allegiances, duties and goals, while the professional organization of writers and journalists at first defined their activities in terms of general participation in cultural creativity.

These activities were most clearly expressed in the settlements and workers' camp, where changes happened very gradually and a growing differentiation and specialization in the various cultural activities and roles slowly occurred.

These changes were not dissimilar to those that took place within other professional groups and which became intensified with the establishment of the state. The main impetus to the change came from the growing tendency towards professionalism and from the intensive developments in the technical and scientific fields.

The continuous increase in the number of scientists in scientific institutions, government research institutions, and industry accelerated these developments, which were similar to the development of the new 'communicative' roles such as journalism and public relations. They all emphasized professionalization and organizational autonomy.

But these tendencies to autonomy and professionalization often evoked, as in the field of social stratification, policies aimed at curbing or regulating these developments according to some collectivist ideological prescription. The struggle between these tendencies is probably among the most important in the field of cultural organization in Israel and provided the background to the debate on the ideological contours of Israeli society.

It was perhaps within this framework that the specific Israeli problem of conservatism versus 'innovation' was most pronounced, caused by the continuous weakening of adherence to the ideology which was, in turn, paradoxically due to the successful institutionalization of some of the major values and symbols implied. These included strong collective identification and the widespread acceptance of the 'pioneering' ideal and of most of the Zionist premises. At the same time, the acceptance of these values often created a lack of patience with fully crystallized ideological formulations which began to seem obvious and trite. This tendency was enhanced by the growth of specialization, professionalization, and emphasis on technical knowledge, and by the emerging autonomy among different professionals. The proponents of ideology were often perceived as representatives of vested interests opposed to the social aspirations and interests of the others.

It was around these problems that the debate about the place of ideology in the cultural format of Israeli society developed.

Ideology in the Cultural Format of Israeli Society

For the two extreme camps the problem virtually did not exist. The extreme religious groups found their solution in the religious tradition and the consequent denial of any secular ideology, though this attitude did not apply to all members of the religious groups, and especially not to members of the religious kibbutzim.

For the more extreme sectarian settlements and movements, and especially for the élite of *Hashomer Hatzair*, the answer was given in the full maintenance of the 'old' socialist ideology. However, this attitude was not necessarily accepted or adhered to by all members of the settlements and, beyond them, more diverse attitudes towards this problem developed.

By its very nature, the ideological camp was more articulate and vocal than the less homogeneous 'non-ideological' one. However, some of the rifts that developed within the 'ideological camp' were themselves contributory causes to the decline of the ideology.

The great dividing point among the ideologically orientated was the attitude towards the state as the full expression of Zionist values and aspirations. To a certain extent the Lavon Affair served as a catalyst accentuating some of the divisions in the ideological camp.

On the one hand there were those ideologues who emphasized adherence to the 'older' socialist, pioneering values upholding the importance of the settlements and, to some extent, the Histadrut, and criticized the 'mass' society tendencies – such as emphasis on consumption – in Israeli society, strongly advocating the belief that adherence to ideology and the continuation of the search for basic ideological solutions would assure moral cohesion and the continuity of Israeli society.

On the other hand there were those ideologues who tended to concern themselves less with such social and cultural issues and to emphasize more the overriding importance of the state as the focus of social and collective values.

Institutional Implications of Ideological Tendencies

If, on the level of contents, the battle on the ideological format of Israeli society was purely 'academic', it had several important repercussions in the institutional sphere, where various attempts were made to impose ideological inference on the organization of cultural life. In the scientific sphere, such attempts stressed the 'social' function of science and the necessity of adhering to the collective aims of the movement. Literature was expected to serve as an expression of the value orientations and realities of the movements.

Similarly, identification with the state was expected from literary and scientific creation, vesting the government with the right to guide the development of scientific and literary activities.

A third more populist ideological orientation emphasized the importance of cultural activities as expressions of 'folk' spirit.

These trends, however, were not very widespread and, on the whole, the tendencies to more autonomous cultural organizations seemed institutionally and ideologically stronger. Strong universalistic criteria of cultural achievement and the diversity of orientations countered any latent totalistic implications. Similarly, the very heterogeneity of orientations in the ideological camp could easily weaken these totalistic institutional and ideological implications.

Moreover, the very existence of continuous tension among the varying ideological orientations on the one hand and between them and the ideological orientations on the other hand – so long as it was not resolved in the granting of undisputed institutional supremacy to the totalistic orientation – could provide points of continuous cultural creativity and crystallization.

Though by no means predominant, these varied totalistic orientations and their institutional implications could not be ignored, especially as they found certain institutional support in the different movements, in the industrial and scientific establishment of the state, and among various groups of officials. Under propitious circumstances, and taken together with the various attempts to establish the supremacy of the state in other spheres as well as with the growing dependence of higher education on state support, they might easily become of great importance in directing the development of Israeli cultural life.

The Place of the Intellectual in Israel: Society and Culture

The debate about the place of ideology touched on a more general problem involved in the contours of Israeli society and culture – namely the place of the intellectual in Israeli society.

As mentioned several times, the Yishuv was initially an ideological society created by intellectuals, who, in their participation in the Zionist movement and in the pioneering groups, epitomized the traditional role of the intellectual as a rebel against the established order. With growing development, with the establishment of the state, and with the growing differentiation of communicative, scientific, and other 'cultural' roles, the place of the intellectual was no longer clear.

While the intellectual's tradition of protest was continuously maintained with regard to the outside – be it the diaspora, the British, or 'capitalist' society in general – it was much more difficult to re-formulate or transpose this on the inside, towards the society created by their own rebellion.

Criticism of their own society was complicated by the lack of coercive power during the mandate, by the strong, sectarian identifications of the pioneer-groups, and by the continuous external dangers. Only marginal 'inter-sectoral' groups like the *Brit Shalom* managed to challenge these common assumptions.

With the establishment of the state the situation both from the point of view of the structural positions of the intellectuals and of their place in the complex of cultural and public life in Israel, has, of course, greatly changed.

The trends described gave rise to a great variety of intellectual 'types', such as the bureaucratic, the professional, the academic, and the freelance intellectual, with overlapping cases between the types.

With regard to public affairs, there were the 'conformers' and the 'critics'. Both can be sub-divided, both from the point of view of articulation, and the scope and target of their criticism, or conformity – and can belong to different ideological or political camps.

387

Beyond these the non-ideological intellectuals emerged who were interested in broader problems and values without being committed to any articulated ideology, and a growing number of apathetic intellectuals appeared who, disinterested in wider public affairs, confined themselves to their professional, technical, and bureaucratic functions.

Although this growing variety of types was similar to other modern or modernizing societies, some of their problems were rooted in the specifically Israeli setting, and especially in the transition of a loosely federated society composed of rebellious intellectual groups.

Here the establishment of the state greatly complicated the possibilities and scope of the critical position of the intellectuals.

Seen at first as the realization of long-standing historical aspirations, the state became the fullest manifestation of the values of Zionism, and sentiments of identification focused on the movements, were transposed on the state. In many literary, journalistic, artistic, and scientific circles the state became the expression of this great historic event which, despite some elements of 'Byzantine' sycophantism, contained the honest efforts of understanding a great historical event, to participate in it, and to find ways in which to define it and make it meaningful.

Inevitably, this tendency to idolize the state gave rise, with the passage of time and the routinization of state activities, to a feeling of emptiness and moral crisis demanding ideological explanations which remained unsatisfied.

Out of these many tendencies the new ideological 'conservatism' emerged, critical to the government, but yet maintaining its allegiance to pioneering values. For at least some intellectuals, this provided a possibility to combine their continuing protest against the established order, with an attachment to other aspects of this social order and to the basic values of the initial ideological rebellion.

However, this development also posed the problem of transforming intellectual criticism beyond the purely ideological, for the strong conservatism contained within the ideology could easily erode the development of non-ideologically committed intellectual criticism, giving rise to apathy and cynicism.

The difficulties in transforming the ideological trends in cultural life were also apparent in the weak development of civic spirit and of civic responsibility in local affairs, voluntary organizations and relations between public bodies and the general public.

Summary – The Development of Israeli Identity

Israel's collective identity has been forged out of the many orientations and attitudes analysed above. Its exact boundaries are not yet fixed although some elements such as strong local patriotism are easily discernible.

Most Israelis would probably agree to the importance of their Jewishness as part of their identification, although it is difficult to know in what way they see this as a basic element in their identity as Israelis. Among most of the older strata of the population there is, in addition, a continuous awareness of the fact that the meaning of being an Israeli or a Jew goes beyond mere patriotism, but refers to wider values, traditions, and orientations, however inarticulate or undefinable these may be.

But whatever the exact definitions of this Israeli self-identity may be, one of its most striking aspects is that it no longer defines Jewish identity in terms of a minority group or culture. Being a Jew in Israel does not necessitate the definition of one's identity in relation to a majority group or culture, and does not involve the problems, uncertainties and anxieties which have constituted such an important part of Jewish life and identity throughout the modern world.

It is perhaps in this aspect of Israel's self-identity that its main novelty lies and it is also this aspect that creates some of the differences and difficulties in the encounter between Israelis and Jews in the diaspora. Further, it is this fact that constitutes the starting point for the Israeli's orientation to Jewish traditions and of forging out his own identity within it.

Every new generation and every new group of immigrants has contributed to the change in Israel's collective identity, which mainly by shifting the emphasis and selection of cultural creativity and tradition showed a high extent of creativity and adaptability. Israel has escaped many of the problems and uncertainties plaguing the identity problem of other new nations facing modernization. However, it does have to cope with problems of provincialism and of the erosion of wider values or orientations, as well as with the possibility of diluting a more specific Zionist component by ceasing to identify with Jewish communities abroad.

This collective identity is, by now, conceived less in terms of explicit ideology, and rather more in terms of continuously shifting orientations, and traditions.

The pure ideology is now only part of the overall cultural scene, and its place and meaning have greatly changed. The values and symbols to which the more active parts of the population adhere are only partly expressed in ideological terms and within all spheres of cultural creativity, tendencies towards autonomy, towards more direct relations (without the mediation of full ideological crystallization) and towards the values of collectivity, are growing.

The adherence to these values and collective commitments has shown great vitality and persistence in the face of many possibilities of erosion, enhanced by the numerous social conflicts for which no adequate regulative norms were found. These possibilities were necessarily intensified by less articulated groups of new immigrants, with different values and commitments who were caught up in the process of social and cultural change and disorganization.

Within this context the development of an original Israeli ideological conservatism may be a great point of strength, though it might well contribute to growing cynicism and apathy. Similarly, the possibility of erosion is rooted in the growing cultural divisions between the religious and the secular.

Among the forces tending to counter the threat of ideological erosion was the flexible relationship to different traditions and the absence of cultural cleavage between different camps.

It is important to note here that, till now, the changing Israeli cultural and collective identity managed to absorb the new tensions and problems which developed from the growing technicalization and professionalization, and, in spite of the many problems and tensions created, did not entirely abandon its commitments to certain values. Some of the ideological and collective orientations even blended with the technical and professional aspect of the new collective image. Thus, for instance, both the development of scientific endeavour and the widespread Israeli aid programmes in Africa and Asia helped to some extent to spread the collective pioneering image to technicians and professionals, incorporating these elements in the emerging Israeli collective identity.

The extent to which such continuous peaceful transformations of Israeli identity will be able to overcome the different eroding tendencies is, perhaps, the most crucial problem facing Israeli society and culture.

11

Non-Jewish Minority Groups in Israel

Introduction

Until now we have dealt almost exclusively with the Jewish section of Israeli society. Analysis of the minority groups was restricted to the general historical background of Palestine, to the political and cultural relations between the Zionist movement, the Yishuv, and the Arab population of Palestine, to a brief description of the exodus of the Arab population from the State of Israel in 1948, and to tracing the trends of development of the Arab and other minority groups in the various institutional fields.

The problems of these minorities and their significance for the State of Israel will be dealt with in somewhat greater detail in this chapter.

However, before analysing the internal structure of the various minority groups and their integration into Israeli society, it may be worth while to outline some of the basic facts connected with these processes.

The Demographic Development of the Arab and Druze Populations

The basic demographic trends of the Arab population in Israel have been aptly summarized as follows, by E. Ben-Amram, and are based on available data, including the results of the 1961 census.[1]

In 1947, the Arab population of Palestine stood at 1,320,000 and constituted 68 per cent of the total population; there were 800,000 non-Jews in the area which today forms part of the State of Israel. However, as a result of the 1948 war, the Arabs became a minority and, out of Israel's population of 2,519,700 at the end of 1964, only 285,400 – or 11 per cent – were non-Jews, mainly Arabs. Though the Arab population grew by 83 per cent since 1948 – 4 per cent per annum – it decreased in the proportion to the total population, mainly due to large-scale Jewish immigration. By 1970 Israel's population is expected to be three million including 350,000 Arabs (11·8 per cent).

The two main concentrations of Arab population are in Galilee and along the Jordan border. Smaller concentrations are to be found in Haifa, Tel Aviv, Jaffa, Ramla, Lydda and in the Jerusalem district. In some areas the Arabs represent a vast majority of the inhabitants; in other areas there are no

[1] Taken from E. Ben-Amram, 'A Demographic Description of the Arab Population in Israel (Hebrew)', *Hamizrah Hehadash (The New East)* Vol. XV, 1965, No. 1–2, pp. II–IV.

Arabs at all. No significant changes have taken place in the geographical distribution of the Arab population since 1948 except for a slight rise in the Haifa sub-district and a decrease in the Southern district.

Whereas in 1963, 87 per cent of the Jews lived in urban settlements, this applied to only 25 per cent of the Arabs, who constitute a mere 3·6 per cent of the total urban population. These urban Arabs inhabit two Arab towns – Nazareth (27,100) and Shafa Amr (8,050), plus six mixed towns (31,000). The flight in 1948 of large numbers of Arabs from the towns, led to a drop in the proportion of town dwellers among the Arabs compared to the mandatory period.

The Arab rural population constitutes 41 per cent of Israel's total rural population and is spread over 101 villages – mainly in the Galilee, on the Carmel and the Samarian Hills. Whereas the main livelihood of the village inhabitatnts used to be agriculture, a recent tendency is to seek employment outside, mainly in the Jewish urban centres.

The Bedouin live mainly in the Negev (20,000) and the Galilee (10,000). Those in the Negev are mainly tent-dwellers, while those in the Galilee are gradually moving into permanent dwellings.

Whereas in 1948 only nine Arab localities, i.e. 27 per cent of the population, had a recognized local government, by the end of 1963 there were fifty-four localities (out of 110), accounting for 71 per cent of the Arab population, with local government institutions: nine municipalities, thirty-one local councils and fifteen villages with regional councils.

At the end of 1963, Islam was the religion of 192,400 Israelis, or 70 per cent of the non-Jewish population. Most of Israel's Muslims are Sunnis, though not all of them are Arabs. Approximately 83 per cent live in rural areas. One-fifth of the Arab population (53,700) are Christians.

There are about seven thousand Christian non-Arabs, of which the Greek Catholics constitute the largest denomination with 42 per cent. Altogether two-thirds of the Christians accept the Pope's authority. In 1961 three-fifths of the Christians lived in urban areas – mainly Nazareth and Shafa Amr.

In 1963 the Druzes constituted one-tenth (27,000) of the Arab population with 91 per cent living in rural areas.

Both marriage and divorce rates among the Arabs have fallen since the days of the Mandate. The drop in the former may be explained by the prohibition of polygamy and the younger age composition of the present day population. The 1961 census showed that three-quarters of the Moslem and Druze women married before the age of twenty-one and the same proportion of men married before the age of twenty-five. The fall in divorce rates can be attributed mainly to the obstacles placed in the path of divorce by the laws of the State of Israel.

The above-mentioned factors, combined with the absence of birth control, account for the high fertility rate among Arab women: the average number of children born to an Arab woman by the age of 45–49 was 7·6 in 1963, as compared with 3·1 among Jews. However, contact with the Jewish population and rising educational standards are resulting in a decreased birth rate among Arab women.

In 1964, there were 49 live births for every 1,000 Arab inhabitants as compared with 22 among the Jews. The birth rate among the Arabs is on the increase, while among Jews the opposite is the case.

The death rate among Arabs is declining and is now similar to that of the Jews: 6 per 1,000 in 1964. Parallel to this, still-births among Arabs are decreasing and amounted to only 38 per 1,000 live births in 1964.

The natural increase (i.e. births minus deaths) of the Arabs has consequently risen from 34 per 1,000 in 1952 to 43 per 1,000 in 1964 (as compared to 16 per thousand among the Jews).

As a result of its age composition, the Arab population contains a relatively large proportion of males.

In 1963 the average Arab family numbered six members as compared to four in Jewish families (a tendency to limit the size of the family can be discerned among Jews of Asian and African origin who, till now, had large families).

According to the 1961 census, half the adult Arab population can read and write (men: 68 per cent; women: 28 per cent), and this percentage will no doubt continue to rise with extended educational facilities. Considerable improvement in educational standards is also reflected in the increased number of years spent at school by Arab youth.

According to the manpower survey of 1963, 47 per cent of the 144,000 Arabs over 14 years of age, belonged to the country's labour force; of these 60,000 were men and 9,000 women (women employed on the family farm apparently did not regard themselves as employed). Unemployment among the Arabs is insignificant; about half of them are employed outside the localities in which they live. The lower overall rate of Arabs belonging to the civilian labour force among the Arabs (44 per cent in 1961 as compared to 53 per cent among the Jews) can be explained by the low rate of employment among Arab women. Other factors are the age structure and the standard of education. The growing demand for labour is expected to raise the future employment rate, especially among women.

Ninety-four per cent of the Arabs are employed in four main economic branches: agriculture (39 per cent), building (22 per cent), industry (22 per cent), and general services (11 per cent). Arabs constitute 22 per cent of all agricultural employees and 18 per cent of all building workers. Parallel to the fall in the proportion of Arabs employed in agriculture since 1954, the proportion of those employed in building and industry has risen. These changes are to be accounted for by changing tendencies in the Jewish economy.

393

The Minorities within the Socio-Economic Framework

The preceding data indicate some of the trends caused through the gradual impact of the State of Israel on the Arab population.

Direct economic ties between Arabs and Jews during the time of the Yishuv consisted mainly of sale of agricultural products by the Arabs to the Jews, employment of Arabs by Jews, and land purchases by Jews. The importance of these ties to the total economy, especially from the standpoint of the Arab sector, was very small.

The establishment of the state considerably changed this situation. The Arab population found itself reduced in size (156,000 in 1948) and stripped of political leadership and power. The economic élite – the urban population of Haifa and Jaffa – fled. Economic institutions were dissolved, and the ties with the Arab countries were severed when government passed into Jewish hands.

Yet with its establishment, the state acquired the responsibility of a welfare state towards a minority group, concerned with the gradual linking of its minority groups in the economic sphere.

Culturally and educationally, the Arabs rank lowest by all criteria, even lagging behind the new immigrants from Asia and Africa who have the lowest educational level among the Jewish population. The large educational gap between men and women is at its worst on the level of literacy and elementary education and is somewhat narrower among persons with secondary and higher education. The inequality in the distribution of education is greatest among women. There is a negative association between level of education and age among men with a sharp decline in the level of education in age groups over forty-five.

Basic Constitutional, Cultural, and Political Problems of the Arab Minority

In order to be able to evaluate fully the constant processes of change within the Arab minority, it is essential to describe not only the basic socio-demographic tendencies, but also the framework within which they are taking place.

A central issue in this problem is the relation between the specifically Jewish orientation of the State of Israel, perceived as the epitomization of Zionist goals, and coupled with the universalistic and secular truths of a modern state based on equality of all its citizens and dissociated from full identification with any one religious or ethnic group. Within the legal-constitutional sphere, universalistic, and secular factors were predominant from the very beginning. The full equality of citizens of all nationalities and religions was fully established with the Declaration of Independence.

394

Similarly, full civil rights and legal equality were granted to all citizens of Israel from the very beginning of the state. This included all Arabs, Druzes, etc., resident in Israel at the time, as well as those permitted to enter later under the policy of family reunion. In addition to their rights as citizens the minority religious communities were granted special communal rights and – in the spheres of personal relations – juridical rights. The various Muslim, Christian Arab, and Druze communities were granted full religious autonomy, with help being given to their religious institutions by the Ministry of Religious Affairs. Arabic is the second-official language, used in the Knesset, and in the Government offices in Arab districts. In Arab schools it is the main language, with Hebrew being taught as the second language from the fourth grade.

Nonetheless, a certain asymmetry developed between Jewish and Arab (or any other minority) groups, rooted in the very essence of the State of Israel. This was evident from the fact that under the 'Law of Return' citizenship was open to all Jews who wanted to come to Israel but was limited with all other groups, to residents or those who obtained special permission to settle.

However if other factors had not intervened, this, in itself, might not have been too great an obstacle to full integration. As it was, the cultural discrepancies and, above all, the complications on the political level all gave rise to a problematic situation.

Although there was full recognition of the minority groups' rights to cultural autonomy, it was not clear what exactly such autonomy implied or what – beyond a general idea of common citizenship – could develop as a common focus of Israeli identity.

The reasons for this were several: the Jewish community was, itself, facing the problems of developing a new collective identity.

The parallel development of Zionist and Arab national movements could only hinder the development of a common identity – even without the hostile political attitudes that developed later. Even in those circles of the Zionist movement (and conversely of the Arab movement) that pleaded for greater mutual understanding, this was done more in political than in cultural terms.

The Arab minority (whether Muslim or Christian) had no distinct cultural Israeli or even Palestinian collective identity, except on the local, traditional level which had survived through centuries of conquest. In so far as a wider identity developed among them (and this began to happen under the Mandate, through contacts with the wider Arab national movement, and paradoxically, through the processes of integration within Israel) it was closely tied to other Arab countries or communities. This did not apply, however, to the non-Arab minorities, especially the Druzes.

All these possibilities were greatly complicated and, to a large degree, negated by the political relations between Israel and its neighbours, the continuous state of hostility between them, the refusal of the Arab countries to recognize the existence of Israel, and their continuous threats to annihilate it. These complexities made an obvious direct and indirect impact on the whole gamut of relations between the state and its minorities.

First and foremost, the Arab community found itself in an ambivalent situation towards the State of Israel, the more negative aspects of this ambivalence being the ones that the Israeli authorities had to cope with and perhaps tended initially to emphasize.

The causes of this ambivalence are, in essence, simple. By ties of kinship, ethnicity, or incipient nationalistic orientation, they were much more closely tied to the Arabs across the border, in countries hostile to Israel. With the exception of very few cases of active participation by small groups of Arabs who fought on the Jewish side in the War of Independence, there was little to foster a positive orientation to the State of Israel, a fact which was geographically reinforced by the high concentration of groups of Arab population in several border-areas.

Their proximity to the borders constituted a grave security problem, which was aggravated by continuous, if intermittent, incursions by infiltrators from the neighbouring countries. In addition, the possibility of the local Arabs being used for the purpose of espionage and sabotage by the hostile states also had to be guarded against. The impact of these facts left its marks on relations between the state and its Arab population, and resulted, first, in the establishment of a Military Government in the border areas.

Although the establishment of a Military Government was necessitated by security reasons, its repercussions were felt also on the legal-constitutional level. Its implementation entailed restrictions on travel, which, though in principle applying to all inhabitants of these areas, in fact mostly affected the Arabs, and did not help much to overcome the ambivalence of the Arab groups, or to develop friendly and 'equal' relations between them and the authorities in day-to-day contact.

A second institutional innovation was the exemption of most of the Arab (though not the Druze) population from Army service, in order to avoid a situation of conflicting loyalties, as well as not to endanger the security of the Israeli Army.

While this might have been seen as a release from an onerous duty, it was also an exclusion from a sphere which epitomized the essence of Israeli citizenship and identity and it therefore emphasized the ambivalent relations between the Arabs and the state. Wider repercussions of this involved the availability of occupational opportunities, as suspicion and a reluctance to employ Arab labour developed in legitimate security areas as well as those not directly affected. As this widespread attitude was not fully articulated, it was also not easy to overcome.

A special and important point here was the problem of admitting Arab workers to the Histadrut, which was originally created to foster the development of modern Jewish labour and which, due to the political hostility between the communities, was an exclusively Jewish organization.

Admittedly, some efforts were made to organize the Arab workers in trade unions, and the *Brit Poalei Eretz Israel* was established for this purpose in 1932. There were also a number of joint Arab-Jewish strikes in the pre-state period. All of this, however, was outside the orbit of the Histadrut.

With the establishment of the state, the proposal was made to annex two Arab organizations to the Histadrut, but this was rejected. The trade union organizations of the Arab workers were the Communist Congress, the Christian *A-Rabita*, and *Brit Poali Eretz Israel*. In 1951 *A-Rabita* merged with *Brit Poalei Eretz Israel* and, at the end of 1953, the Histadrut decided to accept some Arab workers in its trade unions. The Communist Congress voluntarily disbanded a few months later. Finally in 1959, the Histadrut adopted a resolution admitting Arab workers as members with equal rights, and by the middle of 1962, about 16,000 fee-paying Arabs had joined the Histadrut. In 1962 responsibility for dealing with the trade union problems of Arab workers was transferred from the Histadrut Executive to the local labour councils, and the willingness of the Histadrut to grant Arab workers equal status increased. Parallel with this, there was a growth of Arab members in the Histadrut insurance funds.

Problems of Development and Administration

A second major force in the changing Arab society in Israel was the great expansion of administrative services in the Arab sector, which ranged from the provision of health and general services to technical instruction in agriculture and the provision of educational services.[1]

In the health sphere, traditional attitudes and the lack of facilities limited health services in the Arab sector, particularly in the villages. As a result of this, the Ministry of Health had to bear both initial and current expenses for all health projects executed since 1948. These include: health services in fifty-six settlements, two health centres and maternity hospitals, twenty-four clinics and thirty mother-and-child-care centres.

In the educational field, we find that there were sixty elementary schools in the Arab sector before the passing of the Compulsory Education Law. Once this law came into force, the number of pupils increased fourfold, and the problem of insufficient space became ever more acute. Costs of new buildings were supposed to be borne by the local authorities and, where such authority was non-existent, by the local education authority established by the Ministry of Education. In reality however, the local authorities did not

[1] Taken from B. Shidlovsky, 'Changes in the Development of the Arab Village in Israel', *Hamizrah Hehadash*, Vol. XV, 1965, No. 1–2, pp. 25–37.

fully use the sums placed at their disposal for school-building purposes until 1960–1. Today government grants amount to at least 50 per cent of the cost of building a classroom, and IL 2,500 are given for every classroom built in settlements without municipal status. As a result of this, every recognized Arab settlement now has a school building.

Another important field of government activity was the modernization of agriculture. Government investment in agriculture emphasized training and production. Loans are therefore provided to increase the means of production and output has therefore risen considerably in recent years. The Ministry of Agriculture also formulated long-term plans for Arab villages but, for various reasons, these are not always supported by the inhabitants.

Realizing the need to supplement agricultural employment, the Ministry of Commerce and Industry initiated and financed the establishment of small industries in the Arab sector, which are now expanding with the aid of special funds managed principally by the Israel-Arab Bank. The two main funds for this purpose are: (1) The funds for the Encouragement of Manufacturing (IL 300,000) financed equally by the Ministry and the Bank which has authorized 350 loans for the establishment of new firms or the improvement of existing ones; (2) the Fund for the Encouragement of Commerce (IL 300,000) which has authorized 325 requests for loans. In addition the Ministry also grants direct loans to larger enterprises. No apparent budgetary limit exists for future industrial development which is likely to continue on a scale parallel to the development of basic services in the villages.

In this context various public works have been of great importance. Since the establishment of the state, 175 kilometres of approach and inner roads have been constructed in Arab settlements and on completion of the five-year plan almost all Arab villages will have approach roads.

Similarly, various water projects have been initiated by the Ministry of Agriculture since the establishment of the state, as a result of which drinking water is now piped to ninety villages (and is now in the process of being supplied to all Arab localities).

The connexion to the national electricity grid is generally financed by the inhabitants of each settlement. However, the government offers cheap loans for this purpose to any Arab village where a legally constituted municipal body exists.

Until 1962–3 the various Ministries formulated their own development programmes for the Arab sector, subject to the discretion of the Minister concerned. Since then, recognizing the urgency of such development, the budget for the Arab sector has been doubled and funds are now allocated within the framework of an overall five-year plan. The original plan provided for the allocation of IL 25 million which was later increased to IL 33 million. Total investments in the Arab sector including non-government sources are expected to amount to IL 71 million for the period 1962–3 to 1966–7, compared to the total of IL 9,700,000 invested by the government during the period 1957–8 to 1961–2.

Of the IL 71,000,000 to be invested, IL 15,800,000 will be allocated for agriculture, IL 12,500,000 for housing, IL 11,500,000 for water supply, IL 11,000,000 for electricity, IL 7,500,000 for industry, IL 6,000,000 for education and the remainder for roads, health projects, and other municipal services.

The fact that most administrative and even some direct employment services in the Arab sector revolved around the Military Government, created a rather special situation whereby the Arab sector was heavily but separately 'administered'. Though this showed some parallels to the administrative situation among new immigrant groups, the specific implications and the geographical concentrations of the Arabs were quite different.

This, as well as the creation of a special advisory office for minorities, established as part of the Prime Minister's Office, emphasized the separateness of the Arabs and reinforced feelings of ambivalence and of only partial participation in the state. At the same time, however, this office also constituted one of the main factors for change and development.

The Poles of Change in Arab Society

The processes analysed above created the basic dynamics of development for the Arabs in Israel, including the Bedouins in the Negev but excluding the Druze communities. This framework was composed of several basic, sometimes contradictory, starting points, the first of which was the economic one. Though initially distinct and separate from the economy of the Yishuv, the Arab sectors were comparatively quickly drawn into the general framework, although up to this very day agriculture – but greatly changed and to some extent modernized – remains yet their main base. These changes were greatly reinforced by the great demographic increase of the Arab population which was discussed above.

The natural increase of the Arab population brings us to the second administrative-economic aspect of development, which resulted in heavy concentration of administrative services among the Arabs, as well as in the recognition of their equality as citizens and the state's duties to provide them with services.

These economic and administrative demographic processes provided for the change in the traditional pattern of Arab society, for growing modernization, and continuously rising aspirations in the economic, occupational, and socio-political spheres.

Next came the problem of realizing the various aspirations in which the political-administrative aspects were involved.

While the premises of equality, the provision of services and of drawing the Arabs into the Israeli framework predominated the economic-administrative sphere, the ambivalences of the political and security situations were paramount on the political-administrative level.

Thus the Arab and, to a lesser degree, the Druze and other small communities, found themselves in the position of a minority group, whose traditional way of life was changing and whose attitude to these changes was full of ambiguity caused by the assumption of political equality coupled with potentially hostile national-political tendencies.

Patterns of Change in Arab Society

In order to understand the problems analysed above, it is essential to look at the changing Arab society in Israel starting with the village in which the largest part of the Arab population lived.

The traditional Arab village in Palestine, and later in Israel, evinced most of the general characteristics of a peasant society based on agriculture. The internal composition of each village was based on economic and family position and included many large landowners whose families at times married into other villages. It also included many small tenants and landless peasants.

The common institutions of the village were usually those of religion and local government, imposed by the ruling government, be it Turkish, English, or Israeli. Major links with the rest of the country were forged through these institutions.

From the 'twenties and 'thirties on, education began to spread under the Mandate, and was greatly accelerated under Israeli rule, and additional links with the developing urban centres and the various social and national movements and organizations were established through teachers and some advanced urban occupational groups.

Within the village, conformity to the basic economic, social, and political administrative status hierarchies was observed, while, within the families, the family elders ruled. Participation in wider political life, such as social movements and parties, was mediated by the larger family groups, who also organized political activities and represented the link with the central government.

Under the impact of modernization, increased services, and demographic expansion, this traditional structure began to change. Although some specifically Israeli connotations were inherent in these changes, they were not confined to the Israeli Arabs but were common to most peasant societies in a similar state of transition, and particularly to other Arab peasants.

Among the more common breakdowns that occurred in these shifting societies was the relation between the hierarchies of wealth and the status of power with the growth of *nouveaux riches* farmers and politically active individuals not tied to the older order.

Another phenomenon was the growing dissociation of the younger generation from the pattern of the old in religion and in general social attitudes – a dissociation which was largely connected with demographic expansion and with the inability of the traditional structure to meet the growing demands made on it.

In addition, the growing level of education, leading to greater occupational aspirations, contributed largely to the alienation of the young beyond the scope of the home village and the older urban setting.

One of the consequences of these changes was the development of a migrant landless peasant-proletariat consisting of those who went to the cities as part-time workers and developed the traits usual in migrant labour. Such groups tended to concentrate in areas where manpower was most needed, but while some developed into skilled workers helped by the vocational courses of the Histadrut and the government, the great majority of this floating proletariat belonged to the lower categories of unskilled workers.

A special group consisted of youngsters who flocked from the villages into the towns – especially to Jaffa and Acre – without the help of any one institution and who, therefore, drifted into marginal semi-slum, ecological settings.

Another trend was the development of a 'semi-intelligentsia' drawn mostly from the Israeli school system and partly reinforced from existing nuclei in Jaffa and Acre, which had benefited from the expanding educational system. However, even among this group many had received only partial secondary education, due to the high rate of drop-outs and failures, and because the achievement of complete secondary education often did not seem to be worth while economically.

As a general rule, it was easier for rural youths looking for manual labour than for white collar workers to find work in the cities. This fact applied particularly to Arab youths in a Jewish market. While the differences in language and cultural and social backgrounds are not quite so important in manual occupations, they decisively affect eligibility for white-collar jobs. An Arab youth whose formal education is equivalent to that of a Jewish youth cannot, in general, compete for a clerical job in the Jewish area, even if no feelings of discrimination motivate the employer. The fact that, in many instances, workers are taken on the basis of personal connexions and recommendations, in contrast to the non-personal basis on which manual labourers are hired, further weakens the chances of Arab youth, whose employment in clerical jobs in the Jewish sector is insignificant.

In the Arab sector itself the demand for educated manpower is very limited, and as professional and administrative services are partly supplied by the Jewish sector, this leaves only the government services. However, the Arab youth looking for employment in government service in the Jewish sector faces at least the same handicaps as he does in the private sector, with various political and security considerations acting as handicaps. The main single occupation open to the higher ranks of the intelligentsia is therefore teaching, and in 1961 the Ministry of Education employed 1,400 of the 1,800 Arab young people employed by the government.[1]

Tensions and Ambiguities Among the Arab Minority

The problems of integration were fully articulated mainly by the dynamic groups of the intelligentsia who tried to crystallize mutual ambiguities and uncertainties as well as the more positive points of progress and contact.

On the positive side we find growing concern on the part of the authorities and the general Israeli public for the problems of integration of the Arab minority, the relaxation of military rule, the development of new social and cultural meeting points between Arabs and Jews, and the growing concern about the lack of such facilities.

Inevitably, however, the more ambivalent and problematic aspects of these developments were the most fully articulated. Parallel problems to those in the economic sphere also developed in the political field.

Here several different trends become apparent.[2] There is the old 'paternalistic' participation, evinced in the Arab lists close to Mapai, which are essentialy a parliamentary device established to catch the Arab vote with the help of the government machine. Two or three such lists exist at most elections and take into account the personal and family feuds and communal divisions of their electorate. The methods applied to the vote catching are a combination of pressure (often through the military government) or of favours – such as permits, jobs, licences, and land leases – being granted. The wealthier elements in the community who have many dealings with the authorities therefore usually find it expedient to co-operate.

These lists are more concerned with avoiding the possible consequences of 'wrong' votes than they are with attempts to change the regime. The slogans used by their candidates are of various kinds: they may stress the importance of supporting the powers-that-be; or they may be anti-Jewish and nationalist, with such slogans as 'vote for your own people (the Arab lists), against the Jewish parties'. With these means at their disposal, these lists have gathered between half and two-thirds of the Arab vote, giving them four to five members in the Knesset.

Other lists are of the Communist party and the Zionist-left, especially Mapam, though distinction between the two should, of course, be made.

---

[1] This analysis follows Yoram Ben-Porat, *Characteristics of Arab Labour Force in Israel*, Falk Centre for Economic Research.

[2] Taken from Y. Washitz, 'Arabs in Israeli Politics', *New Outlook*, Vol. 5, No. 3, March–April 1962, pp. 33–45.

However, both can be regarded as manifestations of protest and it is doubtful whether either represents a real, even though oppositionist, participation in the political life of Israel.

A new feature which appeared in the elections to the Fourth Knesset was the *El-Ard* group – an Arab Nationalist group without any connexion to any other party. This group emerged from the 'Arab Front', formed in 1958, during the period of enthusiasm over the Syrian-Egyptian union. At that time the Communist Party seemed to be identified with the aims of Arab nationalism, and many of its members were imprisoned following a clash with the police during a Mapai-organized May-Day parade in Nazareth. The 'Arab Front' was formed by Arab Communists and nationalist middle-class intellectuals. Besides making specific demands for the Arabs within the state, its programme also called for the 'right of the refugees to return to Israel'.

The *El-Ard* movement later became semi-illegal and having been declared to be bascially opposed to the existence of the State of Israel, by the Supreme Court, was ordered to disband.[1]

A similarly ambivalent and problematic picture developed on the socio-cultural level. Although many cultural activities and organizations were undertaken by various official and semi-official bodies, the extent to which they were fully accepted by the Arabs seems to be very limited, partly, no doubt, because of their ambiguous political situation, and partly because of their suspicion towards the initiators of these schemes and their difficulties in social and cultural encounter.

These uncertainties necessarily created, or reinforced, existing apathy and no doubt intensified the feelings of alienation and ambiguity. This, in turn, led to various negative attitudes towards the state, sometimes bordering on treason – such as contacts with neighbouring countries, ranging from 'limited' traditional smuggling, to sheltering infiltrators, and even to active participation in espionage activities, anti-Israel demonstrations, and extreme political movements, like the *El-Ard*.

It is extremely difficult to estimate accurately the extent and intensity of these different orientations, as the more vocal and negative ones obviously catch the eye while the more passive, less vocal acceptance of Israel does not as easily become apparent.

A recent survey of Arab writers in Israel shows that most develop rather negative attitudes to Israel with only occasional positive orientations.[2] However, there are many indications that these positive views are growing in daily life, as well as in more articulate literary ways, though it is as yet difficult to gauge their extent and scope.

---

[1] See *The Jerusalem Post*, 12 November 1964.

[2] See Avraham Yinon, 'Some Aspects of Arabic Literature in Israel', *Hamizrah Hehadash*, Vol. XV, 1965, No. 1–2, pp. 57–85.

Problems of Identity in Israel

To illustrate the problems inherent in the search for a national identity on the part of the Arabs in Israel, the following quotations from the writings of two Israeli Arab intellectuals serve to show the serious efforts made in this direction:

. . . Not all the consequences of the encounter with Zionism were positive. The meeting between the Palestinian communities and the nationalist Zionist movement divided the country along nationalist lines, over and above the religious affiliations. Whereas in Lebanon political organization took on a religious character, the Arab national movement in Palestine tended toward Christian-Moslem rapprochement. The Zionist movement provided the impetus and opportunity for this coming together of rival religious groups and signalled the passing of the traditional oriental division by millets or religious groups, which proved inadequate to deal with the new challenge provided by the Zionist settlers. The stage was prepared for a struggle between the national groups in Palestine.

After the establishment of the state of Israel in 1948 European patterns were stimulated through the newly-created instruments of sovereignty. The oriental culture, which was almost hermetically sealed off from its immediate environment, was struck a serious blow. Although half the State's inhabitants came from an oriental background, European culture was dominant because of the social and political character of the Jewish population, the impulse towards contacts with the European continent, and the dynamic force and influence of the highly-industrialized European culture. . . .

While it can be said that Israel's establishment broke down the divisions between Jews from oriental and occidental cultures, and tended to create a single over-all cultural and social unit embracing all the State's Jewish population, this has not been the case with the Arab population. The State's proclamation gave an official stamp to the division of Israel's inhabitants into Jews and Arabs, and ended once and for all the traditional oriental pattern of division into different religious communities. This new division is supported by the different patterns which govern everyday activities. Jewish and Arab schools have separate curricula, based on national differences. The Arab child studies Arabic, Hebrew, and English in that order; the Jewish child studies Hebrew and English, with a choice of Arabic and French. The Arab child studies Arab history at length, and Jewish history only briefly; the reverse is true of the Jewish child. There are indeed cases where Arab children study in Jewish schools; but in effect Jewish and Arab children are set apart by their different major languages – Hebrew and Arabic respectively – which divide the inhabitants into two different nations and perpetuate this situation through a separatist, national-conscious education in different schools.

It is true that, during the final stages of education, at the universities and sometimes even in the high schools in such mixed Jewish-Arab towns as Haifa, Acre and,

[1] From A. Mansour, 'The Modern Encounter between Jews and Arabs', *New Outlook*, Vol. 5, No. 3, 1962, pp. 59–63.

Jaffa – the members of these two different nations meet once more. But even then, under the influence of the general political and cultural climate, the young Jews and Arabs become members of different national groups, far removed from one another both in religious background and general cultural characteristics.

When these two different groups do meet, the result is frequently a clash. The feeling of strangeness is seen at once. The Arab students, who have usually studied in a school attended only by boys (because of the refusal of most Arab parents to allow their daughters to study in co-educational schools), are embarrassed and ill at ease in the co-educational framework prevailing in most Jewish schools. They try to integrate into the new Jewish Society, but are usually rebuffed by the Jewish society's insularity.

The stories of youths who have come into contact with Jewish young people in schools and at places of work often lead to the dismal conclusion that this section of the Arab population is more hostile to the Jewish society than any other Arab element. The young Arab hates the Jewish society because it regards him as strange and different and rejects him, and because of envy for his Jewish counter-part, who outdoes him culturally and intellectually. He also suffers from feelings of inferiority because he comes from a society which has a lower economic and cultural level than most of the Jewish society. He can hardly forget that the Arab minority was the majority in this same land a decade and a half ago, and formed part of a large nation with a deeply-rooted culture, one which might be backward by European standards, but which developed in accordance with its own needs and suffered from no inferiority complex.

The equivocal nature of official policy towards the Israeli Arabs, supplies these young Arabs with emotional justification for hatred and indignation. It prompts them to express their feelings of hatred for Jewish society by fleeing from Israel and 'joining' – in an emotional and practical sense – the Arabs in the neighbouring countries, who hate Israel as a state. A lesser degree of hatred leads some Arab youth to join extremist groups. In many cases this leads them into a cultural and political blind alley, in which they lose all faith in words and action.

The greatest disaster is the considerable deterioration in the thinking of the two generations on both sides of the fence. Most of the older Jewish generation never thought much about the Arabs, and took a fairly liberal attitude towards members of other national groups. In contrast to this, most of the younger Jewish Israelis accept, by and large, the mood of the press reports they read and the comments they hear at home and in school; this is all too frequently chauvinistic and anti-Arab. The young Jew who does not come into contact with the Arabs, although he may live in the centre of an Arab area, thinks of Arabs as strange and peculiar people. The same is true on the Arab side. For the older Arabs, the Jews still represent a *religious* community which was respected as such. (It should not be forgotten that both Christianity and Islam hold Judaism in high regard.) Though anti-Zionist propaganda has created anti-Jewish feelings, the older generation, which is conservative and religious, has remained positive in its attitude towards the Jew as a religious group. Even the most severe critic of the Arab attitude towards the Jews during the British Mandatory period will admit that hatred of the Jews was confined to small strata of political interests, and that the Arab masses were in the main indifferent and moderate. In order to arouse anti-Zionist agitation, emissaries were invariably brought in from the neighbouring countries to introduce a reign of terror, with the aid of local supporters.[1]

A second expression of the Arab point of view reads as follows:

The question remains, therefore, whether Israel's Arabs can integrate into Israel's dynamic society with their present culture, or whether they must adopt another one. To answer this question we must remember that, in addition to the usual difficulties facing developing societies, Israel's Arabs suffer from the extra burden of the vague terminology of 'national loyalty to the Arab Nation' and are subjected to a propaganda of hatred from the neighbouring Arab states. Moreover, Israel's Arabs are leaderless, since those who claim to speak in their name abroad are the product of foreign governments.

Though the economic position of the Arabs has improved since the establishment of Israel, there has been an understandable increase in the proportion of mobile wage-earners. The Five-Year Plan of 1962, intended to accelerate the development of the Arab sector, will hardly keep pace with the natural increase of the Arab population. Any economic progress, however, must be accompanied by parallel social development if the harmful aspects of modernisation are to be avoided.

One method of modernisation is to force changes from above; the other method is to arouse the desire for change, and to achieve this end, the patriarchal structure of the Arab family in which the women's influence is insignificant, must undergo a fundamental transformation. A decisive factor in this direction will be the reform of the educational system. Further, official policy towards the Arabs must include the abolishment of separate treatment for them; in the field of security, Arabs, like any other citizens, must be regarded as innocent unless proved guilty. A special effort must be made towards economic integration. Finally, a clear distinction must be drawn between the foreign policy towards Arab states and internal policy towards Israel's Arabs. These measures will contribute to a great extent to the restoration of the self-confidence of Israel's Arabs, to assisting their social development and to leading them on to a new way of life.[2]

Summary: Problems and Prospects

The preceding analysis shows the great complexity and the tragic elements of the Arabs' situation in Israel. By many standards, those of economic development, administrative services, education, and even political equality (though with the exception of military rule and the expropriation of land for security reasons) the standards of the Israeli Arabs are high – certainly much higher than those of most minorities in Arab countries – and their lot is being improved continuously.

However, this does not always mitigate the potential alienation and

[1] From A. Mansour, 'The Modern Encounter between Jews and Arabs', *New Outlook*, Vol. 5, No. 3, 1962, pp. 59–63.

[2] Quoted from a summary of 'Arab Society in Israel', by R. Bastuni, *Hamizrah Hehadash*, Vol. XV, No. 1–2, 1965, p. II.

hostility, rooted in the historical and political situation which is partly fostered by the initial approaches of the Israeli authorities, both on the administrative and the political-cultural level.

The real tragedy of the problem lies in the fact that, although improved attitudes by the Israeli authorities and public, the assurance of greater freedom, and the increased scope of mutual contact, certainly alleviate many aspects of the problem, yet they may also, as in so many parallel situations in other places, give rise to growing disillusionment on the part of the Arabs.

Naturally, this does not absolve either the Israeli public or the authorities from adopting the best possible policies and the most democratic attitudes with regard to the minorities. However, the success of such measures is to no small degree dependent on broader political-historical and international circumstances, and especially on relations with the surrounding Arab countries and their attitude to Israel.

In many ways the possibility of a fuller and freer encounter between the Arab minority and the Jewish majority in Israel contains important possibilities, not only of political arrangements, but also of variegating the components of Israeli identity. The complexity and tragedy of the situation lies in the fact that these possibilities and potentials are greatly limited by the international political situations.

12

Israel, a Modern Society

Characteristics and Problems of the Yishuv and of Israel as a Modern Society

We have come to the end of our story although, of course, the story itself continues to unfold. After surveying the historical development of Israel's social structure and of its major institutional spheres, it is perhaps worth while to attempt an evaluation of the nature of Israeli society, the specific characteristics and problems, and its potential trends of development.

Two basic problems or questions common to all modern societies also arise here, the first is the nature of the specific structural and organizational characteristics of the Yishuv and the State of Israel as distinct from those of other modern societies. The second is the extent to which these varied social forms can cope with the new problems arising from the continuous development of an emerging society.

We shall, therefore, first attempt to recapitulate briefly the major characteristics of the Yishuv as they developed in its formative stages, to compare them with those of some other modern societies, and then to see how these characteristics influenced its capacity to deal with the new problems which arose in the new stage of its development or modernization on which it entered with the establishment of the State of Israel.

The aim of the first pioneers was, as we have seen, that the Yishuv should become not only a modern society in every sense of the term but also one that embodied wider values and meaning and some transcendental significance. This aim developed, in a transformed way, from the legacy of traditional Jewish society which combined an ardent yearning for universal meaning with the realities of an oppressed minority. As long as this minority remained closed within itself, the tension between this yearning and actuality produced considerable creative activity within its own framework, while relegating any hope that its universal claims would be accepted to the distant future. When the gates of European society were – at least partially – opened, many of its members succeeded in entering fields of general social and cultural activity in which they could be highly creative. But at the same time, they faced the problem of losing their collective Jewish identity and/or of not being fully accepted into the broader European society.

The Zionist movement aimed at providing the opportunity for cultural and social creativity of universal significance within the framework of a free, modern, self-supporting Jewish society – and it is this combination which accounts for the tremendous emphasis placed on socio-cultural creativity and for its strong élitist orientations. This emphasis was further heightened by the external circumstances prevailing in Palestine – the conditions of the country, the absence of capital reserves and suitable manpower resources, as well as the lack of a long tradition of an orderly civil society.

Perhaps the most outstanding characteristic of the Yishuv was that its centre developed first. Its central institutions and symbols crystallized before the emergence of the 'periphery' made up of broader, less creative social groups and strata. This centre – built up through the élitist and future orientations of the pioneering sects – was envisaged as being capable of permeating and absorbing the periphery which (it was hoped) would develop and expand through continuous migration.

The ideological and élitist orientations of the first pioneering groups and the strong transcendental orientations and sense of personal responsibility for the fulfilment of the ideal inherent in the image of the pioneer guided the initial development of this centre, its symbols and institutions.

Far-reaching attempts to develop a specific modern structure were implied in the pioneering ideology. These attempts combined the positive aspects of modern technology with the maintenance of basic human and social values and were oriented especially to their implementation in the fields of economic and social organization. However, these economic orientations were not purely social or ideological. They were closely related to national effort and were conceived not in utopian terms but rather as part and parcel of the building of a new nation.

The encounter between these orientations and the tasks encountered in their implementation in Palestine during the Ottoman and Mandate periods constituted the focal point of the development of the Israeli social structure.

As the development and maintenance of a high standard of living for existing and future waves of immigrants was implicitly assumed, it necessitated a partial separation from the local, traditional Arab economy.

Among basic initial factors which influenced the implementation of these ideals were the lack of adequate capital resources and manpower for primary occupations combined, however, with a high initial educational potential. This latter attribute eventually ensured a relatively smooth transition to a fairly high level of technological development.

These basic exigencies, together with the ideology of the pioneering groups, caused the initial heavy concentration of public capital in the major development sectors while at the same time permitting the continuous expansion of the private sectors. They also gave rise to the specifically Israeli forms of socio-economic organization (above all to the communal and co-operative settlements) and to the proliferation of co-operative

409

enterprises in the urban sector, a feature also found to some extent in other sectarian and colonizing societies. However, most of these co-operative and colonizing bodies were to some extent incorporated into the more unitary framework of the Histadrut to a degree unparalleled in other countries, thus going beyond the initial agrarian orientation of the first pioneering groups. It was here that the major characteristics of the urban social structure of the Yishuv developed. Most important was the attempt to combine unified large-scale organizational frameworks designed for implementing collective goals, with the more totalistic and closed sects or social movements on the one hand, and with the differentiated, functionally specific organizations on the other.

The second aspect of the emerging social structure of the Yishuv was the strong emphasis on equality and deprecation of specialization. It showed itself in two ways – in the strong egalitarian trend in the distribution of rewards allocated to major occupational roles, and in the minimization of differences between them and the presumption of an easy transition from one to the other.

Another aspect of egalitarianism was that of general accessibility to various occupational positions. This aspect was, however, much less explicitly emphasized in the initial ideological tenets. This was due to the fact that in the beginning access to these positions did not constitute a problem; it was assured by the comparative homogeneity of educational and cultural facilities and by the dependence of all groups on external economic and political resources.

In the political field the encounter between the basic ideologies and their implementation in the Zionist movement and the reality of Palestine explains the development of two partly contradictory and partly complementary tendencies in the political organization of the Yishuv and later in the State of Israel.

The first of these tendencies was the totalistic orientation inherent in the sectarian and ideological base of the pioneering sects. The second was the more constitutional pluralistic trend which was part of the federative structure of the Yishuv and which, mitigating the totalistic orientations of the sectarian movements, created the structural framework for constitutional pluralistic institutions and the broader social preconditions required for their continuous functioning.

The federative system proved to be of great importance for the political socialization of the various pioneering and immigrant groups in common democratic procedures and symbols. Moreover, the social structure and composition of the immigrant groups provided some of the broader conditions for the continuous working of a viable pluralistic setting, especially as the relative similarity of background of the immigrants and the constant emphasis on the national importance of immigration facilitated the accessibility of different positions within both the private and the workers' sectors and assured the continuity and development of each of these sectors.

Characteristics of the Yishuv and of the Israeli Society from a Comparative Point of View

It might be worth while at this point to summarize the comparative indications implied in the preceding analysis and to see what characteristics Israeli society shares with other societies in which some of its analytical components may also be found.

Israeli society shares important characteristics with some non-imperial, colonizing societies (especially the United States and the British Dominions): First, a strong emphasis on equality, at least among the initial settler groups, and the consequent lack of any strong hereditary, feudal, aristocratic landowner class. Second, the development of a strong concentration of various types of economic and administrative activities within broad, unified, organizational frameworks in common with other sectarian, colonizing societies. And last, and again in common with other colonizing societies, Zionist settlement emphasized the conquest of wasteland through work – as shown in the expansion of productive, primary occupations and in the expansion of the colonizing frameworks and frontiers.

Such combinations of co-operative endeavours and economic-colonizing enterprise could be found also, for instance, in the settlement of wasteland by the Mormons. The combination of trade unions with the industrial and financial activities of the entrepreneur could also be found in other politically oriented labour movements, especially in Scandinavia and – to a lesser extent – in England.

However, the fusion of these features as developed within the Histadrut seems to be unique and is explained by the Histadrut's political character and outlook. This also explains its political power although it is, economically, by no means the largest sector of the country.

These characteristics became closely interwoven with other components of Israeli society, such as the sectarian or social movements which are evident in the totalistic outlook of the pioneering sects with their strong internal ideological cohesion and in the institutionalization of ideology in the face of growing social differentiation.

Unlike many other sects, the pioneering groups aimed from the beginning at being the trail blazers of a modern society and committed themselves to many institutional frameworks and organizations which might serve as the forerunners of such a development and through which these broader groups of Jewish society could participate in the economic, ideological and political life of the Yishuv.

411

Unlike most modern social and nationalistic movements, however, the Zionist pioneers did not plan for the immediate seizure of power and a new, unitary, political framework. Their primary emphasis was on broad rural and urban colonization which, in itself, weakened the political implications of totalistic orientations.

It was only at the end of the mandatory period, with the intensification of the external political struggle, that some conception of a self-governing polity developed.

It was out of the sectarian and social movement elements of the Yishuv that another crucial trend developed – the strong élitist ideological bent, aiming at the achievement of a new society through the implementation of an ideological programme.

In this, Israel was akin to some revolutionary societies, such as the USSR, Yugoslavia, or Mexico, which attempted to mould relatively traditional societies into a specific modern pattern. However, the ideologies which were developed within the Zionist movement contained more variegated and heterogeneous elements than either those of closed religious sects or of revolutionary political movements. This ideological diversity was greatly reinforced by the co-existence of many different groups within the federative structure of the Yishuv, creating new institutional nuclei with orientations to broader, more universalistic, cultural and social values.

Israeli society also shared many features and problems with other countries which had large-scale immigration. It had to deal with continuous waves of immigrants and with their integration into its emerging institutional framework. But it also developed specific characteristics of its own, rooted in the basic motivations and orientations among the immigrants and their strong emphasis on national and social goals.

As pointed out, Israeli society contained also many elements and problems similar to those of other developing countries. This similarity could also be found in the establishment of a new political framework by the élite of a colonial ruler and the consequent transformation of this élite into a ruling class. However, several important differences stand out.

Unlike many contemporary developing societies, the initial institutional framework in Israel was established by modern élites and along modern lines. These élites had a large pool of educated persons committed by ideology, outlook, or creed to the creation of a modern society. The traditional elements were only taken into these frameworks much later, and the process of their modernization was quicker and more intense than in many other newly independent developing countries. Further, and again unlike most New States, the attainment of independence did not create a sharp break with the past, since the Yishuv and the Zionist movement had already developed manifold political, administrative, and economic organizations. The emphasis on the 'Political Kingdom' was therefore much smaller.

Israel, the United States and the USSR – Comparisons in Modernity

The combination of characteristics listed above was almost unique, as can be seen from a comparison with two major industrial societies: the Puritan colonization in the United States and the ideologically oriented political revolution in the USSR.

Some of the similarities with these societies, such as settlement by sectarian groups in the American colonies and the strong social-ideological emphasis in Russia, though striking, should not obscure the major differences. With regard to the United States there were, of course, the obvious differences in external environment – the differences between a large, sparsely populated, potentially open continent and a small, barren, densely populated country, surrounded by other countries which soon became hostile to the colonizing efforts made and thus created immediate security problems and considerations in the development of the new society.

But beyond this, there were also some important differences between the Puritan groups on the one hand and the Zionist and socialist pioneering sects on the other. Unlike the former, the latter were mostly secular; and it was not within the religious sphere that they were most inventive or re-volutionary. Hence, while American society had to face continuous secularization which had to be related to its initial religious value orientations, Israeli society faced almost opposite problems. It had to transform its totalistic secular ideologies into a value-system of a more differentiated and partly de-ideologized society, and later faced the possibility of erosion of these values by many factors – among them the growing militancy of the newly growing non-Zionist religious groups. On the social and economic side, there was the great difference between the collective orientations and organizational form of the predominant Zionist groups and the more individualistic emphasis and individual recruitment of the American pioneers.

Next came the great difference in the development and expansion beyond the initial phase. Although both cases deal with societies which had to absorb waves of immigrants whose social orientations differed from those of the first settlers, there were basic differences in these problems and the frame-work in which they were set. In America the major common motivation of new immigrants – especially during the second half of the nineteenth century and the beginning of the twentieth – was the attainment of personal security and economic advancement, while in Israel it was more a common national orientation. Thus, while some of the differences between the newer, tradi-tional immigrant groups and the initial settlers were perhaps smaller in Israel than in the United States, they were perceived as more crucial for the unity of the nation.

The differences with the USSR are even more striking. Beyond the obvious differences of scale and the relative backwardness of Russian society, was the fact that in Russia attempts to mould society to an ideological formula came by a highly unified and closely organized élite after the Revolution and after the establishment of a new political framework and that the ideologists were therefore caught up in the establishment and maintenance of a totalitarian regime bent on quick industrialization of a relatively backward country.

In the Yishuv and in the State of Israel, attempts to implement the ideology came long before the establishment of a unified political framework and were mainly concerned with economic, colonizing, and social fields. The establishment of the state continued this process of selective institutionalization in a pluralistic setting and weakened the effectiveness of the monolithic elements in the ideological orientation of the élite. Not only were these attempts set in a pluralistic-constitutional setting but, paradoxically, the emphasis on the pioneering ideology also gave rise to claims for some political influence by some of the older pioneering groups, against those of the state, thus reinforcing the pluralistic tendency. Moreover, these groups were comparatively successful in absorbing new elements which did not, as in Russia, have to be coerced into the new central framework.

Processes and Problems of Israel's New Stage of Development

The differences between the societies mentioned above and the Yishuv help to illuminate the latter's specific structural characteristics and the ways in which it was able to deal with the various problems which it had to face at the new stage of its development which it entered into when the State of Israel was established. It was at this stage that the Yishuv's capacity to grow, to absorb new elements and to deal with new kinds of problems was to be severely tested in many ways.

These problems developed out of the three broad trends which brought about the structural transformation of the Israeli society and which, as it were, ushered in the new stage of development or modernization.

The first of these was the growing differentiation and specialization in all major spheres of society, but especially in the occupational and economic fields, culminating in the 'situation of irreversibility' in occupational mobility – a development which was, to some extent, opposed to the initial pioneering ideology.

The second trend was the transformation, with the establishment of the state, of the élite into a ruling group and the concomitant changes in the structural placement and orientation of all other major groups.

Third, was the large-scale influx of new immigrants, which was one of the major sources for the growing expansion and differentiation of the Israeli social structure but which also brought some of the hardest problems

Israeli society had to face. Here there developed risks of lowering the level of economic, technical, and educational performances and the possibility of creating a whole gamut of new social and cultural tensions and conflicts, leading to the possible cleavage between 'Orientals' and 'Occidentals' and thus giving rise to the possibility of creating 'Two Nations' within Israel.

These three coinciding trends accentuated the problem of the extent to which the existing élites and centre are able to absorb the new broadened periphery within the framework of its basic institutions and symbols.

As in all other modern or modernizing societies which enter a new stage of development and face new problems, the attempts to solve these problems could develop either in a way which could assure the further growth of the society or in a more stagnant and conflict-ridden direction.

In Israel each of these possible developments was based on some combination of the older ideologies and institutions combined with new orientations and organizations.

These encounters created varied possibilities of developing new, broader, universalistic, cultural orientations and patterns of social organizations, and integrating those organizational and institutional nuclei which were the bearers of such orientations into the new organizations developed in the state period. Conversely, there could develop a stronger emphasis on the particularistic and ascriptive frameworks, thus reinforcing the tendencies in the society towards stagnation and contributing to the possible lowering of levels of social, economic, and cultural activity.

Such tendencies towards stagnation could become reinforced by the transformation of many social movements into more constricted interest groups, by the development of restrictive orientations within the 'older' movement groups (the settlements, the Histadrut, the political parties), and by the development of such orientations within several new sectors of the society, such as the new ethnic and religious groups and the various professional organizations.

In the following sections we shall point out briefly the major ways in which new problems – and varied attempts to deal with them – were developed in the major fields of Israeli society, starting with that area in which these problems are in a way most visible – namely, the political one.

Problems in the Political Field

In most general terms, the problems which the Israeli political élite faced were similar to those which develop in other modern or modernizing societies.

In each new stage of development or modernization new groups hitherto politically relatively inert create problems by the expression of demands which necessitate redefining the guiding principles of political activities, institutions, and policies and reconstituting the centre of the society. This always necessitates also the re-formulation of problems and dilemmas of political freedom and causes tensions between legitimacy and efficiency of the political order.

The new centre has to face the problem of the extent to which it can withstand the pressures of different groups, of being able to forge a viable institutional framework and new principles of policy or political activity, without at the same time monopolizing all effective power and legitimation, thus denying or restricting the participation of the broader groups in its formation and work.

Often these two possibilities may become paradoxically combined, thus minimizing both the efficiency of the new élite and the responsible participation of the new groups in the new complex and differentiated political setting.

The ability of the élites to forge a new centre and to maintain both its efficiency and legitimacy is, usually, to no small degree dependent on internal cohesion and on the relations between the old and the new groups.

Although such problems develop in all cases of transition from one stage of modernization to another, some specific features emerge in each modern society.

The Israeli social and political system faced the crucial problem of developing and maintaining effective and legitimate rule within the state which emerged from the pluralistic setting of 'pre-state' institutions, movements and organizations. The legitimation of the new state, torn between the demand for total identification with its collective goals and the perception of the state as a mere provider of facilities to other groups or sectors, became a major problem, greatly impeding the development and legitimation of new viable and flexible political institutions.

This problem was further reinforced by a trend, to be found in many new or established, affluent or welfare societies of the West or in the British Dominions. This was the transformation of labour movements into interest groups, connected with the growing importance of administrative injunctions, regulations, and bargaining procedures in the overall political process.

This resulted in a somewhat paradoxical situation. While the tendency to centralize leadership succeeded in minimizing the autonomy of alternative centres of power, the strength of these centres as pressure groups greatly increased, thus often testing the leadership's ability to forge effective policies in the face of new situations and problems.

Two factors contributed to the growth of such pressures on the political leadership and to its possible inability to forge new consistent policies.

One was the semi-ideological legitimation of demands made in terms of older, federative values and arrangements. This often weakened unity among the leadership without, necessarily, facilitating the development of more adaptive or creative power centres or of a more realistic perception of society.

The second factor was the comparatively successful initial absorption of the many new immigrant groups, a fact which led to increased demands on the ruling group and the potential political dependence of the country's leaders on these groups.

These problems became focused, as we have seen, in the dominant party, Mapai, which had achieved this position through its majority in the Histadrut and its standing in the government.

Mapai and the Israeli political system were faced with the problem of absorbing the growing new forces while maintaining cohesion and solidarity between new technical, bureaucratic, and professional groups and the more diffuse political leadership, as well as between the different echelons and groups of political leaders. These problems affected the other parties by forcing them to exert enough pressure on the dominant party to make it responsive to new problems.

These developments and problems tended to become acute not only in the political centre but also in the broader periphery within which there continuously developed new loci of power and new cleavages which had very heavy repercussions on the centre itself.

Perhaps the most important of these potential cleavages was that between the 'old' and the 'new' immigrants, between the 'Oriental' groups and the 'European' centre and groups. Here the political centre faced the problem of whether it would be able to develop new creative frameworks common to these varied groups and cutting across them, or whether there would develop a continuous cleavage between them, giving rise to political eruptions and conflicts and breakdowns on the one hand and/or to political stagnation with a consequent lowering of the efficiency and legitimation of the political system on the other.

The repercussions of the problems and developments analyzed above were felt in all major spheres of Israeli society – in the economic field, in education, in social organization – in all of which various attempts were made by the élite to deal with them.

As we have seen above, these problems were first tackled through the continuous physical expansion of the basic institutional framework, by the multiplication and segmentation of its major social organizations, and by the absorption of new groups within these frameworks.

Although several basic features of these organizations were transformed by the three processes outlined above, some of the outstanding structural characteristics remained. Among these was the tendency towards monolithic organizations into which smaller, more specialized units could be incorporated and of centralized decision-making, as evident in the activities of the government and the Histadrut.

417

However, new problems severely tested the feasibility of using these frameworks and structures in the new situation and the ability of the élite to solve the new problems which developed in Israeli society.

Often, as we have seen, the policies developed by the élite inadvertently undermined the conditions for existence and the activities of these specific organizations and questioned the élite's ability to deal with the new problems – but at the same time opened up possibilities for new developments.

Major Economic Problems

In the economic field, many difficulties developed in the transition from one economic level to another, especially from an economy in which the main emphasis was on the mobilization and investment of capital for physical expansion to an economy in which much investment has to be put into technological development.

The social and economic structures of the Yishuv were originally geared to the continuous physical expansion of both agriculture and industry and to the mobilization and investment of capital through collective and private channels.

The influx of new immigrants from societies with lower educational and technological levels and the internal dynamics of the economy, with its pressure towards higher standards of living, gave impetus to the growing differentiation and specialization in the occupational and economic sphere, resulting in the establishment of new enterprises and in the continuous physical expansion of the economy, according to the existing pattern and framework.

Within this framework the partial social security provided by the Histadrut, provided important facilities for initial absorption of immigrant manpower, both in agriculture and in industry, to a degree probably unparalleled in most other developing countries.

But these policies were not enough to ensure the attainment of new levels of economic and technological development, and the ability of the élite to deal with continuous economic development and differentiation was severely tested.

Problems and difficulties developed on two levels. On the central political level, they became evident in the attempts made by the government to maintain its overall control of major processes of growth and development, while at the same time attempting to use all available entrepreneurial groups in order to assure the physical expansion of the economy.

This gave rise to the paradoxical development of a strong upsurge of speculation both in the private and public sectors, and the consequent attempts by the élite to control the symptoms (such as conspicuous consumption), though not the deeper causes of such speculation. It also created great difficulties in curbing growing consumption and in putting Israeli economy on a technological level which could compete in the international market.

On the more sectorial level the main impediments to structural trans-formation were rooted in the conservatism of many of the trade unions which, being somewhat similar to those in England, did not have the flexibility of the Swedish unions. This conservatism constituted an obstacle to the mobility of labour and to progress towards higher levels of technical and professional competence.

Similarly the policies of the government tended to discourage the develop-ment of relatively new types of enterpreneurs not dependent on the protection in the local market given to them by government subsidies and customs policy and of a higher level of economic specialization.

Here also many developments connected with the highly politicized electorate which developed continuous pressures for growing consumption gave rise to possible waste of resources needed for economic development.

In contrast to the older non-specialized roles which claimed to be the only legitimate bearers of such wider orientations, it became vital in all these spheres to find new or differentiated, occupational roles, and to find ways of how to connect the more technical aspects of such roles with wider collective and value orientations.

Here also, the problem of the adequacy of the educational system in providing for the needs of a variegated social structure and for higher technical development became very acute.

As in other countries with a strong tradition of humanistic, élitist education, a homogeneous educational system tended to develop, offering a pre-dominantly humanistic education with relatively little variety. This created some rigidity with regard to technological and professional orientation and accentuated the necessity of finding ways of combining general, broad cultural values with more specialized tasks, rejecting both a rigid adherence to the general orientation of the preceding period and an indiscriminate system geared only to the changing, specialized technical needs.

Reinforced by the over-emphasis on public service and the expansion of academic educational facilities, this trend could contribute to the rigidity of the educational system, to the growing bottlenecks within it, and to the possible lowering of general standards of education.

However, it also helped to crystallize the more dynamic possibilities of development, of establishment of new centres of potential creativity, especially in the cultural, scientific, professional, and technological spheres.

Major Changes and Problems in Social Organization

Similar problems and dilemmas arose also in the broader sphere of social organization and stratification. Growing differentiation fundamentally

419

changed the Israeli social organization, destroying the relative equality of different occupational positions and disturbing the homogeneity of status. It also changed the bases of accessibility to various new – and especially higher – occupational positions and created new cleavages and tensions around these avenues of access.

As in most other countries, the increased importance of educational achievements underlined the problems of differential access to educational facilities and institutions.

The establishment of compulsory general state education led to the absorption of strata groups which did not share the social orientations of the originators of the system. At this stage the educational system became an important instrument of occupational selection.

In Israel the most crucial aspect of these problems was the 'ethnic' one, i.e. the problem of the so-called Oriental groups.

In all the spheres of social organization the problem of the possible cleavage between the new Oriental groups and the European old timers became very important. This is evident mostly in the fact that the Oriental groups tended to become concentrated in the lower occupational and educational echelons. Both the economic and the educational systems, while very successful in the initial stages of absorption were very much less successful in transforming themselves in ways that would cut across this distinction and create new levels of specialization and new frameworks and organizations that could be common to old and new Orientals and Europeans alike.

With the possibility of perpetuating their deprivation through continued failure in the educational sphere, a feeling of frustration developed among these groups – not least among their more successful middle echelons.

This problem was to some extent similar to the problem of adjusting traditional groups in other developing societies to modern educational and occupational tasks. However, the acuteness of this problem in Israel was accentuated by the high initial success (as compared with other under-developed or immigrant communities) in absorbing traditional groups into modern surroundings and by the society's overall commitment to their full integration and to the creation of one common nationhood.

The search for solutions to these problems developed, as in other societies, in two different directions – towards increasing flexibility and growth in the social and economic structures on the one hand and towards insoluble tensions and stagnation on the other.

The more growth conducive policies were connected with the development of new specialized and universalistically oriented and organized social, educational, and economic enterprises and frameworks which tended to cut across the different social and ethnic groups. The more stagnant possibilities were connected with the perpetuation of existing frameworks within which the differences between these groups became more pronounced and with the concomitant symbolization of these differences. These in turn gave rise to attempts to overcome these problems not by helping the relatively deprived groups to obtain the qualities needed for achievement in various (old or new) universalistic frameworks but mainly by making membership in various particularistic sectors of the society – political, ethnic or religious – the major criteria of access to different positions and to the emoluments attached to them.

Repercussions on Values and Ideologies and the Continuity of Israel's Identity

All these problems indicative as they were of the ability of Israeli society to deal with the extension of its periphery and with the problems of a new stage of development or modernization, were very closely connected with the transformation of the pioneer image.

This image combined, as we have seen, both asceticism and this-worldliness, together with some broader, potentially transcendental qualities which went beyond any concrete situation and setting. However, it also contained other more stagnative orientations. In this it was not unlike the ideological and religious orientations connected with the famous Protestant Ethic, as well as many other ideological orientations of modern or modernizing countries.

Here also, as in many of these cases, the initial ideology evinced strong totalistic and restrictive orientations which – as in the case of the Protestant Ethic – were initially minimized and transformed through the institutionalization of the religious or pioneering groups within the wider social setting.

But here, as in other cases, the more restrictive and stagnative orientations could reappear or become reinforced in later stages of development – especially when they became embedded in various institutional structures which tended to become foci of vested interests and which tended to restrict and impede the adequate perception of new problems.

As the initial phase of the Yishuv's modernization developed a strong ideological emphasis, this transformation was largely concerned with the transition from predominantly ideological goals to more concrete, varied, and realistic goals, while yet maintaining commitments to broader values and to collective responsibilities.

Thus, in this context, the continuity of Israel's growth centered round the transformation of the image of the pioneer and of the initial symbols of its collective identity.

Many attempts were made to redefine the concrete elements of this pioneering image. Claims made by the various groups that specific new tasks and activities contained certain elements of the collective commitments of the pioneer are significant as attempts to maintain such commitments in the new setting, even though such claims continuously contributed to changing the image of the pioneer and to making it more diffuse.

At the same time there developed the possibility of the expansion of amorphous mass culture, and the possible resurgence of so-called Levantinism and provincialism could greatly weaken the wider cultural and social horizons and erode their institutional bases and nuclei. This could become evident in diminishing orientations towards other centres of culture in the West, in losing contact with other Jewish communities and, accordingly, in increasing the narrow provincial identity and growth of purely instrumental orientations to collective commitments.

A similar range of dilemmas and problems developed around the symbols of collective identity with regard to the possibility of the absorption by the central symbolic sphere of the society of new elements, traditions, and orientations. Here several areas of potential conflict developed which could easily become very disruptive.

The first of these was in the sphere of secular-religious relations. The conflict in this sphere has lately intensified and the growing militancy of the religious groups may well restrict the flexibility of the collective identity and its ability to deal with modern problems. Another was the conflict between over-emphasis on ideology on the one hand, and a more flexible commitment to broader values on the other.

A third area of conflict was that in the 'ethnic' sphere, in the possibility of the development of 'Two Nations', the intensification and symbolization of the cleavage between Orientals and Europeans, and in the development of this cleavage as a major divisive element in the sphere of central social, political, and cultural symbols.

Against these constricting and conflict-ridden possibilities we also find the continuous expansion and recrystallization of the Israeli collective image, its ability to incorporate many new ethnic, traditional and modern (technical and professional) elements, and to adjust the centres of its creativity to new problems and changing situations.

Summary

In the preceding pages we have briefly summarized some of the major problems which Israeli society faces at this stage of its development, their historical and sociological roots as well as the different directions in which solutions to them are being attempted.

All these varied problems tend to converge into the central problem of whether Israeli society will be capable of maintaining some of its major premises and especially of combining the maintenance of a self-supporting modern Jewish society together with the development of social and cultural creativity which has some significance beyond its own confines.

We have seen that many of the problems are largely due to a convergence of expectations and demands for creativity on the one hand and the conditions of development in a small new country with limited population and resources on the other hand.

As we have seen, this society perceived itself as a 'centre' which has its 'periphery' to a large extent outside itself. Although the establishment of the state helped to develop a growing 'natural' internal differentiation between centre and periphery, Israeli society continuously attempted to maintain its 'central' and 'élitist' characteristics and the concomitant specialized institutional arrangements that emphasize its commitments to the creation of a cultural and social order of wider significance.

However, these orientations inevitably face the problems created by the growth of a modern but small society – the smallness of its population may limit the ability to develop differentiated specialized roles and activities and the means by which such roles and activities could be maintained.

This problem has become even more acute with the mass immigration since 1948 which brought in its wake not only a wider but also a different kind of periphery – namely, many groups from relatively lower educational and technical levels of the society. These pressures are manifest in the development of various particularistic orientations and organizations.

These particularistic trends seem to have developed from three roots: The first was the traditional, closed, Jewish-European society from which the veteran half of the population came, and many of whose characteristics could have become perpetuated in the setting of Palestine once their original revolutionary fervour abated and the revolutionary ideology became more and more routinized and institutionalized. Second were the parallel particularistic orientations of the new immigrants which became transformed in the new setting into new types of demands for political and social participation and for economic rewards based on particularistic criteria. But particularistic tendencies could also, thirdly, have developed from the basically élitist orientations of the pioneering groups themselves – rooted as they were in small sects and social movements which could easily become transformed into relatively narrow interest groups and organizations attempting to claim for themselves the right to be the sole bearers of the 'pioneering', social and cultural creativity inherent in the Zionist ideology.

All these tendencies could, of course, become easily reinforced by the smallness of the country and its population and by the attempts to create within it a 'normal' modern economic structure with a differentiated role-structure.

But these new developments could also serve as starting points for new directions of creativity, challenging the existing centre to find, together with the new groups, new ways of creating various nuclei of social and cultural creativity with broader universalistic orientations and attempting to

423

continue to overcome the various limitations inherent in its background and in its setting.

As, due to lack of appropriate social traditions and environmental conditions, it seems doubtful whether Israeli society can develop as a normal small or medium-sized modern country, these problems become even more important and crucial for its future. Israeli society faces now in all its sharpness the dilemma either of declining to a local stagnant structure, lacking both internal and external forces of attraction, or of overcoming this possible stagnation by finding new ways of developing social and cultural creativity which has some significance beyond its own confines.

Beyond this, there looms the more fundamental question of the extent to which it will be possible for a social and cultural tradition which maintained strong orientations to such broader social and cultural creativity throughout its history to maintain them under new conditions. As we have seen, such orientations were maintained by this society both when it was an oppressed or segregated minority in a traditional-religious society and when its members began to enter into the various fields of the majority society or societies when these became modernized. The problem which it faces now, and which constitutes its greatest challenge, is whether it will be able to preserve and develop such orientations now that it has not only ceased to be embedded in a situation of a minority but became also transposed into an autonomous modern society, which has to develop its institutional frameworks and organizations within the confines of a relatively small country.

Selected Bibliography

I. Basic General Data

BENTWICH, N. *Israel*, New York, E. Benn, 1952.

Central Bureau of Statistics. *Statistical Abstract of Israel*, Jerusalem, 1949–66, Nos. 1–17.

'Eretz Israel', *Encyclopedia Hebraica* (Hebrew), Tel Aviv, Massada, 1957, Vol. 6.

Jewish Agency for Palestine. *Statistical Handbook of Jewish Palestine, 1947*, Jerusalem, Jewish Agency, 1947.

Ministry of Foreign Affairs Information Department. *Facts About Israel*, Jerusalem, 1963.

SAFRAN, N. *The U.S. and Israel*, Cambridge, Mass., Harvard University Press, 1963.

II. Historical Development and Institutional Structure of the Yishuv

A. GENERAL

ATTIAS, M. *Knesset Israel in Eretz Israel* (Hebrew), Jerusalem, Information Department of Va'ad HaLeumi (National Commission), 1944.

BEIN, A. *The Return to the Soil* Jerusalem, The Jewish Agency, 1954.

BRESLAVSKI, M. *The Jewish Workers' Movement in Palestine* (Hebrew), Tel Aviv, Hakibbutz Hameuchad, 1959–63, Vols. 1–4.

CHABAS, B. and SHOCHET, A., eds. *The Second Aliya* (Hebrew), Tel Aviv, Am Oved, 1947.

EREZ, V. (ed.). *The Third Aliya* (Hebrew), Tel Aviv, Am Oved, 1964.

JOSEPH, B. *British Rule in Palestine*, Washington, Public Affairs Press, 1948.

KATZNELSON, B. *Collected Works* (Hebrew), Tel Aviv, Mapai, 1949, Vol. 11.

Peel Commission. *Palestine Royal Commission Report*, London, 1937.

POLAK, A. *The Jewish Community at the End of the Second World War* (Hebrew), Merhavia, Sifriat Poalim, 1946.

ROSENSTEIN, Z. *History of the Workers' Movement in Palestine* (Hebrew), Tel Aviv, Am Oved, 1956, Vol. I; 1966, Vols. II, III.

RUPPIN, A. *Thirty Years of Building the Country*, Jerusalem, Shocken, 1937.

B. BASIC STATISTICAL MATERIAL ON THE YISHUV PERIOD

Government of Palestine, Office of Statistics. *Statistical Abstract of Palestine*, Jerusalem, 1937–43.

GUREVITCH, D. *Statistic Book of Eretz Israel* (Hebrew), Jerusalem, The Jewish Agency, 1930.

C. SPECIFIC HISTORICAL SUBJECTS

ARLOZOROV, CH. *Jerusalem Diary* (Hebrew), Tel Aviv, Mapai, 1949.

ATTIAS, M. (ed.). *Havaad Haleumi Book of Documents: 1915–1948* (Hebrew), Jerusalem, 1949.

BANAI, J. *Unknown Soldiers: 'Lehi' Operations* (Hebrew), edited by Y. Elddad, Tel Aviv, Hug-Yedidim, 1957–8.

BEN-GURION, D. *Bama'aracha* (Hebrew), Tel Aviv, Ayanot, 1950.

DINUR, B. *et al* (ed.), *The Haganah History Book* (Hebrew), The Zionist Library and Maarchot, 1954, 1963 (four volumes published to date).

GILAD, Z. (ed.), *Book of the Palmach* (Hebrew), Tel Aviv, Hakibbutz Hameuchad, 1953.

GOLOMB, E., *Defense 'Hidden Strength'* (Hebrew), Tel Aviv, Mapai, 1950.

NIV, D. *Battles of the Irgun* (*National Military Organization*) (Hebrew), Tel Aviv, Klausner Centre, 1965.

SHOCHAT, A. and STORER, H. (eds.). *Chapters on Hapoel Hatzair* (Hebrew), Tel Aviv, Tiversky, 1935–9 (13 volumes).

ZEMACH, S. *In the Beginning* (Hebrew), Tel Aviv, Am Oved, 1946.

D. GENERAL DISCUSSIONS OF THE MAJOR ISSUES IN THE YISHUV PERIOD

ARLOZOROV, CH. *The Class War in Palestinian Reality* (Hebrew), Selected Writings of Arlozorov, Tel Aviv, The Zionist Library and Ayanot, 1959.

BEN-GURION, D. *From Class to Nation* (Hebrew), Tel Aviv, Ayanot, 1956.

MERHAVIA, H. (ed.), *The People and the National Home* (Hebrew), Jerusalem, Halevi Press, 1949.

OPHIR, J. *The National-Worker Book. History of the National Workers' Movement in Palestine* (Hebrew), Tel Aviv, The General Labour Organization Executive Committee, 1958–9.

III. The Establishment of the State

A. THE HISTORICAL SETTING OF THE ESTABLISHMENT OF THE STATE OF ISRAEL

DUNNER, J. *The Republic of Israel, its History and its Promise*, New York, Whittlesey House, 1950.

LEHRMAN, H. *Israel*, New York, Sloane, 1951.

SACHER, H. *Israel: The Establishment of a State*, London, Weidenfeld, 1952.

WEINGROD, A. *Israel*, London, Pall Mall, 1965.

B. THE MAJOR TRENDS OF DEMOGRAPHIC CHANGE

BACCHI, R. 'The Demographic Development of Israel' (Hebrew), *Rivaon Lekalkala*, Vol. III, No. 8, 1955.

Central Bureau of Statistics. *The Jewish Population, 1949–1953*, Jerusalem, 1953. (Special Publication No. 37.)

—— *Statistical Abstract of Israel*, Jerusalem, 1949–65, Nos. 1–16.

MATRAS, J. *Social Change in Israel*, Chicago, Aldine Publishing, 1965.

SIKRON, M. 'Demographic Structure of the Israeli Population', *Megamot*, Vol. 7, No. 2, April 1955.

—— *The Immigration to Israel, 1948–1953*, Jerusalem, Falk Institute and Central Bureau of Statistics, 1957.

C. THE MAJOR INSTITUTIONAL CHANGES IN THE TRANSITION FROM THE YISHUV TO THE STATEHOOD

EISENSTADT, S. N. 'The Social Structure of Israel', in A. Ross (ed.), *The Institutions of Advanced Societies*, Minneapolis, University of Minnesota Press, 1958.

EISENSTADT, S. N., ADLER, H., BAR-YOSEF, R. and KAHANE, R. *The Social Structure of Israel* (Hebrew), Jerusalem, Akademon, 1966.

IV. Economic Structure

A. ECONOMIC DEVELOPMENTS IN THE PERIOD OF THE YISHUV

HOROWITZ, D. *The Palestine Economy in its Development* (Hebrew), Jerusalem, Bialik Institute, 1948.

HOVNE, A. *The Labor Force in Israel*, Jerusalem, Falk Project, 1961.

B. THE DEVELOPMENT OF THE WORKERS' SECTOR

BREIMAN, S. 'The General Labour Organization of Hebrew Workers' (Hebrew), *Encyclopedia Hebraica*, Tel Aviv, Massada, 1962, Vol. 15.

DAN, H. *On an Unpaved Road: The Legend of Solel Boneh* (Hebrew), Jerusalem, Shubin Press, 1963.

General Labour Organization, the Executive Committee, *The Labour Economy: 1959–1962* (Hebrew), Tel Aviv, The Institute for Economic and Social Research, 1963.

MINTZNER, G. *The Economic Structure of the General Labour Organization* (Hebrew), Tel Aviv, General Labour Organization, 1942.

NAPHTALI, P. *Workers' Society* (Hebrew), Tel Aviv, Public Relations Committee, 1956.

Workers' Council of Haifa, *The General Labour Organization in Haifa until 1945* (Hebrew), Haifa, 1945.

ZIDROVITCH, G. *The Workers' Economy in Israel* (Hebrew), Tel Aviv, Am Oved, 1954.

C. MAJOR TRENDS OF ECONOMIC DEVELOPMENT IN ISRAEL

Bank of Israel. *Bank of Israel Report*, Jerusalem, 1955–65.

—— *Economic Development in Israel* (Hebrew), Jerusalem, 1960–4.

Central Bureau of Statistics. *The Israeli Economic Scene* (Monthly).

—— *The Labour Force in Israel: Publications of the 1961 Population and Dwelling Census*, Jerusalem, 1964, Part I.

—— *The National Income and Expenditure of Israel, 1950–1952*, Jerusalem, 1964. (Series of Special Publications, publication No. 153.)

EISENSTADT, S. N. *Essays on Sociological Aspects of Political and Economic Development*, The Hague, Mouton and Co., 1961.

—— 'Israel: Traditional and Modern Social Values and Economic Development', *Annals of American Academy of Political and Social Sciences*, Philadelphia American Academy of Political and Social Sciences, 1956.

GAATON, A. L. 'Economic Growth in Israel in the Years 1948–1962' (Hebrew), *Riveon Lekalkala*, Vol. II, Nos. 41–42, 1964.

HALEVI, N. *Estimates of Israel's International Transactions*, Jerusalem, Falk Project, 1956.

HALEVI, N. and KLINOV-MALUL, R. *The Development of Israeli Economy*, Jerusalem, Bank of Israel Advisory Council for the Israel Economic and Sociological Research Project in co-operation with the Histadrut Institute, Basle, 1965.

HORVITZ, D. *Economic Theory and Economic Policy in Israel* (Hebrew), Tel Aviv, Am Oved, 1958.

—— *The Economy of Israel* (Hebrew), Tel Aviv, Massada, 1954.

—— 'At the End of the Second Decade' (Hebrew), *Riveon Lekalkala*, Vol. 5, No. 19, 1957–8.

—— *Structure and Trend in Israel Economy* (Hebrew), Tel Aviv, Massada, 1964.

LUBELL, H. *Israel's National Expenditure, 1950–1954*, Jerusalem, Falk Project, 1958.

OLITZKI, Y. (ed.), *Histadrut Yearbook* (Hebrew), Tel Aviv, The General Labour Organization, Executive Committee, 1962–3, 1963–4 and 1964–5.

PATINKIN, D. *Israeli Economy in the First Decade* (English and Hebrew), Jerusalem, Falk Project, 1957–8. (Report No. 14.)

RUBNER, A. 'Problems of Israel's Economy', *Commentary*, Vol. 26, No. 3, 1958.

ZWEIG, F. 'The Jewish Trade Union Movement in Israel', *Jewish Journal of Sociology*, Vol. 1, 1959.

D. MANPOWER PROBLEMS

BEN-BARUCH, Y. *Changes in the Input of Manpower Quality in Israel*, Jerusalem, Bank of Israel Survey, 1966.

HOROWITZ, U. and BONNÉ, M. *Development of Manpower in the Natural Sciences and Technology in Israel* (Hebrew), Jerusalem, The National Council for Research and Development, 1964.

KLINOV-MALUL, R. *The Profit from Investment in Education*, Jerusalem, Falk Project, 1966.

Ministry of Labour, Manpower Planning Authority. *Manpower in Israel*, Jerusalem, 1964–5, (Annual Report.)

—— *Manpower Forecast. The Supply for the Years 1964–1969*, Jerusalem, 1964.

—— *Manpower Forecast, Supply and Demand and Suggestions for a Balance from 1964–1969*, Jerusalem, 1964.

E. Agricultural Development in Israel

Ben-David, J. (ed.). *Agricultural Planning and Village Community in Israel*, Paris, UNESCO, 1964. (Arid Zone Research Report XXIII.)

Eisenstadt, S. N. 'Institutional and Social Aspects of Agriculture', paper on development and modernization prepared for Rehovot Conference on Comprehensive Planning of Agriculture in Developing Countries, August 1963 (mimeogr.)

Mundlack, Y. *Supply and Demand for Agricultural Products in Israel*, Jerusalem, Falk Project, 1964.

Weintraub, D. and Lissak, M. *Some Social Aspects of Agricultural Settlement in Israel*, A Research Report, Jerusalem, Department of Sociology, The Hebrew University, 1960.

Weintraub, D., Yuchtman, E. and Weihl, H. *Report on the Role of the Agricultural Producer in Cooperative Settlements*, A Research Report, Jerusalem, Department of Sociology, The Hebrew University, 1962 (mimeogr.).

Weitz, R. 'A Change of Values in Our Agriculture' (Hebrew), *Molad*, Vol. 21, Nos. 177–178, May-June 1963.

Weitz, R. and Rokach, A. *Forecast and Guidance of Agriculture and Settlement in Israel* (Hebrew), Rehovoth, The National and University Institute of Agriculture, 1962.

F. Economic Absorption of Immigrants

Bar-Yosef, R. 'Adaptation of New Immigrants to Factory Work' (Hebrew), *Histadrut Yearbook 1965–1966*, Tel Aviv, 1966, Vol. II.

—— 'Dimona – The Adaptation of Migrant Workers to Industry', *Proceedings of the International Seminar on Migrant Workers in the Industry*, Wiesbaden, OECO, 1963.

Cohen, E. *The Ecological Structure of a Development Town* (Hebrew), A Research Report, Jerusalem, Department of Sociology, The Hebrew University, 1960 (mimeogr.)

—— *Municipal Committees in Development Towns* (Hebrew), Jerusalem, Department of Sociology, The Hebrew University and the Public Committee on Community Development, 1962 (mimeogr.).

—— 'On the Problem of Social Policy in the Planning of the New Urban Settlement in Israel' (Hebrew), *Molad*, Vol. XXII, Nos. 195–196, 1964.

Eisenstadt, S. N. 'Traditional and Modern Social Values and Economic Development', *Annals of American Academy of Political and Social Sciences*, Philadelphia, American Academy of Political and Social Sciences, 1956.

Shuval, J. *Immigrants on the Threshold*, Chicago, Atherton Press, 1963.

—— 'Occupational Interests and Parental Pressures' (Hebrew), *Megamot*, Vol. 13, No. 1, 1964.

—— 'Occupational Interests and Sex Role Congruence', *Human Relations*, Vol. XVI, No. 2, 1963.

V. Social Organization and Stratification

A. General Trends in the Development of Stratification in Israel

Antonovsky, A. 'Ideology and Class in Israel' (Hebrew), *Ammot*, Vol. 2, No. 7, 1963.

—— 'Wishes and Anxieties in Israel' (Hebrew), *Ammot*, Vol. 2, No. 9, 1963.

Bar-Yosef, R. and Padan, D. 'The Oriental Communities in the Class Structure of Israel' (Hebrew), *Molad*, Vol. XXII, Nos. 195–196, 1964.

Cohen, E. *Emigration from Israel* (Hebrew), A Research Report, Jerusalem, Department of Sociology, The Hebrew University, 1959 (mimeogr.)

—— *Economic Gap, Economic Equality and Standard of Living* (Hebrew), Tel Aviv, The General Workers' Organization, Executive Committee, 1963.

Eisenstadt, S. N. 'The Oriental Jews in Israel', *Jewish Social Studies*, Vol. XII, 1950.

—— 'The Social Conditions of Voluntary Associations', Scripta Hierosolomytana, Vol. III, 1956.

—— 'Sociological Aspects of the Economic Adaptation of Oriental Immigrants in Israel: A Case of Study in the Process of Modernization', *Economic Development and Cultural Change*, Vol. IV, No. 3, 1956.

Epstein, S. 'On Social Stratification in Israel' (Hebrew), *Tmurot*, 1962.

Frankenstein, D., Simon, A. E., Rottenstreich, N., Groll, M. and Ben-David, J. 'Discussion on the Problem of Ethnic Differences' (Hebrew), *Megamot*, Vols. II and III, Nos. 3 and 4. (Summary of discussion in *Megamot*, 1951, 1952).

Hanoch, G. *Income Differentials in Israel*, Jerusalem, The Falk Project, 1959–60, Report No. 5.

Matras, J. 'Some Data on Intergenerational Occupational Mobility in Israel', *Population Studies*, XVIII, No. 2, 1963.

Ministry of Labour, Department of Work Relations. *Survey on Work Relations and Department Activities, 1964–1965*, Jerusalem, Ministry of Labour, Department of Work Relations, 1965.

——, Manpower Planning Authority. *Change in Occupational Structure*, Jerusalem, 1965.

Yoseftal, G. *Life and Works* (Hebrew), edited by Sh. Wurm, Tel Aviv, Mapai Press, 1963.

Zloczower, A. 'Mobility Patterns and Status Conceptions in the Urban Israeli Setting' (Hebrew), Unpublished Ph.D. Thesis, Jerusalem, The Hebrew University, (draft) 1967.

B. Developments in the Kibbutzim

Bar-Yosef, R. 'The Pattern of Early Socialization in the Collective Settlements in Israel', *Human Relations*, Vol. XII, No. 4, 1959.

Cohen, E. *Allocation of Consumer Goods in the Kibbutz* (Hebrew), Jerusalem, Department of Sociology, The Hebrew University, A Research Report, 1960 (mimeogr.).

COHEN, E. 'Changes in the Social Structure of Work in the Kibbutz' (Hebrew), *Riveon Lekalkala*, Vol. X, No. 4, 1963.

—— 'Cohesion of Work Groups in the Kibbutz Haartzi, *Hedim*, Vols. 26–27, No. 70, 1962.

—— *The Division of Labour in the Kibbutzim*, A Research Report, Jerusalem, Department of Sociology, The Hebrew University, 1956 (mimeogr.).

—— 'Forms of Institutionalization' (Hebrew), *Niv Hakevutza*, Vol. VII, No. 3, 1958.

—— 'Meetings of Branch Workers in Kibbutzim' (Hebrew), *Hedim*, Vol. 28, No. 75, 1963.

—— *The Social Structure of the Work Process in Kibbutzim of Hashomer Hatzair* (Hebrew), A Research Report, Jerusalem, Department of Sociology, The Hebrew University, Extension Service of the Ministry of Agriculture and Federation of Hashomer Hatzair, forthcoming (mimeogr.).

—— *Survey of Public Activity in the Religious Kibbutz Movement* (Hebrew), Jerusalem, The Department of Sociology, The Hebrew University and the Religious Kibbutz Movement, 1964 (mimeogr.).

COHEN, E. and LEIHMAN, E. 'Attitude to Hired Labour in Kibbutzim of Hashomer Hatzair' (Hebrew), *Hedim*, Vol. 29, No. 77, 1964.

ETZIONI, A. 'The Organizational Structure of the Kibbutz' (Hebrew), Part A, *Niv Hakevutza*, Vol. 6, No. 3, 1957; Part B, *Niv Hakevutza*, Vol. 6, No. 4, 1957.

—— 'Solidarity Work Group in Collective Settlements', *Human Organization*, Vol. 16, No. 3, 1958.

ORLEAN, CH. *The Religious Kibbutz and Its Development* (Hebrew), Tel Aviv, Hakibbutz Hadati, 1946.

PERES, J. 'General Assembly of Members in the Kvutza' (Hebrew), *Ovnaim*, No. 3, 1962.

SARELL, M. 'Conservatism and Change in the Second Generation in the Kibbutzim' (Hebrew), *Megamot*, Vol. 1, No. 2, 1961.

—— *The Second Generation in Israel's Collective Settlements* (Hebrew), Jerusalem, Department of Sociology, The Hebrew University, 1959 (mimeogr.).

TALMON-GARBER, Y. 'Differentiation in Collective Settlements', *Scripta Hierosolymitana*, Vol. 3, 1955.

—— 'The Family in Collective Settlements', *Transactions of the Fifth World Congress of Sociology*, Vol. IV, 1962.

—— 'The Family and Occupational Placement of the Second Generation in Collective Settlements' (Hebrew), *Megamot*, Vol. VIII, No. 4, 1957.

—— 'The Family in a Revolutionary Movement', in M. Nimkoff (ed.), *Comparative Family Systems*, New York, Houghton, Mifflin & Co., 1965.

—— 'Parent-Child Relationship in the Collective Settlement' (Hebrew), *Niv Hakevutza*, Vol. VIII, No. 1, 1959.

—— *Sex-Role Differentiation in an Equalitarian Society*, Jerusalem, Department of Sociology, The Hebrew University, 1959 (mimeogr.).

—— *The Sleeping Arrangements for Children of the Kibbutz* (Hebrew), A Research Report, Jerusalem, Department of Sociology, The Hebrew University, 1956 (mimeogr.).

TALMON-GARBER, Y. and COHEN, E. 'Collective Settlements in the Negev', in

Ben-David, J. (ed.), *Agricultural Planning and Village Community in Israel*, Paris, UNESCO, 1964.

TALMON-GARBER, Y. and STUP, Z. 'Secular Asceticism: Patterns of Ideological Reformulation' (Hebrew), in Sh. Wurm (ed.), *Sefer Busel*, Tel Aviv, Tarbut VeHinuch, 1960.

C. DEVELOPMENTS IN THE MOSHAVIM

ABRAMOV, S. Z. 'Workers' Moshavim – The History of a Social Idea' (Hebrew), *Ammot*, Vol. II, No. 7, 1963.

ASAF, A. *The Workers' Moshavim in Israel* (Hebrew), Tel Aviv, Ayanot and Tenuat Hamoshavim, 1954.

EISENSTADT, S. N. *Essays on Sociological Aspects of Political and Economic Development*, The Hague, Mouton Publications, 1961, Part II.

KOREN, J. *Ingathering of the Exiles and Their Settlement: History of Immigrants' Moshavim in Israel* (Hebrew), Tel Aviv, Am Oved, 1964.

—— *The Path of the Moshav Movement* (Hebrew), Tel Aviv, The General Labour Organization, 1957.

LISSAK, M. *Immigrants' Moshavim in Crisis and Foundation* (Hebrew), A Research Report, Jerusalem, The Kaplan School of Economics and Social Science, The Hebrew University, 1956.

WEINGROD, A. 'Change and Continuity in a Village of Moroccan Immigrants' (Hebrew), *Megamot*, Vol. 10, No. 4, 1960.

WEINTRAUB, D. 'Problems of Absorption and Integration in Immigrants' Moshavim' (Hebrew), *Megamot*, Vol. 5, No. 3, 1953–4.

—— *Social Change in New Immigrants' Smallholders' Co-operative Settlements in Israel*, A Preliminary Research Report, Jerusalem, Development of Sociology, The Hebrew University, 1963 (mimeogr.).

—— 'A Study of New Farmers in Israel', *Sociologia Ruralis*, Vol. IV, No. 2, 1954.

WEINTRAUB, D. and LISSAK, M. 'Problems of Absorption of North African Immigrants in Smallholders' Collective Settlements in Israel', *Jewish Journal of Sociology*, Vol. II, No. 3, 1961.

WEITZ, R. 'Seven Years of New Settling' (Hebrew), *Riveon Lekalkala*, No. 11, Vol. III, 1955–6.

WILLNER, D. 'On Home Industry in Immigrants' Moshavim' (Hebrew), *Megamot*, Vol. 7, No. 3, 1956.

D. DEVELOPMENTS IN THE PROFESSIONS

ADAR, L. 'Attitudes Related to Status Sensitivity among Teachers in Israel' (Hebrew), *Megamot*, Vol. 12, No. 2, 1962.

BEN-DAVID, J. 'Professions and Social Structure in Israel', *Scripta Hierosolymitana*, Vol. III, 1959.

—— 'Social Status of the Israeli Teacher' (Hebrew), *Megamot*, Vol. VIII, No. 2, 1957.

MUHSAM, H. V. *The Supply of Professional Manpower from Israel's Educational System*, Jerusalem, Falk Project, 1959.
The Academic Worker (Hebrew), Tel Aviv, Havaad Hapoel, The Department of Academic Workers, 1956.

E. OCCUPATIONAL SELECTION AND MOBILITY

ADLER, C. 'The Role of Israel's School System in Elite Formation', *Transactions of the Fifth World Congress of Sociology*, 1962 (mimeogr.).
LISSAK, M. *Tendencies in Occupational Choice – Israeli Urban Youth*, Ph.D. Dissertation, Hebrew University, 1961.

F. THE DEVELOPMENT OF STYLES OF LIFE AND CONSUMPTION PATTERNS IN ISRAEL SOCIETY

Bank of Israel Survey. *The Order of Acquiring Durable Goods*, Jerusalem, 1963 (Survey No. 20).
LANDSBERGER, M. *Changes in the Consumption Habits in Israel 1956–7 – 1959–60*, Jerusalem, Bank of Israel Survey, 1964 (Survey No. 23).
LEVIATHAN, N. *Consumption Patterns in Israel*, Jerusalem, Falk Project, 1964.

G. IMMIGRATION AND ABSORPTION OF IMMIGRANTS AND THE RELATIONSHIP BETWEEN ETHNIC GROUPS

ABBAS, A. 'Between Diffusion and Ingathering of Exiles' (Hebrew), *Shevet Veam*, June 1958.
BAR-YOSEF, R. 'Vadi Salib: An Analysis of the Status of the North African Immigrants in Israel' (Hebrew), *Molad*, Jerusalem, Vol. 17, No. 131, 1959.
BERGER, L. 'Dialectics of Immigration and Absorption', *The Israel Year Book*, Jerusalem, Israel Year Book Publications, 1966.
COHEN, E., SHAMGAR, L. and LEVY, Y. *Absorption of Immigrants in a Development Town*, A Final Research Report, Jerusalem, Department of Sociology, The Hebrew University, 1962 (mimeogr.) (two volumes).
DULZIN, L. 'New Epoch of Immigration and Absorption', *The Israel Year Book*, Jerusalem, Israel Year Book Publications, 1966.
EISENSTADT, S. N. *The Absorption of Immigrants*, London, Routledge and Kegan Paul, 1954; Glencoe, III, The Free Press, 1955.
—— 'Communication Processes Among Immigrants in Israel', *Public Opinion Quarterly*, Vol. 16, No. 1, 1952.
—— 'Conditions of Communicative Receptivity', *Public Opinion Quarterly*, Vol. 17, No. 3, 1953.
—— 'Problems of Leadership Among Immigrants' (Hebrew), *Megamot*, Vol. IJ, No. 2, 1953.
—— 'Studies in Reference Group Behaviour, Reference Norms and the Social Structure', *Human Relations*, Vol. 7, No. 2, 1954.

FRANKENSTEIN, C. *Between Past and Future: Essays and Studies on Aspects of Immigrants' Absorption in Israel*, Jerusalem, Szold Institute, 1953.

KATZ, E. and EISENSTADT, S. N. 'Observations on the Response of Israeli Organizations to New Immigrants', *Administrative Science Quarterly*, Vol. V, No. 1, 1960.

LISSAK, M. *The Ethnic Factor in Immigrants' Moshavim* (Hebrew), Jerusalem, Ministry of Education and Culture, 1959 (Pamphlet on oriental communities in Israeli society).

PATAI, R. *Israel Between East and West*, Philadelphia, Jewish Publication Society of America, 1957.

ROSENFELD, H. 'The Immigrants' Town Kiryat Shmoneh' (Hebrew), *Mibifnim*, Vol. 13, No. 4, 1947–9.

SHUMSKY, A. *The Clash of Cultures in Israel*, New York, Columbia University, 1955.

SHUVAL, J. 'Cultural Assimilation and Tension in Israel', *International Social Science Bulletin*, Vol. 8, No. 1, 1956.

—— *Immigrants on the Threshold*, New York, Atherton Press, 1963.

—— 'The Role of Ideology as a Predisposing Frame of Reference for Immigrants', *Human Relations*, Vol. XII, No. 1, 1959.

—— 'Value Orientations of Immigrants to Israel', *Sociometry*, Vol. XXVI, No. 1, 1963.

WEIHL, H. *Shimon – A Yemenite Village in the Judean Hills* (Hebrew), A Research Report, Jerusalem, Department of Sociology, The Hebrew University, 1963 (mimeogr.).

WEINGROD, A. *Reluctant Pioneers*, Ithaca, Cornell University Press, 1966.

—— 'Moroccan Jewry in Transition' (Hebrew), *Megamot*, Vol. 10, No. 3, 1960.

—— *Report to the Advisory Council on Absorption Problems* (Hebrew), Jerusalem, Settlement Department, The Jewish Agency, no year (mimeogr.).

WEINTRAUB, D. 'The Influence of the Demographic Structure of the Immigrant Family on Its Adaptation to the Moshav' (Hebrew), *Megamot*, Vol. 6, No. 2, 1960.

H. SOCIAL POLICY

BARUCH, N. *Major Problems of the Development of the Social Service 1965–1970*, Jerusalem, Ministry of Social Welfare, 1964.

Central Bureau of Statistics. *Survey of Housing Conditions, 1963*, Jerusalem, 1965.

Ministry of Social Welfare, *Saad* (Hebrew), Jerusalem, 1960–6.

—— *Welfare in Israel* (Hebrew), Jerusalem, 1965.

National Insurance Institute, *Report 1954–59, 1961–62* (Hebrew), Jerusalem.

VI. *Education*

A. BASIC DATA ON THE EDUCATIONAL SYSTEM

ARAN, Z. 'Speech to the Knesset on the Budget of the Ministry' (Hebrew), *Bahinuch Uvatarbut*, Vol. 35, No. 11, 1964, and op. cit., Vol. 36, No. 12, 1965.

BENTWICH, J. *Education in the State of Israel*, London, Kegan Paul, 1965.

Central Bureau of Statistics. *Statistical Information on Education* (Hebrew), Jerusalem (Report No. 4), 1963.

EVEN, A. 'Education in Israel' (Hebrew), in *Divrai-Haknesset*, Vol. 20, pp. 1135–1442, March 12–14, 1963.

GOLAN, S. 'Collective Education in the Kibbutz', *Psychiatry, Journal for the Study of Interpersonal Processes*, Vol. 22, No. 2, May 1959.

GOLAN, S. and LEVI, J. 'Communal Education', *Ofakim*, Vol. XI, No. 4, 1957.

GREENBAUM, A. *Report to the Committee on Cultural-Religious Affairs*, Jerusalem, American Joint Distribution Committee, 1963.

MERHAVIA, H. *The Educational System in Israel* (Hebrew), Jerusalem, Achiasaff, 1957.

—— *Educational Encyclopedia* (Hebrew), Jerusalem, Bialik Institute, 1959–67 (4 volumes).

B. HIGHER EDUCATION

National Council for Research and Development. *By-yearly Report 1963–4.* The Prime Minister's Office, Jerusalem, January 1965.

PRAWER, Y. 'Secondary Education, General Education and Higher Education' (Hebrew), in J. Tverski (ed.), *Knowledge and Activity in Education* in memory of A. Arnon, Tel Aviv, Havaad Hatziburi, 1964.

Prime Minister's Office, State of Israel. *Report on Higher Education*, Jerusalem, 1965.

C. ECONOMIC ASPECTS OF THE EDUCATIONAL SYSTEM

BARUCH, J. *Investments in Education and Manpower in Israel*, Jerusalem, Bank of Israel Survey, 1964.

GREENFELD, Y. *The Measurement of Educational Capital in Israel*, Falk Project (forthcoming).

KLINOV-MALUL, R. *The Profit from Investment in Education*, Jerusalem, Falk Project, 1966.

MUHSAM, H. V., HANOCH, G. and MALUL-KLINOV, R. *The Supply of Professional Manpower from Israel's Educational System*, Jerusalem, Falk Project, 1959.

SMILANSKI, M. 'The Social Aspect of the Educational Structure in Israel' (Hebrew), *Megamot*, Vol. 8, No. 3, 1957.

D. PEDAGOGICAL PROBLEMS: A SELECTION

ADAR, L. and ADLER, C. *Education Towards Values in the Schools* (Hebrew), Jerusalem, School of Education, The Hebrew University, 1965.

ADAR, Z. 'Critique of the State Educational Program' (Hebrew), *Megamot*, Vol. 7, No. 1, 1956.

ADLER, Ch. *The Secondary School as a Selective Factor from a Social and Educational Point of View* (Hebrew), Ph.D. Dissertation, Jerusalem, The Hebrew University, 1966.

ARNON, Y. 'The Beer-Sheva Experiment' (Hebrew), *Hachinuch*, Vol. 35, No. 2, 1963.

CHEN, M. 'Statistical Bulletin on Secondary Education Choices by Primary School Graduates in Tel Aviv' (Hebrew), *Megamot*, Vol. II, No. 4, 1961.

EVEN, A. *Education in Israel* (Hebrew), Jerusalem, Ministry of Education and Culture, 1963.

SHAPIRA, M. (ed.). *Theory and Practice in Secondary Education* (Hebrew), Jerusalem, The Hebrew University, 1962.

SHMUELI, A. 'A Developmental Project' (Hebrew), *Davar*, December 5, 1963.

SIMON, A. 'The Scholastic Achievement of Immigrant Children in the Negev' (Hebrew), *Megamot*, Vol. 8, No. 4, 1957.

SMILANSKI, M. 'Proposal for Reforms in the Secondary Education Structure' (Hebrew), *Megamot*, Vol. 11, No. 4, 1961.

TEVETH, S. 'The Beginning of the End of Equality in Education' (Hebrew), *Haaretz*, May 8, 1963.

E. FAMILY STRUCTURE AND YOUTH CULTURE

ADLER, H. *Youth Movements in Israeli Society* (Hebrew), Jerusalem, Szold Foundation, 1962.

BEN-DAVID, J. 'Conforming and Deviant Images of Youth in a New Society', *Transactions of the Fifth World Congress of Sociology*, Louvain, International Sociological Association, 1962.

—— 'Youth Movement Membership and Social Status' (Hebrew), *Megamot*, Vol. 5, No. 3, 1954.

CHEN, M., SCHIFENBAUER, D. and DORON, R. 'Uniformity and Diversity in the Leisure Activities of Secondary School Students in Israel' (Hebrew), *Megamot*, Vol. 13, No. 2, 1964.

EISENSTADT, S. N. 'Youth Culture and Social Structure in Israel', *British Journal of Sociology*, Vol. 2, 1951.

EISENSTADT, S. N. and BEN-DAVID, J. 'Inter-generational Tensions in Israel', *International Soc. Sc. Bulletin*, Vol. VIII, No. 1, 1956.

KREITLER, H. and KREITLER, S. 'The Attitude of Israeli Youth Towards Social Ideals' (Hebrew), *Megamot*, Vol. 13, No. 2, 1964.

LOTAN, M. *Attitudes and Values in the Youth Movement* (Hebrew), Beit Berel, 1964.

—— *Attitudes and Values in the Youth Movement* (*Immigrants*) (Hebrew), Tel Aviv, HaNoar HaOved VeHalomed, 1966.

PERES, J. 'Statistical Bulletin on Youth Movement Membership' (Hebrew), *Megamot*, Vol. 11, No. 2, 1961.

—— 'Youth and Youth Movements in Israel', *Jewish Journal of Sociology*, Vol. V, No. 1, 1963.

F. ADOLESCENT DELINQUENCY

Central Bureau of Statistics. *Judicial Statistics*, 1963 (Special Series No. 182).

MILO, A. 'Statistical Details on Adolescent Delinquency' (Hebrew), *Megamot*, Vol. I, No. 1, 1959.

'Statistical Bulletin on Slum Areas in Jerusalem, Tel Aviv and Haifa' (Hebrew), *Megamot*, Vol. 11, No. 3, 1961.

VII. Political Structure and Institutions

A. Basic Structure of Political Institutions

AKZIN, B. *et al.* 'Governmental and Legal Arrangements in Israel' (Hebrew), *Encyclopedia Hebraica*, Tel Aviv, Massada, Vol. VI, 1957.

AKZIN, B. and DROR, Y. *National Planning in Israel*, Tel Aviv, Hamidrasha Leminhal, 1966.

Civil Service Commission, *Governmental and Legal Arrangements in Israel* (Hebrew), Jerusalem, 1953.

EISENSTADT, S. N. *Essays on the Sociological Aspects of Political and Economic Development*, The Hague, Mouton & Co., 1960.

—— 'Le passage d'une société de pionniers à une société organisée: Aspects de la sociologie politique d'Israel', *Revue Française de Science Politique*, July-September 1954.

FREUDENHEIM, Y. *The Government in the State of Israel* (Hebrew), Jerusalem, 1960, 3rd Edition.

Israel Government Year Book, Jerusalem, Government Press, 1951–66.

JANOWSKY, O. *Foundations of Israel: Emergence of a Welfare State*, Princeton, Van Nostrand, Vol. I, 1959.

KRAINES, O. *Government and Politics in Israel*, Boston, Houghton Mifflin, 1961.

SELIGMAN, L. G. *Leadership in a New Nation: Political Development in Israel*, New York, Atherton Press, 1964.

B. The Legal Structure of Israel

TEDESCHI, G. *Studies in Israel Law*, Jerusalem, Hebrew University Press, 1960.

C. The Structure and Programmes of the Parties

AKZIN, B. 'The Knesset', *International Social Science Journal*, Vol. 13, No. 4, 1961.

—— 'The Role of Parties in Israel Democracy', *Journal of Politics*, Vol. 17, No. 4, 1955.

ANTONOVSKY, A. 'Socio-Political Attitudes in Israel' (Hebrew), *Ammot*, Vol. 1, No. 6, 1963.

BENARI, N. *Socialist Zionism* (Hebrew), Tel Aviv, Hamerkaz LeTarbut VeHinuch (HaHistadrut), 1950.

Central Bureau of Statistics, *Results of the Elections to the Third Knesset and Elections in the Local Municipalities* (Hebrew), 1956.

—— *Results of the Elections to the Fifth Knesset* (Hebrew), Jerusalem, 1964.

GILBOA, Y. 'The Absorptive Capacity of Mapai' (Hebrew), *Maariv*, March 8, 1963.

GUTMAN, E. 'Some Observations on Politics and Parties in Israel', *India Quarterly*, Vol. XVII, No. 1, 1961.

KLEINMAN, M. *The General Zionists* (Hebrew), Jerusalem, Institute for Zionist Knowledge, 1945.

LUBOTZKI. *The Revisionists and Beitar* (Hebrew), Jerusalem, Institute for Zionist Knowledge, 1946.

POLES. 'Retreat from Opposition' (Hebrew), *Haaretz*, September 1, 1964.

—— 'The Failing of the "Club of Four" ' (Hebrew), *Haaretz*, October 6, 1961.

RECHEV (LANDKUTSCH), S. *Hashomer Hatzair* (Hebrew), Sifriat Poalim, 1955.

SHAPIRO, O. *Patterns of Party Activity in an Immigrants' Town* (Hebrew), A Research Report, Jerusalem, The Kaplan School of Economics and Social Sciences, The Hebrew University, 1956.

WOLFSBURG, Y. *The Mizrachi and the Torah VeAvoda Movements* (Hebrew), Jerusalem, Institute for Zionist Knowledge, 1944.

D. GENERAL ASPECTS OF THE HISTADRUT

'Employment Service Law' (Hebrew), (a) *Divrei Haknesset*, Vol. 23, pp. 2020–2025; (b) *Divrei Haknesset*, Vol. 25, pp. 775–795. The Government Press, Jerusalem.

LAVON, P. *Values and Changes* (Hebrew), Tel Aviv, Hamerkaz Letarbut Vehinuch, 1960.

MALKIN, A. *The Histadrut Within the State* (Hebrew), Beit Berel, Ovnaim, 1961.

'Petach' Review. 'Government and Society' (Hebrew), Beit Berel, 1958.

—— 'Socialistic Trends in the Israel Society' (Hebrew), Beit Berel, 1962.

TABB, G. J., AMI, G. and SHAAL, G. *Labour Relations in Israel*, Tel Aviv, Dvir, 1961.

VIII. *Culture, Values and Religion*

A. GENERAL BACKGROUND AND PROBLEMS

AGUDAT ISRAEL. Report submitted to the Delegates of the Fifth World Congress of Agudat Israel (Hebrew), Jerusalem, Information Service of World Agudat Israel Organization, 1963–4.

From the Foundation (Hebrew), Tel Aviv, Amikam, 1962.

GOLDMAN, N. *From Danger of Extermination to Liberation* (Hebrew), Jerusalem, The Zionist Organization, 1958.

Hazut. Pamphlets for Inquiry into the Zionist Question.

Hechal Shlomo. *From Year to Year* (Hebrew), Jerusalem, 1961–2 – 1965–6.

Institute of Contemporary Jewry. *Studies in Contemporary Jewish Life*, Jerusalem, The Hebrew University, 1964.

'Jewish Consciousness' (Hebrew), Reprint from *Divrei Haknesset* in Bahinuch Uvartarbut, Nos. 31–32, 1959.

KURTZWEIL, B. *The Essence and Sources of the Young Hebrew Movement* (Hebrew), Tel Aviv, Haaretz Yearbook, 1952–3.

LEWIN, I. M. *Discourses* (Hebrew), Jerusalem, El-Hamakor, 1951–2.

—— 'What is Judaism? Who is a Jew' (Hebrew), *Beit-Yacov*, No. 5, 1959.

LUFBEN, Y. *Selected Writings*, Tel Aviv, Ayanot, 1953–4.

MEGED, M. 'The Normalization of Israel', *Commentary*, Vol. 32, No. 3, September 1961.

NETUREI KARTA. *Uncover the Mask* (Hebrew), Jerusalem, Hamassora Press, 1949–50.

PATAI, R. (ed.). *Hertzel Year Book*, New York, Hertzel Press, 1958–61 (4 volumes).
ROTENSTREICH, N. *Between Nation and State*, Tel Aviv, HaKibbutz HaMeuchad, 1965.
YZHAR, S. *The Days of Ziklag* (Hebrew), Tel Aviv, Am Oved, 1958.

B. ZIONISM AND NATIONALISM

BUBER, M. *Between a People and Their Nation* (Hebrew), Jerusalem, Shocken, 1945.
HALPERN, B. *The Idea of the Jewish State*, Cambridge, Mass., Harvard University Press, 1961.
—— 'Zionism and Israel', *Jewish Journal of Sociology*, Vol. III, No. 2, 1961.
HERTZBERG, A. *The Zionist Idea*, New York and Tel Aviv, Doubleday and Herzl Press, 1959.
LIVNEH, R. 'Is Israel a Zionist State?' *Midstream*, Vol. 2, 1956.

C. THE TRANSFORMATION OF PIONEERING IDEOLOGY

ALTERMAN, N. Instead of Introduction to 'Kineret Kineret' (Hebrew), *Haaretz*, June 9, 1962.
BITMAN, Y. 'Pioneers to the University' (Hebrew), *Davar*, November 30, 1942.
KATZNELSON, B. *Latent Values* (Hebrew), Tel Aviv, Ayanot, 1954.
LUZ, K. *Milestones* (Hebrew), Tel Aviv, Tarbut Vehinuch, 1962.
Man in the Hityashvut (Kibbutz-Moshav) (Hebrew), Tel Aviv, Mapai Press, 1958.
SHPRINTZAK, Y. *Writing and Speaking* (Hebrew), Tel Aviv, Mapai Press, 1952.
ZAKAI, D. *Short Subjects* (Hebrew), Tel Aviv, Davar, 1956.

D. PATTERNS OF CULTURAL CREATIVITY: INTELLECTUALS AND COMMUNICATION

AVINOAU, L. (ed.). *Parchments of Fire* (Hebrew), Tel Aviv, Ministry of Defense, 1952–61 (three volumes).
BEN-PORAT, Y. 'Intellectuals in Israel' (Hebrew), *Yediot Aharonot*, March 9, 1962, March, 16, 1962, March 30, 1962.
ELLEMERS, J. E. 'Some Sociological Comments on Mass Communication in Israel', *Gazette*, Vol. VII, No. 1, 1961.
'The Essence of the Intellectuals: A Symposium' (Hebrew), *Keshet*, Vol. 1, No. 2, 1959.
Public Committee on Culture and Art. *Two Years of Activity* (Hebrew), Jerusalem, Ministry of Education and Culture, 1962.
SHMUELI, A. 'The Change in Literature and in the Status of Writers' (Hebrew), *Moznaim*, Vol. VIII, Nos. 5–6, 1959.

E. ASPECTS OF THE DEVELOPMENT OF HOLIDAYS, THEATRE AND FOLKLORE

BEN-ZAKAI, T. 'The Israeli Theatre Tries to Find Its Way' (Hebrew), *Maariv*, January 3, 1964.

DONEWITZ, N. 'Not the Same Holiday' (Hebrew), *Haaretz*, April 24, 1964.

KADMAN, G. 'Folk Dances in Israel' (Hebrew), in *Kama*, Jerusalem, Jewish Nation Fund, 1952.

F. THE TRANSFORMATION OF THE RELIGIOUS SCENE: ISSUES AND PROBLEMS

FISHMAN, A. *The Religious Kibbutz Movement: The Revival of the Jewish Religious Community*, Jerusalem, 1957.

GOLDMAN, E. *Religious Issues in Israel's Political Life*, Jerusalem, Jewish Agency, 1964.

Hamodia (Agudat Israel Paper).

Hasbara Press. *The Book of Religious Israel* (Hebrew), Tel Aviv, 1954.

Hatzofe (The National Religious Party Paper).

Hechal Shlomo. *From Year to Year* (Hebrew), Jerusalem, 1963–4, 1964–5, 1965–6.

LEBOVITZ, Y. 'The Crisis of Religion in the State of Israel', *Judaism*, Vol. 2, No. 3, July 1953.

MAIMON, C. L. Y. 'The Reinstitution of the Sanhedrin in Our Renewed State' (Hebrew), Jerusalem, Kook Institute, 1961.

Mizrahi and Hapoel Hamizrahi, *The People of Israel Will See and Will Judge* (Hebrew), Jerusalem, 1958.

NETUREI KARTA. *Drawing Back the Curtain* (Hebrew), Jerusalem, no year.

Sharim (Hebrew) (Poalei Agudat Israel Paper).

WEINER, H. 'Church and State in Israel', *Midstream*, Vol. 8, 1962.

IX. Minorities

ASAF, M. 'The Future of Arab Education in Israel' (Hebrew), *Hamizrah Hehadash*, Vol. 3, No. 3 (II), 1952.

BACHI, R. 'Demography of the Moslem, Christian and Druze Population' (Hebrew), *Encyclopedia Hebraica*, Tel Aviv, Massada, Vol. 6, 1957.

BEN-AMRAM, E. 'Demographic Description of the Arab Community in Israel' (Hebrew), *Hamizrah Hehadash*, Vol. 15, Nos. 1–2, 1965.

BEN-HANANNIAH, Y. 'The Achmadic Community' (Hebrew), *Hamizrah Hehadash*, Vol. 8, No. 3 (26), 1957.

BENOR, Y. L. 'The Arab Education in Israel' (Hebrew), *Hamizrah Hehadash*, Vol. 3, No. 1, Fall 1954.

BEN-PORAT, Y. *Characteristics of the Arab Labour Power in Israel*, Jerusalem, The Falk Project (forthcoming).

BLANK, CH. *The Druzes* (Hebrew), Jerusalem, The Office of the Adviser on Arab Affairs, Prime Minister's Office, 1958.

Central Bureau of Statistics. *Moslems, Christians and Druzes in Israel*, Jerusalem, 1964 (Publication No. 17).

COHEN, A. *Arab Border Villages in Israel*, Manchester, Manchester University Press, 1965.

HAREL, M. *Yanvach – A Druze Village in the Galilee* (Hebrew), Jerusalem, Office of the Adviser on Arab Affairs, The Prime Minister's Office, 1959.

BIBLIOGRAPHY

Lisch, A. 'The Community Jurisdiction of the Druzes in Israel' (Hebrew), *Hamizrah Hehadash*, Vol. 11, No. 4 (44), 1961.

—— 'The Religious Jurisdiction of the Moslems in Israel' (Hebrew), *Hamizrah Hehadash*, Vol. 13, Nos. 1–2 (49–50), 1963.

Liskovsky, A. 'The Arab Refugees – Israel at Present' (Hebrew), *Hamizrah Hehadash*, Vol. 10, No. 3 (39), 1960.

Mansour, A. 'The Modern Encounter Between Jews and Arabs', *New Outlook*, Vol. 5, No. 3, 1962.

Maoz, M. 'The Local Rule in the Arab Settlements' (Hebrew), *Hamizrah Hehadash*, Vol. 12, 1961–2.

Marx, E. 'Bedouins of the Negev' (Hebrew), *Hamizrah Hehadash*, Vol. 7, 1957.

—— 'The Social Structure of the Negev Bedouins' (Hebrew), *Hamizrah Hehadash*, Vol. 8, 1957.

Office of the Adviser on Arab Affairs, *Arab and Druze Settlement in Israel* (Hebrew), Jerusalem, Prime Minister's Office, 1963.

Rosenfeld, H. 'The Arab Village Proletariat', *New Outlook*, Vol. V, No. 3, 1962.

—— 'The Determinants of the Status of Arab Village Women', *Man*, Article 95, Vol. LX, 1960.

—— 'Factors that Determine the Woman's Status in the Arab Village' (Hebrew), *Hamizrah Hehadash*, Vol. 9, Nos. 1–2 (33–34), 1958–9.

—— 'From Rural Peasantry to Rural Proletariat and Residual Peasantry: The Economic-Occupational Transformation of an Arab Village', in Robert A. Manners (ed.), *Patterns and Processes of Culture*, Essays in honour of Julian H. Steward, Chicago, Aldine Press (forthcoming).

—— 'The Problems of Social Planning in an Arab Village' (Hebrew), *Megamot*, Vol. 11, No. 4, 1961.

—— 'Processes of Separation and Division of the Extended Family in the Arab Village' (Hebrew), *Megamot*, Vol. 8, No. 4, 1957.

—— *They Were Peasants* (Hebrew), Tel Aviv, Hakibbutz Hameuhad, 1965.

—— 'Wage, Labour and Status in an Arab Village', *New Outlook*, Vol. VI, No. 1, 1963.

Shamir, S. 'Changes in Leadership in the Village of Ar-Rameh' (Hebrew), *Hamizrah Hehadash*, Vol. 11, No. 4, 1961.

Shidlovsky, B. 'Changes in the Development of the Arab Village in Israel' (Hebrew), *Hamizrah Hehadash*, Vol. 15, Nos. 1–2, 1965.

Shimoni, Y. *The Arabs of Palestine* (Hebrew), Tel Aviv, Am Oved, 1947.

—— 'The Arabs in Anticipation of the Israel-Arab War 1945–1946' (Hebrew), *Hamizrah Hehadash*, Vol. 12, No. 3 (47), 1962.

Washitz, Y. 'Arabs in Israeli Politics', *New Outlook*, Vol. V, No. 3, 1962.

Yinon, A. 'Some Aspects of the Arabic Literature in Israel' (Hebrew), *Hamizrah Hehadash*, Vol. 15, Nos. 1–2, 1965.

Index